CALENDRICAL CALCULATIONS

The Ultimate Edition

An invaluable resource for working programmers, as well as a fount of useful algorithmic tools for computer scientists, astronomers, and other calendar enthusiasts, the Ultimate Edition updates and expands the previous edition to achieve more accurate results and present new calendar variants. The book now includes algorithmic descriptions of nearly forty calendars: the Gregorian, ISO, Icelandic, Egyptian, Armenian, Julian, Coptic, Ethiopic, Akan, Islamic (arithmetic and astronomical forms), Saudi Arabian, Persian (arithmetic and astronomical), Bahá'í (arithmetic and astronomical), French Revolutionary (arithmetic and astronomical), Babylonian, Hebrew (arithmetic and astronomical), Samaritan, Mayan (long count, haab, and tzolkin), Aztec (xihuitl and tonalpohualli), Balinese Pawukon, Chinese, Japanese, Korean, Vietnamese, Hindu (old arithmetic and medieval astronomical, both solar and lunisolar), and Tibetan Phug-lugs. It also includes information on major holidays and on different methods of keeping time. The necessary astronomical functions have been rewritten to produce more accurate results and to include calculations of moonrise and moonset.

The authors frame the calendars of the world in a completely algorithmic form, allowing easy conversion among these calendars and the determination of secular and religious holidays. Lisp code for all the algorithms is available in machine-readable form.

Edward M. Reingold is Professor of Computer Science at the Illinois Institute of Technology.

Nachum Dershowitz is Professor of Computational Logic and Chair of Computer Science at Tel Aviv University.

About the Authors

Edward M. Reingold was born in Chicago, Illinois, in 1945. He has an undergraduate degree in mathematics from the Illinois Institute of Technology and a doctorate in computer science from Cornell University. Reingold was a faculty member in the Department of Computer Science at the University of Illinois at Urbana-Champaign from 1970–2000; he retired as a Professor Emeritus of Computer Science in December 2000 and moved to the Department of Computer Science at the Illinois Institute of Technology as professor and chair, an administrative post he held until 2006. His research interests are in theoretical computer science—especially the design and analysis of algorithms and data structures. A Fellow of the Association for Computing Machinery since 1996, Reingold has authored or coauthored more than 70 research papers and 10 books; his papers on backtrack search, the generation of combinations, weight-balanced binary trees, and the drawing of trees and graphs are considered classics. He has won awards for his undergraduate and graduate teaching. Reingold is intensely interested in calendars and their computer implementation; in addition to *Calendrical Calculations* and *Calendrical Tabulations*, he is the author and former maintainer of the calendar/diary part of GNU Emacs. In the accompanying photograph he is wearing a tie showing the twelve animal totems of the Chinese calendar.

Beyond his expertise in calendars, Nachum Dershowitz is a leading figure in software verification in general and the termination of programs in particular; he is an international authority on equational inference and term rewriting. Other areas in which he has made major contributions include program semantics, analysis of historical manuscripts, and combinatorial enumeration. Dershowitz has authored or coauthored more than 100 research papers and several books and has held visiting positions at prominent institutions around the globe. He has won numerous awards for his research and teaching, including the Herbrand Award for Distinguished Contributions to Automated Reasoning (2011) and Test-of-Time awards for the IEEE Symposium on Logic in Computer Science (2006), for the International Conference on Rewriting Techniques and Applications (2014), and for the International Conference on Automated Deduction (2015). Born in 1951, his graduate degrees in applied mathematics are from the Weizmann Institute in Israel. He is currently Professor of Computational Logic and Chair of Computer Science at Tel Aviv University and was elected to Academia Europaea in 2013.

Calendrical Calculations

THE ULTIMATE EDITION

EDWARD M. REINGOLD
Illinois Institute of Technology, Chicago

NACHUM DERSHOWITZ
Tel Aviv University, Israel

CAMBRIDGE
UNIVERSITY PRESS

University Printing House, Cambridge CB2 8BS, United Kingdom

One Liberty Plaza, 20th Floor, New York, NY 10006, USA

477 Williamstown Road, Port Melbourne, VIC 3207, Australia

314-321, 3rd Floor, Plot 3, Splendor Forum, Jasola District Centre, New Delhi - 110025, India

79 Anson Road, #06-04/06, Singapore 079906

Cambridge University Press is part of the University of Cambridge.

It furthers the University's mission by disseminating knowledge in the pursuit of education, learning and research at the highest international levels of excellence.

www.cambridge.org
Information on this title: www.cambridge.org/9781107057623
DOI: 10.1017/9781107415058

First edition 1997
Second edition 2001
Third edition 2008
Fourth edition 2018

A catalogue record for this publication is available from the British Library

Library of Congress Cataloging in Publication data
Names: Reingold, Edward M., 1945– author. | Dershowitz, Nachum, author.
Title: Calendrical calculations : the ultimate edition / Edward M. Reingold, Illinois Institute of Technology, Chicago, Nachum Dershowitz, Tel Aviv University, Israel.
Description: Fourth edition. | Cambridge : Cambridge University Press, 2017.
Identifiers: LCCN 2017024295| ISBN 9781107057623 (hardback) | ISBN 9781107683167 (paperback)
Subjects: LCSH: Calendar–Mathematics.
Classification: LCC CE12 .R45 2017 | DDC 529/.3–dc23
LC record available at https://lccn.loc.gov/2017024295

ISBN 978-1-107-05762-3 Hardback
ISBN 978-1-107-68316-7 Paperback

Additional resources for this publication available at www.cambridge.org/calendricalcalculations

לקהלות הקדש
שמסרו נפשם על קדשת השם
יהי זכרם ברוך

Contents

I Arithmetical Calendars

List of Frontispieces

List of Figures

List of Tables

List of Calendar Functions

Abbreviations

Abbreviation	Meaning	Explanation
a.d.	ante diem	prior day
A.D.	Anno Domini (= C.E.)	In the year of the Lord
A.H.	Anno Hegiræ	In the year of Mohammed's emigration to Medina
a.m.	ante meridiem	before noon
A.M.	Anno Mundi	In the year of the world since creation
	Anno Martyrum	Era of the Martyrs
A.P.	Anno Persico Anno Persarum	Persian year
A.S.	Anno Samaritanorum	Samaritan year
A.U.C.	Ab Urbe Condita	From the founding of the city of Rome
B.C.	Before Christ (= B.C.E.)	
B.C.E.	Before the Common Era (= B.C.)	
B.E.	Bahá'í Era	
C.E.	Common Era (= A.D.)	
E.E.	Ethiopic Era	
JD	Julian Day number	Elapsed days since noon on Monday, January 1, 4713 B.C.E. (Julian); sometimes J.A.D., Julian Astronomical Day
K.Y.	Kali Yuga	"Iron Age" epoch of the traditional Hindu calendar
m	meters	

continued

Abbreviation	Meaning	Explanation
MJD	Modified Julian Day number	Julian day number minus 2400000.5
p.m.	post meridiem	after noon
R.D.	Rata Die	Fixed date—elapsed days since the onset of Monday, January 1, 1 (Gregorian)
S.E.	Śaka Era	Epoch of the modern Hindu calendar
U.T.	Universal Time	Mean solar time at Greenwich, England (0° meridian), reckoned from midnight; sometimes G.M.T., Greenwich Mean Time
V.E.	Vikrama Era	Alternative epoch of the modern Hindu calendar

Mathematical Notations

Notation	Name	Meaning
$\lfloor x \rfloor$	floor	largest integer not larger than x
$\lceil x \rceil$	ceiling	smallest integer not smaller than x
round(x)	round	nearest integer to x, that is, $\lfloor x + 0.5 \rfloor$
$x \bmod y$	remainder	$x - y\lfloor x/y \rfloor$
$x \bmod [1 \mathinner{..} y]$	adjusted remainder	y if $x \bmod y = 0$, $x \bmod y$ otherwise
$x \bmod [a \mathinner{..} b)$	interval mod	x if $a = b$, $a + (x - a) \bmod (b - a)$ otherwise
$\gcd(x, y)$	greatest common divisor	x if $y = 0$, $\gcd(y, x \bmod y)$ otherwise
$\mathrm{lcm}(x, y)$	least common multiple	$xy/\gcd(x, y)$
$\lvert x \rvert$	absolute value	unsigned value of x
sign(x)	sign	-1 when x is negative, $+1$ when x is positive, 0 when x is 0
$i^\circ j' k''$	angle	i degrees, j arc minutes, and k arc seconds
$\varphi(n)$	totient function	number of positive integers less than n and relatively prime to it
π	pi	ratio of circumference of circle to diameter
$\sin x$	sine	sine of x, given in degrees
$\cos x$	cosine	cosine of x, given in degrees
$\tan x$	tangent	tangent of x, given in degrees
$\arcsin x$	arc sine	inverse sine of x, in degrees

continued

Notation	Name	Meaning
$\arccos x$	arc cosine	inverse cosine of x, in degrees
$\arctan x$	arc tangent	inverse tangent of x, in degrees
$[a\,..\,b]$	closed interval	all real numbers x, $a \leqslant x \leqslant b$
$(a\,..\,b)$	open interval	all real numbers x, $a < x < b$
$[a\,..\,b)$	half-open interval	all real numbers x, $a \leqslant x < b$
$(a\,..\,b]$	half-open interval	all real numbers x, $a < x \leqslant b$
$\neg p$	logical negation	true when p is false and vice versa
$\sum_{i \geqslant k}^{p(i)} f(i)$	summation	the sum of $f(i)$ for all integers $i = k, k+1, \ldots$, continuing only as long as the condition $p(i)$ holds
$\prod_{i \geqslant k}^{p(i)} f(i)$	product	the product of $f(i)$ for all integers $i = k, k+1, \ldots$, continuing only as long as the condition $p(i)$ holds
$\sum f(\tilde{x}, \tilde{y}, \ldots)$	summation	the sum of $f(\tilde{x}_i, \tilde{y}_i \ldots)$ for all like-indexed components of the vectors $\tilde{x}, \tilde{y}, \ldots$
$\mathbf{MAX}_{\xi \geqslant \mu}\{\psi(\xi)\}$	maximum integer value	the largest integer $\xi = \mu, \mu+1, \ldots$ such that $\psi(\mu), \psi(\mu+1), \ldots, \psi(\xi)$ are true
$\mathbf{MIN}_{\xi \geqslant \mu}\{\psi(\xi)\}$	minimum integer value	the smallest integer $\xi = \mu, \mu+1, \ldots$ such that $\psi(\xi)$ is true
$\mathbf{MIN}_{\xi \in [\mu..\nu]}^{p(\mu,\nu)}\{\psi(\xi)\}$	minimum value	the value ξ such that ψ is false in $[\mu\,..\,\xi)$ and is true in $[\xi\,..\,\nu]$; see equation (1.35) on page 24 for details
$f^{-1}(y, [a\,..\,b])$	function inverse	approximate x in $[a\,..\,b]$ such that $f(x) = y$
$\boxed{f_1 \mid f_2 \mid f_3} \cdots$	record formation	the record containing fields $f_1, f_2, f_3, \ldots$
$R_{\mathbf{f}}$	field selection	contents of field **f** of record R
$\langle x_0, x_1, x_2, \ldots \rangle$	list construction	the list containing $x_0, x_1, x_2, \ldots$
$\langle\,\rangle$	empty list	a list with no elements
$L_{[i]}$	list element	the ith element of list L; 0-based
$L_{[i..]}$	sublist	a list of the ith, $(i+1)$st, and so on elements of list L
$A \parallel B$	concatenation	the concatenation of lists A and B

continued

Notation	Name	Meaning
$\tilde{x}$	vector	indexed list of elements $\langle x_0, x_1, \ldots \rangle$
$\{x_0, x_1, x_2, \ldots\}$	set formation	the set containing $x_0, x_1, x_2, \ldots$
$x \in S$	set membership	the element x is a member of set S
$x \in \mathbf{Z}$	integer	the number x is an integer
$A \cap B$	set intersection	the intersection of sets A and B
$A \cup B$	set union	the union of sets A and B
$i \mathinner{..} j$	range of integers	the set $\{i, i+1, \ldots, j\}$
$\langle b_1, \ldots, b_k; b_{k+1}, \ldots, b_n \rangle$	mixed-radix base	each position i takes values in $[0 \mathinner{..} b_i)$, with units in position k
$a \xleftarrow{\text{rad}} b$	mixed-radix number	value of a in base b
$x \xrightarrow{\text{rad}} b$	mixed-radix representation	representation of x in base b
$h : m : s$	time of day	h hours, m minutes, and s seconds
$i^{\text{d}} j^{\text{h}} k^{\text{m}} l^{\text{s}}$	duration of time	i days, j hours, k minutes, and l seconds
bogus	error	invalid calendar date or time

בָּרוּךְ הַגֶּבֶר אֲשֶׁר יִבְטַח בַּה׳ (יִרְמְיָה י״ז : ז׳) ترجمه : مبارك باد كسيكه بر خداوند توكل نمايد (ارميا ١٧ : ٧)

« شكرانهٔ بازوی توانا » « بگرفتن دست ناتوان است »

یادواره حماسه آفرین (اِستر و مُردِخای) و (جشن مذهبی و تاریخی پوریم) را به عموم همکیشان ارجمند مقیم ایران و خارج از کشور تبریک و تهنیت می گوییم.

פּוּרִים פּוּרִים פּוּרִים לָנוּ. בָּרוּךְ אֲשֶׁר בָּחַר בָּנוּ:

20

JOURS DAYS	میلادی مارس מרס MARS 1998	הערות ملاحظات NOTE جامعترین و دقیقترین تقویم چهارگانه ادیان توحیدی	قمری ذیقعده ז׳יקעדה ZIGHADEH ١٤١٨	شمسی اسفند אספ׳נד ESFAND ١٣٧٦	عبری ادار אדר ADAR 5758	ایام ימים
Jeudi THURSDAY روز نیکوکاری (نیایش و شادزی کلیمیان) (סוף זְמַן בִּרְכַּת הַלְּבָנָה)	12	פּוּרִים پوریم (3405 לב׳ אדם) میلا اِستر (جشن پوریم) POURIM מוֹצִיאִים סֵפֶר תּוֹרָה קוֹרְאִים בְּפָרָשַׁת בְּשַׁלַּח – וַיָּבֹא עֲמָלֵק لغو استعماری پیمان سنتو (ایران ١٣٥٧ ش) (מִשְׁלוֹחַ מָנוֹת אִישׁ לְרֵעֵהוּ וּמַתָּנוֹת לָאֶבְיוֹנִים) استعانت به مستمندان و هدیه به دوستان سنتی کلیمیان	١٣ גְּמִילוּת חֲסָדִים: (روز احسان و جشن نیکوکاری) تعطیل کلیمیان اول بردالعجوزه ـ سرمای پیرزن	٢١	14 | יד	پنجشنبه חמישי الخمیس חַג שָׂמֵחַ
Vendredi FRIDAY קַבָּלַת שַׁבָּת: אוֹ הַדְלָקַת הַנֵּר שָׁעָה آغاز شبات ساعت 17/55	13	פּוּרִים שׁוּשָׁן (پوریم شوشن) POURIM SHOUSHAN کشف (سیاره پلوتون) دورترین سیاره منظومه شمسی (1930 میلادی) توسط (لاکول) ستاره‌شناس ومنجم شهیر آمریکائی سالروز درگذشت شادروان مرحومهٔ گوهر کهن‌صدق נ״ע – 5742 عبری (عیال‌شادروان شِلُمو کهن‌صدق ـ سلطان‌سلیمان) (ת׳ נ׳ צ׳ ב׳ ה׳)	١٤ تأسیس بنیاد شهید (ایران ١٣٥٨ ش) אֵין אוֹמְרִים נְפִילַת אַפַּיִם (وید وی نمیخوانند)	٢٢	טו 15	آدینه ששי الجمعه
SAMEDI SATURDAY SHABAT	14 (سرما. پیوسا) מוֹצָאֵי שַׁבָּת پایان شبات 18/40	כִּי תִשָּׂא (פר׳ 21) کی‌تیسا KI TISSA מַפְטִירִים مفطارا וַיִּשְׁלַח אַחְאָב (מְלָכִים א׳ – יח׳ : כ׳) (שַׁבַּת הַפְסָקָה שְׁנִי – ה סִימָן ו״ב׳׳ו) تأسیس ذوب‌آهن ایران در اصفهان (١٣٤٦ ش) מִשְׁמָרָה : میشمارا יִרְמְיָה סִימָן יז׳ עַד לא׳ - כָּל מְגִילַּת אֶסְתֵּר - שְׁקָלִים (סדר ב׳) شب یکشنبه: پایان برگزاری جشن مذهبی و تاریخی (پوریم) کلیمیان	١٥ درگذشت آیت‌الله سیدابوالقاسم کاشانی (تهران ١٣٤٠ ش) (پایان سرما در نقاط معتدله) (نیایش کلیمیان)	٢٣	טז 16	شنبه שַׁבָּת شبات يوم السّبت
Dimanche SUNDAY	15	انتخابات اولین دوره مجلس شورای اسلامی (ایران ١٣٥٨ ش) رحلت حجت‌الاسلام حاج سید احمد خمینی (تهران ١٣٧٣ش)	١٦	٢٤ (انارام روز) زرتشتیان	יז 17	یکشنبه ראשון الاحد
Lundi MONDAY	16 پنجه‌بزرگ زرتشتیان	بمباران شیمیائی (حلبچه) توسط رژیم بعث عراق (١٣٦٦ ش) درگذشت (جورج وستینگهاوس) آمریکائی (مخترع ترمز کمپرسی - 1914 م.) (آغاز گاهنبار 6 ـ هَمِس پَت مَیدیم‌گاه. جشن زرتشتیان تا ٢٩ اسفند) سالروز در گذشت شادروان دکتر ابراهیم ابراهیمیان (5743 عبری) נ״ע	١٧ מִשְׁעָה 5/45 מַגִּיעַ זְמַן בִּרְכַּת צִיצִית: אוֹר עַמּוּד הַשַּׁחַר	٢٥ خَمبه مُشتَرَقه زرتشتیان	יח 18	دوشنبه שני الاثنين
Mardi TUESDAY	17 راهنما صفحه 39	درگذشت (ایرن‌کوری) شیمیدان و فیزیسین فرانسوی کاشف عناصر جدید (رادیواکتیو 1957–1897م.)	١٨ (آخر بردالعجوزه ـ سرمای پیرزن)	٢٦	19 | יט	سه‌شنبه שלישי الثلاثا
Mercredi WEDNESDAY	18	درگذشت (اتوو الاش) یهودی آلمانی (برنده‌جایزه‌شیمی نوبل 1910م.) (1931–1847 میلادی)	١٩ آغاز وَزِش باد و ریزش بارانهای بهاری	٢٧	20 | כ	چهارشنبه רביעי الاربعاء
Jeudi THURSDAY	19	پایان استعمار فرانسه در الجزایر (١٣٤١ ش)	٢٠	٢٨	כא 21	پنجشنبه חמישי الخمیس
Vendredi FRIDAY (وَ هَشتواش زرتشتیان) קַבָּלַת שַׁבָּת آغاز شبات 18/00	20	(آغاز تعطیلات نوروزی دوایر دولتی تاچهارم فروردین) درگذشت (اسحق‌نیوتون) انگلیسی (کاشف قانون جاذبه عمومی 1727 م) درگذشت (پاول‌نیپکو) مخترع تلویزیون (1940-1860 میلادی) (پایان گاهنبار6 ـ پنجه‌بزرگ هَمِس پَت مَیدیم‌گاه زرتشتیان)	٢١ ملی‌شدن صنعت‌نفت درایران (١٣٢٩ شمسی) (آغاز تعطیلات نوروزی مدارس تا ١٤ فروردین در ایران)	٢٩ (عرفه عید)	כב 22	آدینه ששי الجمعه
SAMEDI SATURDAY SHABAT یادآوری: از ساعت ٢٤ نیمه شب (شب یکشنبه) جلو کشیدن یك ساعت عقربه ساعت فصل تابستانی را در ایران	21 نیایش کلیمیان جنگ کرامه (1968م.)	عید نوروز باستانی ١٣٧٧ هجری شمسی (NOWROOZ) וַיַּקְהֵל – פְקוּדֵי (פר׳ 23 – 22) VAYAGHEL — PEKUDEH (وَیَقهِل ـ پِقوده = دو پاراشائی) (מוֹצִיאִים שְׁנֵי סְפָרִים) בָּרִאשׁוֹן קוֹרְאִים שִׁבְעָה גַבְרֵי אוֹ יוֹתֵר וְהַמַּשְׁלִים אוֹ׳ חֲצִי קַדִּישׁ וְהַמַּפְטִיר קוֹרֵא בְּסֵפֶר שֵׁנִי בְּפָרָשַׁת (חוּקַּת 39) זֹאת חֻקַּת עַד – וְהַנֶּפֶשׁ הַנֹּגַעַת תִּטְמָא עַד־הָעָרֶב: (וְאוֹ׳ חֲצִי קַדִּישׁ) מַפְטִירִים مفطارا וַיְהִי דְבַר־ה׳ אֵלַי לֵאמֹר (יְחֶזְקֵאל לו׳ : טז׳) (اورمزد = فروردینماه) (نیایش زرتشتیان) (روز شادزی پارسیان) מוֹצָאֵי שַׁבָּת: אוֹ צֵאת שִׁבְעָה כּוֹכָבִים پایان شبات ساعت 18/45	٢٢ חַג נוֹרוּז לְפַרְסִים שַׁבַּת פָּרָה شباتِ پارا SH. PARAH (سالروز بین‌المللی رفع تبعیضات نژادی) عیدتان شاد باد מְבָרְכִים הַחֹדֶשׁ (آغاز دید و بازدید عمومی پارسیان تا ١٣ فروردین)	فروردین פ׳רורדין FARVARDIN	23 | כג הַתְחָלַת הָאָבִיב	شنبه שַׁבָּת شبات يوم السّبت

מִשְׁמָרָה : میشمارا יִרְמְיָה סִי׳ לא׳ עַד מט׳ - שִׁיר הַשִּׁירִים – מִשְׁלֵי עַד ו׳ – שַׁבָּת (סדר ב׳) טַהֲרוֹת וְיָדַיִם (סדר ו׳)

(عید نوروز باستانی را به عموم هموطنان تبریک و تهنیت می‌گوییم.)

בְּסִימָנָא טָבָא

لحظه تحویل سال نو ١٣٧٧ شمسی (به زمان و ساعت رسمی ایران)
روز آدینه ٢٩ اسفند ١٣٧٦ شمسی، مطابق ٢٠ مارس ١٩٩٨ میلادی، برابر ٢١ ذیقعده ١٤١٨ قمری
و ٢٢ ماه آدار سال ٥٧٥٨ عبری (ساعت ٢٣ و ٢٥ دقیقه و ٣٠ ثانیه) می‌باشد.

Page from an Iranian synagogue calendar for mid-March 1998 showing the Gregorian, Hebrew, Persian, and Islamic calendars. (Collection of E.M.R.)

Preface

No one has the right to speak in public before he has rehearsed what he wants to say two, three, and four times, and learned it; then he may speak ... But if a man ... puts it down in writing, he should revise it a thousand times, if possible.
Maimonides: *The Epistle on Martyrdom* (circa 1165)

This book has developed over a more than 30-year period during which the calendrical algorithms and our presentation of them have continually evolved. Our initial motivation was an effort by one of us (E.M.R.) to create Emacs-Lisp code that would provide calendar and diary features for GNU Emacs [15]; this version of the code included the Gregorian, Islamic, and Hebrew calendars (the Hebrew implemented by N.D.). A deluge of inquiries from around the globe soon made it clear to us that there was keen interest in an explanation that would go beyond the code itself, leading to our article [3] and encouraging us to rewrite the code completely, this time in Common Lisp [16]. The subsequent addition—by popular demand—of the Mayan and French Revolutionary calendars to GNU Emacs prompted a second article [13]. We received many hundreds of reprint requests for these articles. This response far exceeded our expectations and provided the impetus to write a book in which we could more fully address the multifaceted subject of calendars and their implementation.

The subject of calendars has always fascinated us with its cultural, historical, and mathematical wealth, and we have occasionally employed calendars as accessible examples in introductory programming courses. Once the book's plan took shape, our curiosity turned into obsession. We began by extending our programs to include other calendars such as the Chinese, Coptic, modern Hindu, and arithmetic Persian. Then, of course, the code for these newly added calendars needed to be rewritten, in some cases several times, to bring it up to the standards of the earlier material. We have long since lost track of the number of revisions, and, needless to say, we could undoubtedly devote another decade to polishing what we have, tracking down minutiæ, and implementing and refining additional interesting calendars. As much as we might be tempted to, circumstances do not allow us to follow Maimonides' dictum quoted above.

In this book we give a unified algorithmic presentation for more than three dozen calendars of current and historical interest: the Gregorian (current civil), ISO (International Organization for Standardization), Icelandic, Egyptian (and nearly identical Armenian), Julian (old civil), Coptic and virtually identical Ethiopic, Akan, Islamic (Muslim), including the arithmetic, observational, and Saudi Arabian forms, modern Persian (both the astronomical and arithmetic forms), Bahá'í (both the arithmetic and astronomical forms), French Revolutionary (both the astronomical and arithmetic forms), Babylonian, Hebrew (Jewish) standard and observational, Samaritan, Mayan (long count, haab, and tzolkin) and two almost identical Aztec, Balinese Pawukon, Chinese (and nearly identical Japanese, Korean, and Vietnamese), old Hindu (solar and lunisolar), modern Hindu (solar and lunisolar, traditional and astronomical), and Tibetan. Easy conversion among these calendars is a natural outcome of the approach, as is the determination of secular and religious holidays.

Our goal in this book is twofold: to give precise descriptions of each calendar and to make accurate calendrical algorithms readily available for computer use. The complete workings of each calendar are described in prose and in mathematical/algorithmic form. Working computer programs are included in an appendix and are available on the internet (see following).

Calendrical problems are notorious for plaguing software, as shown by the following examples:

1. Since the early days of computers, when storage was at a premium, programmers—especially COBOL programmers—usually allocated only two decimal digits for the internal storage of years [10]; thus billions of dollars were spent fixing untold numbers of programs to prevent their going awry on New Year's Day of 2000 by interpreting "00" as 1900 instead of 2000. This became known as the "Y2K problem."

2. In a Reuters story dated Monday, November 6, 2006, Irene Klotz wrote:

   > A computer problem could force NASA to postpone next month's launch of shuttle Discovery until 2007 to avoid having the spaceship in orbit when the clock strikes midnight on New Year's Eve. The shuttle is due to take off from the Kennedy Space Center in central Florida on December 7 on a 12-day mission to continue construction of the half-built International Space Station. But if the launch is delayed for any reason beyond December 17 or 18, the flight likely would be postponed until next year, officials at the U.S. space agency said on Monday. To build in added cushion, NASA may move up the take off to December 6. "The shuttle computers were never envisioned to fly through a year-end changeover," space shuttle program manager Wayne Hale told a briefing. After the 2003 accident involving space shuttle Columbia, NASA started developing procedures to work around the computer glitch. But NASA managers still do not want to launch Discovery knowing it would be in space when the calendar rolls over to January 1, 2007.

> The problem, according to Hale, is that the shuttle's computers do not reset to day one, as ground-based systems that support shuttle navigation do. Instead, after December 31, the 365th day of the year, shuttle computers figure January 1 is just day 366.

3. Poorly written calendar software in Notify Technology's code to synchronize mobile devices did not correctly handle monthly recurring events on the 29th, 30th, or 31st of the month because these dates do not occur in all months.

4. The change from daylight saving time to standard time in late 2010 (at various dates around the world) caused the failure of certain repeating iPhone alarms. The alarms failed again on January 1, 2011.

5. Many programs err in, or simply ignore, the century rule for leap years on the Gregorian calendar (every 4th year is a leap year, except for every 100th year, which is not, except for every 400th year, which is):

   (a) The *New York Times* of March 1, 1997 reported that the New York City Taxi and Limousine Commission chose March 1, 1996, as the start date for a new, higher fare structure for cabs. Meters programmed by one company in Queens ignored the leap day and charged customers the higher rate on February 29.

   (b) According to the *New Zealand Herald* of January 8, 1997, a computer software error at the Tiwai Point aluminum smelter at midnight on New Year's Eve caused more than A$ 1 million of damage. The software error was the failure to consider 1996 a leap year; the same problem occurred 2 hours later at Comalco's Bell Bay smelter in Tasmania (which was 2 hours behind New Zealand). The general manager of operations for New Zealand Aluminum Smelters, David Brewer, said, "It was a complicated problem and it took quite some time to find the cause."

   (c) Early releases of the popular spreadsheet program Lotus® 1-2-3® treated 2000 as a nonleap year—a problem that was eventually fixed. However, all releases of Lotus® 1-2-3® take 1900 as a leap year, which is a serious problem with historical data; by the time this error was recognized, the company deemed it too late to correct: "The decision was made at some point that a change now would disrupt formulas which were written to accommodate this anomaly" [17]. Excel®, part of Microsoft Office®, suffers from the same flaw; Microsoft acknowledges this error on its "Help and Support" web site, claiming that "the disadvantages of [correcting the problem] outweigh the advantages."

   (d) According to Reuters (March 22, 2004), the computer display in the 2004 Pontiac Grand Prix shows the wrong day of the week because engineers overlooked the fact that 2004 is a leap year.

   (e) Similarly, Zune®, Microsoft's portable media player, failed (according to the *New York Times* of January 1, 2009) because the software did not treat 2008 as a leap year. In fact, Zune's code to compute the present year from the number of days elapsed since January 1, 1980 would go into an infinite loop on the last day of *any* leap year.

(f) Again according to the *New York Times* (March 1, 2010), Sony Playstation 3® code considered 2010 a leap year, an error that caused problems for gamers on March 1—some games would not load, others lost records of trophies, and online connections failed.

6. The calculation of holidays and special dates is a source of confusion:

   (a) According to the *New York Times* of January 12, 1999, for example, Microsoft Windows® 95, 98, and NT get the start of daylight saving time wrong for years, like 2001, in which April 1 is a Sunday; in such cases Windows has daylight saving time starting on April 8. An estimated 40 million to 50 million computers were affected, including some in hotels that were used for wake-up calls.

   (b) Microsoft Outlook® 98 had the wrong date for U.S. Memorial Day in 1999, giving it as May 24, 1999, instead of May 31, 1999. It gave wrong dates for U.S. Thanksgiving Day for 1997–2000. Outlook® 2000 corrected the Memorial Day error, but compounded the Thanksgiving Day error by giving *two dates* for Thanksgiving for 1998–2000. Their 2015 Web App has incorrect dates for the Hebrew calendar fast days Tzom Tammuz and Tishah be-Av.

   (c) Various programs calculate the Hebrew calendar by first determining the date of Passover using Gauss's method [6] (see [14]); this method is correct only when sufficient precision is used, and thus such an approach often leads to errors.

   (d) Delrina Technology's 1994 Daily Planner had three days instead of two for Rosh ha-Shanah.

   (e) Israeli daylight saving time has ended at various dates over the years, but Microsoft's Windows Vista® always ended it on September 2.

7. At least one modern, standard, source for calendrical matters, Parise [12], has many errors, some of which are presumably due not to sloppy editing, but to the algorithms used to produce the tables. For example, the Mayan date 8.1.19.0.0 is given incorrectly as February 14, 80 (Gregorian) on page 290; the dates given on pages 325–327 for Easter for the years 1116, 1152, and 1582 are not Sundays; the epact for 1986 on page 354 is wrongly given as 20; Chinese New Year is wrong for many years; the epoch is wrong for the Ethiopic calendar, and hence that entire table is flawed.

8. Even the Astronomical Applications Department of the U.S. Naval Observatory is not immune to calendrical errors! They gave Sunday, April 9, 2028 and Thursday, March 29, 2029 for Passover on their web site `aa.usno.navy.mil/faq/docs/passover.html`, instead of the correct dates Tuesday, April 11, 2028 and Saturday, March 31, 2029, respectively. The site was corrected on March 10, 2004.

Finally, the computer world is plagued with unintelligible code that seems to work by magic. Consider the following Unix script for calculating the date of Easter:

```
echo $* '[ddsf[lfp[too early]Pq]s@1583>@
ddd19%1+sg100/1+d3*4/12-sx8*5+25/5-sz5*4/lx-10-
sdlg11*20+lz+lx-30%d[30+]s@0>@d[[1+]s@lg11<@]s@25=@d[1+]
s@24=@se44le-d[30+]s@21>@dld+7%-7+
[March ]smd[31-[April ]sm]s@31<@psnlmPpsnlz>p]splpx' | dc
```

We want to provide transparent algorithms to replace the gobbledegook that is so common.

Our algorithms are carefully crafted, fully explained, and (in almost all cases) endogenous. They illustrate all the basic features of calendars: fidelity only to solar events (Gregorian, Persian, French), fidelity only to lunar events (Islamic), and fidelity to both solar and lunar events (Hebrew, Chinese, Hindu); intricate cycles disconnected from solar and lunar events (Mayan, Balinese); simultaneous intercalation and extraculation yielding irregular cycles of days of the month and months of the year (Hindu). We hope that in the process of reworking classical calendrical calculations and rephrasing them in the algorithmic language of the computer age we have also succeeded in affording the reader a glimpse of the beauty and individuality of diverse cultures past and present.

The Ultimate Edition

> *How I labored day and night for almost ten years straight composing this work. Great scholars as yourselves will understand what I have accomplished, having gathered statements that were distant and dispersed among the hills and mountains … For these reasons, it is appropriate for one to examine my statements, to scrutinize, and to investigate after me. The reader of this composition should not say, who am I … I hereby grant him my permission … You, in your wisdom, have done me a great favor. Likewise, anyone who finds a problem and informs me will be rendering me a favor, lest there remain any stumbling block.*
>
> Maimonides: Letter to Jonathan ben David Hakohen of Lunel (1199)

After the first edition of the book was published in 1997 we continued to gather material, polish the algorithms, and keep track of errors. Because the second edition was to be published in the year 2000, some wag at Cambridge University Press dubbed it "The Millennium Edition," and that title got used in prepublication catalogs, creating a *fait accompli*. The Millennium Edition was a comprehensive revision of the first edition, and the third edition was a comprehensive revision of the Millennium Edition. Since the publication of the third edition we have continued to gather new material and polish existing material; this fourth edition is, once again, a comprehensive revision. We have called this "The Ultimate Edition" for several reasons. First, and foremost, we have no intention of ever producing another edition of this book (though minor changes may be made in subsequent printings). Second, because we have strived to be as comprehensive as possible, we are sanguine that we have covered all the world's calendar types (though not, of course, all variations). Finally, this material has undergone continuous refinement for over 30 years and diminishing returns have set in: future refinements are unlikely to yield much benefit.

In preparing this Ultimate Edition we have corrected all known errors (fortunately, only minor errors were ever reported in the third edition), added much new material, reworked and rearranged some discussions to accommodate the new material, improved the robustness of some functions, added many new references, and made an enormous number of small improvements. Among the new material the reader will find much more use of the mixed-radix notation of [9, sec. 4.1], use of the generalized modulo interval notation of [4], and presentations of Unix dates, Italian time, and the Akan, Icelandic, Saudi Arabian *Umm al-Qura* (an approximation of the Observational Islamic calendar), and Babylonian calendars; there are also expanded treatments of the observational Islamic and Hebrew calendars and brief discussions of the Samaritan and Nepalese calendars. Several of the astronomical functions of Chapter 14 have been rewritten to produce more accurate results (causing occasional changes in astronomically-based calendar computations, such as the Persian and the Chinese). We have added calculations of moonrise and moonset, as well as a function to invert the *molad* in the Hebrew calendar chapter. The sample data in Appendix C has been correspondingly updated and expanded (changes in hardware and software since the preparation of the third edition have caused minor changes in some sample values compared with that edition; the revision of what we called the "Future Bahá'í calendar" has caused significant changes to some of those sample values). Sample dates of many of the holidays we discuss have also been added. A cross reference list for the functions has been added (Appendix B) showing the dependencies among the functions. Despite requests from some readers, we have *not* added oddities such as the World Calendar [1], Star Trek's stardate [11], Knuth's Potrzebie calendar [8], the pataphysique calendar [7], or the Martian calendar [5]!

Algorithmically sophisticated readers of the first edition of this book could, with only slight difficulty, jump right into the descriptions of the various calendars, skipping the introductory chapter on "Calendar Basics." With each successive edition such an omission became more difficult as various commonalities were moved to that chapter and the notations became more specialized. As much as we regret it, failing to read the introduction now may cause even a sophisticated reader bafflement in later chapters. So, for those without the patience to read the introductory chapter, we suggest at least a careful perusing of the "Mathematical Notations" table on pages xxvi–xxviii.

> *I determined, therefore, to attempt the reformation; I consulted the best lawyers and the most skilled astronomers, and we cooked up a bill for that purpose. But then my difficulty began: I was to bring in this bill, which was necessarily composed of law jargon and astronomical calculations, to both of which I am an utter stranger. However, it was absolutely necessary to make the House of Lords think that I knew something of the matter; and also to make them believe that they knew something themselves, which they do not. For my own part, I could just as soon have talked Celtic or Sclavonian to them, as astronomy, and could have understood me full as well; so I resolved . . . to please instead of informing them. I gave them, therefore, only an historical account of calendars, from the Egyptian*

down to the Gregorian, amusing them now and then with little episodes… They thought I was informed, because I pleased them; and many of them said, that I had made the whole story very clear to them; when, God knows, I had not even attempted it.

Letter from Philip Dormer Stanhope (Fourth Earl of Chesterfield, the man who in 1751 introduced the bill in Parliament for reforming the calendar in England) to his son, March 18, 1751 C.E. (Julian), the day of the Second Reading debate

Calendrical Tabulations

A man who possessed a calendar and could read it was an important member of the village community, certain to be widely consulted and suitably awarded.

K. Tseng: "Balinese Calendar," *Myths & Symbols in Indonesian Art* (1991)

A companion volume by the authors, *Calendrical Tabulations*, is also available. It contains tables for easy conversion of dates and some holidays on the world's major calendars (Gregorian, Hebrew, Islamic, Hindu, Chinese, Coptic/Ethiopic, and Persian) for the years 1900–2200. These tables were computed using the Lisp functions from Appendix B of the Millennium Edition and typeset directly from LaTeX output produced by driver code. Small changes made to the astronomical code in the interim can cause minor discrepancies in dates and times.[1]

The Cambridge University Press Web Site

Exegi monumentum aere perennius. [*I have created a monument more lasting than bronze.*]

Horace: *Odes,* III, xxx

`www.cambridge.org/calendricalcalculations`

This web site contains links to files related to this book, including the Lisp code from Appendix D for the calendar functions and the sample data from Appendix C.

The Authors' Web Site

The author has tried to indicate every known blemish in [2]*; and he hopes that nobody will ever scrutinize any of his own writings as meticulously as he and others have examined the ALGOL report.*

Donald E. Knuth: "The Remaining Trouble Spots in ALGOL 60," *Communications of the ACM* (1967)

Visit us at

`www.calendarists.com`

[1] The following minor errors regarding lunar phases in *Calendrical Tabulations* bear noting: First, the dust jacket uses a negative image of the calendar pages; this has the effect of interchanging the full/new moon symbols and the first quarter/last quarter symbols visible in the Gregorian calendar at the middle bottom. Second, when a lunar phase (or equinox or solstice) occurs seconds before midnight, the date is correctly indicated, but the time is rounded up to midnight and shown as 0:00 instead of 24:00. Finally, when two lunar phases occur during the same week, the times given in the right margin are in reverse order.

Among other things, one can find errata for this book at this address. Try as we have, at least one error remains in this book.

Acknowledgments

It is traditional for the author to magnanimously accept the blame for whatever deficiencies remain. I don't. Any errors, deficiencies, or problems in this book are somebody else's fault, but I would appreciate knowing about them so as to determine who is to blame.

Steven Skiena: *The Algorithm Design Manual* (1997)

Stewart M. Clamen wrote an early version of the Mayan calendar code. Parts of Section 2.3 are based on suggestions by Michael H. Deckers. Chapters 6 and 21 are based in part on the work of Svante Janson.

Our preparation of the fourth edition was aided considerably by the help of Mark D. Bej, Uri Blass, Irvin L. Bromberg, Assaf Cohen, William P. Collins, Craig Dedo, Ben Denckla, Idan Dershowitz, Surya Prasad Dhungel, Tony Finch, Gedalya Gordon, Julian Gilbey, Eysteinn Guðni Guðnason, Peter Zilahy Ingerman, Svante Janson, Kaboel Karso, Eric Kingston, Kwasi Konadu, Stanislav Koncebovski, Kai Kuhlmann, Jonathan Leffler, Yaaqov Loewinger, Zhuo Meng, Susan Milbrath, Josua Müller, Fabrice Orgogozo, Andy Pepperdine, John Powers, Eugene Quah, Lester A. Reingold, Ruth N. Reingold, Dieter Schuh, Matthew Sheby, Enrico Spinielli, Sacha Stern, Sharad Upadhyay, Robert H. van Gent, Nadia Vidro, Steve Ward, and Alan R. White, all of whom pointed out errors, suggested improvements, and helped gather materials. Special thanks go to our copy editor Susan S. Parkinson who went carefully through every every detail of the book and provided many invaluable corrections. We also thank all those acknowledged in the prior editions for their help.

Gerald M. Browne, Sharat Chandran, Shigang Chen, Jeffrey L. Copeland, Idan Dershowitz, Nazli Goharian, Mayer Goldberg, Getatchew Haile, Shiho Inui, Yoshiyasu Ishigami, Howard Jacobson, Subhash Kak, Claude Kirchner, Sakai Kō, Jungmin Lee, Nabeel Naser El-deen, Gerhard A. Nothmann, Trần Đức Ngọc, Sigurður Örn Stefánsson, Fentahun Tiruneh, Roman Waupotitsch, Daniel Yaqob, and Afra Zomorodian helped us with various translations and foreign language fonts. Charles Hoot labored hard on the original program for automatically transforming Lisp code into arithmetic expressions and provided general expertise in Lisp. Mitchell A. Harris helped with fonts, star names, and the automatic translation; Matthew Carroll, Benita Ulisano, and Upendra Gandhi were our system support people; Marla Brownfield helped with various tables. Herbert Voss modified PSTricks several times to enable us to produce various figures. Erga Dershowitz, Idan Dershowitz, Molly Flesner, Schulamith Halevy, Deborah Klapper, Eve Kleinerman, Rachel Mandel, Ruth Reingold, Christine Mumm, and Joyce Woodworth were invaluable in proofreading tens of thousands of dates, comparing our results with published tables. We are grateful to all of them.

Portions of this book appeared, in a considerably less polished state, in our papers [3] and [13]. We thank John Wiley & Sons for allowing us to use that material here.

The second author is grateful to the Institut d'études avancées de Paris for the conducive environment it provided during the last stages of preparation of this edition.

> *THE END.*
> *This work was completed on the 17th or 27th day of May, 1618; but Book v was reread (while the type was being set) on the 9th or 19th of February, 1619. At Linz, the capital of Austria—above the Enns.*
>
> Johannes Kepler: *Harmonies of the World*

> *I have not always executed my own scheme, or satisfied my own expectations ... [But] I look with pleasure on my book however defective and deliver it to the world with the spirit of a man that has endeavored well ... When it shall be found that much is omitted, let it not be forgotten that much likewise has been performed.*
>
> Samuel Johnson: Preface to his *Dictionary*

R.D. 736520
Chicago, Illinois — E.M.R.
Tel Aviv, Israel — N.D.

References

> *A book without a preface is like a body without a soul.*
>
> Hebrew proverb

[1] The World Calendar Association, www.theworldcalendar.org.

[2] A. Birashk, *A Comparative Calendar of the Iranian, Muslim Lunar, and Christian Eras for Three Thousand Years*, Mazda Publishers (in association with Bibliotheca Persica), Costa Mesa, CA, 1993.

[3] N. Dershowitz and E. M. Reingold, "Calendrical Calculations," *Software—Practice and Experience*, vol. 20, no. 9, pp. 899–928, September 1990.

[4] N. Dershowitz and E. M. Reingold, "Modulo Intervals: A Proposed Notation," *ACM SIGACT News*, vol. 43, no. 3, pp. 60–64, 2012.

[5] N. Dershowitz and E. M. Reingold, "A Terrestrial Calendar for Mars (Abstract)," *Program Book of The Founding Convention of the Mars Society*, The University of Colorado at Boulder, pp. 117–118, 1998.

[6] C. F. Gauss, "Berechnung des jüdischen Osterfestes," *Monatliche Correspondenz zur Beförderung der Erd- und Himmelskunde*, vol. 5 (1802), pp. 435–437. Reprinted in Gauss's *Werke*, Herausgegeben von der Königlichen Gesellschaft der Wissenschaften, Göttingen, vol. VI, pp. 80–81, 1874; republished, Georg Olms Verlag, Hildesheim, 1981.

[7] A. Jarry, *Ubu à l'Anvers*, Rossaert, Antwerp, 1997.

[8] D. E. Knuth, "The Potrzebie System of Weights and Measures," *MAD Magazine*, vol. 1, no. 33, pp. 36–37, June 1957. Reprinted in Knuth's *Selected Papers on Fun & Games*, Center for the Study of Language and Information, Stanford University, Stanford, CA, 2011.

[9] D. E. Knuth, *The Art of Computer Programming, vol. 2: Seminumerical Algorithms*, 3rd edn., Addison-Wesley Publishing Company, Reading, MA, 1998.

[10] P. G. Neumann, "Inside Risks: The Clock Grows at Midnight," *Communications of the ACM*, vol. 34, no. 1, p. 170, January 1991.

[11] M. Okuda, and D. Okuda, *Star Trek Chronology: The History of the Future*, revised edn., Pocket Books, NY, 1996.

[12] F. Parise, ed., *The Book of Calendars*, Facts on File, New York, 1982.

[13] E. M. Reingold, N. Dershowitz, and S. M. Clamen, "Calendrical Calculations, Part II: Three Historical Calendars," *Software—Practice and Experience*, vol. 23, no. 4, pp. 383–404, April 1993.

[14] I. Rhodes, "Computation of the Dates of the Hebrew New Year and Passover," *Computers & Mathematics with Applications*, vol. 3, pp. 183–190, 1977.

[15] R. M. Stallman, *GNU Emacs Manual*, 13th edn., Free Software Foundation, Cambridge, MA, 1997.

[16] G. L. Steele, Jr., G. L. Steele, Jr., COMMON LISP: *The Language*, 2nd edn., Digital Press, Bedford, MA, 1990.

[17] K. Wilkins, Letter to Nachum Dershowitz from a Customer Relations Representative, Lotus Development Corporation, Cambridge, MA, April 21, 1992.

La dernière chose qu'on trouve en faisant un ouvrage, est de savoir celle qu'il faut mettre la première. [*The last thing one settles in writing a book is what one should put in first.*]

Blaise Pascal: *Pensées sur l'esprit et le style* (1660)

Credits

Whoever relates something in the name of its author brings redemption to the world.

Midrash Tanḥuma (Numbers, 27)

Photograph of Edward M. Reingold on the dust jacket is by Photography by Rick & Rich (Northbrook, IL, 2014); used with permission.

Photograph of Nachum Dershowitz on the dust jacket is by Olivier Toussaint (Nancy, 2011); used with permission.

Quote on page xxxi from *Epistles of Maimonides: Crisis and Leadership*, A. Halkin, trans., Jewish Publication Society, 1993; used with permission.

Translation of Scaliger's comment on the Roman calendar on page 75 is from A. T. Grafton, *Joseph Scaliger: A Study in the History of Classical Scholarship, vol. II, Historical Chronography*, Oxford University Press, Oxford, 1993; used with permission.

Translation of Ptolemy III's *Canopus Decree* on page 92 is from page 90 of R. Hannah, *Greek & Roman Calendars*, Gerald Duckworth & Co., London, 2005; used with permission.

Translation on page 114 of Scaliger's comment on the Hebrew calendar (found on page 294 of Book 7 in the 1593 Frankfort edition of *De Emendatione Temporum*) is by H. Jacobson; used with permission.

Translation of "The Synodal Letter" on page 143 (found in Gelasius, *Historia Concilii Nicæni*, book II, Chapter xxxiii) is from J. K. Fotheringham, "The Calendar," in *The Nautical Almanac and Astronomical Ephemeris*, His Majesty's Stationery Office, London, 1931–1934; revised 1935–1938; abridged 1939–1941.

Translation of the extract from Canon 6 of Gregorian reform on page 145 is by M. H. Deckers; used with permission.

Translation of the Quintus Curtius Rufus quotation on page 257 is from J. C. Rolfe, *History of Alexander*, Harvard University Press, Cambridge, MA, 1946.

Translation of Ovid quotation on page 259 is from J. G. Frazer, *Ovid's Fasti*, Harvard University Press, Cambridge, MA, 1931.

Letter on page 273 reprinted with permission.

License and Limited Warranty and Remedy

The Functions (code, formulas, and calendar data) contained in this book and/or provided on the publisher's web site for this book were written by Nachum Dershowitz and Edward M. Reingold (the "Authors"), who retain all rights to them except as granted in the License and subject to the warranty and liability limitations below. These Functions are subject to this book's copyright.

In case there is cause for doubt about whether a use you contemplate is authorized, please contact the Authors.

1. LICENSE. The Authors grant you a license for personal use. This means that for strictly personal use you may copy and use the code and keep a backup or archival copy also. The Authors grant you a license for re-use within non-commercial, non-profit software provided prominent credit is given and the Authors' rights are preserved. Any other uses, including, without limitation, allowing the code or its output to be accessed, used, or available to others, are not permitted.
2. WARRANTY.
   (a) *The Authors and Publisher provide no warranties of any kind, either express or implied, including, without limiting the generality of the foregoing, any implied warranty of merchantability or fitness for a particular purpose.*
   (b) *Neither the Authors nor Publisher shall be liable to you or any third parties for damages of any kind, including without limitation, any lost profits, lost savings, or other incidental or consequential damages arising out of, or related to, the use, inability to use, or accuracy of calculations of the code and functions contained herein, or the breach of any express or implied warranty, even if the Authors or Publisher have been advised of the possibility of those damages.*
   (c) *The foregoing warranty may give you specific legal rights which may vary from state to state in the U.S.A.*
3. LIMITATION OF LICENSEE REMEDIES. You acknowledge and agree that your exclusive remedy (in law or in equity), and Authors' and Publisher's entire liability with respect to the material herein, for any breach of representation or for any inaccuracy shall be a refund of the price of this book. *Some States in the U.S.A. do not allow the exclusion or limitation of liability for incidental or consequential damages, and thus the preceding exclusions or limitation may not apply to you.*

4. DISCLAIMER. Except as expressly set forth above, the Authors and Publisher:

   (a) make no other warranties with respect to the material and expressly disclaim any others;

   (b) do not warrant that the functions contained in the code will meet your requirements or that their operation shall be uninterrupted or error free;

   (c) license this material on an "as is" basis, and the entire risk as to the quality, accuracy, and performance herein is yours should the code or functions prove defective (except as expressly warranted herein). You alone assume the entire cost of all necessary corrections.

MENSIVM DIVISIO.

MENSES ENNEADECAETERICI.

IVDÆORVM	SYROCHALDAEORVM	SYROGRÆCORVM	HAGARENORVM.	CALIPPI ET METONIS.	SAXONVM
TISRI	TISRIN prior	DIVS	RABIE prior	Pyanepsion	Wintyrfyllith
Marche-	Tisrin alter	Apellæus	Rabie alter	Mæmacterion	Blothmonath
schwan	Canum prior	Audynæus	Giumadi prior	Posideon	Giuli prior
Casleu	Canum alter	Peritius	Giumadi alter	Gamelion	Giuli posterior
Tebeth	Aschbat	Dystrus	Regiabu	Anthesterion	Solmonath
Schebat	Adar	Xanthicus	Sahabenu	Elaphebolion	Rethmonath
Adar prior	Nisan	Artemisius	Ramadhan	Munychion	Chosturmonath
Adar po-	Ijar	Dæsius	Schewal	Thargelion	Trimilchi
sterior	HaZiran	Panemus	Dulkaida	Scirrhophoriō	Lida prior
Nisan	Tamuz	Lous	Dulhagia	prior	Lida posterior
Ijar	Ab	Gorpiæus	Muharam	Scirrhophoriō	Lida embolimus
Siwan	Ilul	Dioscurus emb.	Tzephar	alter	Wendenmonath
Tamuz	Teboch embol.	HYPERBE-	Tzephar embol.	HECATOM-	HALEGMO-
Ab		RETÆVS		BÆON	NATH.
Elul				Metagitnion	
				Boedromion	

MENSES ÆQVABILES VAGI

ÆGYPTIORVM	ARMENIORVM	PERSARVM
THOTH	Nawasarni	Behemen
Paophi	Hori	Asphandar
Athyr	Musterak	Musteraka
Choiac	SAHAMI	PHRVRDIN
Tybi	Thert	Adarpahaschth
Mechir	Caguts	Chardad
Phamenoth	Harats	Thir
Pharmuthi	Mahic	Mardad
Pachon	Arich	Scheheriz
Payni	Abeli	Mehar
Epiphi	Mariri	Aban
Mesori	Marcats	Adar
Epagomenæ	Harwatsis	Di

MENSES ÆQVABILES TETRAETERICI

ATTICORVM	MACEDONVM	THEBANORVM
GAMELION	Dystrus	BVCATIVS
Anthesterion	Xanthicus	Hermæus
Elaphebolion	Artemisius	★ ★
Munychion	Dæsius prior	★ ★
Thargelion	Dæsius posterior	★ ★
Scirrhophorion	Ἄναρχοι duæ	
Hecatombæon	PANEMVS	Hippodromius
Metagitnion	Lous	Panemus
Boedromion	Gorpiæus	★ ★
Pyanepsion	Hyperberetæus	Damatrios
Mæmacterion	Dius	Alalcomenios
Posideon prior	Apellæus	★ ★
Posideon alter	Audynæus	Embolimus
Ἄναρχοι duæ	Peritius	Ἄναρχοι duæ

MEN-

MENSES IVLIANI.

ROMANORVM.	ATHENIENSIVM.	SYROGRÆCORVM.	ANTIOCHENORVM.	HAGARENORVM.
IANVARIVS	Pyanepsion	Audynæus	Canum alter	Giumadi alter
Februarius	Mæmacterion	Peritius	Aschbat	Regiab
Martius	Posideon	Dystrus	Adar	Sahaben
Aprilis	Gamelion	Xanthicus	Nisan	Ramadhan
Maius	Anthesterion	Artemisius	Ijar	Schewal
Iunius	Elaphebolion	Dæsius	HaZiran	Dulkaida
Iulius	Munychion	Panemus	Tamuz	Dulchechia
Augustus	Thargelion	Lous	Ab	Muharam
September	Scirrhophorion	Gorpiæus	Elul	Tzephar
October	HECATOM-	HYPERBE-	TISRIN prior	RABIE prior
Nouember	BÆON	RETÆVS	Tisrin alter	Rabie alter
December	Metagitnion	Dius	Canum prior	Giumadi prior
	Boedromion	Apellæus		

MISCELA MENSIVM.

MENSES VAGI LVNARES.	MENSES VITIOSI LVNARES.	MENSES SOLARES IVLIANI æquabiles.	MENSES TROPICI ÆQVABILES Gelalæi.	MENSES COELESTES VITIOSI.
MVHAMETANORVM.	ROMANORVM.	KOPTITARVM.	PERSARVM.	PTOLOMÆI PHILADELPHI.
MVHARAM	MARTIVS	THOTH	Aban	Zygon
Tzephar	Aprilis	Papa	Adar	Scorpion
Rabie prior	Maius	Hathur	Di	Toxon
Rabie alter ❋	Iunius	Chiac	Behemen	Aegon
Giumadi prior	Quintilis	Tuba	Asphander	Hydron
Giumadi alter	Sextilis	Amschir	Musteraka	Ichthyon
Regiab	September	Parmahath	PHRVRDIN	Quadrans diei
Sahaben	October	Parmudá	Adarpahaschth	KRION
Ramadhan	Nouember	Paschnes	Chardad	Tauron
Shewal	December	Penni	Thir	Didymon
Dulkaida	Ianuarius	Epip	Mardad	Karkinon
Dulchegia	Februarius	Musri	Scheheriz	Leonton
	Mercedonius	Nisi	Mehar	Parthenon

Ii 4

Two pages of Joseph Scaliger's, *De Emendatione Temporum* (Frankfort edition, 1593), giving month names on many calendars. (Courtesy of the University of Illinois, Urbana, IL.)

1

Calendar Basics

A learned man once asked me regarding the eras used by different nations, and regarding the difference of their roots, that is, the epochs where they begin, and of their branches, that is, the months and years, on which they are based; further regarding the causes which led to such difference, and the famous festivals and commemoration-days for certain times and events, and regarding whatever else one nation practices differently from another. He urged me to give an explanation, the clearest possible, of all this, so as to be easily intelligible to the mind of the reader, and to free him from the necessity of wading through widely scattered books, and of consulting their authors. Now I was quite aware that this was a task difficult to handle, an object not easily to be attained or managed by anyone, who wants to treat it as a matter of logical sequence, regarding which the mind of the student is not agitated by doubt.

Abū-Raiḥān Muḥammad ibn 'Aḥmad al-Bīrūnī:
Al-Āthār al-Bāqiyah 'an al-Qurūn al-Khāliyah (1000)

Calendrical calculations are ubiquitous. Banks need to calculate interest on a daily basis. Corporations issue paychecks on weekly, biweekly, or monthly schedules. Bills and statements must be generated periodically. Computer operating systems need to switch to and from daylight saving time. Dates of secular and religious holidays must be computed for consideration in planning events. Most of these calculations are not difficult because the rules of our civil calendar (the Gregorian calendar) are straightforward.

Complications begin when we need to know the day of the week on which a given date falls or when various religious holidays based on other calendars occur. These complications lead to difficult programming tasks—not often difficult in an algorithmic sense but difficult because it can be extremely tedious to delve into, for example, the complexities of the Hebrew calendar and its relation to the civil calendar.

The purpose of this book is to present, in a unified, completely algorithmic form, a description of over three dozen calendars and how they relate to one another. Among them are included the present civil calendar (Gregorian); the recent ISO commercial calendar; the old civil calendar (Julian); the ancient Egyptian calendar and its Armenian equivalent; the Coptic and the virtually identical Ethiopic calendars; the Akan (African) calendar, the Islamic (Muslim) calendar (the arithmetical version, one based on calculated lunar observability, and a

Saudi Arabian variant); the modern Persian calendar (both astronomical and arithmetic forms); the Bahá'í calendar, both arithmetic and astronomical forms; the Hebrew (Jewish) calendar, both its present arithmetical form and a speculative observational form; the three Mayan calendars and two virtually identical Aztec calendars; the Pawukon calendar from Bali; the French Revolutionary calendar (both astronomical and arithmetic forms); the Chinese calendar and the virtually identical Japanese, Korean, and Vietnamese calendars; both the old (mean) and new (true) Hindu (Indian) solar and lunisolar calendars; and the Tibetan calendar. Information that is sufficiently detailed to allow computer implementation is difficult to find for most of these calendars because the published material is often inaccessible, ecclesiastically oriented, incomplete, inaccurate, based on extensive tables, overburdened with extraneous material, focused on shortcuts for hand calculation to avoid complicated arithmetic or to check results, or difficult to find in English. Most existing computer programs are proprietary, incomplete, or inaccurate.

The need for such a secular, widely available presentation was made clear to us when we (primarily E.M.R., with contributions by N.D.), in implementing a calendar/diary feature for GNU Emacs [44], found difficulty in gathering and interpreting appropriate source materials that describe the interrelationships among the various calendars and the determination of the dates of holidays. Some of the calendars (Chinese, Japanese, Korean, Vietnamese, Hindu, and Tibetan) had never had full algorithmic descriptions published in English.

The calendar algorithms in this book are presented as mathematical function definitions in standard mathematical format. Appendix A gives the types (ranges and domains) of all functions and constants we use; Appendix B is a cross reference list that gives all dependencies among the functions and constants. In Appendix C we tabulate results of the calendar calculations for 33 sample dates and 44 holidays; this will aid those who develop their own implementations of our calendar functions. To ensure correctness, all calendar functions were automatically typeset[1] directly from the working Common Lisp [46] functions given in Appendix D.[2]

We chose mathematical notation as the vehicle for presentation because of its universality and easy convertibility to any programming language. We have endeavored to simplify the calculations as much as possible without obscuring the intuition. Many of the algorithms we provide are considerably more concise than previously published ones; this is particularly true of the arithmetic Persian, Hebrew, and old Hindu calendars.

We chose Lisp as the vehicle for implementation because it encourages functional programming and has a trivial syntax, nearly self-evident semantics, historical durability, and wide distribution; moreover, Lisp was amenable to translation into ordinary mathematical notation. Except for a few short macros, the code uses

---

[1] This has meant some sacrifice in the typography of the book; we hope readers sympathize with our decision.

[2] The Lisp code is available through a Cambridge University Press web site `www.cambridge.org/calendricalcalculations` under the terms of the License Agreements and Limited Warranty on page xli. Any errata are available over the World Wide Web at `www.calendarists.com`.

only a very simple, side-effect-free, subset of Lisp. We emphasize that our choice of Lisp should be considered irrelevant to most readers, whom we expect to follow the mathematical notation used in the text, not to delve into the code.

It is not the purpose of this book to give a detailed historical treatment of the material, nor, for that matter, a mathematical one; our goal is to give a logical, thorough, *computational* treatment. Thus, although we give much historical, religious, mathematical, and astronomical data to leaven the discussion, the focus of the presentation is algorithmic. Full historical and religious details as well as the mathematical and astronomical underpinnings of the calendars can be pursued in the references.

In this chapter, we describe the underlying unifying theme of all the calculations along with some useful mathematical facts. The details of specific calendars are presented in subsequent chapters. Historically, the oldest calendars that we consider are the Egyptian (more than 3000 years old) and Babylonian. The Chinese and Mayan calendars also derive from millennia-old calendars. Next are the classical (observation-based) Hebrew, the Julian (the roots of which date back to the ancient Roman empire), the Coptic and Ethiopic (third century), the current Hebrew (fourth century) and the old Hindu (fifth century), followed by the Islamic calendar (seventh century), the newer Hindu calendars (tenth century), the Persian and Tibetan calendars (eleventh century), the Gregorian modification to the Julian calendar (sixteenth century), the French Revolutionary calendar (eighteenth century), and the Bahá'í calendar (nineteenth century). Finally, the International Organization for Standardization's ISO calendar and the arithmetic Persian calendar are of twentieth-century origin.

For expository purposes, however, we present the Gregorian calendar first, in Part I, because it is the most popular calendar currently in use. Because the Julian calendar is so close in substance to the Gregorian, we present it next, followed by the very similar Coptic and Ethiopic calendars. Then we give the ISO calendar and the Icelandic calendar, which are trivial to implement and depend wholly on the Gregorian. The arithmetic Islamic calendar, which because of its simplicity is easy to implement, follows. Next, we present the Hebrew calendar, one of the more complicated and difficult calendars to implement. This is followed by a chapter on the computation of Easter, which is lunisolar like the Hebrew calendar. The ancient Hindu solar and lunisolar calendars are described next; these are simple versions of the modern Hindu solar and lunisolar calendars described in Part II. Next come the Mayan and similar Aztec calendars of historical interest, which have several unique computational aspects. These are followed by the Balinese Pawukon calendar. All the calendars described in Part I are "arithmetical" in that they operate by straightforward integer-based rules. We conclude Part I with a chapter describing the generic arithmetic calendar schemata that apply to many calendars in this part.

In Part II we present calendars that are controlled by irregular astronomical events (or close approximations to them), although these calendars may have an arithmetical component as well. Because the calendars in Part II require some understanding of astronomical events such as solstices, equinoxes, and lunar phases, we begin Part II with a chapter introducing the topics and algorithms that will be needed. We then give the modern Persian calendar in its astronomical and arithmetic forms followed by the Bahá'í calendar, also in two versions: the former Western (arithmetic) version, which depends wholly on the Gregorian, and the new astronomical version. Next we describe the original (astronomical) and modified (arithmetic) forms of the French Revolutionary calendar. All these calendars are computationally simple, provided that certain astronomical values are available. Next we describe some astronomical calendars based on the moon: the Babylonian calendar, a proposed astronomical calculation of Easter, the observational Islamic calendar, and the classical Hebrew calendar. We continue with the Chinese lunisolar calendar and its Japanese, Korean, and Vietnamese versions. We then describe the modern Hindu calendars, which are by far the most complicated of the calendars in this book. We conclude with the Tibetan calendar.

We also provide algorithms for computing holidays based on most of the calendars. In this regard we take the ethnocentric view that our task is to compute the dates of holidays in a given *Gregorian year*; there is clearly little difficulty in finding the dates of, say, Islamic New Year in a given Islamic year! In general we have tried to mention significant holidays on the calendars we cover but have not attempted to be exhaustive and to include all variations. The interested reader can find extensive holiday definitions in [22], [23], and [24].

The selection of calendars we present was chosen with two purposes: to include all common modern calendars and to cover all calendrical techniques. We do not give all variants of the calendars we discuss, but we have given enough details to make any calendar easy to implement.

1.1 Calendar Units and Taxonomy

Teach us to number our days, that we may attain a wise heart.
Psalms 90:12

The sun moves from east to west, and night follows day with predictable regularity. This apparent motion of the sun as viewed by an earthbound observer provided the earliest time-keeping standard for humankind. The day is, accordingly, the basic unit of time underlying all calendars, but various calendars use different conventions to structure days into larger units: weeks, months, years, and cycles of years. Different calendars also begin their day at different times: the French Revolutionary day, for example, begins at true (apparent) midnight; the Islamic, Bahá'í, and Hebrew days begin at sunset; the Hindu day begins at sunrise. The various definitions of *day* are surveyed in Section 14.3.

The purpose of a calendar is to give a name to each day. The mathematically simplest naming convention would be to assign an integer to each day; fixing day 1 would determine the whole calendar. The Babylonians had such a day count (in base 60). Such *diurnal* calendars are used by astronomers (see Section 14.3) and by calendarists (see, for example, Section 10.1); we use a day numbering in this book as an intermediate device for converting from one calendar to another (see the following section). Day-numbering schemes can be complicated by using a mixed-radix system [28] in which the day number is given as a sequence of numbers or names (see Section 1.10). The Mayans, for example, utilized such a method (see Section 11.1).

Calendar day names are generally distinct, but this is not always the case. For example, the day of the week is a calendar, in a trivial sense, with infinitely many days having the same day name (see Section 1.12). A 7-day week is almost universal today. In many cultures, the days of the week were named after the seven "wandering stars" (or after the gods associated with those heavenly bodies), namely, the sun, the moon, and the five planets visible to the naked eye—Mercury, Venus, Mars, Jupiter, and Saturn. In some languages—Arabic, Lithuanian, Portuguese, Ukrainian, and Hebrew are examples—some or all of the days of the week are numbered, not named. In the Armenian calendar, for example, the days of the week are named as follows [22, vol. 3, p. 70]:

Sunday	Kiraki (or Miashabathi)
Monday	Erkoushabathi
Tuesday	Erekhshabathi
Wednesday	Chorekhshabathi
Thursday	Hingshabathi
Friday	Urbath (or Vetsshabathi)
Saturday	Shabath

"Shabath" means "day of rest" (from the Hebrew), "Miashabathi" means the first day following the day of rest, "Erkoushabathi" is the second day following the day of rest, and so on. The Armenian Christian church later renamed "Vetsshabathi" as "Urbath," meaning "to get ready for the day of rest." Subsequently, they declared the first day of the week as "Kiraki" or "the Lord's day."

Other cycles of days have also been used, including 4-day weeks (in the Congo), 5-day weeks (in other parts of Africa, in Bali, and in Russia in 1929), 6-day weeks (Japan), 8-day weeks (in yet other parts of Africa and in the Roman Republic), and 10-day weeks (in ancient Egypt and in France at the end of the eighteenth century; see page 282). The mathematics of cycles of days are described in Section 1.12. Many calendars repeat after one or more years. In one of the Mayan calendars (see Section 11.2), and in many preliterate societies, day names are recycled every year. The Chinese calendar uses a repeating 60-name scheme for days and years, and at one time used it to name months.

An interesting variation in some calendars is the use of two or more cycles running simultaneously. For example, the Mayan tzolkin calendar (Section 11.2) combines a cycle of 13 names with a cycle of 20 numbers. The Chinese cycle of 60 names for years is actually composed of cycles of length 10 and 12 (see Section 19.4). The Balinese calendar takes this idea to an extreme; see Chapter 12. The mathematics of simultaneous cycles is described in Section 1.13.

The notions of "month" and "year," like the day, were originally based on observations of heavenly phenomena, namely the waxing and waning of the moon, and the cycle of seasons, respectively. The lunar cycle formed the basis for the palaeolithic marking of time (see [32] and [13]), and many calendars today begin each month with the new moon, when the crescent moon first becomes visible (as in the Hebrew calendar of classical times and in the religious calendar of the Muslims today—see Sections 14.9 and 18.4); others begin the month at full moon (in northern India, for example)—see page 160. For calendars in which the month begins with the observed new moon, beginning the day at sunset is natural.

Over the course of history, many different schemes have been devised for determining the start of the year, usually based on the solar cycle.[3] Some are astronomical, beginning at the autumnal or spring equinox, or at the winter or summer solstice. Solstices are more readily observable; either one can note when the midday shadow of a gnomon is longest (at the winter solstice in the northern hemisphere) or shortest (at the summer solstice) or one can note the point in time when the sun rises or sets the farthest south during the course of the year (which is the start of winter in the northern hemisphere) or the farthest north (the start of summer). The ancient Egyptians began their year with the *heliacal rising* of Sirius—that is, on the day when the Dog Star Sirius (the brightest fixed star in the sky) can first be seen in the morning after a period during which the sun's proximity to Sirius makes the latter invisible to the naked eye. The Pleiades ("Seven Sisters") were used by the Maoris and other peoples for the same purpose. Various other natural phenomena such as harvests or the rutting seasons of certain animals have been used among North American tribes [9] to establish the onset of a new year. And not just humans use such phenomena: the lunar cycle determines life cycle events for certain corals [7], birds [43], and monkeys [30]. It has also been suggested [10] that the pink "skylight" on the crown of the head of leatherback turtles serves to allow them to determine when in late summer the lengths of day and night are equal (taking refraction into account), at which point foraging turtles turn south.

Calendars have, of necessity, an integral number of days in a month and an integral number of months in a year. However, these astronomical periods—day, month, and year—are incommensurate: their periods do not form integral multiples of one another. The lunar month is about $29\frac{1}{2}$ days long, and the solar year is about $365\frac{1}{4}$ days long (Chapter 14 has precise definitions and values). How exactly one coordinates these time periods and the accuracy with which they approximate their astronomical values is what differentiates one calendar from another.

Broadly speaking, solar calendars—including the Egyptian, Armenian, Persian, Gregorian, Julian, Coptic, Ethiopic, ISO, French Revolutionary, and Bahá'í —are based on the yearly solar cycle, whereas lunar and lunisolar calendars—such as the Islamic, Hebrew, Hindu, Tibetan, and Chinese—take the monthly lunar cycle as their basic building block. Most solar calendars are divided into months, but these months are divorced from the lunar events; they are sometimes related to the movement of the sun through the 12 signs of the zodiac, notably in the Hindu solar calendars (see Chapter 20).

Because observational methods suffer from vagaries of weather and chance, they have for the most part been supplanted by calculations. The simplest option

[3] It has been claimed that in equatorial regions, where the tropical year is not of paramount agricultural importance, arbitrary year lengths are more prevalent, such as are found in the 210-day Balinese Pawukon calendar (Chapter 12) and the 260-day Mayan divine year (Section 11.2).

is to approximate the length of the year, of the month, or of both. Originally, the Babylonian solar calendar was based on 12 months of 30 days each (see [26]), overestimating the length of the month and underestimating the year; see Figure 1.1. Such a calendar is easy to calculate, but each month begins at a slightly later lunar phase than the previous, and the seasons move forward slowly through the year. The ancient Egyptian calendar achieved greater accuracy by having 12 months of 30 days plus 5 extra days—Egyptian mythology includes a tale of how the calendar came to have these five extra days [3]. Conversions for this calendar are illustrated in Section 1.11. To achieve better correlation with the motion of the moon, one can instead alternate months of 29 and 30 days. Twelve such months, however, amount to 354 days—more than 11 days short of the solar year.

Almost every calendar in this book and virtually all other calendars incorporate a notion of "leap" year to deal with the cumulative error caused by approximating a year by an integral number of days and months.[4] Solar calendars add a day every few years to keep up with the astronomical year. The calculations are simplest when the leap years are evenly distributed and the numbers involved are small; for instance, the Julian, Coptic, and Ethiopic calendars add 1 day every 4 years. Formulas for the evenly distributed case, such as when one has a leap year every fourth or fifth year, are derived in Section 1.14. The old Hindu solar calendar (Chapter 10) follows such a pattern; the arithmetical Persian calendar almost does (see Chapter 15). The Gregorian calendar, however, uses an uneven distribution of leap years but a relatively easy-to-remember rule (see Chapter 2). The modified French Revolutionary calendar (Chapter 17) included an even more accurate but uneven rule.

Most lunar calendars incorporate the notion of a year. Purely lunar calendars may approximate the solar year with 12 lunar months (as does the Islamic), though this is about 11 days short of the astronomical year. Lunisolar calendars invariably alternate 12- and 13-month years, according either to some fixed rule (as in the Hebrew calendar) or to an astronomically determined pattern (Chinese and modern Hindu). The so-called *Metonic cycle* is based on the observation that 19 solar years contain almost exactly 235 lunar months. This correspondence, named after the Athenian astronomer Meton (who published it in 432 B.C.E.) and known much earlier to ancient Babylonian and Chinese astronomers, makes a relatively simple and accurate fixed solar/lunar calendar feasible. The $235 = 12 \times 12 + 7 \times 13$ months in the cycle are divided into 12 years of 12 months and 7 leap years of 13 months. The Metonic cycle is used in the Hebrew calendar (Chapter 8) and for the calculation of Easter (Chapter 9).

The more precise the mean year, the larger the underlying constants must be. For example the Metonic cycle is currently accurate to within 6.5 minutes a year, but other lunisolar cycles are conceivable: 3 solar years are approximately 37 lunar months with an error of 1 day per year; 8 years are approximately 99 months with an error of 5 hours per year; 11 years are approximately 136 months with

[4] See [6, pp. 677–678] for a discussion of the etymology of the term "leap."

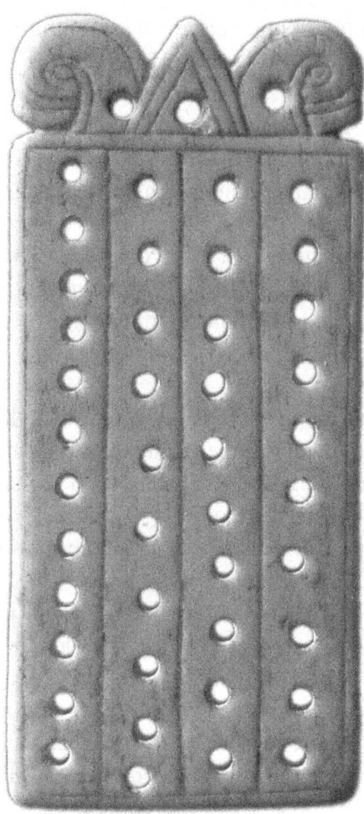

Figure 1.1 A small (6 × 2.7 cm) bone plaque found in Tel ‘Aroer, an Iron Age II (8th–6th century B.C.E.) caravan town in the Negev, Israel. It is conjectured to be a calendar counter: a peg could move daily through the 30 holes in the three right-hand columns of 10 holes each, while another peg moved monthly through the 12 holes in the first column. It could have been used either as a schematic 360-day calendar or as a lunar calendar, in which case some months would end after 29 days [14]. (Reproduced courtesy of the Hebrew Union College, Jerusalem.)

an error of 3 hours per year; and 334 years are 4131 months with an error of 7.27 seconds per year. The old Hindu calendar is even more accurate, comprising 2226389 months in a cycle of 180000 years (see Chapter 10) to which the leap-year formulas of Section 1.14 apply, and errs by less than 8 seconds per year.

The placement of leap years must make a trade-off between two conflicting requirements: small constants defining a simple leap year rule of limited accuracy versus greater accuracy at the expense of larger constants, as the examples in the last paragraph suggest. The choice of the constants is aided by taking the continued fraction (see [27]) of the desired ratio and choosing among the convergents (where to stop in evaluating the fraction). In the case of lunisolar calendars, the solar year is about 365.24244 days, while the lunar month is about 29.53059 days, so we write

$$\frac{365.24244}{29.53059} = 12 + \cfrac{1}{2 + \cfrac{1}{1 + \cfrac{1}{2 + \cfrac{1}{1 + \cfrac{1}{1 + \cfrac{1}{18 + \cfrac{1}{3 + \cdots}}}}}}}.$$

By choosing further and further stopping points, we get better and better approximations to the true ratio. For example,

$$12 + \cfrac{1}{2 + \cfrac{1}{1}} = \frac{37}{3}$$

while

$$12 + \cfrac{1}{2 + \cfrac{1}{1 + \cfrac{1}{2}}} = \frac{99}{8}$$

$$12 + \cfrac{1}{2 + \cfrac{1}{1 + \cfrac{1}{2 + \cfrac{1}{1}}}} = \frac{136}{11}$$

and

$$12 + \cfrac{1}{2 + \cfrac{1}{1 + \cfrac{1}{2 + \cfrac{1}{1 + \cfrac{1}{1}}}}} = \frac{235}{19}$$

These are the ratios of the previous paragraph. Not all approximations must come from continued fractions, however: 84 years are approximately 1039 lunar months with an error of 33 minutes per year, but this is not one of the convergents.

Continued fractions can be used to get approximations to solar calendars too. The number of days per solar year is about 365.242177, which we can write as

$$365.242177 = 365 + \cfrac{1}{4 + \cfrac{1}{7 + \cfrac{1}{1 + \cfrac{1}{2 + \cfrac{1}{1 + \cfrac{1}{5 + \cdots}}}}}}$$

The convergents are $1/4$ (the basis of the Julian, Coptic, and Ethiopic calendars), $7/29$, $8/33$ (possibly used for an ancient Persian calendar), $23/95$, and $31/128$ (used in our implementation of the arithmetical Persian calendar—see Chapter 15).

Table 1.1 gives for comparison the values for the mean length of the year and month as implemented by the various solar, lunar, and lunisolar calendars in this book. The true values change over time, as explained in Chapter 14.

1.2 Fixed Day Numbers

May those who calculate a fixed date ... perish.[5]
Morris Braude: *Conscience on Trial: Three Public Religious Disputations between Christians and Jews in the Thirteenth and Fifteenth Centuries* (1952)

Over the centuries, human beings have devised an enormous variety of methods for specifying dates.[6] None are ideal computationally, however, because all have idiosyncrasies resulting from attempts to coordinate a convenient human labeling with lunar and solar phenomena.

For a computer implementation, the easiest way to reckon time is simply to count days. Fix an arbitrary starting point as day 1 and specify a date by giving a day number relative to that starting point; a single 32-bit integer allows the representation of more than 11.7 million years. Such a reckoning of time is, evidently, extremely awkward for human beings and is not in common use, except among astronomers, who use *julian day numbers* to specify dates (see Section 1.5), and calendarists, who use them to facilitate conversion among calendars—see equation

[5] This is a loose translation of a famous dictum from the Babylonian Talmud *Sanhedrin* 97b. The omitted words from Braude's translation (p. 112 of his book) are "for the coming of the Messiah." The exact Talmudic wording is "Blasted be the bones of those who calculate the end." Braude was the uncle of E.M.R.'s mother-in-law, a connection we discovered long after the first edition of this book was published!

[6] The best reference is still Ginzel's monumental three-volume work [16], in German. An exceptional survey can be found in the *Encyclopædia of Religion and Ethics* [22, vol. III, pp. 61–141 and vol. V, pp. 835–894]. Useful modern summaries are [6], [12], [40], and [45]; [6] and [40] have extensive bibliographies. The incomparable tables of Schram [41] are the best available for converting dates by hand, whereas those in Parise [36] are best avoided because of an embarrassingly large numbers of errors.

Table 1.1 Length in days of mean years on solar and lunisolar calendars and length in days of mean lunar months on lunar and lunisolar calendars. The year length is given in italics when the sidereal, rather than the tropical, value is intended. These may be compared with the astronomical values given for various millennial points—*in solar days current at the indicated time*. No values are given here for the Chinese, astronomical Persian, observational Islamic, astronomical Bahá'í, and (original) French Revolutionary calendars because they are self-adjusting. The implicit Mayan values come from other values that they knew; see the footnote on page 171.

	Calendar (or year)	Mean year (days)	Mean month (days)
Calendrical	Egyptian	365	
	Mayan (haab)	365	
	Mayan (implicit)	365.24204	29.530864
	Julian/Coptic/Ethiopic	365.25	
	Hebrew	365.24682	29.530594
	Easter (Orthodox)	365.25	29.530851
	Islamic (Arithmetic)		29.530556
	Hindu (*Arya*)	*365.25868*	29.530582
	Hindu (*Sūrya*)	*365.25876*	29.530588
	Tibetan (*Phugpa*)	*365.27065*	29.530587
	Gregorian	365.2425	
	Easter (Gregorian)	365.2425	29.530587
	French (Arithmetic)	365.24225	
	Persian (Arithmetic)	365.24220	
Astronomical	Year −1000	365.24257	29.530598
	Year 0	365.24244	29.530595
	Year 1000	365.24231	29.530591
	Year 2000	365.24218	29.530588
	Year 3000	365.24204	29.530584

(10.2) for the ancient Indian method and for a more modern example see [41]. The day-count can be augmented by a fractional part to give a specific moment during the day; for example, noon on day i, where i is an integer, would be specified by $i + 0.5$.

We have chosen midnight at the onset of Monday, January 1, 1 (Gregorian) as our fixed date 1, which we abbreviate as R.D. 1,[7] and we count forward day-by-day from there. Of course, this is anachronistic because there was no year 1 on the Gregorian calendar—the Gregorian calendar was devised only in the sixteenth century—thus by January 1, 1 (Gregorian) we mean the day we get if we extrapolate backwards from the present; this day turns out to be Monday, January 3, 1 C.E.[8] (Julian); this too is anachronistic. We call an R.D. that has a fractional part giving the time of day a "moment."

The date Monday, January 1, 1 (Gregorian), though arbitrarily chosen as our starting point, has a desirable characteristic: It is early enough that almost all dates

[7] *Rata Die*, or fixed date. We are indebted to Howard Jacobson for this coinage.

[8] Common Era, or A.D.

of interest are represented by positive integers of moderate size. We have been careful to write our functions in such a way that all dependencies on this choice of starting point are explicit. To change the origin of the calculations we have provided a function

$$\mathbf{rd}(t) \stackrel{\text{def}}{=} t - \mathit{epoch} \tag{1.1}$$

where

$$\mathit{epoch} = 0$$

which defines the origin, *epoch*. Changing this definition to *epoch* = 710347, for example, would make Monday, November 12, 1945 (Gregorian) the starting point.

We should thus think of the passage of time in terms of a sequence of days numbered ..., −2, −1, 0, 1, 2, 3, ..., which the various human-oriented calendars label differently. For example, R.D. 710347 is called

- Monday, November 12, 1945, on the Gregorian calendar.
- October 30, 1945 C.E., on the Julian calendar, which would be called *ante diem III Kalendas Novembris* in the Roman nomenclature.
- Julian day number 2431772 (at noon).
- Modified julian day number 31771.
- Month 7, day 10, 2694, on the ancient Egyptian calendar.
- Trē 5, 1395, on the Armenian calendar.
- Fodwo on the Akan calendar.
- Day 1 of week 46 of year 1945, on the ISO calendar.
- Mánudagur of week 3 of winter of year 1945, on the Icelandic calendar.
- Athōr 3, 1662, Era of the Martyrs, on the Coptic calendar (until sunset).
- Ḫedār 3, 1938, on the Ethiopic calendar (until sunset).
- Dhu al-Ḥijja 6, 1364, on the arithmetic and observational Islamic calendars (until sunset).
- Kislev 7, 5706, on the Hebrew calendar, but Kislev 6, 5706, on the observational Hebrew calendar (until sunset in both cases).
- 12.16.11.16.9 in the Mayan long count.
- 7 Zac on the Mayan haab calendar.
- 11 Muluc on the Mayan tzolkin calendar.
- Panquetzaliztli 1 on the Aztec xihuitl calendar.
- 11 Atl on the Aztec tonalpohualli calendar.

- Luang, Pepet, Pasah, Sri, Pon, Tungleh, Coma of Gumbreg, Ludra, Urungan, Pati on the Balinese Pawukon calendar.
- Tulā 29, 5046, Kali Yuga Era (elapsed) on the old Hindu solar calendar (after sunrise).
- Day 8 in the bright half of Kārtika, 5046, Kali Yuga Era (elapsed) on the old Hindu lunisolar calendar (after sunrise).
- Abān 21, 1324, on the modern Persian arithmetic and astronomical calendars.
- The day of Asmā', of the month of Qudrat, of the year Abad, of the sixth Vahid, of the first Kull-i-Shay on the Bahá'í calendar (until sunset).
- Décade III, Primidi de Brumaire de l'Année 154 de la République on the arithmetical and astronomical French Revolutionary calendars.
- Day 8 of the tenth month in the year Yĭyŏu on the Chinese calendar.
- Kārtika 27, 1867, Śaka Era (elapsed) on the modern and astronomical Hindu solar calendars (after sunrise).
- Day 7 in the bright half of Kārtika, 2002, Vikrama Era (elapsed) on the modern and astronomical Hindu lunisolar calendars (after sunrise).
- Arakhsamna 6, 2256 on the Babylonian calendar.
- Day 7 of the tenth month, 2072 on the Tibetan calendar.

All that is required for calendrical conversion is to be able to convert each calendar to and from this fixed-date R.D. calendar. Because some calendars begin their day at midnight and others at sunrise or sunset,

We fix the time of day at which conversions are performed to be noon.

Figure 1.2 shows the relationships of various calendar's times for the beginning and ending of days.

In subsequent chapters we give functions to do the conversions for the various calendars. For each calendar x, we write a function **fixed-from-*x***(*x-date*) to convert a given date *x-date* on that calendar to the corresponding R.D. date, and a function ***x*-from-fixed**(*date*) to do the inverse operation, taking the R.D. *date* and computing its representation in calendar x. One direction is often much simpler to calculate than the other, and occasionally we resort to considering a range of possible dates on calendar x, searching for the one that converts to the given R.D. date (see Section 1.8). To convert from calendar x to calendar y, one need only compose these two functions:

y*-from-*x(*x-date*) $\stackrel{\text{def}}{=}$

  y*-from-fixed**(**fixed-from-*x(*x-date*))

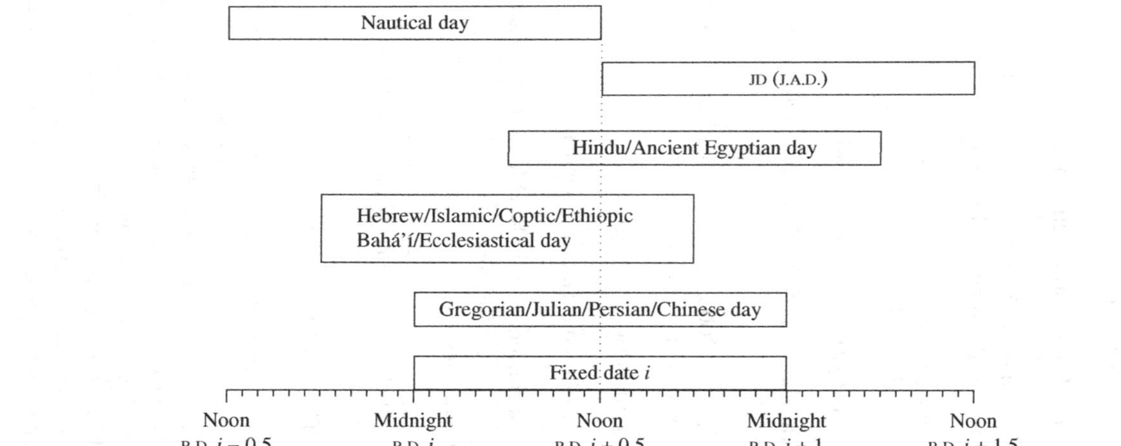

Figure 1.2 Meaning of a "day" in various calendars. Conversion from a date on a calendar to an R.D. date is done as of noon; the rectangles indicate the day of a calendar that gets converted to R.D. i. For example, the Hebrew date corresponding to fixed date i is the Hebrew day that begins at sunset of the evening of fixed date $i - 1$ and ends at sunset of the evening of fixed date i. Similarly, the Hindu date corresponding to fixed date i is the Hindu day that begins at sunrise in the morning of fixed i and ends at sunrise of the morning of fixed date $i + 1$. The JD corresponding to fixed date i begins at noon of fixed date i and ends at noon of fixed date $i + 1$.

Each calendar has an *epoch*, the first day of the first year of that calendar (see Section 1.4). We assign an integer R.D. date to an epoch, even if the calendar in question begins its days at a time other than midnight. Such assignment is done as per Figure 1.2. All the algorithms given in this book give mathematically sensible results for dates prior to a calendar's epoch.

1.3 Negative Years

Quis enim potest intelligere dies et tempora et annos, nisi per numerum? [Who can understand days and seasons and years, save by number?]

Attributed to the Venerable Bede: *De Computo Dialogus*

We cannot avoid dealing with dates before the common era. For example, the Hebrew calendar begins at sunset on Sunday, September 6, –3760 (Gregorian); scholarly literature is replete with such statements. Thus, to aid the reader, we now explain how years before the common era are conventionally handled. This convention is often a source of confusion, even among professional historians.

It is computationally convenient, and mathematically sensible, to label years with the sequence of integers $\ldots, -3, -2, -1, 0, 1, 2, 3, \ldots$, so that year 0 precedes year 1; we do this when extrapolating backward on the Gregorian calendar, so the same leap-year rule based on divisibility by 4, 100, and 400 will apply (see Chapter 2). However, on the Julian calendar it is customary to refer to the year preceding 1 C.E. as 1 B.C.E.,[9] counting it as a leap year in accordance with the every-fourth-year leap-year rule of the Julian calendar. Thus, the beginning of the Hebrew calendar can alternatively be referred to as sunset on October 6, 3761 B.C.E. (Julian). To highlight this asymmetry, in the rest of this book we append "B.C.E." *only* to Julian calendar years, reserving the minus sign for Gregorian calendar years.[10] Care must therefore be taken when doing arithmetic with year numbers. For $n \geqslant 0$, the rough present-day alignment of the Julian and Gregorian calendars gives

year $-n$ (Gregorian) $\approx$ year $(n+1)$ B.C.E. (Julian)

and, for $n \geqslant 1$,

year n (Gregorian) $\approx$ year n C.E. (Julian)

1.4 Epochs

My son, take occasional lessons on calendrical calculations from R. Aaron for it is a necessary wisdom.

Judah ibn Tibbon: *Ethical Will* (circa 1180)

Every calendar has an *epoch* or starting date. This date is virtually never the date the calendar was adopted but rather a hypothetical starting point for the first day. For example, the Gregorian calendar was devised and adopted in the sixteenth century,

[9] Before the Common Era, or B.C.

[10] Historically scholars have mixed the notations, using negative years for the Julian calendar and the B.C.E./C.E. (B.C./A.D.) notation for Gregorian years, so one must be cautious in interpreting what a particular author means. The ambiguity has led to confusion and errors.

but its epoch is January 1, 1. Because days begin at different hours on different calendars, we follow the convention that a calendar's epoch is the onset of the civil day (the mean solar day, beginning at midnight) containing the first noon (see Figure 1.2). For example, we take midnight at the onset of September 7, −3760 (Gregorian) as the epoch of the Hebrew calendar, which was codified in the fourth century, though the first Hebrew day began at sunset the preceding evening. For calendars like the Akan or Balinese Pawukon, in which cycles are unnumbered, the choice of epoch is arbitrary; the first day of any cycle can be used.

Table 1.2 gives the epochs of the calendars discussed in this book. With the exception of the Julian day number, we express the epochs of all the calendars as integer R.D. dates, that is, the integer R.D. day number at *noon* of the first day of the calendar (again, see Figure 1.2). Thus, the epoch for the Gregorian calendar is R.D. 1, and that for the Hebrew calendar is R.D. −1373427. Using this form of calendar epochs is convenient because

$$\text{R.D. } d = (d - \text{calendar epoch}) \text{ days since the start of that calendar}$$

For example,

$$\begin{aligned} 710347 - (\text{Hebrew calendar epoch}) &= 710347 - (-1373427) \\ &= 2083774 \end{aligned}$$

and hence

$$\text{R.D. } 710347 = 2083774 \text{ days since the start of the Hebrew calendar}$$

Because, for the most part, our formulas depend on the number of days elapsed on some calendar, we often use the expression (d − calendar epoch) in our calendar formulas.

For many calendars, including the Gregorian, the same calendar rules were used with different eras and different month names at different times and in different places. In Taiwan, for instance, the Gregorian calendar is used with an era beginning with the founding of the republic in 1912. An often-encountered era from the second century B.C.E. until recent times—used with many calendars—was the Era of Alexander, or the Seleucid Era, in which year 1 corresponds to 312 B.C.E. In general, we will avoid describing the details of trivial variants of calendars.

1.5 Julian Day Numbers

Iulianam vocauimus: quia ad annum Iulianum dumtaxat accommodata est. [*I have called this the Julian period because it is fitted to the Julian year.*]

Joseph Justus Scaliger: *De Emendatione Temporum*, end of introduction to Book V (1583)

Astronomers in recent centuries have avoided the confusing situation of date references on different calendars, each with its idiosyncrasies, by specifying moments in time by giving them in "julian days" or JD (sometimes "julian astronomical days" or J.A.D.). The "Julian period," published in 1583 by Joseph Justus Scaliger, was

Table 1.2 Epochs for various calendars.

Calendar	Epoch (R.D.)	Equivalents
Julian day number	−1721424.5	Noon, November 24, −4713 (Gregorian)
		Noon, January 1, 4713 B.C.E. (Julian)
Hebrew	−1373427	September 7, −3760 (Gregorian)
		October 7, 3761 B.C.E. (Julian)
Mayan	−1137142	August 11, −3113 (Gregorian)
		September 6, 3114 B.C.E. (Julian)
Hindu (Kali Yuga)	−1132959	January 23, −3101 (Gregorian)
		February 18, 3102 B.C.E. (Julian)
Chinese	−963099	February 15, −2636 (Gregorian)
		March 8, 2637 B.C.E. (Julian)
Samaritan	−598573	March 3, −1638 (Gregorian)
		March 15, 1639 B.C.E. (Julian)
Egyptian	−272787	February 18, −746 (Gregorian)
		February 26, 747 B.C.E. (Julian)
Babylonian	−113502	March 29, −310 (Gregorian)
		April 3, 311 B.C.E. (Julian)
Tibetan	−46410	December 7, −127 (Gregorian)
		December 10, 128 B.C.E. (Julian)
Julian	−1	December 30, 0 (Gregorian)
		January 1, 1 C.E. (Julian)
Gregorian	1	January 1, 1 (Gregorian)
		January 3, 1 C.E. (Julian)
ISO	1	January 1, 1 (Gregorian)
		January 3, 1 C.E. (Julian)
Akan	37	February 6, 1 (Gregorian)
		February 8, 1 C.E. (Julian)
Ethiopic	2796	August 27, 8 (Gregorian)
		August 29, 8 C.E. (Julian)
Coptic	103605	August 29, 284 (Gregorian)
		August 29, 284 C.E. (Julian)
Armenian	201443	July 13, 552 (Gregorian)
		July 11, 552 C.E. (Julian)
Persian	226896	March 22, 622 (Gregorian)
		March 19, 622 C.E. (Julian)
Islamic	227015	July 19, 622 (Gregorian)
		July 16, 622 C.E. (Julian)
Zoroastrian	230638	June 19, 632 (Gregorian)
		June 16, 632 C.E. (Julian)
French Revolutionary	654415	September 22, 1792 (Gregorian)
		September 11, 1792 C.E. (Julian)
Bahá'í	673222	March 21, 1844 (Gregorian)
		March 9, 1844 C.E. (Julian)
Modified julian day number	678576	November 17, 1858 (Gregorian)
		November 5, 1858 C.E. (Julian)
Unix	719163	January 1, 1970 (Gregorian)
		December 19, 1969 C.E. (Julian)

originally a counting of *years* in a repeating pattern 7980 years long, starting from 4713 B.C.E. (Julian). It is often claimed ([1, page 431], for example) that Scaliger named the period after his father, the Renaissance physician Julius Cæsar Scaliger, but this claim is not borne out by examination of Scaliger's great work, *De Emendatione Temporum*, from which the section quote above is taken. Grafton [17] gives a full history of *De Emendatione Temporum*. The details of the derivation for the value 7980 are given in [39]; the roots of the 7980-year cycle are much earlier than Scaliger, however, dating back to the twelfth century [38]. In the mid-nineteenth century, Herschel [25, page 532] adapted the system into a strict counting of *days* backward and forward from

$$\begin{aligned}\text{JD } 0 &= \text{noon on Monday, January 1, 4713 B.C.E. (Julian)}\\ &= \text{noon on Monday, November 24, }-4713\text{ (Gregorian)}\end{aligned}$$

A fractional part of a julian[11] date gives the fraction of a day beyond noon; switching dates at noon makes sense for astronomers who work through the night. In this system, for example, sunset on the first day of the Hebrew calendar occurred at about JD 347997.25 (local time), which is 1/4 of a day after noon. The literature on the Mayan calendar commonly specifies the beginning of the calendar in julian days. Because noon of R.D. 0 is JD 1721425, it follows that

$$\text{JD } n = \text{Noon on R.D. } (n - 1721425)$$

In other words,

$$\text{Midnight at the onset of R.D. } d = \text{JD } (d + 1721424.5) \qquad (1.2)$$

We do not use julian days directly, as suggested in [21], because we want our days to begin at civil midnight. *We also use fractional days when we need to calculate with time, but we begin each day at midnight.*

To distinguish clearly between the Julian calendar and julian days in our functions, we use the abbreviation "jd" instead of "julian." We have

$$\textbf{jd-epoch} \stackrel{\text{def}}{=} \text{R.D. } -1721424.5 \qquad (1.3)$$

$$\textbf{moment-from-jd}\,(jd) \stackrel{\text{def}}{=} jd + \textbf{jd-epoch} \qquad (1.4)$$

$$\textbf{jd-from-moment}\,(t) \stackrel{\text{def}}{=} t - \textbf{jd-epoch} \qquad (1.5)$$

where *jd* can be a fraction representing time as well as date. As used by historians, julian day numbers are defined as $jd + 0.5$ (see [33, vol. 3, p. 1064], for example). Thus our function **fixed-from-jd** gives the R.D. date intended by historians when they refer to julian dates.[12]

---

[11] We use lowercase here to avoid any confusion between a julian day number and a date on the Julian calendar.

[12] "Note that Julian date is sometimes used as a synonym for day of year, but this is not correct usage. Day of year ranges from 1 to 365 (366 for leap years) whereas Julian dates are a continuous count of days" [2].

For dates near the present, the julian day number is inconvenient because at least 7-digit accuracy is needed. Astronomers occasionally use *modified julian day numbers*, or MJD, defined as

Modified julian day number = julian day number − 2400000.5

which counts days from midnight, Wednesday, November 17, 1858 (Gregorian). This is equivalent to defining

$$\textbf{mjd-epoch} \stackrel{\text{def}}{=} \text{R.D. } 678576 \tag{1.6}$$

$$\textbf{fixed-from-mjd}\,(mjd) \stackrel{\text{def}}{=} mjd + \textbf{mjd-epoch} \tag{1.7}$$

$$\textbf{mjd-from-fixed}\,(date) \stackrel{\text{def}}{=} date - \textbf{mjd-epoch} \tag{1.8}$$

We do not use modified julian days directly because we want positive numbers for dates within recent history.

1.6 Unix Time Representation

Unix is simple and coherent, but it takes a genius (or at any rate, a programmer) to understand and appreciate the simplicity.

Dennis Ritchie: "Unix: A Dialectic," *The Australian UNIX systems User Group Newsletter* (1989)

In the Unix operating system, and its derivatives, time is measured in seconds after midnight Universal Time (see Section 14.2) on January 1, 1970, ignoring leap seconds. Unix time simply counts 60 seconds per minute, 60 minutes per hour, 24 hours per day. Hence we define

$$\textbf{unix-epoch} \stackrel{\text{def}}{=} \text{R.D. } 719163 \tag{1.9}$$

The equivalent R.D. moment of a Unix time is easily computed,

$$\textbf{moment-from-unix}\,(s) \stackrel{\text{def}}{=} \textbf{unix-epoch} + \frac{s}{24 \times 60 \times 60} \tag{1.10}$$

as is the Unix time of an R.D. moment,

$$\textbf{unix-from-moment}\,(t) \stackrel{\text{def}}{=} 24 \times 60^2 \times (t - \textbf{unix-epoch}) \tag{1.11}$$

On computers that represent integers with signed 32-bit words, only moments from 20:45:53 December 13, 1908 until 3:14:07 on January 19, 2038 can be represented. With 64 bits, the range is greater than ±292 billion years from the present.

1.7 Mathematical Notation

The best notation is no notation.
Paul Halmos: *How to Write Mathematics (1970)*

We use the following mathematical notation (see [18]) when describing the calendar calculations: The *floor function*, $\lfloor x \rfloor$, gives the largest integer less than or equal to x. For example, $\lfloor \pi \rfloor = 3$. The similar *ceiling function*, $\lceil x \rceil$, gives the smallest integer greater than or equal to x. For example, $\lceil \pi \rceil = 4$ and $\lceil -\pi \rceil = -3$. In general, $\lceil x \rceil = -\lfloor -x \rfloor$, so for example $\lfloor -\pi \rfloor = -4$. For integers n, $\lfloor n \rfloor = \lceil n \rceil = n$. Using the floor function, we can convert a moment into an R.D. date by

$$\textbf{fixed-from-moment}\,(t) \stackrel{\text{def}}{=} \lfloor t \rfloor \tag{1.12}$$

Similarly, we can convert a moment given in julian days to an R.D. date, with no fractional part by

$$\textbf{fixed-from-jd}\,(jd) \stackrel{\text{def}}{=} \lfloor \textbf{moment-from-jd}\,(jd) \rfloor \tag{1.13}$$

The inverse is simply the same as **jd-from-moment**:

$$\textbf{jd-from-fixed}\,(date) \stackrel{\text{def}}{=} \textbf{jd-from-moment}\,(date) \tag{1.14}$$

Occasionally we need to *round* values to the nearest integer. We can express this using the floor function as

$$\text{round}(x) \stackrel{\text{def}}{=} \lfloor x + 0.5 \rfloor \tag{1.15}$$

which is either $\lfloor x \rfloor$ or $\lceil x \rceil$.

We use a single large left-hand brace to indicate a conditional expression, one whose value depends on two or more conditions. For example, in

$$x \stackrel{\text{def}}{=} \begin{cases} \textbf{value}_1 & \textbf{condition}_1 \\ \textbf{value}_2 & \textbf{condition}_2 \\ \textbf{value}_3 & \textbf{otherwise} \end{cases}$$

the conditions are examined in order, from top down. Thus the value of x is $\textbf{value}_1$ if $\textbf{condition}_1$ is true, $\textbf{value}_2$ if $\textbf{condition}_1$ is false but $\textbf{condition}_2$ is true, and $\textbf{value}_3$ if both conditions are false. Note that if both conditions are true, the sequential evaluation of them means that the value of the expression is $\textbf{value}_1$. As a simple example of such a conditional expression we define the sign function

$$\text{sign}\,(y) \stackrel{\text{def}}{=} \begin{cases} -1 & \textbf{if } y < 0 \\ 1 & \textbf{if } y > 0 \\ 0 & \textbf{otherwise} \end{cases} \tag{1.16}$$

The *remainder*, or *modulus, function*, $x \bmod y$, is defined for $y \neq 0$ as

$$x \bmod y \stackrel{\text{def}}{=} x - y\lfloor x/y \rfloor \tag{1.17}$$

which is the remainder when x is divided by y (x and y need not be integers). For example, $9 \bmod 5 = 4$, $-9 \bmod 5 = 1$, $9 \bmod -5 = -1$, and $-9 \bmod -5 = -4$. Definition (1.17) makes sense for any nonzero value of y; for example, $5/3 \bmod 3/4 = 1/6$. In particular, when $y = 1$, $x \bmod 1$ is the *fractional part* of x, allowing us to obtain the time of day as a fraction from a moment by

$$\textbf{time-from-moment}\,(t) \stackrel{\text{def}}{=} t \bmod 1 \tag{1.18}$$

In programming languages (including C, C++, and Pascal) without a built-in remainder function that works for nonintegers, the definition given in (1.17) must be used instead.

There are five important consequences of definition (1.17). First,

$$\text{if } y > 0 \text{ then } x \bmod y \geqslant 0$$

for all x, even for negative values of x; we use this property throughout our calculations. Care must thus be exercised in implementing our algorithms in computer languages such as C and C++ in which the mod operator `%` may have $(x \,\%\, y) < 0$ for $x < 0$, $y > 0$. It follows from (1.17) that

$$(-x) \bmod y = y - (x \bmod y)$$

for $y > 0$ and $x \not\equiv 0 \pmod{y}$. The third consequence is that the definition of the mod function implies that for $y \neq 0$ and $z \neq 0$,

$$a = (x \bmod y) \text{ if and only if } az = (xz \bmod yz) \tag{1.19}$$

Setting $z = -1$ then gives

$$(-x) \bmod (-y) = -(x \bmod y)$$

as a special case. Fourth,

$$x - (x \bmod y) \text{ is always an integer multiple of } y \tag{1.20}$$

Finally, the fifth consequence is a generalization of the first consequence: for $y \neq 0$,

$$0 \leqslant \text{sign}(y) \times (x \bmod y) < |y| \tag{1.21}$$

The mod function allows us to define two other important functions, the *greatest common divisor* and the *least common multiple*. The greatest common divisor of two positive integers, x and y is defined as

$$\gcd(x, y) \stackrel{\text{def}}{=} \begin{cases} x & \textbf{if } y = 0 \\ \gcd(y, x \bmod y) & \textbf{otherwise} \end{cases} \tag{1.22}$$

and their least common multiple as

$$\text{lcm}(x, y) \stackrel{\text{def}}{=} \frac{xy}{\gcd(x, y)} \tag{1.23}$$

We make extensive use of an extension of the standard modulus notation of [11] which takes an *interval* as the modulus, rather than a divisor; we use the "double-dot" notation ". ." for interval ranges, as suggested by C. A. R. Hoare and L. Ramshaw; see [18, p. 73]). Then we can write the *interval modulus* as

$$x \bmod [a\,..\,b)$$

which shifts a real-valued x into the half-open (meaning one end point, indicated by the right-hand parenthesis, is not included) real interval $[a\,..\,b)$ by adding a multiple of the length $b - a$. We define

$$x \bmod [a\,..\,b) \stackrel{\text{def}}{=} \begin{cases} x & \textbf{if } a = b \\ a + (x - a) \bmod (b - a) & \textbf{otherwise} \end{cases} \tag{1.24}$$

or, equivalently,

$$x \bmod [a\,..\,b) \stackrel{\text{def}}{=} \begin{cases} x & \textbf{if } a = b \\ x - (b - a)\left\lfloor \dfrac{x - a}{b - a} \right\rfloor & \textbf{otherwise} \end{cases}$$

This definition works perfectly well when the interval is given backward, that is, $a > b$, yielding a modulus in the half-open interval $(b\,..\,a]$. It follows that $a \leqslant x \bmod [a\,..\,b) < b$ if $a < b$, but $b < x \bmod [a\,..\,b) \leqslant a$ when $a > b$. This notation conveniently supports addition and multiplication:

$$c + (x \bmod [a\,..\,b)) = (c + x) \bmod [c + a\,..\,c + b) \tag{1.25}$$

$$c \times (x \bmod [a\,..\,b)) = (c \times x) \bmod [c \times a\,..\,c \times b) \tag{1.26}$$

On a few occasions (especially in Chapter 20) we will want to recenter the remainder; this is easy with the interval modulus notation. For example, to convert an angle α to the range $[-180°\,..\,180°)$, we just write

$$\alpha \bmod [-180\,..\,180) \tag{1.27}$$

We frequently need a special case of the interval modulus in order to shift an integer into the range $[1\,..\,b+1) = [1\,..\,b]$, where b is also an integer. We call this the *adjusted remainder function*, $x \bmod [1\,..\,b]$, and it can be defined for $b \neq 0$ as

$$x \bmod [1\,..\,b] \stackrel{\text{def}}{=} \begin{cases} b & \textbf{if } x \bmod b = 0 \\ x \bmod b & \textbf{otherwise} \end{cases} \tag{1.28}$$

This function is equivalently defined by

$$x \bmod [1\,..\,b] = b + x \bmod (-b) \tag{1.29}$$

$$x \bmod [1\,..\,b] = [(x - 1) \bmod b] + 1$$

$$x \bmod [1\,..\,b] = x - b(\lceil x/b \rceil - 1)$$

Though this definition works equally well for real numbers, we will need this adjusted remainder only for integers x and b.

Finally, we use a special summation operator,

$$\sum_{i\geq k}^{p(i)} f(i) = f(k) + f(k+1) + \cdots$$

whose value is that obtained when $f(i)$ is summed for all $i = k, k+1, \ldots$, continuing only as long as the condition $p(i)$ holds. This operator can be defined recursively as follows:

$$\sum_{i\geq k}^{p(i)} f(i) \stackrel{\text{def}}{=} \begin{cases} f(k) + \sum_{i\geq k+1}^{p(i)} f(i) & \textbf{if } p(k) \\ 0 & \textbf{otherwise} \end{cases} \tag{1.30}$$

Thus, the sum is 0 when $p(k)$ is false. The analogous product operator

$$\prod_{i\geq k}^{p(i)} f(i) = f(k) \times f(k+1) \times \cdots$$

can be defined as follows:

$$\prod_{i\geq k}^{p(i)} f(i) \stackrel{\text{def}}{=} \begin{cases} f(k) \times \prod_{i\geq k+1}^{p(i)} f(i) & \textbf{if } p(k) \\ 1 & \textbf{otherwise} \end{cases} \tag{1.31}$$

1.8 Search

... as two grains of wheat hid in two bushels of chaff: you shall seek all day ere you find them, and when you have them, they are not worth the search.

William Shakespeare: *Merchant of Venice,* Act I, scene i (1600)

In many calendar computations, it is easy to compute an approximate date and easy to check whether a date in question is correct, but difficult to compute the correct date directly. In such cases, we compute a lower bound d_0 on the possible date and then perform a linear search, day by day, until the correct date d is reached. For that purpose we use the operator

$$\mathop{\mathbf{MIN}}_{d\geqslant d_0} \{\psi(d)\}$$

which searches for the smallest d in the sequence d_0, $d_0 + 1$, $d_0 + 2$, ... such that the condition ψ holds true for d. In other words, using the symbol "$\neg$" for logical negation, we have $\neg\psi(d_0)$, $\neg\psi(d_0 + 1)$, $\neg\psi(d_0 + 2)$, ..., $\neg\psi(d - 1)$, but $\psi(d)$. The operator **MIN** is defined formally as

$$\mathop{\mathbf{MIN}}_{d\geqslant k} \{\psi(d)\} \stackrel{\text{def}}{=} \begin{cases} k & \textbf{if } \psi(k) \\ \mathop{\mathbf{MIN}}_{d\geqslant k+1} \{\psi(d)\} & \textbf{otherwise} \end{cases} \tag{1.32}$$

It is undefined and does not terminate if the predicate $\psi(d)$ does not become true eventually, so care must be taken in its use.

Occasionally, we search the sequence for the day prior to the first d' such that $\neg\psi(d')$ and use instead

$$\underset{d \geqslant d_0}{\mathbf{MAX}} \{\psi(d)\}$$

With this operator, we have $\psi(d_0)$, $\psi(d_0 + 1)$, $\psi(d_0 + 2)$, ..., $\psi(d)$, but $\neg\psi(d + 1)$. **MAX** is undefined and its computation does not terminate if the predicate $\psi(d)$ does not eventually become false. This **MAX** operator is defined formally as

$$\underset{d \geqslant k}{\mathbf{MAX}} \{\psi(d)\} \stackrel{\text{def}}{=} \begin{cases} k - 1 & \textbf{if } \neg\psi(k) \\ \underset{d \geqslant k+1}{\mathbf{MAX}} \{\psi(d)\} & \textbf{otherwise} \end{cases} \tag{1.33}$$

When $\psi(d_0)$ is already false, $\underset{d \geqslant d_0}{\mathbf{MAX}} \{\psi(d)\} = d_0 - 1$.

In the absence of explicit methods for calculating the inverse of a function f, that is, for calculating a value x such that $f(x) = y$ given the value of y, we will need to search an interval $[a \,..\, b]$ for the point x, $a \leqslant x \leqslant b$, when $f(x) = y$. To express such a calculation, we write

$$f^{-1}(y, [a \,..\, b])$$

In other words, $f^{-1}(y, [a \,..\, b])$ is a value x_0 such that there is some $x \in [a \,..\, b]$ for which $f(x) = y$, precisely, and $|x - x_0| < \varepsilon$, where $\varepsilon > 0$ is some small tolerance within which the result is acceptable.

When the function in question f is *increasing*, binary search [42, Section 3.2] can be an effective means of inverting f. Hence

$$\overset{\varphi(l,u)}{\underset{\xi \in [\mu..\nu]}{\mathbf{MIN}}} \{\psi(\xi)\} \approx y \quad \text{means} \quad \begin{matrix} \mu \leqslant l < y < u \leqslant \nu, \\ \varphi(l, u), \neg\psi(l), \text{ and } \psi(u) \end{matrix} \tag{1.34}$$

That is, we search for a y satisfying the definiens (defining expression) under the assumption that the region $[\mu \,..\, \nu]$ can be split into two intervals $[\mu \,..\, x)$, up to but not including x, and $[x \,..\, \nu]$, such that ψ is false throughout the former and true in the latter. Then y must be close enough to x that it lies in an interval $[l \,..\, u]$, sandwiching x, small enough to satisfy the test $\varphi(l, u)$. If ψ is true of the midpoint ξ, then we go left and let the new upper bound ν be ξ. On the other hand, if ψ is false, then we go right and let the new lower bound μ be ξ. This process continues until the interval $[\mu \,..\, \nu]$ is small enough that φ is true, at which point the midpoint is returned. At each stage of the search, $\psi(\mu)$ is false and $\psi(\nu)$ is true. We implement the definition using a straightforward binary search of the interval $[\mu \,..\, \nu]$ that behaves as follows:

$$\overset{\varphi}{\underset{\xi \in [\mu..\nu]}{\mathbf{MIN}}} \{\psi(\xi)\} \stackrel{\text{def}}{=} \begin{cases} x & \textbf{if } \varphi(\mu, \nu) \\ \overset{\varphi}{\underset{\xi \in [\mu..x]}{\mathbf{MIN}}} \{\psi(\xi)\} & \textbf{if } \psi(x) \\ \overset{\varphi}{\underset{\xi \in [x..\nu]}{\mathbf{MIN}}} \{\psi(\xi)\} & \textbf{otherwise} \end{cases} \tag{1.35}$$

where

$$x = \frac{\mu + \nu}{2}$$

To determine the time of astronomical events, for example equinoxes or solstices, we need to invert astronomical functions, such as the celestial longitude of the sun in Section 14.4. These astronomical functions f take moments and return values in the range $[0° \,..\, 360°)$. We use binary search to invert such functions. That is, given a desired value y, here in degrees, we search for a moment x, within some given range, such that $f(x) = y$. Since the search interval will always be relatively small, we sidestep the discontinuity at $360° = 0°$ by searching for the first moment at which $f(x) - y$ modulo 360 becomes tiny. Using binary search, this is achieved as follows:

$$f^{-1}(y, [a \,..\, b]) \stackrel{\text{def}}{=} \underset{x \in [a..b]}{\overset{u-l<10^{-5}}{\mathbf{MIN}}} \{(f(x) - y) \bmod 360 < 180°\} \tag{1.36}$$

The process terminates when the moment is ascertained within one ten-thousandth of a day, which is less than one second.

1.9 Dates and Lists

The list could surely go on, and there is nothing more wonderful than a list, instrument of wondrous hypotyposis.

Umberto Eco: *The Name of the Rose* (1983)

We represent calendar dates by fixed-length records with fields (components)—in descending order of significance—which we draw as a sequence of boxes, usually having the form

year	*month*	*day*

in which *year*, *month*, and *day* are all integers. We use boldface subscripts to select fields; for example, if

$d =$

1945	11	12

then $d_{\mathbf{day}} = 12$. The fields of dates differ for some calendars; we explain those particular forms in the individual discussions and use analogously named indices for extracting individual components.

We also have occasion to use lists of dates or of other items. Our use of lists requires manipulations such as forming lists, selecting elements from a list, or concatenating lists. We use the following notation for lists in our calendar functions.

- Angle brackets indicate list construction, that is, the formation of a list from individual components. For example, $\langle 1945, 11, 12\rangle$ is a list of the three components 1945, 11, and 12, respectively.

- Subscripts in square brackets indicate list element selection, with the indices of the elements 0-based. Thus if $b = \langle 1945, 11, 12\rangle$ then $b_{[0]}$ is 1945, $b_{[1]}$ is 11, and $b_{[2]}$ is 12.

- Empty angle brackets, $\langle\ \rangle$, indicate the list with no elements.
- Double bars indicate the concatenation of lists, and thus

$$\langle 1945\rangle \parallel \langle 11, 12\rangle = \langle 1945, 11, 12\rangle$$

The identity under concatenation is $\langle\ \rangle$; that is, the concatenation of $\langle\ \rangle$ with any list leaves the list unchanged.

A recursive traversal of a list can be used, for example, to convert each element of a list of moments into a fixed date, using the earlier function **fixed-from-moment** (1.12):

$$\textbf{list-of-fixed-from-moments}\,(\ell) \stackrel{\text{def}}{=} \tag{1.37}$$

$$\begin{cases} \langle\ \rangle & \textbf{if } \ell = \langle\ \rangle \\ \left\langle \textbf{fixed-from-moment}\left(\ell_{[0]}\right)\right\rangle \parallel \textbf{list-of-fixed-from-moments}\left(\ell_{[1..]}\right) & \\ \qquad \textbf{otherwise} & \end{cases}$$

The empty list $\langle\ \rangle$ gives an empty list, while a nonempty list is composed of its first element, $\ell_{[0]}$, converted to a fixed date, followed by the converted remainder of the list.

We use the notation $[a\,..\,b]$ to represent an interval of time beginning at moment a and ending at moment b (inclusive). To indicate that a given R.D. moment t is within a range $[a\,..\,b]$, in other words, that $a \leqslant t \leqslant b$, we write

$$t \in [a\,..\,b]$$

The same notation is used for an occurrence within half-open intervals:

$$t \in [a\,..\,b) \stackrel{\text{def}}{=} a \leqslant t < b \tag{1.38}$$

The determination of non-Gregorian holidays occurring in a given Gregorian year can require generating a list of the R.D. dates of those holidays over some longer interval and then scanning the list to filter out those not in the given Gregorian year. To cull a list of dates for those that occur in a given (half-open) range, we use the following recursive process:

$$\ell \cap [a\,..\,b) \stackrel{\text{def}}{=} \tag{1.39}$$

$$\begin{cases} \langle\ \rangle & \textbf{if } \ell = \langle\ \rangle \\ \left\langle \ell_{[0]} \right\rangle \parallel r & \textbf{if } \ell_{[0]} \in [a\,..\,b] \\ r & \textbf{otherwise} \end{cases}$$

where

$$r = \ell_{[1..]} \cap [a\,..\,b)$$

To collect all occurrences of events, such as holidays, in an interval of time, like a Gregorian year, we write a generic function to find the first occurrence on or after a given moment of the pth moment in a c-day cycle, $0 \leqslant p < c$, and then recursively find the remaining occurrences:

$$\textbf{positions-in-range}\,(p, c, \Delta, [a \,..\, b)) \stackrel{\text{def}}{=} \tag{1.40}$$

$$\begin{cases} \langle\,\rangle & \textbf{if } \mathit{date} \geqslant b \\ \langle \mathit{date} \rangle \parallel \textbf{positions-in-range}\,(p, c, \Delta, [a + c \,..\, b)) & \textbf{otherwise} \end{cases}$$

where

$$\mathit{date} = (p - \Delta) \bmod [a \,..\, a + c)$$

Here Δ is congruent modulo c to the position of R.D. moment 0 in the repeating cycle, and *date* is the first occurrence of position p in the interval *range*, computed using the interval modulus function (1.24).

1.10 Mixed-Radix Notations

It is interesting to note that nearly all MIX *programs can be expressed without knowing whether binary or decimal notation is being used—even when we are doing calculations involving multiple-precision arithmetic. Thus we find that the choice of radix does not significantly influence computer programming.*

Donald E. Knuth, *The Art of Computer Programming, vol. 2, Seminumerical Algorithms* (1998)

Mixed-radix notation, in which the radix can differ from position to position, is a generalization of ordinary positional notation, such as decimal, binary, and sexagesimal (base 60). We represent numbers in mixed-radix notation as lists, following the notation in [28, Section 4.1]: for example, 4 weeks, 1 day, 12 hours, 44 minutes, and 2.88 seconds is written $\langle 4, 1, 12, 44, 2.88 \rangle$ in base $\langle 7; 24, 60, 60 \rangle$, where the semicolon separates the integer part of the base from the fractional part. Each (rational) number b_i in the base determines the range $[0 \,..\, b_i)$ of values that may appear in position i. There will always be one more element in the number than in the base, for the most significant position; this position has no maximal value. The most significant position of a date given in mixed-radix notation can be negative. Also, the least significant position need not be a whole number, as in the above example, $\langle 4, 1, 12, 44, 2.88 \rangle$.

To evaluate the mixed-radix number

$$a = \langle a_0, a_1, \ldots, a_n \rangle$$

written in base

$$b = \langle b_1, \ldots, b_k; b_{k+1}, \ldots, b_n \rangle$$

we define the symbol $a \stackrel{\text{rad}}{\longleftarrow} b$ by

$$a \stackrel{\text{rad}}{\longleftarrow} b \stackrel{\text{def}}{=} \sum_{i=0}^{k} \left(a_i \times \prod_{j=i+1}^{k} b_j \right) + \sum_{i=k+1}^{n} \left(a_i \middle/ \prod_{j=k+1}^{i} b_j \right) \tag{1.41}$$

In the opposite direction, to convert a number x into base $b = \langle b_1, \ldots, b_k; b_{k+1}, \ldots, b_n \rangle$ we define the symbol $x \xrightarrow{\text{rad}} b$ by

$$x \xrightarrow{\text{rad}} b \stackrel{\text{def}}{=} \langle a_0, a_1, \ldots, a_n \rangle \tag{1.42}$$

where

$$a_0 = \left\lfloor x \Big/ \prod_{j=1}^{k} b_j \right\rfloor$$

$$a_i = \left\lfloor x \Big/ \prod_{j=i+1}^{k} b_j \right\rfloor \bmod b_i, \quad i = 1, \ldots, k$$

$$a_i = \left\lfloor x \times \prod_{j=k+1}^{i} \right\rfloor \bmod b_i, \quad i = k+1, \ldots, n-1$$

$$a_n = \left(x \times \prod_{j=k+1}^{n} \right) \bmod b_n$$

We use mixed-radix numbers for the Gregorian (Section 2.3), Icelandic (Chapter 6), Hebrew (Section 8.3), and Mayan (Section 11.1) calendars.

When referring to durations of time, we use base $\langle ; 24, 60, 60 \rangle$ and indicate positions with superscripts; for example,

$$i^{\text{d}} j^{\text{h}} k^{\text{m}} l^{\text{s}} = \langle i, j, k, l \rangle = i + \cfrac{j + \cfrac{k + \cfrac{l}{60}}{60}}{24} \text{ days}$$

is i days, j hours, k minutes, and l seconds. Thus, a fifth of a day is $0^{\text{d}}4^{\text{h}}48^{\text{m}}0^{\text{s}}$, or $4^{\text{h}}48^{\text{m}}$, for short, and $10^{\text{d}} - 4^{\text{h}}48^{\text{m}} = 9.8^{\text{d}} = 9^{\text{d}}19^{\text{h}}12^{\text{m}}$ is represented as the list $\langle 9, 19, 12 \rangle$.

To convert the usual clock time—also expressed in base $\langle ; 24, 60, 60 \rangle$ but without any whole days—into a fraction of a day, we use

$$\textbf{time-from-clock}\,(hms) \stackrel{\text{def}}{=} \frac{1}{24} \times hms \xleftarrow{\text{rad}} \langle ; 24, 60, 60 \rangle \tag{1.43}$$

The following function converts the fractional part of R.D. moment t into hours, minutes, and seconds on a 24-hour clock, taking midnight as $\langle 0, 0, 0 \rangle$, that is, 0:00:00 hours:

$$\textbf{clock-from-moment}\,(t) \stackrel{\text{def}}{=} \left(t \xrightarrow{\text{rad}} \langle ; 24, 60, 60 \rangle \right)_{[1..]} \tag{1.44}$$

The first component of $t \xrightarrow{\text{rad}} \langle ; 24, 60, 60 \rangle$, which contains whole days, is removed. To round to the nearest second, apply **clock-from-moment** to

$$\frac{\textbf{round}(t \times 24 \times 60 \times 60)}{24 \times 60 \times 60}$$

instead of t.

Angles can be described in terms of a list of degrees, arc minutes, and arc seconds in base $\langle ; 60, 60 \rangle$:

$$\langle d, m, s \rangle = d^\circ m' s'' = d + \frac{m + \frac{s}{60}}{60} \text{ degrees}$$

Given angle α as a real number of degrees, we can convert it to a list of degrees, arc minutes, and arc seconds with

$$\textbf{angle-from-degrees}\,(\alpha) \stackrel{\text{def}}{=} \tag{1.45}$$

$$\begin{cases} dms & \textbf{if } \alpha \geqslant 0 \\ \big\langle -dms_{[0]}, -dms_{[1]}, -dms_{[2]} \big\rangle & \textbf{otherwise} \end{cases}$$

where

$$dms = |\alpha| \xrightarrow{\text{rad}} \langle ; 60, 60 \rangle$$

Negative angles (such as southern latitudes) are given as a list of negative numbers of degrees, arc minutes, and arc seconds. The function $|\alpha|$ returns the absolute value of the angle α.

1.11 A Simple Calendar

This calendar is, indeed, the only intelligent calendar which ever existed in human history.

Otto Neugebauer: *The Exact Sciences in Antiquity* (1952)

A simple solar calendar with 365 days each year and no leap-year rule was in use in Egypt for millennia before the adoption of the Julian calendar in the third century C.E. and was also used in Babylon and Persia.[13] The development of this calendar is discussed in [37] ([8] has extensive source documents); it served as the canonical calendar for astronomers until the sixteenth century, and it is to this calendar that Neugebauer refers in the preceding quotation. Each month had 30 days, except for the last 5 days of the year, called *epagomenæ*, which were considered an unlucky period and which we can treat as a short thirteenth month. The month names with their hieroglyphs, according to [4], were:

---

[13] The ancient Egyptians are also believed to have used a lunar calendar with months beginning the first morning of invisibility of the old moon [37].

	Middle Kingdom	New Kingdom	
(1) Thoth			30 days
(2) Phaophi			30 days
(3) Athyr			30 days
(4) Choiak			30 days
(5) Tybi			30 days
(6) Mechir			30 days
(7) Phamenoth			30 days
(8) Pharmuthi			30 days
(9) Pachon			30 days
(10) Payni			30 days
(11) Epiphi			30 days
(12) Mesori			30 days
(13) (Unnamed)			5 days

Variants of these month names are still used in the Coptic calendar (see Section 4.1). Days began at dawn. We use this calendar as a simple example of calendar conversion functions. Our calendar functions always use numbers to represent months; we provide tables of names, when known, for each calendar.

The epoch chosen by the famous Alexandrian astronomer Ptolemy, author of the *Almagest*, for this calendar, and called the *Nabonassar Era* after the Chaldean king Nabonassar, is given by [33] as JD 1448638:

$$\textbf{egyptian-epoch} \stackrel{\text{def}}{=} \textbf{fixed-from-jd}\,(1448638) \tag{1.46}$$

which corresponds to R.D. −272787, or February 26, 747 B.C.E. (Julian). Because all years have fixed length, converting Egyptian dates into fixed dates is trivial:

$$\textbf{fixed-from-egyptian}\left(\boxed{\,\textit{year} \mid \textit{month} \mid \textit{day}\,}\right) \stackrel{\text{def}}{=} \tag{1.47}$$

$$\textbf{egyptian-epoch} + 365 \times (\textit{year} - 1) + 30 \times (\textit{month} - 1) + \textit{day} - 1$$

The short last month causes no problem, because we only count the number of days in prior months.

In the astronomical code and elsewhere we use a vector notation within summations. For example,

$$\textbf{alt-fixed-from-egyptian}\left(\widetilde{e\text{-}date}\right) \stackrel{\text{def}}{=} \tag{1.48}$$

$$\textbf{egyptian-epoch} + \sum \widetilde{a} \times \left(\widetilde{e\text{-}date} - 1\right)$$

where

$$\widetilde{a} = \langle 365, 30, 1 \rangle$$

performs the same calculation as **fixed-from-egyptian**. Each of the three components of the Egyptian date $\widetilde{e\text{-}date}$ is decremented by 1 and then multiplied by the corresponding element of $\widetilde{a} = \langle 365, 30, 1\rangle$ to give the total number of elapsed days since the epoch.

For the inverse, converting fixed dates to Egyptian dates, we make straightforward use of the floor and mod functions:

$$\textbf{egyptian-from-fixed}\,(date) \stackrel{\text{def}}{=} \boxed{\, year \mid month \mid day \,} \tag{1.49}$$

where

$$days = date - \textbf{egyptian-epoch}$$

$$year = \left\lfloor \frac{days}{365} \right\rfloor + 1$$

$$month = \left\lfloor \frac{1}{30} \times (days \bmod 365) \right\rfloor + 1$$

$$day = days - 365 \times (year - 1) - 30 \times (month - 1) + 1$$

The rules of the Armenian calendar were identical to those of the Egyptian; the only difference is the epoch (see [31]):

$$\textbf{armenian-epoch} \stackrel{\text{def}}{=} \text{R.D. } 201443 \tag{1.50}$$

which corresponds to July 11, 552 C.E. (Julian). To convert R.D. dates to and from the Armenian calendar, we simply adjust by the difference in epochs:

$$\textbf{fixed-from-armenian}\left(\boxed{\, year \mid month \mid day \,}\right) \stackrel{\text{def}}{=} \tag{1.51}$$

$$\textbf{armenian-epoch} + \textbf{fixed-from-egyptian}\left(\boxed{\, year \mid month \mid day \,}\right)$$

$$- \textbf{egyptian-epoch}$$

In the other direction we have

$$\textbf{armenian-from-fixed}\,(date) \stackrel{\text{def}}{=} \tag{1.52}$$

$$\textbf{egyptian-from-fixed}\,(date + \textbf{egyptian-epoch} - \textbf{armenian-epoch})$$

The 12 Armenian months were called

(1) Nawasardi	(7) Mehekani
(2) Hoṝi	(8) Areg
(3) Sahmi	(9) Ahekani
(4) Trē	(10) Mareri
(5) K‘aloch	(11) Margach
(6) Arach	(12) Hrotich

and the epagomenæ were called *aweleach*.

The Zoroastrian calendar has an identical structure to that of the ancient Egyptian calendar, but with a different epoch (see Table 1.2) and different month names. In the past, the Persians used individual names for each of the days of the month; these Persian names were

(1) Hormuz	هرمز	(16) Mehr	مهر
(2) Bahman	بهمن	(17) Sorūsh	سروش
(3) Ordībehesht	اردیبهشت	(18) Rashn	رشن
(4) Shahrīvar	شهریور	(19) Farvardīn	فروردین
(5) Esfandārmud	اسفندارمذ	(20) Bahrām	بهرام
(6) Xordād	خرداذ	(21) Rām	رام
(7) Mordād	مرداذ	(22) Bād	باد
(8) Diy be Āzar	دی باذر	(23) Diy be Dīn	دی بدین
(9) Āzar	آزر	(24) Dīn	دین
(10) Ābān	آبان	(25) Ard	ارد
(11) Xor	خور	(26) Ashtād	اشتاذ
(12) Māh	ماه	(27) Asmān	اسمان
(13) Tīr	تیر	(28) Zāmyād	زامیاد
(14) Goosh	گوش	(29) Māresfand	مارسفند
(15) Diy be Mehr	دی بمهر	(30) Anīrān	انیران

and the epagomenæ were sometimes named:

(1) Ahnad	اهند
(2) Ashnad	اشند
(3) Esfandārmud	اسفندارمد
(4) Axshatar	اخشتر
(5) Behesht	بهشت

The Mandean calendar also follows the same structure, but its epagomenæ lie between the eighth and ninth months [47].

1.12 Cycles of Days

And day by day I'll do this heavy task.
Shakespeare: *Titus Andronicus*, Act V, scene ii (1594)

Because R.D. 1 is a Monday, determining the day of the week amounts to taking the R.D. date modulo 7: 0 is Sunday, 1 is Monday, and so forth. We define the seven constants

$$\textbf{sunday} \stackrel{\text{def}}{=} 0 \tag{1.53}$$

$$\textbf{monday} \stackrel{\text{def}}{=} 1 \tag{1.54}$$

$$\textbf{tuesday} \stackrel{\text{def}}{=} 2 \tag{1.55}$$

$$\textbf{wednesday} \stackrel{\text{def}}{=} 3 \tag{1.56}$$

$$\textbf{thursday} \stackrel{\text{def}}{=} 4 \tag{1.57}$$

$$\textbf{friday} \stackrel{\text{def}}{=} 5 \tag{1.58}$$

$$\textbf{saturday} \stackrel{\text{def}}{=} 6 \tag{1.59}$$

and determine the day of the week with

$$\textbf{day-of-week-from-fixed}\,(date) \stackrel{\text{def}}{=} \tag{1.60}$$
$$(date - \text{R.D. } 0 - \textbf{sunday}) \bmod 7$$

We include the superfluous terms $-$R.D. $0 - \textbf{sunday} = 0$ to make this function independent of any particular choice of epoch for fixed dates, and for that reason we use this function in the formulas that follow.

Many holidays are on the *n*th occurrence of a given day of the week, counted forward or backward from some date. For example, Thanksgiving in the United States is the fourth Thursday in November, that is, the fourth Thursday on or after November 1. We handle such specifications by writing a function that encapsulates the formula

$$k \bmod [date \,..\, date - 7) \tag{1.61}$$

to find the kth day of the week ($k = 0$ for Sunday, and so on) that falls in the 7-day period ending on R.D. *date*. Using equations (1.25) and (1.26) we find that (1.61) is equivalent to

$$\begin{aligned} k \bmod [date \,..\, date - 7) &= date + (k - date) \bmod [0 \,..\, -7) \\ &= date - (date - k) \bmod [0 \,..\, 7) \\ &= date - (date - k) \bmod 7 \end{aligned}$$

To incorporate the possibility that day 0 of the day count is other than a Sunday, we use the function **day-of-week-from-fixed** (1.60):

$$\textbf{kday-on-or-before}\,(k, date) \stackrel{\text{def}}{=} \tag{1.62}$$

$$date - \textbf{day-of-week-from-fixed}\,(date - k)$$

We generally use the parameter *date* for R.D. dates.

Formula (1.61) is an instance of a more general principle for finding the occurrence of the kth day of a repeating m-day cycle that is closest to but not past day number d, where day number 0 is day Δ of the m-day cycle:

$$\boxed{(k - \Delta) \bmod [d \mathinner{..} d - m)} \tag{1.63}$$

This formula works equally well for negative and nonintegral dates d (that is, for a time of day) and for nonintegral positions k, shifts Δ, and periods m. We use such computations extensively for the Hindu calendars (Chapter 10), the Mayan calendars (Chapter 11), and the Balinese Pawukon calendar (Chapter 12).

Note that formula (1.63) for the last k-label day on or before day number d remains correct even if the cycle of labels is $a, a + 1, \ldots, a + m - 1$ (that is, based at a instead of 0). We use this in the Chinese calendar (Chapter 19) for $a = 1$, that is, for 1-based cycles of labels, and also for Balinese dates (Chapter 12).

Similarly, the first k-labeled moment at or after moment d is

$$(k - \Delta) \bmod [d \mathinner{..} d + m) \tag{1.64}$$

We can write a function **kday-on-or-after** R.D. d by applying **kday-on-or-before** to $d + 6$. Similarly, applying it to $d + 3$ gives the **kday-nearest** to R.D. d, applying it to $d - 1$ gives the **kday-before** R.D. d, and applying it to $d + 7$ gives the **kday-after** R.D. d:

$$\textbf{kday-on-or-after}\,(k, date) \stackrel{\text{def}}{=} \textbf{kday-on-or-before}\,(k, date + 6) \tag{1.65}$$

$$\textbf{kday-nearest}\,(k, date) \stackrel{\text{def}}{=} \textbf{kday-on-or-before}\,(k, date + 3) \tag{1.66}$$

$$\textbf{kday-before}\,(k, date) \stackrel{\text{def}}{=} \textbf{kday-on-or-before}\,(k, date - 1) \tag{1.67}$$

$$\textbf{kday-after}\,(k, date) \stackrel{\text{def}}{=} \textbf{kday-on-or-before}\,(k, date + 7) \tag{1.68}$$

Equations (1.62) and (1.65)–(1.68) are specific instances of more general calculations that occur in cyclical calendars such as the Mayan, Aztec, and Balinese. The general form can be expressed as

$$(k - \Delta) \bmod [\delta(d) \mathinner{..} \delta(d) - m) \tag{1.69}$$

where the length of the repeating cycle is m, k is the desired position in the cycle, R.D. 0 is at position Δ in the cycle, and the function $\delta(d)$ is chosen according to Table 1.3.

Table 1.3 Functions $\delta(d)$ for use in formula (1.69).

Relation to date d	$\delta(d)$
before d	$d-1$
on or before d	d
after d	$d+m$
on or after d	$d+m-1$
nearest to d	$d+\lfloor m/2 \rfloor$

1.13 Simultaneous Cycles

In the year 4-House of the eighth sheaf of years of the Mexican era the Emperor Moteçuçuma the Younger had a great fright. We know this year as 1509. The Mexicans counted their time in "sheafs" of fifty-two years, and in order to designate them without error or ambiguity, a system had been adopted which can be best understood by reference to a pack of cards: as if we were to call our years one of spades, two of hearts, three of diamonds, four of clubs, five of spades, six of hearts, seven of diamonds, eight of clubs, etc. It is clear that the series or "sheaf" would begin again every fifty-two years. The Mexican calendar divided the fifty-two years of a "sheaf" into four sets or "colours" of thirteen years, i.e., rabbits, reeds, flints and houses.

Salvador de Madariaga: *Hernán Cortés: Conqueror of Mexico* (1942)

Some calendars employ two cycles running simultaneously. Each day is labeled by a pair of numbers $\langle a, b\rangle$, beginning with $\langle 0, 0\rangle$, followed by $\langle 1, 1\rangle$, $\langle 2, 2\rangle$, and so on. Suppose the first component repeats after c days and the second after d days, with $c < d < 2c$; then after day $\langle c-1, c-1\rangle$ come days $\langle 0, c\rangle$, $\langle 1, c+1\rangle$, and so on until $\langle d-c-1, d-1\rangle$, which is followed by $\langle d-c, 0\rangle$. If day 0 of the calendar is labeled $\langle 0, 0\rangle$ then day n is $\langle n \bmod c, n \bmod d\rangle$. The Chinese use such pairs to identify years (see Section 19.4), with cycles of length $c = 10$ and $d = 12$ but, because the first component ranges from 1 to 10, inclusive, and the second from 1 to 12, we would use the adjusted remainder function: $\langle n \bmod [1 \,..\, 10], n \bmod [1 \,..\, 12]\rangle$

More generally, for arbitrary positive integers c and d, if the label of day 0 is $\langle \Gamma, \Delta\rangle$ then day n is labeled

$$\boxed{\langle (n+\Gamma) \bmod c, (n+\Delta) \bmod d\rangle} \tag{1.70}$$

For the Mayan tzolkin calendar, with $c = 13$, $d = 20$, $\Gamma = 3$, $\Delta = 19$, and beginning the cycles with 1 instead of 0, this is $\langle (n+3) \bmod [1 \,..\, 13], (n+19) \bmod [1 \,..\, 20]\rangle$. It follows that day 1 of the Mayan calendar is labeled $\langle 4, 20\rangle$ (see Section 11.2).

How many distinct day names does such a scheme provide? If m is the least common multiple (lcm) of c and d, then such a calendar repeats after m days. If the cycle lengths c and d are relatively prime (that is, no integer greater than 1 divides both c and d without remainder), then it repeats after $m = c \times d$ days. Thus, for the Mayan tzolkin calendar, with $c = 13$ and $d = 20$, m is 260. For the Chinese year names, $\text{lcm}(10, 12) = 60$ yielding a sexagesimal cycle.

Inverting this representation is harder. Suppose first that $\Gamma = \Delta = 0$. Given a pair $\langle a, b\rangle$, where a is an integer in the range $0 \mathinner{\ldotp\ldotp} c-1$ and b is an integer in the range $0 \mathinner{\ldotp\ldotp} d-1$, we are looking for an n, $0 \leqslant n < m$, such that $a = n \bmod c$ and $b = n \bmod d$. This requires the solution to a pair of simultaneous linear congruences (this is an instance of the Chinese Remainder Theorem; see, for example, [28]):

$$n \equiv a \pmod{c}$$

$$n \equiv b \pmod{d}$$

The first congruence means that

$$n = a + ic \tag{1.71}$$

for some integer i. Substituting this for n in the second congruence and transposing, we get

$$ic \equiv b - a \pmod{d}$$

Let g be the greatest common divisor (gcd) of c and d and let $u = c/g$ and $v = d/g$, so that u and v are relatively prime. Now let k be the multiplicative inverse of u modulo v; that is,

$$ku \bmod v = 1$$

We can use the Fermat-Euler Theorem [19, Theorem 72, p. 63], because u and v are relatively prime:

$$k = u^{\varphi(v)-1} \bmod v \tag{1.72}$$

where the totient function $\varphi(v)$ counts the number of integers i, $1 \leqslant i \leqslant v$, that are relatively prime to v. (The multiplicative inverse k can also be determined using the Euclidean algorithm; see [34] for details.) Now,

$$k\frac{c}{g} \bmod \frac{d}{g} = 1$$

Then

$$i \equiv ik\frac{c}{g} \equiv k\frac{b-a}{g} \left(\bmod \frac{d}{g}\right)$$

Using this value of i in equation (1.71), we get day number

$$a + c\left[k\frac{b-a}{g} \bmod \frac{d}{g}\right] = a + \left[\frac{ck}{g}(b-a) \bmod \frac{cd}{g}\right]$$

When day 0 is labeled $\langle\Gamma, \Delta\rangle$, we must subtract Γ from a and Δ from b. To make sure that n is in the range $0 \mathinner{\ldotp\ldotp} m-1$, we use

$$\boxed{n = \left(a - \Gamma + \frac{ck[b - a + \Gamma - \Delta]}{\gcd(c, d)}\right) \bmod \operatorname{lcm}(c, d)} \tag{1.73}$$

For example, if $c = 10$ and $d = 12$, as in the Chinese calendar, then $\gcd(10, 12) = 2$, $\mathrm{lcm}(10, 12) = 60$, and $k = 5$ because $(5 \times 5) \bmod 6 = 1$. Using $\Gamma = \Delta = 0$, but counting from 1 instead of 0, we find that Chinese year name $\langle a, b\rangle$ corresponds to year number

$$(a + 25(b - a)) \bmod [1 \,..\, 60] \tag{1.74}$$

of the sexagesimal cycle; we use this formula in Section 19.4. We use other derivations of this sort for the Hebrew calendar in Section 8.3, for the Mayan calendars in Section 11.2, and for the Balinese calendar in Chapter 12.

Note that some combinations $\langle a, b\rangle$ are impossible. In general, there is no solution (1.73) unless

$$\boxed{\gcd(c, d) \text{ divides } (b - a + \Gamma - \Delta)} \tag{1.75}$$

or, equivalently,

$$(b - a + \Gamma - \Delta) \bmod \gcd(c, d) = 0$$

For example, with the Chinese scheme, the odd-even parity of the two components must be the same because c and d are both even, and only 60 of the 120 conceivable pairs are possible.

Equation (1.73) is all we need to implement the calendar of the Akan people of Ghana [5], [29], [35], which is based on a 42-day cycle of day names formed by two simultaneous cycles of six prefixes and seven stems. It is similar to the Mayan tzolkin calendar (Section 11.2) and the Chinese sexagesimal names (Section 19.4). The prefixes of the Akan calendar are

(1) Nwona (care, wellness, surpass, innocence)
(2) Nkyi (passing, no restrictions)
(3) Kuru (sacred, complete)
(4) Kwa (ordinary, empty, freedom)
(5) Mono (fresh, new)
(6) Fo (generous, calm, love to another)

and the stems are

(1) Wukuo (cleansing, advocate, mean-spirited)
(2) Yaw (pain, suffering, bravery)
(3) Fie (depart from, come forth, travel)
(4) Memene (digest, satiety, creation, ancient)
(5) Kwasi (freedom, purify, smoke)
(6) Dwo (peaceful, cool, calm)
(7) Bene (well-cooked)

Together these prefixes and suffixes form a sequence of 42 day names, Nwonawukuo, Nkyiyaw, …, Fobene. Representing Akan day names as pairs of positive integers,

$$\boxed{\textit{prefix}}\boxed{\textit{stem}}$$

where *prefix* and *stem* are integers in the ranges 1 to 6 and 1 to 7, respectively, the nth Akan day name is given by

$$\textbf{akan-day-name}\,(n) \stackrel{\text{def}}{=} \boxed{n \bmod [1\,..\,6]}\boxed{n \bmod [1\,..\,7]} \tag{1.76}$$

Applying formula (1.73) with $c = 6$, $d = 7$, $\Gamma = \Delta = 0$ but counting from 1 instead of 0, we find that the Akan name $\boxed{a}\boxed{b}$ corresponds to name number

$$(a + 36(b - a)) \bmod [1\,..\,42]$$

Determination of the number of names between given Akan names is thus given by

$$\textbf{akan-name-difference} \tag{1.77}$$
$$\left(\boxed{\textit{prefix}_1}\boxed{\textit{stem}_1}, \boxed{\textit{prefix}_2}\boxed{\textit{stem}_2}\right) \stackrel{\text{def}}{=}$$
$$(\textit{prefix-difference} + 36 \times (\textit{stem-difference} - \textit{prefix-difference}))$$
$$\bmod [1\,..\,42]$$

where

$$\textit{prefix-difference} = \textit{prefix}_2 - \textit{prefix}_1$$
$$\textit{stem-difference} = \textit{stem}_2 - \textit{stem}_1$$

Computing backwards from known dates in the present, we find that a cycle began on R.D. 37, so that we have

$$\textbf{akan-day-name-epoch} \stackrel{\text{def}}{=} \text{R.D. } 37 \tag{1.78}$$

which allows us to write

$$\textbf{akan-name-from-fixed}\,(\textit{date}) \stackrel{\text{def}}{=} \tag{1.79}$$
$$\textbf{akan-day-name}\,(\textit{date} - \textbf{akan-day-name-epoch})$$

Now we can apply formula (1.63) to compute the R.D. date of the last date with a given Akan name before a given R.D. date:

$$\textbf{akan-day-name-on-or-before}\,(\textit{name}, \textit{date}) \stackrel{\text{def}}{=} \tag{1.80}$$
$$\textbf{akan-name-difference}\,(\textbf{akan-name-from-fixed}\,(0), \textit{name})$$
$$\bmod [\textit{date}\,..\,\textit{date} - 42)$$

1.14 Cycles of Years

An ordinary person cannot count each day, and say this is so many and so many days. Instead, the count uses a significant unit, that is, years.

T. Schvarcz: *Zichron Menachem*, 5673 A.M. (= 1913–14); from a talk given in June 1907 to honor the fortieth anniversary of Franz Josef I's rule of Hungary

We now derive some general formulas that are useful in calendar conversions for the Julian, Islamic, Coptic, Hebrew, arithmetic Persian, and old Hindu lunisolar calendars (although not in the same way for the Gregorian calendar, unfortunately), as well as serving as the basis for the generic solar and lunisolar calendars in Chapter 13. All of these calendars have in common that they follow a simple type of leap-year rule in which leap years are spread as evenly as possible over a cycle of years; the particular constants that define these leap-year rules are given in Table 1.4. The formulas in this section are closely related to Bresenham's "midpoint line algorithm" for drawing lines in two dimensions on a discrete raster graphics image [20], [47].

Suppose we have a sequence of years $\ldots, -2, -1, 0, 1, 2, \ldots$, and we want to place l leap years in a cycle of c years, with year 0 as the first year of the cycle. How can we spread the leap years evenly over the cycle? If l is a divisor of c, our problem is easy: Let year numbers that are multiples of c/l be leap years. If l is not a divisor of c, however, the best we can do is to let year numbers that are *roughly* multiples of c/l be leap years—specifically, we have a leap year whenever the year number has reached, or just passed, a multiple of c/l. Let y be a year number; then it is a leap year if

$$y - 1 < k\frac{c}{l} \leqslant y$$

for some integer k. Rearranging this inequality, we get

$$k\frac{c}{l} \leqslant y < k\frac{c}{l} + 1 \tag{1.81}$$

which is the same as saying that

$$0 \leqslant \left(y \bmod \frac{c}{l}\right) < 1$$

Multiplying by l and using equation (1.19), we obtain

$$0 \leqslant (yl \bmod c) < l$$

Because our cycles always have length $c > 0$, the definition of the mod function guarantees that $(yl \bmod c) \geqslant 0$, so we can drop that part of the inequality to get

$$(yl \bmod c) < l \tag{1.82}$$

For example, on the Julian calendar for years C.E. (see Chapter 3) we want $l = 1$ leap year in the cycle of $c = 4$ years; then year $y > 0$ is a leap year if

$$(y \bmod 4) < 1$$

Table 1.4 Constants describing the simple leap-year structure of various calendars; c is the length of the leap-year cycle, l is the number of leap years in that cycle of c years, Δ is the position in the cycle of year 0, L is the length of an ordinary year (hence $L+1$ is the length of a leap year), $\bar{L} = (cL+l)/c$ is the average length of a year, and $\delta = (\Delta l)/c \bmod 1$ is the time of day or month (as a fraction of the day or month, respectively) when mean year 0 begins. This cyclic pattern also applies to Islamic months, and approximately to the Gregorian/Julian months.

	Calendar	Section	c	l	Δ	L	$\bar{L} = \frac{cL+l}{c}$	$\delta = \frac{\Delta l}{c} \bmod 1$
Years	Julian C.E.	3.1	4	1	0	365 days	$\frac{1461}{4}$ days	0 days
	Julian B.C.E.	3.1	4	1	1	365 days	$\frac{1461}{4}$ days	$\frac{1}{4}$ day
	Coptic	4.1	4	1	1	365 days	$\frac{1461}{4}$ days	$\frac{1}{4}$ day
	Islamic	7.1	30	11	4	354 days	$\frac{10631}{30}$ days	$\frac{7}{15}$ day
	Islamic (variant)	7.1	30	11	15	354 days	$\frac{10631}{30}$ days	$\frac{1}{2}$ day
	Hebrew	8.1	19	7	11	12 months	$\frac{235}{19}$ months	$\frac{1}{19}$ month
	Ecclesiastical	9.1	19	7	13	12 months	$\frac{235}{19}$ months	$\frac{1}{19}$ month
	Old Hindu lunisolar	10.3				12 months	$\frac{2226389}{180000}$ months	$\frac{2093611}{2160000}$ month
	Persian	15.3	128	31	38	365 days	$\frac{46751}{128}$ days	$\frac{13}{64}$ day
Months	Gregorian/Julian (approximate)	2.2	12	7	11	30 days	$\frac{367}{12}$ days	$\frac{5}{12}$ day
	Gregorian/Julian (approximate)	2.3	7	4	6	30 days	$\frac{214}{7}$ days	$\frac{3}{7}$ day
	Gregorian/Julian (March–March)	2.3	5	3	4	30 days	$\frac{153}{5}$ days	$\frac{2}{5}$ day
	Islamic (ordinary year)	7.1	12	6	1	29 days	$\frac{59}{2}$ days	$\frac{1}{2}$ day
	Islamic	7.1	11	6	10	29 days	$\frac{325}{11}$ days	$\frac{5}{11}$ day

or, in other words, if

$$(y \bmod 4) = 0$$

We can complicate the leap-year situation by insisting that year 0 be in position Δ in the cycle of c years. In this case, we have the same analysis but pretend that the cycle begins at year 0 and ask about year $y + \Delta$. Inequality (1.82) becomes

$$\boxed{[(y + \Delta)l \bmod c] < l} \tag{1.83}$$

For example, the Julian calendar for years B.C.E. (Chapter 3) and the Coptic calendar (Chapter 4) have a cycle of $c = 4$ years containing $l = 1$ leap years with $\Delta = 1$. Inequality (1.83) becomes

$$[(y + 1) \bmod 4] < 1$$

this is equivalent to

$$(y \bmod 4) = 3$$

The Islamic calendar (Chapter 7) has a cycle of $c = 30$ years containing $l = 11$ leap years with $\Delta = 4$ (some Muslims have a different leap-year structure, which corresponds to $\Delta = 15$; see page 107), so the test for an Islamic leap year is

$$[(11y + 14) \bmod 30] < 11$$

Spreading 11 leap years evenly over 30 years implies gaps of 2 or 3 years between leap years. Because $\frac{30}{11} = 2\frac{8}{11}$, 3 of the 11 leap years each occur after a gap of only 2 years. If we associate each leap year with the gap preceding it and number the gaps 0, 1, ... 10, these three short gaps are numbers 2, 6, and 9, to which formula (1.83) could also be applied (with $c = 11$, $l = 3$, and $\Delta = 2$).

If $\Delta = 0$, inequality (1.81) implies that

$$k = \left\lfloor \frac{y}{c/l} \right\rfloor \tag{1.84}$$

is the number of leap years in the range of years $1 \mathinner{..} y$. When $\Delta \neq 0$, we again pretend that the cycle begins at year 0 and ask about year $y + \Delta$ instead of year y. Thus, the number of leap years in the range $1 \mathinner{..} y - 1$ for $\Delta \neq 0$ is the same as the number of leap years in the unshifted range of years $\Delta + 1 \mathinner{..} y + \Delta - 1$ (whether y is positive or negative), namely,

$$\boxed{\left\lfloor \frac{y + \Delta - 1}{c/l} \right\rfloor - \left\lfloor \frac{\Delta}{c/l} \right\rfloor = \left\lfloor \frac{ly - l + (\Delta l \bmod c)}{c} \right\rfloor} \tag{1.85}$$

the number of years in the unshifted range $1 \mathinner{..} y + \Delta - 1$ minus the number in the unshifted range $1 \mathinner{..} \Delta$. For example, $\lfloor (y - 1)/4 \rfloor$ is the number of leap years before year y on the Julian calendar (counting from the Julian epoch), $\lfloor (11y + 3)/30 \rfloor$ is the number of leap years prior to year y on the Islamic calendar, and $\lfloor y/4 \rfloor$ is the number of leap years prior to year y on the Coptic calendar.

Using formula (1.85), we immediately get the following formula for the number of days in the years before year y—that is, the number of days in the years 1, 2, 3, ..., $y - 1$, assuming there are L days in an ordinary year and $L + 1$ days in a leap year:

$$\boxed{n = \left\lfloor \frac{ly - l + (\Delta l \bmod c)}{c} \right\rfloor + L(y - 1)} \tag{1.86}$$

For example, for the Julian calendar this yields $\lfloor (y - 1)/4 \rfloor + 365(y - 1)$, for the Coptic calendar this yields $\lfloor y/4 \rfloor + 365(y - 1)$, and for the Islamic calendar it yields $\lfloor (11y + 3)/30 \rfloor + 354(y - 1)$. Because the Hebrew calendar (and lunisolar calendars in general) adds leap months, formula (1.86) does not apply to days, but it does apply to *months*: The number of months prior to year y on the Hebrew calendar is $\lfloor (7y - 6)/19 \rfloor + 12(y - 1)$.

Formula (1.86) works for $y \leqslant 0$. In this case it computes the number of days in years $y \,..\, 0$ as a negative number.

Finally, we can derive an inverse to formula (1.86) to find the year at day n, counting day $n = 0$ as the first day of year 1 (the epoch). Because there are L days in an ordinary year and $L + 1$ days in a leap year, the average year length is

$$\bar{L} = \frac{cL + l}{c}$$

In the simple case that $\Delta = 0$, year y begins on day

$$\begin{aligned} n &= (y - 1)L + (\text{number of leap years in } 1 \,..\, y - 1) \\ &= (y - 1)L + \left\lfloor \frac{y - 1}{c/l} \right\rfloor \\ &= \lfloor (y - 1)\bar{L} \rfloor \end{aligned} \tag{1.87}$$

by using formula (1.84) and simplifying. Day n is in year y provided that it is on or after the first day of year y and before the first day of year $y + 1$; that is,

$$\lfloor (y - 1)\bar{L} \rfloor \leqslant n < \lfloor y\bar{L} \rfloor \tag{1.88}$$

The sequence $\lfloor \bar{L} \rfloor, \lfloor 2\bar{L} \rfloor, \lfloor 3\bar{L} \rfloor, \ldots$ is called the *spectrum* of $\bar{L}$ (see [18, sec. 3.2]); in our case, they are the initial day numbers of successive years. Inequality (1.88) is equivalent to

$$(y - 1)\bar{L} - 1 < n \leqslant y\bar{L} - 1$$

from which it follows that

$$y = \left\lceil \frac{n + 1}{\bar{L}} \right\rceil \tag{1.89}$$

In general, when $\Delta \neq 0$, we must shift Δ years backward; that is, shift the first day of year 1 to the first day of year $-\Delta + 1$. The number of days in the shifted years $-\Delta + 1 \,..\, 0$ is the same as the number of days in the unshifted years $1 \,..\, \Delta$, which is computed by adding the L ordinary days in each of those Δ years, plus the $\lfloor \Delta/(c/l) \rfloor$ leap days in those years as given by (1.84). The shift of Δ years thus corresponds to a shift of $\Delta L + \lfloor \Delta/(c/l) \rfloor$ days. So the shifted form of (1.89) is

$$y + \Delta = \left\lceil \frac{n + 1 + \Delta L + \left\lfloor \frac{\Delta}{c/l} \right\rfloor}{\bar{L}} \right\rceil$$

which is the same as

$$\boxed{\begin{aligned} y &= \left\lceil \frac{cn + c - (l\Delta \bmod c)}{cL + l} \right\rceil \\ &= \left\lfloor \frac{cn + cL + l - 1 + c - (l\Delta \bmod c)}{cL + l} \right\rfloor \end{aligned}} \tag{1.90}$$

We usually prefer the latter form because the floor function is more readily available than the ceiling function in computer languages.

For the Julian calendar, formula (1.90) gives day n occurring in year

$$\left\lceil \frac{4n + 4}{1461} \right\rceil = \left\lfloor \frac{4n + 1464}{1461} \right\rfloor$$

for the Coptic calendar it gives year

$$\left\lceil \frac{4n + 3}{1461} \right\rceil = \left\lfloor \frac{4n + 1463}{1461} \right\rfloor$$

and for the Islamic calendar it gives year

$$\left\lceil \frac{30n + 16}{10631} \right\rceil = \left\lfloor \frac{30n + 10646}{10631} \right\rfloor$$

Formula (1.90) does not apply to days on the Hebrew calendar but rather to months, giving the formula

$$\left\lceil \frac{19n + 18}{235} \right\rceil = \left\lfloor \frac{19n + 252}{235} \right\rfloor \tag{1.91}$$

for the year in which month n occurs; we use this formula in Section 8.3 to get the month/year corresponding to *elapsed-months* in **fixed-from-molad**.

Formula (1.90) makes sense when $n < 0$, too. In this case it gives the correct year as a negative number (but, as discussed earlier, this is off by one for Julian B.C.E. years).

A more general approach to leap-year distribution is to imagine a sequence of *mean years* of (noninteger) length $\bar{L}$, with year 1 starting on day 0 at time δ, $0 \leqslant \delta < 1$, where δ expresses time as a fraction of a day. We define a *calendar year* y to begin at the start of the day on which mean year y begins; that is, mean year y begins at moment $\delta + (y - 1)\bar{L}$, and thus calendar year y begins on day

$$\boxed{n = \lfloor (y - 1)\bar{L} + \delta \rfloor} \tag{1.92}$$

Calendar year y is an ordinary year if

$$\lfloor y\bar{L} + \delta \rfloor - \lfloor (y-1)\bar{L} + \delta \rfloor = \lfloor \bar{L} \rfloor$$

and a leap year if

$$\lfloor y\bar{L} + \delta \rfloor - \lfloor (y-1)\bar{L} + \delta \rfloor = \lfloor \bar{L} \rfloor + 1$$

By definition (1.17), this latter equation tells us that calendar year y is a leap year if

$$\left(\delta + (y-1)(\bar{L} \bmod 1)\right) \bmod 1 \geqslant 1 - \left(\bar{L} \bmod 1\right)$$

or, equivalently, if

$$\boxed{\left(\delta + (y-1)\bar{L}\right) \bmod 1 \geqslant 1 - \left(\bar{L} \bmod 1\right)} \tag{1.93}$$

For the old Hindu lunisolar calendar, with the year count beginning at 0 (not 1), average year length of

$$\bar{L} = \frac{2226389}{180000} \approx 12.368828$$

months, and

$$\delta = \frac{2093611}{2160000}$$

inequality (1.93) means that y is a leap year if

$$\left(\frac{2093611}{2160000} + y\frac{2226389}{180000}\right) \bmod 1 \geqslant 1 - \frac{66389}{180000} = \frac{113611}{180000}$$

or, equivalently,

$$(2093611 + 796668\,y) \bmod 2160000 \geqslant 1363332$$

(See page 163.) However, this test is not needed for other calculations on the old Hindu calendar.

When $\delta = 0$, mean year 1 and calendar year 1 both begin at the same moment, and equation (1.92) tells us that leap years follow the same pattern as for $\Delta = 0$ in our earlier discussion. More generally, given any Δ, if we choose

$$\delta = \frac{\Delta l}{c} \bmod 1 \tag{1.94}$$

the leap-year test (1.93) simplifies to (1.83), and thus we have the same leap-year structure. For example, the Coptic calendar has $\delta = [(1 \times 1)/4] \bmod 1 = 1/4$.

Our δ formulas generalize our Δ formulas because formula (1.94) gives a corresponding value of δ for each Δ. However, there need not be a value of Δ for arbitrary $\bar{L}$ and δ; indeed, there is no such Δ for calendars in which the mean and calendar years never begin at exactly the same moment. Given $\bar{L}$ and δ, we have $l/c = \bar{L} \bmod 1$, and (1.94) means that Δ exists only if δ is an integer multiple, modulo 1, of $\bar{L}$. In the old Hindu lunisolar calendar, for example, formula (1.83) cannot be used directly: $\bar{L}$ mod 1 = 66389/180000, and we must have an integer Δ such that

$$\frac{2093611}{2160000} = \left(\Delta \frac{66389}{180000}\right) \bmod 1$$

or

$$2093611 = (796668\,\Delta) \bmod 2160000$$

No such Δ exists because 796668 and 2160000 are both even, but 2093611 is odd. When $\bar{L}$ is rational, and $\bar{L} = l/c$ for relatively prime l and c, then we *can* use formulas (1.83)–(1.90), with Δ such that $l\Delta \equiv \lfloor c\delta \rfloor \pmod{c}$. For example, for the old Hindu lunisolar calendar we can use $c = 180000$, $l = 66389$, $\lfloor c\delta \rfloor = 174467$ and $\Delta = 147703$. However, the δ formula is more general in that it applies even if average year length is not rational.

The generalization of formula (1.90) in terms of δ follows by solving equation (1.92) for y, to yield

$$\boxed{y = \left\lceil \frac{n + 1 - \delta}{\bar{L}} \right\rceil} \tag{1.95}$$

For the Coptic calendar, this becomes

$$y = \left\lceil \frac{n + 1 - 1/4}{1461/4} \right\rceil = \left\lceil \frac{4n + 3}{1461} \right\rceil$$

as we knew before.

For the old Hindu lunisolar calendar, in every 180000-year cycle there are 66389 evenly distributed leap years of 13 months. Because the year count begins with year 0, month m falls in year

$$y = \left\lceil \frac{m + 1 - \dfrac{2093611}{2160000}}{\dfrac{2226389}{180000}} \right\rceil - 1$$

The application of these formulas to the old Hindu lunisolar calendar is discussed in Chapter 10.

In the foregoing discussion we have counted days beginning with the epoch of the calendars, and thus when formulas (1.86) and (1.90) are used in our calendrical functions, the epoch must be added or subtracted to refer to R.D. dates. For example, to compute the Islamic year of R.D. d, we must write

$$\left\lfloor \frac{30(d - \text{Islamic epoch}) + 10646}{10631} \right\rfloor$$

because R.D. d is (d – Islamic epoch) elapsed days on the Islamic calendar.

1.15 Approximating the Year Number

At the expiration of the years, come challenge me.
Shakespeare: *Love's Labour's Lost*, Act V, scene ii (1598)

For calendars that do not follow the strict paradigm of the previous section, a useful method to determine the exact year number of a fixed date d is to estimate the year number and then correct it if necessary. Let Y be the *average* year length. Given a_1, the (actual or approximate) first day of year 1 on the calendar, the *mean* new year a_j of year j, for any year j, is simply

$$a_j = a_1 + (j - 1)Y$$

Conversely, for any moment d, the *approximate* year number y can be determined by division:

$$y = \left\lfloor \frac{d - a_1}{Y} \right\rfloor + 1$$

For all years j, let n_j be the actual fixed date of the start of the year on the calendar. Assuming that the actual date n_j is within a year of the mean date a_j, we need only check whether the above estimate y is off by 1:

$$year = \begin{cases} y - 1 & \textbf{if } d < n_y \\ y + 1 & \textbf{if } d \geqslant n_{y+1} \\ y & \textbf{otherwise} \end{cases}$$

The calculation of the exact new year can be relatively expensive, so we would like to avoid computing n_y and n_{y+1} whenever possible. Suppose that we can bound the difference between the mean dates, a_j, and the actual dates, n_j, so that it is guaranteed that

$$n_j - \varepsilon \leqslant a_j \leqslant n_j + \delta$$

for bounds $\delta \geqslant 0$ and $\varepsilon \leqslant Y$; suppose further that these bounds hold for all years j—or at least for all years within a 100 centuries of the current date (which is all that we demand of our algorithms). Then, whenever the given date d is far enough away from the two mean new years a_y and $a_y + Y$, we can be sure that the approximation y is accurate.

Let $\Delta = (d - a_1) \bmod Y$. If $\Delta \leqslant \delta$, then d falls in the "twilight zone" and we need to check whether $d < n_y$; if so then the estimate is actually wrong, and the correct year is $y - 1$. Similarly, if $\Delta \geqslant Y - \epsilon$, then d is too close to the end of year y for us to be certain, and we need to check if $d \geqslant n_{y+1}$, in which case the correct year is $y + 1$. The test for $\Delta \leqslant \delta$ may be omitted if $\delta = 0$ (Δ is nonnegative, and if $\Delta = \delta = 0$, then y must be exactly $(d - a_1)/Y + 1$, in which case $n_y = n_y - \varepsilon \leqslant a_y = a_1(y-1)Y = d$). Likewise, the test for $\Delta \geqslant Y - \varepsilon$ may be omitted if $\varepsilon = 0$ (because $\Delta < Y$). By shifting the initial estimate a_1, one can ensure that $\varepsilon = 0$; then we get the precise year number for fixed date d with

$$year = \begin{cases} y - 1 & \textbf{if } (d - a_1) \bmod Y \leqslant \delta \textbf{ and } d < n_y \\ y & \textbf{otherwise} \end{cases} \tag{1.96}$$

where

$$y = \left\lfloor \frac{d - a_1}{Y} \right\rfloor + 1$$

We use this method for Gregorian calendar years in (2.30), for Hebrew calendar years in (8.28), and for arithmetic French Revolutionary calendar years in (17.10).

1.16 Warnings about the Calculations

Caveat emptor. [*Let the buyer beware.*]
Latin motto

We have been careful to ensure that our conversion functions work for at least ±10000 years from the present, if not forever. We have worked hard to make sure that our conversion algorithms do not suffer from a Y10K problem!

Many holiday calculations assume that the Gregorian year and the true solar year, and/or the mean year length of a specific calendar, maintain the same alignment, which will not remain the case over millennia. We have endeavored to make these calculations robust for at least ±2000 years from the present. Of course, the dates of most holidays will not be historically correct over that range.

The astronomical code we use is not the best available but it works quite well in practice, especially for dates near the present time, around which its approximations are centered. More precise code would be more time-consuming and complex and would not necessarily yield more accurate results for those calendars that depended on observations, tables, or less accurate calculations. Thus, the correctness of a date on any of the astronomical calendars is contingent on the historical accuracy of the astronomical code used in its calculation.

We have chosen not to optimize the algorithms at the expense of clarity; consequently, considerable improvements in economy are possible, some of which are pointed out. In particular, our algorithms are designed to convert individual dates from one calendar to another; thus the preparation of monthly or yearly calendars would benefit enormously if intermediate results were stored and used for subsequent days. This standard algorithmic technique (called "caching" or "memoization") is ignored in this book.

We do not do error checking in the code. If one asks for the R.D. date corresponding to a date in Julian year 0, or to February 29, 1990, an answer will be forthcoming despite the nonexistence of such dates. Similarly, the code will not object to the absurdity of asking for the R.D. date corresponding to December 39, or even the thirty-ninth day of the thirteenth month. In other cases, we use the special constant

bogus (1.97)

to indicate that a calendar date, holiday, or astronomical event is nonexistent. For each calendar x, the validity of a date *x-date* on that calendar can be checked by a function

valid-*x*-date(*x-date*) $\stackrel{\text{def}}{=}$

$$x\text{-}date = \textbf{x-from-fixed}(\textbf{fixed-from-x}(x\text{-}date))$$

All our functions give "correct" (mathematically sensible) results for negative years and for dates prior to the epoch of a calendar. However, these results may be *culturally* wrong in the sense that, say, the Copts may not refer to a year 0 or −1. It may be considered heretical on some calendars to refer to years before the creation of the world.

All Gregorian dates before the Common Era that appear in this book follow the astronomical convention of using nonpositive year numbers—including 0 for the year preceding the onset of the era. (The varying conventions with regard to Gregorian year 0 have led to many errors in the converting of historical dates.) Year 0 is assumed to exist for all calendars *except* the Julian (Chapter 3) and the Persian (Chapter 15).

Except for our summation and product operators (page 23) and search functions (page 23), we avoid iteration and instead use recursion, which is natural because we use functional notation. The use of recursion, however, is not essential: it is invariably "tail" recursion and can easily be replaced by iteration.

Our algorithms assume that if $y > 0$, then $(x \bmod y) \geqslant 0$ for all x, even for negative values of x. Thus, as we stated in Section 1.7, care must thus be exercised in implementing our algorithms in computer languages like C or C++, in which the built-in mod function (often the `%` operator) may give $(x \bmod y) < 0$ for $x < 0$, $y > 0$. We also assume, in the case of some functions, that $x \bmod y$ works for real numbers x and y, as well as for integers.

Care must be taken with indices of arrays and cycles. Our arrays are 0-based, while some programming languages begin with index 1. However, when we speak of elements of a sequence as "first," "second," and so on, we intend standard English usage with no zeroth element. Most calendars number their days, months, and years starting with 1, but there are exceptions—Hindu years and Mayan days, for example. Some cycle formulas in this chapter work for arbitrary starting points; others require adjustment when the first element of a cycle is not 0.

Checking the results of conversions against the historical record is sometimes misleading because the different calendars begin their days at different times. For example, a person who died in the evening will have a different Hebrew date of death than if he or she had died in the morning of the same Gregorian calendar date; gravestone inscriptions often err in this. All our conversions are as of noon.

Some of our calculations require extremely large numbers; other calculations depend on numerically accurate approximations to lunar or solar events. All functions for the calendars in Part I, except the old Hindu, work properly (for dates within thousands of years from the present) in 32-bit integer arithmetic; the Hebrew calendar approaches this limit, so we have indicated how to rephrase the calculations to use only small numbers—one exception is **fixed-from–molad** (page 126) which requires 64-bit integers. On the other hand, 64-bit arithmetic is needed to reproduce accurately the results of the astronomical calculations done in Part II. We use exact rational arithmetic, with very large numbers, for the Hindu calendars; 64-bit arithmetic can be used to approximate their calculation.

We use degree-based trigonometric functions throughout for simplicity. For programming languages in which these functions are radian-based, conversions are necessary—see our Lisp code (page 513), for an example of such conversions.

Finally, floating point calculations are platform-dependent. The values given for the sample data of Appendix C will differ slightly for different languages, implementations, or platforms. Double precision is necessary, however, for accurate results; furthermore, in some cases, low precision results when low- and high-precision real numbers are combined—this can have seriously deleterious effects. To avoid such problems, all real numbers should have maximal (double) precision, as they have in our Lisp code. For details, see the introduction to Appendix C.

References

> *I have, however, read enough in the field to know that many of these treatments of the calendar are sound, some of them brilliant, and some purely fantastic. I also know that practically every theory about the calendar which could conceivably have been devised has been proposed by somebody, and that many have been re-invented several times. I know that very little of what I have to say has not been anticipated ...*
>
> Agnes K. Michels: *The Calendar of the Roman Republic* (1967)

[1] *Explanatory Supplement to the Astronomical Ephemeris and the American Ephemeris and Nautical Almanac*, Her Majesty's Stationery Office, London, 1961.

[2] Goddard Earth Sciences Data Information Services Center website, National Aeronautics and Space Administration, `disc.sci.gsfc.nasa.gov/julian_calendar.html`.

[3] *The Larousse Encyclopedia of Mythology*, Barnes & Noble Books, New York, 1994.

[4] J. P. Allen, *Middle Egyptian: An Introduction to the Language and Culture of Hieroglyphs*, Cambridge University Press, Cambridge, 2nd edn., pp. 107–110, 2010.

[5] P. F. W. Bartle, "The Forty Days: The Akan Calendar," *Africa*, vol. 48, pp. 80–84, 1978.

[6] B. Blackburn and L. Holford-Strevens, *The Oxford Companion to the Year*, Oxford University Press, Oxford, 1999.

[7] C. A. Boch, B. Ananthasubramaniam, A. M. Sweeney, F. J. Doyle, and D. E. Morse, "Effects of Light Dynamics on Coral Spawning Synchrony," *Biological Bulletin*, vol. 220, pp. 161–173, 2011.

[8] M. Clagett, *Ancient Egyptian Science*: vol. 2, *Calendars, Clocks, and Astronomy*, American Philosophical Society, Philadelphia, 1995.

[9] L. Cope, "Calendars of the Indians North of Mexico," *American Archaeology and Ethnology*, vol. 16, pp. 119–176, 1919.

[10] J. Davenport, T. T. Jones, T. M. Work, and G. H. Balazs, "Pink Spot, White Spot: The Pineal Skylight of the Leatherback Turtle (*Dermochelys Coriacea* Vandelli 1761) Skull and its Possible Role in the Phenology of Feeding Migrations," *Journal of Experimental Marine Biology and Ecology*, vol. 461, pp. 1–6, 2014.

[11] N. Dershowitz and E. M. Reingold, "Modulo Intervals: A Proposed Notation," *ACM SIGACT News*, vol. 43, no. 3, pp. 60–64, 2012.

[12] L. E. Doggett, "Calendars," *Explanatory Supplement to the Astronomical Almanac*, P. K. Seidelmann, ed., University Science Books, Mill Valley, CA, pp. 575–608, 1992.

[13] J. Elkins, "On the Impossibility of Close Reading," *Current Anthropology*, vol. 37, pp. 185–226, 1996.

[14] N. Fox, "A Bone Carved Calendar," in *Tel 'Aroer: An Iron Age II Caravan Town and the Hellenistic–Early Roman Settlement. Avraham Biran (1975–1982) and Rudolph Cohen (1975–1976) Excavations*, Y. Thareani, ed., Annual of the Nelson Glueck School of Biblical Archaeology, No. VIII, Jerusalem, pp. 255–258, 468, 2011.

[15] T. Galloway and W. S. B. Woolhouse, "Calendar," *The Encyclopædia Britannica*, 11th edn., vol. 4, pp. 987–1004, The Encyclopædia Britannica Co., New York, 1910. The same article also appears in the 8th (1860) through the 13th (1926) editions.

[16] F. K. Ginzel, *Handbuch der mathematischen und technischen Chronologie*, J. C. Hinrichs'sche Buchhandlung, Leipzig, 1906 (vol. 1), 1911 (vol. 2), and 1914 (vol. 3). Reprinted by F. Ullmann Verlag, Zwickau, 1958.

[17] A. T. Grafton, *Joseph Scaliger: A Study in the History of Classical Scholarship, vol. II, Historical Chronography*, Oxford University Press, Oxford, 1993.

[18] R. L. Graham, D. E. Knuth, and O. Patashnik, *Concrete Mathematics*, 2nd edn., Addison-Wesley Publishing Company, Reading, MA, 1994.

[19] G. H. Hardy, and E. M. Wright, *An Introduction to the Theory of Numbers*, 5th edn., Oxford University Press, Oxford, 1979.

[20] M. A. Harris and E. M. Reingold, "Line Drawing, Leap Years, and Euclid," *ACM Computing Surveys*, vol. 36, pp. 68–80, 2004.

[21] O. L. Harvey, *Calendar Conversions by Way of the Julian Day Number*, American Philosophical Society, Philadelphia, 1983.

[22] J. Hastings, edn., *Encyclopædia of Religion and Ethics*, Charles Scribner's Sons, New York, 1908–1922.

[23] H. Henderson and B. Puckett, *Holidays & Festivals Index*, Omnigraphics, Detroit, MI, 1995.

[24] H. Henderson and S. E. Thompson, *Holidays, Festivals & Celebrations of the World Dictionary*, 2nd edn., Omnigraphics, Detroit, MI, 1997.

[25] J. F. W. Herschel, *Outlines of Astronomy*, 3rd edn., Longman, Brown, Green, Longmans, and Roberts, London, 1849.

[26] W. Horowitz, "The 360 and 364 Day Year in Ancient Mesopotamia," *Journal of the Ancient Near Eastern Society* vol. 24 (1996), pp. 35–41.

[27] A. Ya. Khinchin, *Continued Fractions*, translated by P. Wynn, P. Noordhoff, Groningen, 1964. Reprinted by Dover Publications, Mineola, NY, 1997.

[28] D. E. Knuth, *The Art of Computer Programming*, vol. 2: *Seminumerical Algorithms*, 3rd edn., Addison-Wesley Publishing Company, Reading, MA, 1998.

[29] K. Konadu, "The Calendrical Factor in Akan History," *International Journal of African Historical Studies* vol. 45, pp. 217–246, 2012.

[30] N. Kronfeld-Schor, D. Dominoni, H. de la Iglesia, O. Levy, E. D. Herzog, T. Dayan, and C. Helfrich-Forster, "Chronobiology by Moonlight," *Proc. Royal Soc. B* vol. 280, 20123088, 2013.

[31] F. Macler, "Calendar (Armenian)," vol. III, pp. 70–72, *Encyclopædia of Religion and Ethics*, J. Hastings, edn., Charles Scribner's Sons, New York, 1908–1922.

[32] A. Marshack, *The Roots of Civilization*, McGraw-Hill, New York, 1972.

[33] O. Neugebauer, *A History of Ancient Mathematical Astronomy*, Springer-Verlag, Berlin, 1975 (vol. 1, pp. 1–555, vol. 2, pp. 556–1058, vol. 3, pp. 1059–1457).

[34] Ø. Ore, *Number Theory and Its History*, McGraw-Hill., New York, 1948. Reprinted by Dover, Mineola, NY, 1987.

[35] O. K. Osei, *A Discourse on Akan Perpetual Calendar* (*for Religious Ceremonies and Festivals*), Domak Press Ltd., Accra, Ghana, 1997.

[36] F. Parise, ed., *The Book of Calendars*, Facts on File, New York, 1982.

[37] R. A. Parker, *The Calendars of Ancient Egypt*, University of Chicago Press, Chicago, 1950.

[38] R. L. Reese, E. D. Craun, and C. W. Mason, "Twelfth-Century Origins of the 7980-Year Julian Period," *Amer. J. Physics*, vol. 51, p. 73, 1983.

[39] R. L. Reese, S. M. Everett, and E. D. Craun, "The Origin of the Year Julian Period: An Application of Congruences and the Chinese Remainder Theorem," *Amer. J. Physics*, vol. 49, pp. 658–661, 1981.

[40] E. G. Richards, *Mapping Time: The Calendar and its History*, Oxford University Press, Oxford, 1998.

[41] R. G. Schram, *Kalendariographische und chronologische Tafeln*, J. C. Hinrichs'sche Buchhandlung, Leipzig, 1908.

[42] R. D. Skeel and J. B. Keiper, *Elementary Numerical Computing with Mathematica*, McGraw-Hill, New York, 1993.

[43] J. Speicher, L. Schreffler, and D. Speicher, "Lunar Influence on the Fall Migration of Northern Saw-whet Owls," *Wilson J. Ornithology*, vol. 123, pp. 158–160, 2011.

[44] R. M. Stallman, *GNU Emacs Manual*, 13th edn., Free Software Foundation, Cambridge, MA, 1997.

[45] D. Steel, *Marking Time: The Epic Quest to Invent the Perfect Calendar*, John Wiley & Sons, New York, 2000.

[46] G. L. Steele, Jr., Common LISP: *The Language*, 2nd edn., Digital Press, Bedford, MA, 1990.

[47] S. H. Taqizadeh, "An Ancient Persian Practice Preserved by a Non-Iranian People," *Bulletin of the School of Oriental Studies*, vol. 9, no. 3, pp. 603–619, 1938.

[48] A. Troesch, "Interprétation géométrique de l'algorithme d'Euclide et reconnaissance de segments," *Theoret. Comp. Sci.*, vol. 115, pp. 291–319, 1993.

[49] B. L. van der Waerden, "Tables for the Egyptian and Alexandrian Calendar," *ISIS*, vol. 47, pp. 387–390, 1956.

If you steal from one author it's plagiarism; if you steal from many, it's research.
Attributed to Wilson Mizner

Part I

Arithmetical Calendars

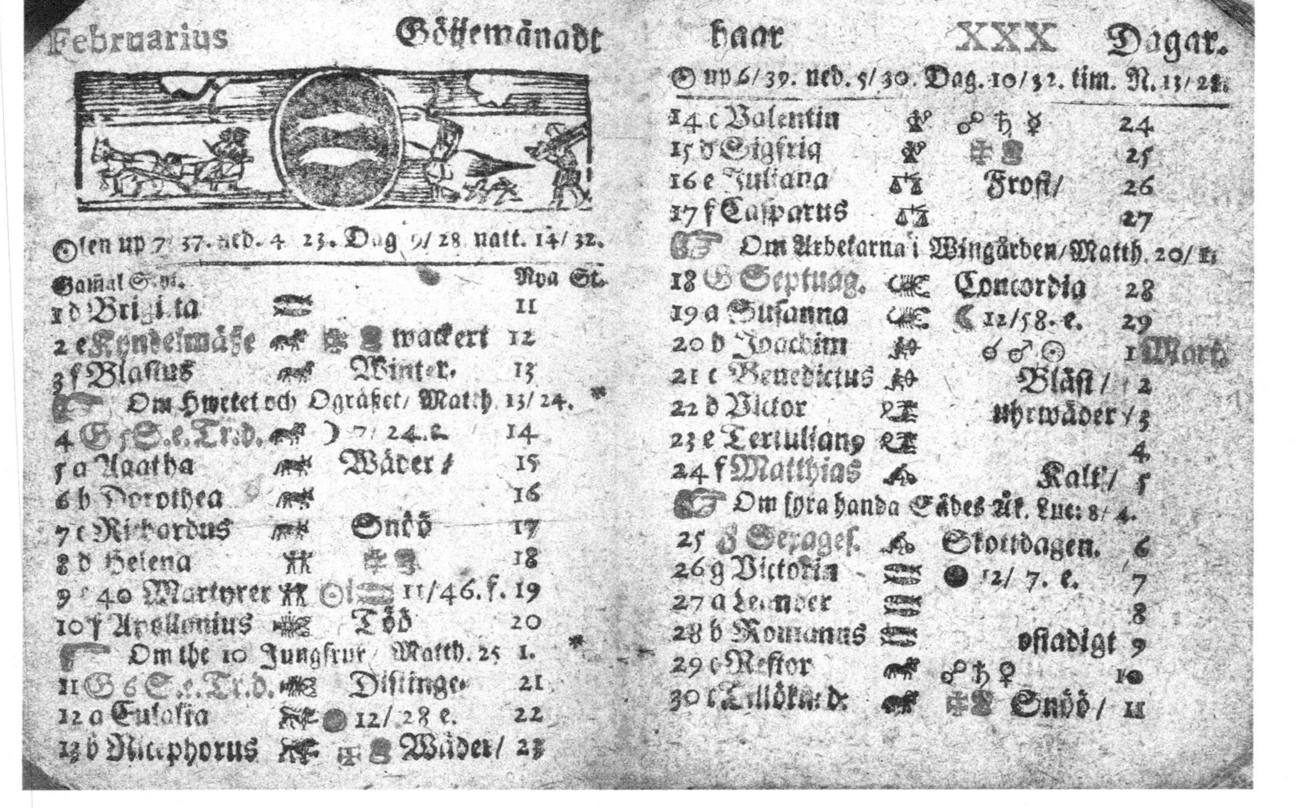
Februarius Göttemånadt

Solen up 7/37. ned. 4/23. Dag 9/28. natt. 14/32.

Gamal St. Nya St.

1 d Brigitta 11

2 e Kyndelmässe wackert 12

3 f Blasius Winter. 13

Om Hwetet och Ogräset/ Matth. 13/24.

4 G 5 S.e.Tr.d.) 7/24. e. 14

5 a Agatha Wäder/ 15

6 b Dorothea 16

7 c Rikardus Snöö 17

8 d Helena 18

9 e 40 Martyrer 11/46. f. 19

10 f Apollonius Töö 20

Om the 10 Jungfrur/ Matth. 25/1.

11 G 6 S.e.Tr.d. Disiinge 21

12 a Eulalia 12/28 e. 22

13 b Nicephorus Wäder/ 23

haar XXX Dagar.

Solen up 6/39. ned. 5/30. Dag. 10/32. tim. N. 13/28.

14 c Valentin 24

15 d Sigfrid 25

16 e Juliana Frost/ 26

17 f Casparus 27

Om Arbetarna i Wingården/ Matth. 20/1.

18 G Septuag. Concordia 28

19 a Susanna 12/58. e. 29

20 b Joachim 1 Mart.

21 c Benedictus Blåst/ 2

22 d Victor ohrwäder/ 3

23 e Tertullianus 4

24 f Matthias Kalt/ 5

Om fyra handa Sädes åker. Luc. 8/4.

25 G Sexages. Stortdagen. 6

26 g Victoria 12/7. e. 7

27 a Leander 8

28 b Romanus ostadigt 9

29 c Nestor 10

30 c Tillökad. Snöö/ 11

Swedish almanac pages for February, 1712, showing a 30-day month. The Swedish date is on the left, the Gregorian on the right. Friday, February 30 (Swedish) is given as March 11 (Gregorian) = February 29 (Julian). The word next to the “30” is “Tillökad,” that is, “added.” The word “Snöö,” that is, the weather prediction “snow,” is to the left of the “11.” (Courtesy of The Royal Library, National Library of Sweden, Stockholm.)

2

The Gregorian Calendar

For some ridiculous reason, to which, however, I've no desire to be disloyal,
Some person in authority, I don't know who, very likely the Astronomer Royal,
Has decided that, although for such a beastly month as February,
twenty-eight as a rule are plenty.
One year in every four his days shall be reckoned as nine-and-twenty.

Gilbert and Sullivan: *Pirates of Penzance*, Act II (1879)

2.1 Structure

The calendar in use today in most of the world is the Gregorian or *new-style* calendar designed by a commission assembled by Pope Gregory XIII[1] in the sixteenth century. The main author of the new system was the Naples astronomer Aloysius Lilius; see [4], [6], [16], and [18] for mathematical and historical details. This strictly solar calendar is based on a 365-day common year divided into 12 months of lengths 31, 28, 31, 30, 31, 30, 31, 31, 30, 31, 30, and 31 days with 366 days in leap years, the extra day being added to make the second month 29 days long:

(1) January	31 days	(7) July	31 days
(2) February	28 {29} days	(8) August	31 days
(3) March	31 days	(9) September	30 days
(4) April	30 days	(10) October	31 days
(5) May	31 days	(11) November	30 days
(6) June	30 days	(12) December	31 days

The leap-year structure is given in curly brackets. A year is a leap year if it is divisible by 4 and is not a century year (a multiple of 100) or if it is divisible by 400. For example, 1900 is not a leap year; 2000 is. The Gregorian calendar differs

[1] Gregory was also responsible for a bull *Vices eius nos* (September 1, 1577) organizing regular missionizing sermons by apostate Jews, which the Jewish community of Rome was forced to attend and subsidize. His bull *Sancta mater ecclesia* (September 1, 1584) specified more precise conditions: beadles armed with rods made sure the Jews paid attention and checked that they had not put wax in their ears. These sermons took place throughout the Papal States and much of the Roman Catholic world, as well in the church nearest the Jewish Quarter in Rome, San Gregorio della Divina Pietà. (The front of this church has an inscription in Hebrew and Latin, beside an image of the crucified Jesus, quoting from Isaiah 65:2–3, "I have spread out My hands all the day unto a rebellious people, that walk in a way that is not good, after their own thoughts; a people that provoke me to my face continually.")

from its predecessor, the old-style or Julian calendar, only in that the Julian calendar did not include the century rule for leap years—all century years were leap years. It is the century rule that causes the leap year structure to fall outside the cycle-of-years paradigm of Section 1.14 (but Gregorian-like leap year rules have their own interesting mathematical properties; see [19]). Days on both calendars begin at midnight.

Although the month lengths seem arbitrarily arranged, they would precisely satisfy the cyclic formulas of Section 1.14 with $c = 12$, $l = 7$, $\Delta = 11$, and $L = 30$, if February always had 30 days. In other words, if we assume February has 30 days, formula (1.86) tells us that there are

$$\left\lfloor \frac{7m - 2}{12} \right\rfloor + 30(m - 1) = \left\lfloor \frac{367m - 362}{12} \right\rfloor \tag{2.1}$$

days in the months $1, \ldots, m - 1$, and formula (1.90) tells us that day n of the year falls in month number

$$\left\lfloor \frac{12n + 373}{367} \right\rfloor \tag{2.2}$$

where, as in the derivation of (1.90), the first day of the year is $n = 0$; that is, n is the number of prior days in the year rather than the day number in the usual sense. The values $c = 12$ and $L = 30$ leading to (2.1) and (2.2) are obvious: There are 12 months and the ordinary length is 30 days. The value $l = 7$ comes from the 7 long months of 31 days; the value $\Delta = 11$ forces January to be month number 1 (rather than 0), necessary for the applicability of formulas (1.86) and (1.90). It is a simple matter to use the formulas (2.1) and (2.2) and to correct for the mistaken assumption that February has 30 days; we do just that in the next section.

The Julian calendar dates from January 1, 709 A.U.C.[2] (45 B.C.E.) and is by Julius Cæsar, with the help of Alexandrian astronomer Sosigenes; it was a modification of the Roman Republican (see [15]) and ancient Egyptian calendars. Because every

---

[2] *Ab Urbe Condita*; from the founding of the city (of Rome). Varro's statements imply that the year of the founding of Rome was 753 B.C.E., which gives 709 A.U.C. = 45 B.C.E. as the year of institution of the Julian calendar; this year is commonly, but not universally, accepted. The counting of years according to the Christian era was instituted by Eusebius, a fourth-century bishop of Cæsarea, and then used by the sixth-century Roman monk and scholar Dionysius Exiguus; it only became commonplace a few centuries later—Eusebius erred by a few years in his determination of the year of Jesus's birth (see D. P. McCarthy, "The Emergence of *Anno Domini*," pp. 31–53 in *Time and Eternity: The Medieval Discourse*, G. Jaritz and G. Moreno-Riaño, eds., Brepols, Turnhout, Belgium, 2003). Much of the Christian world used "Anno Diocletiani" for many years (the Julian calendar with Diocletian's reign as the origin—the same origin as the Coptic calendar discussed in Chapter 4). Eusebius's innovation was to substitute his estimate of Jesus's birth year for the origin, starting his count at 1. The "1 B.C.E. is the year before 1 C.E." problem was a result of the system introduced and popularized by the Venerable Bede around 731. Bede did not know about 0, so he did not use it [Bede's work *De Temporum Ratione* was translated by Faith Wallis as *Bede: The Reckoning of Time*, Liverpool University Press, Liverpool, 1999 (also University of Pennsylvania Press, Philadelphia, 2000)], and the custom of omitting a year 0 in the Julian calendar's year count became well established. Astronomers do use a year 0 preceding year 1 on the Gregorian calendar—this is due to Cassini in 1740 [5]; see also Dick Teresi, "Zero," *The Atlantic Monthly*, vol. 280, no. 1, pp. 88–94, July 1997.

fourth year was a leap year, a cycle of 4 years contained $4 \times 365 + 1 = 1461$ days, giving an average length of year of 365.25 days. This is somewhat more than the mean length of the tropical year (the year measured between successive vernal equinoxes), and over the centuries the calendar slipped with respect to the seasons. By the sixteenth century, the true date of the vernal (spring) equinox had shifted from around March 21 in the fourth century when the date of Easter was fixed (see Chapter 9) to around March 11. If this error were not corrected, then Easter, whose date depends on the ecclesiastical approximation of March 21 for the vernal equinox, would gradually migrate through the seasons, eventually to become a summer holiday.

Pope Gregory XIII instituted only a minor change in the calendar—century years not divisible by 400 would no longer be leap years. (He also modified the rules for Easter; see Chapter 9.) Thus, 3 out of 4 century years are common years, giving a cycle of 400 years containing $400 \times 365 + 97 = 146097$ days and an average year length of $146097/400 = 365.2425$ days. He also corrected the accumulated 10-day error in the date of the equinox by proclaiming that Thursday, October 4, 1582 C.E. according to the calendar then in use (Julian) would be followed by Friday, October 15, 1582, the first day of the new-style (Gregorian) calendar. Catholic countries followed his rule: Spain, Portugal, and Italy adopted it immediately, as did the Catholic states in Germany. However, Protestant countries resisted. The Protestant parts of Germany waited until 1700 to adopt it. The various cantons of Switzerland changed at different times. Sweden began a gradual changeover in 1699, omitting February 29 in 1700. At that point the plan was abandoned, leaving the Swedish calendar one day off from the Julian. This was only rectified in 1712 by adding a February 30 to that year—see the frontispiece for this chapter! The Swedish calendar stayed in tune with the Julian until 1753, when the Gregorian was adopted.[3] Great Britain and her colonies (including the United States) waited until 1752 (see [17] for an interesting description of the effect); Russia held out until 1918, after the Bolshevik Revolution, which is also known as the October Revolution because it occurred on October 25–26, 1917 C.E. (Julian) = November 7–8, 1917 (Gregorian).[4] Different parts of what is now the United States changed over at different dates; Alaska, for example, changed only when it was purchased by the United States in 1867.[5] Turkey did not change to the Gregorian calendar

---

[3] See [9, p. 275]. We are indebted to Tapani Tarvainen and Donald Knuth for pointing out this anomaly.

[4] In 1923 the Congress of the Orthodox Oriental Churches adopted a slightly more accurate leap-year rule: Century years are leap years only if they leave a remainder of 2 or 6 when divided by 9; this "Revised Julian" rule agrees with the usual Gregorian rule for 1700–2700 (see M. Milankovitch, "Das Ende des julianischen Kalenders und der neue Kalender der orientalischen Kirche," *Astronomische Nachrichten*, vol. 220, pp. 379–384, 1924). The Soviet Union and some orthodox churches (the New Calendarists) adopted this rule at that time. Like the rest of the world, we ignore this "improvement."

[5] Alaska skipped only 11 days instead of 12 (as we might expect) but with a repeated weekday because it also jumped the International Date Line when it became United States territory in 1867: Friday, October 6, 1867 C.E. (Julian) was followed by Friday, October 18, 1867 (Gregorian)! Even without the change from the Julian to the Gregorian calendar, jumping the date line causes bizarre situations. In 1892 Samoa jumped the date line and also switched from "Asian Time" to "American Time," causing the Fourth of July to be celebrated for 2 consecutive days; the reverse happened

until 1927. An extensive list of dates of adoption of the Gregorian calendar can be found in [1].

The Gregorian calendar is not fully accurate in its alignment with the solar cycle because its approximation to the year, $365\frac{97}{400} = 365.2425$ is slightly too large (see the discussion in Section 14.4). This was known as early as 1700, so various modifications have been suggested, but none accepted. For example, the astronomer John Herschel (and others) proposed making years divisible by 4000 ordinary years, not leap years; such a modification is simple to incorporate into our functions in the following sections. Isaac Newton had much earlier proposed a radically different approach (see [3]) with a 5000-year cycle in which years divisible by 4 would be leap years (February would have 29 days), except that years divisible by 100 would not be leap years, except that years divisible by 500 would be leap years; furthermore, years divisible by 5000 would be "double leap years" with 30 days in February. Implementing Newton's calendar is a nice exercise for the reader.

By universal current custom, the new Gregorian year number begins on January 1. There have, however, been other beginnings—parts of Europe began the New Year variously on March 1, Easter, September 1, Christmas, and March 25 (see, for example, [11]). This is no small matter in interpreting dates between January 1 and the point at which the number of the year changed. For example, in England under the Julian calendar, the commencement of the ecclesiastical year on March 25 in the sixteenth and seventeenth centuries means that a date like February 1, 1660 leaves the meaning of the year in doubt. Such confusion led to the practice of writing a hyphenated year giving both the legal year first and the calendar year number second: February 1, 1660-1. The same ambiguity occurs even today when we speak of the "fiscal year," which can run from July to July or from October to October, but we would always give the calendar year number, not the fiscal year number in specifying dates.

Although the Gregorian calendar did not exist prior to the sixteenth century, we can extrapolate backwards using its rules to obtain what is sometimes called the "proleptic Gregorian calendar,"[6] which we implement in the next section. Unlike the Julian calendar, we implement this proleptic calendar with a year 0, as is common among astronomers—see the footnote on page 56. By our choice of the starting point of our fixed counting of days, we define

$$\textbf{gregorian-epoch} \stackrel{\text{def}}{=} \text{R.D. } 1 \tag{2.3}$$

when the Philippines jumped the date line in the other direction in 1844: Monday, December 30, 1844, was followed by Wednesday, January 1, 1845. On December 29, 2011 Samoa again changed its time zone to align itself with Australia and New Zealand, moving from the eastern side of the international date line to the western side. Samoans lost a day, going straight from December 29 to December 31.

[6] The name is really a misnomer because "proleptic" refers to the future, not the past.

2.2 Implementation

Les protestants de toutes les communions s'obstinérent à ne pas recevoir des mains du pape une vérité qu'il aurait fallu recevoir des Turcs, s'ils l'avaient proposée. [*The Protestants of all denominations insist on rejecting a truth from the hands of the Pope, which they would have accepted even from the Turks had they proposed it.*]

Voltaire: *Essai sur les Mœurs et l'esprit des nations* (1756)

For convenience, we define 12 numerical constants by which we will refer to the 12 months of the Gregorian and Julian calendars:

$$\textbf{january} \stackrel{\text{def}}{=} 1 \tag{2.4}$$

$$\textbf{february} \stackrel{\text{def}}{=} 2 \tag{2.5}$$

$$\textbf{march} \stackrel{\text{def}}{=} 3 \tag{2.6}$$

$$\textbf{april} \stackrel{\text{def}}{=} 4 \tag{2.7}$$

$$\textbf{may} \stackrel{\text{def}}{=} 5 \tag{2.8}$$

$$\textbf{june} \stackrel{\text{def}}{=} 6 \tag{2.9}$$

$$\textbf{july} \stackrel{\text{def}}{=} 7 \tag{2.10}$$

$$\textbf{august} \stackrel{\text{def}}{=} 8 \tag{2.11}$$

$$\textbf{september} \stackrel{\text{def}}{=} 9 \tag{2.12}$$

$$\textbf{october} \stackrel{\text{def}}{=} 10 \tag{2.13}$$

$$\textbf{november} \stackrel{\text{def}}{=} 11 \tag{2.14}$$

$$\textbf{december} \stackrel{\text{def}}{=} 12 \tag{2.15}$$

To convert from a Gregorian date to an R.D. date, we first need a function that tells us whether a year is a leap year. We write

$$\textbf{gregorian-leap-year?}\,(\textit{g-year}) \stackrel{\text{def}}{=} \tag{2.16}$$
$$(\textit{g-year} \bmod 4) = 0 \text{ and } (\textit{g-year} \bmod 400) \notin \{100, 200, 300\}$$

The calculation of the R.D. date from the Gregorian date (which was described in [12] as "impractical") can now be done by counting the number of days in prior years (both common and leap years), the number of days in prior months of the current year, and the number of days in the current month:

$$\textbf{fixed-from-gregorian}\left(\boxed{\textit{year} \mid \textit{month} \mid \textit{day}}\right) \stackrel{\text{def}}{=} \tag{2.17}$$

$$\textbf{gregorian-epoch} - 1 + 365 \times (\textit{year} - 1) + \left\lfloor \frac{\textit{year} - 1}{4} \right\rfloor - \left\lfloor \frac{\textit{year} - 1}{100} \right\rfloor$$
$$+ \left\lfloor \frac{\textit{year} - 1}{400} \right\rfloor + \left\lfloor \tfrac{1}{12} \times (367 \times \textit{month} - 362) \right\rfloor$$
$$+ \begin{cases} 0 & \textbf{if } \textit{month} \leqslant 2 \\ -1 & \textbf{if gregorian-leap-year?}\ (\textit{year}) \\ -2 & \textbf{otherwise} \end{cases} + \textit{day}$$

The explanation of this function is as follows. We start at the R.D. number of the last day before the epoch (**gregorian-epoch** − 1 = 0, but we do it explicitly so that the dependency on our arbitrary starting date is clear); to this, we add the number of nonleap days (positive for positive years, negative otherwise) between R.D. 0 and the last day of the year preceding the given year, the corresponding (positive or negative) number of leap days, the number of days in prior months of the given year, and the number of days in the given month up to and including the given day. The number of leap days between R.D. 0 and the last day of the year preceding the given year is determined by the mathematical principle of "inclusion and exclusion" [13, chapter 4]: add all Julian-leap-year-rule leap days (multiples of 4), subtract all the century years (multiples of 100), and then add back all multiples of 400. The number of days in prior months of the given year is determined by formula (2.1), corrected by 0, −1, or −2 for the assumption that February always has 30 days.

For example, to compute the R.D. date of November 12, 1945 (Gregorian), we compute $365 \times (1945 - 1) = 709560$ prior nonleap days, $\lfloor (1945-1)/4 \rfloor = 486$ prior Julian-rule leap days (multiples of 4), $-\lfloor (1945-1)/100 \rfloor = -19$ prior century years, $\lfloor (1945-1)/400 \rfloor = 4$ prior 400-multiple years, $\lfloor (367 \times 11 - 362)/12 \rfloor = 306$ prior days, corrected by −2 because November is beyond February and 1945 is not a Gregorian leap year. Adding these values and the day number 12 together gives $709560 + 486 - 19 + 4 + 306 - 2 + 12 = 710347$.

The function **fixed-from-gregorian** allows us to calculate the first and last days of the Gregorian year, and the range of dates between them:

$$\textbf{gregorian-new-year}\ (\textit{g-year}) \stackrel{\text{def}}{=} \tag{2.18}$$
$$\textbf{fixed-from-gregorian}\left(\boxed{\textit{g-year} \mid \textbf{january} \mid 1}\right)$$

$$\textbf{gregorian-year-end}\ (\textit{g-year}) \stackrel{\text{def}}{=} \tag{2.19}$$
$$\textbf{fixed-from-gregorian}\left(\boxed{\textit{g-year} \mid \textbf{december} \mid 31}\right)$$

$$\textbf{gregorian-year-range}\ (\textit{g-year}) \stackrel{\text{def}}{=} \tag{2.20}$$
$$[\textbf{gregorian-new-year}\ (\textit{g-year}) \,..\, \textbf{gregorian-new-year}\ (\textit{g-year} + 1))$$

We will need these functions to determine holidays on other calendars that fall within a specific Gregorian year for example.

Calculating the Gregorian date from the R.D. *date* involves sequentially determining the year, month, and day of the month. Because the century rule for Gregorian leap years allows an occasional 7-year gap between leap years, we cannot use the methods of Section 1.14—in particular, formula (1.90)—to determine the Gregorian year. Rather, exact determination of the Gregorian year from the R.D. *date* involves the decomposition of the number of days into units of 1, 4, 100, and 400 years.

$$\textbf{gregorian-year-from-fixed}\,(\mathit{date}) \stackrel{\text{def}}{=} \tag{2.21}$$

$$\begin{cases} \mathit{year} & \textbf{if } n_{100} = 4 \text{ or } n_1 = 4 \\ \mathit{year} + 1 & \textbf{otherwise} \end{cases}$$

where

$$\begin{aligned}
d_0 &= \mathit{date} - \textbf{gregorian-epoch} \\
n_{400} &= \left\lfloor \frac{d_0}{146097} \right\rfloor \\
d_1 &= d_0 \bmod 146097 \\
n_{100} &= \left\lfloor \frac{d_1}{36524} \right\rfloor \\
d_2 &= d_1 \bmod 36524 \\
n_4 &= \left\lfloor \frac{d_2}{1461} \right\rfloor \\
d_3 &= d_2 \bmod 1461 \\
n_1 &= \left\lfloor \frac{d_3}{365} \right\rfloor \\
\mathit{year} &= 400 \times n_{400} + 100 \times n_{100} + 4 \times n_4 + n_1
\end{aligned}$$

Alternatively, the year may be calculated by means of base conversion in a mixed-radix system (Section 1.10); see formula (2.30) in the next section.

This function can be extended to compute the ordinal day of *date* in its Gregorian year:

$$\text{Ordinal day of } \mathit{date} \text{ in its Gregorian year} \tag{2.22}$$

$$= \begin{cases} (d_3 \bmod 365) + 1 & \textbf{if } n_1 \neq 4 \text{ and } n_{100} \neq 4 \\ 366 & \textbf{otherwise} \end{cases}$$

That is, if $n_{100} = 4$ or $n_1 = 4$, then *date* is the last day of a leap year (day 146097 of the 400-year cycle or day 1461 of a 4-year cycle); in other words, *date* is December 31 of *year*. Otherwise, *date* is the ordinal day $(d_3 \bmod 365) + 1$ in *year* + 1.

This calculation of the Gregorian year of R.D. *date* is correct even for nonpositive years. In that case, n_{400} gives the number of 400-year cycles from *date* until the start of the Gregorian calendar—*including* the current cycle—as a *negative* number because the floor function always gives the largest integer smaller than its argument. Then the rest of the calculation yields the number of years from the *beginning* of that cycle, as a *positive* integer, because the modulus is always nonnegative for positive divisor—see equations (1.20) and (1.21).

Now that we can determine the year of an R.D. date, we can find the month by formula (2.2), corrected by 0, 1, or 2 for the assumption that February always has 30 days. Knowing the year and month, we determine the day of the month by subtraction. Putting these pieces together, we have

$$\textbf{gregorian-from-fixed}\,(date) \stackrel{\text{def}}{=} \boxed{year \mid month \mid day} \tag{2.23}$$

where

$$\begin{aligned}
year &= \textbf{gregorian-year-from-fixed}\,(date)\\
prior\text{-}days &= date - \textbf{gregorian-new-year}\,(year)\\
correction &= \begin{cases} 0 & \textbf{if } date < \textbf{fixed-from-gregorian}\left(\boxed{year \mid \textbf{march} \mid 1}\right)\\ 1 & \textbf{if gregorian-leap-year?}\,(year)\\ 2 & \textbf{otherwise}\end{cases}\\
month &= \left\lfloor \frac{1}{367} \times (12 \times (prior\text{-}days + correction) + 373) \right\rfloor\\
day &= date - \textbf{fixed-from-gregorian}\left(\boxed{year \mid month \mid 1}\right) + 1
\end{aligned}$$

We can use our fixed numbering of days to facilitate the calculation of the number of days difference between two Gregorian dates:

$$\textbf{gregorian-date-difference}\,(g\text{-}date_1, g\text{-}date_2) \stackrel{\text{def}}{=} \tag{2.24}$$

$$\textbf{fixed-from-gregorian}\,(g\text{-}date_2) - \textbf{fixed-from-gregorian}\,(g\text{-}date_1)$$

This function can then be used to compute the ordinal day number of a date on the Gregorian calendar within its year:

$$\textbf{day-number}\,(g\text{-}date) \stackrel{\text{def}}{=} \tag{2.25}$$

$$\textbf{gregorian-date-difference}\left(\boxed{g\text{-}date_{\textbf{year}} - 1 \mid \textbf{december} \mid 31}, g\text{-}date\right)$$

The ordinal day number could also be computed directly using equation (2.22) in a modified version of **gregorian-year-from-fixed**. It is easy to determine the number of days remaining after a given date in the Gregorian year:

$$\textbf{days-remaining}\,(g\text{-}date) \stackrel{\text{def}}{=} \tag{2.26}$$

gregorian-date-difference

$\left(g\text{-}date, \boxed{g\text{-}date_{\mathbf{year}} \mid \mathbf{december} \mid 31} \right)$

Finally, we can compute the last day of a Gregorian month in a similar fashion:

$$\textbf{last-day-of-gregorian-month}\,(g\text{-}year, g\text{-}month) \stackrel{\text{def}}{=} \tag{2.27}$$

gregorian-date-difference

$$\left(\boxed{g\text{-}year \mid g\text{-}month \mid 1}, \boxed{\begin{cases} g\text{-}year + 1 & \textbf{if } g\text{-}month = 12 \\ g\text{-}year & \textbf{otherwise} \end{cases} \mid (g\text{-}month + 1) \bmod [1 \,..\, 12] \mid 1} \right)$$

2.3 Alternative Formulas

... premature, unnecessary, and likely to produce upheavals, and bewilderment of mind and conscience among the people.

Prince Carl Christoph von Lievenin in his denouncement to the Tsar of a plan to switch Russia to the Gregorian calendar (1829)

We noted in Section 2.1 that if we pretend that February always has 30 days and we count months starting from December, the month lengths satisfy the cycle-of-years formulas of Section 1.14 with $c = 12$, $l = 7$, $\Delta = 11$, and $L = 30$; we used the resulting formulas (2.1) and (2.2) to convert Gregorian dates to and from fixed dates. The fraction $7/12$ occurring on the left-hand side of (2.1) is not critical; we will see below that we can use the fraction $4/7$ instead. This leads us to see that the values $c = 7$, $l = 4$, $\Delta = 6$, and $L = 30$ also work, and thus we could substitute

$$\left\lfloor \frac{4m - 1}{7} \right\rfloor + 30(m - 1) = \left\lfloor \frac{214m - 211}{7} \right\rfloor$$

and

$$\left\lfloor \frac{7n + 217}{214} \right\rfloor$$

respectively, for (2.1) and (2.2) in **fixed-from-gregorian** and **gregorian-from-fixed**.

The justification of the change of $7/12$ to $4/7$ is worth examining in detail because it is typical of arguments used to derive and simplify calendrical formulas. Note that formulas (2.1) and (2.2) are applied only to month numbers 1 through 12. The sum on the left-hand side of equation (2.1) has a corrective term, the floor of

$$C(m) = \frac{7m - 2}{12}$$

This has values

m	1	2	3	4	5	6	7	8	9	10	11	12
$\lfloor C(m) \rfloor$	0	1	1	2	2	3	3	4	5	5	6	6

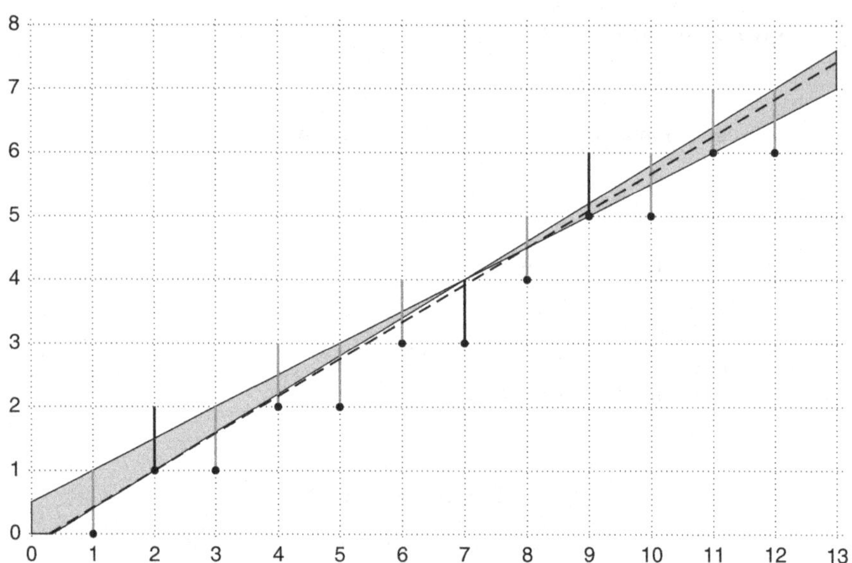

Figure 2.1 The 12 half-open line segments giving the ranges that the corrective line must transect, along with the correction of equation (2.1), that is, the dashed line $C(m) = (7m - 2)/12$. The limiting line segments, $[(2, 1) \mathinner{..} (2, 2))$, $[(7, 3) \mathinner{..} (7, 4))$, and $[(9, 5) \mathinner{..} (9, 6))$, are shown darker than the others. The limiting region, bounded by slopes $1/2$ and $3/5$, is shaded light gray. (Suggested by M. H. Deckers.)

which we show as a set of points $(m, \lfloor C(m) \rfloor)$ in Figure 2.1. Each point can be moved upward by any amount less than 1 without changing the value of $\lfloor C(m) \rfloor$; each range is represented as a half-open vertical line segment in the figure. The problem is to determine lines $L(m) = am + b$ such that $\lfloor L(m) \rfloor = \lfloor C(m) \rfloor$ for the 12 integer values, $1 \leqslant m \leqslant 12$. In other words, we want to determine the lines that transect each of the 12 half-open line segments in the figure. The line we know about, $C(m) = (7m - 2)/12$, is shown dashed. The critical line segments, shown in bold, are $[(2, 1) \mathinner{..} (2, 2))$, $[(7, 3) \mathinner{..} (7, 4))$, and $[(9, 5) \mathinner{..} (9, 6))$. To cut both the half-open line segments $[(7, 3) \mathinner{..} (7, 4))$ and $[(9, 5) \mathinner{..} (9, 6))$, a line $L(m) = am + b$ must have slope $a > 1/2$; to cut both the half-open line segments $[(2, 1) \mathinner{..} (2, 2))$ and $[(7, 3) \mathinner{..} (7, 4))$, a line $L(m) = am + b$ must have slope $a < 3/5$. The fraction $4/7$ has the smallest denominator in the acceptable range. It is clear from the figure that any slope $1/2 < a < 3/5$ (the shaded region) is possible—take the line of the desired slope that goes through the point $(7, 4)$. We make this precise by giving an explicit line for each slope in that range: $a = 1/2 + \varepsilon$, $b = 1/2 - 8\varepsilon$ works for $0 < \varepsilon \leqslant 1/12$, and $a = 3/5 - \varepsilon$, $b = -1/5 + 2\varepsilon$ works for $0 < \varepsilon \leqslant 1/35$. Because $1/2 + 1/12 > 3/5 - 1/35$, there exists a b for each value of a, $1/2 < a < 3/5$.

More significant use of the cycle-of-years formulas is also possible. Instead of pretending that February has 30 days and correcting for the pretense, we could instead consider the annual period from March 1 to the end of February of the following year (see, for example, [2] and [21]). For this shifted year, the cycle-of-years formulas with $c = 12$, $l = 7$, $\Delta = 1$, and $L = 30$ work perfectly because the formulas are never applied in cases for which the length of February matters. Again, as above, the fraction $7/12$ can be replaced by any fraction in the open range $(4/7, 5/8)$; the fraction of smallest denominator in the allowable range, $3/5$, leads to $c = 5$, $l = 3$, $\Delta = 4$, and $L = 30$. The well-known "Zeller's congruence," [22], [23], derived in the next section, is based on this idea, as are calendar formulas such as [20] (see [14, pp. 61–63]), and many others.

The shifted-year formulas are then applied as follows. The number of days in months starting in March prior to month m (where March is $m = 1$, April is $m = 2$, ..., February is $m = 12$) is

$$\left\lfloor \frac{3m-1}{5} \right\rfloor + 30(m-1) = \left\lfloor \frac{153m-151}{5} \right\rfloor$$

To consider March ($month = 3$) of $year$ to be month $m = 1$ of year $y = year + 1$, April ($month = 4$) of $year$ to be month $m = 2$ of year $y = year + 1, \ldots$, February ($month = 2$) of $year + 1$ to be month $m = 12$ of year $y = year + 1$, we shift the month numbers using

$$m = (month - 2) \bmod [1 \,..\, 12]$$

and adjust the year using

$$y = year + \left\lfloor \frac{month+9}{12} \right\rfloor$$

We can simplify this further by expressing the calculations in terms of $m' = m - 1$ and $y' = y - 1$ calculated as

$$m' = (month - 3) \bmod 12$$

$$y' = year - \left\lfloor \frac{m'}{10} \right\rfloor$$

Because there are 306 days in the period March–December, we can write

$$\textbf{alt-fixed-from-gregorian}\left(\boxed{year \mid month \mid day} \right) \stackrel{\text{def}}{=} \qquad (2.28)$$

$$\textbf{gregorian-epoch} - 1 - 306 + 365 \times y' + \sum \widetilde{y} \times \widetilde{a} + \left\lfloor \frac{3 \times m' + 2}{5} \right\rfloor + 30 \times m' + day$$

where

$$m' = (month - 3) \bmod 12$$

$$y' = year - \left\lfloor \frac{m'}{10} \right\rfloor$$

$$\widetilde{y} = y' \xrightarrow{\text{rad}} \langle 4, 25, 4\rangle$$
$$\widetilde{a} = \langle 97, 24, 1, 0\rangle$$

The number of leap years under the Gregorian rule depends on the number of quadrennia, centuries, and 400-year periods. We compute the number of elapsed periods of 4, 100, and 400 years, using the mixed-radix notation of Section 1.10. Accordingly, the approximation for the year is expressed in base $\langle 4, 25, 4\rangle$, there being 4 years in a quadrennium, 25 quadrennia in a century, and 4 centuries in 400 years. Each quadrennium contributes 1 leap day, each century contributes 24, every 400 years contribute 97, while an ordinary year contributes none. So we count the total number of leap days by taking the sum of the products of the individual contributions $\widetilde{a} = \langle 97, 24, 1, 0\rangle$ with the corresponding components of $\widetilde{y} = \langle n_{400}, n_{100}, n_4, n_1\rangle$, which is the year number expressed in base $\langle 4, 25, 4\rangle$ using the same variable names as in equation (2.21) for the counts. To avoid subscripts the formula employs vector notation, $\sum \widetilde{y} \times \widetilde{a}$, with the intention that the operation in the sum is performed on like-indexed elements of $\widetilde{y}$ and $\widetilde{a}$ (as explained on page 31).

In the reverse direction, the same ideas lead to

$$\textbf{alt-gregorian-from-fixed}\,(\textit{date}) \stackrel{\text{def}}{=} \boxed{\textit{year} \mid \textit{month} \mid \textit{day}} \tag{2.29}$$

where

$$\begin{aligned}
y &= \textbf{gregorian-year-from-fixed} \\
&\qquad (\textbf{gregorian-epoch} - 1 + \textit{date} + 306) \\
\textit{prior-days} &= \textit{date} - \textbf{fixed-from-gregorian}\left(\boxed{y-1 \mid \textbf{march} \mid 1}\right) \\
\textit{month} &= \left(\left\lfloor \frac{1}{153} \times (5 \times \textit{prior-days} + 2)\right\rfloor + 3\right) \bmod [1 \,..\, 12] \\
\textit{year} &= y - \left\lfloor \frac{\textit{month} + 9}{12} \right\rfloor \\
\textit{day} &= \textit{date} - \textbf{fixed-from-gregorian}\left(\boxed{\textit{year} \mid \textit{month} \mid 1}\right) + 1
\end{aligned}$$

All these alternative functions are simpler in appearance than our original functions converting Gregorian dates to and from fixed dates, but intuition has been lost with a negligible gain in efficiency. Versions of these alternative functions are the basis for the conversion algorithms in [7] (see [5, p. 604]) and many others because, by using formulas (1.17) and (1.29) to eliminate the modulus and adjusted-remainder operators, **alt-fixed-from-gregorian** and **alt-gregorian-from-fixed** can be written as single arithmetic expressions over the integer operations of addition, subtraction, multiplication, and division with no conditionals.

Finally, we can give an alternative version of **gregorian-year-from-fixed** by doing a simple but approximate calculation and correcting it when needed. The approximate year is found by dividing the number of days from the epoch until 2 days after the given fixed date by the average Gregorian year length. The fixed date of the start of the next year is then found; if the given date is before the start of that next year, then the approximation is correct; otherwise the correct year is the year after the approximation:

$$\textbf{alt-gregorian-year-from-fixed}\,(\mathit{date}) \stackrel{\text{def}}{=} \qquad (2.30)$$

$$\begin{cases} \mathit{approx} & \textbf{if } \mathit{date} < \mathit{start} \\ \mathit{approx} + 1 & \textbf{otherwise} \end{cases}$$

where

$$\begin{aligned} \mathit{approx} &= \left\lfloor \frac{400}{146097} \times (\mathit{date} - \textbf{gregorian-epoch} + 2) \right\rfloor \\ \mathit{start} &= \textbf{gregorian-epoch} + 365 \times \mathit{approx} + \sum \widetilde{y} \times \widetilde{a} \\ \widetilde{y} &= \mathit{approx} \stackrel{\text{rad}}{\longrightarrow} \langle 4, 25, 4 \rangle \\ \widetilde{a} &= \langle 97, 24, 1, 0 \rangle \end{aligned}$$

The adjustment by 2 days is needed because the number of days in years 1 through n of the 400-year cycle can fall short of $365.2425 \times n$ by as much as 1.4775 days (for $n = 303$). Thus 2 is the smallest integer we can add that guarantees that, for the first day of any year n, $\mathit{approx} \geqslant n - 1$.

2.4 The Zeller Congruence

These examples [of errors in published works] show that, even for the possessor of such reference books, formulæ are not completely superfluous, as they make it possible to double check the handbooks by means of calculations, without very much trouble.

Rektor Chr. Zeller: "Kalender-Formeln,"
Mathematisch-naturwissenschaftliche Mitteilungen des mathematisch-naturwissenschaftlichen Vereins in Württemberg (1885)

Zeller's congruence [22], [23] (see [21]), due to Christian Zeller, a Protestant minister and seminary director in Germany in the second half of the nineteenth century, is a relatively simple method—often used in feats of "mental agility"—for determining the day of the week, given any Gregorian calendar date. The main idea is to add up elapsed days from the epoch of the Gregorian until the day in question but, since we are interested only in the day of the week, always discarding multiples of 7, leaving numbers in the range 0–6 to represent Sunday through Saturday.

We can use the simplification of **fixed-from-gregorian** suggested on page 65 to derive Zeller's congruence. We substitute the number of elapsed days into the definition of **day-of-week-from-fixed** from page 33, ignoring the zero-valued

$$\textbf{gregorian-epoch} - 1$$

to obtain the day of the week

$$-306 + 365y' + \left\lfloor \frac{y'}{4} \right\rfloor - \left\lfloor \frac{y'}{100} \right\rfloor + \left\lfloor \frac{y'}{400} \right\rfloor + \left\lfloor \frac{3m' + 2}{5} \right\rfloor + 30m' + day \tag{2.31}$$

taken modulo 7, where

$$m' = (month - 3) \bmod 12$$
$$y' = year - \left\lfloor \frac{m'}{10} \right\rfloor$$

Zeller used month numbers 3–14 for March–February (that is, he renumbered January as 13 and February as 14), and dealt separately with centuries and the year within a century:

$$m = m' + 3 = \begin{cases} month + 12 & \textbf{if } month < \textbf{march} \\ month & \textbf{otherwise} \end{cases}$$
$$y = y' \bmod 100$$
$$c = \lfloor y'/100 \rfloor$$

Making these substitutions in (2.31) we get

$$-306 + 365(100c + y) + \left\lfloor \frac{100c + y}{4} \right\rfloor - c + \left\lfloor \frac{c}{4} \right\rfloor + \left\lfloor \frac{3m - 7}{5} \right\rfloor + 30(m - 3) + day$$

taken modulo 7. Discarding multiples of 7, dividing by 10 instead of 5, and regrouping, this becomes

$$-5 + (2c + y) + 4c + \left\lfloor \frac{y}{4} \right\rfloor - c + \left\lfloor \frac{c}{4} \right\rfloor + \left\lfloor \frac{6m - 14}{10} \right\rfloor + 2m - 6 + day$$

Finally, rearranging terms, we get

$$(day - 1) + \left\lfloor \frac{(m + 1)26}{10} \right\rfloor + y + \left\lfloor \frac{y}{4} \right\rfloor + \left\lfloor \frac{c}{4} \right\rfloor - 2c$$

taken modulo 7, which is Zeller's congruence as he wrote it in [23], except that he numbered the days Sunday–Saturday 1–7 so he had *day* not (*day* – 1).

Other versions of this formula often attributed to Zeller can be obtained by algebraic manipulation. Zeller [23] also gave a similar formula for Julian calendar dates.

2.5 Holidays

The information in this book has been gathered from many sources. Every effort has been made to insure its accuracy. Holidays sometimes are subject to change, however, and Morgan Guaranty cannot accept responsibility should any date or statement included prove to be incorrect.

Morgan Guaranty: *World Calendar* (1978)

Secular holidays on the Gregorian calendar are either on fixed days or on a particular day of the week relative to the beginning or end of a month. (An extensive list of secular holidays can be found in [10].) Fixed holidays are trivial to deal with; for example, to determine the R.D. date of United States Independence Day in a given Gregorian year we would use

$$\textbf{independence-day}\,(\textit{g-year}) \stackrel{\text{def}}{=} \tag{2.32}$$

$$\textbf{fixed-from-gregorian}\left(\boxed{\textit{g-year}}\boxed{\textbf{july}}\boxed{4}\right)$$

Other holidays are on the nth occurrence of a given day of the week, counting from either the beginning or the end of the month. The U.S. Labor Day, for example, is the first Monday in September, and U.S. Memorial Day is the last Monday in May. To find the R.D. date of the nth k-day ($n \neq 0$, k is the day of the week) on, or after or before, a given Gregorian date (counting forward when $n > 0$, backward when $n < 0$), we write

$$\textbf{nth-kday}\,(n, k, \textit{g-date}) \stackrel{\text{def}}{=} \tag{2.33}$$

$$\begin{cases} 7 \times n + \textbf{kday-before}\,(k, \textbf{fixed-from-gregorian}\,(\textit{g-date})) & \textbf{if } n > 0 \\ 7 \times n + \textbf{kday-after}\,(k, \textbf{fixed-from-gregorian}\,(\textit{g-date})) & \textbf{if } n < 0 \\ \textbf{bogus} & \textbf{otherwise} \end{cases}$$

using the functions of Section 1.12 (page 34); when $n = 0$ the special constant **bogus** is returned, signifying a nonexistent value. It is convenient to define two special cases for use with this function:

$$\textbf{first-kday}\,(k, \textit{g-date}) \stackrel{\text{def}}{=} \textbf{nth-kday}\,(1, k, \textit{g-date}) \tag{2.34}$$

gives the fixed date of the first k-day on or after a Gregorian date;

$$\textbf{last-kday}\,(k, \textit{g-date}) \stackrel{\text{def}}{=} \textbf{nth-kday}\,(-1, k, \textit{g-date}) \tag{2.35}$$

gives the fixed date of the last k-day on or before a Gregorian date.

Now we can define holiday dates, such as U.S. Labor Day,

$$\textbf{labor-day}\,(\textit{g-year}) \stackrel{\text{def}}{=} \tag{2.36}$$

$$\textbf{first-kday}\left(\textbf{monday}, \boxed{\textit{g-year}}\boxed{\textbf{september}}\boxed{1}\right)$$

U.S. Memorial Day,

$$\textbf{memorial-day}\,(g\text{-}year) \stackrel{\text{def}}{=} \tag{2.37}$$

$$\textbf{last-kday}\left(\textbf{monday},\ \boxed{g\text{-}year \mid \textbf{may} \mid 31}\right)$$

or U.S. Election Day (the Tuesday falling after the first Monday in November, which is the first Tuesday on or after November 2),

$$\textbf{election-day}\,(g\text{-}year) \stackrel{\text{def}}{=} \tag{2.38}$$

$$\textbf{first-kday}\left(\textbf{tuesday},\ \boxed{g\text{-}year \mid \textbf{november} \mid 2}\right)$$

Further, we can determine the starting and ending dates of U.S. daylight saving time (as of 2007, the second Sunday in March and the first Sunday in November, respectively):

$$\textbf{daylight-saving-start}\,(g\text{-}year) \stackrel{\text{def}}{=} \tag{2.39}$$

$$\textbf{nth-kday}\left(2, \textbf{sunday},\ \boxed{g\text{-}year \mid \textbf{march} \mid 1}\right)$$

$$\textbf{daylight-saving-end}\,(g\text{-}year) \stackrel{\text{def}}{=} \tag{2.40}$$

$$\textbf{first-kday}\left(\textbf{sunday},\ \boxed{g\text{-}year \mid \textbf{november} \mid 1}\right)$$

The main Christian holidays are Christmas, Easter, and various days connected with them (Advent Sunday, Ash Wednesday, Good Friday, and others; see [11, vol. V, pp. 844–853]). The date of Christmas on the Gregorian calendar is fixed and hence easily computed:

$$\textbf{christmas}\,(g\text{-}year) \stackrel{\text{def}}{=} \tag{2.41}$$

$$\textbf{fixed-from-gregorian}\left(\boxed{g\text{-}year \mid \textbf{december} \mid 25}\right)$$

The related dates of Advent Sunday (the Sunday closest to November 30) and Epiphany (the first Sunday after January 1)[7] are computed by

$$\textbf{advent}\,(g\text{-}year) \stackrel{\text{def}}{=} \tag{2.42}$$

$$\textbf{kday-nearest}\left(\textbf{sunday}, \textbf{fixed-from-gregorian}\left(\boxed{g\text{-}year \mid \textbf{november} \mid 30}\right)\right)$$

[7] Outside the United States, Epiphany is celebrated on January 6.

$$\textbf{epiphany}\,(g\text{-}year) \stackrel{\text{def}}{=} \tag{2.43}$$

$$\textbf{first-kday}\left(\textbf{sunday},\ \boxed{g\text{-}year \mid \textbf{january} \mid 2}\right)$$

The date of the Assumption (August 15), celebrated in Catholic countries, is fixed and presents no problem. We defer the calculation of Easter and related "movable" Christian holidays, which depend on lunar events, until Chapter 9.

To find all instances of Friday the Thirteenth within a range of fixed dates *range*, we mimic (1.39) as follows:

$$\textbf{unlucky-fridays-in-range}\,([a\,..\,b)) \stackrel{\text{def}}{=} \tag{2.44}$$

$$\begin{cases} \begin{cases} \langle fri \rangle & \textbf{if } date_{\textbf{day}} = 13 \\ \langle\,\rangle & \textbf{otherwise} \end{cases} \Bigg\} \parallel \textbf{unlucky-fridays-in-range}\,([fri+1\,..\,b)) \\ \qquad \textbf{if } fri \in range \\ \langle\,\rangle \quad \textbf{otherwise} \end{cases}$$

where

$$\begin{aligned} range &= [a\,..\,b) \\ fri &= \textbf{kday-on-or-after}\,(\textbf{friday}, a) \\ date &= \textbf{gregorian-from-fixed}\,(fri) \end{aligned}$$

Then, to list the "unlucky" Fridays in a given Gregorian year, we use that year as the range:

$$\textbf{unlucky-fridays}\,(g\text{-}year) \stackrel{\text{def}}{=} \tag{2.45}$$

$$\textbf{unlucky-fridays-in-range}\,(\textbf{gregorian-year-range}\,(g\text{-}year))$$

References

[1] *Explanatory Supplement to the Astronomical Ephemeris and the American Ephemeris and Nautical Almanac*, Her Majesty's Stationery Office, London, 1961.

[2] J. A. Ball, *Algorithms for RPN Calculators*, John Wiley & Sons, New York, 1978.

[3] A. Belenkiy and E. V. Echagüe, "History of One Defeat: Reform of the Julian calendar as Envisaged by Isaac Newton," *Notes & Records of the Royal Society*, vol. 59, pp. 223–254, 2005.

[4] G. V. Coyne, M. A. Hoskin, and O. Pedersen, *Gregorian Reform of the Calendar: Proceedings of the Vatican Conference to Commemorate Its 400th Anniversary, 1582–1982*, Pontifica Academica Scientiarum, Specola Vaticana, Vatican, 1983.

[5] L. E. Doggett, "Calendars," *Explanatory Supplement to the Astronomical Almanac*, P. K. Seidelmann, ed., University Science Books, Mill Valley, CA, pp. 575–608, 1992.

[6] J. Dutka, "On the Gregorian Revision of the Julian Calendar," *Mathematical Intelligencer*, vol. 10, pp. 56–64, 1988.

[7] H. F. Fliegel and T. C. van Flandern, "A Machine Algorithm for Processing Calendar Dates," *Communications of the ACM*, vol. 11, p. 657, 1968.

[8] J. K. Fotheringham, "The Calendar," *The Nautical Almanac and Astronomical Ephemeris*, His Majesty's Stationery Office, London, 1931–1934; revised 1935–1938; abridged 1939–1941.

[9] F. K. Ginzel, *Handbuch der mathematischen und technischen Chronologie*, vol. 3, J. C. Hinrichs'sche Buchhandlung, Leipzig, 1914. Reprinted by F. Ullmann Verlag, Zwickau, 1958.

[10] R. W. Gregory, *Special Days*, Citadel, Secaucus, NJ, 1975. Previous editions appeared under the title *Anniversaries and Holidays*.

[11] J. Hastings, ed., *Encyclopædia of Religion and Ethics*, Charles Scribner's Sons, New York, 1911.

[12] L. Lamport, "On the Proof of Correctness of a Calendar Program," *Communications of the ACM*, vol. 22, pp. 554–556, 1979.

[13] C. L. Liu, *Introduction to Combinatorial Mathematics*, McGraw-Hill, New York, 1968.

[14] J. Meeus, *Astronomical Algorithms*, 2nd edn., Willmann-Bell, Richmond, VA, 1998.

[15] A. K. Michels, *The Calendar of the Roman Republic*, Princeton University Press, Princeton, NJ, 1967.

[16] G. Moyer, "The Gregorian Calendar," *Scientific American*, vol. 246, no. 5, pp. 144–152, May 1982.

[17] R. Poole, "'Give Us Our Eleven Days!': Calendar Reform in Eighteenth-Century England," *Past and Present*, no. 149, pp. 95–139, November 1995.

[18] V. F. Rickey, "Mathematics of the Gregorian Calendar," *Mathematical Intelligencer*, vol. 7, pp. 53–56, 1985.

[19] J. Shallit, "Pierce Expansions and Rules for the Determination of Leap Years," *Fibonacci Quarterly*, vol. 32, pp. 416–423, 1994.

[20] R. G. Tantzen, "Algorithm 199: Conversions Between Calendar Date and Julian Day Number," *Communications of the ACM*, vol. 6, p. 444, 1963.

[21] J. V. Uspensky and M. A. Heaslet, *Elementary Number Theory*, McGraw-Hill, New York, 1939.

[22] C. Zeller, "Problema duplex Calendarii fundamentale," *Bulletin Société Mathématique*, vol. 11, pp. 59–61, March 1883.

[23] C. Zeller, "Kalender-Formeln," *Acta Mathematica*, vol. 9, pp. 131–136, November 1886.

Illustration from Lichtenberg's 1757 *Göttinger Taschen Kalender*: a reverse copy of a man pouring gin over the head of another, and a flag reading "Give us our eleven days," in protest at the British abandonment of the Julian calendar in September 1752. From the first plate of William Hogarth's 1755 "An Election Entertainment." (Courtesy of the British Museum, London.)

3

The Julian Calendar

Atque hic erat anni Romani status cum C. Cæsar ei manum admovit: qui ex lunari non malo in pessimum a Numa aut alio rupice et rustico depravatus, vitio intercalationis veteres fines suos tamen tueri non potuit. Vt non semel miratus sim, orbis terrarum dominam gentem, quæ generi humano leges dabat, sibi unam legem anni ordinati statuere non potuisse, ut post hominum memoriam nulla gens in terris ineptiore anni forma usa sit. [*Such was the condition of the Roman calendar when Julius Cæsar went about his work on it. Numa or some other rustic clod took a lunar calendar that was not too bad and made it appalling. Thanks to his faulty system of intercalation it could not stay in its original bounds. I have been amazed more than once that the people who ruled the entire world and gave laws to the entire human race could not make one law for itself for an orderly calendar. As a result, no nation in human memory has used a worse calendar than theirs.*]

Joseph Justus Scaliger: *De Emendatione Temporum* (1583)[1]

3.1 Structure and Implementation

The calculations for the Julian calendar, which we described in introducing the Gregorian calendar in Chapter 2, are nearly identical to those for the Gregorian calendar, but we must change the leap-year rule to

$$\textbf{julian-leap-year?}\,(\textit{j-year}) \stackrel{\text{def}}{=} (\textit{j-year} \bmod 4) = \left\{ \begin{array}{ll} 0 & \textbf{if } \textit{j-year} > 0 \\ 3 & \textbf{otherwise} \end{array} \right\} \tag{3.1}$$

The upper part is formula (1.82); the lower part is formula (1.83) with $\Delta = 1$ because there is no year 0 on the Julian calendar. Note that the Julian leap-year rule was applied inconsistently for a period of years prior to 8 C.E. (see [6, pp. 156–158]).

The months of the Julian calendar are the same as those of the Gregorian calendar (see page 55).

Converting from a Julian date to an R.D. date requires a calculation similar to that in the Gregorian case but with two minor adjustments: we no longer need consider century-year leap days, and we must define the epoch of the Julian calendar

[1] *Lectores ne credant huius libri auctores his sententiis subscribere.*

in terms of our fixed dating. For the epoch, we know that R.D. 1 is January 3, 1 C.E. (Julian), and thus the first day of the Julian calendar, January 1, 1 C.E. (Julian) must be December 30, 0 (Gregorian), that is, R.D. −1:

$$\textbf{julian-epoch} \stackrel{\text{def}}{=} \textbf{fixed-from-gregorian}\left(\boxed{0 \mid \textbf{december} \mid 30}\right) \tag{3.2}$$

Now we can write

$$\textbf{fixed-from-julian}\left(\boxed{\textit{year} \mid \textit{month} \mid \textit{day}}\right) \stackrel{\text{def}}{=} \tag{3.3}$$

$$\textbf{julian-epoch} - 1 + 365 \times (y-1) + \left\lfloor \frac{y-1}{4} \right\rfloor + \left\lfloor \tfrac{1}{12} \times (367 \times \textit{month} - 362) \right\rfloor + \begin{cases} 0 & \textbf{if } \textit{month} \leqslant 2 \\ -1 & \textbf{if julian-leap-year?}\ (\textit{year}) \\ -2 & \textbf{otherwise} \end{cases} + \textit{day}$$

where

$$y = \begin{cases} \textit{year} + 1 & \textbf{if } \textit{year} < 0 \\ \textit{year} & \textbf{otherwise} \end{cases}$$

This function is similar in structure to that of **fixed-from-gregorian**. We start at **julian-epoch**−1, the R.D. number of the last day before the epoch; to this, we add the number of nonleap days (positive for positive years, negative otherwise) between the last day before the epoch and the last day of the year preceding the given year, the corresponding (positive or negative) number of leap days, the number of days in prior months of the given year, and the number of days in the given month up to and including the given day. For nonpositive years, we adjust the year to accommodate the lack of year 0.

For the inverse function, we handle the missing year 0 by subtracting 1 from the year as determined by formula (1.90) for dates before the epoch:

$$\textbf{julian-from-fixed}\ (\textit{date}) \stackrel{\text{def}}{=} \boxed{\textit{year} \mid \textit{month} \mid \textit{day}} \tag{3.4}$$

where

$$\textit{approx} = \left\lfloor \frac{1}{1461} \times (4 \times (\textit{date} - \textbf{julian-epoch}) + 1464) \right\rfloor$$

$$\textit{year} = \begin{cases} \textit{approx} - 1 & \textbf{if } \textit{approx} \leqslant 0 \\ \textit{approx} & \textbf{otherwise} \end{cases}$$

$$\textit{prior-days} = \textit{date} - \textbf{fixed-from-julian}\left(\boxed{\textit{year} \mid \textbf{january} \mid 1}\right)$$

$$correction = \begin{cases} 0 & \textbf{if } date < \textbf{fixed-from-julian}\left(\boxed{year \mid \textbf{march} \mid 1}\right) \\ 1 & \textbf{if julian-leap-year?}\,(year) \\ 2 & \textbf{otherwise} \end{cases}$$

$$month = \left\lfloor \frac{1}{367} \times (12 \times (prior\text{-}days + correction) + 373) \right\rfloor$$

$$day = date - \textbf{fixed-from-julian}\left(\boxed{year \mid month \mid 1}\right) + 1$$

We can construct alternative functions in the style of **alt-fixed-from-gregorian** and **alt-gregorian-from-fixed** from Section 2.3 for the functions **fixed-from-julian** and **julian-from-fixed**.

3.2 Roman Nomenclature

Brutus: Is not tomorrow, boy, the ides of March?
Lucius: I know not, sir.
Brutus: Look in the calendar and bring me word.

Shakespeare: *Julius Cæsar*, Act II, scene i (1623)

In ancient Rome it was customary to refer to days of the month by counting down to certain key events in the month: the *kalends*, the *nones*, and the *ides*. This custom, in popular use well past the middle ages, is evidently quite ancient, coming from a time in which the month was still synchronized with the lunar cycle: the kalends were the new moon, the nones the first quarter moon, and the ides the full moon. (Indeed, the word *calendar* is derived from *kalendæ*, meaning "account book," for loans were due on the first of the month.) We define three special constants,

$$\textbf{kalends} \stackrel{\text{def}}{=} 1 \tag{3.5}$$

$$\textbf{nones} \stackrel{\text{def}}{=} 2 \tag{3.6}$$

$$\textbf{ides} \stackrel{\text{def}}{=} 3 \tag{3.7}$$

to identify these events.

The kalends are always the first of the month. The ides are near the middle of the month—the thirteenth of the month, except in March, May, July, and October when they fall on the fifteenth; hence

$$\textbf{ides-of-month}\,(month) \stackrel{\text{def}}{=} \tag{3.8}$$

$$\begin{cases} 15 & \textbf{if } month \in \{\textbf{march, may, july, october}\} \\ 13 & \textbf{otherwise} \end{cases}$$

The nones are always 8 days before the ides:

$$\textbf{nones-of-month}\,(\mathit{month}) \stackrel{\text{def}}{=} \textbf{ides-of-month}\,(\mathit{month}) - 8 \tag{3.9}$$

Dates that fall on the kalends, the nones, or the ides are referred to as such. Thus, March 15 is called "the ides of March," for example, whereas January 1 and 5 are, respectively, the kalends and nones of January. Dates that fall on the day before one of these special days are called *pridie* ("day before" in Latin); for example, July 6, the day before the nones of July, is *pridie Non. Jul.* in Latin. All dates other than the kalends, nones, or ides, or days immediately preceding them are described by the number of days (inclusive) until the next upcoming event: The Roman name for October 30 is *ante diem III Kal. Nov.*, meaning 3 days (inclusive) before the kalends of November; the idiomatic English usage would describe this as "2 days before the first of November," but the Roman custom uses the inclusive count.

In a leap year February has an extra day, and modern authorities understand the Roman custom as intercalating that day after February 24, before February 25 (see [6] for another possibility; see [1, pp. 92–94, 678–680] for a discussion of the placement of the leap day on the Julian calendar). Because February 24 was *ante diem VI Kal. Mar.*, the extra day was called *ante diem bis VI Kal. Mar.* or "the second sixth day before the kalends of March." The phrase *bis VI* was read *bis sextum* which gave rise to the English words *bissextus* for leap day and *bissextile* as an adjective to describe a leap year [3, p. 795]. Despite the official Roman calendar, unofficial and medieval usage made the day after February 23 the leap day. The necessary changes to our functions **fixed-from-roman** and **roman-from-fixed** are simple, should one want to follow that variant rule.

Table 3.1 gives abbreviated names for all the days according to the Roman system. Full spellings of all the names are given for each in [1]; details of the Latin grammar of those names can also be found there [1, pp. 672–673].

We represent the Roman method of referring to a day of the month by a list containing the year number, the month, the next event, a count (inclusive) of days until that event, and a **true/false** leap-day indicator:

year	*month*	*event*	*count*	*leap*

Although the Roman method of referring to days of the month is sometimes used in the context of Gregorian calendar dates, such references are archaic and it is more sensible to tie the Roman nomenclature to the Julian calendar, as we do here. Determining the Roman name for a Gregorian date is easily done by making the appropriate substitutions of **gregorian-from-fixed** and **gregorian-leap-year?** for the corresponding Julian functions.

Determining the fixed date corresponding to a given Roman form involves subtracting the count from the date of the event in the specified month and year, while adjusting for the leap day if the event is the kalends of March in a leap year:

Table 3.1 Roman nomenclature for days of the month on the Julian calendar. The abbreviation "a.d." stands for the Latin *ante diem*. In dates after the ides of a month, "Kal." means the kalends of the coming month; "Non." and "Id." mean the nones and ides, respectively, of the current month. Adapted from [2] and [5].

Day	January August December	February (ordinary)	February (leap)	March May July October	April June September November
1	**Kalends**	**Kalends**	**Kalends**	**Kalends**	**Kalends**
2	a.d. iv Non.	a.d. iv Non.	a.d. iv Non.	a.d. vi Non.	a.d. iv Non.
3	a.d. iii Non.	a.d. iii Non.	a.d. iii Non.	a.d. v Non.	a.d. iii Non.
4	pridie Non.	pridie Non.	pridie Non.	a.d. iv Non.	pridie Non.
5	**Nones**	**Nones**	**Nones**	a.d. iii Non.	**Nones**
6	a.d. viii Id.	a.d. viii Id.	a.d. viii Id.	pridie Non.	a.d. viii Id.
7	a.d. vii Id.	a.d. vii Id.	a.d. vii Id.	**Nones**	a.d. vii Id.
8	a.d. vi Id.	a.d. vi Id.	a.d. vi Id.	a.d. viii Id.	a.d. vi Id.
9	a.d. v Id.	a.d. v Id.	a.d. v Id.	a.d. vii Id.	a.d. v Id.
10	a.d. iv Id.	a.d. iv Id.	a.d. iv Id.	a.d. vi Id.	a.d. iv Id.
11	a.d. iii Id.	a.d. iii Id.	a.d. iii Id.	a.d. v Id.	a.d. iii Id.
12	pridie Id.	pridie Id.	pridie Id.	a.d. iv Id.	pridie Id.
13	**Ides**	**Ides**	**Ides**	a.d. iii Id.	**Ides**
14	a.d. xix Kal.	a.d. xvi Kal.	a.d. xvi Kal.	pridie Id.	a.d. xviii Kal.
15	a.d. xviii Kal.	a.d. xv Kal.	a.d. xv Kal.	**Ides**	a.d. xvii Kal.
16	a.d. xvii Kal.	a.d. xiv Kal.	a.d. xiv Kal.	a.d. xvii Kal.	a.d. xvi Kal.
17	a.d. xvi Kal.	a.d. xiii Kal.	a.d. xiii Kal.	a.d. xvi Kal.	a.d. xv Kal.
18	a.d. xv Kal.	a.d. xii Kal.	a.d. xii Kal.	a.d. xv Kal.	a.d. xiv Kal.
19	a.d. xiv Kal.	a.d. xi Kal.	a.d. xi Kal.	a.d. xiv Kal.	a.d. xiii Kal.
20	a.d. xiii Kal.	a.d. x Kal.	a.d. x Kal.	a.d. xiii Kal.	a.d. xii Kal.
21	a.d. xii Kal.	a.d. ix Kal.	a.d. ix Kal.	a.d. xii Kal.	a.d. xi Kal.
22	a.d. xi Kal.	a.d. viii Kal.	a.d. viii Kal.	a.d. xi Kal.	a.d. x Kal.
23	a.d. x Kal.	a.d. vii Kal.	a.d. vii Kal.	a.d. x Kal.	a.d. ix Kal.
24	a.d. ix Kal.	a.d. vi Kal.	a.d. vi Kal.	a.d. ix Kal.	a.d. viii Kal.
25	a.d. viii Kal.	a.d. v Kal.	a.d. bis vi Kal.	a.d. viii Kal.	a.d. vii Kal.
26	a.d. vii Kal.	a.d. iv Kal.	a.d. v Kal.	a.d. vii Kal.	a.d. vi Kal.
27	a.d. vi Kal.	a.d. iii Kal.	a.d. iv Kal.	a.d. vi Kal.	a.d. v Kal.
28	a.d. v Kal.	pridie Kal.	a.d. iii Kal.	a.d. v Kal.	a.d. iv Kal.
29	a.d. iv Kal.		pridie Kal.	a.d. iv Kal.	a.d. iii Kal.
30	a.d. iii Kal.			a.d. iii Kal.	pridie Kal.
31	pridie Kal.			pridie Kal.	

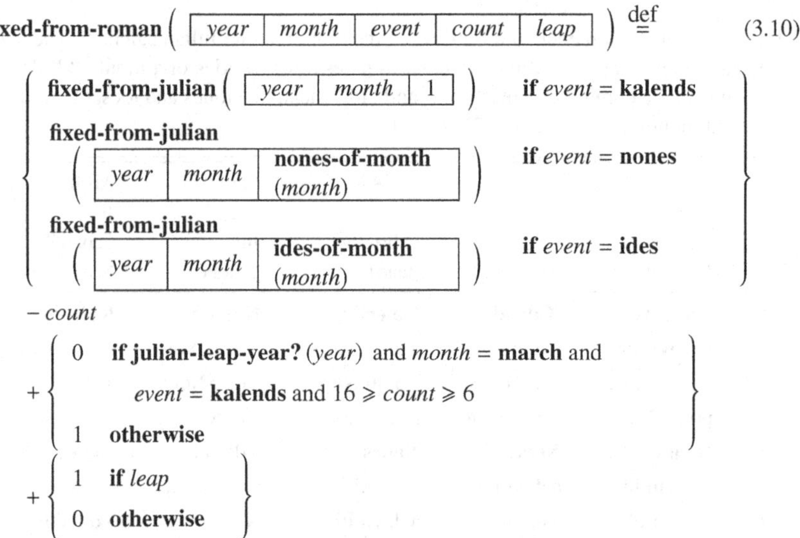

$$\textbf{fixed-from-roman}\left(\boxed{\,year \mid month \mid event \mid count \mid leap\,}\right) \stackrel{\text{def}}{=} \tag{3.10}$$

$$\begin{cases} \textbf{fixed-from-julian}\left(\boxed{\,year \mid month \mid 1\,}\right) & \textbf{if } event = \textbf{kalends} \\ \textbf{fixed-from-julian}\left(\boxed{\,year \mid month \mid \textbf{nones-of-month}\,(month)\,}\right) & \textbf{if } event = \textbf{nones} \\ \textbf{fixed-from-julian}\left(\boxed{\,year \mid month \mid \textbf{ides-of-month}\,(month)\,}\right) & \textbf{if } event = \textbf{ides} \end{cases}$$
$$- count$$
$$+ \begin{cases} 0 & \textbf{if julian-leap-year?}\,(year) \text{ and } month = \textbf{march} \text{ and} \\ & \quad event = \textbf{kalends} \text{ and } 16 \geqslant count \geqslant 6 \\ 1 & \textbf{otherwise} \end{cases}$$
$$+ \begin{cases} 1 & \textbf{if } leap \\ 0 & \textbf{otherwise} \end{cases}$$

Converting a fixed date to the Roman form thus requires converting that fixed date to a Julian year-month-day and then determining the next event. If the month is February of a leap year, the special cases must be handled separately:

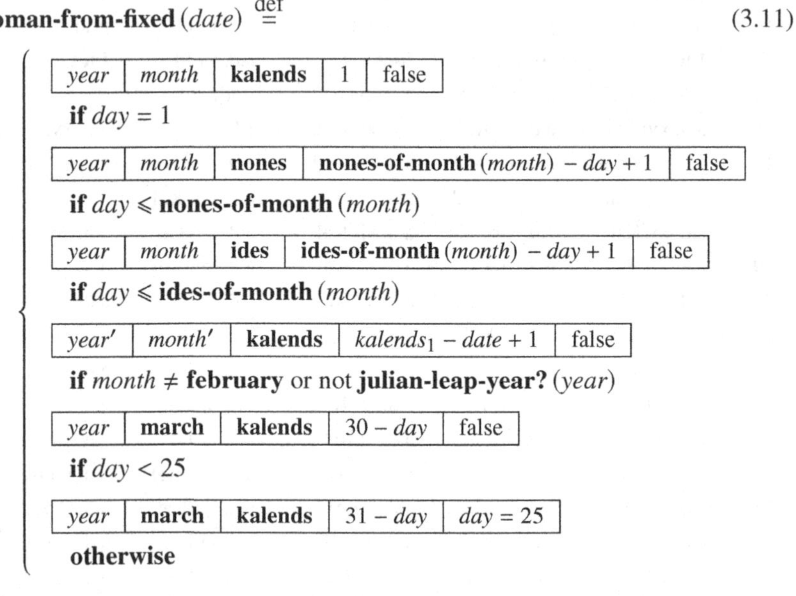

$$\textbf{roman-from-fixed}\,(date) \stackrel{\text{def}}{=} \tag{3.11}$$

$$\begin{cases} \boxed{\,year \mid month \mid \textbf{kalends} \mid 1 \mid \text{false}\,} \\ \quad \textbf{if } day = 1 \\ \boxed{\,year \mid month \mid \textbf{nones} \mid \textbf{nones-of-month}\,(month) - day + 1 \mid \text{false}\,} \\ \quad \textbf{if } day \leqslant \textbf{nones-of-month}\,(month) \\ \boxed{\,year \mid month \mid \textbf{ides} \mid \textbf{ides-of-month}\,(month) - day + 1 \mid \text{false}\,} \\ \quad \textbf{if } day \leqslant \textbf{ides-of-month}\,(month) \\ \boxed{\,year' \mid month' \mid \textbf{kalends} \mid kalends_1 - date + 1 \mid \text{false}\,} \\ \quad \textbf{if } month \neq \textbf{february} \text{ or not } \textbf{julian-leap-year?}\,(year) \\ \boxed{\,year \mid \textbf{march} \mid \textbf{kalends} \mid 30 - day \mid \text{false}\,} \\ \quad \textbf{if } day < 25 \\ \boxed{\,year \mid \textbf{march} \mid \textbf{kalends} \mid 31 - day \mid day = 25\,} \\ \quad \textbf{otherwise} \end{cases}$$

where

$$\begin{aligned} j\text{-}date &= \textbf{julian-from-fixed}\,(date) \\ month &= j\text{-}date_{\textbf{month}} \\ day &= j\text{-}date_{\textbf{day}} \\ year &= j\text{-}date_{\textbf{year}} \end{aligned}$$

$$month' = (month + 1) \bmod [1 \,..\, 12]$$

$$year' = \begin{cases} year & \textbf{if } month' \neq 1 \\ year + 1 & \textbf{if } year \neq -1 \\ 1 & \textbf{otherwise} \end{cases}$$

$$kalends_1 = \textbf{fixed-from-roman}\left(\boxed{year' \mid month' \mid \textbf{kalends} \mid 1 \mid \text{false}} \right)$$

Note that when the upcoming event is the kalends, it is the kalends of the *next* month, not the present month; thus, dates following the ides of a month carry the name of the next month, and after the ides of December dates carry the following year number.

3.3 Roman Years

Cæsar set out the problem before the best philosophers and mathematicians and, from the methods available, he concocted his own correction that was more precise.

Plutarch: *Life of Cæsar* (75 C.E.)

Roman years were specified A.U.C., *Ab Urbe Condita*, from the founding of the city (of Rome). There is some uncertainty about the precise traditional year of the founding of Rome, so we make it a symbolic value:

$$\textbf{year-rome-founded} \stackrel{\text{def}}{=} 753 \text{ B.C.E.} \tag{3.12}$$

We want to convert between A.U.C. years and Julian years. Because years were not counted from zero on the Julian calendar, we assume that they should not be counted from zero A.U.C.; recalling that B.C.E. years are represented internally as negative integers we write

$$\textbf{julian-year-from-auc}\,(year) \stackrel{\text{def}}{=} \tag{3.13}$$

$$\begin{cases} year + \textbf{year-rome-founded} - 1 & \textbf{if } 1 \leqslant year \leqslant -\textbf{year-rome-founded} \\ year + \textbf{year-rome-founded} & \textbf{otherwise} \end{cases}$$

and

$$\textbf{auc-year-from-julian}\,(year) \stackrel{\text{def}}{=} \tag{3.14}$$

$$\begin{cases} year - \textbf{year-rome-founded} + 1 & \textbf{if year-rome-founded} \leqslant year \leqslant -1 \\ year - \textbf{year-rome-founded} & \textbf{otherwise} \end{cases}$$

3.4 Olympiads

Therefore those who prophesied in the time of Darius Hystaspes, about the second year of his reign—Haggai, and Zechariah, and the angel of the twelve, who prophesied about the first year of the forty-eighth Olympiad—are demonstrated to be older than Pythagoras, who is said to have lived in the sixty-second Olympiad, and than Thales, the oldest of the wise men of the Greeks, who lived about the fiftieth Olympiad.

Clement of Alexandria: *The Stromata* (c. 200 C.E.)

Another common historical method of denoting years was in terms of the Olympiad, the four-year cycle of Olympic games, said to have been introduced by either the Greek historian Timaeus or by Eratosthenes. The recently reconstructed Antikythera mechanism included this reckoning, along with eclipse predictions and displays of the phases of the moon and positions of the visible planets.[2] The games were held every fourth year, so each Olympiad comprises four years; we represent an Olympiad by a pair of integers,

cycle	*year*

The first recorded games were in 776 B.C.E., so this was year 1 of cycle 1:

$$\textbf{olympiad-start} \stackrel{\text{def}}{=} 776 \text{ B.C.E.} \tag{3.15}$$

To convert a Julian year into its Olympiad equivalent and vice versa, we need to count quadrenniel periods:

$$\textbf{julian-year-from-olympiad}\,(\textit{o-date}) \stackrel{\text{def}}{=} \begin{cases} \textit{years} & \textbf{if } \textit{years} < 0 \\ \textit{years} + 1 & \textbf{otherwise} \end{cases} \tag{3.16}$$

where

$$\begin{aligned} \textit{cycle} &= \textit{o-date}_{\textbf{cycle}} \\ \textit{year} &= \textit{o-date}_{\textbf{year}} \\ \textit{years} &= \textbf{olympiad-start} + 4 \times (\textit{cycle} - 1) + \textit{year} - 1 \end{aligned}$$

In the other direction

$$\textbf{olympiad-from-julian-year}\,(\textit{j-year}) \stackrel{\text{def}}{=} \tag{3.17}$$

$$\boxed{\left\lfloor \frac{\textit{years}}{4} \right\rfloor + 1} \boxed{(\textit{years} \bmod 4) + 1}$$

where

$$\textit{years} = \textit{j-year} - \textbf{olympiad-start} - \begin{Bmatrix} 0 & \textbf{if } \textit{j-year} < 0 \\ 1 & \textbf{otherwise} \end{Bmatrix}$$

---

[2] For more about this marvelous device, see "The Antikythera Mechanism: A Computer Science Perspective," D. Spinellis, *IEEE Computer* vol. 41, no. 5, pp. 22–27, May 2008. Also, see "Calendars with Olympiad display and eclipse prediction on the Antikythera Mechanism," T. Freeth, A. Jones, J. M. Steele, and Y. Bitsakis, *Nature*, vol. 454, pp. 614–617, July 2008. A popular treatment, with many interesting photographs, is given in J. Marchant's *Decoding the Heavens*, William Heinemann, London, 2008.

3.5 Seasons

Civilized nations in general now agree to begin reckoning the new year from the first of January. Yet it may seem strange to call that a new season, when everything is most inactive and lifeless; when animals are benumbed by the cold, and vegetables are all dead or withered. For this reason, some have thought to begin the year in Spring.

Thomas Gosden: *The Calendar of Nature: Designed for the Instruction and Entertainment of Young Persons* (1822)

As the Julian year of 365.25 days is longer than the Gregorian year of 365.2425 days, the times and dates of the Julian seasons shift over the years with respect to the Gregorian calendar. Let *season* be any value in the range $[0° \,..\, 360°)$; in particular, let the four seasons be defined by the following values:

$$\textbf{spring} \stackrel{\text{def}}{=} 0° \tag{3.18}$$

$$\textbf{summer} \stackrel{\text{def}}{=} 90° \tag{3.19}$$

$$\textbf{autumn} \stackrel{\text{def}}{=} 180° \tag{3.20}$$

$$\textbf{winter} \stackrel{\text{def}}{=} 270° \tag{3.21}$$

(These are the celestial longitudes of the sun at the start of those seasons; see Section 14.4.)

To compute the occurrences of the Julian *season* in the Gregorian year *g-year*, we first define a generic function for calculating occurrences of seasons of a year of any length *L*. We must allow for the possibility of multiple occurrences (if the calendar year is short) or none (if the year is long and the season falls near January 1 on the Gregorian calendar). We use **positions-in-range** (1.40):

$$\textbf{cycle-in-gregorian}\,(\textit{season}, \textit{g-year}, L, \textit{start}) \stackrel{\text{def}}{=} \tag{3.22}$$

$$\textbf{positions-in-range}\,(\textit{pos}, L, \Delta, \textit{year})$$

where

$$\begin{aligned} \textit{year} &= \textbf{gregorian-year-range}\,(\textit{g-year}) \\ \textit{pos} &= \frac{\textit{season}}{360°} \times L \\ \Delta &= \textit{pos} - (\textit{start} \bmod L) \end{aligned}$$

Then, for Julian seasons, we have

$$\textbf{julian-season-in-gregorian}\,(\textit{season}, \textit{g-year}) \stackrel{\text{def}}{=} \tag{3.23}$$

$$\textbf{cycle-in-gregorian}\Big(\textit{season}, \textit{g-year}, Y, \textbf{fixed-from-julian}\Big(\boxed{1\text{ B.C.E.}}\,\boxed{\textbf{march}}\,\boxed{23}\Big) + \textit{offset}\Big)$$

where

$$Y = 365 + 6^{\text{h}}$$

$$\textit{offset} = \frac{\textit{season}}{360^\circ} \times Y$$

This is based on the assumption of a spring equinox on March 23 in 1 B.C.E., as used in computations of Easter. See Chapter 9.

3.6 Holidays

It is related that once a Roman asked a question to Rabbi Yoḥanan ben Zakkai: We have festivals and you have festivals; we have the Kalends, Saturnalia, and Kratesis, and you have Passover, Shavuot, and Sukkot; which is the day whereon we and you rejoice alike? Rabbi Yoḥanan ben Zakkai replied: "It is the day when rain falls."

Deuteronomy Rabbah, VII, 7

Until 1923 the date of the Eastern Orthodox Christmas depended on the Julian calendar. At that time, the Ecumenical Patriarch, Meletios IV, convened a congress at which it was decided to use the Gregorian date instead.[3] By 1968 all but the churches of Jerusalem, Russia, and Serbia had adopted the new date, December 25 on the Gregorian calendar. There remain, however, *Palaioemerologitai* groups, especially in Greece, who continue to use the old calendar. Virtually all Orthodox churches continue to celebrate Easter according to the Julian calendar (see Chapter 9).

The occurrence of the old Eastern Orthodox Christmas in a given Gregorian year is somewhat involved. With the current alignment of the Julian and Gregorian calendars, and because the Julian year is always at least as long as the corresponding Gregorian year, Eastern Orthodox Christmas occurs at most once in a given Gregorian year—in modern times it occurs near the beginning. However, far in the past or the future, there are Gregorian years in which it does not occur at all (1100, for example); as the two calendars get further out of alignment (it will take some 50000 years for them to be a full year out of alignment), Eastern Orthodox Christmas will migrate throughout the Gregorian year.

We can write a general function that gives a list of the corresponding R.D. dates of occurrence, within a specified Gregorian year, of a given month and day on the Julian calendar:

[3] The Congress of the Orthodox Oriental Churches actually adopted a "revised" Gregorian leap-year rule; see footnote on page 57.

$$\textbf{julian-in-gregorian}\,(\textit{j-month}, \textit{j-day}, \textit{g-year}) \stackrel{\text{def}}{=} \tag{3.24}$$

$$\{\textit{date}_0, \textit{date}_1\} \cap \textbf{gregorian-year-range}\,(\textit{g-year})$$

where

$$\begin{aligned}
\textit{jan}_1 &= \textbf{gregorian-new-year}\,(\textit{g-year})\\
y &= (\textbf{julian-from-fixed}\,(\textit{jan}_1))_{\textbf{year}}\\
y' &= \begin{cases} 1 & \textbf{if } y = -1\\ y+1 & \textbf{otherwise}\end{cases}\\
\textit{date}_0 &= \textbf{fixed-from-julian}\left(\boxed{y \mid \textit{j-month} \mid \textit{j-day}}\right)\\
\textit{date}_1 &= \textbf{fixed-from-julian}\left(\boxed{y' \mid \textit{j-month} \mid \textit{j-day}}\right)
\end{aligned}$$

Tens of thousands of years from the present, the alignment of the Gregorian and Julian calendars will be such that some Julian dates occur twice in a Gregorian year—the first example of this is in Gregorian year 41104 when Julian date February 28 occurs twice; the function **julian-in-gregorian** correctly returns a list of two R.D. dates in such cases.

For example, we can use this function to determine a list of R.D. dates of December 25 (Julian) for a given year of the Gregorian calendar:

$$\textbf{eastern-orthodox-christmas}\,(\textit{g-year}) \stackrel{\text{def}}{=} \tag{3.25}$$

$$\textbf{julian-in-gregorian}\,(\textbf{december}, 25, \textit{g-year})$$

Other fixed Orthodox holidays are the Nativity of the Virgin Mary (September 8), the Elevation of the Life-Giving Cross (September 14), the Presentation of the Virgin Mary in the Temple (November 21), Theophany (January 6), the Presentation of Christ in the Temple (February 2), the Annunciation (March 25), the Transfiguration (August 6), and the Repose of the Virgin Mary (August 15). Orthodox periods of fasting include the Fast of the Repose of the Virgin Mary (August 1–14) and the 40-day Christmas Fast (November 15–December 24).

Orthodox movable holidays and fasts are explained in Chapter 9.

The Armenian church celebrates Christmas on January 6 (Julian) in Jerusalem, and on January 6 (Gregorian) elsewhere.

References

[1] B. Blackburn and L. Holford-Strevens, *The Oxford Companion to the Year*, Oxford University Press, Oxford, 1999.

[2] L. E. Doggett, "Calendars," *Explanatory Supplement to the Astronomical Almanac*, P. K. Seidelmann, ed., University Science Books, Mill Valley, CA, pp. 575–608, 1992.

[3] J. K. Fotheringham, "The Calendar," *The Nautical Almanac and Astronomical Ephemeris*, His Majesty's Stationery Office, London, 1931–1934; revised 1935–1938; abridged 1939–1941.

[4] A. K. Michels, *The Calendar of the Roman Republic*, Princeton University Press, Princeton, NJ, 1967.

[5] E. G. Richards, *Mapping Time: The Calendar and its History*, Oxford University Press, Oxford, 1998.

[6] A. E. Samuel, *Greek and Roman Chronology: Calendars and Years in Classical Antiquity*, C. H. Beck'sche Verlagsbuchhandlung, Munich, 1972.

Ethiopic computus (*Baḥrā Ḥassab*) in Ge'ez (1904 E.E.). The third column from the right gives the day of the Ethiopic month (Magābit or Miyāzyā) of Nicæan Easter for years 1417–1435 E.E. (= 1425–1443 C.E.). Other columns give the number of epagomenæ (third column from the left), the epact (sixth column from the left), the day of the Ethiopic month of various fasts, and (nonstandard) dates for Jewish holidays. See [4] for detailed information on such tables. (Courtesy of the Library of Congress, Washington, D.C.; MS 23, Thomas Leiper Kane Manuscript Collection.)

4

The Coptic and Ethiopic Calendars

Kiyahk: ṣabāḥak misāk [*In Kiyahk, your morning is your evening.*]
Coptic rhyme about the short days of winter

Both the Coptic and Ethiopic calendars have the same leap-year structure as does the Julian (1 year out of 4 is a leap year), but their months follow a more regular pattern.

4.1 The Coptic Calendar

The Christian Copts, modern descendants of the Pharaonic Egyptians, use a calendar based on the ancient Egyptian solar calendar (see Section 1.11) but with leap years. The year starts in late summer. Days begin at sunset, and the calendar consists of 12 months of 30 days each, followed by an extra 5-day period. Once every fourth year a leap day is added to this extra period to make it 6 days, making the average year $365\frac{1}{4}$ days long like the Julian calendar of Chapter 3.[1] The months are called by coptized forms of their ancient Egyptian names (see page 30 for the hieroglyphic forms of the names); in Coptic (Sahidic) they are:

(1) Thoout	Ⲑⲟⲟⲩⲧ	30 days
(2) Paope	Ⲡⲁⲟⲡⲉ	30 days
(3) Athōr	Ϩⲁⲑⲱⲣ	30 days
(4) Koiak	Ⲕⲟⲓⲁⲕ	30 days
(5) Tōbe	Ⲧⲱⲃⲉ	30 days
(6) Meshir	Ⲙ̅ϣⲓⲣ	30 days
(7) Paremotep	Ⲡⲁⲣⲙ̅ⲟⲧⲡ̅	30 days
(8) Parmoute	Ⲡⲁⲣⲙⲟⲩⲧⲉ	30 days
(9) Pashons	Ⲡⲁϣⲟⲛⲥ̅	30 days
(10) Paōne	Ⲡⲁⲱⲛⲉ	30 days
(11) Epēp	Ⲉⲡⲏⲡ	30 days
(12) Mesorē	Ⲙⲉⲥⲟⲣⲏ	30 days
(13) Epagomenē	Ⲉⲡⲁⲅⲟⲙⲉⲛⲏ	5 {6} days

[1] The Dionysian calendar, referred to by Ptolemy in the *Almagest*, is believed to have had the same structure; see B. L. van der Waerden, "Greek Astronomical Calendars III: The Calendar of Dionysius," *Archive for History of Exact Sciences*, vol. 29, no. 2, pp. 125–130, 1984.

(The leap-year structure is given in braces.) We treat epagomenæ, the extra 5 or 6 days, as a short thirteenth month. Indeed, they are called "the small month" (*p abot n kouji*) in Coptic.

The day names are

Sunday	Tkyriakē	Ⲧⲕⲩⲣⲓⲁⲕⲏ
Monday	Pesnau	Ⲡⲉⲥⲛⲁⲩ
Tuesday	Pshoment	Ⲡϣⲟⲙⲙ̄ⲧ
Wednesday	Peftoou	Ⲡⲉϥⲧⲟⲟⲩ
Thursday	Ptiou	Ⲡⲧⲟⲩ
Friday	Psoou	Ⲡⲥⲟⲟⲩ
Saturday	Psabbaton	Ⲡⲥⲁⲃⲃⲁⲧⲟⲛ

The Copts count their years from August 29, 284 C.E. (Julian), R.D. 103605, the beginning of year 1 A.M.[2] Thus, we define

$$\textbf{coptic-epoch} \stackrel{\text{def}}{=} \textbf{fixed-from-julian}\left(\boxed{284 \text{ C.E.} \mid \textbf{august} \mid 29}\right) \tag{4.1}$$

Leap years occur whenever the Coptic year number leaves a remainder of 3 when divided by 4; this is $c = 4$, $l = 1$, $\Delta = 1$ in formula (1.83). We can express this rule by

$$\textbf{coptic-leap-year?}\,(c\text{-}year) \stackrel{\text{def}}{=} (c\text{-}year \bmod 4) = 3 \tag{4.2}$$

but we will not need this function.

Considering the epagomenæ as a month, to convert a Coptic date

$$\boxed{year \mid month \mid day}$$

to an R.D. date, we do the same as for the corresponding Gregorian and Julian functions. Start at **coptic-epoch** − 1, the R.D. number of the last day before the epoch. To this add: the number of nonleap days (positive for positive years, negative otherwise) between this date and the last day of the year preceding *year*; the corresponding (positive or negative) number of leap days; the number of days in the prior months in *year*; and the number of days in *month* up to and including *day*. Thus

$$\textbf{fixed-from-coptic}\left(\boxed{year \mid month \mid day}\right) \stackrel{\text{def}}{=} \tag{4.3}$$
$$\textbf{coptic-epoch} - 1 + 365 \times (year - 1) + \left\lfloor \frac{year}{4} \right\rfloor + 30 \times (month - 1) + day$$

To convert an R.D. date to a Coptic date, we use formula (1.90) to determine the year. Then, unlike the Gregorian or Julian calendars, the simple month-length structure

[2] *Anno Martyrum* or "Era of the Martyrs"; this is the year Diocletian ascended the emperorship of Rome.

of the Coptic calendar allows us to determine the month by dividing by 30. As for the other calendars, we determine the day by subtraction:

$$\textbf{coptic-from-fixed}\,(date) \stackrel{\text{def}}{=} \begin{array}{|c|c|c|}\hline \textit{year} & \textit{month} & \textit{day} \\ \hline \end{array} \tag{4.4}$$

where

$$\begin{aligned} \textit{year} &= \left\lfloor \frac{1}{1461} \times (4 \times (\textit{date} - \textbf{coptic-epoch}) + 1463) \right\rfloor \\ \textit{month} &= \left\lfloor \frac{1}{30} \times \left(\textit{date} - \textbf{fixed-from-coptic}\left(\begin{array}{|c|c|c|}\hline \textit{year} & 1 & 1 \\ \hline \end{array} \right) \right) \right\rfloor + 1 \\ \textit{day} &= \textit{date} + 1 - \textbf{fixed-from-coptic}\left(\begin{array}{|c|c|c|}\hline \textit{year} & \textit{month} & 1 \\ \hline \end{array} \right) \end{aligned}$$

4.2 The Ethiopic Calendar

The Ethiopic calendar "Computus" (hasab) is an extremely simple affair: it nowhere requires more than the most elementary arithmetical operations.

Otto Neugebauer: *Orientalia* (1982)

The Ethiopic calendar is identical to the Coptic calendar except for the epoch, the month names, and the day names. Many calendars in this book have similar variants, differing only in month names and year numbers, and can be treated analogously.

The Amharic Ethiopic months are

(1) Maskaram	መስከረም	30 days
(2) Teqemt	ጥቅምት	30 days
(3) H̲edār	ኅዳር	30 days
(4) Tākhśāś	ታሕሣሥ	30 days
(5) Ṭer	ጥር	30 days
(6) Yakātit	የካቲት	30 days
(7) Magābit	መጋቢት	30 days
(8) Miyāzyā	ሚያዝያ	30 days
(9) Genbot	ግንቦት	30 days
(10) Sanē	ሰኔ	30 days
(11) Ḥamlē	ሐምሌ	30 days
(12) Naḥasē	ነሐሴ	30 days
(13) Pāguemēn	ጳጉሜን	5 {6} days

and the day names are

Sunday	Iḥud	እሑድ
Monday	Sanyo	ሰኞ
Tuesday	Maksanyo	ማክሰኞ
Wednesday	Rob/Rabu'e	ሮቡ/ረቡዕ
Thursday	H̲amus	ኀሙስ
Friday	Arb	ዓርብ
Saturday	Kidāmmē	ቅዳሜ

Ethiopic year 1 E.E.[3] starts on August 29, 8 C.E. (Julian), our R.D. 2796:

$$\textbf{ethiopic-epoch} \stackrel{\text{def}}{=} \textbf{fixed-from-julian}\left(\boxed{8\text{ C.E.} \mid \textbf{august} \mid 29}\right) \tag{4.5}$$

To convert Ethiopic dates to and from R.D. dates, we just use our Coptic functions above but adjust for the different epoch:

$$\textbf{fixed-from-ethiopic}\left(\boxed{\mathit{year} \mid \mathit{month} \mid \mathit{day}}\right) \stackrel{\text{def}}{=} \tag{4.6}$$

$$\textbf{ethiopic-epoch} + \textbf{fixed-from-coptic}\left(\boxed{\mathit{year} \mid \mathit{month} \mid \mathit{day}}\right) - \textbf{coptic-epoch}$$

In the other direction,

$$\textbf{ethiopic-from-fixed}\,(\mathit{date}) \stackrel{\text{def}}{=} \tag{4.7}$$

$$\textbf{coptic-from-fixed}\,(\mathit{date} + \textbf{coptic-epoch} - \textbf{ethiopic-epoch})$$

4.3 Holidays

... so that the seasons also may run properly forever in accordance with the present state of the cosmos, and lest it happen that some public festivals which are celebrated in the winter, are ever celebrated in the summer, since the star shifts one day every four years, while others which are celebrated now in the summer, are celebrated in the winter, at the appropriate times hereafter, just as it has happened before, and would have been so now if the organization of the year, from the 360 days and the five days which were deemed later to be intercalated, held good, from the present time one day at the festival of the Benefactor Gods to be intercalated every four years after the five which are intercalated before the new year, so that everyone may see that the correction and restoration of the previous deficiency in the organization of the seasons and of the year and of the customs to do with the whole regulation of the heavenly sphere has happened through the Benefactor Gods.

Ptolemy III's *Canopus Decree* (238 B.C.E.)

Determining the corresponding Gregorian date of a date on the Coptic or Ethiopic calendars is similar to the corresponding determination for the Julian calendar. Indeed, the Coptic and Julian are consistently aligned, except for a fluctuation of one day caused by the difference in leap-year rule and the absence of year 0 on the Julian calendar. For the Coptic calendar, to determine the R.D. dates of a given Coptic month/day during a Gregorian year, we use

$$\textbf{coptic-in-gregorian}\,(\mathit{c\text{-}month}, \mathit{c\text{-}day}, \mathit{g\text{-}year}) \stackrel{\text{def}}{=} \tag{4.8}$$

$$\{\mathit{date}_0, \mathit{date}_1\} \cap \textbf{gregorian-year-range}\,(\mathit{g\text{-}year})$$

[3] Ethiopic Era (of Mercy).

where

$$\begin{aligned} jan_1 &= \textbf{gregorian-new-year}\,(g\text{-}year) \\ y &= (\textbf{coptic-from-fixed}\,(jan_1))_{\textbf{year}} \\ date_0 &= \textbf{fixed-from-coptic}\left(\boxed{y \mid c\text{-}month \mid c\text{-}day}\right) \\ date_1 &= \textbf{fixed-from-coptic}\left(\boxed{y+1 \mid c\text{-}month \mid c\text{-}day}\right) \end{aligned}$$

For example, the Copts celebrate Christmas on Koiak 29 (which is always either December 25 or December 26 on the Julian calendar) and thus we can write

$$\textbf{coptic-christmas}\,(g\text{-}year) \stackrel{\text{def}}{=} \textbf{coptic-in-gregorian}\,(4, 29, g\text{-}year) \tag{4.9}$$

to give us a list of R.D. dates of Coptic Christmas during a given Gregorian year.

Other Coptic holidays include the Building of the Cross (Thoout 17), Jesus's Circumcision (Ṭōbe 6), Epiphany (Ṭōbe 11), Mary's Announcement (Paremotep 29), and Jesus's Transfiguration (Mesorē 13). The date of Easter may be determined by the Orthodox rule (page 146) and converted to the Coptic calendar.

Fixed Ethiopic holidays have the same fixed dates as the Coptic ones, and thus nothing more is needed for their computation. Locating arbitrary Ethiopic dates requires only a straightforward modification of **coptic-in-gregorian**, changing all references from the Coptic calendar to the Ethiopic. Moveable fasts and feasts are determined relative to the date of Nicæan Easter (Section 9.1); see [4].

References

[1] M. Chaîne, *La chronologie des temps Chrétiens de l'Égypte et de l'Éthiopie*, Paul Geuthner, Paris, 1925.

[2] A. Cody, "Coptic Calendar," *The Coptic Encyclopedia*, vol. 2, pp. 433–436, Macmillan, New York, 1991.

[3] F. K. Ginzel, *Handbuch der mathematischen und technischen Chronologie*, vol. 3, J. C. Hinrichs'sche Buchhandlung, Leipzig, section 262, 1914. Reprinted by F. Ullmann Verlag, Zwickau, 1958.

[4] O. Neugebauer, *Ethiopic Astronomy and Computus*, Verlag der Österreichischen Akademie der Wissenschaften, Vienna, 1979.

[5] C. W. Wassef, *Pratiques rituelles et alimentaires des Coptes*, Publications de L'Institut Français d'Archéologie Orientale du Caire, Bibliothèque d'Études Coptes, Cairo, 1971.

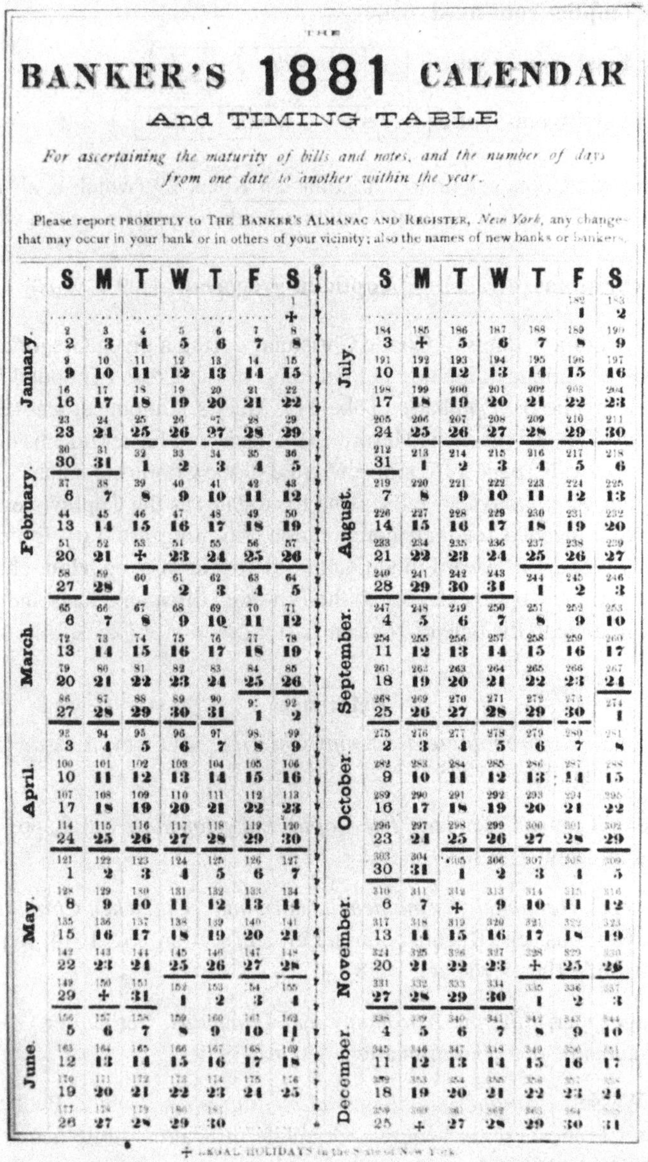

THE

BANKER'S 1881 CALENDAR

And TIMING TABLE

For ascertaining the maturity of bills and notes, and the number of days from one date to another within the year.

Please report PROMPTLY to THE BANKER'S ALMANAC AND REGISTER, *New York*, any changes that may occur in your bank or in others of your vicinity; also the names of new banks or bankers.

	S	M	T	W	T	F	S		S	M	T	W	T	F	S
							1 ✝							182 1	183 2
January.	2 2	3 3	4 4	5 5	6 6	7 7	8 8	July.	184 3	185 ✝	186 5	187 6	188 7	189 8	190 9
	9 9	10 10	11 11	12 12	13 13	14 14	15 15		191 10	192 11	193 12	194 13	195 14	196 15	197 16
	16 16	17 17	18 18	19 19	20 20	21 21	22 22		198 17	199 18	200 19	201 20	202 21	203 22	204 23
	23 23	24 24	25 25	26 26	27 27	28 28	29 29		205 24	206 25	207 26	208 27	209 28	210 29	211 30
	30 30	31 31	32 1	33 2	34 3	35 4	36 5		212 31	213 1	214 2	215 3	216 4	217 5	218 6
February.	37 6	38 7	39 8	40 9	41 10	42 11	43 12	August.	219 7	220 8	221 9	222 10	223 11	224 12	225 13
	44 13	45 14	46 15	47 16	48 17	49 18	50 19		226 14	227 15	228 16	229 17	230 18	231 19	232 20
	51 20	52 21	53 ✝	54 23	55 24	56 25	57 26		233 21	234 22	235 23	236 24	237 25	238 26	239 27
	58 27	59 28	60 1	61 2	62 3	63 4	64 5		240 28	241 29	242 30	243 31	244 1	245 2	246 3
March.	65 6	66 7	67 8	68 9	69 10	70 11	71 12	September.	247 4	248 5	249 6	250 7	251 8	252 9	253 10
	72 13	73 14	74 15	75 16	76 17	77 18	78 19		254 11	255 12	256 13	257 14	258 15	259 16	260 17
	79 20	80 21	81 22	82 23	83 24	84 25	85 26		261 18	262 19	263 20	264 21	265 22	266 23	267 24
	86 27	87 28	88 29	89 30	90 31	91 1	92 2		268 25	269 26	270 27	271 28	272 29	273 30	274 1
April.	93 3	94 4	95 5	96 6	97 7	98 8	99 9	October.	275 2	276 3	277 4	278 5	279 6	280 7	281 8
	100 10	101 11	102 12	103 13	104 14	105 15	106 16		282 9	283 10	284 11	285 12	286 13	287 14	288 15
	107 17	108 18	109 19	110 20	111 21	112 22	113 23		289 16	290 17	291 18	292 19	293 20	294 21	295 22
	114 24	115 25	116 26	117 27	118 28	119 29	120 30		296 23	297 24	298 25	299 26	300 27	301 28	302 29
May.	121 1	122 2	123 3	124 4	125 5	126 6	127 7	November.	303 30	304 31	305 1	306 2	307 3	308 4	309 5
	128 8	129 9	130 10	131 11	132 12	133 13	134 14		310 6	311 7	312 ✝	313 9	314 10	315 11	316 12
	135 15	136 16	137 17	138 18	139 19	140 20	141 21		317 13	318 14	319 15	320 16	321 17	322 18	323 19
	142 22	143 23	144 24	145 25	146 26	147 27	148 28		324 20	325 21	326 22	327 23	328 ✝	329 25	330 26
	149 29	150 ✝	151 31	152 1	153 2	154 3	155 4		331 27	332 28	333 29	334 30	335 1	336 2	337 3
June.	156 5	157 6	158 7	159 8	160 9	161 10	162 11	December.	338 4	339 5	340 6	341 7	342 8	343 9	344 10
	163 12	164 13	165 14	166 15	167 16	168 17	169 18		345 11	346 12	347 13	348 14	349 15	350 16	351 17
	170 19	171 20	172 21	173 22	174 23	175 24	176 25		352 18	353 19	354 20	355 21	356 22	357 23	358 24
	177 26	178 27	179 28	180 29	181 30				359 25	360 ✝	361 27	362 28	363 29	364 30	365 31

✝ LEGAL HOLIDAYS in the State of New York.

Banker's calendar, arranged by weeks and including day numbers. From *The Banker's Almanac and Register*, B. Homans, ed., Homans Publishing Co., New York, 1884. (Courtesy of Northwestern University, Evanston, IL.)

5

The ISO Calendar

O tempora! O mores! [*Oh what times! Oh what standards!*]
Cicero: *In Catilinam* (63 B.C.E.)

The International Organization for Standardization (ISO) calendar, popular in Sweden and other European countries, specifies a date by giving the ordinal day in the week and the "calendar week" in a Gregorian year. The ISO standard [1, sec. 2.2.10] defines the *calendar week number*[1] as the

> ordinal number which identifies a calendar week within its calendar year according to the rule that the first calendar week of a year is that one which includes the first Thursday of that year and that the last calendar week of a calendar year is the week immediately preceding the first calendar week of the next calendar year.

This does not define a new calendar *per se*, but rather a representation of dates on the Gregorian calendar; still, it is convenient for us to treat it as a separate calendar because the representation depends on weeks and the day of the week.

It follows from the ISO standard that an ISO year begins with the Monday between December 29 and January 4 and ends with the Sunday between December 28 and January 3. Accordingly, a year on the ISO calendar consists of 52 or 53 whole weeks, making the year either 364 or 371 days long. The epoch is the same as the Gregorian calendar, namely R.D. 1, because January 1, 1 (Gregorian) was a Monday.

The week number of a given ISO date gives the number of weeks after the first Sunday on or after December 28 of the preceding year. Hence the determination of the R.D. date corresponding to an ISO date is easy using **nth-kday** (page 69). The ISO calendar counts Sunday as the seventh day of the week, and thus we implement this calendar as follows:

$$\textbf{fixed-from-iso}\left(\boxed{\textit{year} \mid \textit{week} \mid \textit{day}}\right) \stackrel{\text{def}}{=} \qquad (5.1)$$

[1] Microsoft Access® and Excel®, have a week numbering function WEEKNUM that can be set to number weeks starting on either Sunday or Monday. However, these week numbers are not always the same as the ISO week because Microsoft defines the first week in the year as the week containing January 1.

$$\textbf{nth-kday}\left(\mathit{week}, \textbf{sunday}, \boxed{\mathit{year}-1 \,|\, \textbf{december} \,|\, 28}\right) + \mathit{day}$$

In the other direction,

$$\textbf{iso-from-fixed}\,(\mathit{date}) \stackrel{\text{def}}{=} \boxed{\mathit{year} \,|\, \mathit{week} \,|\, \mathit{day}} \qquad (5.2)$$

where

$$\mathit{approx} = \textbf{gregorian-year-from-fixed}\,(\mathit{date} - 3)$$

$$\mathit{year} = \begin{cases} \mathit{approx} + 1 & \textbf{if } \mathit{date} \geqslant \textbf{fixed-from-iso}\left(\boxed{\mathit{approx}+1 \,|\, 1 \,|\, 1}\right) \\ \mathit{approx} & \textbf{otherwise} \end{cases}$$

$$\mathit{week} = \left\lfloor \frac{1}{7} \times \left(\mathit{date} - \textbf{fixed-from-iso}\left(\boxed{\mathit{year} \,|\, 1 \,|\, 1}\right)\right)\right\rfloor + 1$$

$$\mathit{day} = (\mathit{date} - \text{R.D. } 0) \bmod [1 \,..\, 7]$$

We use the adjusted remainder function, defined on page 22, to assign 7 to *day* for Sundays.

The calculation of the ISO day and week numbers from the fixed date is clear once the ISO year has been found. Because the ISO year can extend as much as 3 days into the following Gregorian year, we find the Gregorian year for *date* – 3; this approximation is guaranteed to be either the desired ISO year or the prior ISO year. We determine which is the case by comparing the *date* to the R.D. date of the start of the year after the approximate ISO year.

To avoid using the Gregorian year in **iso-from-fixed**, thus making the ISO implementation self-contained, we can calculate the approximation to the ISO year as

$$\mathit{approx} = \left\lfloor \frac{\mathit{date} - 4}{\frac{146097}{400}} \right\rfloor + 1$$

The ISO calendar has "short" (52-week) and "long" (53-week) years,[2] which appear in a mixture to give the Gregorian cycle. The Gregorian cycle of 400 years contains $146097 = 7 \times 20871$ days which is exactly 20871 weeks. Thus the ISO cycle of short or long years repeats after 400 years. Let s be the number of short years and l be the number of long years in the cycle; we have

$$\begin{aligned} s + l &= 400 \\ 52s + 53l &= 20871 \end{aligned}$$

whose solution is $s = 329$, $l = 71$. In other words, short ISO years occur $329/400 = 82\frac{1}{4}\%$ of the time and long ISO years occur $71/400 = 17\frac{3}{4}\%$ of the time. Long years usually occur at 5 or 6 year intervals (27 times versus 43 times, respectively), but are 7 years apart once in each 400 year cycle.

[2] This is reminiscent of the tenth-century Icelandic calendar described in the next chapter.

An ISO year is long if and only if January 1 or December 31 is a Thursday. Thus we can write

$$\textbf{iso-long-year?}\,(\textit{i-year}) \stackrel{\text{def}}{=} \tag{5.3}$$

$$\textit{jan}_1 = \textbf{thursday} \text{ or } \textit{dec}_{31} = \textbf{thursday}$$

where

$$\textit{jan}_1 = \textbf{day-of-week-from-fixed}\,(\textbf{gregorian-new-year}\,(\textit{i-year}))$$
$$\textit{dec}_{31} = \textbf{day-of-week-from-fixed}\,(\textbf{gregorian-year-end}\,(\textit{i-year}))$$

Reference

[1] *Data Elements and Interchange Formats – Information Interchange – Representation of Dates and Times*, ISO 8601, International Organization for Standardization, 3rd edn., 2004. This standard replaced ISO 2015, the original document describing the ISO calendar.

Cave ab homine unius libri. [*Beware the man of one book.*]
Latin motto

Oak wheels carved with the names of months, weekdays, dominical letters, and golden numbers. The device, from Þórðarstaðir in Fnjóskadalur, Iceland, was first mentioned in 1871, but is probably older. (Courtesy of the National Museum of Iceland, Reykjavik.)

6

The Icelandic Calendar

> *Kæstur hákarl . . . is the rotten, aged meal of the Greenland shark . . . it is still consumed . . . in Thorrablot, a modem Icelandic holiday that attempts to recreate the ancient midwinter pagan feast during* Thorri, *a month on the old Icelandic calendar which begins in late January. Anthony Bourdain called it the "worst, worst, worst, worst thing" that he had ever tasted . . .*
>
> Sidra Durst: *They Eat That*? (2012)[1]

Like the ISO calendar described in the previous chapter, the Icelandic ("Viking") calendar—still used in Iceland today—centers around the week. Ordinary years have 52 weeks and leap years have 53. In the tenth-century version every seventh year was leap [1], [4]. The weekdays are

Sunday	Sunnudagur
Monday	Mánudagur
Tuesday	Þriðjudagur
Wednesday	Miðvikudagur
Thursday	Fimmtudagur
Friday	Föstudagur
Saturday	Laugardagur

Years are divided into two seasons, summer (which includes much of spring) and winter (which includes much of autumn). Seasons are divided into 30-day months, but we do not include them in dates since they are secondary. Like the Qumran 364-day calendar, the months begin on fixed days of the week [2]. The months and the day of the week on which they invariably begin are

Summer	1.	Harpa	Thursday
	2.	Skerpla	Saturday
	3.	Sólmánuður	Monday
	4.	Heyannir	Sunday
	5.	Tvímánuður	Tuesday
	6.	Haustmánuður	Thursday

[1] Þær skoðanir sem fram koma í tilvitnunum endurspegla ekki nauðsynlega skoðanir höfunda.

Winter	1.	Gormánuður	Saturday
	2.	Ýlir	Monday
	3.	Mörsugur	Wednesday
	4.	Þorri	Friday
	5.	Góa	Sunday
	6.	Einmánuður	Tuesday

The extra four days in a 364-day year are not part of any month and are placed between the third and fourth summer months.

In the version after the Gregorian switchover in 1700, summer begins on the first Thursday on or after April 19, and winter 180 days earlier. As in the ISO calendar, there is a leap week every 5–7 years, in midsummer. The year count parallels the Gregorian, except that the year begins with the summer season in April. The modern version has been described algorithmically in [3].

The epoch of the Icelandic calendar is Thursday, April 19, in year 1 of the Gregorian calendar, the onset of Icelandic summer:

$$\textbf{icelandic-epoch} \stackrel{\text{def}}{=} \textbf{fixed-from-gregorian}\left(\boxed{1 \mid \textbf{april} \mid 19}\right) \tag{6.1}$$

The start of summer in subsequent years may be calculated by adding up days and leap days, just as was done in **alt-gregorian-year-from-fixed** (page 67):

$$\textbf{icelandic-summer}\,(i\text{-}year) \stackrel{\text{def}}{=} \textbf{kday-on-or-after}\,(\textbf{thursday}, apr_{19}) \tag{6.2}$$

where

$$\begin{aligned} apr_{19} &= \textbf{icelandic-epoch} + 365 \times (i\text{-}year - 1) + \sum \vec{y} \times \vec{a} \\ \vec{y} &= i\text{-}year \xrightarrow{\text{rad}} \langle 4, 25, 4 \rangle \\ \vec{a} &= \langle 97, 24, 1, 0 \rangle \end{aligned}$$

Winter begins 6 months before summer:

$$\textbf{icelandic-winter}\,(i\text{-}year) \stackrel{\text{def}}{=} \textbf{icelandic-summer}\,(i\text{-}year + 1) - 180 \tag{6.3}$$

We represent a date as a quadruple: the Gregorian year number at the start of summer; the season, for which we use the two constants, **summer** (3.19) and **winter** (3.21), defined in Section 3.5; the week within the season, as an integer in the range [1 .. 27]; and the day of week, with our usual numbering of 0 for Sunday, and so on.

Conversions are straightforward:

$$\textbf{fixed-from-icelandic}\left(\boxed{year \mid season \mid week \mid weekday}\right) \stackrel{\text{def}}{=} \tag{6.4}$$

$$start + 7 \times (week - 1) + ((weekday - shift) \bmod 7)$$

where

$$start = \begin{cases} \textbf{icelandic-summer}\,(year) & \textbf{if } season = \textbf{summer} \\ \textbf{icelandic-winter}\,(year) & \textbf{otherwise} \end{cases}$$

$$shift = \begin{cases} \textbf{thursday} & \textbf{if } season = \textbf{summer} \\ \textbf{saturday} & \textbf{otherwise} \end{cases}$$

$$\textbf{icelandic-from-fixed}\,(date) \stackrel{\text{def}}{=} \boxed{year \mid season \mid week \mid weekday} \tag{6.5}$$

where

$$approx = \left\lfloor \frac{400}{146097} \times (date - \textbf{icelandic-epoch} + 369) \right\rfloor$$

$$year = \begin{cases} approx & \textbf{if } date \geqslant \textbf{icelandic-summer}\,(approx) \\ approx - 1 & \textbf{otherwise} \end{cases}$$

$$season = \begin{cases} \textbf{summer} & \textbf{if } date < \textbf{icelandic-winter}\,(year) \\ \textbf{winter} & \textbf{otherwise} \end{cases}$$

$$start = \begin{cases} \textbf{icelandic-summer}\,(year) & \textbf{if } season = \textbf{summer} \\ \textbf{icelandic-winter}\,(year) & \textbf{otherwise} \end{cases}$$

$$week = \left\lfloor \frac{date - start}{7} \right\rfloor + 1$$

$$weekday = \textbf{day-of-week-from-fixed}\,(date)$$

The approximate year is computed in the usual way, starting from an approximation close to the beginning of year 0.

To test whether a year is leap, we can count the number of days in the year:

$$\textbf{icelandic-leap-year?}\,(i\text{-}year) \stackrel{\text{def}}{=} \tag{6.6}$$

$$\textbf{icelandic-summer}\,(i\text{-}year + 1) - \textbf{icelandic-summer}\,(i\text{-}year) \neq 364$$

Ordinary years, with 52 weeks, have 364 days; leap years have 371 days (53 weeks).

The months of each season are numbered 1 .. 6 and can be determined from the date by counting in units of 30 days from the start of the season:

$$\textbf{icelandic-month}\,(i\text{-}date) \stackrel{\text{def}}{=} \left\lfloor \frac{date - start}{30} \right\rfloor + 1 \tag{6.7}$$

where

$$date = \textbf{fixed-from-icelandic}\,(i\text{-}date)$$

$$year = i\text{-}date_{\textbf{year}}$$

$$season = i\text{-}date_{\textbf{season}}$$

$$midsummer = \textbf{icelandic-winter}\,(year) - 90$$

$$start = \begin{cases} \textbf{icelandic-winter}\,(year) & \\ & \textbf{if } season = \textbf{winter} \\ midsummer - 90 & \textbf{if } date \geqslant midsummer \\ \textbf{icelandic-summer}\,(year) & \\ & \textbf{if } date < \textbf{icelandic-summer}\,(year) + 90 \\ midsummer & \textbf{otherwise} \end{cases}$$

For days of the year that do not belong to any of the twelve months, those days lying between the end of the third month of summer and the beginning of the fourth month, this function returns 0.

References

[1] Ari the Learned, *Libellum Islandorum* [The Book of Icelanders], c. 1130, in J. Benediktsson, ed., *Íslenzk fornrit I: Ískebdubgabók, Landnámabók fyrri hluti* [The Book of Icelanders and the Book of Settlements], Hiðíslenzka fornritafélag, Reykjavik, 1968.

[2] J. Ben-Dov and S. Saulnier, "Qumran Calendars: A Survey of Scholarship 1980–2007," *Currents in Biblical Research*, vol. 7, pp. 124–168, 2008.

[3] S. Janson, "The Icelandic Calendar," *Scripta Islandica*, vol. 62, pp. 53–104, 2011.

[4] Þ. Vilhjálmsson, "Time-Reckoning in Iceland before Literacy," in *Archaeoastronomy in the 1990s*, C. L. N. Ruggles, ed., pp. 69–76, UK Group D Publications, Loughborough, 1991.

[illegible] Bibliothèque Nationale de France, Paris.

Page containing a discussion of months in the pre-Islamic Arab, Hebrew, Islamic, and Hindu calendars, along with an illustration of Mohammed instituting the purely lunar calendar. From a seventeenth-century copy of an illuminated fourteenth-century manuscript of the eleventh-century work *Al-Āthār al-Bāqiyah ʻan al-Qurūn al-Khāliyah* by the great Persian scholar and scientist Abū-Raiḥān Muḥammad ibn ʼAḥmad al-Bīrūnī. (Courtesy of Bibliothèque Nationale de France, Paris.)

7

The Islamic Calendar

The number of months with God is twelve in accordance with God's law since the day he created the heavens and the Earth ... Intercalating a month is adding to unbelief.

Koran (IX, 36–37)

7.1 Structure and Implementation

The Islamic calendar is a straightforward, strictly lunar calendar, with no intercalation of months (unlike lunisolar calendars). The average lunar year is about $354\frac{11}{30}$ days, so the Islamic calendar's independence of the solar cycle means that its months do not occur in fixed seasons but migrate through the solar year over a period of about 32 solar years.[1] Days begin at sunset. In this chapter, we describe the arithmetic Islamic calendar in which months follow a set pattern; for religious purposes, virtually all Muslims (except the Ismāʿīlīs and a few other sects) follow an observation-based calendar (described in Section 14.9) and use the arithmetic calendar only for estimation.

The week begins on Sunday; the days Sunday–Thursday are numbered, not named:

Sunday	yaum al-aḥad (the first day)	يَوْم الأَحد
Monday	yaum al-ithnayna (the second day)	يَوْم الاثنين
Tuesday	yaum ath-thalāthā' (the third day)	يَوْم الثلَاثاء
Wednesday	yaum al-arbaʿā' (the fourth day)	يَوْم الأَربعاء

[1] There was an interesting consequence to the strict lunar nature of the calendar in the Ottoman Empire. The Islamic calendar, as the official calendar, was used for expenditures, but revenue collecting generally followed the solar year because seasons affected income-producing activities such as agriculture, shipping, and mining. For every 32 solar years there are 33 Islamic years; thus every 33 Islamic years had one "skip" year, called a *sıvış* year in Turkish, for which there was no income. Such years precipitated crises, such as in 852 A.H. (1448 C.E.) in which the troops' pay was six months in arrears, resulting in a lack of resistance on their part when Hungarian and Serbian forces entered the Ottoman Empire. A detailed analyis of the phenomenon is given in H. Sahillioğlu's article, "*Sıvış* Year Crises in the Ottoman Empire," *Studies in the Economic History of the Middle East*, M. A. Cook, ed., Oxford University Press, London, pp. 230–252, 1970.

Thursday	yaum al-h̲amīs (the fifth day)	يَوْم الخَميس
Friday	yaum al-jum'a (the day of assembly)	يَوْم الجُمعة
Saturday	yaum as-sabt (the sabbath day)	يَوْم السَبْت

The calendar is computed, by the majority of the Muslim world, starting at sunset of Thursday, July 15, 622 C.E. (Julian), the year of Mohammed's migration to Medina from Mecca.[2] The introduction of the calendar is often attributed to the Caliph 'Umar in 639 C.E., but there is evidence that it was in use before his succession. In essence, Muslims count R.D. 227015 = Friday, July 16, 622 C.E. (Julian) as the beginning of the Islamic year 1, that is, as Muḥarram 1, A.H.[3] 1, and thus we define

$$\textbf{islamic-epoch} \stackrel{\text{def}}{=} \textbf{fixed-from-julian}\left(\boxed{622\text{ C.E.} \mid \textbf{july} \mid 16}\right) \tag{7.1}$$

There are 12 Islamic months, which contain, alternately, 29 or 30 days:

(1) Muḥarram	مُحَرَّم	30 days
(2) Ṣafar	صَفَر	29 days
(3) Rabī' I (Rabī' al-Awwal)	رَبيع الأَوَّل	30 days
(4) Rabī' II (Rabī' al-Āḥir)	رَبيع الآخِر	29 days
(5) Jumādā I (Jumādā al-Ūlā)	جُمَادَى الأُولَى	30 days
(6) Jumādā II (Jumādā al-Āḥira)	جُمَادَى الآخِرة	29 days
(7) Rajab	رَجَب	30 days
(8) Sha'bān	شَعبَان	29 days
(9) Ramaḍān	رَمَضَان	30 days
(10) Shawwāl	شَوَّال	29 days
(11) Dhu al-Qa'da	ذو القَعدة	30 days
(12) Dhu al-Ḥijja	ذو الحِجَّة	29 {30} days

The leap-year structure is given in curly brackets—the last month, Dhu al-Ḥijja, contains 30 days in years 2, 5, 7, 10, 13, 16, 18, 21, 24, 26, and 29 of a 30-year cycle. This gives an average month of $29.5305555\cdots$ days and an average year of $354.3666\cdots = 354\frac{11}{30}$ days. The cycle of common and leap years can be expressed concisely by observing that an Islamic year y is a leap year if and only if $(11y + 14) \bmod 30$ is less than 11; this is an instance of formula (1.83) with $c = 30$, $l = 11$, and $\Delta = 4$:

[2] The Arabic term *hijra*, used to denote the beginning of the Islamic epoch, signifies "emigration," "abandonment," or "flight."

[3] *Anno Hegiræ*; in the year of the Hegira (Mohammed's emigration to Medina)—see the previous footnote.

$$\textbf{islamic-leap-year?}\,(\textit{i-year}) \stackrel{\text{def}}{=} ((14 + 11 \times \textit{i-year}) \bmod 30) < 11 \tag{7.2}$$

We will never need this function, however.

Some Muslims take year 15 of the 30-year cycle as a leap year instead of year 16. This variant structure, which was used by Bar Hebræus (Gregory Abu'l-Faraj), John Greaves (1650; based on tables of Ulugh Beg), Birashk [1], and some Microsoft products,[4] corresponds to $L = 354$, $c = 30$, $l = 11$, and $\Delta = 15$ in the cycle formulas from Section 1.14; our functions thus require only minor modification for this variant leap-year rule.[5] The Bohras (an Ismailite Muslim sect of about 1 million in India) follow a book called *Sahifa*, giving leap years 2, 5, 8, 10, 13, 16, 19, 21, 24, 27, and 29; this corresponds to $\Delta = 1$. Their epoch is Thursday, July 15, 622 C.E. (Julian).

To convert an Islamic date to its R.D. equivalent, start at **islamic-epoch** − 1, the R.D. number of the last day before the epoch; to this add the number of days between that date and the last day of the year preceding the given year [using formula (1.86)], the number of days in prior months in the given year, and the number of days in the given month, up to and including the given day. The number of days in months prior to the given month is also computed by (1.86) because the pattern of Islamic month lengths in an ordinary year satisfies the cycle formulas of Section 1.14 with $c = 12$, $l = 6$, $\Delta = 1$ (to count months from 1 instead of 0), and $L = 29$; because the leap day is day 30 of month 12, this works for leap years also:

$$\textbf{fixed-from-islamic}\left(\boxed{\textit{year} \mid \textit{month} \mid \textit{day}}\right) \stackrel{\text{def}}{=} \tag{7.3}$$

$$\textbf{islamic-epoch} - 1 + (\textit{year} - 1) \times 354 + \left\lfloor \frac{1}{30} \times (3 + 11 \times \textit{year}) \right\rfloor$$
$$+ 29 \times (\textit{month} - 1) + \left\lfloor \frac{\textit{month}}{2} \right\rfloor + \textit{day}$$

Computing the Islamic date equivalent to a given R.D. date is slightly more complicated (though it is more straightforward than the computations for the Gregorian calendar or the Julian). We can calculate the exact value of the year using formula (1.90). We want to determine the month number in the same way; unfortunately, determining the month cannot be done directly from (1.90) using the values $c = 12$, $l = 6$, $\Delta = 1$, and $L = 29$, because these values describe the common-year month lengths, not those for the leap year. Indeed, no set of values with $c = 12$ can work properly in the cycle-length formulas for the leap year because there are three 30-day months in a row (months 11, 12, and 1). However, the values $c = 11$, $l = 6$, $\Delta = 10$, $L = 29$ actually do work—not completely, but over the range $0 \leqslant n \leqslant 354$ in (1.90), which is all we care about; thus (7.3) remains correct if $\lfloor \textit{month}/2 \rfloor$ is replaced with $\lfloor (6 \times \textit{month} - 1)/11 \rfloor$. Hence the month can be determined using (1.86), the day of the month is determined by subtraction, and we obtain:

---

[4] Microsoft inexplicably calls this version the "Kuwaiti algorithm."

[5] Specifically, the following three changes are needed: replacing 14 by 15 in **islamic-leap-year?**, replacing the numerator $3 + 11 \times \textit{year}$ by $4 + 11 \times \textit{year}$ in **fixed-from-islamic**, and replacing the 10646 by 10645 in the numerator of the value for *year* in **islamic-from-fixed**.

$$\textbf{islamic-from-fixed}\,(date) \stackrel{\text{def}}{=} \boxed{year \mid month \mid day} \tag{7.4}$$

where

$$year = \left\lfloor \frac{1}{10631} \times (30 \times (date - \textbf{islamic-epoch}) + 10646) \right\rfloor$$

$$prior\text{-}days = date - \textbf{fixed-from-islamic}\left(\boxed{year \mid 1 \mid 1} \right)$$

$$month = \left\lfloor \frac{1}{325} \times (11 \times prior\text{-}days + 330) \right\rfloor$$

$$day = date - \textbf{fixed-from-islamic}\left(\boxed{year \mid month \mid 1} \right) + 1$$

It is important to realize that, to a great extent, the foregoing calculations are merely hypothetical because there are many disparate forms of the Islamic calendar [6]. Furthermore, much of the Islamic world relies not on the calculations of this *arithmetical* calendar at all but on proclamation of the new moon, by religious authorities, based on the visibility of the lunar crescent. Consequently, the dates given by the functions here can be in error by a day or two from what will actually be observed in various parts of the Islamic world; this is unavoidable.

One could use astronomical functions (see Chapter 14) to determine the likely date of visibility of a new moon (see [5]). The calculation of such an astronomical Islamic calendar—sketched in Section 18.3—is quite intricate and not generally accepted.

7.2 Holidays

Only approximate positions have been used for predicting the commencement of a Hijri month, as accurate places cannot be computed without a great amount of labour . . . Users of this Diglott Calendar must, therefore, at the commencement of each year correct the dates with those in the official Block Calendar issued by the Nizamiah Observatory.

Director of Nizamiah Observatory, quoted by Mazhar Husain:
Diglott Calendar, vol. II, p. iii (1961)

Determining the R.D. dates of holidays occurring in a given Gregorian year is complicated, because an Islamic year is always shorter than the Gregorian year, and thus each Gregorian year contains parts of at least 2 and sometimes 3 successive Islamic years. Hence, any given Islamic date occurs at least once and possibly twice in any given Gregorian year. For example, Islamic New Year (Muḥarram 1) occurred twice in 1943: on January 8 and again on December 28. Accordingly, we approach the problem of the Islamic holidays by writing a general function to return a list of the R.D. dates of a given Islamic date occurring in a given Gregorian year:

$$\textbf{islamic-in-gregorian}\,(i\text{-}month, i\text{-}day, g\text{-}year) \stackrel{\text{def}}{=} \tag{7.5}$$

$$\{date_0, date_1, date_2\} \cap \textbf{gregorian-year-range}\,(g\text{-}year)$$

where

$$jan_1 = \textbf{gregorian-new-year}\,(g\text{-}year)$$

$$y = (\textbf{islamic-from-fixed}\,(jan_1))_{\textbf{year}}$$

$$date_0 = \textbf{fixed-from-islamic}\left(\boxed{y \mid i\text{-}month \mid i\text{-}day}\right)$$

$$date_1 = \textbf{fixed-from-islamic}\left(\boxed{y+1 \mid i\text{-}month \mid i\text{-}day}\right)$$

$$date_2 = \textbf{fixed-from-islamic}\left(\boxed{y+2 \mid i\text{-}month \mid i\text{-}day}\right)$$

There is little uniformity among the Islamic sects and countries as to holidays. In general, the principal holidays of the Islamic year are Islamic New Year (Muḥarram 1), ‘Ashūrā’ (Muḥarram 10), Mawlid (Rabī‘ I 12), Lailat-al-Mi‘rāj (Rajab 27), Lailat-al-Barā’a (Sha‘bān 15), Ramadan (Ramaḍān 1), Lailat-al-Kadr (Ramaḍān 27), Eid ul-Fitr (Shawwāl 1), and Eid ul-Adha (Dhu al-Ḥijja 10). Other days, too, have religious significance—for example, the entire month of Ramaḍān. Like all Islamic days, an Islamic holiday begins at sunset the prior evening. We can determine a list of the corresponding R.D. dates of occurrence in a given Gregorian year by using **islamic-in-gregorian** above, as in

$$\textbf{mawlid}\,(g\text{-}year) \stackrel{\text{def}}{=} \textbf{islamic-in-gregorian}\,(3, 12, g\text{-}year) \tag{7.6}$$

It bears reiterating that the determination of the Islamic holidays cannot be fully accurate because the actual day of their occurrence depends on proclamation by religious authorities.

References

[1] A. Birashk, *A Comparative Calendar of the Iranian, Muslim Lunar, and Christian Eras for Three Thousand Years*, Mazda Publishers (in association with Bibliotheca Persica), Costa Mesa, CA, 1993.

[2] F. C. de Blois and B. van Dalen, “Ta’rikh” (Part I), in *The Encyclopaedia of Islam*, 2nd edn., vol. 10, E. J. Brill, Leiden, pp. 257–271, 1998.

[3] S. B. Burnaby, *Elements of the Jewish and Muhammadan Calendars, with Rules and Tables and Explanatory Notes on the Julian and Gregorian Calendars*, George Bell and Sons, London, 1901.

[4] G. S. P. Freeman-Grenville, *The Muslim and Christian Calendars*: *Being Tables for the Conversion of Muslim and Christian Dates from the Hijra to the Year A.D. 2000*, 2nd edn., Rex Collings, London, 1977. A new edition has been published as *The Islamic and Christian Calendars* A.D. 622–2222 (A.H. 1–1650): *A Complete Guide for Converting Christian and Islamic Dates and Dates of Festivals*, Garnet Publications, Reading, MA, 1995.

[5] M. Ilyas, *A Modern Guide to Astronomical Calculations of Islamic Calendar, Times & Qibla*, Berita Publishing, Kuala Lumpur, 1984.

[6] V. V. Tsybulsky, *Calendars of Middle East Countries*, Institute of Oriental Studies, USSR Academy of Sciences, Moscow, 1979.

[7] W. S. B. Woolhouse, *Measures, Weights, & Moneys of All Nations: and an Analysis of the Christian, Hebrew, and Mahometan Calendars*, 7th edn., Crosby Lockwood, London, 1890. Reprinted by Ares Publishers, Chicago, 1979.

[8] F. Wüstenfeld and E. Mahler, *Wüstenfeld-Mahler'sche Vergleichungs-Tabellen zur muslimischen und iranischen Zeitrechung: mit Tafeln zur Umrechnung orient-christlicher Ären*, 3rd edn. revised by J. Mayr and B. Spuler, Deutsche Morgenländische Gesellschaft, Wiesbaden, 1961.

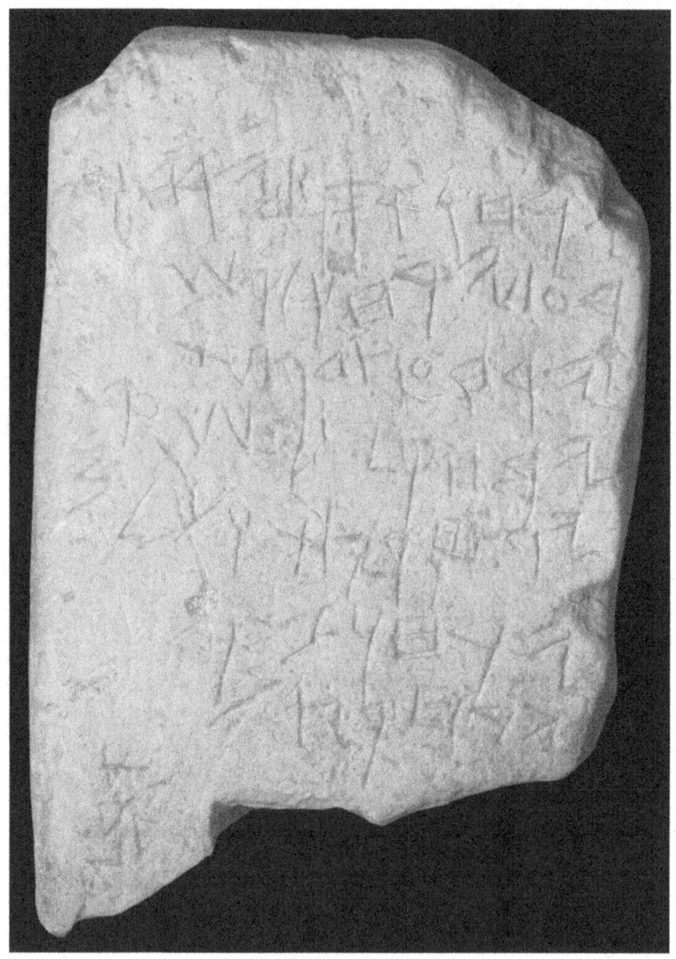

The "Gezer calendar," a tenth century B.C.E. limestone tablet discovered in 1908 in excavations of the Cannanite city of Gezer, 20 miles west of Jerusalem. It lists, in paleo-Hebrew, the months named according to their agricultural activities; for example, month 4 (late winter/early spring) is called ירח קצר שערמ, month of the barley harvest. The scribe's name is given as אביה, Abiyah. (Courtesy of the Istanbul Archaeological Museums, Istanbul.)

8

The Hebrew Calendar

Do not take these [*visibility*] *calculations lightly ... for they are deep and difficult and constitute the "secret of intercalation" that was* [*only*] *known to the great sages ... On the other hand, this computation that is calculated nowadays ... even school children can master in three or four days.*

Maimonides: *Mishneh Torah, Book of Seasons* (1178)

The Hebrew calendar, promulgated by the patriarch Hillel II in the mid-fourth century[1] and attributed by Sa'adia Gaon to Mosaic revelation, is more complicated than the other calendars we have considered so far. Its complexity is inherent in the requirement that calendar months be strictly lunar whereas Passover must always occur in the spring. Because the seasons depend on the solar year, the Hebrew calendar must harmonize simultaneously with both lunar and solar events, as do all lunisolar calendars, including the Hindu and Chinese calendars described in Chapters 10, 19, and 20. The earliest extant description of the Hebrew calendar is by the famous al-Khowārizmī [13], after whom the words *algebra* and *algorithm* were coined. The most comprehensive early work is by Savasorda of the eleventh century [19]. Much information about the Hebrew calendar in the early modern period can be found in [6].

The earlier, observation-based, Hebrew calendar is described in Section 18.4.

As in the Islamic calendar, days begin at sunset, the week begins on Sunday, and the days for the most part are numbered, not named, as follows:

Sunday	yom rishon (first day)	יום ראשון
Monday	yom sheni (second day)	יום שני
Tuesday	yom shelishi (third day)	יום שלישי
Wednesday	yom revi'i (fourth day)	יום רביעי
Thursday	yom ḥamishi (fifth day)	יום חמישי
Friday	yom shishi (sixth day)	יום ששי
Saturday	yom shabbat (sabbath day)	יום שבת

[1] Bornstein [3] and others dispute the assertion of the tenth-century Hai Gaon that the current calendar was formulated in 359 C.E. (year 670 of the Seleucid Era); see also [17, p. 118]. Stern [23] argues that the Hebrew calendar calculations were not standardized or fixed until at least the ninth century.

8.1 Structure and History

Iudaicus computus, omnium qui hodie extant antiquissimus, articiosissimus, et elegantissimus. [*Of all methods of intercalation which exist today the Jewish calculation is the oldest, the most skillful, and the most elegant.*]

Joseph Justus Scaliger: *De Emendatione Temporum* (1593)[2]

The Hebrew year consists of 12 months in a common year and 13 in a leap ("gravid" or "embolismic") year:

(1) Nisan	30 days	ניסן
(2) Iyyar	29 days	אייר
(3) Sivan	30 days	סיון
(4) Tammuz	29 days	תמוז
(5) Av	30 days	אב
(6) Elul	29 days	אלול
(7) Tishri	30 days	תשרי
(8) Marḥeshvan	29 or 30 days	מרחשון or חשון
(9) Kislev	29 or 30 days	כסלו
(10) Tevet	29 days	טבת
(11) Shevat	30 days	שבט
{(12) Adar I	30 days	{אדר ראשון
(12) {(13)} Adar {II}	29 days	אדר {שני}

The leap-year structure is given in braces—in a leap year there is an interpolated twelfth month of 30 days called Adar I to distinguish it from the final month, Adar II. The lengths of the eighth and ninth months vary from year to year according to criteria that will be explained below. Our ordering of the Hebrew months follows biblical convention (Leviticus 23:5) in which (what is now called) Nisan is the first month. This numbering causes the Hebrew New Year (Rosh ha-Shanah) to begin on the first of Tishri, which by our ordering is the seventh month—but this too agrees with biblical usage (Leviticus 23:24).

Adding up the lengths of the months, we see that a normal year has 353–355 days, whereas a leap year has 383–385 days. These are the same year lengths as would be possible with an astronomical lunisolar calendar; see Section 18.4.

It will be convenient to have the following constants defined for the Hebrew months:

$$\textbf{nisan} \stackrel{\text{def}}{=} 1 \tag{8.1}$$

$$\textbf{iyyar} \stackrel{\text{def}}{=} 2 \tag{8.2}$$

$$\textbf{sivan} \stackrel{\text{def}}{=} 3 \tag{8.3}$$

$$\textbf{tammuz} \stackrel{\text{def}}{=} 4 \tag{8.4}$$

$$\textbf{av} \stackrel{\text{def}}{=} 5 \tag{8.5}$$

[2] המובאות אינן מיצגות בהכרח את דעות המחברים.

$$\textbf{elul} \stackrel{\text{def}}{=} 6 \tag{8.6}$$

$$\textbf{tishri} \stackrel{\text{def}}{=} 7 \tag{8.7}$$

$$\textbf{marheshvan} \stackrel{\text{def}}{=} 8 \tag{8.8}$$

$$\textbf{kislev} \stackrel{\text{def}}{=} 9 \tag{8.9}$$

$$\textbf{tevet} \stackrel{\text{def}}{=} 10 \tag{8.10}$$

$$\textbf{shevat} \stackrel{\text{def}}{=} 11 \tag{8.11}$$

$$\textbf{adar} \stackrel{\text{def}}{=} 12 \tag{8.12}$$

$$\textbf{adarii} \stackrel{\text{def}}{=} 13 \tag{8.13}$$

In the Hebrew calendar, leap years occur in years 3, 6, 8, 11, 14, 17, and 19 of the 19-year Metonic cycle. This sequence can be computed concisely by noting that Hebrew year y is a leap year if and only if $(7y + 1) \bmod 19$ is less than 7—another instance of formula (1.83)[3] with $c = 19$, $l = 7$, and $\Delta = 11$. Thus, we determine whether a year is a Hebrew leap year by

$$\textbf{hebrew-leap-year?}\,(\textit{h-year}) \stackrel{\text{def}}{=} ((7 \times \textit{h-year} + 1) \bmod 19) < 7 \tag{8.14}$$

and the number of months in a Hebrew year by

$$\textbf{last-month-of-hebrew-year}\,(\textit{h-year}) \stackrel{\text{def}}{=} \tag{8.15}$$

$$\begin{cases} \textbf{adarii} & \textbf{if hebrew-leap-year?}\,(\textit{h-year}) \\ \textbf{adar} & \textbf{otherwise} \end{cases}$$

The biblically mandated sabbatical years (Exodus 23:10–11) are—by current reckoning—those whose Hebrew year number is a multiple of 7:

$$\textbf{hebrew-sabbatical-year?}\,(\textit{h-year}) \stackrel{\text{def}}{=} (\textit{h-year} \bmod 7) = 0 \tag{8.16}$$

Sabbatical years no longer bear calendrical significance.

The number of days in a Hebrew month is a more complex issue. The twelfth month, Adar or Adar I, has 29 days in a common year and 30 days in a leap year, but the numbers of days in the eighth month (Marḥeshvan) and ninth month (Kislev) depend on the overall length of the year, which in turn depends on factors discussed later in this section.

---

3 An equivalent formula appears in Slonimski [20, p. 21]; see [21] for a fascinating article about this polymath.

The beginning of the Hebrew New Year is determined by the occurrence of the mean new moon (conjunction) of the seventh month (Tishri), subject to possible postponements of 1 or 2 days. The new moon of Tishri A.M.[4] 1, the first day of the first year for the Hebrew calendar, is fixed at Sunday night at 11:11:20 p.m. Because Hebrew days begin at sunset, whereas our fixed dates begin at midnight, we define the epoch of the Hebrew calendar (that is, Tishri 1, A.M. 1) to be Monday, September 7, −3760 (Gregorian) or October 7, 3761 B.C.E. (Julian).

The Hebrew day is traditionally divided into 24 hours, and the hour is divided into 1080 *parts* (*ḥalaqim*), and thus a day has 25920 parts of $3\frac{1}{3}$ seconds duration each. These divisions are of Babylonian origin. The new moon of Tishri A.M. 1, which occurred 5 hours and 204 parts after sunset (6 p.m.) on Sunday night, is called *molad* ***beharad***, because the numerical value of the letter ***beth*** is 2, signifying the second day of the week; ***heh*** is 5 (hours); ***resh*** = 200 parts; ***daleth*** = 4 parts. Other epochs and leap-year distributions appear in classical and medieval literature. In particular, the initial conjunction of the epoch starting 1 year later, called ***weyad*** (signifying 6 days, 14 hours), occurred on Friday at exactly 8 a.m. on the morning when Adam and Eve were created according to the traditional chronology.[5]

The length of a mean lunar period in the traditional representation is 29 days, 12 hours, and 793 parts, or $29\frac{13753}{25920} \approx 29.530594$ days. This is a classical value for the lunar (synodic) month, attributed to Cidenas in about 383 B.C.E. and was an integral part of what is called "System B" of Babylonian astronomy [16]; it was used by Ptolemy in his *Almagest*.[6] With $354^{d}8^{h}48^{m}40^{s}$ for an ordinary year and $383^{d}21^{h}32^{m}43\frac{1}{3}^{s}$ for a leap year, this value gives an average Hebrew year length of about 365.2468 days. The start of each New Year, Rosh ha-Shanah (Tishri 1), coincides with the calculated day of the mean conjunction (new moon) of Tishri—12 months after the previous New Year conjunction in ordinary years, and 13 in leap years—unless one of 4 delays is mandated:

1. If the time of mean conjunction is at midday or after, then the New Year is delayed.[7]

---

[4] *Anno Mundi*; in the (traditional) year of the world (since creation).

[5] The ambiguities in the Hebrew epoch have led to some confusion in medieval, as well as modern, times. For example, M. Kantor's *The Jewish Time Line Encyclopedia*, Jason Aronson, Northvale, NJ (1989), erroneously gives 69 C.E., rather than 70 C.E., as the date on which Titus captured Jerusalem. Similarly, Sephardic Jews, every Tishah be-Av (see page 130), announce in the synagogue the wrong number of elapsed years since the fall of Jerusalem.

[6] The astronomer and mathematician Abraham bar Ḥiyya Savasorda (eleventh century) suggested that the reason for the choice of 1080 parts per hour is that it is the smallest number that allows this particular value of the length of a month to be expressed with an integral number of parts (in other words, 793/1080 is irreducible).

[7] According to Maimonides [15, 6:2] (cf. al-Bīrūnī [2, p. 149]), seasonal time is used in which "daylight hours" and "nighttime hours" have different lengths, which vary according to the seasons (see Section 14.8). Postponement occurs if the conjunction is 18 variable-length hours or more after sunset. Others use fixed-length hours, but the computation is unaffected, because true noon is 18 temporal (seasonal) hours after true sunset just as mean local noon is 18 civil hours after mean local sunset (6 p.m. local mean time). Savasorda and others say that equal-length hours, not variable-length hours, are intended in the Hebrew calendar calculations; dates would be unaffected.

2. In no event may the New Year (Rosh ha-Shanah) be on a Sunday, Wednesday, or Friday. (This rule is called *lo iddo rosh*.)[8] If the conjunction is on Saturday, Tuesday, or Thursday afternoon, then this rule combines with the previous rule and results in a 2-day delay.

3. In some cases (about once in 30 years) an additional delaying factor may need to be employed to keep the length of a year within the allowable ranges. It is the irregular effect of the second delay that makes this necessary: if the conjunction is before noon on a Tuesday of a common year, and the conjunction of the following year is at noon on Saturday or later (possibly after sunset), then the previous rules would delay Rosh ha-Shanah until Monday (a Saturday afternoon conjunction is put off by the first rule and Rosh ha-Shanah on Sunday is precluded by the second rule). This would require a unacceptable year length of 356 days, and thus instead the *current* Rosh ha-Shanah is delayed (skipping Wednesday) until Thursday, giving a 354-day year. For the following year's conjunction to fall on a Saturday afternoon, the current year's must have occurred after 3:11:20 a.m. The prior year cannot become too long because of this delay, for its New Year conjunction must have been on Friday (in a common year) or Wednesday (in a leap year) and would have been delayed a day by the second rule.

4. In rare cases (about once in 186 years), Rosh ha-Shanah on a Monday after a leap year can pose a similar problem by causing the year just ending to be too short—when the *prior* New Year conjunction was after midday on Tuesday and was, therefore, delayed until Thursday. If the conjunction were after midday Tuesday the previous year, then in the current year it would be after $9{:}32{:}43\frac{1}{3}$ a.m. on Monday. In this case, Rosh ha-Shanah is postponed from Monday to Tuesday, extending the leap year just ending from 382 days to 383. The current year cannot become too short because of this delay; it is shortened from 355 days to 354, the following Rosh ha-Shanah being delayed until Saturday.

The precise rules for delays were the subject of a short-lived dispute (921–923 C.E.) between Palestinian and Babylonian Jewish authorities (the best source in English for details of the controversy is [23, pp. 264–275]). In 923 C.E. the calculated conjunction fell just after midday, but the Palestinian authority, Aaron ben Meir, insisted that the first delaying rule applied only when the conjunction was at 12:35:40 p.m. (that is, noon plus 624 parts) or later, presumably because they (the Palestinians) did their calculations from Nisan instead of Tishri, and rounded the time of the epochal new moon differently. Because of the retroactive effect of the third delay, this had already affected the dates in 921 (see the sample calculation beginning on page 124). In the end, the Babylonian gaon, Sa'adia ben

[8] Excluding Wednesday and Friday serves the ritual purpose of preventing Yom Kippur (Tishri 10) from falling on Friday or Sunday; excluding Sunday prevents Hoshana Rabba (Tishri 21) from falling on Saturday. Maimonides [15, 7:8] ascribes this correction in the calendar of approximately half a day, on the average, to the need to better match the mean date of appearance of the new moon of the month of Tishri; al-Bīrūnī [2] attributes it to astrological considerations. The real purpose of the delay is a moot point.

Joseph al-Fayyūmi, prevailed, and the rules have since been fixed as given above. (Some scant details can be found in [17, vol. III, p. 119] and [10, col. 539–540]; [3] gives a full discussion of the controversy; see also [12].) Interestingly, according to Maimonides [15, 5:13], the final authority in calendrical matters is vested in the residents of the Holy Land, and their decision—even if erroneous—should be followed worldwide:

> Our own calculations are solely for the purpose of making the matter available to public knowledge. Since we know that residents of the Land of Israel use the same method of calculation, we perform the same operations in order to find out and ascertain what day it is that has been determined by the people of Israel.

One fairly common misconception regarding the Hebrew calendar is that the correspondence with the Gregorian calendar repeats every 19 years. This, however, is usually not the case because of the irregular Gregorian leap-year rule and the irregular applicability of the delays. Nor does the Hebrew calendar repeat its pattern every 247 years. In the seventeenth century, Hezekiah ben David da Silva of Jerusalem complained about published tables for the Hebrew calendar:[9]

> I have seen disaster and scandal [on the part] of some intercalators who are of the [erroneous] opinion that the character [of years] repeats every thirteen cycles [$13 \times 19 = 247$ years]. For the sake of God, do not rely and do not lean on them. "Far be it from thee to do after this manner," which will—perish the thought—cause the holy and awesome fast to be nullified, leaven to be eaten on Passover, and the holidays to be desecrated. Therefore, you the reader, "Hearken now unto my voice, I will give thee counsel, and God be with thee." Be cautious and careful lest you forget ... what I am writing regarding this matter, since it is done according to exact arithmetic, "divided well," and is precise on all counts ... from the 278th cycle [1521 C.E.] until the end of time. "Anyone who separates from it, it is as if he separates [himself] from life [itself]."

By the "character" of a year da Silva means the day of the week on which New Year falls and the length of the year. In fact, the Hebrew calendar repeats only after 689472 years (as was pointed out by the celebrated Persian Muslim writer, al-Bīrūnī [2, p. 154] in 1000 C.E.): The 19-year cycle contains exactly

$$\begin{aligned}&\text{991 weeks, 2 days, 16 hours, and 595 parts}\\ &\qquad = \text{991 weeks and 69715 parts}\end{aligned}$$

A week has 181440 parts, so it takes

$$\begin{aligned}\frac{\text{lcm}(69715,\ 181440)\text{ parts}}{69715\text{ parts/cycle}} &= \frac{2529817920\text{ parts}}{69715\text{ parts/cycle}}\\ &= 36288\text{ cycles}\\ &= 689472\text{ years}\end{aligned}$$

[9] *Peri Ḥadash, Oraḥ Ḥayyim*, 428. For a recent study of the early origin of this imagined cycle, see "The Origins of the 247-year Calendar Cycle," N. Vidro, *Aleph: Historical Studies in Science and Judaism*, vol. 17, pp. 95–137, 2017.

for the excess parts to accumulate into an integer number of weeks, and for the calendar to return to the same pattern of delays. Thus, the exact correspondence of Hebrew dates (which has a mean year length of $365\frac{24311}{98496}$ days) and dates on the Gregorian calendar (which has a 400-year cycle) repeats only after

$$\begin{aligned}\text{lcm}\left(689472 \times 365\tfrac{24311}{98496}, 400 \times 365\tfrac{97}{400}\right)\\ &= 5255890855047 \text{ days}\\ &= 14390140400 \text{ Gregorian years}\\ &= 14389970112 \text{ Hebrew years}\end{aligned}$$

Similar astronomically long periods are needed for other pairs of calendars to match up exactly.

8.2 Implementation

You have already seen … how much computation is involved, how many additions and subtractions are still necessary, despite our having exerted ourselves greatly to invent approximations that do not require complicated calculations. For the path of the moon is convoluted. Hence wise men have said: the sun knows its way, the moon does not…

Maimonides: *Mishneh Torah, Book of Seasons* (1178)

The epoch of the Hebrew calendar is R.D. −1373427:

$$\textbf{hebrew-epoch} \stackrel{\text{def}}{=} \qquad (8.17)$$

$$\textbf{fixed-from-julian}\left(\boxed{3761 \text{ B.C.E.}}\,\boxed{\textbf{october}}\,\boxed{7}\right)$$

We can calculate the time elapsed on the Hebrew calendar from the Hebrew epoch until the new moon of Tishri for Hebrew year y by computing

$$m \times \left(29^{\text{d}}12^{\text{h}}44^{\text{m}}3\tfrac{1}{3}^{\text{s}}\right) - (48^{\text{m}}40^{\text{s}}) \qquad (8.18)$$

where m is the number of months before year y, because the first mean conjunction was $48^{\text{m}}40^{\text{s}}$(= 876 parts) before midnight on the epoch, or 5 hours 204 parts after nominal sunset (see page 116). To compute the total number of months, leap and regular, we just apply formula (1.86) with $c = 19$, $l = 7$, and $\Delta = 11$:[10]

$$\lfloor (7y - 6)/19 \rfloor + 12(y - 1) = \lfloor (235y - 234)/19 \rfloor$$

More generally, the fixed moment of the mean conjunction, called the *molad* (plural, *moladot*), of any month of the Hebrew calendar is computed by

$$\textbf{molad}\,(\textit{h-year}, \textit{h-month}) \stackrel{\text{def}}{=} \qquad (8.19)$$

$$\textbf{hebrew-epoch} - \frac{876}{25920} + \textit{months-elapsed} \times \left(29 + 12^{\text{h}} + \frac{793}{25920}\right)$$

---

[10] An analogous formula for the number of nonleap years was used by Gauss [9].

where

$$y = \begin{cases} \textit{h-year} + 1 & \textbf{if } \textit{h-month} < \textbf{tishri} \\ \textit{h-year} & \textbf{otherwise} \end{cases}$$

$$\textit{months-elapsed} = \textit{h-month} - \textbf{tishri} + \left\lfloor \frac{1}{19} \times (235 \times y - 234) \right\rfloor$$

readjusting for the year starting with Tishri. The degree to which **molad** approximates the astronomical new moon can be seen in Figure 8.1, which shows a scatter plot of the error (in hours) for Nisan for Gregorian years −1000 to 5000 (= 2760 − −8760 A.M.). Indeed, any arithmetic calendar that uses a mean value for the lunar month, such as the Old Hindu lunisolar calendar (Section 10.3), must show similar deviations, since the true length of the month varies greatly (see Section 14.6).

To implement the first of the four delays (putting off the New Year if the calculated conjunction is in the afternoon), all we need to do is add 12 hours to the time of the epochal conjunction and let the day be the integer part (the floor) of the value obtained. This is analogous to equation (1.92), except that we are counting the days in months of average length $29\frac{13753}{25920}$ days rather than in years. The initial conjunction is $11^{h}11^{m}20^{s}$—that is, 12084 parts—into the determining period, which began at noon on the day before the epoch.

To test for Sunday, Wednesday, and Friday, as required by the second delay, we can use $(3d \bmod 7) < 3$, as in equation (1.82) with $c = 7$ and $l = 3$, to determine

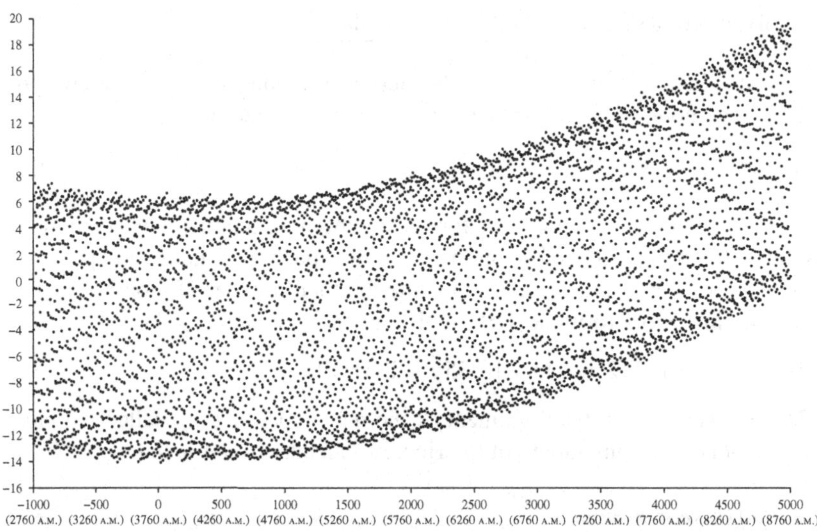

Figure 8.1 Molad of Nisan minus the actual moment of the new moon, Jerusalem local time, in hours, for Gregorian years −1000 to 5000 (= 2760–8760 A.M.). (Suggested by I. L. Bromberg.)

whether d is one of the three evenly spaced excluded days. These two delays are incorporated in the following function:

$$\textbf{hebrew-calendar-elapsed-days}\,(\textit{h-year}) \stackrel{\text{def}}{=} \tag{8.20}$$

$$\begin{cases} \textit{days} + 1 & \textbf{if } ((3 \times (\textit{days} + 1)) \bmod 7) < 3 \\ \textit{days} & \textbf{otherwise} \end{cases}$$

where

$$\begin{aligned} \textit{months-elapsed} &= \left\lfloor \frac{1}{19} \times (235 \times \textit{h-year} - 234) \right\rfloor \\ \textit{parts-elapsed} &= 12084 + 13753 \times \textit{months-elapsed} \\ \textit{days} &= 29 \times \textit{months-elapsed} + \left\lfloor \frac{\textit{parts-elapsed}}{25920} \right\rfloor \end{aligned}$$

Because the count of elapsed days begins with Sunday evening (which is already the second day of the week from the point of view of the Hebrew calendar), we use $\textit{days} + 1$ for the number of days since the Sunday before the first molad. Whole days and fractional days (parts) are computed separately, so that 32 bits suffice for dates in the foreseeable future; however, this calculation comes close to the 32-bit limit. To avoid such large numbers one can compute days, hours, and parts separately:

$$\begin{aligned} \textit{parts-elapsed} &= 204 + 793 \times (\textit{months-elapsed} \bmod 1080) \\ \textit{hours-elapsed} &= 11 + 12 \times \textit{months-elapsed} \\ &\quad + 793 \times \left\lfloor \frac{\textit{months-elapsed}}{1080} \right\rfloor + \left\lfloor \frac{\textit{parts-elapsed}}{1080} \right\rfloor \\ \textit{days} &= 29 \times \textit{months-elapsed} + \left\lfloor \frac{\textit{hours-elapsed}}{24} \right\rfloor \end{aligned}$$

When one can work directly with rational numbers, one may just let

$$\textit{days} = \left\lfloor \textbf{molad}(\textbf{tishri}, \textit{h-year}) - \textbf{hebrew-epoch} + 12^{\text{h}} \right\rfloor$$

using the **molad** function.

The two remaining delays depend on the lengths of the prior and current years that would result from the putative New Year dates suggested by the previous function. If the current year were 356 days then it would be too long, and we would delay its start by 2 days. If the prior year were 382 days long then we delay its end by 1 day. Rather than check the day of the week, the time of conjunction, and the leap-year status of the prior and current year, as in the traditional formulation of these delays, we just check for unacceptable year lengths:

$$\textbf{hebrew-year-length-correction}\,(\textit{h-year}) \stackrel{\text{def}}{=} \tag{8.21}$$

$$\begin{cases} 2 & \textbf{if } ny_2 - ny_1 = 356 \\ 1 & \textbf{if } ny_1 - ny_0 = 382 \\ 0 & \textbf{otherwise} \end{cases}$$

where

$$\begin{aligned} ny_0 &= \textbf{hebrew-calendar-elapsed-days}\,(\textit{h-year} - 1) \\ ny_1 &= \textbf{hebrew-calendar-elapsed-days}\,(\textit{h-year}) \\ ny_2 &= \textbf{hebrew-calendar-elapsed-days}\,(\textit{h-year} + 1) \end{aligned}$$

Adding the value of this function to the number of elapsed days determines the day on which the year begins. To get the R.D. date of the New Year, we have to add the (negative) epoch:

$$\textbf{hebrew-new-year}\,(\textit{h-year}) \stackrel{\text{def}}{=} \tag{8.22}$$

$$\begin{aligned} &\textbf{hebrew-epoch} + \textbf{hebrew-calendar-elapsed-days}\,(\textit{h-year}) \\ &\quad + \textbf{hebrew-year-length-correction}\,(\textit{h-year}) \end{aligned}$$

As already mentioned, the length of the year determines the lengths of the two varying months, Marḥeshvan and Kislev. Marḥeshvan is long (30 days) if the year has 355 or 385 days; Kislev is short (29 days) if the year has 353 or 383 days. The length of the year, in turn, is determined by the dates of the Hebrew New Years (Tishri 1) preceding and following the year in question:

$$\textbf{last-day-of-hebrew-month}\,(\textit{h-year}, \textit{h-month}) \stackrel{\text{def}}{=} \tag{8.23}$$

$$\begin{cases} 29 & \textbf{if } \textit{h-month} \in \{\textbf{iyyar}, \textbf{tammuz}, \textbf{elul}, \textbf{tevet}, \textbf{adarii}\} \text{ or} \\ & \quad \{\textit{h-month} = \textbf{adar} \text{ and not } \textbf{hebrew-leap-year?}\,(\textit{h-year})\} \text{ or} \\ & \quad \left\{ \begin{array}{l} \textit{h-month} = \textbf{marheshvan} \text{ and} \\ \text{not } \textbf{long-marheshvan?}\,(\textit{h-year}) \end{array} \right\} \text{ or} \\ & \quad \{\textit{h-month} = \textbf{kislev} \text{ and } \textbf{short-kislev?}\,(\textit{h-year})\} \\ 30 & \textbf{otherwise} \end{cases}$$

Here,

$$\textbf{long-marheshvan?}\,(\textit{h-year}) \stackrel{\text{def}}{=} \tag{8.24}$$

$$\textbf{days-in-hebrew-year}\,(\textit{h-year}) \in \{355, 385\}$$

Also,

$$\textbf{short-kislev?}\,(\textit{h-year}) \stackrel{\text{def}}{=} \tag{8.25}$$

$$\textbf{days-in-hebrew-year}\,(\textit{h-year}) \in \{353, 383\}$$

and

$$\textbf{days-in-hebrew-year}\,(\textit{h-year}) \stackrel{\text{def}}{=} \tag{8.26}$$
$$\textbf{hebrew-new-year}\,(\textit{h-year}+1) - \textbf{hebrew-new-year}\,(\textit{h-year})$$

With the foregoing machinery, we are now ready to convert from any Hebrew date to an R.D. date:

$$\textbf{fixed-from-hebrew}\left(\boxed{\textit{year} \mid \textit{month} \mid \textit{day}}\right) \stackrel{\text{def}}{=} \tag{8.27}$$
$$\textbf{hebrew-new-year}\,(\textit{year}) + \textit{day} - 1$$
$$+ \begin{cases} \left(\sum\limits_{m \geqslant \textbf{tishri}}^{p(m)} \textbf{last-day-of-hebrew-month}\,(\textit{year}, m)\right) & \textbf{if } \textit{month} < \textbf{tishri} \\ \quad + \left(\sum\limits_{m \geqslant \textbf{nisan}}^{m<\textit{month}} \textbf{last-day-of-hebrew-month}\,(\textit{year}, m)\right) & \\ \sum\limits_{m \geqslant \textbf{tishri}}^{m<\textit{month}} \textbf{last-day-of-hebrew-month}\,(\textit{year}, m) & \textbf{otherwise} \end{cases}$$

where

$$p(m) = m \leqslant \textbf{last-month-of-hebrew-year}\,(\textit{year})$$

To the fixed date of the start of the given year we add the number of elapsed days in the given month and the length of each elapsed month. We distinguish between months before and after Tishri, which is the seventh month, though the New Year begins with its new moon. For dates in the second half of the year (months 1 through 6) we need to include the lengths of all months from Tishri until **last-month-of-hebrew-year** (month 12 or 13).

Conversion to Hebrew dates is done as follows:

$$\textbf{hebrew-from-fixed}\,(\textit{date}) \stackrel{\text{def}}{=} \boxed{\textit{year} \mid \textit{month} \mid \textit{day}} \tag{8.28}$$

where

$$\textit{approx} = \left\lfloor \frac{98496}{35975351} \times (\textit{date} - \textbf{hebrew-epoch}) \right\rfloor + 1$$

$$\textit{year} = \underset{y \geqslant \textit{approx}-1}{\textbf{MAX}} \left\{ \textbf{hebrew-new-year}\,(y) \leqslant \textit{date} \right\}$$

$$\textit{start} = \begin{cases} \textbf{tishri} & \textbf{if } \textit{date} < \textbf{fixed-from-hebrew}\left(\boxed{\textit{year} \mid \textbf{nisan} \mid 1}\right) \\ \textbf{nisan} & \textbf{otherwise} \end{cases}$$

$$\textit{month} = \underset{m \geqslant \textit{start}}{\textbf{MIN}} \left\{ \textit{date} \leqslant \textbf{fixed-from-hebrew}\left(\boxed{\textit{year} \mid m \mid \begin{array}{c}\textbf{last-day-of-}\\ \textbf{hebrew-month}\\ (\textit{year}, m)\end{array}}\right) \right\}$$

$$\textit{day} = \textit{date} - \textbf{fixed-from-hebrew}\left(\boxed{\textit{year} \mid \textit{month} \mid 1}\right) + 1$$

We first approximate the Hebrew year by dividing the number of elapsed days by the average year length, 35975351/98496 days. (A simpler value—even 365.25—can be used instead.) The irregularity of the year lengths means that the estimate *approx* can be off by 1 in either direction. Thus we search for the right year, adding 1 to *approx* − 1 for each year *y* whose New Year is not after *date*. To determine the Hebrew month, we search forward from Nisan or Tishri until we reach the first month that ends on or after *date*.

Consider, as an example, the calculation of the date of Passover in 922 C.E.—that is, Nisan 15, A.M. 4682 (see page 117 for the historical significance of this year). The mean conjunction of the preceding Tishri fell on Wednesday, September 5, 921 C.E. (Julian), R.D. 336276, at 5:51:46$\frac{2}{3}$ a.m. The mean conjunction of the following Tishri fell on Tuesday, September 29, 922 C.E. (Julian), at 3:24:30 a.m. At the latter time, $57909 = (235 \times 4683 - 234)/19$ months of mean length $29\frac{13753}{25920}$ had elapsed since the primeval conjunction, to which we add 12084/25920 to count from noon on the Sunday before the epoch. By the traditional reckoning, that is Tuesday, 9 hours and 441 parts since sunset the preceding evening. Hebrew year 4683 was year 9 of the 247th 19-year cycle, which is not a leap year, making 4683 an instance of the third delay. Because this conjunction was later than 9 hours and 204 parts, the conjunction of the following year, 4684, fell on Saturday afternoon, just 237 parts (13.167 minutes) after midday, for which time the first two delays apply. Specifically, equation (8.20) yields

hebrew-calendar-elapsed-days(4682) = 1709704
hebrew-calendar-elapsed-days(4683) = 1710087
hebrew-calendar-elapsed-days(4684) = 1710443

With the first two delays, but without the third delay, year 4683 would be of $1710443 - 1710087 = 356$ days in duration, an unacceptable length. Thus, the first of Tishri 4683 is put off 2 days to Thursday, September 26, R.D. 336662. The start of year 4682 is delayed until Thursday, making 4682 a "long" leap year with a total of 385 days. Tishri (month 7) and Shevat (month 11) are always 30 days long, Tevet (month 10) is 29 days, Marḥeshvan (month 8) and Kislev (month 9) both have 30 days in a long year, and in a leap year Adar I (month 12) has 30 days and Adar II (month 13) has 29. Adding these ($5 \times 30 + 2 \times 29 = 208$), plus the 14 days of Nisan (month 1), to the R.D. date of Rosh ha-Shanah of 4682, we arrive at R.D. $336277 + 208 + 14 = 336499$ as the starting date of Passover.[11] That date is Tuesday, April 16, 922 C.E. (Julian) and April 21, 922 (Gregorian). Were the first delay not applied in 4684, there would have been no need for the third delay in 4683. Were it not for the third delay, Hebrew year 4682 would have been "short," and Passover in 922—as well as all other dates between Tevet 1 in late 921 and

[11] Dates during the second half of the Hebrew year (from Nisan through Elul) depend *only* on the date of the following Rosh ha-Shanah, because the intervening months are all of fixed length, and thus for hand calculations it is easier to count backwards from the following Rosh ha-Shanah, subtracting 30 days for Sivan and Av, 29 days for Iyyar, Tammuz, and Elul, and 16 for the remainder of Nisan, rather than always starting with the preceding Rosh ha-Shanah, as in our algorithm.

Elul 29 in the summer of 922—would have occurred 2 days earlier. Dates in Kislev would have been 1 day earlier.

8.3 Inverting the Molad[12]

If you see such calculations in other tables, which differ from what I say—as I have seen that what I have calculated in my tables does not agree with them—ignore their reckonings and do not consent to their calculations, but rely on what I have counted for you, no less no more.

Issachar ben Mordecai Susan: *Tikkun Yissakhar* (1564)

Suppose we are told at what time of day and on which day of the week the molad of some Hebrew month occurs; can we determine the date (month and year) of that molad? Surprisingly, the answer is yes, if we assume that the date is within a range of about 14000 years.

Recall that the interval from molad to molad is $29\frac{1}{2}$ days and 793 parts of an hour. There are 1080 parts per hour, so there are $w = 7 \times 24 \times 1080 = 181440$ parts in a week; there are four weeks plus $r = 36 \times 1080 + 793 = 39673$ parts in a molad, so each successive molad advances in the week by r parts. Because r and w are relatively prime, a molad will recur on the same day of the week and at the same time of day as another molad only after w months, about 14670 years—this means that since the epoch of the Hebrew calendar and for more than 8000 years into the future the day/time combination of the molad uniquely determines the Hebrew month and year.

Imagine time as a sequence of Hebrew calendar parts numbered $0, 1, 2, \ldots$, each labeled with a pair of numbers $\langle a, b\rangle$, where a is the part number within the molad and b is the part number within the week. Thus the first component repeats after $4\times w+r = 765433$ parts and the second repeats after 181440 parts. Because 765433 and 181440 are relatively prime, there are $765433 \times 181440 = 138880163520$ labels; we want to determine n, $0 \leqslant n < 138880163520$, from the pair $\langle a, b\rangle$ such that $a = n \bmod 765433$ and $b = n \bmod 181440$. This is precisely the matter discussed in Section 1.13, where equation (1.70) gives us the answer by setting the cycle lengths $c = 765433$ and $d = 181440$ and the values $a = 0$ (a specifies that it is the start of the molad), $\Gamma = 0$ (the offset Γ specifies that part 0 is the start of a molad), $\Delta = (18 + 5) \times 1080 + 204 = 25044$ [the offset Δ specifies that the cycle began 5 hours, 204 parts after sunset on weekday 0 (Sunday)], and b to the given position in the week of the molad we seek to determine. We need the multiplicative inverse of c modulo d, which by equation (1.72) is

$$k = c^{\varphi(d)-1} \bmod d = 74377$$

The ordinal position of the specified molad in the sequence of 138880163520 labels is hence

$$n = (56930610241b - 1425770202875604) \bmod 138880163520$$

Because the greatest common divisor of the three integers is 765433, this becomes

$$n/765433 = (74377b - 34548) \bmod 181440$$

[12] This problem was suggested by Sacha Stern. Tabular methods have been around at least since the work of Isaac Israeli [11] in the early fourteenth century.

Of course, since n is in parts and 765433 is the number of parts per molad, $n/765433$ is the number of moladot; that is, $74377b - 34548$ is the residue class of the desired molad (one occurring at part b in the week), modulo the cycle of 181440 moladot after which the moladot repeat their positions.

Working with the rationals, we can express everything in terms of days, rather than parts. Let $m = b/25920$, where 25920 is the number of parts in a 24-hour day. We divide the previous equation through by 25920, giving

$$r = (74377m - 2879/2160) \bmod 7$$

where $r \times 765433 = n/25920$ counts the number of elapsed days and fractional days until the desired occurrence of a molad. Assuming that we want the first occurrence since the Hebrew epoch, we add this to the epoch—adjusted 876 parts (expressed in days) backward to the moment of the initial molad **beharad**,

$$\textbf{hebrew-epoch} - \frac{876}{25920} = \textbf{molad}(1, \textbf{tishri})$$

giving

$$\textbf{fixed-from-molad}\,(moon) \stackrel{\text{def}}{=} \tag{8.29}$$

$$\textbf{fixed-from-moment}\,(\textbf{molad}\,(1, \textbf{tishri}) + r \times 765433)$$

where

$$r = \left(74377 \times moon - \frac{2879}{2160}\right) \bmod 7$$

(This calculation requires exact rational arithmetic and 64-bit integers.) One could just as easily choose an arbitrary starting point, **molad**(*year*, *month*), instead of **molad**(1, **tishri**), by replacing the offset 2879/2160 in (8.29) with

$$[74377 \times \textbf{molad}(year, month)] \bmod 7$$

Then the calculation would compute the first occurrence of a molad at the given time starting from that point onward.

The time of the molad is nowadays specified as the day of the week, d, together with h hours measured from midnight, m minutes, and p parts. To convert such a molad to a point in the weekly cycle, we express the time as a fraction of a day, using mixed-radix notation (Section 1.10):

$$moon = \langle d, h, m, p \rangle \stackrel{\text{rad}}{\longleftarrow} \langle ; 24, 60, 18 \rangle$$

For example, a molad of Wednesday, 18 hours, 35 minutes, 11 parts is specified by

$$\textbf{wednesday} + \frac{18}{24} + \frac{35}{24 \times 60} + \frac{11}{24 \times 60 \times 18} = \frac{97841}{25920}$$

and **fixed-from-molad**(97841/25920) is R.D. 735913 = Kislev 28, 5776 A.M. = November 11, 2015 (Gregorian), the day of the molad of the coming month, Tevet, 5776 A.M. To display a molad occurring at moment t in this traditional format, we use the inverse radix operation

$$(t \bmod 7) \xrightarrow{\text{rad}} \langle ; 24, 60, 18 \rangle$$

Traditionally the molad was specified by the day of the week, d, together with h hours measured from sunset not midnight, and p parts of an hour. To convert such a molad to a point in the weekly cycle, we would use

$$moon = \langle d, h-6, p \rangle \xleftarrow{\text{rad}} \langle ; 24, 1080 \rangle$$

because sunset is 6 hours before midnight. For example, the undated Oxford Bodleian manuscript, Pococke 368, folio 221 recto, refers to a traditional molad on a Sunday, at 2 hours and 240 parts:

$$\textbf{sunday} - \frac{4}{24} + \frac{240}{24 \times 1080} = -\frac{17}{108}$$

and **fixed-from-molad**($-17/108$) is R.D. 292452 = Elul 28, 4561 A.M. = September 11, 801 C.E. (Julian), meaning that this is the molad of the coming month, Tishri, 4562 A.M. For the moment t of a molad in traditional format, one computes the inverse:

$$(t + 6^{\text{h}}) \bmod 7 \xrightarrow{\text{rad}} \langle ; 24, 1080 \rangle$$

The easiest way to extract the coming Hebrew month and year from the result of **fixed-from-molad** is to apply **hebrew-from-fixed** to a few days afterwards, since the molad often precedes the first day of a month:

$$\begin{aligned} year &= \textbf{hebrew-from-fixed}(\textbf{fixed-from-molad}(moon) + 5)_{\textbf{year}} \\ month &= \textbf{hebrew-from-fixed}(\textbf{fixed-from-molad}(moon) + 5)_{\textbf{month}} \end{aligned}$$

Because **fixed-from-molad** inverts **molad**, we have the identity

$$\textbf{molad}(year, month) = moon$$

The year and month can also be derived directly from $k = n/765433$, the number of elapsed months. Applying formula (1.90) with $c = 19$, $\ell = 7$, $\Delta = 11$, and $L = 12$, we get

$$year = \lfloor 19k + 253 - ([7 \times 11] \bmod 19)/235 \rfloor = \lfloor (19k + 252)/235 \rfloor$$

The number of months unaccounted for is

$$m = \lfloor ([19k + 252] \bmod 235)/19 \rfloor = \lfloor ([19k + 17] \bmod 235)/19 \rfloor$$

To obtain the corresponding month number, considering that years begin with the seventh month, Tishri, we need to adjust m:

$$month = (\textbf{tishri} + m) \bmod [1 \,..\, \textbf{last-month-of-hebrew-year}(year)]$$

8.4 Holidays and Fast Days

In the days of wicked Trajan, a son was born to him on Tishah be-Av and they fasted; his daughter died on Hanukkah and they lit candles. His wife sent to him and said, rather than conquer the Barbarians, come and conquer the Jews who have revolted ... He came ... and the blood flowed in the sea until Cyprus.

Jerusalem Talmud (Succah 5:1)

As throughout this book, we consider our aim to be the determination of holidays that occur in a specified Gregorian year. Because the Hebrew year is, within thousands of years of the present, consistently aligned with the Gregorian year, each Jewish holiday occurs just once in a given Gregorian year (with a minor exception noted below). The major holidays of the Hebrew year occur on fixed days on the Hebrew calendar but only in fixed seasons on the Gregorian calendar. They are easy to determine on the Gregorian calendar with the machinery developed above provided that we observe that the Hebrew year beginning in the Gregorian year y is given by

Hebrew New Year occurring in the fall of Gregorian year y

$$= y + 1 - \textbf{gregorian-year-from-fixed}(\textbf{hebrew-epoch})$$

The Hebrew year that began in the fall of 1 (Gregorian) was A.M. 3762. This implies that holidays occurring in the fall and early winter of the Gregorian year y occur in the Hebrew year $y + 3761$, but holidays in the late winter, spring, and summer occur in Hebrew year $y + 3760$. For example, to find the R.D. date of Yom Kippur (Tishri 10) in a Gregorian year, we would use

$$\textbf{yom-kippur}\,(g\text{-}year) \stackrel{\text{def}}{=} \qquad (8.30)$$

$$\textbf{fixed-from-hebrew}\left(\boxed{h\text{-}year \mid \textbf{tishri} \mid 10}\right)$$

where

$$h\text{-}year = g\text{-}year - \textbf{gregorian-year-from-fixed}\,(\textbf{hebrew-epoch}) + 1$$

The R.D. dates of Rosh ha-Shanah (Tishri 1), Sukkot (Tishri 15), Hoshana Rabba (Tishri 21), Shemini Aẓeret (Tishri 22), and Simḥat Torah (Tishri 23, outside Israel) are determined identically.[13] As on the Islamic calendar, all Hebrew holidays begin at sunset the prior evening.

The dates of the other major holidays—Passover (Nisan 15), the ending of Passover (Nisan 21), and Shavuot (Sivan 6)—are determined similarly but, because these holidays occur in the spring, the year corresponding to Gregorian year y is $y + 3760$. Conservative and Orthodox Jews observe two days of Rosh ha-Shanah—Tishri 1 and 2. Outside Israel, they also observe Tishri 16, Nisan 16, Nisan 22, and Sivan 7 as holidays.

---

[13] See [1, p. 800] for another way to determine the date of Rosh ha-Shanah.

Thus, for example, we determine the R.D. date of Passover by

$$\textbf{passover}\,(\textit{g-year}) \stackrel{\text{def}}{=} \textbf{fixed-from-hebrew}\left(\boxed{\textit{h-year}}\boxed{\textbf{nisan}}\boxed{15}\right) \tag{8.31}$$

where

$$\textit{h-year} = \textit{g-year} - \textbf{gregorian-year-from-fixed}\,(\textbf{hebrew-epoch})$$

Gauss [9] developed an interesting alternative formula to determine the Gregorian date of Passover in a given year.

The 7-week period beginning on the second day of Passover is called the *omer* (sheave offering); the days of the omer are counted from 1 to 49, and the count is expressed in completed weeks and excess days. The following function tells the omer count for an R.D. date, returning a list of weeks (an integer 0–7) and days (an integer 0–6) if the date is within the omer period and returning **bogus** if not:

$$\textbf{omer}\,(\textit{date}) \stackrel{\text{def}}{=} \begin{cases} \left\langle \left\lfloor \frac{c}{7} \right\rfloor, c \bmod 7 \right\rangle & \textbf{if } 1 \leqslant c \leqslant 49 \\ \textbf{bogus} & \textbf{otherwise} \end{cases} \tag{8.32}$$

where

$$c = \textit{date} - \textbf{passover}\,(\textbf{gregorian-year-from-fixed}\,(\textit{date}))$$

The minor holidays of the Hebrew year are the "intermediate" days of Sukkot (Tishri 16–21) and of Passover (Nisan 16–20); Hanukkah (8 days, beginning on Kislev 25); Tu-B'Shevat (Shevat 15); and Purim (Adar 14 in normal years, Adar II 14 in leap years). Hanukkah occurs in late fall or early winter, and thus Hanukkah of the Gregorian year y occurs in the Hebrew year $y + 3761$, whereas Tu-B'Shevat occurs in late winter or early spring, and hence Tu-B'Shevat of Gregorian year y occurs in Hebrew year $y + 3760$. Thus, these two holidays are handled as were Yom Kippur and Passover, respectively. Purim also always occurs in late winter or early spring, in the last month of the Hebrew year (Adar or Adar II); hence its R.D. date is computed by

$$\textbf{purim}\,(\textit{g-year}) \stackrel{\text{def}}{=} \tag{8.33}$$

$$\textbf{fixed-from-hebrew}\left(\boxed{\textit{h-year}}\boxed{\textit{last-month}}\boxed{14}\right)$$

where

$$\begin{aligned} \textit{h-year} &= \textit{g-year} - \textbf{gregorian-year-from-fixed}\,(\textbf{hebrew-epoch}) \\ \textit{last-month} &= \textbf{last-month-of-hebrew-year}\,(\textit{h-year}) \end{aligned}$$

The Hebrew year contains several fast days that, though specified by particular Hebrew calendar dates, are shifted when those days occur on a Saturday. The fast days are Tzom Gedaliah (Tishri 3), Tzom Tevet (Tevet 10), Ta'anit Esther (the day before Purim), Tzom Tammuz (Tammuz 17), and Tishah be-Av (Av 9). When Purim is on a Sunday, Ta'anit Esther occurs on the preceding Thursday and thus we can write

$$\textbf{ta-anit-esther}\,(\textit{g-year}) \stackrel{\text{def}}{=} \tag{8.34}$$

$$\begin{cases} \textit{purim-date} - 3 & \textbf{if day-of-week-from-fixed}\,(\textit{purim-date}) = \textbf{sunday} \\ \textit{purim-date} - 1 & \textbf{otherwise} \end{cases}$$

where

$$\textit{purim-date} = \textbf{purim}\,(\textit{g-year})$$

Each of the other fast days, as well as Shushan Purim (the day after Purim, celebrated in Jerusalem), is postponed to the following day (Sunday) when it occurs on a Saturday. Because Tzom Gedaliah is always in the fall and Tzom Tammuz and Tishah be-Av are always in the summer, their determination is easy. For example,

$$\textbf{tishah-be-av}\,(\textit{g-year}) \stackrel{\text{def}}{=} \tag{8.35}$$

$$\begin{cases} \textit{av}_9 + 1 & \textbf{if day-of-week-from-fixed}\,(\textit{av}_9) = \textbf{saturday} \\ \textit{av}_9 & \textbf{otherwise} \end{cases}$$

where

$$\textit{h-year} = \textit{g-year} - \textbf{gregorian-year-from-fixed}\,(\textbf{hebrew-epoch})$$

$$\textit{av}_9 = \textbf{fixed-from-hebrew}\left(\boxed{\textit{h-year}\;|\;\textbf{av}\;|\;9}\right)$$

Tzom Tevet, which can never occur on Saturday, must be handled with (8.42) in Section 8.5 below, because Tevet 10 can fall on either side of January 1, and thus a single Gregorian calendar year can have 0, 1, or 2 occurrences of Tzom Tevet. For example, Tzom Tevet occurred twice in 1982 but not at all in 1984. We leave it to the reader to work out the details. For the foreseeable future, other Jewish holidays and fasts occur exactly once in each Gregorian year, because the Hebrew leap months and Gregorian leap days keep the two calendars closely aligned.

Yom ha-Shoah (Holocaust Memorial Day) is Nisan 27, unless that day is a Sunday (it cannot be a Saturday), in which case it is postponed by 1 day.[14] Yom ha-Zikkaron (Israel Memorial Day), nominally on Iyyar 4, is advanced to Wednesday if it falls on a Thursday or Friday, and delayed to Monday if it falls on a Sunday.[15]

---

[14] This exception was introduced by the Israeli Knesset in May 1997.

[15] This delay was instituted by the Israeli government in 2004, when it was decided that Yom ha-Zikkaron, as well as Israel Independence Day (normally on Iyyar 5), should be postponed by one day whenever Iyyar 4 falls on a Sunday.

Since Iyyar 4 can never fall on Monday, Wednesday, or Saturday, Yom ha-Zikkaron falls on Iyyar 4 only if the latter is a Tuesday. Thus, we write

$$\textbf{yom-ha-zikkaron}\,(\textit{g-year}) \stackrel{\text{def}}{=} \tag{8.36}$$

$$\begin{cases} \textbf{kday-before}\,(\textbf{wednesday}, \textit{iyyar}_4) & \\ \qquad\qquad \textbf{if day-of-week-from-fixed}\,(\textit{iyyar}_4) \in \{\textbf{thursday}, \textbf{friday}\} & \\ \textit{iyyar}_4 + 1 \quad \textbf{if sunday} = \textbf{day-of-week-from-fixed}\,(\textit{iyyar}_4) & \\ \textit{iyyar}_4 \quad \textbf{otherwise} & \end{cases}$$

where

$$\textit{h-year} = \textit{g-year} - \textbf{gregorian-year-from-fixed}\,(\textbf{hebrew-epoch})$$

$$\textit{iyyar}_4 = \textbf{fixed-from-hebrew}\left(\boxed{\textit{h-year} \mid \textbf{iyyar} \mid 4}\right)$$

On the Hebrew calendar, the first day of each month is called Rosh Ḥodesh and has a minor ritual significance. When the preceding month has 30 days, Rosh Ḥodesh includes also the last day of the preceding month. The determination of these days is elementary (except for the months of Kislev and Tevet, because of the varying length of the months that precede those two).

Some other dates of significance depend on the Julian-Coptic approximation of the tropical year (equinox to equinox), in which each of the four seasons is taken to be $91\frac{5}{16}$ days long: The beginning of *sh'ela* (request for rain) outside Israel, meant to correspond to the start of the sixtieth Hebrew day after the autumnal equinox, corresponds to Athōr 26 on the Coptic calendar and follows the same leap-year structure. (See Chapter 4.) Hence, we write

$$\textbf{sh-ela}\,(\textit{g-year}) \stackrel{\text{def}}{=} \textbf{coptic-in-gregorian}\,(3, 26, \textit{g-year}) \tag{8.37}$$

which is either December 5 or 6 (Gregorian) during the twentieth and twenty-first centuries (see [22]). As with most other Jewish holidays and events, sh'ela actually begins on the prior evening. In Israel, sh'ela begins on Marḥeshvan 7.

By one traditional Hebrew reckoning, attributed to the second century scholar Samuel of Nehardea, the vernal equinox of A.M. 5685 was at 6 p.m. on the eve of Wednesday, Paremotep 30, 1641, which is March 26, 1925 C.E. (Julian). It recurs on that day of the Coptic and Julian calendars and at that hour of the week every 28 years in what is called the *solar cycle* and is celebrated as *birkath haḥama*. Because 1641 mod 28 = 17, we can write

$$\textbf{birkath-ha-hama}\,(\textit{g-year}) \stackrel{\text{def}}{=} \tag{8.38}$$

$$\begin{cases} \textit{dates} \quad \textbf{if } \textit{dates} \neq \langle\,\rangle \text{ and} & \\ \qquad \left(\left(\textbf{coptic-from-fixed}\,(\textit{dates}_{[0]})\right)_{\textbf{year}} \bmod 28\right) = 17 & \\ \langle\,\rangle \quad \textbf{otherwise} & \end{cases}$$

where

$$dates = \textbf{coptic-in-gregorian}\,(7, 30, \textit{g-year})$$

(The bracketed subscript 0 extracts the first element of a list.) This function returns an empty list for the 27 out of 28 years in which this event does not occur.

These two functions, **sh-ela** and **birkath-ha-hama**, could alternatively be implemented as part of a Hebrew solar calendar, thereby avoiding the use of the Coptic calendar. First, we find when spring occurs according to Samuel of Nehardea's reckoning:

$$\textbf{samuel-season-in-gregorian}\,(\textit{season}, \textit{g-year}) \stackrel{\text{def}}{=} \tag{8.39}$$

$$\textbf{cycle-in-gregorian}\left(\textit{season}, \textit{g-year}, Y, \textbf{fixed-from-hebrew}\left(\boxed{1 \mid \textbf{adar} \mid 21}\right) + 18^{\text{h}} + \textit{offset}\right)$$

where

$$Y = 365 + 6^{\text{h}}$$

$$\textit{offset} = \frac{\textit{season}}{360^\circ} \times Y$$

Then it is an easy matter to check whether it meets the criteria for *birkath haḥama*:

$$\textbf{alt-birkath-ha-hama}\,(\textit{g-year}) \stackrel{\text{def}}{=} \tag{8.40}$$

$$\begin{cases} \langle \textbf{fixed-from-moment}\,(\textit{moments}_{[0]}) \rangle & \textbf{if } \textit{moments} \neq \langle\,\rangle \text{ and} \\ & \quad \textbf{day-of-week-from-fixed}\,(\textit{moments}_{[0]}) = \textbf{wednesday} \text{ and} \\ & \quad \textbf{time-from-moment}\,(\textit{moments}_{[0]}) = 0^{\text{h}} \\ \langle\,\rangle & \textbf{otherwise} \end{cases}$$

where

$$Y = 365 + 6^{\text{h}}$$

$$\textit{season} = \textbf{spring} + 6^{\text{h}} \times \frac{360^\circ}{Y}$$

$$\textit{moments} = \textbf{samuel-season-in-gregorian}\,(\textit{season}, \textit{g-year})$$

A similar function can be constructed for sh'ela.

Another traditional Hebrew determination of seasons is attributed to one Rabbi Adda bar Ahava by Savasorda. It derives the year length from the assumption that the Metonic cycle provides a perfect correspondence between 19 solar years and 225 lunar months of length $29^{\text{d}}12^{\text{h}}44^{\text{m}}3\frac{1}{3}^{\text{s}}$. That gives a value of $365^{\text{d}}5^{\text{h}}55^{\text{m}}25\frac{25}{57}^{\text{s}}$

for the length of one year. Taking 6 p.m. in the evening on Adar 28, 1 A.M., to be a spring equinox leads to the following:

$$\textbf{adda-season-in-gregorian}\,(\textit{season}, \textit{g-year}) \stackrel{\text{def}}{=} \tag{8.41}$$

$$\textbf{cycle-in-gregorian}\left(\textit{season}, \textit{g-year}, Y, \textbf{fixed-from-hebrew}\left(\boxed{1 \mid \textbf{adar} \mid 28}\right) + 18^{\text{h}} + \textit{offset}\right)$$

where

$$Y = 365 + 5\tfrac{3791}{4104}{}^{\text{h}}$$

$$\textit{offset} = \frac{\textit{season}}{360^\circ} \times Y$$

8.5 The Drift of the Hebrew Calendar

I've been on a calendar, but never on time.
Marilyn Monroe: *Look* (1957)

The average Hebrew year length of about 365.2468 days (page 116) is slightly too long, meaning that the Hebrew year will drift slowly through the Gregorian year (which closely approximates the mean tropical year). This drift means, for example, that Passover will get later and later in the Gregorian year, as illustrated in Figure 8.2, which shows the advancing difference between the first day of Passover and the spring equinox. Although this will not be of practical concern for millennia, in general, in determining when a given Hebrew date will fall in a given Gregorian year, one needs to consider three Hebrew years for the given Gregorian year, just as we did for Islamic dates at the end of the previous chapter. We thus write:

$$\textbf{hebrew-in-gregorian}\,(\textit{h-month}, \textit{h-day}, \textit{g-year}) \stackrel{\text{def}}{=} \tag{8.42}$$

$$\{\textit{date}_0, \textit{date}_1, \textit{date}_2\} \cap \textbf{gregorian-year-range}\,(\textit{g-year})$$

where

$$\textit{jan}_1 = \textbf{gregorian-new-year}\,(\textit{g-year})$$

$$y = (\textbf{hebrew-from-fixed}\,(\textit{jan}_1))_{\textbf{year}}$$

$$\textit{date}_0 = \textbf{fixed-from-hebrew}\left(\boxed{y \mid \textit{h-month} \mid \textit{h-day}}\right)$$

$$\textit{date}_1 = \textbf{fixed-from-hebrew}\left(\boxed{y+1 \mid \textit{h-month} \mid \textit{h-day}}\right)$$

$$\textit{date}_2 = \textbf{fixed-from-hebrew}\left(\boxed{y+2 \mid \textit{h-month} \mid \textit{h-day}}\right)$$

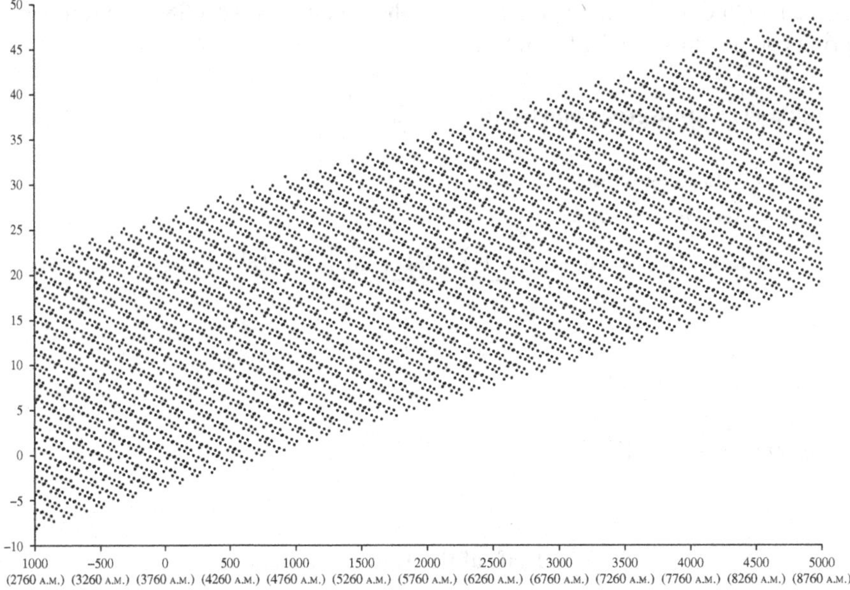

Figure 8.2 Number of days after the spring equinox that the first day of Passover occurs for Gregorian years −1000 to 5000 (= 2760–8760 A.M.). By Gregorian year 5000, Passover will occur, on the average, more than a full month after the spring equinox, whereas it should always occur within 30 days or so.

For example, in the Gregorian year 22336 (but not before), Yom Kippur occurs on January 11 and again on December 30, neither in the same Hebrew year as January 1.

Using the above robust function, we would compute the occurrences of the first day of Hanukkah as follows:

$$\textbf{hanukkah}\,(g\text{-}year) \stackrel{\text{def}}{=} \textbf{hebrew-in-gregorian}\,(\textbf{kislev}, 25, g\text{-}year) \tag{8.43}$$

Because of the drift, there are no occurrences of Kislev 25 in the year 4999, but two in 5000.

8.6 Personal Days

Most modern calendars mar the sweet simplicity of our lives by reminding us that each day that passes is the anniversary of some perfectly uninteresting event.

Oscar Wilde: "A New Calendar," *Pall Mall Gazette* (February 1887)

The Hebrew calendar contains what we might term "personal" days: one's birthday according to the Hebrew calendar determines the day of one's *Bat Mitzvah* (for girls) or *Bar Mitzvah* (for boys) (the 12th or 13th birthday). Dates of death determine when *Kaddish* is recited (*yahrzeit*, *naḥala*) for parents (and sometimes for other relatives). These are ordinarily just anniversary dates, but the leap-year structure and the varying number of days in some months require that alternative days be used in certain years, just as someone born on February 29 on the Gregorian calendar has to celebrate on an alternative day in common years.

The birthday of someone born in Adar of an ordinary year or Adar II of a leap year is also always in the last month of the year, be that Adar or Adar II. The birthday in an ordinary year of someone born during the first 29 days of Adar I in a leap year is on the corresponding day of Adar; in a leap year, the birthday occurs in Adar I, as expected. Someone born on the thirtieth day of Marḥeshvan, Kislev, or Adar I has his or her birthday postponed until the first of the following month, in years when that day does not occur. First, we write a function to determine the anniversary date in a given Hebrew year:

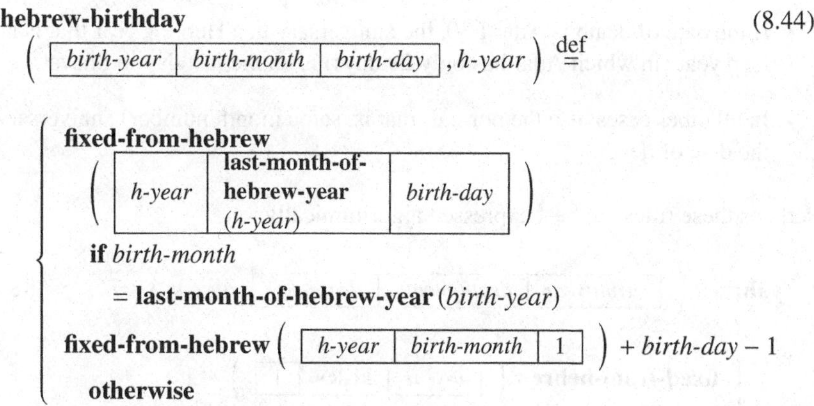

$$\textbf{hebrew-birthday}\left(\boxed{\textit{birth-year} \mid \textit{birth-month} \mid \textit{birth-day}}, \textit{h-year}\right) \stackrel{\text{def}}{=} \tag{8.44}$$

$$\begin{cases} \textbf{fixed-from-hebrew}\left(\boxed{\textit{h-year} \mid \textbf{last-month-of-hebrew-year}\,(\textit{h-year}) \mid \textit{birth-day}}\right) & \textbf{if } \textit{birth-month} = \textbf{last-month-of-hebrew-year}\,(\textit{birth-year}) \\ \textbf{fixed-from-hebrew}\left(\boxed{\textit{h-year} \mid \textit{birth-month} \mid 1}\right) + \textit{birth-day} - 1 & \textbf{otherwise} \end{cases}$$

Unlike for the Islamic calendar, it will be many millennia before the Hebrew and Gregorian New Years coincide. Hence, a Gregorian year always comprises part of two (and eventually, millennia from now, three) Hebrew years. Thus we can collect a list of anniversaries in the possible Hebrew years:

$$\textbf{hebrew-birthday-in-gregorian}\,(\textit{birthdate}, \textit{g-year}) \stackrel{\text{def}}{=} \tag{8.45}$$

$$\{\textit{date}_0, \textit{date}_1, \textit{date}_2\} \cap \textbf{gregorian-year-range}\,(\textit{g-year})$$

where

$$\begin{aligned} \textit{jan}_1 &= \textbf{gregorian-new-year}\,(\textit{g-year}) \\ y &= (\textbf{hebrew-from-fixed}\,(\textit{jan}_1))_{\textbf{year}} \\ \textit{date}_0 &= \textbf{hebrew-birthday}\,(\textit{birthdate}, y) \\ \textit{date}_1 &= \textbf{hebrew-birthday}\,(\textit{birthdate}, y+1) \\ \textit{date}_2 &= \textbf{hebrew-birthday}\,(\textit{birthdate}, y+2) \end{aligned}$$

Similar functions for birthdays can be written for other calendars with variable-length years.

The customary anniversary date of a death is more complicated and depends also on the character of the year in which the first anniversary occurs. There are several cases:

- If the date of death is Marḥeshvan 30, the anniversary in general depends on when the *first* anniversary occurs; if that first anniversary was not on Marḥeshvan 30, use the day before Kislev 1.
- If the date of death is Kislev 30, in general the anniversary again depends on the first anniversary—if that was not Kislev 30, use the day before Tevet 1.
- If the date of death is in Adar II, the anniversary is on the same day in the last month of the Hebrew year (Adar or Adar II).
- If the date of death is Adar I 30, the anniversary in a Hebrew year that is not a leap year (in which Adar has only 29 days) is on the last day in Shevat.
- In all other cases, use the normal (that is, same month number) anniversary of the date of death.

Perhaps these rules are best expressed algorithmically:

$$\mathbf{yahrzeit}\left(\boxed{\textit{death-year} \mid \textit{death-month} \mid \textit{death-day}}, \textit{h-year}\right) \stackrel{\text{def}}{=} \tag{8.46}$$

$$\begin{cases}
\mathbf{fixed\text{-}from\text{-}hebrew}\left(\boxed{\textit{h-year} \mid \mathbf{kislev} \mid 1}\right) - 1 \\
\quad \textbf{if } \textit{death-month} = \mathbf{marheshvan} \text{ and } \textit{death-day} = 30 \text{ and} \\
\qquad \text{not } \mathbf{long\text{-}marheshvan?}\,(\textit{death-year} + 1) \\
\mathbf{fixed\text{-}from\text{-}hebrew}\left(\boxed{\textit{h-year} \mid \mathbf{tevet} \mid 1}\right) - 1 \\
\quad \textbf{if } \textit{death-month} = \mathbf{kislev} \text{ and } \textit{death-day} = 30 \text{ and} \\
\qquad \mathbf{short\text{-}kislev?}\,(\textit{death-year} + 1) \\
\mathbf{fixed\text{-}from\text{-}hebrew} \\
\quad \left(\boxed{\textit{h-year} \mid \begin{array}{l}\mathbf{last\text{-}month\text{-}of\text{-}} \\ \mathbf{hebrew\text{-}year} \\ (\textit{h-year})\end{array} \mid \textit{death-day}}\right) \\
\quad \textbf{if } \textit{death-month} = \mathbf{adarii} \\
\mathbf{fixed\text{-}from\text{-}hebrew}\left(\boxed{\textit{h-year} \mid \mathbf{shevat} \mid 30}\right) \\
\quad \textbf{if } \textit{death-day} = 30 \text{ and } \textit{death-month} = \mathbf{adar} \text{ and} \\
\qquad \text{not } \mathbf{hebrew\text{-}leap\text{-}year?}\,(\textit{h-year}) \\
\mathbf{fixed\text{-}from\text{-}hebrew}\left(\boxed{\textit{h-year} \mid \textit{death-month} \mid 1}\right) + \textit{death-day} - 1 \\
\quad \textbf{otherwise}
\end{cases}$$

There are minor variations in custom regarding the anniversary date in some of these cases.[16] For example, Spanish and Portuguese Jews never observe the anniversary of a common-year date in Adar I.

As with birthdays, anniversaries all occurring in a given Gregorian year must be collected together:

$$\textbf{yahrzeit-in-gregorian}\,(\textit{death-date}, \textit{g-year}) \stackrel{\text{def}}{=} \tag{8.47}$$

$$\{\textit{date}_0, \textit{date}_1, \textit{date}_2\} \cap \textbf{gregorian-year-range}\,(\textit{g-year})$$

where

$$\begin{aligned}
\textit{jan}_1 &= \textbf{gregorian-new-year}\,(\textit{g-year})\\
y &= (\textbf{hebrew-from-fixed}\,(\textit{jan}_1))_{\textbf{year}}\\
\textit{date}_0 &= \textbf{yahrzeit}\,(\textit{death-date}, y)\\
\textit{date}_1 &= \textbf{yahrzeit}\,(\textit{death-date}, y+1)\\
\textit{date}_2 &= \textbf{yahrzeit}\,(\textit{death-date}, y+2)
\end{aligned}$$

8.7 Possible Days of the Week

These budget numbers are not just estimates; these are the actual results for the fiscal year that ended February the 30th.

George W. Bush: President Bush Discusses the Economy and Budget (October 2006)

As described on page 117, the Hebrew calendar rule *lo iddo rosh* precludes Tishri 1 (Rosh ha-Shanah) from occurring on a Sunday, Wednesday, or Friday. This restriction means that, throughout the year, some dates are precluded from occurring on certain weekdays. In this section, we examine the consequences of the restriction, developing a function that gives, for each Hebrew calendar date, a list of the possible weekdays on which it can occur. It turns out that, though a Hebrew year can begin on any of four weekdays, can be leap or ordinary, and can be long (355 for ordinary years and 385 for leap years), short (353 or 383), or regular (354 or 384), only 14 of the $4 \times 2 \times 3 = 24$ combinations are actually possible.

The Tishri 1 restriction means that that date can occur only on a Monday, Tuesday, Thursday, or Saturday. Because the lengths of the months Nisan through Tishri are unvarying, the $177 \equiv 2 \pmod 7$ days separating the previous Nisan 1 from the following Tishri 1 mean that Nisan 1 occurs only on a Saturday, Sunday, Tuesday, or Thursday. Thus, we can determine the possible weekdays for a given Hebrew date by working forward from Nisan 1. The fixed lengths of the months Nisan through Tishri mean that for any date *h-month*, *h-day* from Nisan 1 through Marheshvan 29,

[16] The rules described accord with Ashkenazic practice as given in [22] and in the *Talmudic Encyclopedia: A Digest of Halachic Literature from the Tannaitic Period to the Present Time Alphabetically Arranged*, Talmudic Encyclopedia Publishing, Jerusalem, vol. I (1951), p. 93; vol. XXIII (1997), cols. 153–154. However, M. Feinstein (*Iggerot Moshe*, vol. 6, *Yoreh Deah*, part 3, p. 426) rules that *yahrzeit* anniversaries of the last day of a month follow the rules for birthdays.

the list of possible weekdays can be obtained by adding the number of days from Nisan 1 to *h-month*, *h-day* to each value in the list

$$\langle \textbf{sunday}, \textbf{tuesday}, \textbf{thursday}, \textbf{saturday} \rangle \tag{8.48}$$

and applying **day-of-week-from-fixed** to the sum. We use the function

$$\textbf{shift-days}\,(l, \Delta) \stackrel{\text{def}}{=} \tag{8.49}$$

$$\begin{cases} \langle\,\rangle & \textbf{if } l = \langle\,\rangle \\ \langle (l_{[0]} + \Delta) \bmod 7 \rangle \parallel \textbf{shift-days}\,(l_{[1..]}, \Delta) & \textbf{otherwise} \end{cases}$$

to shift a list such as (8.48) by a given increment.

Marheshvan 30 is exceptional, however. Although Marheshvan 29 can be a Thursday, Marheshvan 30 cannot fall on a Friday: for Marheshvan 29 to be on a Thursday, Tishri 1 must have been on a Tuesday. Marheshvan has 30 days only when the year is 355 or 385 days long. But if a 355-day year began on a Tuesday, the following year would start on a Sunday, violating *lo iddo rosh*. And for a leap year to be extended to 385 days, it would have to begin on a permissible day that is preceded by an excluded day, so that the molad of the year following the leap year—which is just under 384 days after the molad of the leap year—falls on the excluded day and is thereby delayed. Tuesday is not such a day, since Monday is also a permissible day, so a long leap year cannot begin on a Tuesday.

In a year in which Marheshvan has 30 days, there are $236 \equiv 2 \bmod 7$ days between Nisan 1 and Marheshvan 30; that date falling on a Friday would correspond to Nisan 1 falling on a Sunday. So, the possible weekdays for any Hebrew date Nisan–Marheshvan can be found by including **sunday** in the list (8.48) only for dates from Nisan 1 through Marheshvan 29, finding the number of days from Nisan 1 to *h-month*, *h-day*, and applying **shift-days** with that increment to the list.

Other dates in the year are affected by three factors: whether Marheshvan is long (30 days) or short (29 days), whether Kislev is long or short, and whether the year is a leap year. For example, the calculations described in the previous paragraph hold for days in Kislev when Marheshvan does not have 30 days. When Marheshvan does have 30 days, the calculation is off by one day, meaning that it is as though Nisan 1 occurred on a Wednesday, Friday, or Sunday, the days following the days in the list (8.48) with Sunday omitted. Thus, for dates in Kislev, we can find possible weekdays by augmenting (8.48) with

$$\langle \textbf{sunday}, \textbf{wednesday}, \textbf{friday} \rangle$$

and applying **shift-days** to the augmented list. Similar considerations apply for the months Tevet through Adar or Adar II in leap years.

We can calculate the interval between Nisan 1 and *h-month*, *h-day* in any leap year in which both Marheshvan and Kislev are long (a maximal 385-day Hebrew year, so that every month-day combination occurs), adjusting the contents of the list of weekdays equivalent to Nisan 1 as needed. We arbitrarily choose the 385-day Hebrew year 5–6 A.M. The resulting calculation is thus

$$\textbf{possible-hebrew-days}\,(\textit{h-month}, \textit{h-day}) \stackrel{\text{def}}{=} \tag{8.50}$$

$$\textbf{shift-days}\,(\textit{basic} \parallel \textit{extra}, n)$$

where

$$\textit{h-date}_0 = \boxed{5 \mid \textbf{nisan} \mid 1}$$

$$\textit{h-year} = \begin{cases} 6 & \textbf{if } \textit{h-month} > \textbf{elul} \\ 5 & \textbf{otherwise} \end{cases}$$

$$\textit{h-date} = \boxed{\textit{h-year} \mid \textit{h-month} \mid \textit{h-day}}$$

$$n = \textbf{fixed-from-hebrew}\,(\textit{h-date}) - \textbf{fixed-from-hebrew}\,(\textit{h-date}_0)$$

$$\textit{basic} = \langle \textbf{tuesday}, \textbf{thursday}, \textbf{saturday} \rangle$$

$$\textit{extra} = \begin{cases} \langle\,\rangle & \textbf{if } \textit{h-month} = \textbf{marheshvan} \text{ and } \textit{h-day} = 30 \\ \langle \textbf{monday}, \textbf{wednesday}, \textbf{friday} \rangle & \\ & \textbf{if } \textit{h-month} = \textbf{kislev} \text{ and } \textit{h-day} < 30 \\ \langle \textbf{monday} \rangle & \textbf{if } \textit{h-month} = \textbf{kislev} \text{ and } \textit{h-day} = 30 \\ \langle \textbf{sunday}, \textbf{monday} \rangle & \textbf{if } \textit{h-month} \in \{\textbf{tevet}, \textbf{shevat}\} \\ \langle \textbf{sunday}, \textbf{monday} \rangle & \textbf{if } \textit{h-month} = \textbf{adar} \text{ and } \textit{h-day} < 30 \\ \langle \textbf{sunday} \rangle & \textbf{otherwise} \end{cases}$$

This function produces an unsorted list of possible weekdays for the specified Hebrew date. For example, it tells us that Tu B'Shevat (Shevat 15) can occur only on a Thursday, Saturday, Monday, Tuesday, or Wednesday; that is, it can never occur on a Sunday or Friday.

The above function combines those weekdays on which a given date can occur in leap years with those on which it can occur in nonleap years. In particular, there is a difference in possible dates during the twelfth month, depending on whether it is Adar in a plain (common) year or Adar I in a leap year, that is not reflected in **possible-hebrew-days**. One can write a similar function that gives weekdays for leap and nonleap years separately.

References

[1] E. R. Berlekamp, J. H. Conway, and R. K. Guy, *Winning Ways, vol. 2, Games in Particular*, Academic Press, New York, 1982.

[2] al-Bīrūnī (= Abū-Raiḥān Muḥammad ibn 'Aḥmad al-Bīrūnī), *Al-Āthār al-Bāqiyah 'an al-Qurūn al-Khāliyah*, 1000. Translated and annotated by C. E. Sachau as *The Chronology of Ancient Nations*, William H. Allen and Co., London, 1879; reprinted by Hijra International Publishers, Lahore, Pakistan, 1983.

[3] H. Y. Bornstein, *Maḥloket Rav Sa'adyah Ga'on u-Ven Me'ir bi-Kevi'at Shenot 4672–4674* (= *The Dispute Between Sa'adia Gaon and Ben-Meir Regarding the Character of Years 4672–4674*), Warsaw, 1904.

[4] S. B. Burnaby, *Elements of the Jewish and Muhammadan Calendars, with Rules and Tables and Explanatory Notes on the Julian and Gregorian Calendars*, George Bell and Sons, London, 1901.

[5] N. Bushwick, *Understanding the Jewish Calendar*, Moznaim Publishing Corp., New York, 1989.

[6] E. Carlebach, *Palaces of Time: Jewish Calendar and Culture in Early Modern Europe*, Belknap Press of Harvard University Press, Cambridge, MA, 2011.

[7] W. M. Feldman, *Rabbinical Mathematics and Astronomy*, M. L. Cailingold, London, 1931; 3rd, corrected, edn., Sepher-Hermon Press, New York, 1978.

[8] M. Friedländer, "Calendar," in *The Jewish Encyclopedia*, I. Singer, ed., Funk and Wagnalls, New York, 1906.

[9] C. F. Gauss, "Berechnung des jüdischen Osterfestes," *Monatliche Correspondenz zur Beförderung der Erd- und Himmels-Kunde*, Herausgegeben vom Freiherrn von Zach (May 1802). Reprinted in Gauss's *Werke*, Herausgegeben von der Königlichen Gesellschaft der Wissenschaften, Göttingen, vol. 6, pp. 80–81, 1874.

[10] N. Golb, "Ben-Meir, Aaron," in *Encyclopædia Judaica*, C. Roth, ed., vol. 4, Macmillan, New York, 1971. Translated from *Encyclopædia Hebraica*, Jerusalem, 1960.

[11] I. Israeli, *Yesod Olam*, 1310. Published as *Liber Jesod Olam seu Fundamentum Mundi: Opus Astronomicum Celeberrimum, ex codice manuscripto denuo ediderunt, rextum emendarunt, notas adjecerunt, nec non versionem epiromariam vernacuam addendam curaverunt*, B. Goldberg & L. Rosenkranz, Berolini (Berlin), 1846/1848.

[12] M. M. Kasher, Appendix to "Exodus," *Torah Shelemah* (= *Complete Torah*): *Talmudic-Midrashic Encyclopedia of the Pentateuch*, vol. 13, American Biblical Encyclopedia Society, New York, 1949.

[13] al-Khowārizmī (= Abu Ja'far Mohammed ibn Mūsā al-Khowārizmī), *Fi istikhraj ta'rikh al-yahud*. Translated by T. Langermann, *Assufoth*, Jerusalem, pp. 159–168, 1987.

[14] L. Levi, *Jewish Chrononomy: The Calendar and Times of Day in Jewish Law*, Gur Aryeh Institute for Advanced Jewish Scholarship, Brooklyn, NY, 1967. Revised edition published under the title *Halachic Times for Home and Travel*, Rubin Mass, Ltd., Jerusalem, 1992; expanded 3rd edn., 2000.

[15] Maimonides (= Moshe ben Maimon), *Mishneh Torah: Sefer Zemanim–Hilḥot Kiddush HaḤodesh*, 1178. Translated by S. Gandz

(with commentary by J. Obermann and O. Neugebauer), as *Code of Maimonides, Book Three, Treatise Eight, Sanctification of the New Moon*, Yale Judaica Series, vol. XI, Yale University Press, New Haven, CT, 1956. Addenda and corrigenda by E. J. Wiesenberg appear at the end of *Code of Maimonides, Book Three, The Book of Seasons*, translated by S. Gandz and H. Klein, Yale Judaica Series, vol. XIV, Yale University Press, New Haven, CT, 1961.

[16] O. Neugebauer, "The origin of 'System B' of Babylonian astronomy," *Centaurus*, vol. 14, pp. 209–214, 1968.

[17] S. A. Poznański, "Calendar (Jewish)," in *Encyclopædia of Religion and Ethics*, J. Hastings, edn., vol. III, pp. 117–124, Charles Scribner's Sons, New York, 1911.

[18] L. A. Resnikoff, "Jewish Calendar Calculations," *Scripta Mathematica*, vol. 9, pp. 191–195, 274–277, 1943.

[19] Savasorda (= Abraham bar Ḥiyya al-Bargeloní), *Sefer ha-'Ibbūr*, 1122. Edited and printed by H. Filipowski, Longman, Brown, Green, and Longmans, London, 1851.

[20] H. S. Slonimski, *Yesōde ha-'Ibbūr* (= *Basic Intercalation*), H. N. Schriftgisser, Warsaw, 1852. Second edn., I. Bakst, Zitomir, 1865.

[21] N. Slonimski, "My Grandfather Invented the Telegraph," *Commentary*, vol. 63, no. 1, pp. 56–60, 1977.

[22] A. Spier, *The Comprehensive Hebrew Calendar: Its Structure, History, and One Hundred Years of Corresponding Dates: 5660–5760, 1900–2000*, Behrman House, New York, 1952. Revised 2nd edition published with the new subtitle *Up to the Twenty-Second Century 5703–5860, 1943–2100*, Feldheim Publishers, New York, 1981. Revised 3rd edition published with the new subtitle *Twentieth to Twenty-Second Centuries, 5660–5860, 1900–2100*, Feldheim Publishers, New York, 1986.

[23] S. Stern, *Calendar and Community: A History of the Jewish Calendar, 2nd Century BCE to 10th Century CE*, Oxford University Press, Oxford, 2001.

[24] E. J. Wiesenberg, "Calendar," in *Encyclopædia Judaica*, C. Roth, ed., Macmillan, New York, 1971.

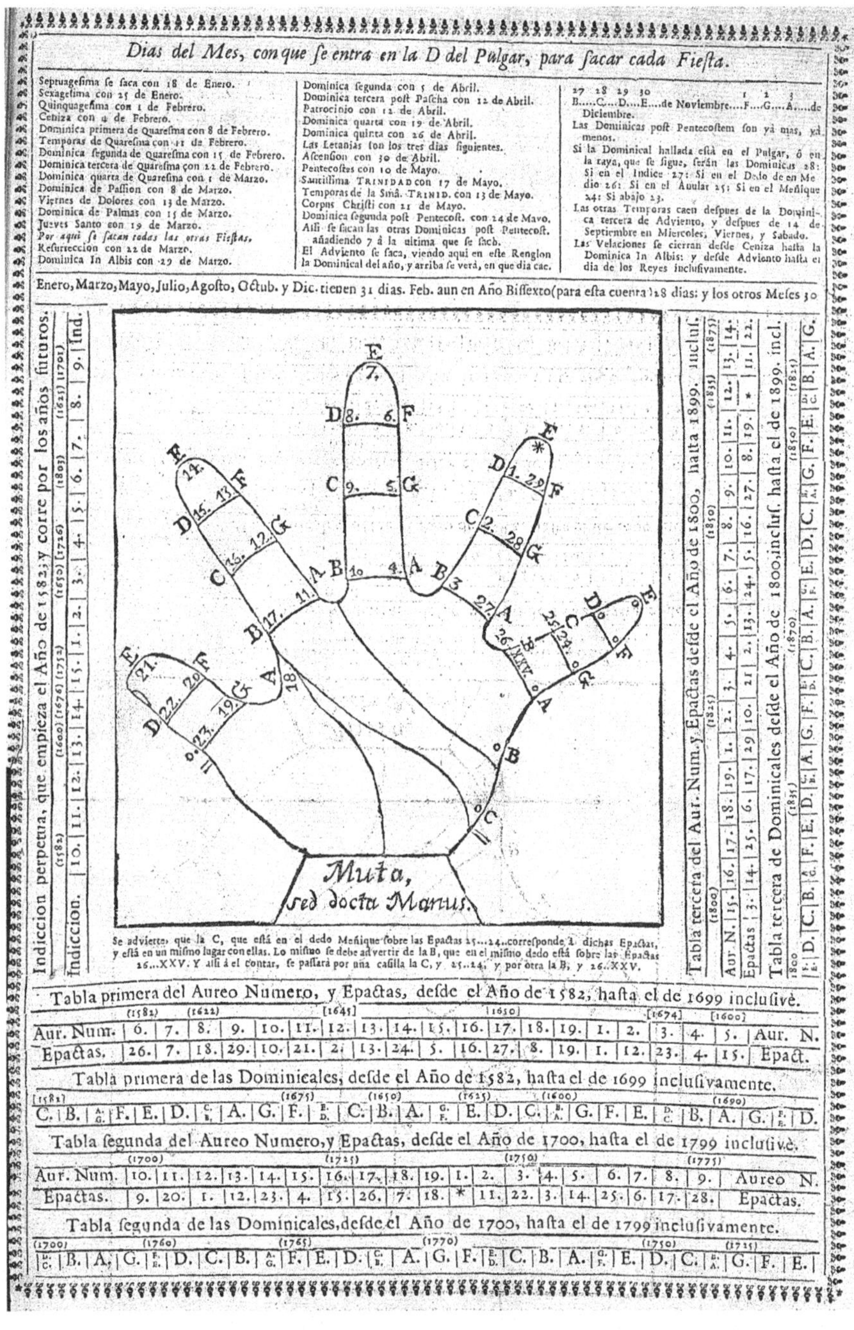

Dias del Mes, con que se entra en la D del Pulgar, para sacar cada Fiesta.

Septuagesima se saca con 18 de Enero.
Sexagesima con 25 de Enero.
Quinquagesima con 1 de Febrero.
Ceniza con 4 de Febrero.
Dominica primera de Quaresma con 8 de Febrero.
Temporas de Quaresma con 11 de Febrero.
Dominica segunda de Quaresma con 15 de Febrero.
Dominica tercera de Quaresma con 22 de Febrero.
Dominica quarta de Quaresma con 1 de Marzo.
Dominica de Passion con 8 de Marzo.
Viernes de Dolores con 13 de Marzo.
Dominica de Palmas con 15 de Marzo.
Jueves Santo con 19 de Marzo.
Por aqui se sacan todas las otras Fiestas,
Resurreccion con 22 de Marzo.
Dominica In Albis con 29 de Marzo.

Dominica segunda con 5 de Abril.
Dominica tercera post Pascha con 12 de Abril.
Patrocinio con 12 de Abril.
Dominica quarta con 19 de Abril.
Dominica quinta con 26 de Abril.
Las Letanias son los tres dias siguientes.
Ascension con 30 de Abril.
Pentecostes con 10 de Mayo.
Santissima TRINIDAD con 17 de Mayo.
Temporas de la Smâ. TRINID. con 13 de Mayo.
Corpus Christi con 21 de Mayo.
Dominica segunda post Pentecost. con 24 de Mayo.
Assi se sacan las otras Dominicas post Pentecost. añadiendo 7 à la ultima que se sacò.
El Adviento se saca, viendo aqui en este Renglon la Dominical del año, y arriba se verá, en que dia cae.

27 28 29 30 1 2 3
B.....C....D....E....de Noviembre....F....G....A.....de Diciembre.
Las Dominicas post Pentecostem son yà mas, yà menos.
Si la Dominical hallada està en el Pulgar, ò en la raya, que se sigue, serán las Dominicas 28: Si en el Indice 27: Si en el Dedo de en Medio 26: Si en el Anular 25: Si en el Meñique 24: Si abajo 23.
Las otras Temporas caen despues de la Dominica tercera de Adviento, y despues de 14 de Septiembre en Miercoles, Viernes, y Sabado.
Las Velaciones se cierran desde Ceniza hasta la Dominica In Albis: y desde Adviento hasta el dia de los Reyes inclusivamente.

Enero, Marzo, Mayo, Julio, Agosto, Octub. y Dic. tienen 31 dias. Feb. aun en Año Bissexto (para esta cuenta) 28 dias: y los otros Meses 30

Indiccion perpetua, que empieza el Año de 1582, y corre por los años futuros.

Indiccion.	10.	11.	12.	13.	14.	15.	1.	2.	3.	4.	5.	6.	7.	8.	9.	Ind.

Se advierte, que la C, que està en el dedo Meñique sobre las Epactas 25...24..corresponde à dichas Epactas, y està en un mismo lugar con ellas. Lo mismo se debe advertir de la B, que en el mismo dedo està sobre las Epactas 26...XXV. Y assi à el contar, se passarà por una casilla la C, y 25..24, y por otra la B, y 26..XXV.

Tabla tercera del Aur. Num. y Epactas desde el Año de 1800, hasta 1899. inclus.

Aur. N.	15.	16.	17.	18.	19.	1.	2.	3.	4.	5.	6.	7.	8.	9.	10.	11.	12.	13.	14.
Epactas	3.	14.	25.	6.	17.	29	10.	21	2.	13.	24.	5.	16.	27.	8.	19.	*	11.	22.

Tabla tercera de Dominicales desde el Año de 1800, inclus. hasta el de 1899. incl.

F/E.	D.	C.	B.	A/G.	F.	E.	D.	C/B.	A.	G.	F.	E/D.	C.	B.	A.	G/F.	E.	D.	C.	B/A.	G.	F.	E.	D/C.	B.	A.	G.

Tabla primera del Aureo Numero, y Epactas, desde el Año de 1582, hasta el de 1699 inclusivè.

Aur. Num.	6.	7.	8.	9.	10.	11.	12.	13.	14.	15.	16.	17.	18.	19.	1.	2.	3.	4.	5.	Aur. N.
Epactas.	26.	7.	18.	29.	10.	21.	2.	13.	24.	5.	16.	27.	8.	19.	1.	12.	23.	4.	15.	Epact.

Tabla primera de las Dominicales, desde el Año de 1582, hasta el de 1699 inclusivamente.

C.	B.	A/G.	F.	E.	D.	C/B.	A.	G.	F.	E/D.	C.	B.	A.	G/F.	E.	D.	C.	B/A.	G.	F.	E.	D/C.	B.	A.	G.	F/E.	D.

Tabla segunda del Aureo Numero, y Epactas, desde el Año de 1700, hasta el de 1799 inclusivè.

Aur. Num.	10.	11.	12.	13.	14.	15.	16.	17.	18.	19.	1.	2.	3.	4.	5.	6.	7.	8.	9.	Aureo N.
Epactas.	9.	20.	1.	12.	23.	4.	15.	26.	7.	18.	*	11.	22.	3.	14.	25.	6.	17.	28.	Epactas.

Tabla segunda de las Dominicales, desde el Año de 1700, hasta el de 1799 inclusivamente.

D/C.	B.	A.	G.	F/E.	D.	C.	B.	A/G.	F.	E.	D.	C/B.	A.	G.	F.	E/D.	C.	B.	A.	G/F.	E.	D.	C.	B/A.	G.	F.	E.

Finger calculation for the date of Easter, according to the Gregorian rule, from page 14 of *Astronómica y Harmoniosa Mano* by Buenaventura Francisco de Ossorio, Bibliotheca Mexicana, Mexico, 1757. For an explanation of the calculation, see F. Cajori's "A Notable Case of Finger-Reckoning in America," *ISIS*, vol. 8, pp. 325–327, 1926. (Courtesy of the Bancroft Library, University of California, Berkeley.)

9

The Ecclesiastical Calendars

We send you the good news concerning the unanimous consent of all in reference to the celebration of the most solemn feast of Easter, for this difference also has been made up by the assistance of your prayers, so that all the brethren in the East, who formerly celebrated this festival at the same time as the Jews, will in future conform to the Romans and to us and to all who have from of old kept Easter with us.

Synodal Letter of the Council of Nicæa to the Church of Alexandria (325 C.E.)

The calculation of the date of Easter has a fascinating history, and algorithms and computer programs abound (for example, [1], [2], [9], [10], [14], and [17]); there are also oddities such as the "finger algorithm" shown in the frontispiece of this chapter and the nomogram of Figure 9.1. Many of the computations rely on the formulas of Gauss [5], [6] (see also [8]).[1] Our fixed-date approach allows considerable simplification of "classical" algorithms.

The history of the establishment of the date of Easter is long and complex; good discussions can be found in [3], [7], and [12]. The Council of Nicæa convened in 325 C.E. by Constantine the Great, was concerned with uniformity across various Christian groups. At the time of Nicæa, almost everyone in the official Church agreed to the definition that Easter was the first Sunday after the first full moon occurring on or after the vernal equinox [3] (a rule promulgated by Dionysius Exiguus and the Venerable Bede, who attributed it to the Council of Nicæa). By this definition, Easter is delayed one week if the full moon is on a Sunday, lessening the likelihood of its being on the same day as the Jewish Passover. This was contrary to the practice of the Quartodecimans, who celebrated Easter on the day of the full moon, 14 days into the month, regardless of the day of the week.

The concern that the date of Passover would influence the date of Easter goes back to the earliest days of Christianity. For example, Eusebius (*Vita Constantini*, book iii, pp. 18–20) gives a letter of the Emperor sent to those not present at the Council of Nicæa:

[1] Gauss's original paper contained an error (which he later corrected) that affects the date of Easter first in 4200 C.E.; see [14].

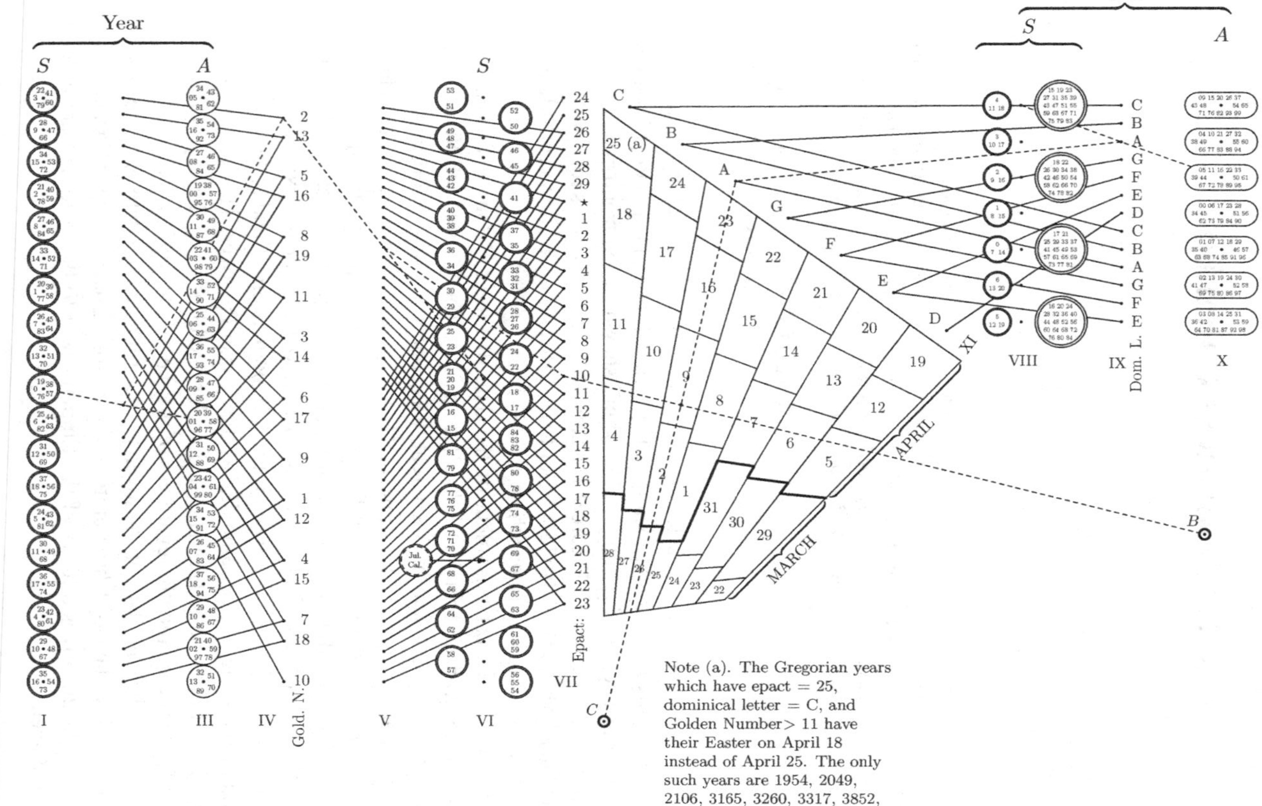

Figure 9.1 Garrigues' nomogram for finding the date of Easter in the Julian and Gregorian calendars. For an explanation, see D. Roegel, "An Introduction to Nomography," *TUGboat*, vol. 30, pp. 88–104, 2009. (Courtesy of D. Roegel.)

> When the question relative to the sacred festival of Easter arose … [i]t was declared to be particularly unworthy for this, the holiest of all festivals, to follow the custom of the Jews … We ought not, therefore, to have anything in common with the Jews … we desire, dearest brethren, to separate ourselves from the detestable company of the Jews, for it is truly shameful for us to hear them boast that without their direction we could not keep this feast. How can they be in the right, they who, after the death of the Saviour, have no longer been led by reason but by wild violence, as their delusion may urge them? They do not possess the truth in this Easter question … it would still be your duty not to tarnish your soul by communications with such wicked people.

Avoiding Passover was also evident in the Gregorian reform of the Easter calculation. Canon 6 of the Gregorian calendar, published in 1582 and probably written by the German Jesuit astronomer Christopher Clavius, says so twice: in the last sentence of the first paragraph

> *ne cum Iudaeis conveniamus, si forte dies XIV lunae caderet in diem dominicum* [so that we would not come together with the Jews if by chance day 14 of the moon may fall on a Sunday]

and in the middle of the second paragraph

> *Ne igitur cum Iudaeis conveniamus, qui Pascha celebrant die XIV lunae* … [Hence so that we would not come together with the Jews who celebrate Passover on day 14 of the moon …]

The definition of Easter as "the first Sunday after the first full moon occurring on or after the vernal equinox" seems precise, but accurate determination of the full moon and the vernal equinox is quite complex, and simpler approximations are used in practice.

9.1 Orthodox Easter

> *The rules given in Protestant Episcopal Prayer Book for computing Easter, if applied to any almanac of the present year, would make the Roman and Greek Easter come on the same day, namely, April 14, since the full moon next after the 21st of March comes on the 4th of April according to our calendar, or the 27th of March according to the Greek. But the Roman Easter this year is on the 10th of April, and the Greek is one week later … The Jewish passover this year occurs on the 9th of April, which agrees better with the Western than the Eastern Easter.*
>
> *Sunday School Times* (1887)

As implemented by Dionysius Exiguus in 525 C.E., the date of Easter is based on the presumption that the vernal equinox is always March 21 and on ecclesiastical approximations to the lunar phases called *epacts*. Epacts are computed on the basis of the fact that new moons occur on about the same day of the solar year (adjusted for leap years) in a cycle of 19 years, called the *Metonic cycle*, comprising 235 lunations (see page 7).

Before the Gregorian reform of the Julian calendar, the approximations were fairly crude. If the Metonic cycle were perfectly accurate, the phase of the moon on January 1 would be the same every 19 years. Hence, the epact can be approximated by multiplying the number of years since the start of the current Metonic cycle (the so-called golden number) by the 11-day difference between a common year of 365 days and 12 lunar months of $29\frac{1}{2}$ days and adjusting by the epact of January 1, 1 C.E. (Julian)—all this done modulo 30. To find the last full moon (that is, day 14 of the monthly cycle) prior to April 19, we subtract the phase of the moon on April 5 (14 days earlier) from the fixed date of April 19. (The number of days between full moon and April 19 is equal to the days between new moon and April 5.) The moon's phase (in days) on April 5, called the *shifted-epact* in the function below, increases by 11 days each year, modulo 30, taking on the values 14, 25, 6, 17, 28, 9, 20, 1, 12, 23, 4, 15, 26, 7, 18, 29, 10, 21, 2 in sequence. Going back that number of days from April 19 gives a date between March 21 and April 18, inclusive, for the (ecclesiastical) "paschal full moon."

Thus, the equivalent of the following calculation was used to determine Easter from the end of the eighth century until the adoption of the Gregorian calendar, and it is still used by all Orthodox churches except those in Finland and Estonia:

$$\textbf{orthodox-easter}\,(\textit{g-year}) \stackrel{\text{def}}{=} \textbf{kday-after}\,(\textbf{sunday}, \textit{paschal-moon}) \tag{9.1}$$

where

$$\textit{shifted-epact} = (14 + 11 \times (\textit{g-year} \bmod 19)) \bmod 30$$

$$\textit{j-year} = \begin{cases} \textit{g-year} & \textbf{if } \textit{g-year} > 0 \\ \textit{g-year} - 1 & \textbf{otherwise} \end{cases}$$

$$\textit{paschal-moon} = \textbf{fixed-from-julian}\left(\boxed{\textit{j-year} \mid \textbf{april} \mid 19} \right) - \textit{shifted-epact}$$

Because the shifted epact is never 0, the calculated full moon is never on April 19. The earliest date for Easter Sunday is therefore March 22 (Julian), and the latest is April 25 (Julian). By this rule, Easter and Passover have not coincided since 783 C.E.

The Julian leap-year cycle of 4 years contains 208 weeks and 5 days. Only after 28 years do all dates on the Julian calendar return to the same day of the week. The combination of this "solar" cycle and the 19-year lunar cycle gives rise to the 532-year "Victorian" or "Dionysian" cycle for the date of Orthodox Easter. The average length of a lunar month according to this method is

$$\frac{19 \times 365\frac{1}{4}}{235} \approx 29.530851 \text{ days}$$

The number of full moons between April 19 of 2 successive years can be either 12 or 13. The distribution of leap years of 13 lunar cycles and ordinary years of 12 follows the regular pattern described by formula (1.85) with $c = 19$, $l = 7$, and $\Delta = 13$, namely

$$\left\lfloor \frac{7 \times \textit{g-year} + 8}{19} \right\rfloor$$

This observation leads to an alternative formula for the fixed date of the paschal moon:

$$\textbf{alt-orthodox-easter}\,(\textit{g-year}) \stackrel{\text{def}}{=} \qquad (9.2)$$

$$\textbf{kday-after}\,(\textbf{sunday}, \textit{paschal-moon})$$

where

$$\textit{paschal-moon} = 354 \times \textit{g-year} + 30 \times \left\lfloor \tfrac{1}{19} \times (7 \times \textit{g-year} + 8) \right\rfloor + \left\lfloor \frac{\textit{g-year}}{4} \right\rfloor - \left\lfloor \frac{\textit{g-year}}{19} \right\rfloor - 273 + \textbf{gregorian-epoch}$$

The minimum 12 lunar months per year contribute 354 days; 7 out of 19 years include a thirteenth lunar month of 30 days; each leap year contributes an extra day to the total number of elapsed days; but every 19 years the lunar cycle is reset to begin one day earlier in a shift called *saltus lunae*, the "moon's leap." Subtracting 273 accounts for the fixed date of the Paschal full moon in 1 C.E., when *g-year* = 1.

9.2 Gregorian Easter

If yet your Lordship think it necessary that the seat of Easter should be rectified, that may easily be done, without altering the Civil Year. For if in the Rule of Easter, instead of saying, next after the one & twentieth of March, you say, next after the Vernal Equinox, the work is done. For then every Almanack will tell you when it is Equinox and when it is Full Moon for the present Year without disturbing the Civil Account, and this Pope Gregory might as well have done without troubling the Civil Account of Christendom.

John Wallis: Letter to the Bishop of Worcester (June 30, 1699)

The Gregorian reform of 1582 C.E. included a more accurate approximation to the lunar phases for the calculation of Easter developed by Clavius and based on the suggestions of Naples astronomer Aloysius Lilius. Two corrections and two adjustments are employed in the Gregorian rule for Easter:

- In 3 out of 4 century years, the Gregorian leap-year rule causes a shift of 1 day forward in the date of the full moon. This is taken into account in the calculation of epacts by subtracting 1 for each nonleap century year.

- The first correction keeps the lunar cycle synchronized with the Julian calendar. But 19 Julian years of 365.25 days are a fraction longer than 235 mean lunations. Thus, a corrective factor of 1 day is added to the epact in 8 out of 25 century years. The epacts of centuries 3, 6, 9, 12, 15, 19, 22, and 25 are affected by this correction. A 1-day bias is said to have been introduced deliberately in the initial sixteenth-century epact value of 5 to minimize the coincidences of Easter and Passover (which is likewise based on the 19-year Metonic cycle; see Section 8.4) [14].

- The old limits on the dates of the ecclesiastical full moon were preserved in the reformed calendar. Unfortunately, with the new century-year rule a shifted epact of 0 becomes possible, which, if used, would place the full moon on April 19. Whenever that occurs, the epact is, therefore, adjusted to 1, which pushes the full moon date back to April 18.
- Clavius also strived to retain the property that the date of the Easter moon never repeats within a single 19-year cycle. The problem is that when the previous adjustment is made and the shifted epact is set to 1 instead of 0, the same shifted epact may also occur 11 years later. The solution is again to increase any shifted epact of 1 occurring in the second half (after year 10) of a cycle.

These adjustments give the method now used by Catholic and Protestant churches:

$$\textbf{easter}\,(\textit{g-year}) \stackrel{\text{def}}{=} \textbf{kday-after}\,(\textbf{sunday}, \textit{paschal-moon}) \tag{9.3}$$

where

$$\textit{century} = \left\lfloor \frac{\textit{g-year}}{100} \right\rfloor + 1$$

$$\textit{shifted-epact} = \Big(14 + 11 \times (\textit{g-year} \bmod 19) - \left\lfloor \tfrac{3}{4} \times \textit{century} \right\rfloor + \left\lfloor \tfrac{1}{25} \times (5 + 8 \times \textit{century}) \right\rfloor \Big) \bmod 30$$

$$\textit{adjusted-epact} = \begin{cases} \textit{shifted-epact} + 1 & \textbf{if } \textit{shifted-epact} = 0 \text{ or } \{\textit{shifted-epact} = 1 \text{ and } 10 < (\textit{g-year} \bmod 19)\} \\ \textit{shifted-epact} & \textbf{otherwise} \end{cases}$$

$$\textit{paschal-moon} = \textbf{fixed-from-gregorian}\left(\boxed{\textit{g-year} \mid \textbf{april} \mid 19} \right) - \textit{adjusted-epact}$$

The sequence of dates of Easter repeats only after 5700000 years, the least common multiple of the 19-year Metonic cycle, the 400 years it takes for the Gregorian calendar to return to the same pattern of days of the week, the 4000 years it takes for the Gregorian leap-year corrections to add up to 30 days, and the 9375 years it takes for the correction to the Metonic cycle to amount to 30 days. This cycle comprises 2081882250 days and 70499183 months for an average lunar month of approximately 29.530587 days.

With the new method, over the entire 5700000 year cycle, the most likely date of Easter is April 19 (almost 4% of the years), while the least likely date is March 22 (less than 0.5%); the full distribution of dates is shown in Figure 9.2. By the

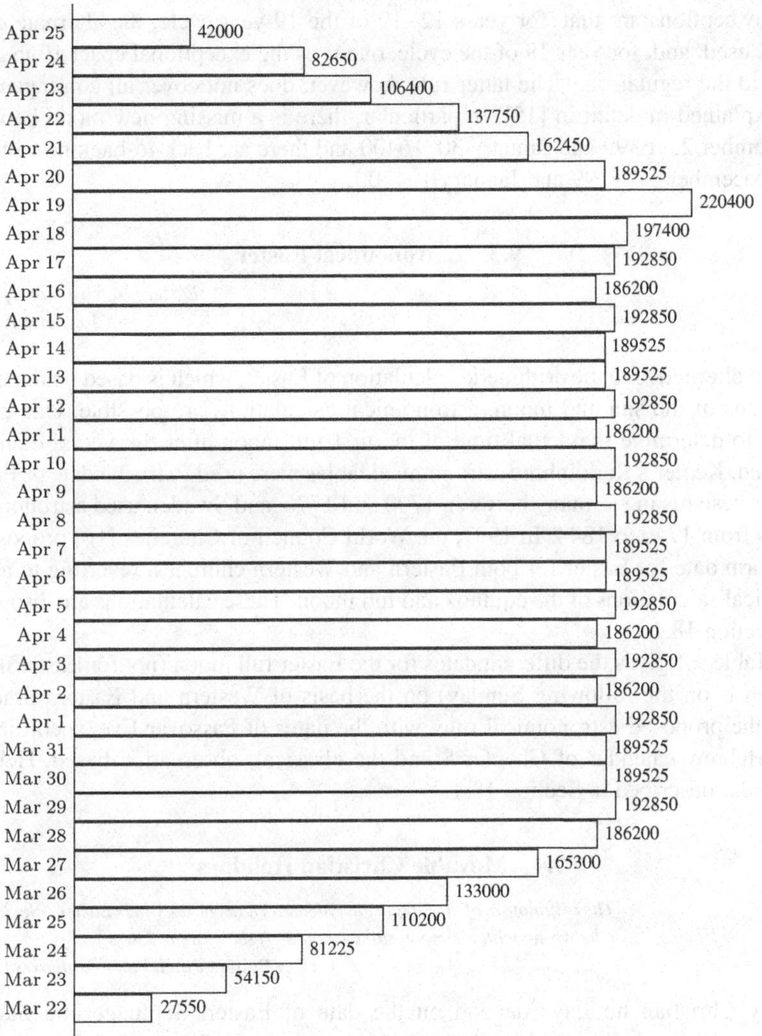

Figure 9.2 Distribution of Gregorian Easter dates over the full 5700000-year cycle.

new rule, Easter and Passover coincided once in the seventeenth century (in 1609), twice in the nineteenth (1805 and 1825), and 5 times in the twentieth century, but will not do so again until 2123.

The ecclesiastical calendar is more than just a rule for calculating the date of Easter; it is a fully-fledged lunisolar calendar, with 12 or 13 months per year. The golden number and the epact of the year determine its structure. There are 32 possible values for the epact: 1–30 (usually given as a roman numeral i–xxx), representing the age of the moon on January 30 (which is one less than its age on January 1, assuming a month length of 30), plus two exceptional alternate values for epacts 19 and 25. Our *shifted-epact* is the epact shifted by 6 (modulo 30). The two exceptions are that, for years 12–19 of the 19-year cycle, the alternate epact 25 is used, and, for year 19 of the cycle, one uses the exceptional epact 19 in addition to the regular one. The latter rule, however, does not cover all contingencies, as explained in detail in [15]. In particular, there is a missing new moon between December 2, 16399 and January 30, 16400 and there are back-to-back new moons on December 31, 4199 and January 1, 4200.

9.3 Astronomical Easter

Easter is a feast, not a planet.
Johannes Kepler[2]

As an alternative to the arithmetic calculation of Easter, which is based on the mean motions of the sun and moon, astronomical calculations are possible. One needs only to determine the actual time of the first full moon after the vernal equinox. Indeed, Kepler's Rudolphine astronomical tables were used to fix the date of Easter by Protestants in Germany between 1700 and 1776, and Sweden used astronomical rules from 1740 to 1844. In 1997, the World Council of Churches [16] proposed a uniform date for Easter for both Eastern and Western churches, reverting to astronomical calculations of the equinox and full moon. These calculations are discussed in Section 18.2.

Table 9.1 gives the different dates for the Easter full moon (not for Easter itself, which is on the following Sunday) on the basis of Western and Eastern practice and the proposed astronomical rule, with the dates of Passover Eve, according to the Hebrew calendar of Chapter 8 and the classical, observation-based, Hebrew calendar described in Section 18.4.

9.4 Movable Christian Holidays

[*The originators of the Gregorian calendar*] *had chosen* [*their Easter calculation*] *to be wrong with the moon rather than be right with the Jews.*
T. H. O'Beirne: *Puzzles and Paradoxes* (1965)

Many Christian holidays depend on the date of Easter: Septuagesima Sunday (63 days before), Sexagesima Sunday (56 days before), Shrove Sunday (49 days before), Shrove Monday (48 days before), Shrove Tuesday or Mardi Gras (47 days

[2] The source of this quotation (in German, "Ostern ist ein Fest vnd khein Stern") is an unpublished paper *Ein Gespräch von der Reformation des alten Kalenders worauff die Correctio Gregoriana gegründet*, written in German by Kepler in 1613; a Latin translation of this paper was published by M. G. Hansch as *Liber singularis de Calendario Gregoriano sive de reformatione Calendarii Juliani necessaria et de fundamentis atque ratione correctionis Gregorianae*, (Leipzig, 1726). The German text of this paper has been published only as the *Dialogus de Calendario Gregoriano* in the C. Frisch edition (1858–1871) of Kepler's collected works, *Joannis Kepleri Opera Omnia*, vol. 4, p. 37, 1863. Kepler's paper is a dialogue between a "Mathematicus" (Kepler), two Catholics ("Confessarius" and "Cancellarius") and two Protestants ("Ecclesiastes" and "Syndicus"), who argue the desirability of the Gregorian reform. Kepler, the imperial mathematician of Emperor Matthias, wrote this dialogue for the Emperor who wanted to be informed about this subject. Kepler was a proponent of the Gregorian calendar but cared little about theological disputes and argued that the date of Easter, like other days of observance, should not depend on long and arduous calculations such as are necessary for predicting the positions of the planets. We are indebted to Robert H. van Gent for this information.

Table 9.1 Julian dates of Passover Eve (Nisan 14), for the years 9–40 C.E., according to the Hebrew arithmetic and [illegible] the Easter full moon preceding Easter Sunday, according to the Orthodox, Gregorian, and proposed astronomical rules. (For the futility of attempting to determine the date of the crucifixion from such data, see chap. 9 of R. T. Beckwith, *Calendar and Chronology, Jewish and Christian: Biblical, Intertestamental and Patristic Studies*, E. J. Brill, Leiden, 1996.)

Julian	Passover Eve		Easter Full Moon		
Year	Classical	Arithmetic	Orthodox	Gregorian	Astronomical
9 C.E.	Saturday, March 30	Friday, March 29	Wednesday, March 27	Friday, March 29	Friday, March 29
10 C.E.	Friday, April 18	Wednesday, April 16	Tuesday, April 15	Thursday, April 17	Thursday, April 17
11 C.E.	Tuesday, April 7	Monday, April 6	Saturday, April 4	Monday, April 6	Monday, April 6
12 C.E.	Saturday, March 26	Friday, March 25	Thursday, March 24	Saturday, March 26	Saturday, March 26
13 C.E.	Friday, April 14	Friday, April 14	Wednesday, April 12	Friday, April 14	Friday, April 14
14 C.E.	Tuesday, April 3	Monday, April 2	Sunday, April 1	Tuesday, April 3	Wednesday, April 4
15 C.E.	Sunday, March 24	Friday, March 22	Thursday, March 21	Saturday, March 23	Sunday, March 24
16 C.E.	Saturday, April 11	Friday, April 10	Thursday, April 9	Saturday, April 11	Saturday, April 11
17 C.E.	Wednesday, March 31	Wednesday, March 31	Monday, March 29	Wednesday, March 31	Wednesday, March 31
18 C.E.	Tuesday, April 19	Saturday, March 19	Sunday, April 17	Tuesday, April 19	Monday, April 18
19 C.E.	Sunday, April 9	Friday, April 7	Wednesday, April 5	Friday, April 7	Saturday, April 8
20 C.E.	Thursday, March 28	Wednesday, March 27	Monday, March 25	Wednesday, March 27	Wednesday, March 27
21 C.E.	Wednesday, April 16	Monday, April 14	Sunday, April 13	Tuesday, April 15	Tuesday, April 15
22 C.E.	Sunday, April 5	Saturday, April 4	Thursday, April 2	Saturday, April 4	Sunday, April 5
23 C.E.	Thursday, March 25	Wednesday, March 24	Monday, March 22	Wednesday, March 24	Friday, March 26
24 C.E.	Wednesday, April 12	Wednesday, April 12	Monday, April 10	Wednesday, April 12	Wednesday, April 12
25 C.E.	Monday, April 2	Monday, April 2	Friday, March 30	Sunday, April 1	Sunday, April 1
26 C.E.	Friday, March 22	Friday, March 22	Thursday, April 18	Saturday, April 20	Saturday, April 20
27 C.E.	Thursday, April 10	Wednesday, April 9	Monday, April 7	Wednesday, April 9	Wednesday, April 9
28 C.E.	Tuesday, March 30	Monday, March 29	Saturday, March 27	Monday, March 29	Monday, March 29
29 C.E.	Sunday, April 17	Saturday, April 16	Friday, April 15	Sunday, April 17	Sunday, April 17
30 C.E.	Thursday, April 6	Wednesday, April 5	Tuesday, April 4	Thursday, April 6	Thursday, April 6
31 C.E.	Tuesday, March 27	Monday, March 26	Saturday, March 24	Monday, March 26	Tuesday, March 27
32 C.E.	Sunday, April 13	Monday, April 14	Saturday, April 12	Monday, April 14	Monday, April 14
33 C.E.	Friday, April 3	Friday, April 3	Wednesday, April 1	Friday, April 3	Friday, April 3
34 C.E.	Wednesday, March 24	Monday, March 22	Sunday, March 21	Tuesday, March 23	Tuesday, March 23
35 C.E.	Tuesday, April 12	Monday, April 11	Saturday, April 9	Monday, April 11	Monday, April 11
36 C.E.	Saturday, March 31	Friday, March 30	Thursday, March 29	Saturday, March 31	Friday, March 30
37 C.E.	Thursday, March 21	Wednesday, March 20	Wednesday, April 17	Friday, April 19	Thursday, April 18
38 C.E.	Tuesday, April 8	Monday, April 7	Saturday, April 5	Monday, April 7	Tuesday, April 8
39 C.E.	Saturday, March 28	Friday, March 27	Wednesday, March 25	Friday, March 27	Saturday, March 28
40 C.E.	Friday, April 15	Friday, April 15	Wednesday, April 13	Friday, April 15	Friday, April 15

before), Ash Wednesday (46 days before), Passion Sunday (14 days before), Palm Sunday (7 days before), Holy or Maundy Thursday (3 days before), Good Friday (2 days before), Rogation Sunday (35 days after), Ascension Day (39 days after), Pentecost (also called Whitsunday—49 days after), Whit Monday (50 days after), Trinity Sunday (56 days after), and Corpus Christi (60 days after, or 63 days after, in the Catholic Church in the United States.).[3] All these are easily computed; for example

$$\textbf{pentecost}\,(g\text{-}year) \stackrel{\text{def}}{=} \textbf{easter}\,(g\text{-}year) + 49 \tag{9.4}$$

The 40 days of Lent, or *Quadragesima*, begin on Ash Wednesday. Orthodox Christians begin Lent 7 weeks (48 days) before Eastern Orthodox Easter, on a Monday. The Eastern Orthodox Church celebrates the Feast of Orthodoxy on the following Sunday (42 days before Eastern Orthodox Easter). The Orthodox Fast of the Apostles begins 8 days after Orthodox Pentecost and ends on June 28 on the Julian calendar.

The ecclesiastical year begins with Advent Sunday (see page 71).

References

[1] E. R. Berlekamp, J. H. Conway, and R. K. Guy, *Winning Ways, vol. 2, Games in Particular*, Academic Press, New York, 1982.

[2] R. Bien, "Gauß and Beyond: The Making of Easter Algorithms," *Archive for History of Exact Sciences*, vol. 58, no. 5, pp. 439–452, July 2004.

[3] G. Declercq, *Anno Domini: The Origins of the Christian Era*, Brepols Publishers, Turnhout, Belgium, 2000.

[4] J. K. Fotheringham, "The Calendar," *The Nautical Almanac and Astronomical Ephemeris*, His Majesty's Stationery Office, London, 1931–1934; revised 1935–1938; abridged 1939–1941.

[5] C. F. Gauss, "Berechnung des Osterfestes," *Monatliche Correspondenz zur Beförderung der Erd- und Himmels-Kunde*, Herausgegeben vom Freiherrn von Zach (August 1800). Reprinted in Gauss's *Werke*, Herausgegeben von der Königlichen Gesellschaft der Wissenschaften, Göttingen, vol. 6, pp. 73–79, 1874.

[6] C. F. Gauss, "Noch etwas über die Bestimmung des Osterfestes," *Braunschweigisches Magazin* (September 12, 1807). Reprinted in Gauss's *Werke*, Herausgegeben von der Königlichen Gesellschaft der Wissenschaften, Göttingen, vol. 6, pp. 82–86, 1874.

[7] J. L. Heilbron, *The Sun in the Church: Cathedrals as Solar Observatories*, Harvard University Press, Cambridge, MA, 1999.

[3] Because of the extensive liturgical changes after the Second Vatican Council, the Catholic Church no longer observes Septuagesima, Sexagesima, and Shrove Sunday through Tuesday.

[8] H. Kinkelin, "Die Berechnung des christlichen Osterfestes," *Zeitschrift für Mathematik und Physik,* vol. 15, pp. 217–228, 1870.

[9] D. E. Knuth, "The Calculation of Easter," *Communications of the ACM*, vol. 5, pp. 209–210, 1962.

[10] D. E. Knuth, *The Art of Computer Programming, vol. 1, Fundamental Algorithms*, 3rd edn., Addison-Wesley, Reading, MA, 1997.

[11] J. Meeus, *Mathematical Astronomy Morsels*, Willmann-Bell, Richmond, VA, 1997.

[12] A. A. Mosshammer, *The Easter Computus and the Origins of the Christian Era*, Oxford University Press, Oxford, 2008.

[13] G. Moyer, "The Gregorian Calendar," *Scientific American*, vol. 246, no. 5, pp. 144–152, May 1982.

[14] T. H. O'Beirne, *Puzzles and Paradoxes*, Oxford University Press, Oxford, 1965. Reprinted by Dover Publications, New York, 1984.

[15] D. Roegel, "The missing new moon of A.D. 16399 and other anomalies of the Gregorian calendar," INRIA internal report A04-R-436, 2004. Available at `hal.inria.fr/inria-00099868/document`.

[16] World Council of Churches, "The Date of Easter: Science Offers Solution to Ancient Religious Problem," Press release, March 24, 1997.

[17] J. V. Uspensky and M. A. Heaslet, *Elementary Number Theory*, McGraw-Hill, New York, 1939.

Stone astrolabe from India. (Courtesy of Adler Planetarium & Astronomy Museum, Chicago, IL.)

10

The Old Hindu Calendars

Scientists with advanced computers have sometimes failed to predict major earthquakes, but ancient Indian astrology does have the tools to roughly foretell the time and sometimes even the exact date and time of an earthquake.

Murli Manohar Joshi: *The Irish Times* (August 4, 2003)

10.1 Structure and History

The Hindus have both solar and lunisolar calendars. In the Hindu lunisolar system, as in other lunisolar calendars, months follow the lunar cycle and are synchronized with the solar year by introducing occasional leap months. Unlike the Hebrew lunisolar calendar (described in Chapter 8), Hindu intercalated months do not follow a short cyclical pattern. Moreover, unlike other calendars, a day can be *omitted* any time in a lunar month.

Modern Hindu calendars are based on close approximations to the *true* times of the sun's entrance into the signs of the zodiac and of lunar conjunctions (new moons). Before about 1100 C.E., however, Hindu calendars used *mean* times. Though the basic structure of the calendar is similar for both systems, the mean (*madhyama*) and true (*spaṣṭa*) calendars can differ by a few days or can be shifted by a month. In this chapter we implement the mean system, as described in [4, pp. 360–446], which is arithmetical; Chapter 20 is devoted to the more recent astronomical version. For an ancient description of Hindu astronomy, calendars, and holidays, see the book on India by al-Bīrūnī [1];[1] a more modern reference is [3].

There are various epochs that are, or have been, used as starting points for the enumeration of years in India. For a list of eras, see [5, pp. 39–47, civ–cvi]. In this chapter, we use the expired Kali Yuga ("Iron Age") epoch. The *expired* year number is the number of years that have *elapsed* since the onset of the Kali Yuga.[2] As van Wijk [6] explains:

---

[1] There is some confusion of dates in the note (on p. 358) attributed to Schram in Sachau's translation of this book where the following equivalences are given: Thursday, February 25, 1031 C.E. (Julian) = 1 Caitra 953 Śaka Era = 28 Ṣafar 422 A.H. = 19 Ispandārmadh-Māh 399 Anno Persarum, and New Year 400 Anno Persarum = March 9, 1031 C.E. (Julian) = JD 2097686. In fact, February 25, 1031 C.E. (Julian) = 29 Ṣafar 422 A.H. = JD 2097686.

[2] For each epoch, there is also a *current* year number, beginning with year 1.

> We count the years of human life in expired years. A child of seven years has already lived more than seven years; but on the famous *18 Brumaire de l'An VIII de la République Française une et indivisible* only 7 years and 47 days of the French Era had elapsed.

The first day of year 0 K.Y.[3] is Friday, January 23, −3101 (Gregorian) or February 18, 3102 B.C.E. (Julian), that is, R.D. −1132959:

$$\textbf{hindu-epoch} \stackrel{\text{def}}{=} \qquad (10.1)$$

$$\textbf{fixed-from-julian}\left(\begin{array}{|c|c|c|}\hline 3102\ \text{B.C.E.} & \textbf{february} & 18 \\ \hline\end{array}\right)$$

Time is measured in days and fractions since this epoch.

The Kali Yuga epoch marks—in Hindu chronology—the onset of the fourth and final stage (lasting 432000 years) of the 4320000-year era beginning with the last recreation of the world. Civil days begin at mean sunrise, reckoned as one quarter of a day past midnight—that is, at 6:00 a.m. The midnight just prior to day 1 of the Hindu calendar is considered to have been the start of a new lunar month; indeed, in Hindu astronomy it was the time of the most recent *mean* conjunction of all the visible planets (the sun, moon, Mercury, Venus, Mars, Jupiter, and Saturn).

The Hindus also have a day count beginning with the first day of the Kali Yuga. To compute it we simply add the R.D. date to the number of days from the onset of the Kali Yuga until R.D. 0; that is, we subtract the epoch:

$$\textbf{hindu-day-count}\,(\mathit{date}) \stackrel{\text{def}}{=} \mathit{date} - \textbf{hindu-epoch} \qquad (10.2)$$

A day's number is called its *ahargaṇa* ("heap of days") and is traditionally used to determine the day of the week by casting off sevens just as we have done with our R.D. numbering.

The names of the days of the week (going back to the third or fourth century C.E.) are

Sunday	Ravivāra or Ādityavāra	रविवार or आदित्यवार
Monday	Somavāra or Candravāra	सोमवार or चन्द्रवार
Tuesday	Maṅgalavāra or Bhaumavāra	मङ्गलवार or भौमवार
Wednesday	Budhavāra or Saumyavāra	बुधवार or सौम्यवार
Thursday	Bṛihaspatvāra or Guruvāra	बृहस्पतिवार or गुरवार
Friday	Śukravāra	शुक्रवार
Saturday	Śanivāra	शनिवार

The Hindu value for the (sidereal) year (the mean number of days it takes for the sun to return to the same point vis-à-vis the celestial globe—see Section 14.4) is

[3] Kali Yuga (Iron Age).

Table 10.1 The names of the samvatsaras of the Hindu Jovian cycle of 60 years.

(1) Prabhava	प्रभव	(31) Hemalamba	हेमलम्ब
(2) Vibhava	विभव	(32) Vilamba	विलम्ब
(3) Śukla	शुक्ल	(33) Vikārin	विकारिन्
(4) Pramoda	प्रमोद	(34) Śarvarī	शर्वरी
(5) Prajāpati	प्रजापति	(35) Plava	प्लव
(6) Aṅgiras	अङ्गिरस्	(36) Śubhakṛt	शुभकृत्
(7) Śrīmukha	श्रीमुख	(37) Śobhana	शोभन
(8) Bhāva	भाव	(38) Krodhin	क्रोधिन्
(9) Yuvan	युवन्	(39) Viśvāvasu	विश्वावसु
(10) Dhātṛ	धातृ	(40) Parābhava	पराभव
(11) Īśvara	ईश्वर	(41) Plavaṅga	प्लवङ्ग
(12) Bahudhānya	बहुधान्य	(42) Kīlaka	कीलक
(13) Pramāthin	प्रमाथिन्	(43) Saumya	सौम्य
(14) Vikrama	विक्रम	(44) Sādhāraṇa	साधारण
(15) Vṛṣa	वृष	(45) Virodhakṛt	विरोधकृत्
(16) Citrabhānu	चित्रभानु	(46) Paridhāvin	परिधाविन्
(17) Subhānu	सुभानु	(47) Pramāthin	प्रमाथिन्
(18) Tāraṇa	तारण	(48) Ānanda	आनन्द
(19) Pārthiva	पार्थिव	(49) Rākṣasa	राक्षस
(20) Vyaya	व्यय	(50) Anala	अनल
(21) Sarvajit	सर्वजित्	(51) Piṅgala	पिङ्गल
(22) Sarvadhārin	सर्वधारिन्	(52) Kālayukta	कालयुक्त
(23) Rākṣasa	राक्षस	(53) Siddhārthin	सिद्धार्थिन्
(24) Vikṛta	विकृत	(54) Rāudra	रौद्र
(25) Khara	खर	(55) Durmati	दुर्मति
(26) Nandana	नन्दन	(56) Dundubhi	दुन्दुभि
(27) Vijaya	विजय	(57) Rudhirodgārin	रुधिरोद्गारिन्
(28) Jaya	जय	(58) Raktākṣa	रक्ताक्ष
(29) Manmatha	मन्मथ	(59) Krodhana	क्रोधन
(30) Durmukha	दुर्मुख	(60) Kṣaya	क्षय

$$\textbf{arya-solar-year} \stackrel{\text{def}}{=} \frac{1577917500}{4320000} \tag{10.3}$$

or $365\frac{149}{576} = 365.258680555\cdots$ civil days.

A Jovian cycle is also employed. It takes Jupiter about 12 years to circle the sun; the Hindu value is

$$\textbf{arya-jovian-period} \stackrel{\text{def}}{=} \frac{1577917500}{364224} \tag{10.4}$$

days. The Jovian period is divided into 12 equal periods of time, one for each sign of the zodiac. Five revolutions of Jupiter give a 60-year cycle of year names, called *samvatsaras*, listed in Table 10.1. The Jovian year number corresponding to the start of a solar year is computed from the fixed date as follows:

$$\textbf{jovian-year}\,(\mathit{date}) \stackrel{\text{def}}{=} \tag{10.5}$$

$$\left(27 + \left\lfloor \frac{\textbf{hindu-day-count}\,(date)}{\frac{1}{12} \times \textbf{arya-jovian-period}} \right\rfloor\right) \bmod [1\,..\,60]$$

Because a Jovian "year" is somewhat shorter than a solar year, consecutive solar years do not necessarily carry consecutive Jovian names. In that case, every 86 years or so the samvatsara for that year is said to be "expunged."

The Jovian cycle and all other figures are given in traditional Hindu astronomy as rational numbers. The numerators and denominators of the rational numbers obtained during the intermediate calculations exceed 32 binary digits but remain below 2^{63}; thus, they can be reformulated as integer calculations on 64-bit computers.

Different Indian astronomical treatises give slightly varying astronomical constants; in this chapter we follow the (First) *Ārya Siddhānta* of Āryabhaṭa (499 C.E.), as amended by Lalla (circa 720–790 C.E.). There are also many variations in detail of the calendars; we describe only one version.

10.2 The Solar Calendar

Sometimes I cannot help regretting that only so very few readers can rejoice with me in the simplicity of the method and the exactness of its results.

Walther E. van Wijk: "On Hindu Chronology III," *Acta Orientalia* (1924)

A solar month is one-twelfth of a year:

$$\textbf{arya-solar-month} \stackrel{\text{def}}{=} \frac{1}{12} \times \textbf{arya-solar-year} \tag{10.6}$$

or 30.438 ⋯ days. The solar (*saura*) months are sometimes named in Sanskrit after the signs of the zodiac corresponding to the position of the mean sun; these signs are given in Table 10.2. In most locations, however, the same names are used as in the lunisolar scheme. These are given in the last column; see the list on page 160.

The solar New Year is called *Mesha saṃkrānti*. Each solar month is 30 or 31 days long and begins on the day of the first sunrise after the calculated time of the mean sun's entry into the next zodiacal sign. If that calculated time is after midnight but before or at sunrise, then the day of entry is the first day of the new month; otherwise, it is the last day of the previous month. Hence, even though the mean month is a constant, months vary in length. Our R.D. 0 is Makara 19, 3101 K.Y. on the mean solar calendar.

Converting a solar date according to this old Hindu calendar into an R.D. date is straightforward:

$$\textbf{fixed-from-old-hindu-solar}\left(\boxed{year \mid month \mid day}\right) \stackrel{\text{def}}{=} \tag{10.7}$$

$$\left\lceil \textbf{hindu-epoch} + year \times \textbf{arya-solar-year} + (month - 1) \times \textbf{arya-solar-month} + day - 30^{\text{h}} \right\rceil$$

Table 10.2 Hindu solar (*saura*) months, named after the signs of the zodiac corresponding to the position of the mean sun.

	Vedic	Sanskrit		Zodiacal sign	Lunisolar month
(1)	Madhu	Meṣa	मेष	Aries	Vaiśākha
(2)	Mādhava	Vṛṣabha	वृषभ	Taurus	Jyeṣṭha
(3)	Śukra	Mithuna	मिथुन	Gemini	Āṣāḍha
(4)	Śuchi	Karka	कर्क	Cancer	Śrāvaṇa
(5)	Nabhas	Siṃha	सिंह	Leo	Bhādrapada
(6)	Nabhasya	Kanyā	कन्या	Virgo	Āśvina
(7)	Issa	Tulā	तुला	Libra	Kārtika
(8)	Ūrja	Vṛścika	वृश्चिक	Scorpio	Mārgaśīrṣa
(9)	Sahas	Dhanus	धनुस्	Sagittarius	Pauṣa
(10)	Sahasya	Makara	मकर	Capricorn	Māgha
(11)	Tapas	Kumbha	कुम्भ	Aquarius	Phālguna
(12)	Tapasya	Mīna	मीन	Pisces	Caitra

Because *year* is the number of years that have *elapsed* since the epoch, we multiply it by the average length of a year, which is a fraction, and add the number of days (and fractions of a day) in the elapsed months of the current year. That gives the time at which the current month began, to which is added the fixed date of the epoch and the number of days up to and including the given *day*. If the resultant moment is after mean sunrise (6 a.m.), then we have the correct fixed date; if it is before sunrise, we need to subtract 1. Subtracting 30^{h} from the resultant moment and taking the ceiling has this effect.

Inverting the process is not much harder:

$$\textbf{old-hindu-solar-from-fixed}\,(date) \stackrel{\text{def}}{=} \boxed{\textit{year} \mid \textit{month} \mid \textit{day}} \qquad (10.8)$$

where

$$sun = \textbf{hindu-day-count}\,(date) + 6^{\text{h}}$$

$$year = \left\lfloor \frac{sun}{\textbf{arya-solar-year}} \right\rfloor$$

$$month = \left(\left\lfloor \frac{sun}{\textbf{arya-solar-month}} \right\rfloor \bmod 12 \right) + 1$$

$$day = \lfloor sun \bmod \textbf{arya-solar-month} \rfloor + 1$$

Here, *sun* is the number of days and the fraction of a day (6^{h}) that have elapsed since the Hindu epoch at mean sunrise—the decisive moment—on fixed *date*; *year* is the number of mean years that have elapsed at that moment; *month* is the number of the current solar month, counting mean months from the beginning of that solar year; and *day* is the number of the civil day, counting from the beginning of the solar month.

10.3 The Lunisolar Calendar

I sincerely hope that leading Indian pañcāṅg-makers, astronomers and mathematicians will keep their Siddhāntic reckoning as pure as possible and not use the old works for purposes they can never be able to serve, mindful of the sage word: no man putteth a piece of undressed cloth upon an old garment; for that which should fill it up taketh from the garment, and a worse rent is made.

Walther E. van Wijk: "On Hindu Chronology IV," *Acta Orientalia*, vol. IV (1926)

We will follow the south-India method in which months begin and end at new moons (the *amānta* scheme); in the north, months go from full moon to full moon (the *pūrṇimānta* scheme). The name of a lunar month depends on the solar month that begins during that lunar month. A month is leap and takes the following month's name when no solar month begins within it. See Figure 10.1.

The Sanskrit names themselves are based on the longitudinal position of the moon at mid-month:

(1) Caitra	चैत्र	(7) Āśvina	आश्विन
(2) Vaiśākha	वैशाख	(8) Kārtika	कार्तिक
(3) Jyeṣṭha	ज्येष्ठ	(9) Mārgaśīrṣa	मार्गशीर्ष
(4) Āṣāḍha	आषाढ	(10) Pauṣa	पौष
(5) Śrāvaṇa	श्रावण	(11) Māgha	माघ
(6) Bhādrapada	भाद्रपद	(12) Phālguna	फाल्गुन

Some regions of India begin the year with Kārtika and use different or shifted month names.

Because a solar month (see Section 14.6) is longer than a lunar month, a lunar month is intercalated whenever the latter is wholly contained within the former. That lunar month and the following take the same name except that the first is leap, called *adhika* ("added," or *prathama*, first), and the second is *nija* ("regular," or *dvitīya*, second).[4] In the rare event (at the onset of K.Y. 0, and every 180000 years later) that both the lunar and solar month end at the same moment and, hence, that the following lunar and solar months both begin at the same moment, we follow the explicit statement of al-Bīrūnī [1, vol. 2, pp. 20–21] that the former lunar month is the intercalated one.

Two constants play a major rôle in lunar computations: the length of a solar month **arya-solar-month** (page 158) and that of the lunar month:

$$\textbf{arya-lunar-month} \stackrel{\text{def}}{=} \frac{1577917500}{53433336} \tag{10.9}$$

that is, $29.53058181\cdots$ days. Though a month on the lunisolar calendar can consist of 29 or 30 civil days, it is always divided into 30 "lunar days,"[5] called *tithis*:

$$\textbf{arya-lunar-day} \stackrel{\text{def}}{=} \frac{1}{30} \times \textbf{arya-lunar-month} \tag{10.10}$$

[4] In the northern, full-moon scheme, the intercalated month is inserted between the two halves of the ordinary month [2, p. 405].

[5] This should not be confused with what astronomers call a "lunar day."

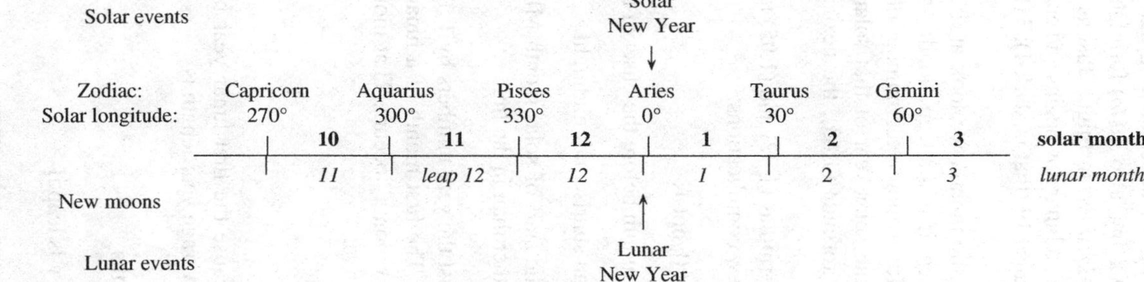

Figure 10.1 The old Hindu lunisolar calendar. Solar events (entry into zodiac constellations) are shown above the time line; lunar events (lunar conjunctions) are shown below; longitudes are sidereal. Solar months are shown in boldface numbers, lunar months in italic numbers.

Because a mean lunar month is less than 30 (civil) days long, a lunar day is about 0.98435 days, somewhat shorter than a full day.

Days within a lunar month are numbered by the lunar day current at sunrise, which is usually referred to by an ordinal number within one fortnight or the other (except that the last day of the second fortnight is numbered 30). We simply use the ordinal numbers from 1 to 30, with the understanding that the first 15 lunar days belong to the *suddha* ("bright," waxing, also *śukla*) fortnight and the second 15 to the *bahula* ("dark," waning, also *kṛishna*) fortnight. Just as there are leap months, there are also "lost" days whenever a lunar day begins and ends between one sunrise and the next. The date R.D. 0 is Pauṣa 19 (that is, dark 4), 3101 K.Y. on the lunisolar calendar.

To determine the number of the month, we look at the next occurrence of a new moon—the second occurrence, if it is a leap month—see where the sun is at that moment, and then give the lunar month the number of that solar month. For the lunar year number, we use the solar year of that solar month. The previous mean new moon is found using formula (1.63); the next new moon is 1 month later.

We can apply our leap year formulas (1.92) and (1.95) to the calculation of the old Hindu calendar subject to a few complications:

1. The K.Y. year count begins at 0, not 1.
2. The first lunar year began 1 month before the onset of the Kali Yuga.
3. The determining time is mean sunrise, not midnight.
4. The relevant solar event—the start of solar month Mīna—occurs in the last month of a lunisolar year rather than in the first.

Accordingly, we need to adjust the year numbers by 1, the month enumeration by 1, and the day count by 1/4. The first month of a lunar year is that in which the moment "Mīna plus 1 (lunar) month" occurs. That moment in year 0 was an amount

$$\delta = 2 - \frac{\textbf{arya-solar-month}}{\textbf{arya-lunar-month}}$$

of days into the first month because the first lunar year began exactly 1 month before the solar New Year. The average year length is

$$\bar{L} = \frac{\textbf{arya-solar-year}}{\textbf{arya-lunar-month}} \text{ months}$$

By inequality (1.93), Hindu year y is leap if

$$\left(2 - \frac{\textbf{arya-solar-month}}{\textbf{arya-lunar-month}} + y\frac{\textbf{arya-solar-year}}{\textbf{arya-lunar-month}}\right) \bmod 1$$

$$\geqslant 1 - \frac{\textbf{arya-solar-year}}{\textbf{arya-lunar-month}} \bmod 1$$

Multiplying by **arya-lunar-month** and simplifying, we get the following test:

$$\textbf{old-hindu-lunar-leap-year?}\ (\textit{l-year}) \stackrel{\text{def}}{=} \tag{10.11}$$

$$((\textit{l-year} \times \textbf{arya-solar-year} - \textbf{arya-solar-month}) \bmod \textbf{arya-lunar-month}) \geqslant \frac{23902504679}{1282400064}$$

We do not, however, require this test for the conversion functions that follow.

Let $sun = n + 1/4$ be the moment of sunrise on day n since the onset of the Kali Yuga. The number of months m that have elapsed since the start of the first lunar year is

$$m = \lfloor sun/\textbf{arya-lunar-month} \rfloor + 1$$

which amounts to

$$sun - (sun \bmod \textbf{arya-lunar-month}) + \textbf{arya-lunar-month}$$

days. By equation (1.95), the year number (starting from 0) is

$$\left\lceil \frac{m + 1 - \delta}{\bar{L}} \right\rceil - 1$$

Using the preceding values for m, δ, and $\bar{L}$ yields

$$y = \left\lceil \frac{m + 1 - \left(2 - \dfrac{\textbf{arya-solar-month}}{\textbf{arya-lunar-month}}\right)}{\dfrac{\textbf{arya-solar-year}}{\textbf{arya-lunar-month}}} \right\rceil - 1$$

$$= \left\lceil \frac{(m - 1) \times \textbf{arya-lunar-month} + \textbf{arya-solar-month}}{\textbf{arya-solar-year}} \right\rceil - 1$$

$$= \left\lceil \frac{\textit{new-moon} + \textbf{arya-solar-month}}{\textbf{arya-solar-year}} \right\rceil - 1$$

where

$$\textit{new-moon} = (m - 1) \times \textbf{arya-lunar-month}$$

$$= \left\lfloor \frac{sun}{\textbf{arya-lunar-month}} \right\rfloor \times \textbf{arya-lunar-month}$$

Intuitively, the lunisolar year number y is the solar year number in effect at the end of the current month.

The same leap-year formula can be used to determine the lunar month name. For this purpose, however, we consider "years" to be a period of either 1- or 2-month duration: 1 for ordinary months and 2 when the month name is shared by a leap month. The average length of such periods, measured in lunar months, is

$$A = \frac{\textbf{arya-solar-month}}{\textbf{arya-lunar-month}}$$

Formula (1.95) tells us that after m lunar months the number of elapsed periods is

$$\begin{aligned}\left\lceil \frac{m+1-\delta}{A} \right\rceil - 1 &= \left\lceil \frac{\textit{new-moon} + \textbf{arya-solar-month}}{\textbf{arya-solar-month}} \right\rceil - 1 \\ &= \left\lceil \frac{\textit{new-moon}}{\textbf{arya-solar-month}} \right\rceil \end{aligned} \tag{10.12}$$

The inverse, deriving the fixed date from the Hindu lunar date, is a bit more complicated. By equation (1.92), there are $\lfloor 12yA + \delta \rfloor$ months from the beginning of year 0 until the end of elapsed year $y - 1$. Accordingly, the number of months since the Kali Yuga (which began 1 month after lunar year 0) is

$$\begin{aligned}\lfloor 12 \times y \times A + \delta \rfloor - 1 &= \left\lfloor 12 \times y \times \frac{\textbf{arya-solar-month}}{\textbf{arya-lunar-month}} \right. \\ &\quad \left. + \left(2 - \frac{\textbf{arya-solar-month}}{\textbf{arya-lunar-month}}\right) \right\rfloor - 1 \\ &= \left\lfloor \frac{(12 \times y - 1) \times \textbf{arya-solar-month}}{\textbf{arya-lunar-month}} \right\rfloor + 1 \\ &= \left\lfloor \frac{\textit{mina}}{\textbf{arya-lunar-month}} \right\rfloor + 1\end{aligned}$$

where

$$\begin{aligned}\textit{mina} &= (12 \times y - 1) \times \textbf{arya-solar-month} \\ &= y \times \textbf{arya-solar-year} - \textbf{arya-solar-month}\end{aligned}$$

is the moment of the determining solar event.

We use a boolean (true/false) value to indicate whether a month is leap. A date is represented as

year	*month*	*leap-month*	*day*

where *year* is an integer, *month* is an integer in the range 1 through 12, *leap-month* is either true or false, and *day* is an integer in the range 1 through 30. We convert R.D. dates as follows:

$$\textbf{old-hindu-lunar-from-fixed}\,(\mathit{date}) \stackrel{\text{def}}{=} \tag{10.13}$$

year	*month*	*leap*	*day*

where

$$\begin{aligned}
\mathit{sun} &= \textbf{hindu-day-count}\,(\mathit{date}) + 6^{\text{h}}\\
\mathit{new\text{-}moon} &= \mathit{sun} - (\mathit{sun} \bmod \textbf{arya-lunar-month})\\
\mathit{leap} &= \textbf{arya-solar-month} - \textbf{arya-lunar-month} \geqslant\\
&\quad (\mathit{new\text{-}moon} \bmod \textbf{arya-solar-month}) > 0\\
\mathit{month} &= \left(\left\lceil \frac{\mathit{new\text{-}moon}}{\textbf{arya-solar-month}} \right\rceil \bmod 12\right) + 1\\
\mathit{day} &= \left(\left\lfloor \frac{\mathit{sun}}{\textbf{arya-lunar-day}} \right\rfloor \bmod 30\right) + 1\\
\mathit{year} &= \left\lceil \frac{\mathit{new\text{-}moon} + \textbf{arya-solar-month}}{\textbf{arya-solar-year}} \right\rceil - 1
\end{aligned}$$

To determine the lunar month, we use equation (10.12) and discard multiples of twelve. A month is leap when it begins closer to the solar month's beginning than the excess of a solar month over a lunar month.

The lunar New Year begins with the first lunar month to begin in the last solar month (*Mīna*) of the prior solar year. To compute the R.D. date from an old Hindu lunar date, we count lunar months and elapsed lunar days, taking care to check whether there is a leap month in the interim. This value is added to the moment of the New Year, as determined above:

$$\textbf{fixed-from-old-hindu-lunar}\left(\boxed{\mathit{year}\;|\;\mathit{month}\;|\;\mathit{leap}\;|\;\mathit{day}}\right) \stackrel{\text{def}}{=} \tag{10.14}$$

$$\left\lfloor \begin{aligned}
&\textbf{hindu-epoch} + \mathit{lunar\text{-}new\text{-}year}\\
&+ \textbf{arya-lunar-month}\\
&\quad \times \left\{\begin{array}{ll}
\mathit{month} & \textbf{if } \text{not } \mathit{leap} \text{ and}\\
& \left\lceil \dfrac{\mathit{lunar\text{-}new\text{-}year} - \mathit{mina}}{\textbf{arya-solar-month} - \textbf{arya-lunar-month}} \right\rceil\\
& \leqslant \mathit{month}\\
\mathit{month} - 1 & \textbf{otherwise}
\end{array}\right\}\\
&+ (\mathit{day} - 1) \times \textbf{arya-lunar-day} - 6^{\text{h}}
\end{aligned} \right\rfloor$$

where

$$\textit{mina} = (12 \times \textit{year} - 1) \times \textbf{arya-solar-month}$$

$$\textit{lunar-new-year} = \textbf{arya-lunar-month} \times \left(\left\lfloor \frac{\textit{mina}}{\textbf{arya-lunar-month}} \right\rfloor + 1 \right)$$

We subtract 6^h before taking the ceiling because the date at midnight is determined by the lunar day that was current at the prior sunrise.

This lunisolar calendar repeats after $4320000/\gcd(432000, 53433336) = 180000$ years.

References

[1] al-Bīrūnī (= Abū-Raiḥān Muḥammad ibn 'Aḥmad al-Bīrūnī), *India: An Accurate Description of all Categories of Hindu Thought, as Well those Which are Admissible as those Which Must be Rejected*, circa 1030. Translated and annotated by C. E. Sachau, *Alberûnî's India: An Account of the Religion, Philosophy, Literature, Geography, Chronology, Astronomy, Customs, Laws and Astrology of India*, William H. Allen and Co., London, 1910; reprinted under the Authority of the Government of West Pakistan, Lahore, 1962, and by S. Chand & Co., New Delhi, 1964.

[2] H. G. Jacobi, "The Computation of Hindu Dates in Inscriptions, &c.," *Epigraphia Indica: A Collection of Inscriptions Supplementary to the Corpus Inscriptionum Indicarum of the Archæological Survey of India*, J. Burgess, ed., Calcutta, pp. 403–460, p. 481, 1892.

[3] D. Pingree, "History of Mathematical Astronomy in India," *Dictionary of Scientific Biography*, C. C. Gillispie, ed., vol. XV, suppl. I, pp. 533–633, 1978.

[4] R. Sewell, *The Siddhantas and the Indian Calendar, Being a Continuation of the Author's "Indian Chronography," with an Article by the Late Dr. J. F. Fleet on the Mean Place of the Planet Saturn*, Government of India Central Publication Branch, Calcutta, 1924. This is a reprint of a series of articles in *Epigraphia Indica*.

[5] R. Sewell and S. B. Dîkshit, *The Indian Calendar, with Tables for the Conversion of Hindu and Muhammadan into* A.D. *Dates, and Vice Versa, with Tables of Eclipses Visible in India by R. Schram*, Motilal Banarsidass Publishers, Delhi, 1995. Originally published in 1896.

[6] W. E. van Wijk, *Decimal Tables for the Reduction of Hindu Dates from the Data of the Sūrya-Siddhānta*, Martinus Nijhoff, The Hague, 1938.

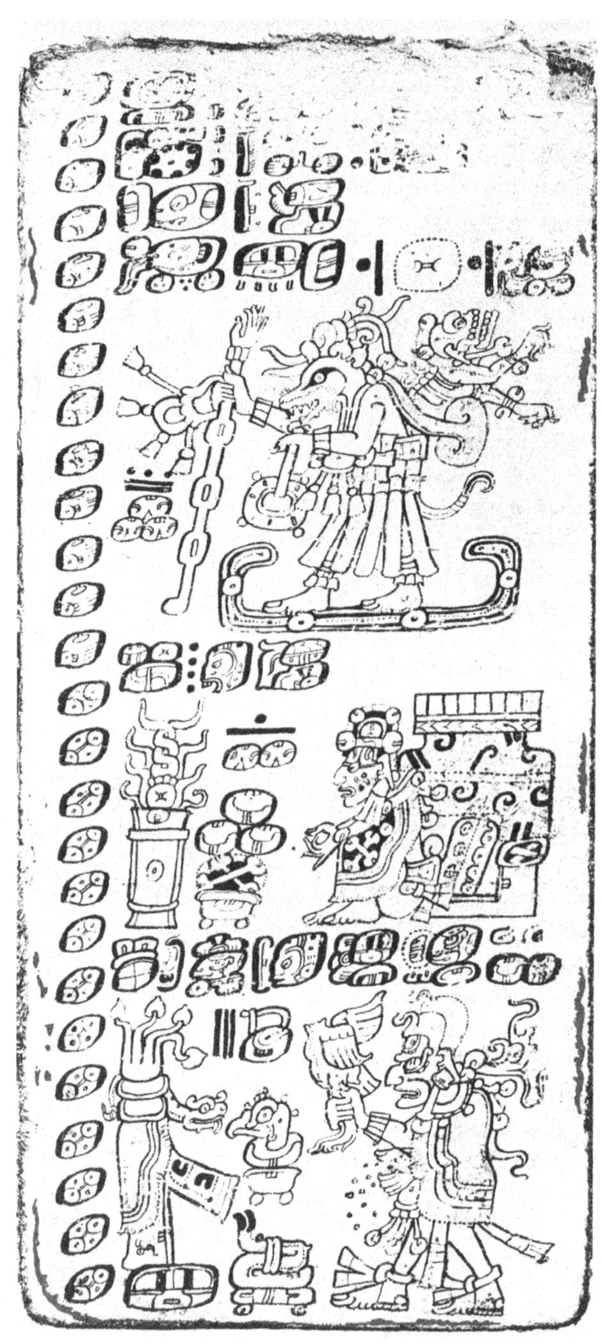

Mayan New Year ceremonies. (Reproduced, with permission, from Plate 28 in *A Commentary on the Dresden Codex: A Maya Hieroglyphic Book*, by J. E. S. Thompson, American Philosophical Society, Philadelphia, PA, 1972.)

11

The Mayan Calendars[1]

The invention of the Central American calendar in the Seventh century before Christ may be described with all propriety as one of the outstanding intellectual achievements in the history of man. This calendar solved with conspicuous success the great problem of measuring and defining time which confronts all civilized nations. Moreover it required the elaboration of one of the four or five original systems of writing the parts of speech in graphic symbols, and it conjoined with this supplementary invention of hieroglyphs the earliest discovery of the device of figures with place values in the notation of numbers. This time machine of ancient America was distinctly a scientific construction, the product of critical scrutiny of various natural phenomena by a master mind among the Mayas. It permitted a school of astronomer-priests to keep accurate records of celestial occurrences over a range of many centuries, with the ultimate reduction of the accumulated data through logical inferences to patterns of truth.

Herbert J. Spinden: *The Reduction of Mayan Dates* (1924)

The Mayans, developers of an ancient Amerindian civilization in Central America, employed three separate, overlapping, calendrical systems called by scholars the *long count*, the *haab*, and the *tzolkin*. Their civilization reached its zenith during the period 250–900 C.E., and the Mayans survive to this day in Guatemala and in the Yucatan peninsula of Mexico and Belize; some groups have preserved parts of the calendar systems. What is known today has been recovered through astroarcheological and epigraphic research (see, for example, [10]). There is general agreement on the Mayan calendrical rules and the correspondence between the three Mayan calendars; however, the exact correspondence between the Mayan calendars and Western calendars is still a matter of some slight dispute (see [1]). Correspondences are proposed by date equivalences in Spanish sources and by interpreting Mayan recordings of astronomical phenomena, such as new moons. Here we give the details for the most popular (and nearly universally accepted) correspondence, the *Goodman-Martinez-Thompson correlation* [20]. Another correlation was used by Spinden [17], [18], [19].[2] A superb discussion of Mayan mathematics, astronomy, and calendrical matters was given by Lounsbury [9] (see also [8]). Other good

[1] Stewart M. Clamen wrote an early version of some Mayan calendar functions given here.

[2] Some of Spinden's date calculations are wrong. Here are three examples: on p. 46 of "Maya Dates and What They Reveal" [19], he gives the equivalence JD 1785384 = February 10, 176 (Gregorian), but it should be February 11, 176 (Gregorian); at the top of p. 55 several Gregorian dates are off by 1 day; on p. 57 he gives the equivalence JD 2104772 = August 30, 1050 (Gregorian), but it should be July 27, 1050 (Gregorian).

general sources are [11] and [16]. Extensive discussions of the regional variations of the calendars of Mesoamerica are contained in [6]; however, its correlations are considered speculative, not authoritative.

The Aztecs had calendars analogous to the haab and tzolkin, borrowed from the Mayans who long predated them. We discuss these two calendars in Section 11.3.

11.1 The Long Count

But the biggest question of all is this: "What happens when the Long Count ends?"

Andrea Klosterman Harris: *The Long Count* (2010)

The long count is a strict counting of days from the beginning of the current cycle, each cycle containing 2880000 days (about 7885 solar years); the Mayans believed that the universe is destroyed and recreated at the start of every cycle.[3] The units of the long count are

1 kin	=	1 day	
1 uinal	=	20 kin	(20 days)
1 tun	=	18 uinal	(360 days)
1 katun	=	20 tun	(7200 days)
1 baktun	=	20 katun	(144000 days)

Thus, the long count date 12.16.11.16.6 means 12 baktun, 16 katun, 11 tun, 16 uinal, and 6 kin, giving a total of 1847486 days from the start of the Mayan calendar epoch. (It is uncertain when the Mayan day began; there is evidence that the tzolkin day began at sunset and the haab day at sunrise, or, in any case, that they began at different times of the day.)

Although not relevant here, the Mayans used the following larger units for longer time periods:

1 pictun	=	20 baktun	(2880000 days)
1 calabtun	=	20 pictun	(57600000 days)
1 kinchiltun	=	20 calabtun	(1152000000 days)
1 alautun	=	20 kinchiltun	(23040000000 days)

An alautun is about 63081377 solar years! To accommodate arbitrary dates, we allow the number of baktun in a long count to be any positive or negative integer.

The starting epoch of the long count, according to the Goodman-Martinez-Thompson correlation, is taken as Monday, August 11, −3113 (Gregorian). This

[3] On the approach of the end of the cycle on December 21, 2012 there was, in some circles, panic that the world would end. See, for example, E. C. Krupp, "The Great 2012 Scare," *Sky & Telescope*, Nov. 2009, pp. 22–26, and E. Barry, "In Panicky Russia, It's Official: End of World Is Not Near," *New York Times*, December 1, 2012. The attention paid to this misinterpretation of a "baktun" led to its being used as the name of a Mayan soap opera!

date equals September 6, 3114 B.C.E. (Julian),[4] which was (at noon) JD 584283, that is, R.D. −1137142:[5]

$$\textbf{mayan-epoch} \stackrel{\text{def}}{=} \textbf{fixed-from-jd}\,(584283) \tag{11.1}$$

In other words, our R.D. 0 is long count 7.17.18.13.2.

Since the components of the long count all begin with zero, we simply apply the mixed-radix formulas of Section 1.10, using the basis $\langle 20, 20, 18, 20 \rangle$. Thus, to convert from a Mayan long count date to an R.D. date, we compute the total number of days given by the long count and subtract the number of days before R.D. 0 by adding the epoch:

$$\textbf{fixed-from-mayan-long-count}\,(count) \stackrel{\text{def}}{=} \tag{11.2}$$

$$\textbf{mayan-epoch} + count \stackrel{\text{rad}}{\longleftarrow} \langle 20, 20, 18, 20 \rangle$$

In the opposite direction, converting an R.D. date to a Mayan long count date, we need to add the number of days in the long count before R.D. 0 and then divide the result into baktun, katun, tun, uinal, and kin:

$$\textbf{mayan-long-count-from-fixed}\,(date) \stackrel{\text{def}}{=} \tag{11.3}$$

$$(date - \textbf{mayan-epoch}) \stackrel{\text{rad}}{\longrightarrow} \langle 20, 20, 18, 20 \rangle$$

11.2 The Haab and Tzolkin Calendars

They made a clay image of the demon of evil Uuayayab, that is u-uayab-haab, "He by whom the year is poisoned," confronted it with the deity who had supreme power over the coming year, and then carried it out of the village in the direction of that cardinal point to which, on the system of the Mayan calendar, the particular year was supposed to belong.

Sir James George Frazer: *The Golden Bough* (1890)

The Mayans used a civil calendar, the haab, based approximately on the solar year and consisting of 18 "months" of 20 days each together with 5 additional days at the end. Because the haab calendar accounts for only 365 days (as compared with the mean length of the solar tropical year, 365.2422 days), the civil calendar slowly drifted with respect to the seasons,[6] as did the Egyptian calendar (see Section 1.11). The months were called[7]

---

[4] Thompson [20] errs in referring to this date as "3113 B.C.," confusing the two systems of dealing with years before the common era (see page 15). His error has been reproduced by many scholars.

[5] Almost all experts believe this correlation, or possibly JD 584285, is correct; in [10] the sources of these two main contenders are discussed. Spinden's value, now no longer used, is JD 489384.

[6] Mayan astronomers had remarkably precise values for the durations of the mean lunar month and tropical year, as well as for the periods of some of the planets. For example, they took 46 tzolkins (see below) to be 405 lunations, giving a value of $46 \times 260/405 \approx 29.530864$ days for the mean synodic month; they took 7.13.0.0.0 = 1101600 to be the number of days for the 365-day haab calendar to move twice through the tropical year, implying a mean tropical year of approximately 365.242036 days. See [3].

[7] The haab month names and tzolkin day names are transliterated from the Yucatan (Yucatec) Mayan language. The Guatemalan (Quiché) Mayans used slightly different names. The translations here are according to [6].

Figure 11.1 The haab month signs. Adapted from Spinden [18, fig. 3].

(1) Pop (Mat)
(2) Uo (Frog)
(3) Zip (Stag)
(4) Zotz (Bat)
(5) Tzec (Skull)
(6) Xul (End)
(7) Yaxkin (Green time)
(8) Mol (Gather)
(9) Chen (Well)
(10) Yax (Green)
(11) Zac (White)
(12) Ceh (Deer)
(13) Mac (Cover)
(14) Kankin (Yellow time)
(15) Muan (Owl)
(16) Pax (Drum)
(17) Kayab (Turtle)
(18) Cumku (Dark god)
(19) Uayeb

The last of these, Uayeb, was not really a month, but a 5-day unlucky period. The pictographs for the haab names are shown in Figure 11.1. Unlike Gregorian months, the days of the haab months begin at 0 and indicate the number of *elapsed days* in the current month. Thus, 0 Uo follows 19 Pop, and the fifth monthless day is followed by 0 Pop. This method of counting is also used for years in the Hindu calendar, as discussed in Chapters 10 and 20.

We represent haab dates as pairs,

month	*day*

where *month* and *day* are integers in the ranges 1 to 19 and 0 to 19, respectively; we thus treat Uayeb as a defective nineteenth month. We can count how many days after the first day of a cycle any given haab date occurs as follows:

$$\textbf{mayan-haab-ordinal}\left(\boxed{\textit{month} \mid \textit{day}}\right) \stackrel{\text{def}}{=} \tag{11.4}$$

$$(\textit{month} - 1) \times 20 + \textit{day}$$

The long count date 0.0.0.0.0 is considered to be haab date 8 Cumku (there is no disagreement here between the various correlations), which we specify by giving the starting R.D. date of the haab cycle preceding the start of the long count:

$$\textbf{mayan-haab-epoch} \stackrel{\text{def}}{=} \tag{11.5}$$

$$\textbf{mayan-epoch} - \textbf{mayan-haab-ordinal}\left(\boxed{18 \mid 8}\right)$$

We can convert an R.D. date to a haab date by using

$$\textbf{mayan-haab-from-fixed}\,(\textit{date}) \stackrel{\text{def}}{=} \boxed{\textit{month} \mid \textit{day}} \tag{11.6}$$

where

$$\begin{aligned} \textit{count} &= (\textit{date} - \textbf{mayan-haab-epoch}) \bmod 365 \\ \textit{day} &= \textit{count} \bmod 20 \\ \textit{month} &= \left\lfloor \frac{\textit{count}}{20} \right\rfloor + 1 \end{aligned}$$

It is not possible to convert a Mayan haab date to an R.D. date because without a "year" there is no unique corresponding R.D. date. We can ask, though, for the R.D. date of the haab date on or before a given R.D. date:

$$\textbf{mayan-haab-on-or-before}\,(\textit{haab}, \textit{date}) \stackrel{\text{def}}{=} \tag{11.7}$$

$$\begin{aligned} &(\textbf{mayan-haab-ordinal}\,(\textit{haab}) + \textbf{mayan-haab-epoch}) \\ &\bmod [\textit{date} \,..\, \textit{date} - 365) \end{aligned}$$

This is an instance of formula (1.63) for which the ordinal position of R.D. 0 is

$$\Delta = (0 - \textbf{mayan-haab-epoch}) \bmod 365$$

The third Mayan calendar, the tzolkin (or sacred) calendar, was a religious calendar consisting of two cycles: a 13-day count and a cycle of 20 names:

(1) Imix (Alligator)
(2) Ik (Wind)
(3) Akbal (Night)
(4) Kan (Iguana)
(5) Chicchan (Serpent)
(6) Cimi (Death)
(7) Manik (Deer)
(8) Lamat (Rabbit)
(9) Muluc (Rain)
(10) Oc (Foot)
(11) Chuen (Monkey)
(12) Eb (Tooth)
(13) Ben (Cane)
(14) Ix (Jaguar)
(15) Men (Eagle)
(16) Cib (Owl)
(17) Caban (Quake)
(18) Etznab (Flint)
(19) Cauac (Storm)
(20) Ahau (Lord)

(The translations are according to [6].) The pictographs for the tzolkin names are shown in Figure 11.2. According to [11], the tzolkin calendar's length is roughly that of human gestation and approximates the crop cycle, hence it was used for prediction of human destiny and to determine planting and harvesting times. This calendar is still in use among the Guatemalan Mayans.

Unlike the haab months and days, the counts and names cycle *simultaneously* and thus, for example, 13 Etznab precedes 1 Cauac, which precedes 2 Ahau, which

	Carving	Codex		Carving	Codex
Imix			Chuen		
Ik			Eb		
Akbal			Ben		
Kan			Ix		
Chicchan			Men		
Cimi			Cib		
Manik			Caban		
Lamat			Eznab		
Muluc			Cauac		
Oc			Ahau		

Figure 11.2 The tzolkin name signs. Adapted from Spinden [18, fig. 1].

precedes 3 Imix, and so on. Because 20 and 13 are relatively prime, this progression results in 260 unique dates, forming the "divine" year.

The long count date 0.0.0.0.0 is taken to be tzolkin date 4 Ahau. (The different correlations agree on this, too.) Representing tzolkin dates as pairs of positive integers

$$\boxed{number \mid name}$$

where *number* and *name* are integers in the ranges 1 to 13 and 1 to 20, respectively, we specify

$$\textbf{mayan-tzolkin-epoch} \stackrel{\text{def}}{=} \tag{11.8}$$

$$\textbf{mayan-epoch} - \textbf{mayan-tzolkin-ordinal}\left(\boxed{4 \mid 20}\right)$$

where the function **mayan-tzolkin-ordinal** is explained below.

We can convert from an R.D. date to a tzolkin date with

$$\textbf{mayan-tzolkin-from-fixed}\,(date) \stackrel{\text{def}}{=} \boxed{number \mid name} \tag{11.9}$$

where

$$count = date - \textbf{mayan-tzolkin-epoch} + 1$$

$$number = count \bmod [1\,..\,13]$$

$$name = count \bmod [1\,..\,20]$$

Just as with the haab calendar, it is impossible to convert a tzolkin date to an R.D. date. Unlike the haab calendar, however, because day numbers and day names cycle simultaneously, to calculate the number of days between two given tzolkin dates requires the solution to a pair of simultaneous linear congruences, as in Section 1.13. (See [13] for a general discussion of this topic and [9] for a specific discussion relating to the Mayan calendars.)

Suppose that we want to know the number of days x from tzolkin date $\boxed{1 \mid 1}$ until the next occurrence of tzolkin date $\boxed{m \mid n}$. We apply formula (1.73) with $a = m - 1$, $b = n - 1$, $c = 13$, $d = 20$, $\Gamma = \Delta = 0$. Because $k = -3$ is the multiplicative inverse of 13 modulo 20, we get

$$x = (m - 1 + 13[-3(n - m)]) \bmod 260$$

Accordingly, we define

$$\textbf{mayan-tzolkin-ordinal}\left(\boxed{number \mid name}\right) \stackrel{\text{def}}{=} \tag{11.10}$$

$$(number - 1 + 39 \times (number - name)) \bmod 260$$

As with the haab calendar, this function can be used to compute the R.D. date of the Mayan tzolkin date on or before a given R.D. date:

$$\textbf{mayan-tzolkin-on-or-before}\,(tzolkin, date) \stackrel{\text{def}}{=} \tag{11.11}$$

$$(\textbf{mayan-tzolkin-ordinal}\,(tzolkin) + \textbf{mayan-tzolkin-epoch})$$
$$\bmod\,[date\,..\,date - 260)$$

This is another instance of formula (1.63).

The Mayans referred to haab years by their "year bearer," the tzolkin day name of 0 Pop (the first day of that haab year).[8] Because the haab year is 365 days and the tzolkin is 260, only tzolkin day names Ik, Manik, Eb, and Caban can occur as year bearers in this scheme. The year bearer for a given R.D. date is computed by

$$\textbf{mayan-year-bearer-from-fixed}\,(date) \stackrel{\text{def}}{=} \tag{11.12}$$
$$\begin{cases} \textbf{bogus} & \textbf{if}\ \left(\textbf{mayan-haab-from-fixed}\,(date)\right)_{\textbf{month}} = 19 \\ (\textbf{mayan-tzolkin-from-fixed}\,(x))_{\textbf{name}} & \textbf{otherwise} \end{cases}$$

where

$$x = \textbf{mayan-haab-on-or-before}\left(\boxed{1\,|\,0}\,, date\right)$$

Dates in Uayeb are not in a haab year and hence have no year bearer; in such cases **bogus** is returned.

A popular way for the Mayans to specify a date was to use the haab and tzolkin dates together, forming a cycle of the least common multiple of 365 and 260 days: 18980 days or approximately 52 solar years. This cycle is called a *calendar round*, and we seek the latest date, on or before a given R.D. *date*, that falls on a specified date of the calendar round with Haab date *haab* and Tzolkin date *tzolkin*. Again we apply formula (1.73), this time with $c = 365$ and $d = 260$ and no shifts. The greatest common divisor of c and d is 5. The inverse of $365/5 = 73$ modulo $260/5 = 52$ is (by coincidence) also 5. Substituting these values into (1.73), we get

$$(a + 365[b - a]) \bmod 18980$$

for the position of the pair of dates, a and b, in the calendar round. Using formula (1.63) to go back to the last occurrence of *haab* and *tzolkin* before *date*, with k and Δ determined in this way—once with a = **mayan-haab-ordinal**(*haab*) and b = **mayan-tzolkin-ordinal**(*tzolkin*) and again with a = **mayan-haab-epoch** and b = **mayan-tzolkin-epoch**—and simplifying, we have

$$\textbf{mayan-calendar-round-on-or-before}\,(haab, tzolkin, date) \stackrel{\text{def}}{=} \tag{11.13}$$
$$\begin{cases} (haab\text{-}count + 365 \times diff) \bmod [date\,..\,date - 18980) & \textbf{if}\ (diff \bmod 5) = 0 \\ \textbf{bogus} & \textbf{otherwise} \end{cases}$$

[8] This is the Tikal custom; however, some scholars believe that the tzolkin name of the last day of the previous year was used, and some data is consistent with this.

where

$$\begin{aligned} \textit{haab-count} &= \textbf{mayan-haab-ordinal}\,(\textit{haab}) + \textbf{mayan-haab-epoch} \\ \textit{tzolkin-count} &= \textbf{mayan-tzolkin-ordinal}\,(\textit{tzolkin}) + \textbf{mayan-tzolkin-epoch} \\ \textit{diff} &= \textit{tzolkin-count} - \textit{haab-count} \end{aligned}$$

For impossible combinations **bogus** is returned.

This function can be used to compute the number of days between a pair of dates on the calendar round or to write a function **mayan-calendar-round-on-or-after**; we leave these possibilities to the reader to investigate.

11.3 The Aztec Calendars

The import of calendrics for Mesoamerican culture cannot be overstated.
Kay Read: *Time and Sacrifice in the Aztec Cosmos* (1998)

The Aztecs (more properly called Mexica-Tenochca) used two calendars, the *xihuitl* which is nearly identical to the Mayan haab and the *tonalpohualli* which is akin to the Mayan tzolkin; in both cases the names are in Nahuatl, however. There are many idiosyncrasies in the Aztec calendar (associating dates, days, or years with colors, directions, patrons, auspiciousness, and so on), but these are computationally trivial and so we will ignore them.

The precise correlation between Aztec dates and our R.D. dates is based on the recorded Aztec dates of the fall of (what later became) Mexico City to Hernán Cortés, August 13, 1521 (Julian). Thus we define

$$\textbf{aztec-correlation} \stackrel{\text{def}}{=} \textbf{fixed-from-julian}\left(\boxed{1521 \mid \textbf{august} \mid 13}\right) \tag{11.14}$$

which was R.D. 555403.

The xihuitl calendar approximated the solar year; like the Mayan haab, it was 365 days long, broken down into 18 "months" of 20 days each, followed by 5 unnamed worthless days called *nemontemi*. Scholars believe that the Aztecs used intercalation on the xihuitl calendar to keep it synchronized with the solar seasons, but the details of how they added days are a matter of speculation. The Nahuatl (Aztec) names of the xihuitl months are:

(1) Izcalli (Sprout)
(2) Atlcahualo (Water left)
(3) Tlacaxipehualiztli (Man flaying)
(4) Tozoztontli (1-Vigil)
(5) Huei Tozoztli (2-Vigil)
(6) Toxcatl (Drought)
(7) Etzalcualiztli (Eating bean soup)
(8) Tecuilhuitontli (1-Lord's feast)
(9) Huei Tecuilhuitl (2-Lord's feast)
(10) Tlaxochimaco (Give flowers)

(11) Xocotlhuetzi (Fruit falls)
(12) Ochpaniztli (Road sweeping)
(13) Teotleco (God arrives)
(14) Tepeilhuitl (Mountain feast)
(15) Quecholli (Macaw)
(16) Panquetzaliztli (Flag raising)
(17) Atemoztli (Falling water)
(18) Tititl (Storm)
(19) Nemontemi (Full in vain)

(Following [5]; the translations are from [6, calendar E, p. 222]. The placement of the nemontemi differs in different communities.) But, while in the Mayan haab the day count is of elapsed days (that is, it goes from 0 to 19), the xihuitl day count goes from 1 to 20. Thus we represent a xihuitl date as a pair

$$\boxed{\textit{month} \mid \textit{day}}$$

where *month* and *day* are integers in the ranges 1 to 19 and 1 to 20, respectively, and we treat the nemontemi as a defective nineteenth month. We can count the number of elapsed days in the cycle of Aztec xihuitl dates as follows:

$$\textbf{aztec-xihuitl-ordinal}\left(\boxed{\textit{month} \mid \textit{day}}\right) \stackrel{\text{def}}{=} \tag{11.15}$$

$$(\textit{month} - 1) \times 20 + \textit{day} - 1$$

The only difference from the haab computation is the subtraction of 1 from *day* to compensate for the shift in range.

According to [5, Table 3], the xihuitl date at the correlation point is 2 Xocotlhuetzi, so the start of a xihuitl cycle is

$$\textbf{aztec-xihuitl-correlation} \stackrel{\text{def}}{=} \tag{11.16}$$

$$\textbf{aztec-correlation} - \textbf{aztec-xihuitl-ordinal}\left(\boxed{11 \mid 2}\right)$$

or R.D. 555202. Then we can compute the xihuitl date of an R.D. by

$$\textbf{aztec-xihuitl-from-fixed}\,(\textit{date}) \stackrel{\text{def}}{=} \tag{11.17}$$

$$\boxed{\textit{month} \mid \textit{day}}$$

where

$$\textit{count} = (\textit{date} - \textbf{aztec-xihuitl-correlation}) \bmod 365$$
$$\textit{day} = (\textit{count} \bmod 20) + 1$$
$$\textit{month} = \left\lfloor \frac{\textit{count}}{20} \right\rfloor + 1$$

Again, the only difference from the haab computation is the addition of 1 to *day* to compensate for the shift in range.

As with the Mayan haab, because there is no count of the cycles, we cannot invert this function and find the R.D. of a xihuitl date, but we can use equation (1.63) to find the R.D. of the xihuitl date on or before a given R.D.:

$$\textbf{aztec-xihuitl-on-or-before}\,(\textit{xihuitl}, \textit{date}) \stackrel{\text{def}}{=} \tag{11.18}$$

$$(\textbf{aztec-xihuitl-correlation} + \textbf{aztec-xihuitl-ordinal}\,(\textit{xihuitl}))$$
$$\bmod\ [\textit{date} \,..\, \textit{date} - 365)$$

The Aztec tonalpohualli (divinatory) calendar is identical, except for the names in the cycle of days, to that of the Mayan tzolkin: two simultaneous cycles run, a 13-day count and a cycle of 20 names [6, p. 221]:

(1) Cipactli (Alligator)	(11) Ozomatli (Monkey)
(2) Ehecatl (Wind)	(12) Malinalli (Grass)
(3) Calli (House)	(13) Acatl (Cane)
(4) Cuetzpallin (Iguana)	(14) Ocelotl (Jaguar)
(5) Coatl (Serpent)	(15) Quauhtli (Eagle)
(6) Miquiztli (Death)	(16) Cozcaquauhtli (Buzzard)
(7) Mazatl (Deer)	(17) Ollin (Quake)
(8) Tochtli (Rabbit)	(18) Tecpatl (Flint)
(9) Atl (Water)	(19) Quiahuitl (Rain)
(10) Itzcuintli (Dog)	(20) Xochitl (Flower)

The implementation is identical to the Mayan tzolkin; we represent tonalpohualli dates as

number	*name*

where *number* and *name* are integers in the ranges 1 to 13 and 1 to 20, respectively, and we compute the ordinal number in the cycle of a given tonalpohualli date by

$$\textbf{aztec-tonalpohualli-ordinal}\left(\boxed{\textit{name}}\boxed{\textit{number}}\right) \stackrel{\text{def}}{=} \tag{11.19}$$

$$(\textit{number} - 1 + 39 \times (\textit{number} - \textit{name})) \bmod 260$$

According to [5, Table 3] the date at the correlation is 1 Coatl, so the start of a tonalpohualli cycle is given by

$$\textbf{aztec-tonalpohualli-correlation} \stackrel{\text{def}}{=} \tag{11.20}$$

$$\textbf{aztec-correlation} - \textbf{aztec-tonalpohualli-ordinal}\left(\boxed{1}\boxed{5}\right)$$

or R.D. 555299. Mimicking our tzolkin conversions we have

$$\textbf{aztec-tonalpohualli-from-fixed}\,(\textit{date}) \stackrel{\text{def}}{=} \tag{11.21}$$

$$\boxed{\textit{number}}\boxed{\textit{name}}$$

where

$$\begin{aligned} count &= date - \textbf{aztec-tonalpohualli-correlation} + 1 \\ number &= count \bmod [1 \,..\, 13] \\ name &= count \bmod [1 \,..\, 20] \end{aligned}$$

and

$$\textbf{aztec-tonalpohualli-on-or-before}\,(tonalpohualli, date) \stackrel{\text{def}}{=} \tag{11.22}$$

$$\big(\textbf{aztec-tonalpohualli-correlation} + \textbf{aztec-tonalpohualli-ordinal}\,(tonalpohualli)\big) \bmod [date \,..\, date - 260)$$

According to [5] and [14], the Aztec, like the Maya, used "calendar rounds" of 52 xihuitl years—the time it takes for the xihuitl and tonalpohualli to realign; these were called *xiuhmolpilli*. The 52 xihuitl years of a calendar round were designated by names and numbers using four of the twenty tonalpohualli day signs, Calli (3), Tochtli (8), Acatl (13), Tecpatl (18), which are similar to the "year bearer" of the Mayan calendar, and numbers 1 through 13. Thus we represent xiuhmolpilli designations as

number	*name*

where *number* is an integer in the range 1 to 13 and *name* is an integer, 3, 8, 13, or 18. The xihuitl year designation was taken from the tonalpohualli date of the last day of that xihuitl year (excluding the nemontemi, of course). The name of the xihuitl year containing a given R.D. is thus given by

$$\textbf{aztec-xiuhmolpilli-from-fixed}\,(date) \stackrel{\text{def}}{=} \tag{11.23}$$

$$\begin{cases} \textbf{bogus} & \textbf{if } month = 19 \\ \textbf{aztec-tonalpohualli-from-fixed}\,(x) & \textbf{otherwise} \end{cases}$$

where

$$\begin{aligned} x &= \textbf{aztec-xihuitl-on-or-before}\left(\boxed{18 \mid 20}, date + 364\right) \\ month &= (\textbf{aztec-xihuitl-from-fixed}\,(date))_{\textbf{month}} \end{aligned}$$

This returns **bogus** for the nemontemi.

We can determine the combination of xihuitl and tonalpohualli dates on or before an R.D. by using (1.73):

$$\textbf{aztec-xihuitl-tonalpohualli-on-or-before}\,(xihuitl, tonalpohualli, date) \stackrel{\text{def}}{=} \tag{11.24}$$

$$\begin{cases} (\textit{xihuitl-count} + 365 \times \textit{diff}) \bmod [\textit{date} \mathinner{..} \textit{date} - 18980) \\ \qquad \textbf{if } (\textit{diff} \bmod 5) = 0 \\ \textbf{bogus} \quad \textbf{otherwise} \end{cases}$$

where

$$\begin{aligned} \textit{xihuitl-count} &= \textbf{aztec-xihuitl-ordinal}\,(\textit{xihuitl}) \\ &\quad + \textbf{aztec-xihuitl-correlation} \\ \textit{tonalpohualli-count} &= \textbf{aztec-tonalpohualli-ordinal}\,(\textit{tonalpohualli}) \\ &\quad + \textbf{aztec-tonalpohualli-correlation} \\ \textit{diff} &= \textit{tonalpohualli-count} - \textit{xihuitl-count} \end{aligned}$$

References

[1] G. Aldana, "The Maya Calendar Correlation Problem," *Calendars and Years, vol. II*, J. M. Steele, ed., Oxbow Books, Oxford and Oakville, CT, pp. 127–179, 2011.

[2] A. F. Aveni, *Empires of Time: Calendars, Clocks, and Cultures*, Basic Books, New York, 1989. Republished by Kondasha America, New York, 1995.

[3] W. Bietenholz, "Should We Revitalize the Maya Numerals?," *Math. Intelligencer*, vol. 35, no. 4, pp. 21–26, 2013.

[4] C. P. Bowditch, *The Numeration, Calendar Systems and Astronomical Knowledge of the Mayas*, Cambridge University Press, Cambridge, 1910.

[5] A. Caso, "Calendrical Systems of Central Mexico," in *Handbook of Middle American Indians*, R. Wauchope, general ed., vol. 10, pt. 1 (G. F. Ekholm and I. Bernal, vol. eds.), University of Texas Press, Austin, Texas, Chap. 13, pp. 333–348, 1971.

[6] M. S. Edmundson, *The Book of the Year: Middle American Calendrical Systems*, University of Utah Press, Salt Lake City, Utah, 1988.

[7] J. T. Goodman, *The Archaic Maya Inscriptions*, appendix to vol. VIII of *Biologia Centrali-Americanna*, F. D. Godman and O. Salvin, eds., R. H. Porter and Dulau & Co., London, 1897.

[8] J. S. Justeson, "Ancient Mayan Ethnoastronomy: An Overview of Epigraphic Sources," *World Archeoastronomy* (Selected Papers from the 2nd Oxford International Conference on Archaeoastronomy, Merida, Yucatan, Mexico, January 13–17 1986), A. F. Aveni, ed., Chap. 8, pp. 76–129, 1989.

[9] F. G. Lounsbury, "Maya Numeration, Computation, and Calendrical Astronomy," in *Dictionary of Scientific Biography, vol. 15*, suppl. 1, Charles Scribner's Sons, New York, pp. 759–818, 1978.

[10] F. G. Lounsbury, "A Derivation of the Mayan-to-Julian Calendar Correlation from the Dresden Codex Venus Chronology," in *The Sky in Mayan Literature*, A. F. Aveni, ed., Oxford University Press, pp. 184–206, Oxford, 1992.

[11] S. Milbrath, *Star Gods of the Maya: Astronomy in Art, Folklore, and Calendars*, University of Texas Press, Austin, Texas, 1999.

[12] S. G. Morley, *The Ancient Maya*, revised by G. W. Brainerd, Stanford University Press, Stanford, CA, 1963.

[13] Ø. Ore, *Number Theory and Its History*, McGraw-Hill, New York, 1948. Reprinted by Dover Publications, Mineola, NY, 1987.

[14] K. Read, *Time and Sacrifice in the Aztec Cosmos*, Indiana University Press, Bloomington Indiana, 1998.

[15] L. Satterwaite, "Concepts and Structures of Maya Calendrical Arithmetics," Ph.D. thesis, University of Pennsylvania, Philadelphia, 1947.

[16] L. Satterwaite, "Calendarics of the Maya Lowlands," *Handbook of Middle American Indians*, R. Wauchope, general ed., vol. 3, pt. 2 (G. R. Willey, vol. ed.), University of Texas Press, Austin, Texas, chap. 24, pp. 603–631, 1965.

[17] H. J. Spinden, "Central American Calendars and the Gregorian Day," *Proceedings of the National Academy of Sciences* (*USA*), vol. 6, pp. 56–59, 1920.

[18] H. J. Spinden, "The Reduction of Maya Dates," *Peabody Museum Papers*, vol. VI, no. 4, 1924.

[19] H. J. Spinden, "Maya Dates and What They Reveal," *Science Bulletin* (The Museum of the Brooklyn Institute of Arts and Sciences), vol. IV, no. 1, 1930.

[20] J. E. S. Thompson, *Maya Hieroglyphic Writing*, 3rd edn., University of Oklahoma Press, Norman, OK, 1971.

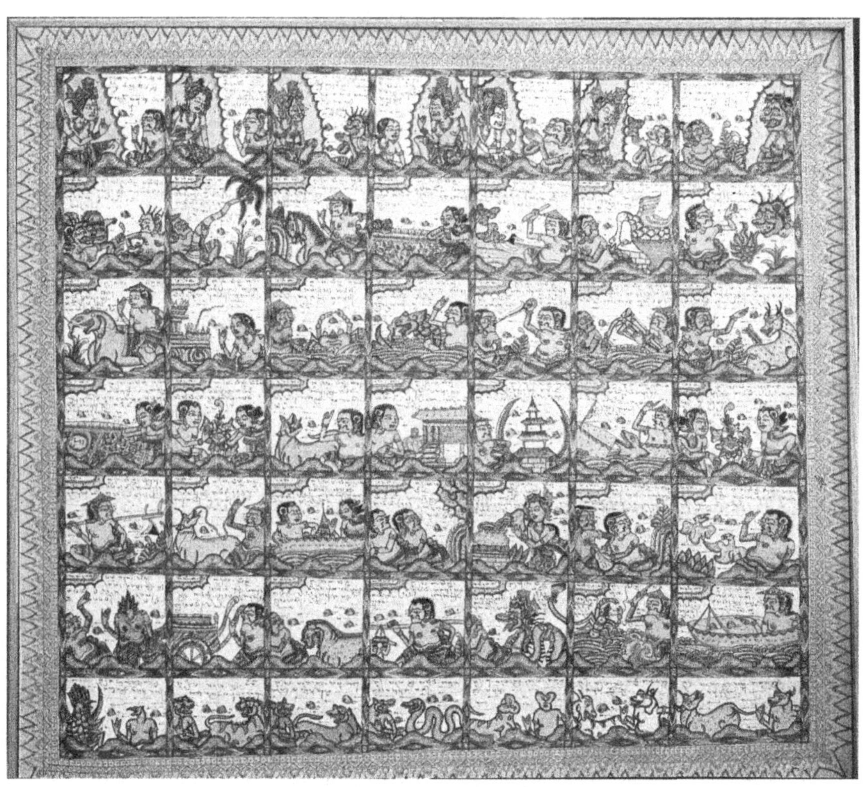

Balinese *plintangen* calendar, by Ni Made Widiarki of Kamasan, Klungkung, Bali, showing a combination of the 5-day market week (*pancawara* cycle) and the 7-day week (*saptawara* cycle). (Reproduced, with permission, from *Myths & Symbols in Indonesian Art*, curated by M.-A. Milford-Lutzker, Antonio Prieto Memorial Gallery, Mills College, Oakland, CA, 1991.)

12

The Balinese Pawukon Calendar

What is "really real" is the name ... of the day, its place in the transempirical taxonomy of days, not its epiphenomenal reflection in the sky.

Clifford Geertz: *The Interpretation of Cultures* (1973)

The Pawukon (*wuku*) calendar of Bali is a complex example of a calendar based on concurrent cycles (see Section 1.13). The whole calendar repeats every 210 days, but these 210-day "years" are unnumbered. In addition to this *small year* comprising one cycle of 210 days, there is a two-cycle *full year* of 420 days [4, p. 110] (see also [1]). The calendar comprises 10 subcycles of lengths 1 through 10, all running simultaneously. The subcycles that determine the calendar are those of lengths 5, 6, 7; the others are altered to fit by repetitions or other complications.

Like many other cultures in the region, the Balinese also have a lunisolar calendar of the old Hindu style (see Chapter 10), but leap months have been added erratically; we do not describe its details. This lunisolar calendar is used to determine only one holiday: Nyepi, a "New Year's Day" marking the start of the tenth lunar month, near the onset of spring.

12.1 Structure and Implementation

The cycles and supercycles are endless, unanchored, unaccountable, and, as their internal order has no significance, without climax. They do not accumulate, they do not build, and they are not consumed. They don't tell you what time it is; they tell you what kind of time it is.

Clifford Geertz: *The Interpretation of Cultures* (1973)

The main subcycles of the Pawukon calendar are those of lengths 5, 6, and 7, and the whole calendar repeats every 210 days, the least common multiple of 5, 6, and 7. The names of the various cycles and of the days in each are given in Table 12.1. There is no notion of a calendar month; rather any 35-day interval is called a *bulan*.

Each day is named according to the value assigned to the day in each of the 10 cycles:

bali-pawukon-from-fixed (*date*) $\stackrel{\text{def}}{=}$ (12.1)

bali-luang-from-fixed (*date*)	**bali-dwiwara-from-fixed** (*date*)	**bali-triwara-from-fixed** (*date*)	**bali-caturwara-from-fixed** (*date*)	**bali-pancawara-from-fixed** (*date*)
bali-sadwara-from-fixed (*date*)	**bali-saptawara-from-fixed** (*date*)	**bali-asatawara-from-fixed** (*date*)	**bali-sangawara-from-fixed** (*date*)	**bali-dasawara-from-fixed** (*date*)

Table 12.1 Names of the days in each of the 10 simultaneous cycles of the Pawukon calendar.

Cycle length										
1	2	3	4	5	6	7	8	9	10	
Ekawara	*Dwiwara*	*Triwara*	*Caturwara*	*Pancawara*	*Sadwara*	*Saptawara*	*Asatawara*	*Sangawara*	*Dasawara*	
Luang	Menga	Pasah	Sri	Umanis	Tungleh	Redite	Sri	Dangu	Pandita	1
	Pepet	Beteng	Laba	Paing	Aryang	Coma	Indra	Jangur	Pati	2
		Kajeng	Jaya	Pon	Urukung	Anggara	Guru	Gigis	Suka	3
			Menala	Wage	Paniron	Buda	Yama	Nohan	Duka	4
				Keliwon	Was	Wraspati	Ludra	Ogan	Sri	5
					Maulu	Sukra	Brahma	Erangan	Manuh	6
						Saniscara	Kala	Urungan	Manusa	7
							Uma	Tulus	Raja	8
								Dadi	Dewa	9
									Raksasa	0

The day names for the periods of length 3, 6, and 7 cycle in their natural order. In particular, the 7-day cycle corresponds to the day of the week on other calendars. The 30 weeks of a full 210-day cycle are also named (see Table 12.2).

Cycles on the Pawukon calendar—like the Mayan haab and tzolkin calendars (see Chapter 11)—are unnumbered, and thus we can take any start of the 210-day period as its epoch; for example:

$$\textbf{bali-epoch} \stackrel{\text{def}}{=} \textbf{fixed-from-jd}\,(146) \tag{12.2}$$

We can determine the position (beginning with 0) of any fixed date within the full 210-day cycle easily:

$$\textbf{bali-day-from-fixed}\,(\textit{date}) \stackrel{\text{def}}{=} (\textit{date} - \textbf{bali-epoch}) \bmod 210 \tag{12.3}$$

The simple cycles of length 3 (*triwara*), 6 (*sadwara*), and 7 (*saptawara*) are then trivial to implement:

$$\textbf{bali-triwara-from-fixed}\,(\textit{date}) \stackrel{\text{def}}{=} \tag{12.4}$$
$$(\textbf{bali-day-from-fixed}\,(\textit{date}) \bmod 3) + 1$$

$$\textbf{bali-sadwara-from-fixed}\,(\textit{date}) \stackrel{\text{def}}{=} \tag{12.5}$$
$$(\textbf{bali-day-from-fixed}\,(\textit{date}) \bmod 6) + 1$$

$$\textbf{bali-saptawara-from-fixed}\,(\textit{date}) \stackrel{\text{def}}{=} \tag{12.6}$$
$$(\textbf{bali-day-from-fixed}\,(\textit{date}) \bmod 7) + 1$$

The only complication of the 5-day (*pancawara*) cycle is that the Pawukon cycle begins with day 2 of the 5-day cycle, and thus we need to add 2 before taking the (adjusted) modulus:

$$\textbf{bali-pancawara-from-fixed}\,(\textit{date}) \stackrel{\text{def}}{=} \tag{12.7}$$
$$(\textbf{bali-day-from-fixed}\,(\textit{date}) + 2) \bmod [1\,..\,5]$$

Calculating the week number is also trivial:

$$\textbf{bali-week-from-fixed}\,(\textit{date}) \stackrel{\text{def}}{=} \tag{12.8}$$
$$\left\lfloor \tfrac{1}{7} \times \textbf{bali-day-from-fixed}\,(\textit{date}) \right\rfloor + 1$$

The position of a day in the 10-day cycle depends on numbers, called *urips*, that are associated with the 5- and 7-day cycles by the sacred palm-leaf scriptures.

Taking the sum of the two appropriate *urips*, modulo 10, gives the position in the 10-day (*dasawara*) cycle:[1]

$$\textbf{bali-dasawara-from-fixed}\,(\mathit{date}) \stackrel{\text{def}}{=} \tag{12.9}$$

$$\left(1 + \langle 5, 9, 7, 4, 8\rangle_{[i]} + \langle 5, 4, 3, 7, 8, 6, 9\rangle_{[j]}\right) \bmod 10$$

where

$$i = \textbf{bali-pancawara-from-fixed}\,(\mathit{date}) - 1$$
$$j = \textbf{bali-saptawara-from-fixed}\,(\mathit{date}) - 1$$

The position of a day on the 2-day (*dwiwara*) cycle is simply the parity of its position on the 10-day cycle:

$$\textbf{bali-dwiwara-from-fixed}\,(\mathit{date}) \stackrel{\text{def}}{=} \tag{12.10}$$

$$\textbf{bali-dasawara-from-fixed}\,(\mathit{date}) \bmod [1\,..\,2]$$

Similarly, the "1-day" (*ekawara*) cycle names only the even days of the 10-day cycle, which are called Luang. We use a boolean function to indicate whether a day is Luang:

$$\textbf{bali-luang-from-fixed}\,(\mathit{date}) \stackrel{\text{def}}{=} \tag{12.11}$$

$$(\textbf{bali-dasawara-from-fixed}\,(\mathit{date}) \bmod 2) = 0$$

Because 210 is not divisible by 8 or 9, to squeeze in subcycles of lengths 8 and 9, certain values must be repeated. The 9-day (*sangawara*) cycle begins with 4 occurrences of the value 1, which can be computed as follows:

$$\textbf{bali-sangawara-from-fixed}\,(\mathit{date}) \stackrel{\text{def}}{=} \tag{12.12}$$

$$(\max\{0, \textbf{bali-day-from-fixed}\,(\mathit{date}) - 3\} \bmod 9) + 1$$

The 8-day (*asatawara*) cycle runs normally except that days 70, 71, and 72 are all given the value 7. This is a bit more complicated to compute:

$$\textbf{bali-asatawara-from-fixed}\,(\mathit{date}) \stackrel{\text{def}}{=} \tag{12.13}$$

$$(\max\{6, 4 + ((\mathit{day} - 70) \bmod 210)\} \bmod 8) + 1$$

---

[1] The sequence 5, 9, 7, 4, 8 can be calculated as

$$a + \begin{cases} 4 & \textbf{if } a \leqslant 1 \\ 5 & \textbf{otherwise} \end{cases}$$

where $a = (3d) \bmod 5$, and $d = \textbf{bali-day-from-fixed}\,(\mathit{date}) - 2$.

where

$$\textit{day} = \textbf{bali-day-from-fixed}\,(\textit{date})$$

Finally, the 4-day (*caturwara*) cycle depends directly on the 8-day cycle:

$$\textbf{bali-caturwara-from-fixed}\,(\textit{date}) \stackrel{\text{def}}{=} \qquad (12.14)$$
$$\textbf{bali-asatawara-from-fixed}\,(\textit{date}) \bmod [1\,..\,4]$$

The full 210-day cycle is shown in Table 12.2. A traditional calendar, called a *tika*, uses symbols to mark the days of each of the 8 cycles shown in the chart.

Without numbering the cycles, there is no way to convert a Pawukon date into a fixed date. Instead, as for the Mayan calendars of Chapter 11, we use formulas (1.73) and (1.63) to determine the last occurrence of a Pawukon date before a given fixed date. The 10 components of the Pawukon date are fully determined by their values on the cycles of relatively prime lengths 5, 6, and 7. Thus we apply (1.73) twice: first to compute the position b_{35} of a Pawukon date within a 35-day subcycle from its position a_5 in the 5-day week and b_7 in the 7-day week, and then to combine its position a_6 in the 6-day week with b_{35}. Recalling the offset of 1 in the 5-day cycle, we let $c = 5$ and $d = 7$ be the cycle lengths, $\Gamma = 1$ and $\Delta = 0$ be the offsets, and $k = 3$ be the inverse of 5 modulo 7 in (1.73), to obtain

$$\begin{aligned} b_{35} &= (a_5 - 1 + 5 \times 3(b_7 - a_5 + 1)) \bmod 35 \\ &= (a_5 + 14 + 15(b_7 - a_5)) \bmod 35 \end{aligned}$$

For the full cycle of 210 days, we let $c = 6$, $d = 35$, $\Gamma = \Delta = 0$, and $k = 6$, to get

$$n = (a_6 + 36(b_{35} - a_6)) \bmod 210$$

Before applying (1.63), we also need to find the offset Δ of the Pawukon cycle vis-à-vis R.D. dates:

bali-on-or-before (12.15)

luang	*dwiwara*	*triwara*	*caturwara*	*pancawara*
sadwara	*saptawara*	*asatawara*	*sangawara*	*dasawara*

, *date*) $\stackrel{\text{def}}{=}$

$$\textit{date} - ((\textit{date} + \Delta - \textit{days}) \bmod 210)$$

where

$$\begin{aligned} a_5 &= \textit{pancawara} - 1 \\ a_6 &= \textit{sadwara} - 1 \\ b_7 &= \textit{saptawara} - 1 \\ b_{35} &= (a_5 + 14 + 15 \times (b_7 - a_5)) \bmod 35 \\ \textit{days} &= a_6 + 36 \times (b_{35} - a_6) \\ \Delta &= \textbf{bali-day-from-fixed}\,(\text{R.D. } 0) \end{aligned}$$

There is no need to take *days* modulo 210 before applying (1.63).

12.2 Conjunction Days

The main ... ceremony occurs on each temple's "birthday," every 210 days, at which time the gods descend from their homes atop the great volcano in the center of the island, enter iconic figurines placed on an altar in the temple, remain three days, and then return.

Clifford Geertz: *The Interpretation of Cultures* (1973)

The holidays on the Balinese Pawukon calendar are based on conjunctions of dates on individual cycles. The ninth day of every 15-day subcycle is important: on this day, called Kajeng Keliwon, the last day of the 3-day cycle (Kajeng) and last day of the 5-day cycle (Keliwon) coincide. (It is the ninth day because the first day of the Pawukon cycle is day 2 of the 5-day cycle.) With the utility function **positions-in-range** (1.40), it is easy to collect all occurrences in a given Gregorian year:

$$\textbf{kajeng-keliwon}\,(g\text{-}year) \stackrel{\text{def}}{=} \textbf{positions-in-range}\,(8, 15, \Delta, year) \tag{12.16}$$

where

$$\begin{aligned} year &= \textbf{gregorian-year-range}\,(g\text{-}year) \\ \Delta &= \textbf{bali-day-from-fixed}\,(\textsc{r.d.}\ 0) \end{aligned}$$

Since **positions-in-range** measures the desired position, starting with 0, the ninth day is at position 8; **bali-day-from-fixed**(R.D. 0) provides it with the position in the cycle of our R.D. epoch.

The 5-day and 7-day cycles together create a 35-day cycle. The second Saturday of the Pawukon cycle, and every subsequent fifth Saturday, is both the last day of the week and the last day of the 5-day cycle. Each such conjunction is called a Tumpek and is computed as follows:

$$\textbf{tumpek}\,(g\text{-}year) \stackrel{\text{def}}{=} \textbf{positions-in-range}\,(13, 35, \Delta, year) \tag{12.17}$$

where

$$\begin{aligned} year &= \textbf{gregorian-year-range}\,(g\text{-}year) \\ \Delta &= \textbf{bali-day-from-fixed}\,(\textsc{r.d.}\ 0) \end{aligned}$$

The six Tumpeks in each Pawukon cycle are named Tumpek Landep (day 14 of the 210-day cycle), Tumpek Uduh (day 49), Tumpek Kuningan (day 84), Tumpek Krulut (day 119), Tumpek Kandang (day 154), and Tumpek Ringgit (day 189).

Other significant conjunctions occur on days 4 (Buda-Keliwon), 18 (Buda-Cemeng), 24 (Anggara Kasih), and 29 (Pengembang) of each 35-day subcycle.

Day 74 of the Pawukon is Galungan; day 84 is Kuningan Day, which is both a Tumpek day and Kajeng Keliwon; and the period from Galungan through Kuningan Day is called the Galungan Days, during which the most important celebrations are held.

[illegible] of each day on the cycles of length 3, 5, 4, 2, 9, 8, 10, and 6 are given. Italics and boldface are used to indicate important conjunctions. Kajeng Keliwon is in italics, [illegible] is bold face. For example, consider the box Saniscara (Saturday) for the twelfth week (Kuningan): The italic *3* in the upper left means that the day is in position 3 in the 3-day (triwara) cycle; it is italic because that day is the conjunction Kajeng Keliwon. The boldface **5** at upper right means that the day is in position 5 in the 5-day (pancawara) cycle; it is in bold because that day is the conjunction Tumpek. The 2 below the boldface **5** means that the day is the second day of the 4-day (caturwara) cycle, and so on. Traditional calendars, called *tika*, use symbols rather than numbers to punctuate each cycle; modern calendars would use the names instead of numbers and are typically arranged in a circular order as displayed here.

Week	1	2	3	4	5	6	7	8	9	10	11	12	13	14	15	16	17	18	19	20	21	22	23	24	25	26	27	28	29	30
Week name	Sinta	Landep	Ukir	Kulantir	Taulu	Gumbreg	Wariga	Warigadian	Jukungwangi	Sungsang	Dunggulan	Kuningan	Langkir	Medangsia	Pujut	Pahang	Krulut	Merakih	Tambir	Medangkungan	Matal	Uye	Menail	Parangbakat	Bala	Ugu	Wayang	Kelawu	Dukut	Watugunung
Redite (Sunday)	1 2	2 4	3 1	1 3	2 5	3 2	1 4	2 1	3 3	1 5	2 2	3 4	1 1	2 3	*3 5*	1 2	2 4	3 1	1 3	2 5	3 2	1 4	2 1	3 3	1 5	2 2	3 4	1 1	2 3	*3 5*
	1 1	2 4	3 3	4 2	5 1	6 4	1 3	2 2	3 1	4 4	5 3	6 4	1 3	2 2	3 1	4 4	5 3	6 2	1 1	2 4	3 3	4 2	5 1	6 4	1 3	2 2	3 1	4 4	5 3	6 2
	5 1	0 2	1 1	3 1	4 2	5 1	0 2	1 1	3 1	4 2	5 1	0 2	1 1	3 1	4 2	5 1	0 2	1 1	3 1	4 2	5 1	0 2	1 1	3 1	4 2	5 1	0 2	1 1	3 1	4 2
	1 1	8 5	7 3	6 1	5 8	4 6	3 4	2 2	1 9	8 7	7 5	4 3	3 1	2 8	1 6	8 4	7 2	6 9	5 7	4 5	3 3	2 1	1 8	8 6	7 4	6 2	5 9	4 7	3 5	2 3
Coma (Monday)	2 3	*3 5*	1 2	2 4	3 1	1 3	2 5	3 2	1 4	2 1	3 3	1 5	2 2	3 4	1 1	2 3	*3 5*	1 2	2 4	3 1	1 3	2 5	3 2	1 4	2 1	3 3	1 5	2 2	3 4	1 1
	2 2	3 1	4 4	5 3	6 2	1 1	2 4	3 3	4 2	5 1	6 3	1 1	2 4	3 3	4 2	5 1	6 4	1 3	2 2	3 1	4 4	5 3	6 2	1 1	2 4	3 3	4 2	5 1	6 4	1 3
	2 2	3 1	4 2	9 1	0 2	2 2	3 1	4 2	9 1	0 2	2 2	3 1	4 2	9 1	0 2	2 2	3 1	4 2	9 1	0 2	2 2	3 1	4 2	9 1	0 2	2 2	3 1	4 2	9 1	0 2
	2 1	1 6	8 4	7 2	6 9	5 7	4 5	3 3	2 1	1 8	7 6	5 4	4 2	3 9	2 7	1 5	8 3	7 1	6 8	5 6	4 4	3 2	2 9	1 7	8 5	7 3	6 1	5 8	4 6	3 4
Anggara (Tuesday)	3 4	1 1	2 3	*3 5*	1 2	2 4	3 1	1 3	2 5	3 2	1 4	2 1	3 3	1 5	2 2	3 4	1 1	2 3	*3 5*	1 2	2 4	3 1	1 3	2 5	3 2	1 4	2 1	3 3	1 5	2 2
	3 3	4 2	5 1	6 4	1 3	2 2	3 1	4 4	5 3	6 2	1 3	2 2	3 1	4 4	5 3	6 2	1 1	2 4	3 3	4 2	5 1	6 4	1 3	2 2	3 1	4 4	5 3	6 2	1 1	2 4
	8 2	9 1	1 1	2 2	3 1	8 2	9 1	1 1	2 2	3 1	8 2	9 1	1 1	2 2	3 1	8 2	9 1	1 1	2 2	3 1	8 2	9 1	1 1	2 2	3 1	8 2	9 1	1 1	2 2	3 1
	3 1	2 7	1 5	8 3	7 1	6 8	5 6	4 4	3 2	2 9	7 7	6 5	5 3	4 1	3 8	2 6	1 4	8 2	7 9	6 7	5 5	4 3	3 1	2 8	1 6	8 4	7 2	6 9	5 7	4 5
Buda (Wednesday)	1 5	2 2	3 4	1 1	2 3	*3 5*	1 2	2 4	3 1	1 3	2 5	3 2	1 4	2 1	3 3	1 5	2 2	3 4	1 1	2 3	*3 5*	1 2	2 4	3 1	1 3	2 5	3 2	1 4	2 1	3 3
	4 4	5 3	6 2	1 1	2 4	3 3	4 2	5 1	6 4	1 3	2 4	3 3	4 2	5 1	6 4	1 3	2 2	3 1	4 4	5 3	6 2	1 1	2 4	3 3	4 2	5 1	6 4	1 3	2 2	3 1
	6 2	7 1	2 2	3 1	5 1	6 2	7 1	2 2	3 1	5 1	6 2	7 1	2 2	3 1	5 1	6 2	7 1	2 2	3 1	5 1	6 2	7 1	2 2	3 1	5 1	6 2	7 1	2 2	3 1	5 1
	4 1	3 8	2 6	1 4	8 2	7 9	6 7	5 5	4 3	3 1	8 8	7 6	6 4	5 2	4 9	3 7	2 5	1 3	8 1	7 8	6 6	5 4	4 2	3 9	2 7	1 5	8 3	7 1	6 8	5 6
Wraspati (Thursday)	2 1	3 3	1 5	2 2	3 4	1 1	2 3	*3 5*	1 2	2 4	3 1	1 3	2 5	3 2	1 4	2 1	3 3	1 5	2 2	3 4	1 1	2 3	*3 5*	1 2	2 4	3 1	1 3	2 5	3 2	1 4
	5 1	6 4	1 3	2 2	3 1	4 4	5 3	6 2	1 1	2 4	3 1	4 4	5 3	6 2	1 1	2 4	3 3	4 2	5 1	6 4	1 3	2 2	3 1	4 4	5 3	6 2	1 1	2 4	3 3	4 2
	4 2	6 2	7 1	8 2	3 1	4 2	6 2	7 1	8 2	3 1	4 2	6 2	7 1	8 2	3 1	4 2	6 2	7 1	8 2	3 1	4 2	6 2	7 1	8 2	3 1	4 2	6 2	7 1	8 2	3 1
	5 2	4 9	3 7	2 5	1 3	8 1	7 8	6 6	5 4	4 2	1 9	8 7	7 5	6 3	5 1	4 8	3 6	2 4	1 2	8 9	7 7	6 5	5 3	4 1	3 8	2 6	1 4	8 2	7 9	6 7
Sukra (Friday)	3 2	1 4	2 1	3 3	1 5	2 2	3 4	1 1	2 3	*3 5*	1 2	2 4	3 1	1 3	2 5	3 2	1 4	2 1	3 3	1 5	2 2	3 4	1 1	2 3	*3 5*	1 2	2 4	3 1	1 3	2 5
	6 2	1 1	2 4	3 3	4 2	5 1	6 4	1 3	2 2	3 1	4 2	5 1	6 4	1 3	2 2	3 1	4 4	5 3	6 2	1 1	2 4	3 3	4 2	5 1	6 4	1 3	2 2	3 1	4 4	5 3
	6 2	1 1	2 2	4 2	5 1	6 2	1 1	2 2	4 2	5 1	6 2	1 1	2 2	4 2	5 1	6 2	1 1	2 2	4 2	5 1	6 2	1 1	2 2	4 2	5 1	6 2	1 1	2 2	4 2	5 1
	6 3	5 1	4 8	3 6	2 4	1 2	8 9	7 7	6 5	5 3	2 1	1 8	8 6	7 4	6 2	5 9	4 7	3 5	2 3	1 1	8 8	7 6	6 4	5 2	4 9	3 7	2 5	1 3	8 1	7 8
Saniscara (Saturday)	1 3	2 **5**	3 2	1 4	2 1	3 3	1 **5**	2 2	3 4	1 1	2 3	*3* **5**	1 2	2 4	3 1	1 3	2 **5**	3 2	1 4	2 1	3 3	1 **5**	2 2	3 4	1 1	2 3	*3* **5**	1 2	2 4	3 1
	1 3	2 2	3 1	4 4	5 3	6 2	1 1	2 4	3 3	4 2	5 3	6 2	1 1	2 4	3 3	4 2	5 1	6 4	1 3	2 2	3 1	4 4	5 3	6 2	1 1	2 4	3 3	4 2	5 1	6 4
	7 1	8 2	9 1	4 2	5 1	7 1	8 2	9 1	4 2	5 1	7 1	8 2	9 1	4 2	5 1	7 1	8 2	9 1	4 2	5 1	7 1	8 2	9 1	4 2	5 1	7 1	8 2	9 1	4 2	5 1
	7 4	6 2	5 9	4 7	3 5	2 3	1 1	8 8	7 6	6 4	3 2	2 9	1 7	8 5	7 3	6 1	5 8	4 6	3 4	2 2	1 9	8 7	7 5	6 3	5 1	4 8	3 6	2 4	1 2	8 9

References

[1] S. K. Chatterjee, "Balinese Traditional Calendar," *Indian J. of History of Science*, vol. 32, no. 4, pp. 325–347, 1997.

[2] F. B. Eiseman, Jr., *Bali: Sekala and Niskala, vol. I, Essays on Religion, Ritual, and Art, with two chapters by Margaret Eiseman*, Chap. 17, Periplus Editions, Berkeley, CA, 1989.

[3] M. Kudlek, "Calendar Systems," *Mitteilungen der mathematischen Gesellschaft in Hamburg*, vol. XII, no. 2, pp. 395–428, 1991.

[4] K. E. Mershon, *Seven Plus Seven: Mysterious Life-Rituals in Bali*, Vantage Press, 1971.

Oil painting of Joseph Scaliger in the Senate Hall at Leiden. (Courtesy of Academisch Historisch Museum, Universiteit Leiden, Leiden.)

13

Generic Cyclical Calendars

> One who is capable of making astronomical calculations, but does not make them, is unworthy of being spoken to.
>
> *Babylonian Talmud* (Sabbath, 75a)

In this chapter, we use formulas from Section 1.14 to cast a number of the calendars presented in Part I into a unified framework. To do this, years must be determined by the occurrence of some "critical" mean annual event, such as a mean equinox or mean solstice. Months must also follow a uniform pattern. In single-cycle calendars, new years begin on the day the critical annual event happens before (or possibly at) some critical time of day. In double-cycle calendars, months begin on the day of a critical mensual event, and years begin with the month associated with the critical annual event.

13.1 Single Cycle Calendars

> *The wheel is come full circle.*
>
> William Shakespeare:
> *King Lear*, Act V, scene iii (1605)

There are four "single-cycle" paradigms for calendars, as we independently allow

1. the determining critical annual event to occur either *strictly before* or *at or before* some critical time of day, and
2. the pattern of months to follow either a *fixed* yearly pattern, according to equations (1.92)–(1.95), or a mean monthly pattern in tune with the yearly pattern.

Five parameters describe such a calendar:

n_0 = the R.D. calendar epoch, an integer

Y = the average year length in days, $Y \geqslant 1$

δ_Y = the offset (fraction of a day) of the first critical annual event from the critical time of the first day of the first year, $0 \leqslant \delta_Y < 1$

M = the average month length in days, $1 \leqslant M \leqslant Y$ (the last month of the year need not be included in the average)

δ_M = the offset (fraction of a day) for the first month, $0 \leqslant \delta_M < 1$

Years are described by equations (1.92)–(1.95); some will have $\lfloor Y \rfloor$ days, and some $\lceil Y \rceil$.

In the "at or before" case, the critical yearly event for the epochal year occurs δ_Y days *before* the critical moment of the day of the epoch. In the "strictly before" case, the critical event occurs δ_Y days *after* the critical moment of the day before the epoch, which is why the previous day is not the start of the first year. If y years of average length Y have elapsed then the number of elapsed days since the epoch is given by $\lfloor yY + \delta_Y \rfloor$ in the "strictly before" case and by $\lceil yY - \delta_Y \rceil$ in the "at or before" case.

Months may or may not be described by equations (1.92)–(1.95); if they are, the critical monthly event for the first month of the calendar is assumed to occur δ_M fractional days late for the first month of the year to begin a day earlier.

In the "strictly before" case, if months are described by equations (1.92)–(1.95), with average length M and offset δ_M, we convert a *year-month-day* date on such a strictly-before-fixed-month single-cycle calendar to a fixed *date* as follows. Add to the epoch n_0 the days before the *year* computed by equation (1.92), the days before *month* in *year* again computed by equation (1.92), and the days before *day* in *month*:

$$date = n_0 + \lfloor (year - 1)Y + \delta_Y \rfloor + \lfloor (month - 1)M + \delta_M \rfloor + day - 1 \tag{13.1}$$

For the inverse calculation of the single-cycle-unvarying-month date from R.D. *date*, we determine the year from the start of the mean year using (1.95), the month from (1.95) applied to the month parameters, and the day by taking the remainder:

$$d = date - n_0 + 1 - \delta_Y \tag{13.2}$$

$$year = \lceil d/Y \rceil \tag{13.3}$$

$$n = \lceil d - (year - 1)Y \rceil - \delta_M \tag{13.4}$$

$$month = \lceil n/M \rceil \tag{13.5}$$

$$day = \lceil n \bmod [1\,..\,M] \rceil \tag{13.6}$$

where d counts the days since the epochal critical moment, and n counts the days from the critical time at the beginning of *year*.

The Coptic calendar of Section 4.1 is of this type, with constants

$$n_0 = 103605$$

$$Y = 365\tfrac{1}{4}$$

$$\delta_Y = \frac{1}{4}$$

$$M = 30$$

$$\delta_M = 0$$

For example, R.D. 710347 yields the Coptic date *year* = 1662, *month* = 3, *day* = 3 (= Athōr 3, 1662 A.M.). This uses a fictitious average month length of 30 to accommodate twelve 30-month days, which are followed by an extra "month," not included in the average, of epagomenæ lasting 5 or 6 days.

If the critical event is allowed to occur up to *and including* the critical time, in the fixed-month case we simply use the ceiling function instead of the floor function for the year part of the computation:

$$date = n_0 + \lceil (year - 1)Y - \delta_Y \rceil + \lfloor (month - 1)M + \delta_M \rfloor + day - 1 \qquad (13.7)$$

In the other direction, we have

$$d = date - n_0 + \delta_Y \qquad (13.8)$$
$$year = \lfloor d/Y \rfloor + 1 \qquad (13.9)$$
$$n = \lfloor d \bmod Y \rfloor + 1 - \delta_M \qquad (13.10)$$
$$month = \lceil n/M \rceil \qquad (13.11)$$
$$day = \lceil n \bmod [1 \,..\, M] \rceil \qquad (13.12)$$

where δ_Y is the fraction of the day *before* the critical moment of the epoch at which the event occurred. This version, an at-or-before-fixed-month single-cycle calendar, also works for the Coptic calendar, but then we take $\delta_Y = 1/2$.

If we have a mean-month scheme in which we determine the start of each month individually, on the basis of the critical time of day, then $L = Y/M$, the number of months per year, should be an integer and there is no month offset δ_M. To convert between R.D. dates and dates on such a mean-month calendar, we again apply formulas (1.92)–(1.95), but with minor variations. If the critical event must occur strictly before the critical time, corresponding to a strictly-before-mean-month calendar, we convert from a date on this calendar to an R.D. date by adding the days before the mean *month* in *year* and the days before *day* in *month*:

$$date = n_0 + \lfloor (year - 1)Y + \delta_Y + (month - 1)M \rfloor + day - 1 \qquad (13.13)$$

In the other direction, we compute the strictly-before-mean-month date from an R.D. date by determining the year from the start of the mean year using (1.95), the month from (1.95) applied to the month parameters, and the day by subtraction:

$$d = date - n_0 + 1 - \delta_Y \qquad (13.14)$$
$$year = \lceil d/Y \rceil \qquad (13.15)$$
$$L = Y/M \qquad (13.16)$$
$$m = \lceil d/M \rceil - 1 \qquad (13.17)$$
$$month = m \bmod L + 1 \qquad (13.18)$$
$$day = \lceil d \bmod [1 \,..\, M] \rceil \qquad (13.19)$$

If the critical event may occur at the critical time in the mean-month case, then we have an at-or-before-mean-month calendar; conversions are made by

$$date = n_0 + \lceil (year - 1)Y - \delta_Y + (month - 1)M \rceil + day - 1 \qquad (13.20)$$

and

$$
\begin{aligned}
d &= date - n_0 + \delta_Y && (13.21)\\
year &= \lfloor d/Y \rfloor + 1 && (13.22)\\
L &= Y/M && (13.23)\\
month &= \lfloor d/M \rfloor \bmod L + 1 && (13.24)\\
day &= \lfloor d \bmod M \rfloor + 1 && (13.25)
\end{aligned}
$$

Finally, we note that the formulas of this section can be applied in the 364-day Qumran calendar[1] and the similar calendars of the books of Jubilees and I Enoch. Each "season" consists of three months of lengths 30, 30, 31, repeated four times to make a year. Thus every year has exactly 52 weeks, and every calendrical holiday always falls on the same day of the week. The appropriate parameters are $Y = 364$, $M = Y/12$, and $\delta_Y = \delta_M = 0$ in (13.1)–(13.6). No correlation, however, is known between this calendar and any other, so n_0 is unknown and the calendar cannot be implemented for date conversion. The Qumran calendar also had a cycle of 24 weeks (based on Chronicles I, 2:4), resulting in a 6-year repeating calendar, as well as a lunar cycle of alternating 29- and 30-day months, with one exceptional 30 day month at the end of the third year of the cycle. These too can be represented with the formulas of this section.

13.2 Double Cycle Calendars

Their appearance and their work was as it were a wheel within a wheel.

Ezekiel 1:16

We can also design a schematic double-cycle "lunisolar" calendar in which years follow one cyclic pattern and months another, with leap months added to synchronize the two patterns. In this case, years are composed of an integral number of months, and δ_Y is a fraction of a *month*, rather than of a day. The remainder $Y/M \bmod 1$ is the fraction of years that include a leap month.

There are two versions of the double-cycle calendar. If both the monthly event and the yearly event must occur *strictly before* the critical time, then δ_Y represents the fraction of a month after the critical moment of the month prior to the epoch at which the monthly event occurs and δ_M represents the fraction of the day at which the annual event occurs for the day prior to the epoch. Then, we can convert a *year-month-day* date to a fixed *date* by

$$date = n_0 + \lfloor mM + \delta_M \rfloor + day - 1 \qquad (13.26)$$

where

$$
\begin{aligned}
L &= Y/M && (13.27)\\
m &= \lfloor (year - 1)L + \delta_Y \rfloor + month - 1 && (13.28)
\end{aligned}
$$

[1] J. Ben-Dov and S. Saulnier, "Qumran Calendars: A Survey of Scholarship 1980–2007," *Currents in Biblical Research*, vol. 7, pp. 124–168, 2008.

and m is the total number of months that have elapsed since the epoch. In the other direction, we have:

$$d = n - n_0 + 1 - \delta_M \tag{13.29}$$

$$L = Y/M \tag{13.30}$$

$$m = \lceil dL \rceil - \delta_Y \tag{13.31}$$

$$year = \lceil m/L \rceil \tag{13.32}$$

$$month = \lceil m \bmod [1\,..\,L] \rceil \tag{13.33}$$

$$day = \lceil d \bmod [1\,..\,M] \rceil \tag{13.34}$$

Finally, when the months follow an "at or before" scheme, we can convert a *year-month-day* date to a fixed *date* by

$$date = n_0 + \lceil mM - \delta_M \rceil + day - 1 \tag{13.35}$$

where

$$L = Y/M$$
$$m = \lfloor (year - 1)L + \delta_Y \rfloor + month - 1$$

In the other direction, we have

$$d = n - n_0 + \delta_M \tag{13.36}$$

$$m = \lfloor d/M \rfloor + 1 - \delta_Y \tag{13.37}$$

$$L = Y/M \tag{13.38}$$

$$year = \lceil m/L \rceil \tag{13.39}$$

$$month = \lceil m \bmod [1\,..\,L] \rceil \tag{13.40}$$

$$day = \lfloor d \bmod M \rfloor + 1 \tag{13.41}$$

The old Hindu lunisolar calendar of Section 10.3, for example, is of this type, with constants

$$n_0 = -1132988$$
$$Y = 365\tfrac{149}{576}$$
$$\delta_Y = \frac{2093611}{2160000}$$
$$M = 29\tfrac{2362563}{4452778}$$
$$\delta_M = 0$$

These values give the current year number, one more than the elapsed year. Month numbers are consecutive, with no indication of which month is a leap month. Day numbers are a straight count rather than lunar days.

Table 13.1 Constants for generic arithmetic calendars.

Calendar	Formulas	Y	δ_Y	M	δ_M
Gregorian (March–March; approximate)	(13.1)–(13.6)	$365\frac{97}{400}$	$\frac{3}{4}$	$30\frac{3}{5}$	$\frac{2}{5}$
Julian (March–March; C.E.)	(13.1)–(13.6)	$365\frac{1}{4}$	$\frac{1}{4}$	$30\frac{3}{5}$	$\frac{2}{5}$
Coptic/Ethiopic	(13.1)–(13.6)	$365\frac{1}{4}$	$\frac{1}{4}$	30	0
Coptic/Ethiopic	(13.7)–(13.12)	$365\frac{1}{4}$	$\frac{1}{2}$	30	0
Islamic	(13.1)–(13.6)	$354\frac{11}{30}$	$\frac{7}{15}$	$29\frac{6}{11}$	$\frac{5}{11}$
Hebrew (Nisan–Nisan; approximate)	(13.26)–(13.34)	$\frac{235}{19}M$	$\frac{2}{19}$	$29\frac{13753}{25920}$	$\frac{1127}{1440}$
Old Hindu solar (current year)	(13.20)–(13.25)	$365\frac{149}{576}$	$\frac{1}{4}$	$\frac{1}{12}Y$	0
Old Hindu lunisolar (current year)	(13.35)–(13.41)	$365\frac{149}{576}$	$\frac{2093611}{2160000}$	$29\frac{2362563}{4452778}$	0

13.3 Summary

Table 13.1 summarizes the parameters that describe the various calendars considered in Part I of this book. The formulas match a March–March Gregorian calendar, for example, only to within a day, because of the uneven spacing (4–8 years) of Gregorian leap years.

All the calculations in this chapter require exact arithmetic in order to work properly, so that fractions add up to integers when they should.

You will find it a very good practice always to verify your references, sir.
Martin Joseph Routh: *Memoir of Dr. Routh* (1878)

Part II

Astronomical Calendars

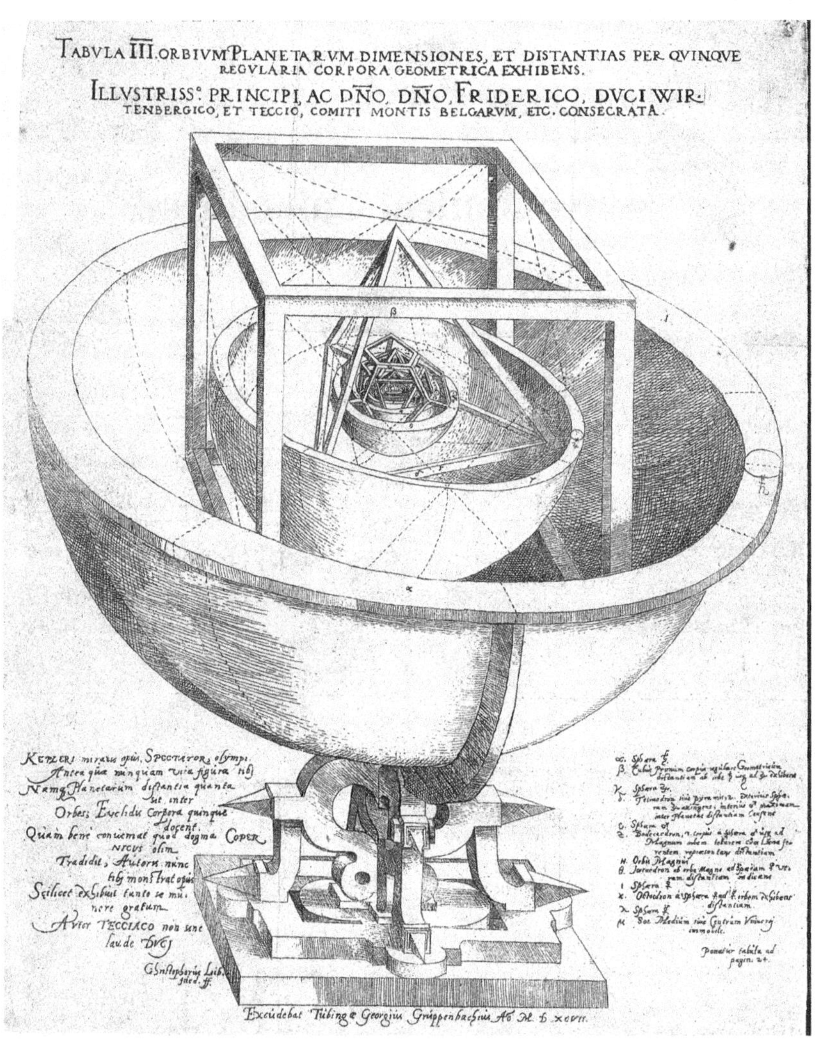

Geometrical explanation of the planetary distances—the mystical harmony of the spheres. From Johannes Kepler's *Prodromus Dissertationum Cosmographicarum Continens Mysterium Cosmographicum* (1596). (Courtesy of the University of Illinois, Urbana, IL.)

14

Time and Astronomy

Ask my friend l'Abbé Sallier to recommend to you some meagre philomath, to teach you a little geometry and astronomy; not enough to absorb your attention, and puzzle your intellects, but only enough, not to be grossly ignorant of either. I have of late been a sort of an astronome malgré moy, *by bringing last Monday, into the house of Lords, a bill for reforming our present Calendar, and taking the New Style. Upon which occasion I was obliged to talk some astronomical jargon, of which I did not understand one word, but got it by heart, and spoke it by rote from a master. I wished that I had known a little more of it myself; and so much I would have you know.*

Letter from Philip Dormer Stanhope (Fourth Earl of Chesterfield)
to his son, February 28, 1751 C.E. (Julian)

The calendars in the second part of this book are based on accurate astronomical calculations. This chapter defines the essential astronomical terms and describes the necessary astronomical functions. A fuller treatment can be found in the references—an especially readable discussion is given in [14].

We begin with an explanation of how the positions of locations on Earth and of heavenly bodies are specified, followed by an examination of the notion of time itself. After discussing the 24-hour day, we summarize the different types of years and months used by various calendars along with algorithms that closely approximate the times of astronomical events—notably equinoxes, solstices, and new moons. These astronomical functions are adapted from those in [18] and [4] and require 64-bit arithmetic.

Most of the algorithms are centered around the present date, for which they are accurate to within about 2 minutes. Their accuracy decreases for the far-distant past or future. More accurate algorithms exist [3] but are extremely complex and not needed for our purposes.

Chapter 18 applies the methods of this chapter to several "speculative" astronomical calendars.

14.1 Position

The cause of the error is very simple ... In journeying eastward he had gone towards the sun, and the days therefore diminished for him as many times four minutes as he crossed degrees in this direction. There are three hundred and sixty degrees in the circumference of the Earth; and these three hundred and sixty degrees, multiplied by four minutes, gives precisely twenty-four hours—that is, the day unconsciously gained.

Jules Verne: *Around the World in Eighty Days* (1873)

Locations on Earth are specified by giving their latitude and longitude. The (*terrestrial*) *latitude* of a geographic location is the angular distance on the Earth, measured in degrees from the equator, along the meridian of the location. Similarly, the (*terrestrial*) *longitude* of a geographic location is the angular distance on the Earth measured in degrees from the Greenwich meridian (which is defined as 0°), on the outskirts of London. Thus, for example, the location of Jerusalem is described as being 31.8° north, 35.2° east. In the algorithms, we take northern latitudes as positive and southern latitudes as negative. For longitudes, we take east from Greenwich as positive and west as negative;[1] thus a positive longitude means a time later than at Greenwich, and a negative longitude means a time earlier than at Greenwich.

As we will see in the next section, locations on Earth are also associated with a *time zone*, which is needed for determining the local clock time. For some calculations (local sunrise and sunset, in particular), the elevation above sea level is also a factor. Thus, the complete specification of a location that we use is

latitude	*longitude*	*elevation*	*zone*

We specify the time zone as the difference from Universal Time (U.T.; see Section 14.2) as a fraction of a day, and we measure the elevation above sea level in meters. For example, the specification of Urbana, Illinois, is

urbana $\stackrel{\text{def}}{=}$

40.1°	−88.2°	225 m	-6^{h}

(14.1)

because Urbana is at latitude 40.1° north, longitude 88.2° west, 225 meters above sea level, and 6 hours before U.T.; Greenwich is specified by

greenwich $\stackrel{\text{def}}{=}$

51.4777815°	0°	46.9 m	0^{h}

(14.2)

Muslims turn towards Mecca for prayer, Jews face Jerusalem, and the Bahá'í face Acre. Their locations are, respectively,

mecca $\stackrel{\text{def}}{=}$

21°25′24″	39°49′24″	298 m	3^{h}

(14.3)

jerusalem $\stackrel{\text{def}}{=}$

31.78°	35.24°	740 m	2^{h}

(14.4)

acre $\stackrel{\text{def}}{=}$

32.94°	35.09°	22 m	2^{h}

(14.5)

[1] This is in agreement with the standard of the International Astronomical Union but inconsistent with common sense and a century of common practice. See [18, p. 93].

If a spherical Earth is assumed, the direction (measured in degrees east of due north) of a location at latitude φ' and longitude ψ', along a great circle, when one stands at another location with latitude φ and longitude ψ, can be determined by spherical trigonometry[2] (see [16] for details):

$$\mathbf{direction}\left(\boxed{\varphi \mid \psi \mid - \mid -}, \boxed{\varphi' \mid \psi' \mid - \mid -}\right) \stackrel{\text{def}}{=} \tag{14.6}$$

$$\begin{cases} 0^\circ & \mathbf{if}\ x = y = 0 \text{ or } \varphi' = 90^\circ \\ 180^\circ & \mathbf{if}\ \varphi' = -90^\circ \\ \mathbf{arctan}\,(y, x) & \mathbf{otherwise} \end{cases}$$

where

$$y = \sin(\psi' - \psi)$$
$$x = \cos\varphi \times \tan\varphi' - \sin\varphi \times \cos(\psi - \psi')$$

This formula uses the two-argument arctangent function

$$\mathbf{arctan}\,(y, x) \stackrel{\text{def}}{=} \tag{14.7}$$

$$\begin{cases} \mathbf{bogus} & \mathbf{if}\ x = y = 0 \\ \left\{\begin{array}{ll} \operatorname{sign}(y) \times 90^\circ & \mathbf{if}\ x = 0 \\ \alpha & \mathbf{if}\ x \geqslant 0 \\ \alpha + 180^\circ & \mathbf{otherwise} \end{array}\right\} \bmod 360 & \mathbf{otherwise} \end{cases}$$

where

$$\alpha = \arctan\left(\frac{y}{x}\right)$$

to find the arctangent of y/x in the appropriate quadrant; this angle changes when the two locations are on opposite sides of the globe. For example, in Urbana, Illinois, the *qibla* (direction of Mecca) is about 49° east of due north whereas Jerusalem is at 45° east.[3]

The positions of heavenly bodies can be measured in a manner corresponding to terrestrial longitude and latitude by reference to meridians (great circles passing through the two poles) of the celestial sphere. In this *equatorial* coordinate system, *right ascension* corresponds to longitude and *declination* to latitude. For marking the positions of the sun and moon, however, astronomers normally use an alternative coordinate system in which (*celestial* or *ecliptical*) *longitude* is measured along the ecliptic (the sun's apparent path among the stars) and (*celestial*) *latitude* is measured from the ecliptic. Zero longitude is at a position called the *First Point of Aries* (see page 219).

---

[2] Imperfect arithmetic accuracy can result in meaningless values of **direction** when *location* and *focus* are nearly coincident or antipodal.

[3] Despite the antiquity of such great-circle calculations in Muslim and Jewish sources, many mosques and synagogues are designed according to other conventions. See [1].

14.2 Time

What, then, is time? I know well enough what it is, provided that nobody asks me; but if I am asked what it is and try to explain, I am baffled.

Saint Augustine: *Confessions* (circa 400)

Three distinct methods of measuring time are in use today:[4]

- *Solar time* is based on the solar day, which measures the time between successive transits of the sun across the meridian (the north-south line, through the zenith, the point overhead in the sky). As we will see, this period varies because of the nonuniform motion of the Earth.
- *Sidereal time* varies less than solar time and indicates the orientation of the rotating Earth with respect to the stars. It is measured as the right ascension at a given moment of those points in the sky just crossing the meridian. Thus, *local* sidereal time depends on terrestrial longitude and differs from observatory to observatory.
- *Dynamical Time* is a uniform measure taking the frequency of oscillation of certain atoms as the basic building block. Various forms of Dynamical Time use different frames of reference, which makes a difference in a universe governed by relativity.

The ordinary method of measuring time is called *Universal Time* (U.T.). It is the local mean solar time, reckoned from midnight, at the observatory in Greenwich, England, the location of the 0° meridian.[5] The equivalent designation "Greenwich Mean Time," abbreviated G.M.T., has fallen into disfavor with astronomers because of confusion as to whether days begin at midnight or noon (before 1925, 00:00 G.M.T. meant noon; from 1925 onward it has meant midnight).

There are several closely related types of Universal Time. Civil time keeping uses Coordinated Universal Time (U.T.C.), which since 1972 has been atomic time adjusted periodically by leap seconds to keep it close to the prime meridian's mean solar time; see [17] and [25]. We use U.T.C. for calendrical purposes (except that we insert all leap seconds at the end of the year, whereas in actual practice they are often added during the year[6]) expressed as a fraction of a solar day.

From the start of the spread of clocks and pocket watches in Europe until the early 1800s, each locale would set its clocks to local mean time. Each longitudinal degree of separation gives rise to a 4 minute difference in local time. For example,

---

[4] Ephemeris time, which takes the orbital motions in the solar system as the basic building block, is an outdated time scale as of 1984.

[5] The formal recognition of Greenwich as the "prime meridian" dates from the International Meridian Conference of 1884, but it had been informal practice from 1767. The French, however, continued to treat Paris as the prime meridian until 1911, when they switched to Greenwich, referring to it as "Paris Mean Time, minus nine minutes twenty-one seconds." France did not formally switch to Universal Time until 1978; see [30] and [11].

[6] The International Telecommunications Union states in ITU-R TF.460-6, sec. 2.1, that "A positive or negative leap-second should be the last second of a UTC month, but first preference should be given to the end of December and June, and second preference to the end of March and September." See [5] for a concise history of leap seconds.

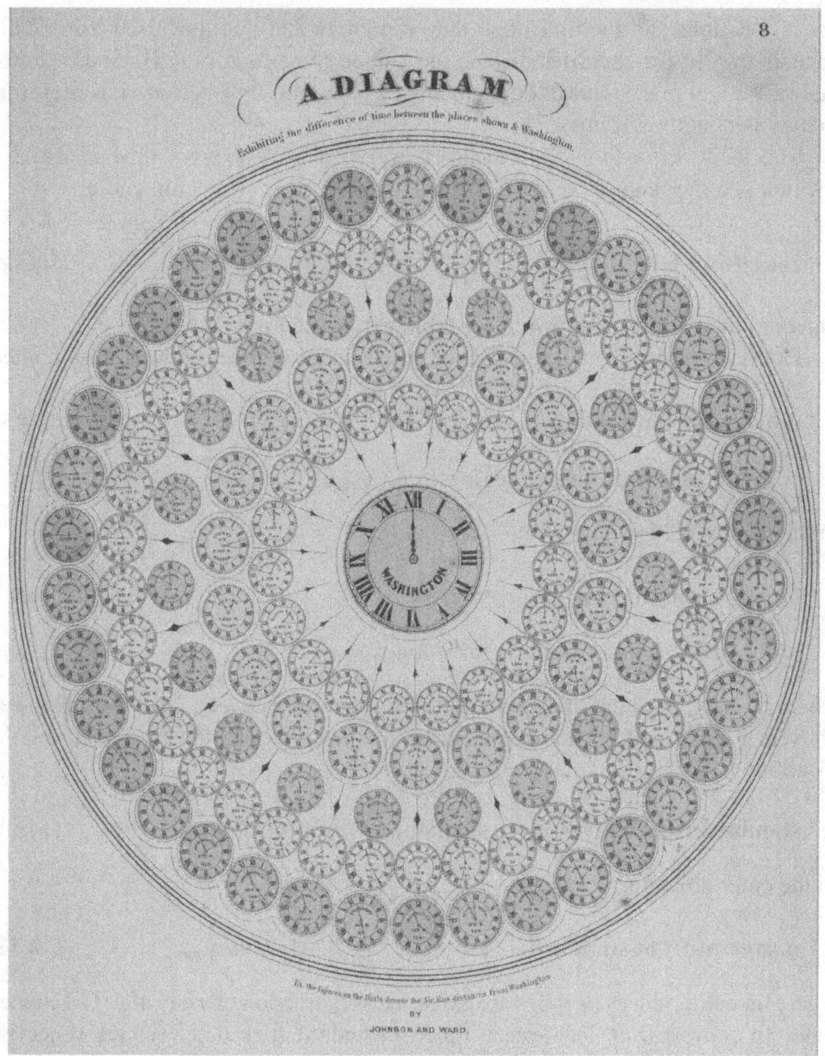

Figure 14.1 Differences in local time between Washington, D.C., and cities around the world: *Johnson's New Illustrated Family Atlas*, 1862. (Collection of E.M.R.)

because the meridian of Paris is 2°20′15″ east, its local mean time is 9 minutes, 21 seconds, ahead of U.T. As another example, Beijing is 116°25′ east; the time difference from U.T. is $7^{h}45^{m}40^{s}$. Figure 14.1 shows a helpful 1862 atlas page showing differences in local time before the advent of time zones.

"Standard time" was first used by British railway companies in 1840; time zones were first adopted by North American railway companies in the late 1800s [11]. The history of time measurement and time zones in the United States is discussed at length in [24]. Most of Western Europe is today in one zone; the 48 contiguous states of the United States are divided into four zones. A very extensive list of locations and the times that they use today and that they used historically appears in [29] for countries outside the United States and in [28] for the United States. We ignore the issue of daylight-saving (summer) time because it is irrelevant to the calendars we discuss.

The local *mean* time zone changes every 15°. We express time zones as a fraction of a day, and so we simply divide the longitude φ by a full circle:

$$\textbf{zone-from-longitude}\,(\varphi) \stackrel{\text{def}}{=} \frac{\varphi}{360^\circ} \tag{14.8}$$

Standard time zones are drawn more arbitrarily—see Figure 14.2.

Converting between Universal Time and local mean time is now an easy matter:

$$\textbf{universal-from-local}\,(t_\ell, \mathit{location}) \stackrel{\text{def}}{=} \tag{14.9}$$

$$t_\ell - \textbf{zone-from-longitude}\,(\mathit{location}_{\textbf{longitude}})$$

In the other direction,

$$\textbf{local-from-universal}\,(t_\mathrm{u}, \mathit{location}) \stackrel{\text{def}}{=} \tag{14.10}$$

$$t_\mathrm{u} + \textbf{zone-from-longitude}\,(\mathit{location}_{\textbf{longitude}})$$

where t_ℓ and t_u are local time and Universal Time, respectively. To convert between Universal Time and standard zone time, we need to use the time zone of the location:

$$\textbf{standard-from-universal}\,(t_\mathrm{u}, \mathit{location}) \stackrel{\text{def}}{=} t_\mathrm{u} + \mathit{location}_{\textbf{zone}} \tag{14.11}$$

In the other direction,

$$\textbf{universal-from-standard}\,(t_\mathrm{s}, \mathit{location}) \stackrel{\text{def}}{=} t_\mathrm{s} - \mathit{location}_{\textbf{zone}} \tag{14.12}$$

where time differences or zones are expressed as a fraction of a day after Greenwich time. To convert from local mean time to standard zone time, or vice versa, we combine the differences between Universal Time and standard time and between local mean time and Universal Time:

$$\textbf{standard-from-local}\,(t_\ell, \mathit{location}) \stackrel{\text{def}}{=} \tag{14.13}$$

$$\textbf{standard-from-universal}\,(\textbf{universal-from-local}\,(t_\ell, \mathit{location}), \mathit{location})$$

and in the other direction

$$\textbf{local-from-standard}\,(t_\mathrm{s}, \mathit{location}) \stackrel{\text{def}}{=} \tag{14.14}$$

$$\textbf{local-from-universal}\,(\textbf{universal-from-standard}\,(t_\mathrm{s}, \mathit{location}), \mathit{location})$$

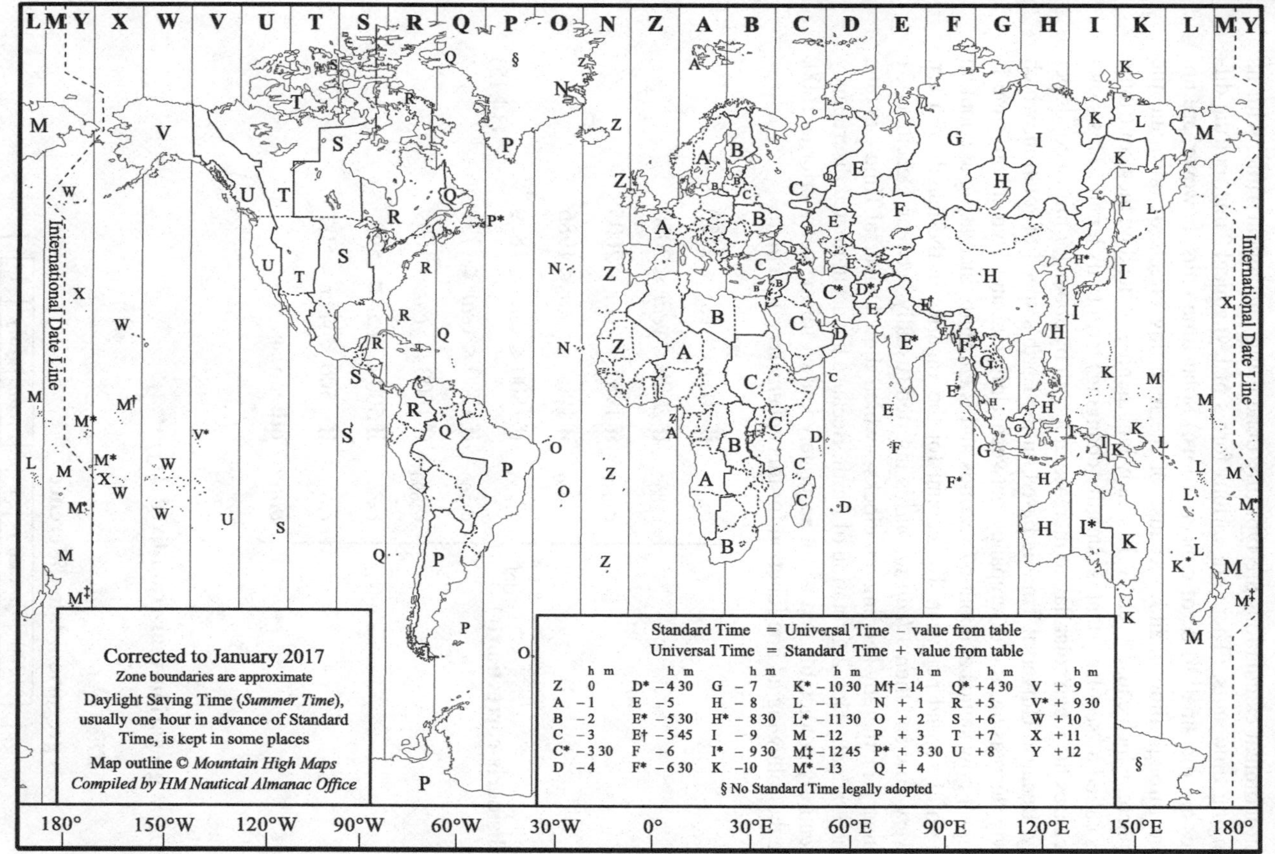

Figure 14.2 Standard time zones of the world as of January, 2017. © Crown Copyright and/or database rights. (Reproduced by permission of the Controller of Her Majesty's Stationery Office and the UK Hydrographic Office, gov.uk/ukho.)

For example, Jerusalem is 35.2° east of Greenwich; its time zone is U.T.+2^h. Therefore, to obtain standard time in Jerusalem from the local mean time, a net offset of 20^m48^s is added.

Astronomical calculations are typically done using Dynamical Time, with its unchanging time units. (There are various forms of Dynamical Time, but the differences are too small to be of concern to us.) Solar time units, however, are not constant through time, mainly because of the retarding effects of tides and the atmosphere, which cause a relatively steady lengthening of the day; they contribute what is called a "secular" (that is, steadily changing) term to its length. This slowdown causes the mean solar day to increase in length by about 1.7 milliseconds per century. Because Universal Time is based on the Earth's speed of rotation, which is slowly decreasing, the discrepancy between Universal and Dynamical Time is growing. It now stands at about 67 seconds and is currently increasing at about an average of 1 second per year. To account for the vagaries in the length of a U.T. day, every now and then a *leap second* is inserted (usually between December 31 and January 1), thereby keeping our clocks—which show Universal Time—in tune with the gradually slowing rotation of Earth. Because the accumulated discrepancy is not entirely predictable and is not accurately known for the years prior to 1600, we use the following ad hoc function for this *ephemeris correction*:

$$\textbf{ephemeris-correction}\,(t) \stackrel{\text{def}}{=} \begin{cases} c_{2051} & \textbf{if } 2051 \leqslant year \leqslant 2150 \\ c_{2006} & \textbf{if } 2006 \leqslant year \leqslant 2050 \\ c_{1987} & \textbf{if } 1987 \leqslant year \leqslant 2005 \\ c_{1900} & \textbf{if } 1900 \leqslant year \leqslant 1986 \\ c_{1800} & \textbf{if } 1800 \leqslant year \leqslant 1899 \\ c_{1700} & \textbf{if } 1700 \leqslant year \leqslant 1799 \\ c_{1600} & \textbf{if } 1600 \leqslant year \leqslant 1699 \\ c_{500} & \textbf{if } 500 \leqslant year \leqslant 1599 \\ c_{0} & \textbf{if } -500 < year < 500 \\ other & \textbf{otherwise} \end{cases} \tag{14.15}$$

where

$$year = \textbf{gregorian-year-from-fixed}\,(\lfloor t \rfloor)$$

$$c = \frac{1}{36525} \times \textbf{gregorian-date-difference}\left(\boxed{1900 \mid \textbf{january} \mid 1}, \boxed{year \mid \textbf{july} \mid 1}\right)$$

$$c_{2051} = \frac{1}{86400} \times \left(-20 + 32 \times \left(\frac{year - 1820}{100}\right)^2 + 0.5628 \times (2150 - year)\right)$$

$$
\begin{aligned}
y_{2000} &= year - 2000 \\
c_{2006} &= \frac{1}{86400} \times \left(62.92 + 0.32217 \times y_{2000} + 0.005589 \times y_{2000}^2 \right) \\
c_{1987} &= \frac{1}{86400} \times \Big(63.86 + 0.3345 \times y_{2000} - 0.060374 \times y_{2000}^2 \\
&\qquad + 0.0017275 \times y_{2000}^3 + 0.000651814 \times y_{2000}^4 \\
&\qquad + 0.00002373599 \times y_{2000}^5 \Big) \\
c_{1900} &= -0.00002 + 0.000297 \times c + 0.025184 \times c^2 \\
&\quad - 0.181133 \times c^3 + 0.553040 \times c^4 - 0.861938 \times c^5 \\
&\quad + 0.677066 \times c^6 - 0.212591 \times c^7 \\
c_{1800} &= -0.000009 + 0.003844 \times c + 0.083563 \times c^2 \\
&\quad + 0.865736 \times c^3 + 4.867575 \times c^4 + 15.845535 \times c^5 \\
&\quad + 31.332267 \times c^6 + 38.291999 \times c^7 + 28.316289 \times c^8 \\
&\quad + 11.636204 \times c^9 + 2.043794 \times c^{10} \\
y_{1700} &= year - 1700 \\
c_{1700} &= \frac{1}{86400} \times \Big(8.118780842 - 0.005092142 \times y_{1700} \\
&\qquad + 0.003336121 \times y_{1700}^2 - 0.0000266484 \times y_{1700}^3 \Big) \\
y_{1600} &= year - 1600 \\
c_{1600} &= \frac{1}{86400} \times \Big(120 - 0.9808 \times y_{1600} - 0.01532 \times y_{1600}^2 \\
&\qquad + 0.000140272128 \times y_{1600}^3 \Big) \\
y_{1000} &= \frac{year - 1000}{100} \\
c_{500} &= \frac{1}{86400} \times \Big(1574.2 - 556.01 \times y_{1000} + 71.23472 \times y_{1000}^2 \\
&\qquad + 0.319781 \times y_{1000}^3 - 0.8503463 \times y_{1000}^4 \\
&\qquad - 0.005050998 \times y_{1000}^5 + 0.0083572073 \times y_{1000}^6 \Big) \\
y_0 &= \frac{year}{100} \\
c_0 &= \frac{1}{86400} \\
&\quad \times \Big(10583.6 - 1014.41 \times y_0 + 33.78311 \times y_0^2 \\
&\qquad - 5.952053 \times y_0^3 - 0.1798452 \times y_0^4 + 0.022174192 \times y_0^5 \\
&\qquad + 0.0090316521 \times y_0^6 \Big)
\end{aligned}
$$

$$y_{1820} = \frac{year - 1820}{100}$$
$$other = \frac{1}{86400} \times \left(-20 + 32 \times y_{1820}^2 \right)$$

We are using **gregorian-date-difference** (page 62) to calculate the number of centuries c before or after the beginning of 1900. The factor $1/86400$ converts seconds into a fraction of a day.

To convert from Universal Time to Dynamical Time, we add the correction

$$\textbf{dynamical-from-universal}\,(t_u) \stackrel{\text{def}}{=} t_u + \textbf{ephemeris-correction}\,(t_u) \qquad (14.16)$$

where t is an R.D. moment measured in U.T. We approximate the inverse of (14.16) by

$$\textbf{universal-from-dynamical}\,(t) \stackrel{\text{def}}{=} t - \textbf{ephemeris-correction}\,(t) \qquad (14.17)$$

The function **gregorian-date-difference** is given on page 62 and **gregorian-year-from-fixed** on page 61.

Figures 14.3 and 14.4 plot the difference between Universal Time and Dynamical Time for ancient and modern eras, respectively.

To keep the numbers within reasonable bounds, our astronomical algorithms usually convert dates and times (given in Universal Time) into "Julian centuries," that is, into the number (and fraction) of uniform-length centuries (36525 days, measured in Dynamical Time) before or after noon on January 1, 2000 (Gregorian):

$$\textbf{julian-centuries}\,(t) \stackrel{\text{def}}{=} \qquad (14.18)$$
$$\frac{1}{36525} \times (\textbf{dynamical-from-universal}\,(t) - \textbf{j2000})$$

$$\textbf{j2000} \stackrel{\text{def}}{=} 12^{\text{h}} + \textbf{gregorian-new-year}\,(2000) \qquad (14.19)$$

Sidereal time is discussed in the following section.

14.3 The Day

How could David have known exactly when [*true*] *midnight occurs? Even Moses didn't know!*

Babylonian Talmud (Beraḥot, 3a)

The Earth rotates around its axis, causing the sun, moon, and stars to move across the sky from east to west in the course of a day. The most obvious way of measuring days is from sunrise to sunrise or from sunset to sunset because sunrise and sunset are unmistakable. The Islamic, Hebrew, and Bahá'í calendars begin their days at sunset, whereas the Hindu day starts and ends with sunrise. The disadvantage of these methods of reckoning days is the wide variation over the year in the beginning and ending times. For example, in London sunrise occurs anywhere from 3:42 a.m.

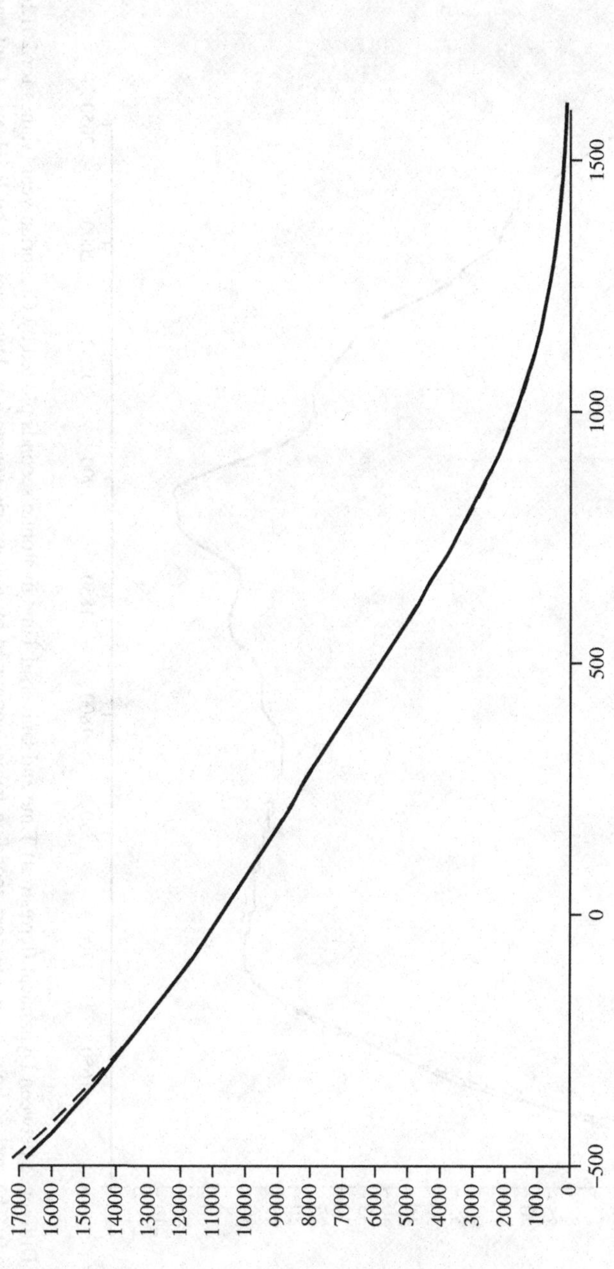

Figure 14.3 Difference between Dynamical (terrestrial) Time and Universal Time in atomic seconds plotted by Gregorian year. The dashed line shows the values of **ephemeris-correction**. Suggested by R. H. van Gent and based on [31, chap. 14].

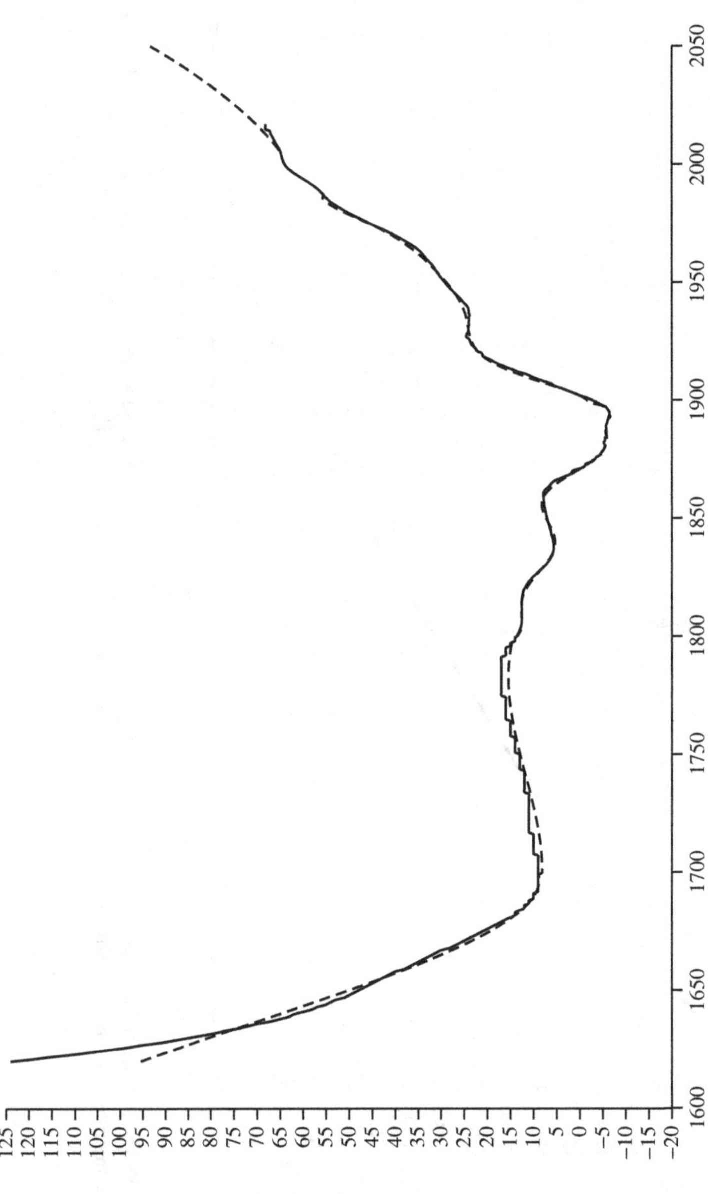

Figure 14.4 Difference between Dynamical (terrestrial) Time and Universal Time in atomic seconds plotted by Gregorian year (values for 2012–2017 are extrapolated). The dashed line shows the corresponding values computed by **ephemeris-correction**. Data supplied by R. H. van Gent based on *Astronomical Almanac for the Year 2014*, Nautical Almanac Office, United States Naval Observatory, Washington, D.C., pp. K8–K9.

to 8:06 a.m. and sunset varies from 3:51 p.m. to 8:21 p.m. By contrast, noon (the middle point of the day) and midnight (the middle point of the night) vary only by about half an hour in London or elsewhere (see below). Thus, in many parts of the world, sunset or sunrise definitions of the day have been superseded by a midnight-to-midnight day. For instance, the Chinese in the twelfth century B.C.E. began their day with the crowing of the rooster at 2 a.m., but more recently they have been using midnight. A noon-to-noon day is also plausible and indeed is used in the julian day system described in Section 1.5, but it has the disadvantage that the date changes in the middle of the working day.

Even with solar days measured from midnight to midnight there are seasonal variations. With the advent of mechanical clocks, introduced in the 1600s, the use of *mean* solar time, in which a day is 24 equal-length hours,[7] was preferred over the *apparent* (that is, true) time as measured by a sundial[8] (during the daytime, at least). The elliptical orbit of the Earth and the obliquity (inclination) of the Earth's equator with respect to its orbit cause a difference between the time the sun crosses the upper celestial meridian and 12 noon on a clock—the difference can be more than 16 minutes. This discrepancy is called the *equation of time*, where the term *equation* has its medieval meaning of "additive corrective factor."

The equation of time gives the difference between apparent midnight (when the sun crosses the lower meridian that passes through the nadir; this is virtually the same as the midpoint between sunset and sunrise) and mean midnight (0 hours on the 24-hour clock). Similarly, at other times of day the equation of time gives the difference between mean solar time and apparent solar time. In the past, when apparent time was the more readily available, the equation of time conventionally had the opposite sign.

The periodic pattern of the equation of time, shown in Figures 14.5 and 14.6, is sometimes inscribed as part of the analemma on sundials (usually in mirror image); the frontispiece for Chapter 18 (page 217) shows a three-dimensional image of the equation of time. During the twentieth century, the equation of time had zeroes around April 15, June 14, September 1, and December 25; it is at its maximum at the beginning of November and at its minimum in mid-February. The equation of time is needed for the French Revolutionary and Persian astronomical calendars, and a rough approximation is used in the modern Hindu calendars. We use the following function for the equation of time:

$$\textbf{equation-of-time}\,(t) \stackrel{\text{def}}{=} \tag{14.20}$$

$$\text{sign}\,(\mathit{equation}) \times \min\left\{|\mathit{equation}|, 12^{\text{h}}\right\}$$

where

$$c = \textbf{julian-centuries}\,(t)$$

$$\lambda = 280.46645° + 36000.76983° \times c + 0.0003032° \times c^2$$

[7] The 24-hour day is sometimes called a *nychthemeron* to distinguish it from the shorter period of daylight.

[8] The hands on early mechanical clocks were imitating the movement of the shadow of the gnomon (in the northern hemisphere where clocks were developed) as the sun crosses the sky. This is the origin of our notion of "clockwise." See "The Last Word," *New Scientist*, March 27, 1999.

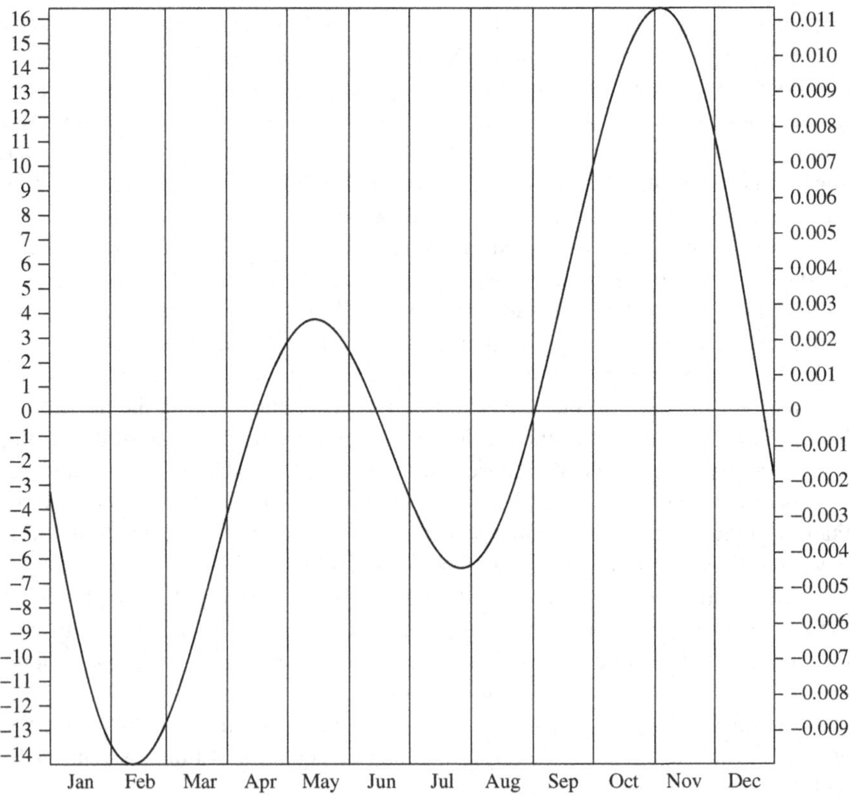

Figure 14.5 The current equation of time, as computed by **equation-of-time**. The left-hand vertical axis is marked in minutes and the right-hand vertical axis is marked in fractions of a day.

$$\begin{aligned}
anomaly &= 357.52910^\circ + 35999.05030^\circ \times c \\
&\quad - 0.0001559^\circ \times c^2 - 0.00000048^\circ \times c^3 \\
eccentricity &= 0.016708617 - 0.000042037 \times c - 0.0000001236 \times c^2 \\
\varepsilon &= \textbf{obliquity}\,(t) \\
y &= \tan^2\left(\frac{\varepsilon}{2}\right) \\
equation &= \frac{1}{2 \times \pi} \\
&\quad \times \Big(y \times \sin(2 \times \lambda) - 2 \times eccentricity \times \sin anomaly \\
&\quad\quad + 4 \times eccentricity \times y \times \sin anomaly \times \cos(2 \times \lambda) \\
&\quad\quad - 0.5 \times y^2 \times \sin(4 \times \lambda) \\
&\quad\quad - 1.25 \times eccentricity^2 \times \sin(2 \times anomaly) \Big)
\end{aligned}$$

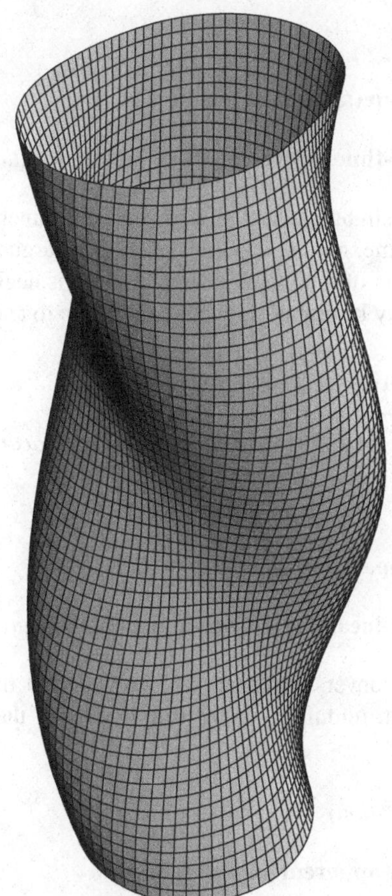

Figure 14.6 The equation of time wrapped onto a cylinder. The rotational range is 1 year; the axial range is Gregorian years 1500–12500. This rendering was converted into a three-dimensional cam by Stewart P. Dickson to be used as a mechanical cam in the "Clock of the Long Now" by W. Daniel Hillis and the Long Now Foundation. The clock is designed to keep local, absolute, and astronomical time over a span of 10000 years. The cam resynchronizes the clock at local solar noon via a thermal trigger. See *The Clock of the Long Now: Time and Responsibility* by Stewart Brand, Basic Books, New York, 1999 for more information. (Reproduced by permission.)

The parameter t is a moment (R.D. day and fraction); it is converted to "Julian centuries," c. The function for obliquity is given below (page 220). The preceding approximation of the equation of time is not valid for dates that are many millennia in the past or future; hence, for robustness, we limit the accuracy of the calculated value to half a day.

The equation of time permits us to convert easily to and from apparent time:

$$\textbf{apparent-from-local}\,(t_\ell, \mathit{location}) \stackrel{\text{def}}{=} \qquad (14.21)$$

$$t_\ell + \textbf{equation-of-time}\,(\textbf{universal-from-local}\,(t_\ell, \mathit{location}))$$

In the other direction,

$$\textbf{local-from-apparent}\,(t, \textit{location}) \stackrel{\text{def}}{=} \tag{14.22}$$

$$t - \textbf{equation-of-time}\,(\textbf{universal-from-local}\,(t, \textit{location}))$$

The latter function is slightly inaccurate because the function **equation-of-time** takes the local mean time, not the apparent time, as its argument; the difference in the value of the equation of time in those few minutes is negligible, however.

These functions may be composed with conversion to and from local time:

$$\textbf{apparent-from-universal}\,(t_{\text{u}}, \textit{location}) \stackrel{\text{def}}{=} \tag{14.23}$$

$$\textbf{apparent-from-local}\,(\textbf{local-from-universal}\,(t_{\text{u}}, \textit{location}), \textit{location})$$

and

$$\textbf{universal-from-apparent}\,(t, \textit{location}) \stackrel{\text{def}}{=} \tag{14.24}$$

$$\textbf{universal-from-local}\,(\textbf{local-from-apparent}\,(t, \textit{location}), \textit{location})$$

Using these time conversion functions, we can find the true middle of the night (true, or apparent, midnight) or the true middle of the day (apparent noon) in Universal Time:

$$\textbf{midnight}\,(\textit{date, location}) \stackrel{\text{def}}{=} \tag{14.25}$$

$$\textbf{universal-from-apparent}\,(\textit{date, location})$$

and

$$\textbf{midday}\,(\textit{date, location}) \stackrel{\text{def}}{=} \tag{14.26}$$

$$\textbf{universal-from-apparent}\left(\textit{date} + 12^{\text{h}}, \textit{location}\right)$$

The Earth's *rotation period* with respect to the fixed celestial sphere is approximately equal to $23^{\text{h}}56^{\text{m}}4.09890^{\text{s}}$. This is marginally more than the length of a (*mean*) *sidereal* (or *tropical*) *day*, namely, $23^{\text{h}}56^{\text{m}}4.09054^{\text{s}}$, which is the time of rotation relative to the First Point of Aries. In the course of one rotation on its axis, the Earth has also revolved somewhat in its orbit around the sun, and thus the sun is not quite in the same position as it was one rotation prior. This accounts for the difference of almost 4 minutes with respect to the solar day. The sidereal day is employed in the Hindu calendar.

Like the solar day, the sidereal day is not constant; it is steadily growing longer. In practice, *sidereal time* is measured by the *hour angle* between the meridian (directly overhead) and the position of the First Point of Aries (see page 219). This definition of sidereal time is affected by the precession of the equinoxes—see page 219. Converting between mean solar and mean sidereal time amounts to evaluating a polynomial:

$$\textbf{sidereal-from-moment}\,(t) \stackrel{\text{def}}{=} \tag{14.27}$$

$$\left(280.46061837^\circ + 36525 \times 360.98564736629^\circ \times c + 0.000387933^\circ \times c^2 - \frac{1^\circ}{38710000} \times c^3\right) \bmod 360$$

where

$$c = \frac{t - \textbf{j2000}}{36525}$$

The modern Hindu lunar calendar uses an approximation to this conversion.

14.4 The Year

And the sun rises and the sun sets—then to its place it rushes; there it rises again. It goes toward the south and veers toward the north.[10]

Ecclesiastes 1, 5–6

The *vernal equinox* occurs at the moment when the sun's position crosses the *true celestial equator* (the line in the sky above the Earth's equator) from south to north, on approximately March 20 each year. At that time day and night are each 12 hours all over the world, and the Earth's axis of rotation is perpendicular to the line connecting the centers of the Earth and sun.[11] The point of intersection of the ecliptic (the sun's apparent path through the constellations of the zodiac), inclined from south to north, and the celestial equator is called the *true vernal equinox* or the "First Point of Aries," but it is currently in the constellation Pisces, not Aries, on account of a phenomenon called the *precession of the equinoxes*. In its gyroscopic motion, the Earth's rotational axis migrates in a slow circle mainly as a consequence of the moon's pull on a nonspherical Earth. This nearly uniform motion causes the position of the equinoxes to move backwards along the ecliptic in a period of about 25725 years. This precession has caused the vernal equinox to cease to coincide with the day when the sun enters Aries, as it did some 2300 years ago (however, since the absolute length of a day is getting longer—see page 210—the sun will be in the same position in calendar year 24500 as it was in 2000). Celestial longitude is measured from the First Point of Aries. As a consequence, the longitudes of the stars are constantly changing (in addition to the measurable motions of many of the "fixed" stars). This precession of the equinoxes also causes the celestial pole to rotate slowly in a circular pattern. This is why the identity of the "pole star" has changed over the course of history. In 13000 B.C.E., Vega was

[10] This translation follows the interpretation of Solomon ben Isaac.

[11] Perhaps this perpendicularity explains the odd belief that fresh eggs balance more easily on the day of the vernal equinox. This turned into a minor craze in the United States; see Martin Gardner's "Notes of a Fringe Watcher," *The Skeptical Inquirer*, May/June 1996.

near the pole; currently it is near the star Polaris. In contrast, the Hindu calendar is based on calculations in terms of the *sidereal* longitude, which ignores precession and remains fixed against the backdrop of the stars.

The equator is currently inclined at approximately

$$23.4443291^\circ = 23^\circ 26' 21.448''$$

with respect to the plane of revolution of the Earth (the ecliptic) around the sun.[12] As a result, the sun, in the course of a year, traces a path through the stars that moves towards the celestial North Pole, back towards the celestial equator, then towards the celestial South Pole and back again. The value of this inclination, called the *obliquity*, varies in a 100000-year cycle, ranging from 24.2° 10000 years ago to 22.6° in another 10000 years. The following function gives an approximate value:

$$\mathbf{obliquity}\,(t) \stackrel{\text{def}}{=} \tag{14.28}$$

$$23^\circ 26' 21.448'' + \left(-46.8150'' \times c - 0.00059'' \times c^2 + 0.001813'' \times c^3 \right)$$

where

$$c = \mathbf{julian\text{-}centuries}\,(t)$$

Given the obliquity, one can compute the declination and right ascension corresponding to celestial latitude β and longitude λ:

$$\mathbf{declination}\,(t, \beta, \lambda) \stackrel{\text{def}}{=} \tag{14.29}$$

$$\arcsin\,(\sin\beta \times \cos\varepsilon + \cos\beta \times \sin\varepsilon \times \sin\lambda)$$

where

$$\varepsilon = \mathbf{obliquity}\,(t)$$

and

$$\mathbf{right\text{-}ascension}\,(t, \beta, \lambda) \stackrel{\text{def}}{=} \tag{14.30}$$

$$\mathbf{arctan}\,(\sin\lambda \times \cos\varepsilon - \tan\beta \times \sin\varepsilon, \cos\lambda)$$

where

$$\varepsilon = \mathbf{obliquity}\,(t)$$

which is measured in degrees, not hours.

In addition to the precession, the axis of rotation of the Earth wobbles like a top in an 18.6-year period about its mean position. This effect is called *nutation*

[12] There has recently been much worry in the fringe science community about the change in the tilt of the Earth's axis causing a global calamity *New Scientist* (August 9, 2008, p. 56) refers to this as "fruitloopery."

and is caused by the gravitational pull of the moon and sun on the unevenly shaped Earth. Nutation causes slight changes in the celestial latitudes and longitudes of stars and planets. It also causes a periodic variation in the lengths of the sidereal and solar days of up to about 0.01 second. The *mean sidereal time* smoothes out (subtracts) this nutation, which can accumulate to a difference of about 1 second from the actual sidereal time. The moon also causes small oscillations in the length of the day, with periods ranging from 12 hours to 1 (sidereal) month, but these can safely be ignored.

The true position of the sun differs from the "mean sun" in both longitude and latitude. The (angular) speed of the longitude of the true sun oscillates markedly within a year, so that the lengths of the four annual seasons differ by as much as 5 days. The sun's mean latitude is 0°, but the true sun does not always stay on the ecliptic.

The *tropical year* is the time it takes for the "mean sun" to travel from one mean vernal equinox to the next. As the speed of the mean sun on the ecliptic is slowly increasing over the centuries, the tropical year as determined from the instantaneous speed of the mean sun for an arbitrary instant is slowly decreasing. The length of a tropical year is defined today with respect to a "dynamical" equinox [21];[13] its current value is 365.242177 mean solar days, and it is decreasing by about 1.3×10^{-5} solar days per century. We use the following older value in our calculations for estimation purposes:

$$\textbf{mean-tropical-year} \stackrel{\text{def}}{=} 365.242189 \tag{14.31}$$

The time intervals between successive vernal equinoxes differ from those between successive autumnal equinoxes and also from the tropical year. Figure 14.7 shows for comparison the fluctuating equinox-to-equinox and solstice-to-solstice year lengths, measured in mean solar days at the same point in time, together with the mean year length used in various arithmetical calendars.

A *sidereal year* is the time it takes for the Earth to revolve once around the sun, that is, for the mean sun to return to the same position relative to the background of the fixed stars. The sidereal year is about 20 minutes more than the tropical:

$$\textbf{mean-sidereal-year} \stackrel{\text{def}}{=} 365.25636 \tag{14.32}$$

The modern Hindu calendar (Chapter 20) uses approximations of the sidereal and tropical year.

To determine the times of equinoxes or solstices, as required for the French Revolutionary (Chapter 17), Chinese (Chapter 19), Persian astronomical (Chapter 15), and proposed Bahá'í (Section 16.3) calendars, we must calculate the longitude of the sun at any given time. The following function takes an astronomical time, given as an R.D. moment *t*, converts it to Julian centuries, sums a long sequence of periodic terms, and adds terms to compensate for aberration (the effect of the sun's

---

[13] This dynamical equinox is the intersection of the mean celestial equator with the ecliptic, where the movement of the ecliptic is derived from a dynamical model of the movement of the Earth-moon barycenter (center of gravity) within the solar system.

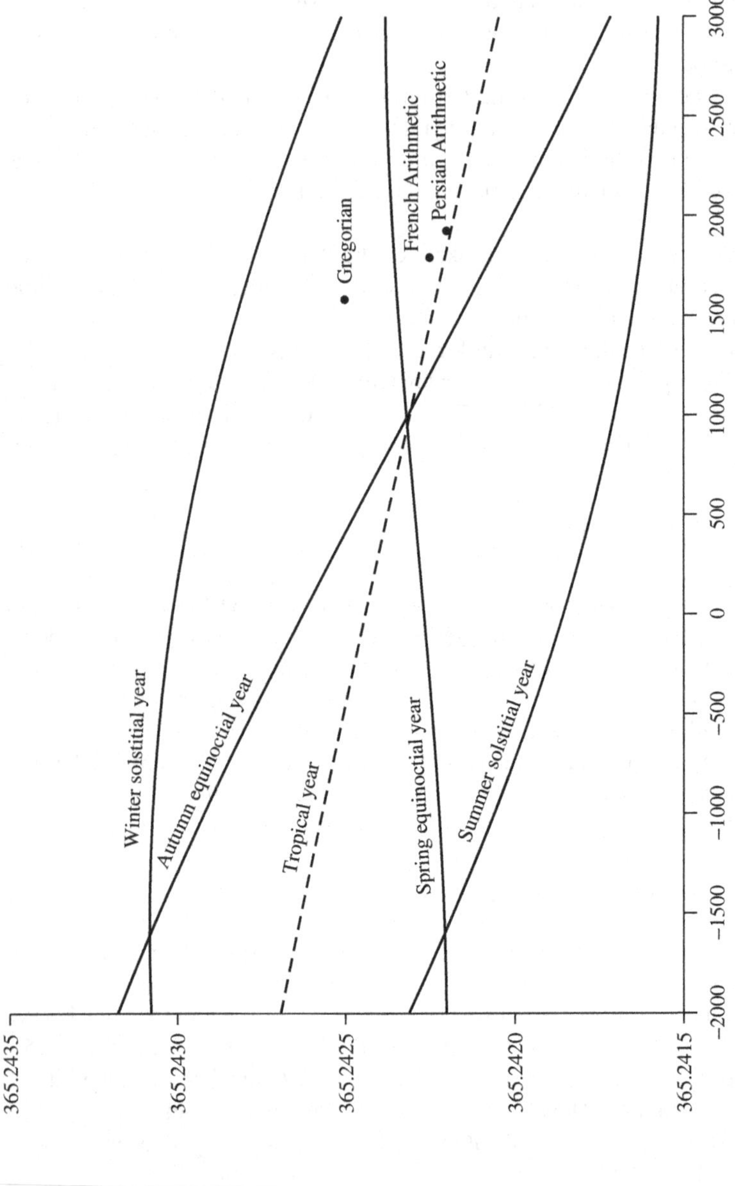

Figure 14.7 Length of the year, in contemporaneous mean solar days, plotted by Gregorian year. (The value for the Julian/Coptic/Ethiopic calendars, 365.25, is omitted because it is far above the values plotted.) Suggested by R. H. van Gent and based on formulas from [18, chap. 27] and the parabolic approximation from Figure 14.3.

apparent motion while its light is traveling towards Earth) and nutation (caused by the wobble of the Earth):

$$\textbf{solar-longitude}\,(t) \stackrel{\text{def}}{=} (\lambda + \textbf{aberration}\,(t) + \textbf{nutation}\,(t)) \bmod 360 \qquad (14.33)$$

where

$$c = \textbf{julian-centuries}\,(t)$$
$$\lambda = 282.7771834° + 36000.76953744° \times c$$
$$+\, 0.000005729577951308232° \times \sum (\overline{x} \times \sin(\overline{y} + \overline{z} \times c))$$
$$\overline{x} = \text{(see Table 14.1)}$$
$$\overline{y} = \text{(see Table 14.1)}$$
$$\overline{z} = \text{(see Table 14.1)}$$

To avoid cluttering the page with subscripts, we will use vector notation, with the intention that the operations within a sum are performed on like-indexed elements of $\overline{x}$, $\overline{y}$, and $\overline{z}$, displayed in the rows of Table 14.1. This function is accurate to within 2 minutes of arc for current times.

The effect of nutation on the longitude is approximately

$$\textbf{nutation}\,(t) \stackrel{\text{def}}{=} -0.004778° \times \sin A - 0.0003667° \times \sin B \qquad (14.34)$$

where

$$c = \textbf{julian-centuries}\,(t)$$
$$A = 124.90° - 1934.134° \times c + 0.002063° \times c^2$$
$$B = 201.11° + 72001.5377° \times c + 0.00057° \times c^2$$

The *aberration*—the effect of the sun's moving about 20.47 seconds of arc during the 8 minutes during which its light is *en route* to Earth—is calculated as follows:

$$\textbf{aberration}\,(t) \stackrel{\text{def}}{=} \qquad (14.35)$$

$$0.0000974° \times \cos(177.63° + 35999.01848° \times c) - 0.005575°$$

where

$$c = \textbf{julian-centuries}\,(t)$$

We determine the time of an equinox or solstice by giving a generic function that takes a moment t (in U.T.) and a number of degrees λ, indicating the season, and searches for the moment when the longitude of the sun is next equal to λ degrees. In effect, we search for the inverse of **solar-longitude**, using equation (1.36) on page 25, within an interval beginning 5 days before the estimate τ (or at the given moment, whichever comes later) and ending 5 days after:

Table 14.1 Values of the arguments $\widetilde{x}$, $\widetilde{y}$, and $\widetilde{z}$ in **solar-longitude** (page 223).

$\widetilde{x}$	$\widetilde{y}$	$\widetilde{z}$	$\widetilde{x}$	$\widetilde{y}$	$\widetilde{z}$
403406	270.54861	0.9287892	46	8	107997.405
195207	340.19128	35999.1376958	38	197.1	−4444.176
119433	63.91854	35999.4089666	37	250.4	151.771
112392	331.26220	35998.7287385	32	65.3	67555.316
3891	317.843	71998.20261	29	162.7	31556.080
2819	86.631	71998.4403	28	341.5	−4561.540
1721	240.052	36000.35726	27	291.6	107996.706
660	310.26	71997.4812	27	98.5	1221.655
350	247.23	32964.4678	25	146.7	62894.167
334	260.87	−19.4410	24	110	31437.369
314	297.82	445267.1117	21	5.2	14578.298
268	343.14	45036.8840	21	342.6	−31931.757
242	166.79	3.1008	20	230.9	34777.243
234	81.53	22518.4434	18	256.1	1221.999
158	3.50	−19.9739	17	45.3	62894.511
132	132.75	65928.9345	14	242.9	−4442.039
129	182.95	9038.0293	13	115.2	107997.909
114	162.03	3034.7684	13	151.8	119.066
99	29.8	33718.148	13	285.3	16859.071
93	266.4	3034.448	12	53.3	−4.578
86	249.2	−2280.773	10	126.6	26895.292
78	157.6	29929.992	10	205.7	−39.127
72	257.8	31556.493	10	85.9	12297.536
68	185.1	149.588	10	146.1	90073.778
64	69.9	9037.750			

$$\textbf{solar-longitude-after}\,(\lambda, t) \stackrel{\text{def}}{=} \textbf{solar-longitude}^{-1}(\lambda, [a\,..\,b]) \tag{14.36}$$

where

$$\begin{aligned} rate &= \frac{\textbf{mean-tropical-year}}{360^\circ} \\ \tau &= t + rate \times ((\lambda - \textbf{solar-longitude}\,(t)) \bmod 360) \\ a &= \max\{t, \tau - 5\} \\ b &= \tau + 5 \end{aligned}$$

Equinoxes and solstices occur when the sun's longitude is a multiple of 90°. Specifically, Table 14.2 gives the names, solar longitudes, and approximate Gregorian dates. The constants for the four seasons were defined in Chapter 3.

It will be convenient to be able to determine the times of the seasons within a given Gregorian year. So, we define

$$\textbf{season-in-gregorian}\,(season, g\text{-}year) \stackrel{\text{def}}{=} \tag{14.37}$$

$$\textbf{solar-longitude-after}\,(season, jan_1)$$

Table 14.2 The solar longitudes and approximate current dates of equinoxes and solstices, along with the approximate length of the following season.

Name	Solar longitude	Approximate date	Season length
Vernal (spring) equinox	0°	March 20	92.76 days
Summer solstice	90°	June 21	93.65 days
Autumnal (fall) equinox	180°	September 22–23	89.84 days
Winter solstice	270°	December 21–22	88.99 days

where

$$jan_1 = \textbf{gregorian-new-year}\,(g\text{-}year)$$

To use this function to determine, say, the standard time of the winter solstice in Urbana, Illinois, we write

$$\textbf{urbana-winter}\,(g\text{-}year) \stackrel{\text{def}}{=} \qquad (14.38)$$
$$\textbf{standard-from-universal}\,(\textbf{season-in-gregorian}\,(\textbf{winter}, g\text{-}year), \textbf{urbana})$$

For year 2000 this gives us the answer R.D. 730475.31751, which is 7:37:13 a.m. on December 21.

To calculate sidereal longitude, we use the following computation for precession:

$$\textbf{precession}\,(t) \stackrel{\text{def}}{=} (p + P - arg) \bmod 360 \qquad (14.39)$$

where

$$c = \textbf{julian-centuries}\,(t)$$
$$\eta = \left(47.0029'' \times c - 0.03302'' \times c^2 + 0.000060'' \times c^3\right) \bmod 360$$
$$P = \left(174.876384° - 869.8089'' \times c + 0.03536'' \times c^2\right) \bmod 360$$
$$p = \left(5029.0966'' \times c + 1.11113'' \times c^2 + 0.000006'' \times c^3\right) \bmod 360$$
$$A = \cos\eta \times \sin P$$
$$B = \cos P$$
$$arg = \textbf{arctan}\,(A, B)$$

To use **precession**, one needs to choose some moment, called **sidereal-start** [such as formula (20.41)], at which one considers that sidereal and ecliptic longitude coincide. Then we have

$$\textbf{sidereal-solar-longitude}\,(t) \stackrel{\text{def}}{=} \qquad (14.40)$$
$$\left(\textbf{solar-longitude}\,(t) - \textbf{precession}\,(t) + \textbf{sidereal-start}\right) \bmod 360$$

Astronomical Hindu calendars (see Section 20.5) require the determination of this solar attribute.

Finally, the altitude of the sun above the horizon at any given time depends on the ecliptical position of the sun at that time and on the latitude φ and longitude ψ of the viewing location:

$$\textbf{solar-altitude}\left(t, \boxed{\varphi \mid \psi \mid - \mid -}\right) \stackrel{\text{def}}{=} \qquad (14.41)$$

$$\textit{altitude} \bmod [-180\,..\,180)$$

where

$$\begin{aligned}
\lambda &= \textbf{solar-longitude}\,(t) \\
\alpha &= \textbf{right-ascension}\,(t, 0, \lambda) \\
\delta &= \textbf{declination}\,(t, 0, \lambda) \\
\theta_0 &= \textbf{sidereal-from-moment}\,(t) \\
H &= (\theta_0 + \psi - \alpha) \bmod 360 \\
\textit{altitude} &= \arcsin(\sin\varphi \times \sin\delta + \cos\varphi \times \cos\delta \times \cos H)
\end{aligned}$$

Here α is the sun's right ascension, δ is its declination, and H is the local sidereal hour angle. The result is not corrected for parallax (the shift in observed position due to the change in position of the observer) or refraction, and ranges from −90° to +90°.

14.5 Astronomical Solar Calendars

Astronomy [lit. seasons] and geometry are accoutrements of wisdom.
Pirkei Avoth III, 23

Astronomical solar calendars are based on the precise solar longitude at a specified time. For example, the astronomical Persian calendar begins its New Year on the day when the vernal equinox occurs before true noon (the middle point of the day, sundial time, not clock time) in Tehran; the start of the New Year is postponed to the next day if the equinox is after noon (see Chapter 15). Other calendars of this type include the astronomical form of the Bahá'í calendar (Chapter 16) and the original French Revolutionary calendar (Chapter 17).

The key to implementing an astronomical solar calendar is to determine the day of the New Year on or before a given fixed date. In general, the New Year begins on the day when the solar longitude reaches a certain value φ at some critical moment, such as noon or midnight. For this purpose, we first estimate the time using the current solar longitude:

$$\textbf{estimate-prior-solar-longitude}\,(\lambda, t) \stackrel{\text{def}}{=} \min\{t, \tau - \textit{rate} \times \Delta\} \qquad (14.42)$$

where

$$\begin{aligned}
\textit{rate} &= \frac{\textbf{mean-tropical-year}}{360^\circ} \\
\tau &= t - \textit{rate} \times ((\textbf{solar-longitude}\,(t) - \lambda) \bmod 360) \\
\Delta &= (\textbf{solar-longitude}\,(\tau) - \lambda) \bmod [-180\,..\,180)
\end{aligned}$$

This is done in a two-step process. First we go back to the time when the sun, traveling at mean speed, was last at longitude φ; then the error Δ in the longitude is used to refine the estimate to within a day of the correct time. The only complication is handling the discontinuity from 360° to 0°; this is done using interval modulus.

Since this estimate is within a day of the actual occurrence, to determine when the year actually starts we need only carry out a short search of the form

$$\underset{day \geqslant \lfloor approx \rfloor - 1}{\mathbf{MIN}} \{\varphi \leqslant \textbf{solar-longitude}(f(day)) \leqslant \varphi + 2^\circ\} \tag{14.43}$$

where f is a function that returns the critical time of *day* for measuring longitude for the specific calendar. The upper bound $\varphi + 2^\circ$ is only needed when one is looking for the spring equinox ($\varphi = 0^\circ$), so that values close to 360°, which precede the equinox, do not stop the search prematurely. We use this method for the astronomical Persian, the astronomical Bahá'í, the original French Revolutionary, and Chinese calendars.

14.6 The Month

Should someone rather less skilled in calculation nonetheless be curious about the course of the moon, we have also for his sake devised a formula adapted to the capacity of his intelligence, so that he might find what he seeks.

The Venerable Bede: *De Temporum Ratione*

The *new moon* occurs when the sun and moon have the same celestial longitude; it is not necessarily the time of their closest encounter, as viewed from Earth, because the orbits of the Earth and moon are not coplanar. The time from new moon (the *conjunction* of the sun and the moon) to new moon, a *lunation*, is called the *synodic month*. Its value today ranges from approximately 29.27 to 29.84 days [19], with a mean of currently about 29.530588 mean solar days:

$$\textbf{mean-synodic-month} \stackrel{\text{def}}{=} 29.530588861 \tag{14.44}$$

in days of 86400 atomic seconds. Approximations to this value are used in many lunar and lunisolar calendars. The Chinese calendar, however, uses actual astronomical values in its determinations. The mean and true times of the new moon can differ by up to about 14 hours. Figure 14.8 shows for comparison the changing length of the month, measured in mean solar days at the same point in time, with the values used in several arithmetic calendars.

The synodic month is not constant but is decreasing in mean length by about 3.6×10^{-7} solar days per century (though it is *increasing* in length by about 0.021 atomic seconds per century). The net effect of the decreases in synodic month and tropical year is to increase the number of months from its current value of about 12.3682670 per year by 0.3×10^{-6} months per century.

The full moon is the most visible feature of the night sky and has thus long fascinated human observers. Some cultures give names to the full moons—the "Harvest Moon" is the full moon closest to the autumnal equinox, for example. For obscure reasons, when four full moons occur within one solar season (from equinox to solstice or solstice to equinox), the third is termed a *blue moon*; see [23]. This event

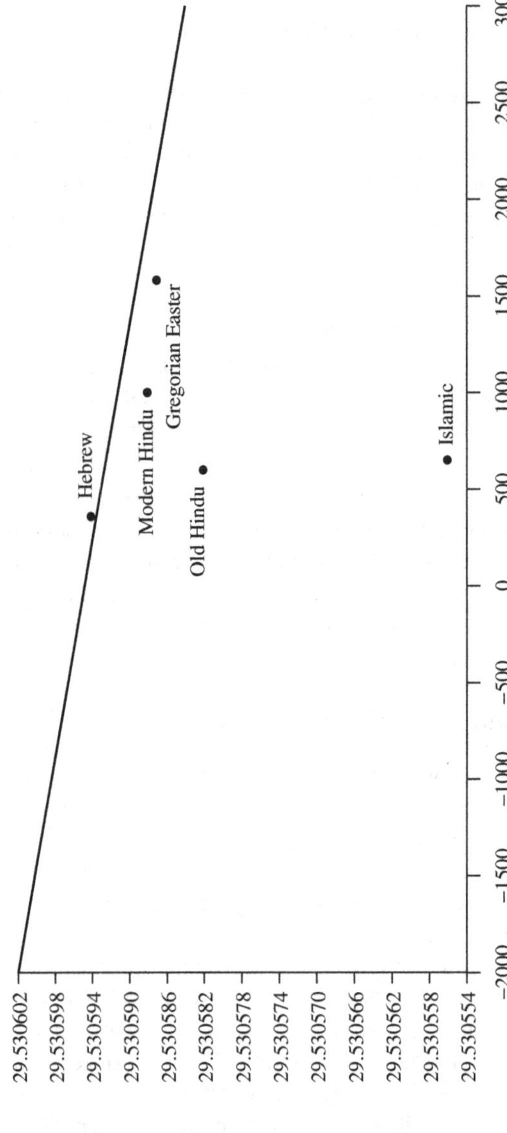

Figure 14.8 Length of the synodic month, in contemporaneous mean solar days, plotted by Gregorian year. (The value for Orthodox Easter, 29.530851, is omitted because it is far above the values plotted.) Suggested by R. H. van Gent and based on data from [18, Chap. 49] and [31, Chap. 14].

is similar to the conditions for a leap month on the Chinese calendar and Hindu lunisolar calendars, which mandate a leap month whenever two new moons occur within the same solar month (see Chapters 19 and 20).

The *sidereal month* is the time it takes the moon to make one revolution around the Earth. Its mean value is 27.32166 days. In the interim, the Earth has moved in its orbit around the sun, and thus the difference in longitude between the sun and moon has increased, which is why the synodic month is longer. The mean values of these types of month should satisfy the equation

$$\frac{1}{\text{sidereal month}} - \frac{1}{\text{synodic month}} = \frac{1}{\text{sidereal year}}$$

The *anomalistic month* is the time between consecutive perigees (points at which the moon is closest to Earth). The anomalistic month averages 27.55455 days. Approximations to these values are used in calculating the position of the moon for the modern Hindu lunisolar calendar.

We also use the notion of a *solar month*, the time for the sun's position in the sky to traverse one sign of the zodiac (30° of longitude). Its mean value is one-twelfth of a solar year and ranges from 29.44 days in Northern Hemisphere winter (to traverse Capricorn) to 31.43 days in Northern Hemisphere summer. Solar months play an important rôle in the Chinese calendar (which uses tropical longitude) and in the Hindu calendar (which uses sidereal longitude).

The time of new moon can be determined directly using sums of periodic terms. We use the following function for the moment (in U.T.) of the nth new moon after (before, if n is negative) the new moon of January 11, 1 (Gregorian), the first new moon after R.D. 0:

$$\textbf{nth-new-moon}\,(n) \stackrel{\text{def}}{=} \qquad (14.45)$$

$$\textbf{universal-from-dynamical}\,(\mathit{approx} + \mathit{correction} + \mathit{extra} + \mathit{additional})$$

where

$$n_0 = 24724$$

$$k = n - n_0$$

$$c = \frac{k}{1236.85}$$

$$\mathit{approx} = \textbf{j2000} + \Big(5.09766 + \textbf{mean-synodic-month} \times 1236.85 \times c + 0.00015437 \times c^2 - 0.000000150 \times c^3 + 0.00000000073 \times c^4\Big)$$

$$E = 1 - 0.002516 \times c - 0.0000074 \times c^2$$

$$\mathit{solar\text{-}anomaly} = 2.5534° + 1236.85 \times 29.10535670° \times c - 0.0000014° \times c^2 - 0.00000011° \times c^3$$

$$
\begin{aligned}
\textit{lunar-anomaly} &= 201.5643^\circ + 385.81693528 \times 1236.85^\circ \times c \\
&\quad + 0.0107582^\circ \times c^2 + 0.00001238^\circ \times c^3 \\
&\quad - 0.000000058^\circ \times c^4 \\
\textit{moon-argument} &= 160.7108^\circ + 390.67050284 \times 1236.85^\circ \times c \\
&\quad - 0.0016118^\circ \times c^2 - 0.00000227^\circ \times c^3 \\
&\quad + 0.000000011^\circ \times c^4 \\
\Omega &= 124.7746^\circ + (-1.56375588 \times 1236.85)^\circ \times c \\
&\quad + 0.0020672^\circ \times c^2 + 0.00000215^\circ \times c^3 \\
\textit{correction} &= -0.00017 \times \sin \Omega \\
&\quad + \sum \left(\widetilde{v} \times E^{\widetilde{w}} \right. \\
&\qquad \times \sin \left(\widetilde{x} \times \textit{solar-anomaly} + \widetilde{y} \times \textit{lunar-anomaly} \right. \\
&\qquad\qquad \left.\left. + \widetilde{z} \times \textit{moon-argument} \right) \right) \\
\textit{extra} &= 0.000325 \times \sin \left(299.77^\circ + 132.8475848^\circ \times c \right. \\
&\qquad \left. - 0.009173^\circ \times c^2 \right) \\
\textit{additional} &= \sum \left(\widetilde{l} \times \sin(\widetilde{i} + \widetilde{j} \times k) \right) \\
\widetilde{v} &= \text{(see Table 14.3)} \\
\widetilde{w} &= \text{(see Table 14.3)} \\
\widetilde{x} &= \text{(see Table 14.3)} \\
\widetilde{y} &= \text{(see Table 14.3)} \\
\widetilde{z} &= \text{(see Table 14.3)} \\
\widetilde{i} &= \text{(see Table 14.4)} \\
\widetilde{j} &= \text{(see Table 14.4)} \\
\widetilde{l} &= \text{(see Table 14.4)}
\end{aligned}
$$

There were $n_0 = 24724$ months between January, 1 and January, 2000, upon which time this function is centered. The first new moon after **j2000** occurred 5.25952 days later. The value of E depends on the eccentricity of Earth's elliptical orbit; Ω is the longitude of the moon's "ascending node."

To find the time of the new moon preceding a given date or moment, we can use

$$
\textbf{new-moon-before}\,(t) \stackrel{\text{def}}{=} \tag{14.46}
$$

$$
\textbf{nth-new-moon}\left(\underset{k \geqslant n-1}{\textbf{MAX}} \left\{ \textbf{nth-new-moon}\,(k) < t \right\} \right)
$$

Table 14.3 Values of the arguments $\widetilde{v}$, $\widetilde{w}$, $\widetilde{x}$, $\widetilde{y}$, and $\widetilde{z}$ in **nth-new-moon** (page 229).

$\widetilde{v}$	$\widetilde{w}$	$\widetilde{x}$	$\widetilde{y}$	$\widetilde{z}$	$\widetilde{v}$	$\widetilde{w}$	$\widetilde{x}$	$\widetilde{y}$	$\widetilde{z}$
−0.40720	0	0	1	0	0.00038	1	1	0	−2
0.17241	1	1	0	0	−0.00024	1	−1	2	0
0.01608	0	0	2	0	−0.00007	0	2	1	0
0.01039	0	0	0	2	0.00004	0	0	2	−2
0.00739	1	−1	1	0	0.00004	0	3	0	0
−0.00514	1	1	1	0	0.00003	0	1	1	−2
0.00208	2	2	0	0	0.00003	0	0	2	2
−0.00111	0	0	1	−2	−0.00003	0	1	1	2
−0.00057	0	0	1	2	0.00003	0	−1	1	2
0.00056	1	1	2	0	−0.00002	0	−1	1	−2
−0.00042	0	0	3	0	−0.00002	0	1	3	0
0.00042	1	1	0	2	0.00002	0	0	4	0

Table 14.4 Values of the arguments $\widetilde{i}$, $\widetilde{j}$, and $\widetilde{l}$ in **nth-new-moon** (page 229).

$\widetilde{i}$	$\widetilde{j}$	$\widetilde{l}$	$\widetilde{i}$	$\widetilde{j}$	$\widetilde{l}$
251.88	0.016321	0.000165	34.52	27.261239	0.000047
251.83	26.651886	0.000164	207.19	0.121824	0.000042
349.42	36.412478	0.000126	291.34	1.844379	0.000040
84.66	18.206239	0.000110	161.72	24.198154	0.000037
141.74	53.303771	0.000062	239.56	25.513099	0.000035
207.14	2.453732	0.000060	331.55	3.592518	0.000023
154.84	7.306860	0.000056			

where

$$t_0 = \textbf{nth-new-moon}\,(0)$$
$$\varphi = \textbf{lunar-phase}\,(t)$$
$$n = \text{round}\left(\frac{t - t_0}{\textbf{mean-synodic-month}} - \frac{\varphi}{360^\circ}\right)$$

For the following new moon, we have

$$\textbf{new-moon-at-or-after}\,(t) \stackrel{\text{def}}{=} \tag{14.47}$$
$$\textbf{nth-new-moon}\left(\underset{k \geqslant n}{\textbf{MIN}}\left\{\textbf{nth-new-moon}\,(k) \geqslant t\right\}\right)$$

where

$$t_0 = \textbf{nth-new-moon}(0)$$
$$\varphi = \textbf{lunar-phase}(t)$$
$$n = \text{round}\left(\frac{t - t_0}{\textbf{mean-synodic-month}} - \frac{\varphi}{360^\circ}\right)$$

Alternatively, one can determine the time of new moon indirectly from the longitude of the moon. The moon's longitude is significantly more difficult to compute than that of the sun, because it is affected in a nonnegligible way by the pull of the sun, Venus, and Jupiter. The function for the longitude of the moon is given by

$$\textbf{lunar-longitude}(t) \stackrel{\text{def}}{=} \tag{14.48}$$
$$\left(L' + \mathit{correction} + \mathit{venus} + \mathit{jupiter} + \mathit{flat\text{-}earth} + \textbf{nutation}(t)\right) \bmod 360$$

where

$$c = \textbf{julian-centuries}(t)$$
$$L' = \textbf{mean-lunar-longitude}(c)$$
$$D = \textbf{lunar-elongation}(c)$$
$$M = \textbf{solar-anomaly}(c)$$
$$M' = \textbf{lunar-anomaly}(c)$$
$$F = \textbf{moon-node}(c)$$
$$E = 1 - 0.002516 \times c - 0.0000074 \times c^2$$
$$\mathit{correction} = \frac{1^\circ}{1000000} \times \sum\left(\widetilde{v} \times E^{|\widetilde{x}|} \times \sin(\widetilde{w} \times D + \widetilde{x} \times M + \widetilde{y} \times M' + \widetilde{z} \times F)\right)$$
$$\mathit{venus} = \frac{3958^\circ}{1000000} \times \sin(119.75^\circ + c \times 131.849^\circ)$$
$$\mathit{jupiter} = \frac{318^\circ}{1000000} \times \sin(53.09^\circ + c \times 479264.29^\circ)$$
$$\mathit{flat\text{-}earth} = \frac{1962^\circ}{1000000} \times \sin(L' - F)$$
$$\widetilde{v} = (\text{see Table 14.5})$$
$$\widetilde{w} = (\text{see Table 14.5})$$
$$\widetilde{x} = (\text{see Table 14.5})$$
$$\widetilde{y} = (\text{see Table 14.5})$$
$$\widetilde{z} = (\text{see Table 14.5})$$

This function and other lunar functions use the following auxiliary functions giving mean values of the moon's longitude, its elongation (angular distance from

Table 14.5 Values of the arguments $\widetilde{v}$, $\widetilde{w}$, $\widetilde{x}$, $\widetilde{y}$, and $\widetilde{z}$ in **lunar-longitude** (page 232).

$\widetilde{v}$	$\widetilde{w}$	$\widetilde{x}$	$\widetilde{y}$	$\widetilde{z}$	$\widetilde{v}$	$\widetilde{w}$	$\widetilde{x}$	$\widetilde{y}$	$\widetilde{z}$
6288774	0	0	1	0	−2348	1	0	1	0
1274027	2	0	−1	0	2236	2	−2	0	0
658314	2	0	0	0	−2120	0	1	2	0
213618	0	0	2	0	−2069	0	2	0	0
−185116	0	1	0	0	2048	2	−2	−1	0
−114332	0	0	0	2	−1773	2	0	1	−2
58793	2	0	−2	0	−1595	2	0	0	2
57066	2	−1	−1	0	1215	4	−1	−1	0
53322	2	0	1	0	−1110	0	0	2	2
45758	2	−1	0	0	−892	3	0	−1	0
−40923	0	1	−1	0	−810	2	1	1	0
−34720	1	0	0	0	759	4	−1	−2	0
−30383	0	1	1	0	−713	0	2	−1	0
15327	2	0	0	−2	−700	2	2	−1	0
−12528	0	0	1	2	691	2	1	−2	0
10980	0	0	1	−2	596	2	−1	0	−2
10675	4	0	−1	0	549	4	0	1	0
10034	0	0	3	0	537	0	0	4	0
8548	4	0	−2	0	520	4	−1	0	0
−7888	2	1	−1	0	−487	1	0	−2	0
−6766	2	1	0	0	−399	2	1	0	−2
−5163	1	0	−1	0	−381	0	0	2	−2
4987	1	1	0	0	351	1	1	1	0
4036	2	−1	1	0	−340	3	0	−2	0
3994	2	0	2	0	330	4	0	−3	0
3861	4	0	0	0	327	2	−1	2	0
3665	2	0	−3	0	−323	0	2	1	0
−2689	0	1	−2	0	299	1	1	−1	0
−2602	2	0	−1	2	294	2	0	3	0
2390	2	−1	−2	0					

the sun), the solar anomaly (angular distance from perihelion), the lunar anomaly (angular distance from perigee), and the moon's "argument of latitude" (the distance from the moon's node, that point at which the moon's path crosses the ecliptic from the south to the north):

mean-lunar-longitude $(c) \stackrel{\text{def}}{=}$ (14.49)

$$\left(218.3164477^\circ + 481267.88123421^\circ \times c - 0.0015786^\circ \times c^2 + \frac{1^\circ}{538841} \times c^3 - \frac{1^\circ}{65194000} \times c^4\right) \bmod 360$$

lunar-elongation $(c) \stackrel{\text{def}}{=}$ (14.50)

$$\left(297.8501921^\circ + 445267.1114034^\circ \times c - 0.0018819^\circ \times c^2 + \frac{1^\circ}{545868} \times c^3 - \frac{1^\circ}{113065000} \times c^4\right) \bmod 360$$

solar-anomaly $(c) \stackrel{\text{def}}{=}$ (14.51)

$$\left(357.5291092^\circ + 35999.0502909^\circ \times c - 0.0001536^\circ \times c^2 + \frac{1^\circ}{24490000} \times c^3\right) \bmod 360$$

lunar-anomaly $(c) \stackrel{\text{def}}{=}$ (14.52)

$$\left(134.9633964^\circ + 477198.8675055^\circ \times c + 0.0087414^\circ \times c^2 + \frac{1^\circ}{69699} \times c^3 - \frac{1^\circ}{14712000} \times c^4\right) \bmod 360$$

moon-node $(c) \stackrel{\text{def}}{=}$ (14.53)

$$\left(93.2720950^\circ + 483202.0175233^\circ \times c - 0.0036539^\circ \times c^2 - \frac{1^\circ}{3526000} \times c^3 + \frac{1^\circ}{863310000} \times c^4\right) \bmod 360$$

These all take, as their argument, a moment expressed in Julian centuries. (Several of these values also appear in **nth-new-moon**, but there they are centered around the year 2000.)

The following function shifts the distance from the equinoctial point into the range [−90 .. 90):

lunar-node (*date*) $\stackrel{\text{def}}{=}$ (14.54)

(**moon-node** (**julian-centuries** (*date*))) mod [−90 .. 90)

If one wants the sidereal, rather than the equinoctial, lunar longitude, the following correction for precession may be used:

sidereal-lunar-longitude $(t) \stackrel{\text{def}}{=}$ (14.55)

(**lunar-longitude** (t) − **precession** (t) + **sidereal-start**) mod 360

Using **solar-longitude** and **lunar-longitude**, one can determine the phase of the moon—defined as the difference in longitudes of the sun and moon—at any moment t:

$$\textbf{lunar-phase}(t) \stackrel{\text{def}}{=} \begin{cases} \varphi' & \textbf{if } |\varphi - \varphi'| > 180^\circ \\ \varphi & \textbf{otherwise} \end{cases} \tag{14.56}$$

where

$$\begin{aligned}
\varphi &= (\textbf{lunar-longitude}(t) - \textbf{solar-longitude}(t)) \bmod 360 \\
t_0 &= \textbf{nth-new-moon}(0) \\
n &= \text{round}\left(\frac{t - t_0}{\textbf{mean-synodic-month}}\right) \\
\varphi' &= 360^\circ \times \left(\frac{t - \textbf{nth-new-moon}(n)}{\textbf{mean-synodic-month}} \bmod 1\right)
\end{aligned}$$

To ensure the robustness of our code, this function checks whether the phase obtained in this way conflicts with the time of new moon as calculated by the more precise **nth-new-moon** function. If it does, that is, if one method puts the time just before a new moon and the other just after, then an approximation based on the **nth-new-moon** moment is preferred.

To determine the time of the new moon, or other phases of the moon, we search using (1.36) for a time before moment t when the solar and lunar longitudes differ by the desired amount, φ:

$$\textbf{lunar-phase-at-or-before}(\varphi, t) \stackrel{\text{def}}{=} \textbf{lunar-phase}^{-1}(\varphi, [a \,..\, b]) \tag{14.57}$$

where

$$\begin{aligned}
\tau &= t - \textbf{mean-synodic-month} \times \frac{1}{360^\circ} \times ((\textbf{lunar-phase}(t) - \varphi) \bmod 360) \\
a &= \tau - 2 \\
b &= \min\{t, \tau + 2\}
\end{aligned}$$

The search is centered around the last time the *mean* moon had that phase. That moment τ is calculated by a variant of equation (1.63) based on the average rate at which the phase changes by 1°.

The search for the next time the moon has a given phase is analogous:

$$\textbf{lunar-phase-at-or-after}(\varphi, t) \stackrel{\text{def}}{=} \textbf{lunar-phase}^{-1}(\varphi, [a \,..\, b]) \tag{14.58}$$

where

$$\begin{aligned}
\tau &= t + \textbf{mean-synodic-month} \times \frac{1}{360^\circ} \times ((\varphi - \textbf{lunar-phase}(t)) \bmod 360) \\
a &= \max\{t, \tau - 2\} \\
b &= \tau + 2
\end{aligned}$$

For the computation of specific phases of the moon, that is, new moon, first quarter, full moon, and last quarter, we can use **lunar-phase-at-or-before** and **lunar-phase-at-or-after**, along with the following set of constants:

$$\textbf{new} \stackrel{\text{def}}{=} 0° \tag{14.59}$$

$$\textbf{first-quarter} \stackrel{\text{def}}{=} 90° \tag{14.60}$$

$$\textbf{full} \stackrel{\text{def}}{=} 180° \tag{14.61}$$

$$\textbf{last-quarter} \stackrel{\text{def}}{=} 270° \tag{14.62}$$

Lunar latitude is computed in nearly the same way as longitude:

$$\textbf{lunar-latitude}\,(t) \stackrel{\text{def}}{=} \beta + \mathit{venus} + \mathit{flat\text{-}earth} + \mathit{extra} \tag{14.63}$$

where

$$\begin{aligned}
c &= \textbf{julian-centuries}\,(t)\\
L' &= \textbf{mean-lunar-longitude}\,(c)\\
D &= \textbf{lunar-elongation}\,(c)\\
M &= \textbf{solar-anomaly}\,(c)\\
M' &= \textbf{lunar-anomaly}\,(c)\\
F &= \textbf{moon-node}\,(c)\\
E &= 1 - 0.002516 \times c - 0.0000074 \times c^2\\
\beta &= \frac{1°}{1000000}\\
&\quad \times \sum \left(\widetilde{v} \times E^{|\widetilde{x}|} \times \sin(\widetilde{w} \times D + \widetilde{x} \times M + \widetilde{y} \times M' + \widetilde{z} \times F) \right)\\
\mathit{venus} &= \frac{175°}{1000000} \times \big(\sin(119.75° + c \times 131.849° + F)\\
&\qquad + \sin(119.75° + c \times 131.849° - F) \big)\\
\mathit{flat\text{-}earth} &= -\frac{2235°}{1000000} \times \sin L' + \frac{127°}{1000000} \times \sin(L' - M')\\
&\quad - \frac{115°}{1000000} \times \sin(L' + M')\\
\mathit{extra} &= \frac{382°}{1000000} \times \sin(313.45° + c \times 481266.484°)\\
\widetilde{v} &= \text{(see Table 14.6)}\\
\widetilde{w} &= \text{(see Table 14.6)}\\
\widetilde{x} &= \text{(see Table 14.6)}\\
\widetilde{y} &= \text{(see Table 14.6)}\\
\widetilde{z} &= \text{(see Table 14.6)}
\end{aligned}$$

Lunar latitude ranges from −6° to +6°.

Table 14.6 Values of the arguments $\widetilde{v}$, $\widetilde{w}$, $\widetilde{x}$, $\widetilde{y}$, and $\widetilde{z}$ in **lunar-latitude** (page 236).

$\widetilde{v}$	$\widetilde{w}$	$\widetilde{x}$	$\widetilde{y}$	$\widetilde{z}$	$\widetilde{v}$	$\widetilde{w}$	$\widetilde{x}$	$\widetilde{y}$	$\widetilde{z}$
5128122	0	0	0	1	777	0	0	1	−3
280602	0	0	1	1	671	4	0	−2	1
277693	0	0	1	−1	607	2	0	0	−3
173237	2	0	0	−1	596	2	0	2	−1
55413	2	0	−1	1	491	2	−1	1	−1
46271	2	0	−1	−1	−451	2	0	−2	1
32573	2	0	0	1	439	0	0	3	−1
17198	0	0	2	1	422	2	0	2	1
9266	2	0	1	−1	421	2	0	−3	−1
8822	0	0	2	−1	−366	2	1	−1	1
8216	2	−1	0	−1	−351	2	1	0	1
4324	2	0	−2	−1	331	4	0	0	1
4200	2	0	1	1	315	2	−1	1	1
−3359	2	1	0	−1	302	2	−2	0	−1
2463	2	−1	−1	1	−283	0	0	1	3
2211	2	−1	0	1	−229	2	1	1	−1
2065	2	−1	−1	−1	223	1	1	0	−1
−1870	0	1	−1	−1	223	1	1	0	1
1828	4	0	−1	−1	−220	0	1	−2	−1
−1794	0	1	0	1	−220	2	1	−1	−1
−1749	0	0	0	3	−185	1	0	1	1
−1565	0	1	−1	1	181	2	−1	−2	−1
−1491	1	0	0	1	−177	0	1	2	1
−1475	0	1	1	1	176	4	0	−2	−1
−1410	0	1	1	−1	166	4	−1	−1	−1
−1344	0	1	0	−1	−164	1	0	1	−1
−1335	1	0	0	−1	132	4	0	1	−1
1107	0	0	3	1	−119	1	0	−1	−1
1021	4	0	0	−1	115	4	−1	0	−1
833	4	0	−1	1	107	2	−2	0	1

Finally, the altitude of the moon is determined in a similar fashion to that of the sun (page 226).

$$\textbf{lunar-altitude}\left(t, \boxed{\varphi \mid \psi \mid \text{—} \mid \text{—}}\right) \stackrel{\text{def}}{=} \tag{14.64}$$

altitude mod [−180 .. 180)

where

$$\begin{aligned}
\lambda &= \textbf{lunar-longitude}\,(t)\\
\beta &= \textbf{lunar-latitude}\,(t)\\
\alpha &= \textbf{right-ascension}\,(t, \beta, \lambda)\\
\delta &= \textbf{declination}\,(t, \beta, \lambda)\\
\theta_0 &= \textbf{sidereal-from-moment}\,(t)\\
H &= (\theta_0 + \psi - \alpha) \bmod 360\\
\mathit{altitude} &= \arcsin\,(\sin\varphi \times \sin\delta + \cos\varphi \times \cos\delta \times \cos H)
\end{aligned}$$

The result has not been corrected for parallax or refraction.

To convert geocentric altitude (viewed from the center of the Earth), as computed by **lunar-altitude**, into topocentric altitude (viewed from the surface), we first need to compute the parallax, for which we need to know the distance in meters between the centers of the Earth and the moon:

$$\textbf{lunar-distance}\,(t) \stackrel{\text{def}}{=} 385000560\text{ m} + \mathit{correction} \tag{14.65}$$

where

$$\begin{aligned}
c &= \textbf{julian-centuries}\,(t)\\
D &= \textbf{lunar-elongation}\,(c)\\
M &= \textbf{solar-anomaly}\,(c)\\
M' &= \textbf{lunar-anomaly}\,(c)\\
F &= \textbf{moon-node}\,(c)\\
E &= 1 - 0.002516 \times c - 0.0000074 \times c^2\\
\mathit{correction} &= \sum\left(\widetilde{v} \times E^{|\widetilde{x}|} \times \cos\,(\widetilde{w} \times D + \widetilde{x} \times M + \widetilde{y} \times M' + \widetilde{z} \times F)\right)\\
\widetilde{v} &= \text{(see Table 14.7)}\\
\widetilde{w} &= \text{(see Table 14.7)}\\
\widetilde{x} &= \text{(see Table 14.7)}\\
\widetilde{y} &= \text{(see Table 14.7)}\\
\widetilde{z} &= \text{(see Table 14.7)}
\end{aligned}$$

Now, we have:

$$\textbf{lunar-parallax}\,(t, \mathit{location}) \stackrel{\text{def}}{=} \arcsin \mathit{arg} \tag{14.66}$$

where

$$\begin{aligned}
\mathit{geo} &= \textbf{lunar-altitude}\,(t, \mathit{location})\\
\Delta &= \textbf{lunar-distance}\,(t)
\end{aligned}$$

Table 14.7 Values of the arguments $\widetilde{v}$, $\widetilde{w}$, $\widetilde{x}$, $\widetilde{y}$, and $\widetilde{z}$ in **lunar-distance** (page 238).

$\widetilde{v}$	$\widetilde{w}$	$\widetilde{x}$	$\widetilde{y}$	$\widetilde{z}$	$\widetilde{v}$	$\widetilde{w}$	$\widetilde{x}$	$\widetilde{y}$	$\widetilde{z}$
−20905355	0	0	1	0	6322	1	0	1	0
−3699111	2	0	−1	0	−9884	2	−2	0	0
−2955968	2	0	0	0	5751	0	1	2	0
−569925	0	0	2	0	0	0	2	0	0
48888	0	1	0	0	−4950	2	−2	−1	0
−3149	0	0	0	2	4130	2	0	1	−2
246158	2	0	−2	0	0	2	0	0	2
−152138	2	−1	−1	0	−3958	4	−1	−1	0
−170733	2	0	1	0	0	0	0	2	2
−204586	2	−1	0	0	3258	3	0	−1	0
−129620	0	1	−1	0	2616	2	1	1	0
108743	1	0	0	0	−1897	4	−1	−2	0
104755	0	1	1	0	−2117	0	2	−1	0
10321	2	0	0	−2	2354	2	2	−1	0
0	0	0	1	2	0	2	1	−2	0
79661	0	0	1	−2	0	2	−1	0	−2
−34782	4	0	−1	0	−1423	4	0	1	0
−23210	0	0	3	0	−1117	0	0	4	0
−21636	4	0	−2	0	−1571	4	−1	0	0
24208	2	1	−1	0	−1739	1	0	−2	0
30824	2	1	0	0	0	2	1	0	−2
−8379	1	0	−1	0	−4421	0	0	2	−2
−16675	1	1	0	0	0	1	1	1	0
−12831	2	−1	1	0	0	3	0	−2	0
−10445	2	0	2	0	0	4	0	−3	0
−11650	4	0	0	0	0	2	−1	2	0
14403	2	0	−3	0	1165	0	2	1	0
−7003	0	1	−2	0	0	1	1	−1	0
0	2	0	−1	2	0	2	0	3	0
10056	2	−1	−2	0	8752	2	0	−1	−2

$$alt = \frac{6378140\text{ m}}{\Delta}$$

$$arg = alt \times \cos geo$$

and

$$\textbf{topocentric-lunar-altitude}\,(t, location) \stackrel{\text{def}}{=} \tag{14.67}$$

$$\textbf{lunar-altitude}\,(t, location) - \textbf{lunar-parallax}\,(t, location)$$

14.7 Rising and Setting of the Sun and Moon

Some, like the Chaldees and the ancient Jews, define such a day as the time between two sunrises; others, like the Athenians, as that between two sunsets; or, like the Romans, from midnight to midnight; or like the Egyptians, from noon to noon ... It was necessary ... to choose some mean and equal day, by which it would be possible to measure regularity of movement without trouble.

Nicolaus Copernicus: *De revolutionibus orbium coelestium* (1543)

We occasionally need the time of sunrise or sunset for a location. Astronomical sunrise is nowadays defined as the time of first appearance of the upper limb of the sun; sunset is the moment of disappearance, again of the upper limb. This is also the definition used for calendars that begin their day at sunset (for example, the Islamic and Hebrew calendars) or sunrise (the Hindu calendar, according to some authorities). Because of the asymmetry involved, on the day of the equinox the intervals from sunrise to sunset and from sunset to sunrise differ by a few minutes. This discrepancy is further compounded by atmospheric refraction (the bending of the sun's light by the Earth's atmosphere), which makes the sun visible 2 to 3 minutes before a straight line to it is actually above the horizon and keeps it visible for a few minutes after it is geometrically below the horizon at sunset time.

We first write a general function to calculate the moment, in local mean time, when the "depression angle" of the geometric center of the sun is α degrees below (above, if the angle is negative) the *geometric horizon* at sea level at a given location around a fixed moment t. The same depression angle occurs both in the east (at around sunrise) and the west (at around sunset), so we use the variable *early?* to specify which we want: *early?* is **true** for the eastern horizon and **false** for the western horizon. First, an approximation is determined:

$$\textbf{approx-moment-of-depression}\,(t, \mathit{location}, \alpha, \mathit{early?}) \stackrel{\text{def}}{=} \tag{14.68}$$

$$\begin{cases} \textbf{local-from-apparent} & \\ \quad \left(\mathit{date} + \begin{cases} 6^{\text{h}} - \mathit{offset} & \textbf{if } \mathit{early?} \\ 18^{\text{h}} + \mathit{offset} & \textbf{otherwise} \end{cases}, \mathit{location}\right) & \textbf{if } |\mathit{value}| \leqslant 1 \\ \textbf{bogus} & \textbf{otherwise} \end{cases}$$

where

$$\mathit{try} = \textbf{sine-offset}\,(t, \mathit{location}, \alpha)$$

$$\mathit{date} = \textbf{fixed-from-moment}\,(t)$$

$$\mathit{alt} = \begin{cases} \mathit{date} & \textbf{if } \alpha \geqslant 0 \text{ and } \mathit{early?} \\ \mathit{date} + 1 & \textbf{if } \alpha \geqslant 0 \\ \mathit{date} + 12^{\text{h}} & \textbf{otherwise} \end{cases}$$

$$\mathit{value} = \begin{cases} \textbf{sine-offset}\,(\mathit{alt}, \mathit{location}, \alpha) & \textbf{if } |\mathit{try}| > 1 \\ \mathit{try} & \textbf{otherwise} \end{cases}$$

$$\mathit{offset} = \frac{\arcsin \mathit{value}}{360^{\circ}} \bmod \left[-12^{\text{h}} \,..\, 12^{\text{h}}\right)$$

Here, we have

$$\textbf{sine-offset}\,(t, location, \alpha) \stackrel{\text{def}}{=} \tan\varphi \times \tan\delta + \frac{\sin\alpha}{\cos\delta \times \cos\varphi} \tag{14.69}$$

where

$$\begin{aligned}\varphi &= location_{\textbf{latitude}}\\ t' &= \textbf{universal-from-local}\,(t, location)\\ \delta &= \textbf{declination}\,(t', 0^\circ, \textbf{solar-longitude}\,(t'))\end{aligned}$$

The function **sine-offset** gives the sine of the angle α between where the sun is at *t* and where it is at its position of interest. An impossible value (that is, outside the range of [−1 .. 1]) is returned if the angle α is not reachable. That approximation is then repeatedly refined:

$$\textbf{moment-of-depression}\,(approx, location, \alpha, early?) \stackrel{\text{def}}{=} \tag{14.70}$$

$$\begin{cases}\textbf{bogus} & \textbf{if } t = \textbf{bogus}\\ t & \textbf{if } |approx - t| < 30^{\text{s}}\\ \textbf{moment-of-depression}\,(t, location, \alpha, early?) & \textbf{otherwise}\end{cases}$$

where

$$t = \textbf{approx-moment-of-depression}\,(approx, location, \alpha, early?)$$

In polar regions, when the sun does not reach the stated depression angle this function returns the constant **bogus**.

The function **moment-of-depression** may then be used in the determination of the local time in the morning or evening when the sun reaches a specified angle below the true horizon. The result (for nonpolar regions) is then converted to standard time, using **standard-from-local** (page 208):

$$\textbf{morning} \stackrel{\text{def}}{=} \text{true} \tag{14.71}$$

$$\textbf{dawn}\,(date, location, \alpha) \stackrel{\text{def}}{=} \tag{14.72}$$

$$\begin{cases}\textbf{bogus} & \textbf{if } result = \textbf{bogus}\\ \textbf{standard-from-local}\,(result, location) & \textbf{otherwise}\end{cases}$$

where

$$result = \textbf{moment-of-depression}\left(date + 6^{\text{h}}, location, \alpha, \textbf{morning}\right)$$

Similarly for the evening we have:

$$\textbf{evening} \stackrel{\text{def}}{=} \text{false} \tag{14.73}$$

$$\textbf{dusk}\,(\textit{date, location}, \alpha) \stackrel{\text{def}}{=} \tag{14.74}$$

$$\begin{cases} \textbf{bogus} & \textbf{if } \textit{result} = \textbf{bogus} \\ \textbf{standard-from-local}\,(\textit{result, location}) & \textbf{otherwise} \end{cases}$$

where

$$\textit{result} = \textbf{moment-of-depression}\left(\textit{date} + 18^{\text{h}}, \textit{location}, \alpha, \textbf{evening}\right)$$

The *visible horizon* depends on the elevation of the observer. The half-diameter of the sun is $16'$, while the average effect of refraction is $34'$, for a total depression angle of $50'$. If the observer is above sea level then the sun is even lower when its upper limb touches the observer's horizon.

A standard value of the refraction, taking elevation into account, is computed as follows:

$$\textbf{refraction}\,(t, \textit{location}) \stackrel{\text{def}}{=} 34' + \textit{dip} + 19'' \times \sqrt{h} \tag{14.75}$$

where

$$\begin{aligned} h &= \max\{0\text{ m}, \textit{location}_{\textbf{elevation}}\} \\ R &= 6.372 \times 10^{6}\text{ m} \\ \textit{dip} &= \arccos\left(\frac{R}{R+h}\right) \end{aligned}$$

The value for R is the radius of the Earth; $\textit{dip} + 19''\sqrt{h}$ is the approximate contribution (in degrees) to the depression angle caused by an elevation of h meters [34]. This function ignores "elevations" that are below sea level or obstructions of the line of sight to the horizon. Also, it cannot be perfectly accurate because the observed position of the sun depends on atmospheric conditions, such as atmospheric temperature, humidity, and pressure (see [26] and [32]). The time parameter t is not used here, but could be used in a more refined calculation that takes average atmospheric conditions into account.

Hence, for sunrise we write

$$\textbf{sunrise}\,(\textit{date, location}) \stackrel{\text{def}}{=} \textbf{dawn}\,(\textit{date, location}, \alpha) \tag{14.76}$$

where

$$\alpha = \textbf{refraction}\left(\textit{date} + 6^{\text{h}}, \textit{location}\right) + 16'$$

The extra $16'$ is needed because we want the time when the upper limb of the sun first becomes visible. Similarly, for sunset we have

$$\textbf{sunset}\,(\textit{date, location}) \stackrel{\text{def}}{=} \textbf{dusk}\,(\textit{date, location}, \alpha) \tag{14.77}$$

where

$$\alpha = \textbf{refraction}\left(date + 18^{\text{h}}, location\right) + 16'$$

For example, to calculate the standard time of sunset in Urbana, Illinois on a given Gregorian date we could write

$$\textbf{urbana-sunset}\,(g\text{-}date) \stackrel{\text{def}}{=} \qquad (14.78)$$

$$\textbf{time-from-moment}\,(\textbf{sunset}\,(d, \textbf{urbana}))$$

where

$$d = \textbf{fixed-from-gregorian}\,(g\text{-}date)$$

On November 12, 1945, this gives sunset at 4:42 p.m. At the Canadian Forces Station Alert in Nunavut, the northernmost settled point in the western hemisphere, for which

cfs-alert $\stackrel{\text{def}}{=}$ (14.79)

82°30′	− 62°19′	0 m	-5^{h}

we get **bogus** for an answer on the same date.

The contribution of 34′ to the depression angle, used above, is based on the average effect of refraction, but—as already mentioned—the refraction varies greatly, depending on atmospheric conditions. Thus, the times of sunrise and sunset can be calculated only to the nearest minute; for polar regions the uncertainty will be several minutes.[14] Furthermore, at high latitudes, because of the discrepancies between apparent, local, and standard time, dawn—or even sunrise—on *date* can actually occur on $date-1$ before midnight, and dusk or sunset can occur on $date+1$. There may even be two occurrences on the same civil day.

The times of occurrence of certain depression angles have religious significance for Jews and Muslims. Some Jews, for example, end Sabbath on Saturday night when the sun reaches a depression angle of 7°5′,

$$\textbf{jewish-sabbath-ends}\,(date, location) \stackrel{\text{def}}{=} \textbf{dusk}\,(date, location, 7°5') \qquad (14.80)$$

but for other purposes they consider dusk to end earlier:

$$\textbf{jewish-dusk}\,(date, location) \stackrel{\text{def}}{=} \textbf{dusk}\,(date, location, 4°40') \qquad (14.81)$$

Table 14.8 gives some depression angles and their significance.

The rising and setting times of the moon, for nonpolar regions, can be determined in a similar fashion to that of the sun. Refraction is used to adjust the topocentric altitude:

$$\textbf{observed-lunar-altitude}\,(t, location) \stackrel{\text{def}}{=} \qquad (14.82)$$

$$\textbf{topocentric-lunar-altitude}\,(t, location) + \textbf{refraction}\,(t, location) + 16'$$

16′ being the approximate average half-diameter of the moon.

---

14 A 12-minute discrepancy between the calculated and observed times of sunrise is documented in [26].

Table 14.8 Significance of various solar depression angles. The Islamic values are derived from [13]; the Jewish values are from [15], primarily, and from [8].

	Angle	Significance
Morning	20°	Alternative Jewish dawn (Rabbenu Tam)
	18°	Astronomical and Islamic dawn
	16°	Jewish dawn (Maimonides)
	15°	Alternative Islamic dawn
	12°	Nautical twilight begins
	6°	Civil twilight begins
	0°50′	Sunrise
Evening	0°50′	Sunset
	4°40′	Jewish dusk (Vilna Gaon)
	6°	Civil twilight ends
	7° 5′	Jewish sabbath ends (Cohn)
	8°30′	Alternative Jewish sabbath ends (Tykocinski)
	12°	Nautical twilight ends
	15°	Alternative Islamic dusk
	18°	Astronomical and Islamic dusk
	20°	Alternative Jewish dusk (Rabbenu Tam)

Moonrise and moonset are found by binary search, after estimating the time of the event, based on altitude at midnight and on whether the moon is waxing or waning:

$$\textbf{moonrise}\,(\mathit{date}, \mathit{location}) \stackrel{\text{def}}{=} \tag{14.83}$$

$$\begin{cases} \max\,\{\textbf{standard-from-universal}\,(\mathit{rise}, \mathit{location}), \mathit{date}\} & \textbf{if } \mathit{rise} < t + 1 \\ \textbf{bogus} & \textbf{otherwise} \end{cases}$$

where

$$t = \textbf{universal-from-standard}\,(\mathit{date}, \mathit{location})$$

$$\mathit{waning} = \textbf{lunar-phase}\,(t) > 180^\circ$$

$$\mathit{alt} = \textbf{observed-lunar-altitude}\,(t, \mathit{location})$$

$$\mathit{lat} = \mathit{location}_{\textbf{latitude}}$$

$$\mathit{offset} = \frac{\mathit{alt}}{4 \times (90^\circ - |\mathit{lat}|)}$$

$$\mathit{approx} = \begin{cases} t + 1 - \mathit{offset} & \textbf{if } \mathit{waning} \text{ and } \mathit{offset} > 0 \\ t - \mathit{offset} & \textbf{if } \mathit{waning} \\ t + \frac{1}{2} + \mathit{offset} & \textbf{otherwise} \end{cases}$$

$$\mathit{rise} = \underset{x \in [\mathit{approx} - 6^{\text{h}} .. \mathit{approx} + 6^{\text{h}})}{\overset{u - l < 1^{\text{m}}}{\textbf{MIN}}} \left\{ \textbf{observed-lunar-altitude}\,(x, \mathit{location}) > 0^\circ \right\}$$

$$\textbf{moonset}\,(\mathit{date}, \mathit{location}) \stackrel{\text{def}}{=} \tag{14.84}$$

$$\begin{cases} \max\left\{\textbf{standard-from-universal}\,(\mathit{set}, \mathit{location}), \mathit{date}\right\} & \textbf{if } \mathit{set} < t+1 \\ \textbf{bogus} & \textbf{otherwise} \end{cases}$$

where

$$\begin{aligned}
t &= \textbf{universal-from-standard}\,(\mathit{date}, \mathit{location}) \\
\mathit{waxing} &= \textbf{lunar-phase}\,(t) < 180^\circ \\
\mathit{alt} &= \textbf{observed-lunar-altitude}\,(t, \mathit{location}) \\
\mathit{lat} &= \mathit{location}_{\textbf{latitude}} \\
\mathit{offset} &= \frac{\mathit{alt}}{4 \times (90^\circ - |\mathit{lat}|)} \\
\mathit{approx} &= \begin{cases} t + \mathit{offset} & \textbf{if } \mathit{waxing} \text{ and } \mathit{offset} > 0 \\ t + 1 + \mathit{offset} & \textbf{if } \mathit{waxing} \\ t - \mathit{offset} + \frac{1}{2} & \textbf{otherwise} \end{cases} \\
\mathit{set} &= \underset{x \in [\mathit{approx}-6^{\text{h}}..\mathit{approx}+6^{\text{h}})}{\overset{u-l<1^{\text{m}}}{\mathbf{MIN}}} \left\{ \begin{array}{l} \textbf{observed-lunar-altitude} \\ \qquad (x, \mathit{location}) < 0^\circ \end{array} \right\}
\end{aligned}$$

A **bogus** value is returned if, on the day in question, the event does not occur, as happens about once a month: since the search for the moment when the moon is at the horizon can return a moment just before midnight of the day in question, we need to take the maximum of the result and the start of the day. This function is not robust in the sense that it returns the time at which the moon gets closest to the horizon in those cases where it does not appear to cross the horizon at all, as happens in polar latitudes.

We will need **moonset** for the Babylonian calendar (Section 18.1).

14.8 Times of Day

> *May the gods destroy that man who first discovered hours and who first set up a sundial here; who cut up my day piecemeal, wretched me.*
>
> Plautus: *The Boeotian Woman*

> *Now Peter and John went up together into the temple at the hour of prayer, being the ninth hour.*
>
> The Acts of the Apostles 3:1

> *This singular and inconvenient method*[16] *had its defenders, and that even among the French; who have found that with pencil, and a little astronomical calculation, one may fix the hour of dinner with very little embarrassment.*
>
> Jacques Ozanam: *Recreations in Science and Natural Philosophy* (1851)

---

[16] Counting hours from zero at sunset.

Our civil day is divided into 24 hours, counting from zero at midnight (so-called "French time"); each hour is divided into 60 minutes, and each minute is divided into 60 seconds (if we assume no leap second is added to that day). Accordingly, we represent the time of day as a triple

$$hour : minute : second$$

where *hour* is an integer in the range 0 to 23, *minute* is an integer in the range 0 to 59, and *second* is a nonnegative real number less than 60. (Sometimes we omit the third component and give only the hour and minute.) Other cultures subdivided the day differently. For instance, the ancient Egyptians—as well as the Greeks and Romans in classical times—divided the day and night *separately* into 12 equal "hours" each. Because, except at the equator, the lengths of daylight and nighttime vary with the seasons, the lengths of such daytime and nighttime hours also vary with the season. These seasonally varying *temporal* (or *seasonal*) hours (*horæ temporales*) are still used for ritual purposes among Jews. In London, for example, the length of such an hour varies from about 39 minutes in December to about 83 minutes in June.

Ancient Chinese civilization divided a day into 10 *shí* and 100 *kè* based on marks on dripping pot. In the first century B.C.E., Chinese astronomers started to divide a day into 12 *shí*, beginning at midnight. Although 100 *kè* cannot be divided equally into 12 *shí*, the *kè* was not changed until 1670, during the early Qīng dynasty, when it was redefined as an eighth of a *shí*, making 96 *kè* per day.

The Hindus divide the civil day into 60 *ghaṭikás* of 24-minute duration, each of which is divided into 60 *palas*, each of which is 24 seconds. They also divide the sidereal day into 60 *nádís*, each *nádí* into 60 *vinadis*, and each of the latter into 6 *asus*. The Hebrew calendar divides hours into 1080 *ḥalaqim* (parts) of $3\frac{1}{3}$ seconds each; each part is divided into 76 *regaim* (moments). The French Revolutionary calendar divided each day into 10 "hours," each "hour" into 100 "minutes," and each "minute" into 100 "seconds."

There have been various conventions for the start of the hour count of a day. In many places in the past, town clocks were reset to 0 h at sunset or at dusk. This is usually referred to as "Italian time" [7], but was the convention in many other places in Europe and the Middle East. An alternate convention, often seen on sundials, was to begin counting hours at sunrise; these were called "Babylonian hours." We can convert between Italian time and local time. For example the clock in Padua,

$$\textbf{padua} \stackrel{\text{def}}{=} \boxed{45°24'28'' \mid 11°53'9'' \mid 18\text{ m} \mid 1^{\text{h}}} \qquad (14.85)$$

was reset every day at the moment of local dusk, taken to be 30 minutes after sunset (which was sometimes computed to occur at a solar depression angle of 16′). Thus we define

$$\textbf{local-zero-hour}\,(t) \stackrel{\text{def}}{=} \qquad (14.86)$$

$$\textbf{local-from-standard}\,(\textbf{dusk}\,(\mathit{date}, \textbf{padua}, 16') + 30^{\text{m}}, \textbf{padua})$$

where

$$date = \textbf{fixed-from-moment}\,(t)$$

To convert local time, measured from midnight, to and from Italian time, measured from dusk, we use:

$$\textbf{local-from-italian}\,(t) \stackrel{\text{def}}{=} t - date + z \tag{14.87}$$

where

$$\begin{aligned} date &= \textbf{fixed-from-moment}\,(t) \\ z &= \textbf{local-zero-hour}\,(t-1) \end{aligned}$$

In the opposite direction,

$$\textbf{italian-from-local}\,(t_\ell) \stackrel{\text{def}}{=} \begin{cases} t_\ell + date + 1 - z & \textbf{if } t_\ell > z \\ t_\ell + date - z_0 & \textbf{otherwise} \end{cases} \tag{14.88}$$

where

$$\begin{aligned} date &= \textbf{fixed-from-moment}\,(t_\ell) \\ z_0 &= \textbf{local-zero-hour}\,(t_\ell - 1) \\ z &= \textbf{local-zero-hour}\,(t_\ell) \end{aligned}$$

Thus when the clock struck 2:00 according to Italian apparent time in Padua on November 12, 1732 (Gregorian), it was 19:16 according to French apparent time, which was 7:01 p.m. by local mean time; this would be 7:13 p.m. on today's standard time clocks.

In Ethiopia and some neighboring regions, this style of time reckoning is still in use. Twelve daytime hours are counted from 6 a.m. until 6 p.m., and twelve nightime hours are counted from 6 p.m. until the next morning.

With the functions for local sunrise and sunset times of the previous section, we can also compute the time based on temporal (seasonal) hours, still used by Jews and Hindus. At a specified *location* on a particular fixed *date*, the lengths of daytime and nighttime temporal hours are given by

$$\textbf{daytime-temporal-hour}\,(date, location) \stackrel{\text{def}}{=} \tag{14.89}$$

$$\begin{cases} \textbf{bogus} & \textbf{if sunrise}\,(date, location) = \textbf{bogus} \text{ or} \\ & \quad \textbf{sunset}\,(date, location) = \textbf{bogus} \\ \frac{1}{12} \times (\textbf{sunset}\,(date, location) - \textbf{sunrise}\,(date, location)) & \\ & \textbf{otherwise} \end{cases}$$

and

$$\textbf{nighttime-temporal-hour}\,(date, location) \stackrel{\text{def}}{=} \tag{14.90}$$

$$\begin{cases} \textbf{bogus} \quad \textbf{if sunrise}\,(date+1, location) = \textbf{bogus} \text{ or} \\ \qquad\qquad \textbf{sunset}\,(date, location) = \textbf{bogus} \\ \frac{1}{12} \times (\textbf{sunrise}\,(date+1, location) - \textbf{sunset}\,(date, location)) \\ \qquad \textbf{otherwise} \end{cases}$$

This allows us to convert "sundial time" to standard time with

$$\textbf{standard-from-sundial}\,(t, location) \stackrel{\text{def}}{=} \tag{14.91}$$

$$\begin{cases} \textbf{bogus} & \textbf{if } h = \textbf{bogus} \\ \textbf{sunrise}\,(date, location) + (hour - 6) \times h & \textbf{if } 6 \leqslant hour \leqslant 18 \\ \textbf{sunset}\,(date - 1, location) + (hour + 6) \times h & \textbf{if } hour < 6 \\ \textbf{sunset}\,(date, location) + (hour - 18) \times h & \textbf{otherwise} \end{cases}$$

where

$$\begin{aligned} date &= \textbf{fixed-from-moment}\,(t) \\ hour &= 24 \times \textbf{time-from-moment}\,(t) \\ h &= \begin{cases} \textbf{daytime-temporal-hour}\,(date, location) & \textbf{if } 6 \leqslant hour \leqslant 18 \\ \textbf{nighttime-temporal-hour}\,(date - 1, location) & \textbf{if } hour < 6 \\ \textbf{nighttime-temporal-hour}\,(date, location) & \textbf{otherwise} \end{cases} \end{aligned}$$

which in turn allows us to determine, say, the end of morning according to Jewish ritual:

$$\textbf{jewish-morning-end}\,(date, location) \stackrel{\text{def}}{=} \tag{14.92}$$

$$\textbf{standard-from-sundial}\left(date + 10^{\text{h}}, location\right)$$

Temporal hours were also used for the canonical hours of the Church breviary: Matins (midnight), Lauds (dawn), Prime (sunrise), Terce (9 a.m.), Sext (noon), None (3 p.m.), Vespers (sunset), and Compline (dusk).

The times of apparent noon and midnight could be calculated using temporal hours, but the times can differ by a few seconds from **midday** (14.26) and **midnight** (14.25) because the times of sunrise and sunset sometimes change relatively quickly.

An important time of day for Muslim prayer is *asr*, which is defined for Hanafi Muslims as the moment in the afternoon when the shadow of a gnomon has increased by double its own length over the shadow length at noon. By trigonometry, we get the following determination:

$$\textbf{asr}\,(\textit{date, location}) \stackrel{\text{def}}{=} \begin{cases} \textbf{bogus} & \textbf{if } \textit{altitude} \leqslant 0^\circ \\ \textbf{dusk}\,(\textit{date, location}, -h) & \textbf{otherwise} \end{cases} \tag{14.93}$$

where

$$\begin{aligned} \textit{noon} &= \textbf{midday}\,(\textit{date, location}) \\ \varphi &= \textit{location}_{\textbf{latitude}} \\ \delta &= \textbf{declination}\,(\textit{noon}, 0^\circ, \textbf{solar-longitude}\,(\textit{noon})) \\ \textit{altitude} &= \arcsin(\cos\delta \times \cos\varphi + \sin\delta \times \sin\varphi) \\ h &= \textbf{arctan}\,(\tan \textit{altitude}, 2 \times \tan \textit{altitude} + 1) \bmod [-90\,..\,90) \end{aligned}$$

and where δ is the solar declination at noon. Shafi'i Muslims use the moment when the length of the shadow doubles:

$$\textbf{alt-asr}\,(\textit{date, location}) \stackrel{\text{def}}{=} \tag{14.94}$$

$$\begin{cases} \textbf{bogus} & \textbf{if } \textit{altitude} \leqslant 0^\circ \\ \textbf{dusk}\,(\textit{date, location}, -h) & \textbf{otherwise} \end{cases}$$

where

$$\begin{aligned} \textit{noon} &= \textbf{midday}\,(\textit{date, location}) \\ \varphi &= \textit{location}_{\textbf{latitude}} \\ \delta &= \textbf{declination}\,(\textit{noon}, 0^\circ, \textbf{solar-longitude}\,(\textit{noon})) \\ \textit{altitude} &= \arcsin(\cos\delta \times \cos\varphi + \sin\delta \times \sin\varphi) \\ h &= \textbf{arctan}\,(\tan \textit{altitude}, \tan \textit{altitude} + 1) \\ &\quad \bmod [-90\,..\,90) \end{aligned}$$

On certain dates in polar regions, there is no shadow.

14.9 Lunar Crescent Visibility

So patent are the evils of a purely lunar year whose length varies, owing to primitive methods of observation and determination of the new moon, that efforts to correct them have never ceased from the beginning to the present day.

K. Vollers: *Encyclopædia of Religion and Ethics*, vol. III, p. 127 (1911)[17]

Astronomical methods, as well as rules of thumb, for predicting the time of first visibility of the crescent moon (the *phasis*) have been developed over the millennia

---

[17] المؤلفون ليس بالضرورة موافقون للآراء الموجودة في الأقتباس.

by the ancient Babylonians, medieval Muslim and Hindu scientists, and by modern astronomers. We will require such a method to simulate the observation-based calendars of Chapter 18.

One simple criterion for likely visibility of the crescent moon, proposed by S. K. Shaukat [2], requires a minimum difference in altitudes between the setting sun and moon (ignoring parallax and refraction, for simplicity), and a minimum-size crescent, which depends on the elongation (angular separation), *arc-of-light*, between the two bodies. The elongation is computed as follows:

$$\textbf{arc-of-light}\,(t) \stackrel{\text{def}}{=} \tag{14.95}$$

$$\arccos\left(\cos\left(\textbf{lunar-latitude}\,(t)\right) \times \cos\left(\textbf{lunar-phase}\,(t)\right)\right)$$

A good time for viewing the young moon is when the sun is 4.5° below the horizon:

$$\textbf{simple-best-view}\,(\mathit{date}, \mathit{location}) \stackrel{\text{def}}{=} \tag{14.96}$$

$$\textbf{universal-from-standard}\,(\mathit{best}, \mathit{location})$$

where

$$\mathit{dark} = \textbf{dusk}\,(\mathit{date}, \mathit{location}, 4.5^\circ)$$

$$\mathit{best} = \begin{cases} \mathit{date} + 1 & \textbf{if } \mathit{dark} = \textbf{bogus} \\ \mathit{dark} & \textbf{otherwise} \end{cases}$$

The following boolean function checks whether the moon was visible on the *eve* of *date* at *location*, according to Shaukat's method:

$$\textbf{shaukat-criterion}\,(\mathit{date}, \mathit{location}) \stackrel{\text{def}}{=} \tag{14.97}$$

$$\textbf{new} < \mathit{phase} < \textbf{first-quarter} \text{ and } 10.6^\circ \leqslant \mathit{ARCL} \leqslant 90^\circ \text{ and } h > 4.1^\circ$$

where

$$\begin{aligned} t &= \textbf{simple-best-view}\,(\mathit{date} - 1, \mathit{location}) \\ \mathit{phase} &= \textbf{lunar-phase}\,(t) \\ h &= \textbf{lunar-altitude}\,(t, \mathit{location}) \\ \mathit{ARCL} &= \textbf{arc-of-light}\,(t) \end{aligned}$$

This definition is not designed for high altitudes and polar regions (where dusk may not occur or where the moon may only become visible late in the month).

Scientists have continued working on improved criteria for predicting visibility. For example, one may prefer to base visibility on the topocentric altitude (page 239), rather than the geocentric altitude (page 237). Some proposed criteria use what is called the *arc of vision*, the angular difference in altitudes of the sun and moon at a given time and place:

$$\textbf{arc-of-vision}\,(t, location) \stackrel{\text{def}}{=} \qquad (14.98)$$

$$\textbf{lunar-altitude}\,(t, location) - \textbf{solar-altitude}\,(t, location)$$

In particular, B. D. Yallop [33] suggested using the following ideal time for visibility, based on [6]:

$$\textbf{bruin-best-view}\,(date, location) \stackrel{\text{def}}{=} \qquad (14.99)$$

$$\textbf{universal-from-standard}\,(best, location)$$

where

$$\begin{aligned} sun &= \textbf{sunset}\,(date, location) \\ moon &= \textbf{moonset}\,(date, location) \\ best &= \begin{cases} date + 1 & \textbf{if } sun = \textbf{bogus} \text{ or } moon = \textbf{bogus} \\ \frac{5}{9} \times sun + \frac{4}{9} \times moon & \textbf{otherwise} \end{cases} \end{aligned}$$

Yallop's criterion is as follows:

$$\textbf{yallop-criterion}\,(date, location) \stackrel{\text{def}}{=} \qquad (14.100)$$

$$\textbf{new} < phase < \textbf{first-quarter} \text{ and } ARCV > q_1 + e$$

where

$$\begin{aligned} t &= \textbf{bruin-best-view}\,(date - 1, location) \\ phase &= \textbf{lunar-phase}\,(t) \\ D &= \textbf{lunar-semi-diameter}\,(t, location) \\ ARCL &= \textbf{arc-of-light}\,(t) \\ W &= D \times (1 - \cos ARCL) \\ ARCV &= \textbf{arc-of-vision}\,(t, location) \\ e &= -0.14 \\ q_1 &= 11.8371 - 6.3226 \times W + 0.7319 \times W^2 - 0.1018 \times W^3 \end{aligned}$$

To determine the angular width of the crescent, Yallop's criterion takes into account the moon's topocentric semi-diameter (in degrees):

$$\textbf{lunar-semi-diameter}\,(t, location) \stackrel{\text{def}}{=} \qquad (14.101)$$

$$0.27245 \times p \times (\sin h \times \sin p + 1)$$

where

$$h = \textbf{lunar-altitude}\,(t, \textit{location})$$
$$p = \textbf{lunar-parallax}\,(t, \textit{location})$$

An approximation for the geocentric apparent lunar diameter is used, for example, by [22]:

$$\textbf{lunar-diameter}\,(t) \stackrel{\text{def}}{=} \frac{1792367000^\circ}{9 \times \textbf{lunar-distance}\,(t)} \tag{14.102}$$

For a recent synthesis of modern methods of determining visibility, see [10].

Adopting Shaukat's relatively simple criterion for the determination of first visibility, we define

$$\textbf{visible-crescent}\,(\textit{date}, \textit{location}) \stackrel{\text{def}}{=} \tag{14.103}$$
$$\textbf{shaukat-criterion}\,(\textit{date}, \textit{location})$$

Other criteria may, of course, be used instead.

With the function **visible-crescent**, we can calculate the day on which the new moon is first observable before—or after—any given *date* by checking for first visibility after the relevant new moon:

$$\textbf{phasis-on-or-before}\,(\textit{date}, \textit{location}) \stackrel{\text{def}}{=} \tag{14.104}$$
$$\underset{d \geqslant \tau}{\textbf{MIN}} \left\{ \textbf{visible-crescent}\,(d, \textit{location}) \right\}$$

where

$$\textit{moon} = \textbf{fixed-from-moment}\,(\textbf{lunar-phase-at-or-before}\,(\textbf{new}, \textit{date}))$$
$$\textit{age} \quad = \textit{date} - \textit{moon}$$
$$\tau \quad = \begin{cases} \textit{moon} - 30 & \textbf{if } \textit{age} \leqslant 3 \text{ and not } \textbf{visible-crescent}\,(\textit{date}, \textit{location}) \\ \textit{moon} & \textbf{otherwise} \end{cases}$$

$$\textbf{phasis-on-or-after}\,(\textit{date}, \textit{location}) \stackrel{\text{def}}{=} \tag{14.105}$$
$$\underset{d \geqslant \tau}{\textbf{MIN}} \left\{ \textbf{visible-crescent}\,(d, \textit{location}) \right\}$$

where

$$\textit{moon} = \textbf{fixed-from-moment}\,(\textbf{lunar-phase-at-or-before}\,(\textbf{new}, \textit{date}))$$

$$
\begin{aligned}
\mathit{age} &= \mathit{date} - \mathit{moon}\\
\tau &= \begin{cases} \mathit{moon} + 29 & \textbf{if } 4 \leqslant \mathit{age} \text{ or } \textbf{visible-crescent}\,(\mathit{date} - 1, \mathit{location})\\ \mathit{date} & \textbf{otherwise} \end{cases}
\end{aligned}
$$

This method will be used in Chapter 18 for the observation-based Islamic (Section 18.3) and Hebrew (Section 18.4) calendars.

References

[1] S. K. Abdali, "The Correct Qibla," manuscript, 1997. Available at cs-www.bu.edu/ftp/amass/Islam/qibla.ps.Z.

[2] K. Abdali, O. Afzal, I. A. Ahmad, M. Durrani, A. Salama, and S. K. Shaukat, "Crescent Moon Visibility: Consensus on Moon-Sighting and Determination of an Islamic Calendar," manuscript, 1996.

[3] P. Bretagnon and G. Francou, "Planetary Theories in Rectangular and Spherical Coordinates—VSOP87 Solutions," *Astronomy and Astrophysics*, vol. 202, pp. 309–315, 1988.

[4] P. Bretagnon and J.-L. Simon, *Planetary Programs and Tables from* −4000 *to* +2800, Willmann-Bell, Richmond, VA, 1986.

[5] M. Brooks, "Stop All the Clocks ... and Then Start Them Again," *New Scientist*, vol. 226, no. 3027, pp. 28–33, 2015.

[6] F. Bruin, "The First Visibility of the Lunar Crescent," *Vistas in Astronomy*, vol. 21, part 4, pp. 331–358, 1977.

[7] D. Camuffo, "Errors in Early Temperature Series Arising from Changes in Style of Measuring Time, Sampling Schedule and Number of Observations." *Climatic Change*, vol. 53, issues 1–3, pp. 331–352, 2002.

[8] B. Cohn, *Tabellen enthaltend die Zeitangaben für den Beginn der Nacht und des Tages für die Breitengrade* +66° *bis* −38°. *Zum Gebrauch für den jüdischen Ritus*, Verlag von Josef Singer, Strasbourg, 1899.

[9] N. Dershowitz and E. M. Reingold, "Implementing Solar Astronomical Calendars," *Birashknāme*, M. Akrami, ed., Shahid Beheshti University, Tehran, pp. 477–487, 1998.

[10] R. E. Hoffman, "Rational Design of Lunar-Visibility Criteria," *The Observatory*, vol. 125, no. 1186, pp. 156–168, 2005.

[11] D. Howse, *Greenwich Time and the Discovery of the Longitude*, Oxford University Press, Oxford, 1980. Republished (with some variations in the appendices) as *Greenwich Time and the Longitude*, Philip Wilson Publishers, London, 1997.

[12] M. Ilyas, *A Modern Guide to Astronomical Calculations of Islamic Calendar, Times & Qibla*, Berita Publishing, Kuala Lampur, 1984.

[13] M. Ilyas, *Astronomy of Islamic Times for the Twenty-First Century*, Mansell Publishing, London, 1988.

[14] J. B. Kaler, *The Ever-Changing Sky*, Cambridge University Press, Cambridge, 1996.

[15] L. Levi, *Jewish Chrononomy: The Calendar and Times of Day in Jewish Law*, Gur Aryeh Institute for Advanced Jewish Scholarship, Brooklyn, NY, 1967. Revised edition published under the title *Halachic Times for Home and Travel*, Rubin Mass, Jerusalem, 1992; expanded 3rd edn., 2000.

[16] D. Z. Levin, "Which Way Is Jerusalem? Which Way Is Mecca? The Direction-Facing Problem in Religion and Geography," *J. Geography*, vol. 101, pp. 27–37, 2002.

[17] D. D. McCarthy, "Astronomical Time," *Proc. IEEE*, vol. 79, pp. 915–920, 1991.

[18] J. Meeus, *Astronomical Algorithms*, 2nd edn., Willmann-Bell, Richmond, VA, 1998.

[19] J. Meeus, "Les durées extrêmes de la lunaison," *L'Astronomie* (Société Astronomique de France), vol. 102, pp. 288–289, July–August 1988.

[20] J. Meeus, *Mathematical Astronomy Morsels*, Willmann-Bell, Richmond, VA, 1997.

[21] J. Meeus and D. Savoie, "The History of the Tropical Year," *Journal of the British Astronomical Association*, vol. 102, no. 1, pp. 40–42, 1992.

[22] M. Odeh, "New Criterion for Lunar Crescent Visibility," *Experimental Astronomy*, vol. 18, pp. 39–64, 2004.

[23] D. W. Olson, R. T. Fienberg, and R. W. Sinnott, "What's a Blue Moon?," *Sky & Telescope*, vol. 97, pp. 36–39, 1999.

[24] M. O'Malley, *Keeping Watch: A History of American Time*, Viking, New York, 1990.

[25] T. J. Quinn, "The BIPM and the Accurate Measure of Time," *Proc. IEEE*, vol. 79, pp. 894–905, 1991.

[26] R. D. Sampson, E. P. Lozowski, A. E. Peterson, and D. P. Hube, "Variability in the Astronomical Refraction of the Rising and Setting Sun," *Astronomical Society of the Pacific*, vol. 115, pp. 1256–1261, 2003.

[27] P. K. Seidelmann, B. Guinot, and L. E. Doggett, "Time," Chapter 2 in *Explanatory Supplement to the Astronomical Almanac*, P. K. Seidelmann, ed., U.S. Naval Observatory, University Science Books, Mill Valley, CA, 1992.

[28] T. G. Shanks, *The American Atlas: U.S. Longitudes & Latitudes Time Changes and Time Zones*, 5th edn., ACS Publications, San Diego, CA, 1996.

[29] T. G. Shanks, *The International Atlas: World Longitudes & Latitudes Time Changes and Time Zones*, 5th edn., ACS Publications, San Diego, CA, 1999.

[30] D. Sobel, *Longitude*, Walker, New York, 1995.

[31] F. R. Stephenson, *Historical Eclipses and Earth's Rotation*, Cambridge University Press, Cambridge, 1997.

[32] M. D. Stern and N. S. Ellis, "Sunrise, Sunset—a Modelling Exercise in Iteration," *Teaching Math. and Its Appl.* vol. 9, pp. 159–164, 1990.

[33] B. D. Yallop, "A Method for Predicting the First Sighting of the New Crescent Moon," NAO Technical Note No. 69, HM Nautical Almanac Office, 1997, updated 1998.

[34] B. D. Yallop and C. Y. Hohenkerk, "Astronomical Phenomena," Chapter 9 in *Explanatory Supplement to the Astronomical Almanac*, P. K. Seidelmann, ed., U.S. Naval Observatory, University Science Books, Mill Valley, CA, 1992.

First 14 of 28 Arabian lunar stations from a late fourteenth-century manuscript of *Kitāb al-Bulhān* by the celebrated ninth-century Muslim astrologer Abu-Ma'shar al-Falaki (Albumazar) of Balkh, Khurasan, Persia. (Courtesy of the Bodleian Libraries, University of Oxford, Oxford; MS Bodley Or. 133, fol. 27b.)

15

The Persian Calendar

It was the custom of the Persians not to begin a march before sunrise. When the day was already bright, the signal was given from the king's tent with the horn; above the tent, from which it might be seen by all, there gleamed an image of the sun enclosed in crystal. Now the order of march was as follows. In front on silver altars was carried the fire which they called sacred and eternal. Next came the Magi, chanting their traditional hymn. These were followed by three hundred and sixty five young men clad in purple robes, equal in number to the days of the whole year; for the Persians also divided the year into that number of days.

Quintus Curtius Rufus: *History of Alexander*, III, iii (circa 35 C.E.)

The modern Persian calendar, adopted in 1925, is a solar calendar based on the Jalālī calendar designed in the eleventh century by a committee of astronomers, including a young Omar Khayyām, the noted Persian mathematician, astronomer, and poet. The Jalālī calendar had 12 months of 30 days each, followed by a 5-day period (6 in leap years), just like the Coptic and Ethiopic calendars described in Chapter 4. In addition to the Jalālī calendar, the Zoroastrian calendar, whose structure is described in Section 1.11, was also used historically in Persia. The lengthy history of Persian calendars is discussed in [3], [5], and [7]; [2] gives a briefer history, together with tables and computational rules for the arithmetic form of the calendar to be discussed in Section 15.3. A calendar identical to the modern Persian calendar, but with different month names, was adopted in Afghanistan in 1957.

15.1 Structure

Epochæ celebriores, astronomis, historicis, chronologis, Chataiorvm, Syro-Græcorvm Arabvm, Persarvm, Chorasmiorvm, usitatæ [Famous epochs customarily in use by astronomers, historians, chronologists, Hittites, Syrian-Greeks, Arabs, Persians, and Chorasmians]

Title of John Greaves' Latin/Persian edition (1650) of a work by the fourteenth-century Persian astronomer Ulugh Beg, grandson of Tamerlane

The epoch of the modern Persian calendar is the date of the vernal equinox prior to the epoch of the Islamic calendar; that is, 1 A.P.[1] began on

[1] *Anno Persico* or *Anno Persarum*; Persian year.

$$\textbf{persian-epoch} \stackrel{\text{def}}{=} \textbf{fixed-from-julian}\left(\boxed{622\text{ C.E.} \mid \textbf{march} \mid 19}\right) \tag{15.1}$$

According to Birashk [2], there is no Persian year 0 (as on the Julian calendar).

The year begins on the day when the vernal equinox (approximately March 20) occurs before true noon (midday) and it is postponed to the next day if the equinox is on or after true noon.

There are 12 Persian months, containing 29, 30, or 31 days, as follows:

(1) Farvardīn	فروردین	31 days
(2) Ordībehesht	اردیبهشت	31 days
(3) Xordād	خرداد	31 days
(4) Tīr	تیر	31 days
(5) Mordād	مرداد	31 days
(6) Shahrīvar	شهریور	31 days
(7) Mehr	مهر	30 days
(8) Ābān	آبان	30 days
(9) Āzar	آذر	30 days
(10) Dey	دی	30 days
(11) Bahman	بهمن	30 days
(12) Esfand	اسفند	29 {30} days

The leap-year structure is given in braces; the last month, Esfand, contains 30 days in leap years. Thus, an ordinary year has 365 days, and a leap year has 366 days.

Days begin at local-zone midnight just like Gregorian days. The week begins on Saturday; the days of the week are numbered, not named:

Saturday	Shanbēh	شنبه
Sunday	Yek-shanbēh	یکشنبه
Monday	Do-shanbēh	دوشنبه
Tuesday	Se-shanbēh	سه شنبه
Wednesday	Chār-shanbēh	چهارشنبه
Thursday	Panj-shanbēh	پنجشنبه
Friday	Jom'ēh	جمعه

The 1925 law establishing the modern Persian calendar is silent on the matter of leap-year determination, possibly intending a purely astronomical calendar in which the accurate determination of the vernal equinox defines the calendar—a leap year occurs when successive spring equinoxes are separated by 366 days. Various commentators ([2] and [7], for example) have suggested arithmetic cycles approximating such a calendar. Taqizadeh [5] rejects arithmetic cycles altogether, claiming that the correct rule is astronomical, both for the medieval and modern calendars. (Cycles may have been used in the past, or present, for limited periods to implement or approximate the astronomical rule.) Like Birashk, Taqizadeh was an influential politican, a member of parliament, a government minister, and a member of the parliamentary committee that introduced the new calendar in 1925; we rely on him for the intentions of the 1925 law.

In this chapter we give implementations of the pure astronomical form favored by Taqizadeh and Birashk's complex arithmetic form [2]. Implementing other arithmetic rules [5, pp. 115–116] would be similar to the arithmetic implementation we present.

15.2 The Astronomical Calendar

Die, age, frigoribus quare novus incipit annus, qui melius per ver incipiendus erat? [*Come, say, why doth the new year begin in the cold season? Better had it begun in spring.*]

Ovid: *Fasti,* I, lines 149–150

Because the occurrence of the New Year depends on true (apparent) noon in Iran, we define

$$\textbf{tehran} \overset{\text{def}}{=} \boxed{35.68^\circ \mid 51.42^\circ \mid 1100\text{ m} \mid 3\tfrac{1}{2}^{\text{h}}} \tag{15.2}$$

and

$$\textbf{midday-in-tehran}\,(date) \overset{\text{def}}{=} \textbf{midday}\,(date, \textbf{tehran}) \tag{15.3}$$

Historically, Isfahan might have been used, but because the 1925 law does not give a location, we opt for the capital, Tehran. The difference in longitudes is only a negligible 11′ of arc.[2]

We find the date of the New Year (the vernal equinox) on or before a given fixed date using (14.43):

$$\textbf{persian-new-year-on-or-before}\,(date) \overset{\text{def}}{=} \tag{15.4}$$

$$\underset{day \geqslant \lfloor approx \rfloor - 1}{\textbf{MIN}} \left\{ \textbf{solar-longitude}\,(\textbf{midday-in-tehran}\,(day)) \leqslant \textbf{spring} + 2^\circ \right\}$$

where

$$approx = \textbf{estimate-prior-solar-longitude}\,(\textbf{spring}, \textbf{midday-in-tehran}\,(date))$$

---

[2] We have read that the location used for the Persian calendar calculations was not fixed in the 1925 law. However, in a letter dated March 7, 1998 to E.M.R., Masahallah Ali-Ahyaie of Tehran said, "The exact time of equinox (in Iranian Standard Time, i.e., U.T. + 3.5 hours) is compared to the time of the apparent or true solar noon on longitude 52.5 E (3.5 hours). Then if the time of the equinox (to the nearest second) is before the true solar noon, that year is not a leap year. But if the equinox time happens exactly at the time of the true solar noon, as defined above, or after the true solar noon, that particular year will be considered as a leap year (366 days)." He repeated this claim in email messages on October 2–3, 2003, saying that the fixing of the longitude *is* part of the 1925 law; however, a French translation of the law does not specify the location. There are a number of years in the range 0–3000 C.E. in which the difference causes the date of Persian New Year—according to the astronomical functions we are using—to be one day later. By Ali-Ahyaie's claim, in Gregorian years 428, 1600, 1699, 1798, 2091, 2157, and 2648 Persian New Year would occur on March 21 instead of March 20; in 395, 1406, and 2714 it would occur on March 22 instead of March 21. One should bear in mind that more accurate astronomical functions might lead to other differences: these calculations are sensitive.

Once we know the date of the New Year it is straightforward to convert to an R.D. date from a Persian date by finding the R.D. date of the appropriate Persian year (correcting for the absence of a year 0) and adding the elapsed days so far that year:

$$\textbf{fixed-from-persian}\left(\boxed{\textit{year} \mid \textit{month} \mid \textit{day}}\right) \stackrel{\text{def}}{=} \tag{15.5}$$

$$\textit{new-year} - 1 + \left\{\begin{array}{ll} 31 \times (\textit{month} - 1) & \textbf{if } \textit{month} \leqslant 7 \\ 30 \times (\textit{month} - 1) + 6 & \textbf{otherwise} \end{array}\right\} + \textit{day}$$

where

$$\begin{aligned}\textit{new-year} = {} & \textbf{persian-new-year-on-or-before} \\ & \Bigg(\textbf{persian-epoch} + 180 \\ & + \left\lfloor \textbf{mean-tropical-year} \times \left\{\begin{array}{ll} \textit{year} - 1 & \textbf{if } 0 < \textit{year} \\ \textit{year} & \textbf{otherwise} \end{array}\right\}\right\rfloor\Bigg)\end{aligned}$$

Similarly, to convert an R.D. date to a Persian date, we find the Persian New Year preceding the R.D. date and base our calculations on that (again, correcting for the absence of a year 0):

$$\textbf{persian-from-fixed}\,(\textit{date}) \stackrel{\text{def}}{=} \boxed{\textit{year} \mid \textit{month} \mid \textit{day}} \tag{15.6}$$

where

$$\begin{aligned}
\textit{new-year} &= \textbf{persian-new-year-on-or-before}\,(\textit{date}) \\
y &= \text{round}\left(\frac{\textit{new-year} - \textbf{persian-epoch}}{\textbf{mean-tropical-year}}\right) + 1 \\
\textit{year} &= \left\{\begin{array}{ll} y & \textbf{if } 0 < y \\ y - 1 & \textbf{otherwise} \end{array}\right. \\
\textit{day-of-year} &= \textit{date} - \textbf{fixed-from-persian}\left(\boxed{\textit{year} \mid 1 \mid 1}\right) + 1 \\
\textit{month} &= \left\{\begin{array}{ll} \left\lceil \frac{1}{31} \times \textit{day-of-year} \right\rceil & \textbf{if } \textit{day-of-year} \leqslant 186 \\ \left\lceil \frac{1}{30} \times (\textit{day-of-year} - 6) \right\rceil & \textbf{otherwise} \end{array}\right. \\
\textit{day} &= \textit{date} - \textbf{fixed-from-persian}\left(\boxed{\textit{year} \mid \textit{month} \mid 1}\right) + 1
\end{aligned}$$

15.3 The Arithmetical Calendar

One of the most remarkable peculiarities of the Persians is their fondness for arithmetical puzzles, and their expertise in the secrets of figures.

Charles Dickens: *All the Year Round* (1863)

Birashk [2, p. 38], [1], explicitly rejects the determination of leap years by the occurrence of the astronomical equinox. He favors the fixed arithmetic intercalation scheme we now describe.[3]

The intricate arithmetic leap-year pattern chosen by Birashk follows a cycle of 2820 years, containing a total of 683 leap years, with the following structure. The 2820-year cycle consists of twenty-one 128-year subcycles followed by a 132-year subcycle:

$$2820 = 21 \times 128 + 132$$

Each 128-year subcycle is divided into one 29-year sub-subcycle followed by three 33-year sub-subcycles:

$$128 = 29 + 3 \times 33$$

Similarly, the 132-year subcycle is divided into one 29-year sub-subcycle followed by two 33-year sub-subcycles, followed by one 37-year sub-subcycle:

$$132 = 29 + 2 \times 33 + 37$$

Finally, a year y in a sub-subcycle is a leap year if $y > 1$ and $y \bmod 4 = 1$. That is, years 5, 9, 13, ... of a sub-subcycle are leap years. Thus, a 29-year sub-subcycle has 7 leap years, a 33-year sub-subcycle has 8 leap years, and a 37-year sub-subcycle has 9 leap years for a total of

$$21 \times (7 + 3 \times 8) + (7 + 2 \times 8 + 9) = 683$$

leap years and a total of

$$2820 \times 365 + 683 = 1029983$$

days in the 2820-year cycle. The true number of days in 2820 tropical years is

$$2820 \times 365.242199 = 1029983.00118$$

and thus Birashk claims that the arithmetic Persian calendar is in error by only a few minutes in 2820 years.[4]

Years 475 A.P., 3295 A.P., ... are the first years of the cycle. To facilitate the use of modular arithmetic, however, it is more convenient for us to view the cycles as beginning in the years 474 A.P., 3294 A.P., ..., which we consider the zeroth years of the cycle rather than the 2820th years of the cycle.

---

[3] Birashk [2] contains some significant numerical errors in the treatment of negative Persian years. For example, the leap-year test in his sec. 2.5.2 works only for positive years. His Table 2.2 shows the subcycle −41 .. 86, which contains only 127 years because there is no year 0; this leads to errors in his examples in his sec. 2.6.2. His Table I shows −1260 as a leap year, which it is not. There are various other minor errors in his Table I as well.

[4] Birashk's calculation is overly simplistic: the length of the spring equinoctial year (currently 365.242374 days) is not the same as the tropical year, and in either case the year length is slowly changing, as is the length of a day. See Section 14.4.

Unfortunately, the distribution of the 683 leap years in the cycle of 2820 years does not obey the cycle-of-years formulas from Section 1.14, and thus our implementation must be more complex than that for, say, the Islamic calendar, described in Chapter 7. Fortunately, the distribution of the leap years in the range of 443–3293 A.P. *does* satisfy the cycle-of-years formulas with c=128, l=31, and Δ=38, a leap-year rule noted by Abdollahy [7, p. 672].[5] This range of years contains a full cycle of 2820 Persian years, 474–3293 A.P.; consequently, by shifting into that range we *can* use the cycle-of-years formulas from Section 1.14. First we find the number of years since the zeroth year of the Persian cycle that started in 474 A.P.; then we find the equivalent position to that year in the range 474–3293 A.P.; and finally we apply formula (1.83). Our test for a Persian leap year according to Birashk's cycle is thus

$$\textbf{arithmetic-persian-leap-year?}\ (\textit{p-year}) \stackrel{\text{def}}{=} \tag{15.7}$$

$$(((\textit{year} + 38) \times 31) \bmod 128) < 31$$

where

$$y = \begin{cases} \textit{p-year} - 474 & \textbf{if } 0 < \textit{p-year} \\ \textit{p-year} - 473 & \textbf{otherwise} \end{cases}$$

$$\textit{year} = (y \bmod 2820) + 474$$

However, we do not need this function to convert arithmetic Persian dates to and from R.D. dates. We include it because it is much simpler than the rule given in [2].

To convert an arithmetic Persian date to an R.D. date we first find the equivalent year in the 2820-year cycle 474–3293 A.P.; then we use *that* year and imitate our function for converting from an Islamic date to an R.D. date (page 107). We add together: the number of days before the epoch of the calendar; the number of days in 2820-year cycles since 474 A.P.; the number of nonleap days in prior years; the number of leap days in prior years, computed using formula (1.85); the number of days in prior months of the given date; and the number of days in the given month up to and including the given date. Thus, we have

$$\textbf{fixed-from-arithmetic-persian}\left(\boxed{\textit{p-year} \mid \textit{month} \mid \textit{day}}\right) \stackrel{\text{def}}{=} \tag{15.8}$$

$$\textbf{persian-epoch} - 1 + 1029983 \times \left\lfloor \frac{y}{2820} \right\rfloor + 365 \times (\textit{year} - 1) + \left\lfloor \frac{31 \times \textit{year} - 5}{128} \right\rfloor + \begin{cases} 31 \times (\textit{month} - 1) & \textbf{if } \textit{month} \leqslant 7 \\ 30 \times (\textit{month} - 1) + 6 & \textbf{otherwise} \end{cases} + \textit{day}$$

where

$$y = \begin{cases} \textit{p-year} - 474 & \textbf{if } 0 < \textit{p-year} \\ \textit{p-year} - 473 & \textbf{otherwise} \end{cases}$$

$$\textit{year} = (y \bmod 2820) + 474$$

[5] Abdollahy's rule repeats the pattern of the first 128-year cycle of Birashk's rule, so it does not work directly to implement Birashk's rule. A direct implemention of an arithmetic Persian calendar based on Abdollahy's leap-year rule involves a simple combination of the ideas used in implementing the arithmetic Islamic calendar in Chapter 7 together with the method used below.

The inverse problem, determining the arithmetic Persian date corresponding to a given R.D. date, must be handled as for the Gregorian calendar (page 62). First we must determine the Persian year in which a given R.D. date occurs. This calculation is done as in the Gregorian calendar (page 61), but by taking the number of days elapsed since Farvardīn 1, 475 A.P., dividing by 1029983 to get the number of completed 2820-year cycles, and using the remainder of that division to get the number of prior days since the start of the last 2820-year cycle. Then we add together 474 (the number of years before the 2820-year cycles started), $2820 \times n_{2820}$ (the number of years in prior 2820-year cycles), and the number of years since the start of the last 2820-year cycle. This last value is computed from formula (1.90), but with $\Delta = 474 + 38 = 512$ to account for the shift of the range of years to 474–3293 A.P. Moreover, formula (1.90) is based on a cycle of years numbered $1, 2, \ldots, c = 2820$, whereas the range of applicability of our cycle structure is 474–3293 A.P., which corresponds to years in the cycle numbered $0, 1, \ldots, 2819$; hence, (1.90) does not apply to the last year. The last year differs from the cycle-of-years formula only because it is a leap year, and thus it is only to the last day of that year that the formula does not apply—that is, day 1029982, the last day of a 2820-year cycle—and we must handle that as an exception. Therefore we have

$$\textbf{arithmetic-persian-year-from-fixed}\,(\textit{date}) \stackrel{\text{def}}{=} \tag{15.9}$$

$$\begin{cases} \textit{year} & \textbf{if } 0 < \textit{year} \\ \textit{year} - 1 & \textbf{otherwise} \end{cases}$$

where

$$d_0 = \textit{date} - \textbf{fixed-from-arithmetic-persian}\left(\boxed{475 \mid 1 \mid 1}\right)$$

$$n_{2820} = \left\lfloor \frac{d_0}{1029983} \right\rfloor$$

$$d_1 = d_0 \bmod 1029983$$

$$y_{2820} = \begin{cases} 2820 & \textbf{if } d_1 = 1029982 \\ \left\lfloor \frac{1}{46751} \times (128 \times d_1 + 46878) \right\rfloor & \textbf{otherwise} \end{cases}$$

$$\textit{year} = 474 + 2820 \times n_{2820} + y_{2820}$$

Now that we can determine the Persian year of an R.D. date, we can easily find the day number in the Persian year of an R.D. date; from that we can compute the Persian month number by division. Knowing the year and month, we determine the day of the month by subtraction. Putting these pieces together, we have

$$\textbf{arithmetic-persian-from-fixed}\,(\textit{date}) \stackrel{\text{def}}{=} \tag{15.10}$$

$$\boxed{\textit{year} \mid \textit{month} \mid \textit{day}}$$

where

$$\textit{year} = \textbf{arithmetic-persian-year-from-fixed}\,(\textit{date})$$

Table 15.1 Years in the range 1000–1800 A.P. (1621–2421 Gregorian) for which the astronomical Persian calendar differs from the arithmetic Persian calendar.

Persian	Astronomical New Year			Arithmetic New Year		
Year	R.D.		Gregorian	R.D.		Gregorian
1016	597616	=	March 20, 1637	597617	=	March 21, 1637
1049	609669	=	March 20, 1670	609670	=	March 21, 1670
1078	620261	=	March 20, 1699	620262	=	March 21, 1699
1082	621722	=	March 21, 1703	621723	=	March 22, 1703
1111	632314	=	March 20, 1732	632315	=	March 21, 1732
1115	633775	=	March 20, 1736	633776	=	March 21, 1736
1144	644367	=	March 20, 1765	644368	=	March 21, 1765
1177	656420	=	March 20, 1798	656421	=	March 21, 1798
1210	668473	=	March 21, 1831	668474	=	March 22, 1831
1243	680526	=	March 20, 1864	680527	=	March 21, 1864
1404	739331	=	March 21, 2025	739330	=	March 20, 2025
1437	751384	=	March 21, 2058	751383	=	March 20, 2058
1532	786082	=	March 21, 2153	786081	=	March 20, 2153
1565	798135	=	March 21, 2186	798134	=	March 20, 2186
1569	799596	=	March 21, 2190	799595	=	March 20, 2190
1598	810188	=	March 22, 2219	810187	=	March 21, 2219
1631	822241	=	March 21, 2252	822240	=	March 20, 2252
1660	832833	=	March 21, 2281	832832	=	March 20, 2281
1664	834294	=	March 21, 2285	834293	=	March 20, 2285
1693	844886	=	March 22, 2314	844885	=	March 21, 2314
1697	846347	=	March 22, 2318	846346	=	March 21, 2318
1726	856939	=	March 22, 2347	856938	=	March 21, 2347
1730	858400	=	March 22, 2351	858399	=	March 21, 2351
1759	868992	=	March 21, 2380	868991	=	March 20, 2380
1763	870453	=	March 21, 2384	870452	=	March 20, 2384
1788	879584	=	March 21, 2409	879583	=	March 20, 2409
1792	881045	=	March 21, 2413	881044	=	March 20, 2413
1796	882506	=	March 21, 2417	882505	=	March 20, 2417

$$\textit{day-of-year} = 1 + \textit{date} - \textbf{fixed-from-arithmetic-persian}\left(\boxed{\textit{year} \mid 1 \mid 1}\right)$$

$$\textit{month} = \begin{cases} \left\lceil \frac{1}{31} \times \textit{day-of-year} \right\rceil & \textbf{if } \textit{day-of-year} \leqslant 186 \\ \left\lceil \frac{1}{30} \times (\textit{day-of-year} - 6) \right\rceil & \textbf{otherwise} \end{cases}$$

$$\textit{day} = \textit{date} - \textbf{fixed-from-arithmetic-persian}\left(\boxed{\textit{year} \mid \textit{month} \mid 1}\right) + 1$$

Comparing the dates of the Persian New Year on the astronomical calendar with those of the arithmetic calendar, for 1000–1800 A.P. (= 1637–2417 Gregorian), we find that they disagree on the 28 years shown in Table 15.1. Outside this range disagreement is far more common, occurring almost every fourth year. Notice that there is complete agreement for the range of Gregorian years 1865–2024 (1244–1403 A.P.); over that same range, a simple 33-year arithmetic cycle with $c = 33$, $l = 8$, $\Delta = 16$ is in phase with Birashk's cycle. Because $365\frac{8}{33}$ is an excellent approximation to the present equinoctial year, this 33-year cycle agrees with the astronomical calendar over an even longer period, 1046–1468 A.P. (1621–2421 Gregorian).

15.4 Holidays

A philosopher of the Ḥashwiyya-school relates that when Solomon the son of David had lost his seal and his empire, but was reinstated after forty days, he at once regained his former majesty, the princes came before him, and the birds were busy in his service. Then the Persians said, "Naurôz âmadh," i.e. *the new day has come. Therefore that day was called Naurôz.*

Abū-Raiḥān Muḥammad ibn 'Aḥmad al-Bīrūnī:
Al-Āthār al-Bāqiyah 'an al-Qurūn al-Khāliyah (1000)

As throughout this book, we consider our problem to be the determination of holidays that occur in a specified Gregorian year. Because the Persian year is almost consistently aligned with the Gregorian year, each Persian holiday (as long as it is not very near January 1) occurs just once in a given Gregorian year. Holidays that occur on fixed days on the Persian calendar are almost fixed on the Gregorian calendar—such holidays are easy to determine on the Gregorian calendar by observing that the Persian year beginning in Gregorian year y is given by

$$\text{Persian New Year occurring in March of Gregorian year } y$$
$$= y + 1 - \textbf{gregorian-year-from-fixed}(\textbf{persian-epoch}),$$

but we must compensate for the lack of year 0 by subtracting 1 if the above value is not positive. Thus, to find the R.D. date of *Nowruz* (Persian New Year, Farvardīn 1), according to the astronomical Persian calendar, that falls in a specified Gregorian year, we would use

$$\textbf{nowruz}\,(\textit{g-year}) \overset{\text{def}}{=} \textbf{fixed-from-persian}\left(\boxed{y \mid 1 \mid 1}\right) \tag{15.11}$$

where

$$\textit{persian-year} = \textit{g-year} - \textbf{gregorian-year-from-fixed}\,(\textbf{persian-epoch}) + 1$$

$$y = \begin{cases} \textit{persian-year} - 1 & \textbf{if } \textit{persian-year} \leqslant 0 \\ \textit{persian-year} & \textbf{otherwise} \end{cases}$$

If we want the date of Nowruz according to the arithmetic Persian calendar, we would substitute the function **fixed-from-arithmetic-persian** for **fixed-from-persian** in (15.11).

References

[1] Letter to Edward Reingold from A. Birashk, editor of *Dāneshnāme-ye Bozorg-e Farsi* (*The Larger Persian Encyclopædia*), Tehran, June 21, 1996.

[2] A. Birashk, *A Comparative Calendar of the Iranian, Muslim Lunar, and Christian Eras for Three Thousand Years*, Mazda Publishers (in association with Bibliotheca Persica), Costa Mesa, CA, 1993.

[3] F. C. de Blois, "The Persian Calendar," *Iran*, vol. 34, pp. 39–54, 1996.

[4] F. C. de Blois and B. van Dalen, "Ta'rikh" (Part I), *The Encyclopaedia of Islam*, 2nd edn., E. J. Brill, Leiden, vol. 10, pp. 257–271, 1998.

[5] S. H. Taqizadeh, "Various Eras and Calendars Used in the Countries of Islam," *Bulletin of the School of Oriental Studies* (*University of London*), vol. 9, pp. 903–922, 1937–1939, and vol. 10, pp. 107–132, 1939.

[6] S. H. Taqizadeh, "Djalali," *The Encyclopaedia of Islam*, 2nd edn., vol. 2, E. J. Brill, Leiden, pp. 397–400, 1962.

[7] E. Yarshater, ed., *Encyclopædia Iranica*, Routledge & Kegan Paul, London, 1990.

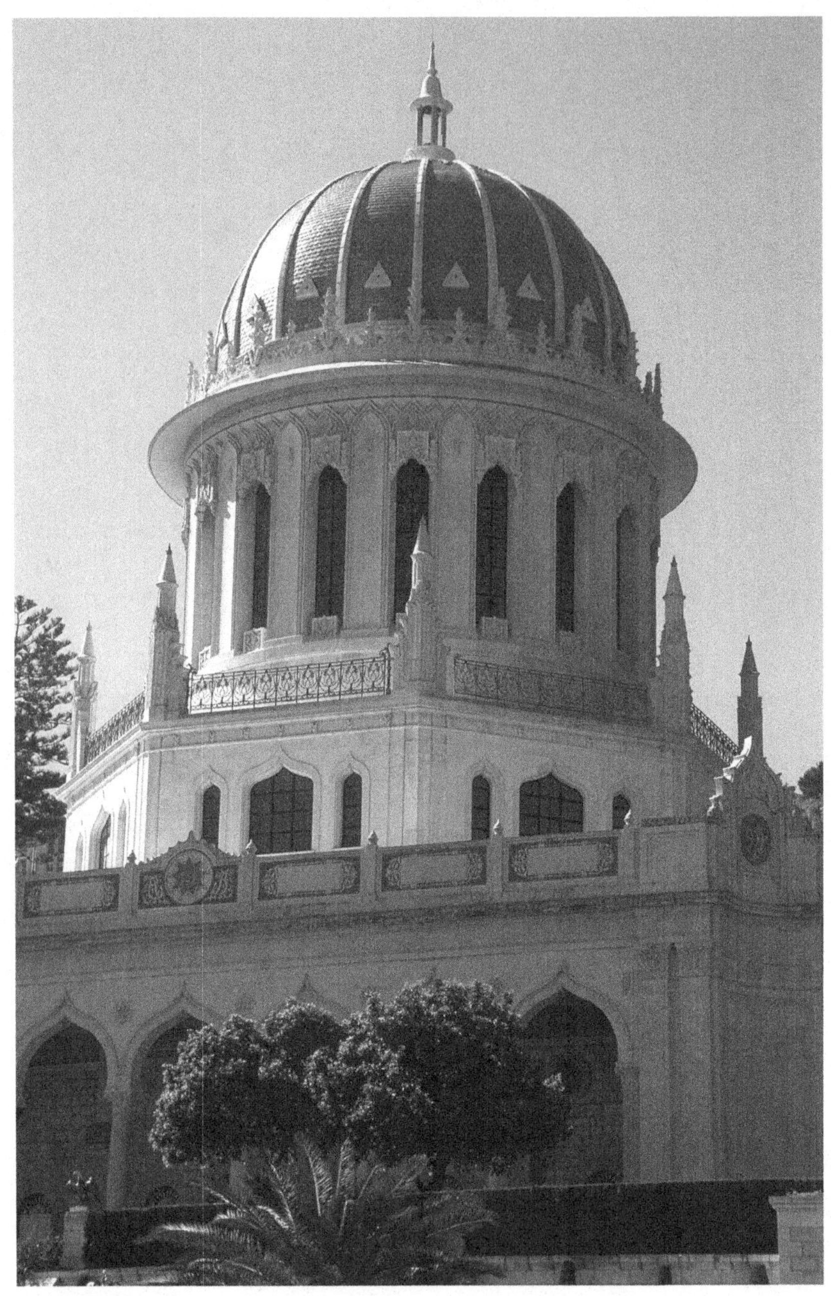

Shrine of the Bāb, located on Mount Carmel, Israel, and built in stages from 1899 to 1953. The Bāb (Mīrzā 'Alī Moḥammad of Shiraz), who was executed in 1850, was the originator of the 19-year cycle of the Bahá'í calendar. (Photograph by N. Wong, © 2006 Bahá'í International Community, used with permission.)

16

The Bahá'í Calendar

In the not far distant future it will be necessary that all peoples in the world agree on a common calendar. It seems, therefore, fitting that the new age of unity should have a new calendar free from the objections and associations which make each of the older calendars unacceptable to large sections of the world's population, and it is difficult to see how any other arrangement could exceed in simplicity and convenience that proposed by the Báb.

John Ebenezer Esslemont: *Bahá'u'lláh and the New Era: An Introduction to the Bahá'í Faith* (1923)[1]

16.1 Structure

The Bahá'í (or Badī') calendar begins its years on the day of the vernal equinox. If the actual time of the equinox in Tehran occurs after sunset, then the year begins a day later [3]. This astronomical version of the Bahá'í calendar [4] is described in Section 16.3. Until recently, practice in the West had been to begin years on March 21 of the Gregorian calendar, regardless. This arithmetical version is described in Section 16.2. The calendar, based on cycles of 19, was established by the Bāb (1819–1850), the martyred forerunner of Bahā'u'llāh, founder of the Bahá'í faith.

As in the Hebrew and Islamic calendars, days are from sunset to sunset. Unlike those calendars, years are solar; they are composed of 19 months of 19 days each with an additional period of 4 or 5 days after the eighteenth month. Until recently, leap years in the Western version of the calendar followed the same pattern as in the Gregorian calendar. As on the Persian calendar, the week begins on Saturday; weekdays have the following names (in Arabic):

Saturday	Jalāl	جلال	(Glory)
Sunday	Jamāl	جمال	(Beauty)
Monday	Kamāl	كمال	(Perfection)
Tuesday	Fiḍāl	فضال	(Grace)
Wednesday	'Idāl	عدال	(Justice)
Thursday	Istijlāl	استجلال	(Majesty)
Friday	Istiqlāl	استقلال	(Independence)

[1] نویسندگان لزوماً با نقطه نظرهای در عبارت موافقت ندارند.

The months are called

(1) Bahā'	بهاء	(Splendor)	19 days
(2) Jalāl	جلال	(Glory)	19 days
(3) Jamāl	جمال	(Beauty)	19 days
(4) 'Aẓamat	عظمت	(Grandeur)	19 days
(5) Nūr	نور	(Light)	19 days
(6) Raḥmat	رحمت	(Mercy)	19 days
(7) Kalimāt	كلمات	(Words)	19 days
(8) Kamāl	كمال	(Perfection)	19 days
(9) Asmā'	اسماء	(Names)	19 days
(10) 'Izzat	عزّت	(Might)	19 days
(11) Mashīyyat	مشيئت	(Will)	19 days
(12) 'Ilm	علم	(Knowledge)	19 days
(13) Qudrat	قدرت	(Power)	19 days
(14) Qawl	قَول	(Speech)	19 days
(15) Masā'il	مسائل	(Questions)	19 days
(16) Sharaf	شرف	(Honor)	19 days
(17) Sulṭān	سلطان	(Sovereignty)	19 days
(18) Mulk	مُلك	(Dominion)	19 days
Ayyām-i-Hā	ايّام ها	(Days of God)	4 {5} days
(19) 'Alā'	علاء	(Loftiness)	19 days

The leap-year variation is given in braces. The 19 days of each month have the same names as the months, except that there is no intercalary Ayyām-i-Hā.

Years are also named in a 19-year cycle, called *Vāḥid*, meaning "unity" and having a numerological value of 19 in Arabic letters:

(1) Alif	الف	(letter A)
(2) Bā'	باء	(letter B)
(3) Ab	أب	(Father)
(4) Dāl	دال	(letter D)
(5) Bāb	باب	(Gate)
(6) Vāv	واو	(letter V)
(7) Abad	ابد	(Eternity)
(8) Jād	جاد	(Generosity)
(9) Bahā'	بهاء	(Splendor)
(10) Ḥubb	حُبّ	(Love)
(11) Bahhāj	بهّاج	(Delightful)
(12) Javāb	جواب	(Answer)
(13) Aḥad	احد	(Single)
(14) Vahhāb	وهّاب	(Bountiful)

(15) Vidād	وداد	(Affection)
(16) Badī'	بدى	(Beginning)
(17) Bahī	بهى	(Luminous)
(18) Abhā	ابهى	(Most Luminous)
(19) Vāḥid	واحد	(Unity)

There is also a 361-year major cycle, called *Kull-i-Shay* (the name has the numerological value $361 = 19^2$ in Arabic). Thus, for example, Monday, April 21, 1930 would be called "Kamāl (Monday), the day of Qudrat (the thirteenth), of the month of Jalāl, of the year Bahhāj (the eleventh), of the fifth Vāḥid, of the first Kull-i-Shay, of the Bahá'í Era."

Accordingly, we represent a Bahá'í date by a list

major	*cycle*	*year*	*month*	*day*

The first component, *major*, is an integer (positive for real Bahá'í dates); the components *cycle*, *year*, and *day*, take on integer values in the range 1 .. 19; because the intercalary period interrupts the sequence of month numbers, *month* is either an integer between 1 and 19 or else the special constant value

$$\textbf{ayyam-i-ha} \stackrel{\text{def}}{=} 0 \tag{16.1}$$

The epoch of the calendar, day 1 of year 1 B.E.,[2] is March 21, 1844 (Gregorian):

$$\textbf{bahai-epoch} \stackrel{\text{def}}{=} \textbf{fixed-from-gregorian}\left(\boxed{1844 \mid \textbf{march} \mid 21}\right) \tag{16.2}$$

which is R.D. 673222.

16.2 The Arithmetical Calendar

Mr. Frank E. Osborne read a complete Bahai calendar on which he has been working for the past four or five years. Abdul-Baha gave it his verbal sanction. It was referred to the executive board.

Star of the West, vol. 8 (1917)

The Bahá'í calendar used in the West until 2015 was based on the Gregorian calendar, and thus its functions are relatively straightforward:

$$\textbf{fixed-from-bahai} \tag{16.3}$$

$$\left(\boxed{\textit{major} \mid \textit{cycle} \mid \textit{year} \mid \textit{month} \mid \textit{day}}\right) \stackrel{\text{def}}{=}$$

$$\textbf{fixed-from-gregorian}\left(\boxed{\textit{g-year} \mid \textbf{march} \mid 20}\right) + \left\{\begin{array}{ll} 342 & \textbf{if } \textit{month} = \textbf{ayyam-i-ha} \\ \left\{\begin{array}{ll} 347 & \textbf{if gregorian-leap-year?}\,(\textit{g-year}+1) \\ 346 & \textbf{otherwise} \end{array}\right\} & \\ & \textbf{if } \textit{month} = 19 \\ 19 \times (\textit{month}-1) & \textbf{otherwise} \end{array}\right\} + \textit{day}$$

[2] Bahá'í Era

where

$$g\text{-}year = 361 \times (major - 1) + 19 \times (cycle - 1) + year - 1 + \textbf{gregorian-year-from-fixed}\,(\textbf{bahai-epoch})$$

We first find the corresponding Gregorian year by counting how many years (361 for each major cycle and 19 for each minor cycle) have elapsed since the epoch in 1844. Starting with the R.D. date of the last day (March 20) of the prior Bahá'í year, we add the number of days in the given month plus 19 days for each month, except that the intercalary period has only 4 or 5 days (for a total of 346 or 347 days), depending on whether February of the Gregorian calendar had a leap day or not.

The inverse function is

$$\textbf{bahai-from-fixed}\,(date) \stackrel{\text{def}}{=} \qquad (16.4)$$

$$\boxed{major \mid cycle \mid year \mid month \mid day}$$

where

$$g\text{-}year = \textbf{gregorian-year-from-fixed}\,(date)$$

$$start = \textbf{gregorian-year-from-fixed}\,(\textbf{bahai-epoch})$$

$$years = g\text{-}year - start - \begin{cases} 1 & \textbf{if } date \leqslant \textbf{fixed-from-gregorian}\left(\boxed{g\text{-}year \mid \textbf{march} \mid 20}\right) \\ 0 & \textbf{otherwise} \end{cases}$$

$$major = \left\lfloor \frac{years}{361} \right\rfloor + 1$$

$$cycle = \left\lfloor \frac{1}{19} \times (years \bmod 361) \right\rfloor + 1$$

$$year = (years \bmod 19) + 1$$

$$days = date - \textbf{fixed-from-bahai}\left(\boxed{major \mid cycle \mid year \mid 1 \mid 1}\right)$$

$$month = \begin{cases} 19 & \textbf{if } date \geqslant \textbf{fixed-from-bahai}\left(\boxed{major \mid cycle \mid year \mid 19 \mid 1}\right) \\ \textbf{ayyam-i-ha} & \textbf{if } date \geqslant \textbf{fixed-from-bahai}\left(\boxed{major \mid cycle \mid year \mid \textbf{ayyam-i-ha} \mid 1}\right) \\ \left\lfloor \frac{days}{19} \right\rfloor + 1 & \textbf{otherwise} \end{cases}$$

$$\begin{aligned} day &= date + 1 \\ &\quad - \textbf{fixed-from-bahai}\left(\boxed{major \mid cycle \mid year \mid month \mid 1}\right) \end{aligned}$$

Here we compute the number of years that have elapsed since the start of the Bahá'í calendar by looking at the Gregorian year number, considering whether the date is before or after Bahá'í New Year, and then using the result to get the number of elapsed major and minor cycles and years within the cycle. Division of the remaining days by 19, the length of a month, gives the month number, but again special consideration must be given for the intercalary period and for the last month of the Bahá'í year.

16.3 The Astronomical Calendar

The chief element of the day after to-morrow in the political calendar will be All Europe as One. There can be no doubt on this point. Unhappily, however, no European nation seems yet to have realized the fact.

German contributor to *Revue de Genéve*, quoted in *The Literary Digest*, vol. 75 (1922)

The Bahá'í year was intended [3] to begin at the sunset preceding the vernal equinox, which is frequently a day before or after March 21. The location at which sunset occurs for this purpose had been undetermined for some time, as explained in the following explanatory letter [2] written in 1974:

> Until the Universal House of Justice decides upon the spot on which the calculations for establishing the date of Naw-Rúz each year are to be based it is not possible to state exactly the correspondence between Bahá'í dates and Gregorian dates for any year. Therefore for the present the believers in the West commemorate Bahá'í events on their traditional Gregorian anniversaries. Once the necessary legislation to determine Naw-Rúz has been made, the correspondence between Bahá'í and Gregorian dates will vary from year to year depending upon whether the Spring Equinox falls on the 20th, 21st or 22nd of March. In fact in Persia the friends have been, over the years, following the Spring Equinox as observed in Tehran, to determine Naw-Rúz, and the National Spiritual Assembly has to issue every year a Bahá'í calendar for the guidance of the friends. The Universal House of Justice feels that this is not a matter of urgency and, in the meantime, is having research conducted into such questions.

Thus, the version of the Bahá'í calendar employed in the Near East (which included, besides Iran, also Israel, Persian Gulf countries, and the Arabian Peninsula) used Tehran for determining the time of sunset on the day of the equinox, which in turn fixes the first day of the year. In 2014, the decision was taken to use Tehran as the determining location the world over [4]:

> "The Festival of Naw-Rúz falleth on the day that the sun entereth the sign of Aries," Bahá'u'lláh explains in His Most Holy Book, "even should this

> occur no more than one minute before sunset." However, details have, until now, been left undefined. We have decided that Ṭihrán, the birthplace of the Abhá Beauty, will be the spot on the earth that will serve as the standard for determining, by means of astronomical computations from reliable sources, the moment of the vernal equinox in the northern hemisphere and thereby the day of Naw-Rúz for the Bahá'í world.

This change took effect with the year that began on March 21, 2015.

For fixing the time of sunset in Tehran, these coordinates are used:[3]

bahai-location $\stackrel{\text{def}}{=}$ (16.5)

35.696111°	51.423056°	0 m	$3\frac{1}{2}^{\text{h}}$

The determination of the U.T. moment of sunset on any specified day is straightforward:

bahai-sunset (*date*) $\stackrel{\text{def}}{=}$ (16.6)

universal-from-standard
(**sunset** (*date*, **bahai-location**), **bahai-location**)

The first day of the year on the new, astronomical, Bahá'í calendar is the day on which the vernal equinox occurs before sunset. To implement the astronomical form of the calendar, we imitate the method used for the astronomical Persian calendar in Section 15.2. The date of the new year is computed using formula (14.43), analogously to what was done for the Persian calendar (page 259), by beginning shortly before the equinox and searching for the sunset when the longitude of the sun first switches from large (close to 360°) to small (less than 2°):

astro-bahai-new-year-on-or-before (*date*) $\stackrel{\text{def}}{=}$ (16.7)

$$\underset{day \geqslant \lfloor approx \rfloor - 1}{\textbf{MIN}} \left\{ \textbf{solar-longitude}\,(\textbf{bahai-sunset}\,(day)) \leqslant \textbf{spring} + 2° \right\}$$

where

$$approx = \textbf{estimate-prior-solar-longitude}\,(\textbf{spring}, \textbf{bahai-sunset}\,(date))$$

Because of the unequal distribution of leap years on the Gregorian calendar, the equinox will be as early as 5:27 p.m. in Tehran on March 19 in 2096, which is before sunset, and it was as late as 10:41 p.m. on March 21 in 1903, long after sunset. By the new rule, the year would begin on March 19 in the former case and March 22 in the latter.

[3] The elevation of Tehran (1180 m) is not taken into account in the sunset calculation, because the mountains to its west are at about the same height, so apparent sunset occurs at approximately the same time as astronomical sunset at zero elevation [1].

To convert a Bahá'í date on the new calendar into a fixed date, we take the R.D. date of the Bahá'í New Year and add 19 days for each full month plus the number of elapsed days in the current month. The intercalary days and last month of the year must be treated as exceptions: days in Ayyām-i-Hā are preceded by 18 full months (that is, 342 days); because the length of that period differs in ordinary and leap years, for dates in the last month, we count backwards from the following New Year. In the following function, we multiply the number of years since the epoch by the mean tropical year length, plus or minus half a year, and then use **astro-bahai-new-year-on-or-before** to get the R.D. date of the subsequent or prior Bahá'í New Year:

$$\textbf{fixed-from-astro-bahai}\left(\boxed{\textit{major} \mid \textit{cycle} \mid \textit{year} \mid \textit{month} \mid \textit{day}}\right) \stackrel{\text{def}}{=} \tag{16.8}$$

$$\begin{cases} \textbf{astro-bahai-new-year-on-or-before} \\ \quad \left(\textbf{bahai-epoch} + \left\lfloor \textbf{mean-tropical-year} \times \left(\textit{years} + \frac{1}{2}\right)\right\rfloor\right) \\ \quad - 20 + \textit{day} \\ \quad \textbf{if } \textit{month} = 19 \\ \textbf{astro-bahai-new-year-on-or-before} \\ \quad \left(\textbf{bahai-epoch} + \left\lfloor \textbf{mean-tropical-year} \times \left(\textit{years} - \frac{1}{2}\right)\right\rfloor\right) \\ \quad + 341 + \textit{day} \\ \quad \textbf{if } \textit{month} = \textbf{ayyam-i-ha} \\ \textbf{astro-bahai-new-year-on-or-before} \\ \quad \left(\textbf{bahai-epoch} + \left\lfloor \textbf{mean-tropical-year} \times \left(\textit{years} - \frac{1}{2}\right)\right\rfloor\right) \\ \quad + (\textit{month} - 1) \times 19 + \textit{day} - 1 \\ \quad \textbf{otherwise} \end{cases}$$

where

$$\textit{years} = 361 \times (\textit{major} - 1) + 19 \times (\textit{cycle} - 1) + \textit{year}$$

The inverse function is

$$\textbf{astro-bahai-from-fixed}\,(\textit{date}) \stackrel{\text{def}}{=} \tag{16.9}$$

$$\boxed{\textit{major} \mid \textit{cycle} \mid \textit{year} \mid \textit{month} \mid \textit{day}}$$

where

$$\textit{new-year} = \textbf{astro-bahai-new-year-on-or-before}\,(\textit{date})$$

$$\textit{years} = \text{round}\left(\frac{\textit{new-year} - \textbf{bahai-epoch}}{\textbf{mean-tropical-year}}\right)$$

$$major = \left\lfloor \frac{years}{361} \right\rfloor + 1$$

$$cycle = \left\lfloor \frac{1}{19} \times (years \bmod 361) \right\rfloor + 1$$

$$year = (years \bmod 19) + 1$$

$$days = date - \textit{new-year}$$

$$month = \begin{cases} 19 & \textbf{if } date \geqslant \textbf{fixed-from-astro-bahai}\left(\boxed{major \mid cycle \mid year \mid 19 \mid 1}\right) \\ \textbf{ayyam-i-ha} & \textbf{if } date \geqslant \textbf{fixed-from-astro-bahai}\left(\boxed{major \mid cycle \mid year \mid \textbf{ayyam-i-ha} \mid 1}\right) \\ \left\lfloor \frac{days}{19} \right\rfloor + 1 & \textbf{otherwise} \end{cases}$$

$$day = date + 1 - \textbf{fixed-from-astro-bahai}\left(\boxed{major \mid cycle \mid year \mid month \mid 1}\right)$$

Here we compute the number of years that have elapsed since the start of the Bahá'í calendar by dividing the numbers of days since the epoch by the mean tropical year length and then using the result to get the number of elapsed major and minor cycles and years within the cycle. Division of the remaining days by 19 (the length of a Bahá'í month) gives the month number but, again, consideration must be given to the intercalary days and for the last month of the Bahá'í year.[4]

[4] The published tables of the ad hoc calendar committee at the Bahá'í World Centre for the years 172–221 B.E. (2015–2064 C.E.) were prepared "using data provided by Her Majesty's Nautical Almanac Office in the United Kingdom" and are available at `wilmetteinstitute.org/wp-content/uploads/2014/11/Bahai-Dates-172-to-221-B-E-_UK-December-2014.pdf`. There is almost complete correspondence between the dates calculated with our functions and those in the table. The only divergence is for 2026, for which the table has New Year occurring on March 21, and our calculations place it on the previous day. This is, however, a very close call, since both sunset and the equinox will occur on March 20 between 6:15 and 6:16 p.m. local standard time in Tehran. On account of the very close proximity of the two events, the decision was made to set Bahá'í New Year to be March 21 [1].

16.4 Holidays and Observances

In all, there are 58 excusable days of observance for various religions on the state's academic calendar – which requires schools to open 180 days a year. It should be noted that in many schools, Christmas and Hanukkah are losing ground to Birth of the Bab Day (Baha'i), and the Rama Navami (Hindu) and Eid El Fitr (Islamic) holy days.

Lisa Suhay: "Want the Day Off? Get Some Religion,"
The New York Times (September 19, 1999)

When the Bahá'í calendar used in the West was synchronized with the Gregorian, holidays were a trivial matter. Bahá'í New Year was always celebrated on March 21, the assumed date of the spring equinox. It is called the Feast of Naw-Rūz, like the Persian New Year, which also celebrates the vernal equinox (see Chapter 15). The computation is trivial:

$$\textbf{bahai-new-year}\,(g\text{-}year) \stackrel{\text{def}}{=} \tag{16.10}$$

$$\textbf{fixed-from-gregorian}\left(\boxed{g\text{-}year \mid \textbf{march} \mid 21}\right)$$

The only holiday that was not aligned with the Gregorian calendar was Ayyām-i-Hā 4, which fell on March 1 in ordinary years, but on February 29 in leap years.

The other major holidays are the Birth of the Bāb (which was celebrated on 'Ilm 5 = October 20), the Birth of Bahā'u'llāh (which was celebrated on Qudrat 9 = November 12), the Feast of Riḍvān (Jalāl 13 = April 21 with the old Western version), Riḍvān 9 (Jamāl 2 = April 29), Riḍvān 12 (Jāmal 5 = May 2), the Declaration of the Bāb ('Aẓamat 8 = May 24), the Ascension of Bahā'u'llāh ('Aẓamat 13 = May 29), and the Martyrdom of the Bāb (Raḥmat 17 = July 10). Two other obligatory observances are the Day of the Covenant (Qawl 4 = November 26) and the Ascension of 'Abdu'l-Bahā (Qawl 6 = November 28). There are additional days of significance, including the first day of each month (known as the Nineteen Day Feast) and the whole last month (comprising fast days).

With the new calendar, which depends on the actual time at which the equinox occurs, Bahá'í Naw-Rūz, on Bahá 1, coincides with Persian Nowruz unless the equinox occurs between noon and sunset in Tehran. A straightforward way to determine the date of Bahá'í Naw-Rūz is as follows:

$$\textbf{naw-ruz}\,(g\text{-}year) \stackrel{\text{def}}{=} \tag{16.11}$$

$$\textbf{astro-bahai-new-year-on-or-before}\,(\textbf{gregorian-new-year}\,(g\text{-}year + 1))$$

Determining the date of holidays, apart from Birth of the Bāb and the Birth of Bahā'u'llāh, on the new astronomical calendar (as previously for the Eastern version) is simply a matter of counting a fixed number of days from Naw-Rūz, or before Naw-Rūz in the case of the month of 'Alā'. For example, we have

$$\textbf{feast-of-ridvan}\,(g\text{-}year) \stackrel{\text{def}}{=} \textbf{naw-ruz}\,(g\text{-}year) + 31 \tag{16.12}$$

The other major holidays on the Bahá'í calendar are also observed on Bahá'í dates (given above), except for four that had been linked in the East to the Islamic calendar (Chapter 7) instead: Declaration of the Bāb (Islamic date Jamādā I 5), Martyrdom of the Bāb (Sh'abān 28), Birth of the Bāb (Muḥarram 1), and the Birth of Bahā'u'llāh (Muḥarram 2). (At the Bahá'í World Centre in Israel, these four had been observed on their Islamic dates whereas the other holidays had been observed on their Gregorian dates.) Following the recent decision Bahá'í dates are to be used for the first two of these four holidays, Declaration of the Bāb (on 'Aẓamat 8) and Martyrdom of the Bāb (Raḥmat 17), while astronomical lunisolar dates are to be used everywhere for the other two: The rule is that the Birth of the Bāb and the Birth of Bahā'u'llāh are observed on the first and second day, respectively, of the eighth lunisolar month, counting new moons from sunset at the end of Naw-Rūz. Using **new-moon-at-or-after** (page 231) for this purpose, we have:

$$\textbf{birth-of-the-bab}\,(g\text{-}year) \stackrel{\text{def}}{=} \begin{cases} day + 1 & \textbf{if } m_8 < set_8 \\ day + 2 & \textbf{otherwise} \end{cases} \tag{16.13}$$

where

$$\begin{aligned} ny &= \textbf{naw-ruz}\,(g\text{-}year) \\ set_1 &= \textbf{bahai-sunset}\,(ny) \\ m_1 &= \textbf{new-moon-at-or-after}\,(set_1) \\ m_8 &= \textbf{new-moon-at-or-after}\,(m_1 + 190) \\ day &= \textbf{fixed-from-moment}\,(m_8) \\ set_8 &= \textbf{bahai-sunset}\,(day) \end{aligned}$$

and m_8 is the moment of the eighth new moon of the year. If new moon is before sunset, then the eighth month begins at sunset; if the new moon is after sunset, the month begins one day later.

References

[1] Email communication from the Bahá'í World Centre, July 22, 2015.

[2] Letter written on behalf of the Universal House of Justice to the National Spiritual Assembly of the Bahá'í of the United States, October 30, 1974.

[3] Universal House of Justice, *The Bahá'í World: An International Record*, vol. xviii, Bahá'í World Center, Haifa, pp. 598–601, 1986.

[4] Universal House of Justice, "Regarding the implementation of the Badí' calendar," July 10, 2014. Available at `universalhouseofjustice.bahai.org/activities-bahai-community/20140710_001`.

Print of the French Revolutionary calendar month of Vendémiaire by Laurent Guyot, after Jean-Jacques Lagrenée, the younger, Paris. (Courtesy of Bibliothèque Nationale de France, Paris.)

17

The French Revolutionary Calendar

Of the Republican calendar, the late John Quincy Adams said: "This system has passed away and is forgotten. This incongruous composition of profound learning and superficial frivolity, of irreligion and morality, of delicate imagination and coarse vulgarity, is dissolved." Unfortunately the effects of this calendar, though it was used for only about twelve years, have not passed away. It has entailed a permanent injury on history and on science.

Joseph Lovering: *Proceedings of the American Academy of Arts and Sciences*, p. 350 (1872)[1]

The French Revolutionary calendar (*Le Calendrier Républicain*) was instituted by the National Convention of the French Republic in October 1793. Its epoch is R.D. 654415, that is, Saturday, September 22, 1792 (Gregorian), the day of the autumnal equinox of that year and also the first day following the establishment of the Republic. The calendar went into effect on Sunday, November 24, 1793 (Gregorian) and was used by the French until Tuesday, December 31, 1805 (Gregorian); on Wednesday, January 1, 1806 (Gregorian), the Revolutionary calendar was abandoned by Napoleonic edict and France reverted to the Gregorian calendar, but the Revolutionary calendar was used again during the "Paris Commune" of May 6–23, 1871 (Gregorian), an insurrection that occurred after the collapse of Napoleon III's Second Empire.

Following the example of several ancient calendars, including the Coptic and Ethiopic (see Chapter 4), the French Revolutionary calendar divided the year into 12 months containing exactly 30 days each, followed by a period of 5 monthless days (6 in leap years). The poetic names of the months, coined by Fabre d'Églantine, were taken from the seasons in which they occurred:[2]

---

[1] *Les auteurs ne souscrivent pas nécessairement aux opinions des auteurs des citations.*

[2] We have spelled the month names Nivôse, Pluviôse, and Ventôse in modern French; in the original proclamation establishing the calendar, these names are written without a circumflex. Native American, old Vedic, Ukrainian, and Gezer (see page 112) names of months have similar phenological flavor, as do the names of the 24 "solar terms" on the Chinese calendar (see Table 19.1 on page 307). Also, in the mid-eighteenth century Linnæus published *The Calendar of Flora* consisting of the 12 months Reviving Winter (December 22–March 19), Thawing (March 19–April 12), Budding (April 12–May 9), Leafing (May 9–May 25), Flowering (May 25–June 20), Fruiting (June 20–July 12), Ripening (July 12–August 4), Reaping (August 4–August 28), Sowing (August 28–September 22),

(1) Vendémiaire (vintage)
(2) Brumaire (fog)
(3) Frimaire (sleet)
(4) Nivôse (snow)
(5) Pluviôse (rain)
(6) Ventôse (wind)
(7) Germinal (seed)
(8) Floréal (blossom)
(9) Prairial (pasture)
(10) Messidor (harvest)
(11) Thermidor (heat)
(12) Fructidor (fruit)

An English wit who was "disgusted with the 'namby pamby' style of the French calendar" dubbed them Slippy, Drippy, Nippy, Showery, Flowery, Bowery, Hoppy, Croppy, Poppy, Wheezy, Sneezy, Freezy [2, vol. I, pp. 38–39].

As usual, we use

year	*month*	*day*

to represent the date, treating the monthless days as a thirteenth month, as in the Mayan haab calendar (Chapter 11).

Although not relevant to our calculations, each month was divided into 3 *décades* (decades) of 10 days each; the tenth day was considered a day of rest. This made the new calendar unpopular because, under the Gregorian calendar, the workers had had every seventh day off. The 10 days were named by their ordinal position in the decade:

(1) Primidi
(2) Duodi
(3) Tridi
(4) Quartidi
(5) Quintidi
(6) Sextidi
(7) Septidi
(8) Octidi
(9) Nonidi
(10) Décadi

The 5 or 6 monthless days that were added at the end of each year were holidays called *sansculottides* celebrating various attributes of the Revolution:

(1) Fête de la Vertu (Virtue Day)
(2) Fête du Génie (Genius Day)
(3) Fête du Travail (Labor Day)
(4) Fête de l'Opinion (Opinion Day)
(5) Fête de la Récompense (Reward Day)
{(6) Jour de la Révolution (Revolution Day)}

The leap-year intercalary day is given in curly brackets.

Shedding (September 22–October 28), Freezing (October 28–November 5), and Dead Winter (November 5–December 22). See *Miscellaneous Tracts Relating to Natural History, Husbandry, and Physick to which is added the Calendar of Flora*, by B. Stillingfleet, R. and J. Dodsley, London, 1762. Stillingfleet is today best remembered as the original "bluestocking"; see the *Oxford English Dictionary*, 2nd edn., Oxford University Press, Oxford, 1989. We are indebted to Evan Melhado for pointing out the Linnæus and Stillingfleet references.

17.1 The Original Form

... je ne regrette presque plus le calendrier républicain [... *I almost no longer regret the French Revolutionary calendar*]

Stendhal: *Journal* (January 20, 1806)

Originally, the calendar was kept in synchronization with the solar year by setting the first day of Vendémiaire to occur at the autumnal equinox, just as the Persian astronomical calendar fixes the start of the year according to the spring equinox (see Chapter 15). That is, there was no leap-year rule per se; a leap year occurred when successive autumnal equinoxes were 366 days apart, which happens roughly every 4 years. However, the pattern is not regular, and the precise calculation of the equinox is not easy, and thus the original rule was changed to the simple Gregorian-like rule that we discuss in the following section. In this section we give the original form of the calendar.

To implement the original form of the calendar we need to determine the moment of the autumnal equinox in Paris. The Paris Observatory is 48°50′11″ (= 175811°/3600) north, 2°20′15″ (= 187°/80) east, 27 meters above sea level, and 1 hour after Universal Time, so we define

$$\textbf{paris} \stackrel{\text{def}}{=} \boxed{48°50'11'' \mid 2°20'15'' \mid 27\text{ m} \mid 1^{\text{h}}} \tag{17.1}$$

Because eighteenth-century France used apparent solar time, days began at true (apparent) midnight. The New Year began on the day on which the autumnal equinox occurs after true midnight. That is, the "critical moment" (in the sense of Section 14.5) for the French Revolutionary calendar is

$$\textbf{midnight-in-paris}\,(date) \stackrel{\text{def}}{=} \textbf{midnight}\,(date + 1, \textbf{paris}) \tag{17.2}$$

We find the date of the New Year (the autumnal equinox) on or before a given fixed date using (14.43):

$$\textbf{french-new-year-on-or-before}\,(date) \stackrel{\text{def}}{=} \tag{17.3}$$

$$\underset{day \geqslant \lfloor approx \rfloor - 1}{\textbf{MIN}} \left\{ \textbf{autumn} \leqslant \textbf{solar-longitude}\,(\textbf{midnight-in-paris}\,(day)) \right\}$$

where

$$approx = \textbf{estimate-prior-solar-longitude}\,(\textbf{autumn}, \textbf{midnight-in-paris}\,(date))$$

We define

$$\textbf{french-epoch} \stackrel{\text{def}}{=} \tag{17.4}$$

$$\textbf{fixed-from-gregorian}\left(\boxed{1792 \mid \textbf{september} \mid 22} \right)$$

Now we can convert from a French Revolutionary date to an R.D. date by finding the preceding New Year and doing some simple arithmetic:

$$\textbf{fixed-from-french}\left(\boxed{\textit{year} \mid \textit{month} \mid \textit{day}}\right) \stackrel{\text{def}}{=} \tag{17.5}$$

$$\textit{new-year} - 1 + 30 \times (\textit{month} - 1) + \textit{day}$$

where

$$\textit{new-year} = \textbf{french-new-year-on-or-before}\\ (\lfloor \textbf{french-epoch} + 180 + \textbf{mean-tropical-year} \times (\textit{year} - 1) \rfloor)$$

In the other direction we have

$$\textbf{french-from-fixed}\,(\textit{date}) \stackrel{\text{def}}{=} \boxed{\textit{year} \mid \textit{month} \mid \textit{day}} \tag{17.6}$$

where

$$\begin{aligned}
\textit{new-year} &= \textbf{french-new-year-on-or-before}\,(\textit{date})\\
\textit{year} &= \text{round}\left(\frac{\textit{new-year} - \textbf{french-epoch}}{\textbf{mean-tropical-year}}\right) + 1\\
\textit{month} &= \left\lfloor \frac{1}{30} \times (\textit{date} - \textit{new-year}) \right\rfloor + 1\\
\textit{day} &= ((\textit{date} - \textit{new-year}) \bmod 30) + 1
\end{aligned}$$

To determine whether a year is leap on this calendar, we can count the days between successive New Years:

$$\textbf{french-leap-year?}\,(\textit{f-year}) \stackrel{\text{def}}{=} \tag{17.7}$$

$$\textbf{fixed-from-french}\left(\boxed{\textit{f-year} + 1 \mid 1 \mid 1}\right)\\ - \textbf{fixed-from-french}\left(\boxed{\textit{f-year} \mid 1 \mid 1}\right) > 365$$

The same sort of leap-year calculation could be done for other astronomical solar calendars, such as the Persian (Section 15.2) and Bahá'í (Section 16.3).

17.2 The Modified Arithmetical Form

We are informed, that the present French Calendar will soon be abolished, it being found productive of endless inconvenience in mercantile transactions, in comparing dates of letters and bills of exchange, and possessing not one advantage in return, as it was not even astronomically just, and actually separated us from all the rest of Europe.

The Times (London; August 8, 1805)

A simpler, arithmetical, leap-year rule for the French Revolutionary calendar was proposed by Gilbert Romme in 1795:

every 4th year is a leap year, except that
every 100th year is not a leap year, except that
every 400th year is a leap year, except that
every 4000th year is not a leap year,

giving an average of 1460969/4000 = 365.24225 days per year, which is an error of about 1 day in 14000 years compared to the present mean tropical year length. Although the calendar was abandoned before this rule could be adopted, we show how to implement this strictly arithmetical form of the calendar.

We do not need to test for leap years for the date conversions, but we give the definition anyway:

$$\textbf{arithmetic-french-leap-year?}\ (\textit{f-year}) \stackrel{\text{def}}{=} \tag{17.8}$$

$$(\textit{f-year} \bmod 4) = 0 \text{ and } (\textit{f-year} \bmod 400) \notin \{100, 200, 300\} \text{ and } (\textit{f-year} \bmod 4000) \neq 0$$

Conversion of a French Revolutionary date to an R.D. date is thus done by summing all days before that date, including the number of days before the calendar began, 365 days for each prior year, all prior leap days (using the inclusion/exclusion method described for the Gregorian calendar—see page 60), and the number of prior days in the present year:

$$\textbf{fixed-from-arithmetic-french}\left(\boxed{\textit{year} \mid \textit{month} \mid \textit{day}}\right) \stackrel{\text{def}}{=} \tag{17.9}$$

$$\textbf{french-epoch} - 1 + 365 \times (\textit{year} - 1) + \left\lfloor \frac{\textit{year} - 1}{4} \right\rfloor - \left\lfloor \frac{\textit{year} - 1}{100} \right\rfloor + \left\lfloor \frac{\textit{year} - 1}{400} \right\rfloor - \left\lfloor \frac{\textit{year} - 1}{4000} \right\rfloor + 30 \times (\textit{month} - 1) + \textit{day}$$

Calculating the French Revolutionary date from the R.D. *date* involves sequentially determining the year, month, and day of the month. The year number is first approximated to within one year of its true value and then is found precisely by checking the two possible years. The month is then found exactly by division, and the day of the month is determined by subtraction:

$$\textbf{arithmetic-french-from-fixed}\ (\textit{date}) \stackrel{\text{def}}{=} \tag{17.10}$$

$$\boxed{\textit{year} \mid \textit{month} \mid \textit{day}}$$

where

$$\textit{approx} = \left\lfloor \frac{4000}{1460969} \times (\textit{date} - \textbf{french-epoch} + 2) \right\rfloor + 1$$

$$\textit{year} = \begin{cases} \textit{approx} - 1 & \textbf{if } \textit{date} < \textbf{fixed-from-arithmetic-french}\left(\boxed{\textit{approx} \mid 1 \mid 1}\right) \\ \textit{approx} & \textbf{otherwise} \end{cases}$$

$$\textit{month} = 1 + \left\lfloor \frac{1}{30} \times \left(\textit{date} - \textbf{fixed-from-arithmetic-french}\left(\boxed{\textit{year} \mid 1 \mid 1}\right)\right)\right\rfloor$$

$$\textit{day} = 1 + \textit{date} - \textbf{fixed-from-arithmetic-french}\left(\boxed{\textit{year} \mid \textit{month} \mid 1}\right)$$

References

[1] *Le Calendrier Républicain*, Bureau des Longitudes et Observatoire de Paris, Paris, 1994.

[2] J. Brady, *Clavis Calendaria; or, a Compendious Analysis of the Calendar: Illustrated with Ecclesiastical, Historical, and Classical Anecdotes*, 2nd edn., printed privately for the author, London, 1812.

[3] M. Hamer, "A Calendar for All Seasons," *New Scientist*, vol. 124, no. 1696/1697, pp. 9–12, December 23/30, 1989.

Neo-Sumerian list (in cuneiform script) of month names for the Lagash, Babylonia calendar, including the extra 13th month; 2000–1600 B.C.E. (MS 4151, The Schøyen Collection, London & Oslo; reproduced with permission.)

18

Astronomical Lunar Calendars

He spent his days and half his nights writing a book on the history of calendars.
Isaac Bashevis Singer: *The Family Moskat* (1950)

In this chapter, we apply the methods of Chapter 14 to compute the old Babylonian calendar, the proposed uniform date of Easter, the observational Islamic lunar calendar, the classical Hebrew lunisolar calendar, and the Samaritan calendar. All but the calculation of Easter and the Samaritan calendar share the feature that the start of the month is determined by the first visibility of the crescent moon after new moon.

Around the time of the new moon, when the sun and moon are close to each other in the sky, the moon cannot be seen with the naked eye. Leading up to that time, a crescent moon is visible in the morning sky near the eastern horizon, while shortly after the new moon conjunction a crescent moon appears in the evening just after sunset, low in the western sky. On very rare occasions, the moon can be seen in the morning one day and in the evening the next [5]; usually, it is invisible for 1 to 3 days.

18.1 The Babylonian Calendar

In the house of history studying chronology is like puttering about the basement working on the plumbing or furnace instead of joining the conversation in the dining room. But it is occasionally useful to check the basic apparatus.
Leo Depuydt: "On the Consistency of the Wandering Year as Backbone of Egyptian Chronology," *Journal of the American Research Center in Egypt* (1995)

The classical Babylonian calendar, from about 380 B.C.E., or earlier, was of the lunisolar type, with a fixed 19-year Metonic cycle. Prior to that date, leap years were irregular (see [6], [9]). The month names are

(1) Nisanu	(7) Tashritu
(2) Ayaru	(8) Arakhsamna
(3) Simanu	(9) Kislimu
(4) Du'uzu	(10) Tebetu
(5) Abu	(11) Shabatu
(6) Ululu	(12) Adaru

The day of the new moon was often determined by an approximate calculation based on the lag time between sunset and moonset. The lag time is simply the difference between the times of the setting of the moon (14.84) and the sun (14.77). Taking into account the possibility of the nonoccurrence of sunset or moonset, we have:

$$\textbf{moonlag}\ (\mathit{date}, \mathit{location}) \stackrel{\text{def}}{=} \begin{cases} \textbf{bogus} & \textbf{if } \mathit{sun} = \textbf{bogus} \\ 24^{\text{h}} & \textbf{if } \mathit{moon} = \textbf{bogus} \\ \mathit{moon} - \mathit{sun} & \textbf{otherwise} \end{cases} \tag{18.1}$$

where

$$\mathit{sun} = \textbf{sunset}\,(\mathit{date}, \mathit{location})$$
$$\mathit{moon} = \textbf{moonset}\,(\mathit{date}, \mathit{location})$$

We take Babylon

$$\textbf{babylon} \stackrel{\text{def}}{=} \boxed{32.4794° \mid 44.4328° \mid 26\text{ m} \mid 3\tfrac{1}{2}^{\text{h}}} \tag{18.2}$$

as the determining location. The precise method of prediction seems to have varied [9]. Requiring that the month be at least a day old and that the lag be at least 48 minutes [3], we have

$$\textbf{babylonian-criterion}\,(\mathit{date}) \stackrel{\text{def}}{=} \tag{18.3}$$

$$\textbf{new} < \mathit{phase} < \textbf{first-quarter} \text{ and}$$
$$\textbf{new-moon-before}\,(t) \leqslant t - 24^{\text{h}} \text{ and}$$
$$\textbf{moonlag}\,(\mathit{date} - 1, \textbf{babylon}) > 48^{\text{m}}$$

where

$$\mathit{set} = \textbf{sunset}\,(\mathit{date} - 1, \textbf{babylon})$$
$$t = \textbf{universal-from-standard}\,(\mathit{set}, \textbf{babylon})$$
$$\mathit{phase} = \textbf{lunar-phase}\,(t)$$

Now, the start of the new month is found by linear search, in a similar fashion to **phasis-on-or-before** (page 252):

$$\textbf{babylonian-new-month-on-or-before}\,(\mathit{date}) \stackrel{\text{def}}{=} \tag{18.4}$$

$$\underset{d \geqslant \tau}{\textbf{MIN}} \left\{ \textbf{babylonian-criterion}\,(d) \right\}$$

where

$$\mathit{moon} = \textbf{fixed-from-moment}\,(\textbf{lunar-phase-at-or-before}\,(\textbf{new}, \mathit{date}))$$

$$age = date - moon$$

$$\tau = \begin{cases} moon - 30 & \textbf{if } age \leqslant 3 \text{ and not } \textbf{babylonian-criterion}\,(date) \\ moon & \textbf{otherwise} \end{cases}$$

We use the beginning of the Seleucid era, April 3, 311 B.C.E. (Julian), as the calendar's epoch:

$$\textbf{babylonian-epoch} \stackrel{\text{def}}{=} \tag{18.5}$$

$$\textbf{fixed-from-julian}\left(\boxed{311\text{ B.C.E.} \mid \textbf{april} \mid 3}\right)$$

The leap-year rule follows the same pattern as that of the Hebrew calendar (8.14), but the cycle is shifted 7 years:

$$\textbf{babylonian-leap-year?}\,(b\text{-}year) \stackrel{\text{def}}{=} ((7 \times b\text{-}year + 13) \bmod 19) < 7 \tag{18.6}$$

The last month of the year, Adaru, was intercalated in years 1, 4, 7, 9, 12, and 15 of the cycle; the sixth month, Ululu, was intercalated instead during the 18th year. Taking this anomaly into account, the conversions are straightforward:

$$\textbf{fixed-from-babylonian} \tag{18.7}$$

$$\left(\boxed{year \mid month \mid leap \mid day}\right) \stackrel{\text{def}}{=}$$

$$\textbf{babylonian-new-month-on-or-before}\,(midmonth) + day - 1$$

where

$$month_1 = \begin{cases} month & \textbf{if } leap \text{ or } \{(year \bmod 19) = 18 \text{ and } month > 6\} \\ month - 1 & \textbf{otherwise} \end{cases}$$

$$months = \left\lfloor \frac{1}{19} \times ((year - 1) \times 235 + 13) \right\rfloor + month_1$$

$$midmonth = \textbf{babylonian-epoch}$$
$$+ \text{round}\,(\textbf{mean-synodic-month} \times months) + 15$$

In the other direction,

$$\textbf{babylonian-from-fixed}\,(date) \stackrel{\text{def}}{=} \tag{18.8}$$

$$\boxed{year \mid month \mid leap \mid day}$$

where

$$crescent = \textbf{babylonian-new-month-on-or-before}\,(date)$$

$$months = \text{round}\left(\frac{crescent - \textbf{babylonian-epoch}}{\textbf{mean-synodic-month}}\right)$$

$$
\begin{aligned}
\textit{year} &= \left\lfloor \frac{1}{235} \times (19 \times \textit{months} + 5) \right\rfloor + 1 \\
\textit{approx} &= \textbf{babylonian-epoch} \\
&\quad + \text{round}\left(\left\lfloor \tfrac{1}{19} \times ((\textit{year} - 1) \times 235 + 13) \right\rfloor \right. \\
&\qquad\qquad \left. \times\, \textbf{mean-synodic-month} \right) \\
\textit{new-year} &= \textbf{babylonian-new-month-on-or-before}\,(\textit{approx} + 15) \\
\textit{month}_1 &= \text{round}\left(\frac{1}{29.5} \times (\textit{crescent} - \textit{new-year}) \right) + 1 \\
\textit{special} &= (\textit{year} \bmod 19) = 18 \\
\textit{leap} &= \begin{cases} \textit{month}_1 = 7 & \textbf{if } \textit{special} \\ \textit{month}_1 = 13 & \textbf{otherwise} \end{cases} \\
\textit{month} &= \begin{cases} \textit{month}_1 - 1 & \textbf{if } \textit{leap} \text{ or } \{\textit{special} \text{ and } \textit{month}_1 > 6\} \\ \textit{month}_1 & \textbf{otherwise} \end{cases} \\
\textit{day} &= \textit{date} - \textit{crescent} + 1
\end{aligned}
$$

Since it is not always certain how the evening of the occurrence of the new moon was actually determined, these dates should be considered approximate. See [6].

18.2 Astronomical Easter

Snout: Doth the moon shine that night we play our play?
Bottom: A calendar, a calendar! look in the almanac;
find out moonshine, find out moonshine.
Quince: Yes, it doth shine that night.

William Shakespeare: *A Midsummer Night's Dream,*
Act III, scene i (1600)

In 1997, the World Council of Churches [1] proposed a uniform date for Easter for the Eastern and Western churches (see Chapter 9). With the algorithms of Chapter 14, the proposed astronomical determination of Easter is straightforward. We need to find the first Sunday in Jerusalem[1] after the first true full moon after the true vernal equinox:

$$
\textbf{astronomical-easter}\,(\textit{g-year}) \stackrel{\text{def}}{=} \textbf{kday-after}\,(\textbf{sunday}, \textit{paschal-moon}) \tag{18.9}
$$

where

$$
\begin{aligned}
\textit{equinox} &= \textbf{season-in-gregorian}\,(\textbf{spring}, \textit{g-year}) \\
\textit{paschal-moon} &= \left\lfloor \textbf{apparent-from-universal} \right. \\
&\qquad \left. (\textbf{lunar-phase-at-or-after}\,(\textbf{full}, \textit{equinox}), \textbf{jerusalem}) \right\rfloor
\end{aligned}
$$

[1] "Astronomical observations, of course, depend upon the position on Earth which is taken as the point of reference. This consultation believes that it is appropriate to employ the meridian of Jerusalem ..." [1].

Table 9.1 in Chapter 9 (page 151) gives the traditional dates of Passover and Easter along with those obtained by the preceding astronomical calculations.

18.3 The Observational Islamic Calendar

It is He who gave the sun its radiance, the moon its luster, and appointed its stations so that you may compute years and numbers. God did not create them but with deliberation. He distinctly explains His signs for those who can understand.

Koran (X, 5)

Muslims in India, Pakistan, and Bangladesh base their calendar on reported moon sightings. In Egypt, they require moonset to be at least 5 minutes after sunset on the first day of the month. In the United States, according to S. K. Shaukat (who was national coordinator and consultant for America): "A confirmed crescent sighting report in North America will be accepted as long as such a report does not contradict indisputable astronomical information." In Saudi Arabia and most of the Gulf countries, the rule is that the moon must set after the sun on the last day of the month as seen from Mecca.

With the functions of Section 14.9, we can approximate the observation-based Islamic calendars that are used in practice. Suppose that we take Cairo, site of Al-Azhar University, a major Islamic religious center, as the location of observation:[2]

$$\textbf{islamic-location} \stackrel{\text{def}}{=} \boxed{30.1^\circ \mid 31.3^\circ \mid 200\text{ m} \mid 2^{\text{h}}} \tag{18.10}$$

Then we calculate the calendar as follows:

$$\textbf{fixed-from-observational-islamic}\left(\boxed{\textit{year} \mid \textit{month} \mid \textit{day}}\right) \stackrel{\text{def}}{=} \tag{18.11}$$

$$\textbf{phasis-on-or-before}\,(\textit{midmonth}, \textbf{islamic-location}) + \textit{day} - 1$$

where

$$\textit{midmonth} = \textbf{islamic-epoch} + \left\lfloor\left((\textit{year} - 1) \times 12 + \textit{month} - \frac{1}{2}\right) \times \textbf{mean-synodic-month}\right\rfloor$$

---

[2] In our *Calendrical Tabulations*, we made the less-than-obvious choice of Los Angeles as the location for the Islamic calendar based on the following advice of S. K. Shaukat [8]:

> The reason I pick Los Angeles is that according to the known practices these dates would be closest to Middle Eastern countries' practices although the visibility would not be in the Middle East. Moreover, in many cases, if the visibility is not in Los Angeles then most of the world would see it the next day and that would be reflected in the calculated dates for Los Angeles. The dates for Los Angeles would also be good for the rest of North America if an aided eye is used, which will also be in line with actual practice and I think these dates would be the closest to practices all around the world.

In other words, the actual observance of Ramadan, and other Islamic events frequently precedes dates as calculated astronomically, for various nonscientific reasons. Thus, choosing Los Angeles gave dates that are both scientifically and religiously reasonable for the United States *and* in good agreement with actual observance in the Middle East.

In the other direction,

$$\textbf{observational-islamic-from-fixed}\,(\mathit{date}) \stackrel{\text{def}}{=} \boxed{\mathit{year} \mid \mathit{month} \mid \mathit{day}} \qquad (18.12)$$

where

$$\begin{aligned}
\mathit{crescent} &= \textbf{phasis-on-or-before}\,(\mathit{date}, \textbf{islamic-location}) \\
\mathit{elapsed\text{-}months} &= \text{round}\left(\frac{\mathit{crescent} - \textbf{islamic-epoch}}{\textbf{mean-synodic-month}}\right) \\
\mathit{year} &= \left\lfloor \frac{1}{12} \times \mathit{elapsed\text{-}months} \right\rfloor + 1 \\
\mathit{month} &= (\mathit{elapsed\text{-}months} \bmod 12) + 1 \\
\mathit{day} &= \mathit{date} - \mathit{crescent} + 1
\end{aligned}$$

These functions for the Islamic calendar are approximate at best for many reasons: The phenomenon of visibility is still an area of astronomical research and is not yet fully understood; this criterion is just one of many suggestions. It ignores the variation in the distance to the moon and also in the clarity of the atmosphere, which depends on location and season as well as on unpredictable factors. Muslim countries base the calendar on reported observations, not calculated observability. The best location for seeing the new moon varies from month to month (western locations are always better), and different religious authorities accept testimony from within different regions.

The above functions allow for a 31st day of an Islamic month, which is longer than is actually allowed by the rules.[3] Instead, that day would be the first of the following month—were the moon actually observed when the simple criterion we are using says it becomes visible. This shift can cascade for several months. We have not taken this into account because there is no way to determine when in fact the new moons are actually observed, and which months are affected.

Imagining that the functions precisely capture observability, the following functions do take this rule into account by checking month after month:

$$\textbf{month-length}\,(\mathit{date}, \mathit{location}) \stackrel{\text{def}}{=} \mathit{moon} - \mathit{prev} \qquad (18.13)$$

where

$$\begin{aligned}
\mathit{moon} &= \textbf{phasis-on-or-after}\,(\mathit{date} + 1, \mathit{location}) \\
\mathit{prev} &= \textbf{phasis-on-or-before}\,(\mathit{date}, \mathit{location})
\end{aligned}$$

$$\textbf{early-month?}\,(\mathit{date}, \mathit{location}) \stackrel{\text{def}}{=} \qquad (18.14)$$

[3] It is possible for there to be 31 days from first visibility to first visiblity. For example, using Yallop's criterion (page 251), there would be have been a 31-day observation-based lunar month in Babylon extending from August 27, 2006 through September 26, 2006. As R. H. van Gent points out [2], there is also a 31-day month in the 10th year of Darius I according to the tables of [6, p. 30].

$$date - start \geqslant 30 \text{ or } \textbf{month-length}\,(prev, location) > 30 \text{ or}$$
$$\{\, \textbf{month-length}\,(prev, location) = 30 \text{ and } \textbf{early-month?}\,(prev, location) \,\}$$

where

$$start = \textbf{phasis-on-or-before}\,(date, location)$$
$$prev = start - 15$$

$$\textbf{alt-fixed-from-observational-islamic}\left(\boxed{year \mid month \mid day}\right) \stackrel{\text{def}}{=} \tag{18.15}$$

$$\begin{cases} date - 1 & \textbf{if early-month?}\,(midmonth, \textbf{islamic-location}) \\ date & \textbf{otherwise} \end{cases}$$

where

$$midmonth = \textbf{islamic-epoch} + \left\lfloor \left((year - 1) \times 12 + month - \frac{1}{2}\right) \times \textbf{mean-synodic-month} \right\rfloor$$
$$moon = \textbf{phasis-on-or-before}\,(midmonth, \textbf{islamic-location})$$
$$date = moon + day - 1$$

$$\textbf{alt-observational-islamic-from-fixed}\,(date) \stackrel{\text{def}}{=} \tag{18.16}$$

$$\boxed{year \mid month \mid day}$$

where

$$early = \textbf{early-month?}\,(date, \textbf{islamic-location})$$
$$long = early \text{ and } \textbf{month-length}\,(date, \textbf{islamic-location}) > 29$$
$$date' = \begin{cases} date + 1 & \textbf{if } long \\ date & \textbf{otherwise} \end{cases}$$
$$moon = \textbf{phasis-on-or-before}\,(date', \textbf{islamic-location})$$
$$elapsed\text{-}months = \text{round}\left(\frac{moon - \textbf{islamic-epoch}}{\textbf{mean-synodic-month}}\right)$$
$$year = \left\lfloor \frac{1}{12} \times elapsed\text{-}months \right\rfloor + 1$$
$$month = (elapsed\text{-}months \bmod 12) + 1$$
$$day = date' - moon - \begin{cases} -2 & \textbf{if } early \text{ and not } long \\ -1 & \textbf{otherwise} \end{cases}$$

Saudi Arabia employs the *Umm al-Qura* calendar for some secular purposes, as an approximation of the observational Islamic calendar. The rule—since March 2002—is that the month begins on the first evening after the conjunction on which the moon sets after the sun.[4] This criterion can be expressed as

$$\textbf{saudi-criterion}\,(date) \stackrel{\text{def}}{=} \tag{18.17}$$

$$\textbf{new} < phase < \textbf{first-quarter} \text{ and } \textbf{moonlag}\,(date - 1, \textbf{mecca}) > 0$$

where

$$\begin{aligned} set &= \textbf{sunset}\,(date - 1, \textbf{mecca}) \\ t &= \textbf{universal-from-standard}\,(set, \textbf{mecca}) \\ phase &= \textbf{lunar-phase}\,(t) \end{aligned}$$

$$\textbf{saudi-new-month-on-or-before}\,(date) \stackrel{\text{def}}{=} \tag{18.18}$$

$$\underset{d \geqslant \tau}{\textbf{MIN}} \left\{ \textbf{saudi-criterion}\,(d) \right\}$$

where

$$\begin{aligned} moon &= \textbf{fixed-from-moment}\,(\textbf{lunar-phase-at-or-before}\,(\textbf{new}, date)) \\ age &= date - moon \\ \tau &= \begin{cases} moon - 30 & \textbf{if } age \leqslant 3 \text{ and not } \textbf{saudi-criterion}\,(date) \\ moon & \textbf{otherwise} \end{cases} \end{aligned}$$

The functions **fixed-from-saudi-islamic** and **saudi-islamic-from-fixed** below are analogous to **fixed-from-observational-islamic** and **observational-islamic-from-fixed**, respectively, except that **saudi-new-month-on-or-before** is used:

$$\textbf{fixed-from-saudi-islamic}\left(\boxed{year \mid month \mid day} \right) \stackrel{\text{def}}{=} \tag{18.19}$$

$$\textbf{saudi-new-month-on-or-before}\,(midmonth) + day - 1$$

where

$$\begin{aligned} midmonth = {} & \textbf{islamic-epoch} \\ & + \left\lfloor \left((year - 1) \times 12 + month - \frac{1}{2} \right) \times \textbf{mean-synodic-month} \right\rfloor \end{aligned}$$

In the other direction,

$$\textbf{saudi-islamic-from-fixed}\,(date) \stackrel{\text{def}}{=} \boxed{year \mid month \mid day} \tag{18.20}$$

[4] See www.kacst.edu.sa/en/services/ummalqura on the King Abdulaziz City for Science and Technology web site.

where

$$\begin{aligned}
\textit{crescent} &= \textbf{saudi-new-month-on-or-before}\,(\textit{date})\\
\textit{elapsed-months} &= \text{round}\left(\frac{\textit{crescent} - \textbf{islamic-epoch}}{\textbf{mean-synodic-month}}\right)\\
\textit{year} &= \left\lfloor \frac{1}{12} \times \textit{elapsed-months} \right\rfloor + 1\\
\textit{month} &= (\textit{elapsed-months} \bmod 12) + 1\\
\textit{day} &= \textit{date} - \textit{crescent} + 1
\end{aligned}$$

18.4 The Classical Hebrew Calendar

O, swear not by the moon, th' inconstant moon,
That monthly changes in her circle orb . . .

William Shakespeare: *Romeo and Juliet*, Act II, scene ii (1591)

In classical times, the Hebrew month began with the reported observation of the crescent new moon, just like the Islamic religious calendar of the previous section.[5] Unlike in the Islamic calendar, leap months were intercalated in such a way that the spring equinox always fell before the onset of Nisan 16 [4, 4:2]. The exact method of determining the day of the equinox and the exact cutoff date are uncertain; also, the courts had leeway to declare a leap year when spring came late.

We will take Haifa, a city at the western edge of Israel, as the location from which observations are made (being at the west makes visibility more likely):

$$\textbf{hebrew-location} \stackrel{\text{def}}{=} \boxed{32.82^\circ \mid 35^\circ \mid 0\text{ m} \mid 2^{\text{h}}} \qquad (18.21)$$

With the methods of this chapter, it is straightforward to convert dates for this classical Hebrew observational calendar. The first of Nisan is determined on the basis of the vernal equinox:

$$\textbf{observational-hebrew-first-of-nisan}\,(\textit{g-year}) \stackrel{\text{def}}{=} \qquad (18.22)$$

$$\textbf{phasis-on-or-after}\left(\lfloor \textit{equinox} \rfloor - \begin{cases} 14 & \textbf{if } \textit{equinox} < \textit{set} \\ 13 & \textbf{otherwise} \end{cases}, \textbf{hebrew-location}\right)$$

where

$$\begin{aligned}
\textit{equinox} &= \textbf{season-in-gregorian}\,(\textbf{spring}, \textit{g-year})\\
\textit{set} &= \textbf{universal-from-standard}\\
&\quad\left(\textbf{sunset}\,(\lfloor \textit{equinox} \rfloor, \textbf{hebrew-location}),\right.\\
&\quad\left.\textbf{hebrew-location}\right)
\end{aligned}$$

[5] Karaite Jews still use this form of the Hebrew calendar and intercalate based on the state of the barley crop.

The start of each month is determined by the observability (visibilty) of the new moon:

$$\textbf{observational-hebrew-from-fixed}\,(\mathit{date}) \stackrel{\text{def}}{=} \boxed{\mathit{year} \mid \mathit{month} \mid \mathit{day}} \tag{18.23}$$

where

$$\begin{aligned}
\mathit{crescent} &= \textbf{phasis-on-or-before}\,(\mathit{date}, \textbf{hebrew-location})\\
\mathit{g\text{-}year} &= \textbf{gregorian-year-from-fixed}\,(\mathit{date})\\
\mathit{ny} &= \textbf{observational-hebrew-first-of-nisan}\,(\mathit{g\text{-}year})\\
\mathit{new\text{-}year} &= \begin{cases} \textbf{observational-hebrew-first-of-nisan}\,(\mathit{g\text{-}year} - 1) & \textbf{if } \mathit{date} < \mathit{ny}\\ \mathit{ny} & \textbf{otherwise} \end{cases}\\
\mathit{month} &= \text{round}\left(\frac{1}{29.5} \times (\mathit{crescent} - \mathit{new\text{-}year})\right) + 1\\
\mathit{year} &= (\textbf{hebrew-from-fixed}\,(\mathit{new\text{-}year}))_{\textbf{year}} + \left\{\begin{array}{ll} 1 & \textbf{if } \mathit{month} \geqslant \textbf{tishri}\\ 0 & \textbf{otherwise} \end{array}\right\}\\
\mathit{day} &= \mathit{date} - \mathit{crescent} + 1
\end{aligned}$$

The inverse computation is

$$\textbf{fixed-from-observational-hebrew}\left(\boxed{\mathit{year} \mid \mathit{month} \mid \mathit{day}}\right) \stackrel{\text{def}}{=} \tag{18.24}$$

$$\textbf{phasis-on-or-before}\,(\mathit{midmonth}, \textbf{hebrew-location}) + \mathit{day} - 1$$

where

$$\begin{aligned}
\mathit{year}_1 &= \begin{cases} \mathit{year} - 1 & \textbf{if } \mathit{month} \geqslant \textbf{tishri}\\ \mathit{year} & \textbf{otherwise} \end{cases}\\
\mathit{start} &= \textbf{fixed-from-hebrew}\left(\boxed{\mathit{year}_1 \mid \textbf{nisan} \mid 1}\right)\\
\mathit{g\text{-}year} &= \textbf{gregorian-year-from-fixed}\,(\mathit{start} + 60)\\
\mathit{new\text{-}year} &= \textbf{observational-hebrew-first-of-nisan}\,(\mathit{g\text{-}year})\\
\mathit{midmonth} &= \mathit{new\text{-}year} + \text{round}\,(29.5 \times (\mathit{month} - 1)) + 15
\end{aligned}$$

Using the above functions, we can approximate the classical date of Passover Eve (Nisan 14) in any given Gregorian year:

$$\textbf{classical-passover-eve}\,(\mathit{g\text{-}year}) \stackrel{\text{def}}{=} \tag{18.25}$$

$$\textbf{observational-hebrew-first-of-nisan}\,(\mathit{g\text{-}year}) + 13$$

As we did for the observational Islamic calendar of the previous section, we can take into account the rule disallowing 31-day months:

$$\textbf{alt-observational-hebrew-from-fixed}\ (\mathit{date}) \stackrel{\text{def}}{=} \tag{18.26}$$

$$\boxed{\mathit{year} \mid \mathit{month} \mid \mathit{day}}$$

where

$$
\begin{aligned}
\mathit{early} &= \textbf{early-month?}\ (\mathit{date}, \textbf{hebrew-location}) \\
\mathit{long} &= \mathit{early} \text{ and } \textbf{month-length}\ (\mathit{date}, \textbf{hebrew-location}) > 29 \\
\mathit{date}' &= \begin{cases} \mathit{date} + 1 & \textbf{if } \mathit{long} \\ \mathit{date} & \textbf{otherwise} \end{cases} \\
\mathit{moon} &= \textbf{phasis-on-or-before}\ (\mathit{date}', \textbf{hebrew-location}) \\
\mathit{g\text{-}year} &= \textbf{gregorian-year-from-fixed}\ (\mathit{date}') \\
\mathit{ny} &= \textbf{observational-hebrew-first-of-nisan}\ (\mathit{g\text{-}year}) \\
\mathit{new\text{-}year} &= \begin{cases} \textbf{observational-hebrew-first-of-nisan}\ (\mathit{g\text{-}year} - 1) \\ \qquad \textbf{if } \mathit{date}' < \mathit{ny} \\ \mathit{ny} \quad \textbf{otherwise} \end{cases} \\
\mathit{month} &= \text{round}\left(\frac{\mathit{moon} - \mathit{new\text{-}year}}{29.5} \right) + 1 \\
\mathit{year} &= (\textbf{hebrew-from-fixed}\ (\mathit{new\text{-}year}))_{\textbf{year}} \\
&\quad + \begin{Bmatrix} 1 & \textbf{if } \mathit{month} \geqslant \textbf{tishri} \\ 0 & \textbf{otherwise} \end{Bmatrix} \\
\mathit{day} &= \mathit{date}' - \mathit{moon} - \begin{Bmatrix} -2 & \textbf{if } \mathit{early} \text{ and not } \mathit{long} \\ -1 & \textbf{otherwise} \end{Bmatrix}
\end{aligned}
$$

In the other direction,

$$\textbf{alt-fixed-from-observational-hebrew} \left(\boxed{\mathit{year} \mid \mathit{month} \mid \mathit{day}} \right) \stackrel{\text{def}}{=} \tag{18.27}$$

$$\begin{cases} \mathit{date} - 1 & \textbf{if early-month?}\ (\mathit{midmonth}, \textbf{hebrew-location}) \\ \mathit{date} & \textbf{otherwise} \end{cases}$$

where

$$\mathit{year}_1 = \begin{cases} \mathit{year} - 1 & \textbf{if } \mathit{month} \geqslant \textbf{tishri} \\ \mathit{year} & \textbf{otherwise} \end{cases}$$

$$\begin{aligned}
\mathit{start} &= \textbf{fixed-from-hebrew}\left(\boxed{\mathit{year}_1 \mid \textbf{nisan} \mid 1}\right)\\
\mathit{g\text{-}year} &= \textbf{gregorian-year-from-fixed}\,(\mathit{start} + 60)\\
\mathit{new\text{-}year} &= \textbf{observational-hebrew-first-of-nisan}\,(\mathit{g\text{-}year})\\
\mathit{midmonth} &= \mathit{new\text{-}year} + \text{round}\,(29.5 \times (\mathit{month} - 1)) + 15\\
\mathit{moon} &= \textbf{phasis-on-or-before}\,(\mathit{midmonth}, \textbf{hebrew-location})\\
\mathit{date} &= \mathit{moon} + \mathit{day} - 1
\end{aligned}$$

18.5 The Samaritan Calendar

The last of such tables ever written was sent by Shalmah ... in 1820 ... As it is, most probably, the last document of its kind that ever will be drawn up by a Samaritan priest, I shall here subjoin it.

John Mills: *Three Months' Residence at Nablus, and an Account of the Modern Samaritans* (1864)

The Samaritan calendar is lunisolar, like the Hebrew. Months are numbered, as in most of the Bible. The first day of each month is that on which the new moon occurs, unless it occurs after apparent noon, in which case the next day is the first of the month. The moment of new moon is determined according to their traditional method, referred to as the "True Reckoning," which agrees with the medieval tables of al-Battānī [7] for finding the true positions of the sun and moon.

Time is measured in temporal hours beginning at sunset and sunrise. The critical time for determining the beginning of the month is apparent noon on Mount Gerizim, for which we have

$$\textbf{samaritan-location} \stackrel{\text{def}}{=} \quad (18.28)$$

32.1994°	35.2728°	881 m	2^{h}

and

$$\textbf{samaritan-noon}\,(\mathit{date}) \stackrel{\text{def}}{=} \textbf{midday}\,(\mathit{date}, \textbf{samaritan-location}) \quad (18.29)$$

Rather than replicate these traditional approximations of the true times, we use our astronomical code to find the actual day of the new moon:

$$\textbf{samaritan-new-moon-after}\,(t) \stackrel{\text{def}}{=} \quad (18.30)$$

$$\left\lceil \textbf{apparent-from-universal}\;(\textbf{new-moon-at-or-after}\,(t), \textbf{samaritan-location}) - 12^{\text{h}} \right\rceil$$

and

$$\textbf{samaritan-new-moon-at-or-before}\,(t) \stackrel{\text{def}}{=} \quad (18.31)$$

$$\left\lceil \textbf{apparent-from-universal}\,(\textbf{new-moon-before}\,(t), \textbf{samaritan-location}) - 12^{\text{h}} \right\rceil$$

(Since we are working with high precision reals, we can ignore the possibility of a new moon occurring precisely at noon.)

The first month of the year is that which begins on or after March 12 (Julian); this ensures that the Festival of the Unleavened Bread, which runs from the 15th through the 21st of the first month, occurs after the Julian vernal equinox, which was March 25 when the Julian calendar was instituted. A leap month is added when necessary at the end of the year. Years begin with the *sixth* lunar month. (The Hebrew calendar of Chapter 8 begins its calendar year with the *seventh* month.) They are counted from the summer of 1639 B.C.E., the traditional year when the Israelites entered the Promised Land. As epoch, we take month 1, day 1 of year 0 A.S.:[6]

$$\textbf{samaritan-epoch} \stackrel{\text{def}}{=} \tag{18.32}$$

$$\textbf{fixed-from-julian}\left(\boxed{1639 \text{ B.C.E.} \mid \textbf{march} \mid 15}\right)$$

The conversions are not difficult:

$$\textbf{samaritan-new-year-on-or-before}\ (\mathit{date}) \stackrel{\text{def}}{=} \tag{18.33}$$

$$\textbf{samaritan-new-moon-after}\ (\textbf{samaritan-noon}\ (\mathit{dates}_{[n]}))$$

where

$$\mathit{g\text{-}year} = \textbf{gregorian-year-from-fixed}\ (\mathit{date})$$

$$\mathit{dates} = \textbf{julian-in-gregorian}\ (\textbf{march}, 11, \mathit{g\text{-}year} - 1)$$
$$\parallel \textbf{julian-in-gregorian}\ (\textbf{march}, 11, \mathit{g\text{-}year}) \parallel \langle \mathit{date} + 1 \rangle$$

$$n = \underset{i \geqslant 0}{\textbf{MAX}} \left\{ \begin{array}{l} \textbf{samaritan-new-moon-after} \\ \quad (\textbf{samaritan-noon}\ (\mathit{dates}_{[i]})) \leqslant \mathit{date} \end{array} \right\}$$

We search for the relevant March 11 from the list *dates*.

$$\textbf{fixed-from-samaritan}\left(\boxed{\mathit{year} \mid \mathit{month} \mid \mathit{day}}\right) \stackrel{\text{def}}{=} \tag{18.34}$$

$$\mathit{nm} + \mathit{day} - 1$$

where

$$\mathit{ny} = \textbf{samaritan-new-year-on-or-before}$$
$$\left(\left\lfloor \textbf{samaritan-epoch} + 50 + 365.25 \times \left(\mathit{year} - \left\lceil \frac{\mathit{month} - 5}{8} \right\rceil \right) \right\rfloor \right)$$

$$\mathit{nm} = \textbf{samaritan-new-moon-at-or-before}\ (\mathit{ny} + 29.5 \times (\mathit{month} - 1) + 15)$$

---

[6] Anno Samaritanorum.

In the other direction,

$$\textbf{samaritan-from-fixed}\,(date) \stackrel{\text{def}}{=} \qquad (18.35)$$

year	*month*	*day*

where

$$
\begin{aligned}
moon &= \textbf{samaritan-new-moon-at-or-before}\,(\textbf{samaritan-noon}\,(date))\\
new\text{-}year &= \textbf{samaritan-new-year-on-or-before}\,(moon)\\
month &= \text{round}\left(\frac{moon - new\text{-}year}{29.5}\right) + 1\\
year &= \text{round}\left(\tfrac{1}{365.25} \times (new\text{-}year - \textbf{samaritan-epoch})\right)\\
&\quad + \left\lceil \frac{month - 5}{8} \right\rceil\\
day &= date - moon + 1
\end{aligned}
$$

The term $\lceil(month - 5)/8\rceil$ serves to adjust for the fact that the calendar year begins with the sixth month.

The major holidays are those listed in the Pentateuch: Passover (month 1, day 14), Festival of the Unleavened Bread (month 1, days 15–21), Festival of Pentecost (the eighth Sunday after Passover), Festival of the Seventh Month (month 7, day 1), Day of Atonement (month 7, day 10), Festival of Tabernacles (month 7, days 15–21), and the Eighth Day (month 7, day 22). All holidays begin on the prior evening. There are two additional, preparatory feast days: Ṣimmut of Passover, which occurs on the Sabbath that falls seven weeks before Passover, and Ṣimmut of Tabernacles, which occurs on the Sabbath seven weeks before Tabernacles. On these days, the semi-annual calendar is delivered to the community by the high priest.

References

[1] World Council of Churches, "The Date of Easter: Science Offers Solution to Ancient Religious Problem," Press release, March 24, 1997.

[2] R. H. van Gent, "The Babylonian Calendar," `www.staff.science.uu.nl/~gent0113/babylon/babycal.htm`.

[3] M. Ilyas, *A Modern Guide to Astronomical Calculations of Islamic Calendar, Times & Qibla*, Berita Publishing, Kuala Lampur, 1984.

[4] Maimonides (= Moshe ben Maimon), *Mishneh Torah: Sefer Zemanim—Hilḥot Kiddush HaḤodesh*, 1178. Translated by S. Gandz (with commentary by J. Obermann and O. Neugebauer), as *Code of Maimonides, Book Three, Treatise Eight, Sanctification of the New Moon*, Yale Judaica Series, vol. XI, Yale University Press, New Haven, CT, 1956. Addenda and corrigenda by E. J.

Wiesenberg appear at the end of *Code of Maimonides, Book Three, The Book of Seasons*, translated by S. Gandz and H. Klein, Yale Judaica Series, vol. XIV, Yale University Press, New Haven, CT, 1961.

[5] S. J. O'Meara, "Sighting the Opposing Crescents," *Sky & Telescope*, vol. 89, p. 105, 1995.

[6] R. A. Parker and W. H. Dubberstein, *Babylonian Chronology 626 B.C.–A.D. 75*, Brown University Press, Providence, RI, fourth printing, 1971.

[7] S. Powels, "The Samaritan Calendar and the Roots of Samaritan Chronology," in *The Samaritans*, A. D. Crown, ed., Mohr, Tübingen, pp. 691–742, 1989.

[8] S. K. Shaukat, personal communication, April 2000.

[9] S. Stern, "The Babylonian Calendar," Chapter 2 in *Calendars in Antiquity: Empires, States, and Societies*, Oxford University Press, 2012.

Pottery figurines of the 12 traditional Chinese calendrical animals (terrestrial branches) excavated from a Táng Dynasty (618–907 C.E.) tomb. These figures, shown left to right in the order given on page 319, have animal faces on human bodies with long robes; such funerary use of the 12 animals is still in practice. (Image © The Metropolitan Museum of Art, New York. Image source: Art Resource, New York.)

19

The Chinese Calendar

The complexity of calendars is due simply to the incommensurability of the fundamental periods on which they are based... Calendars based on [the synodic month], depending only on lunations, make the seasons unpredictable, while calendars based on [the tropical year] cannot predict the full moons, the importance of which in ages before the introduction of artificial illuminants was considerable. The whole history of calendar-making, therefore, is that of successive attempts to reconcile the irreconcilable, and the numberless systems of intercalated months, and the like, are thus of minor scientific interest. The treatment here will therefore be deliberately brief.

Joseph Needham: *Science and Civilisation in China* (1959)[1]

The Chinese calendar is a lunisolar calendar based on astronomical events, not arithmetical rules. Days begin at civil midnight. Months are lunar, beginning on the day of the new moon and ending on the day before the next new moon. Years contain 12 or 13 such months, with the number of months determined by the number of new moons between successive winter solstices. The details of the Chinese calendar have varied greatly—there have been more than 50 calendar reforms—since its inception in the fourteenth century B.C.E.; some of its history, in particular its effect on the development of mathematics in China, is described in [14]; other historical details can be found in [6], [18], and [25].[2] The version we implement here is the 1645 version, established in the second year of the Qīng dynasty;[3] detailed calculations of earlier forms of the Chinese calendar are given in [17] (see also

[1] 作者可以不认同引文的见解

[2] The three most significant of calendar reforms were the following. In 104 B.C.E., the rule that the lunar month without a major solar term is intercalary was established (page 311), and *mean* values were used for both solar and lunar months, much like the old Hindu lunisolar calendar described in Chapter 10. In 619 C.E., the use of *true* new moons was introduced. In 1645 C.E., the use of *true* solar months was introduced.

[3] Specifically, we follow the principles of Baolin Liú, the former calendrist of the Purple Mountain Observatory, Nanjing, China, as given in [15]; for a summary of this manuscript, see [7]. Our functions accurately reproduce the third printing of [2], of which Liú is the primary author, for 1907 onward; they reproduce Xú's table [34] for 1907 onward, except for 2033; Xú used the first printing of [2], which was later corrected (Xú takes the month beginning on August 25 as a leap month, forcing the solstice into the tenth month, thus violating Liú's basic principle given on page 310).

For years 1645–1906, our functions very occasionally err because of disagreements by a few minutes in the astronomical calculations (the Chinese used seventeenth-century models of the solar system until

[24]). We discuss some common misconceptions about the Chinese calendar later in Section 19.5. The Japanese, Korean, and Vietnamese lunisolar calendars are nearly identical to the Chinese; we describe them in Sections 19.9–19.11.

19.1 Solar Terms

It is better to have no decent calendar than have Westerners in China.
Yáng Guāngxiān (1664)[4]

The Chinese year, called a nián (年), consists of true lunar months, but the arrangement of those months depends on the sun's course through the 12 zodiacal signs. Specifically, the Chinese divide the solar year into 24 solar terms or *jiéqì*: 12 *major solar terms* called *zhōngqì* (中气) and 12 *minor solar terms* known by the general term jiéqì (节气). These terms correspond to 15° segments of solar longitude, with the major terms starting at $k \times 30°$ of solar longitude and the minor terms starting at $k \times 30° + 15°$ of solar longitude, $k = 0, 1, \ldots, 11$; the names of the 24 terms are shown in Table 19.1.

The dates of the terms in Table 19.1 are only approximate; the true motion of the sun varies, and thus to implement the Chinese calendar we need to calculate the precise date of a given solar longitude. We use the solar longitude function (14.33) to determine the index of the last major solar term on or before a given date:

$$\textbf{current-major-solar-term}\,(\mathit{date}) \stackrel{\text{def}}{=} \left(2 + \left\lfloor \frac{s}{30°} \right\rfloor\right) \bmod [1 \,..\, 12] \tag{19.1}$$

where

$$s = \textbf{solar-longitude} \\ \quad (\textbf{universal-from-standard}\,(\mathit{date}, \textbf{chinese-location}\,(\mathit{date})))$$

We define

$$\textbf{chinese-location}\,(t) \stackrel{\text{def}}{=} \tag{19.2}$$

$$\begin{cases} \boxed{39°55' \mid 116°25' \mid 43.5\text{ m} \mid \frac{1397}{180}^{\text{h}}} & \textbf{if } \mathit{year} < 1929 \\ \boxed{39°55' \mid 116°25' \mid 43.5\text{ m} \mid 8^{\text{h}}} & \textbf{otherwise} \end{cases}$$

where

$$\mathit{year} = \textbf{gregorian-year-from-fixed}\,(\lfloor t \rfloor)$$

because before 1929 the local mean time of Beijing was used—since Beijing is at longitude 116°25′ east, the time difference from U.T. was $7^{\text{h}}45^{\text{m}}40^{\text{s}} = 1397/180$

1913, and thus their calculated times of solar and lunar events were not as accurate as ours); nevertheless, our calculated dates for Chinese New Year agree with Xú's table for 1644–2050.

[4] Yáng had attempted to amend the calendar, but his inadequate knowledge resulted in frequent errors [14]. He had had the Jesuits, who had—through superior astronomical calculations—achieved positions of importance in determining the calendar, framed and sentenced to death before the errors caused by his ignorance caused him to be sent into exile and the Jesuits to be released [3].

Table 19.1 The solar terms of the Chinese year: major solar terms, zhōngqì (中气), are given in boldface; minor solar terms, jiéqì (节气), are given in lightface. Adapted from [7].

Index	Chinese Name	Japanese Pronunciation	English Meaning	Solar Longitude	Approximate Starting Date
1.	Lìchūn (立春)	Risshun	Beginning of Spring	315°	February 4
1.	**Yǔshuǐ** (雨水)	Usui	**Rain Water**	**330°**	**February 19**
2.	Jīngzhé (惊蛰)	Keichitsu	Waking of Insects	345°	March 6
2.	**Chūnfēn** (春分)	Shunbun	**Spring Equinox**	**0°**	**March 21**
3.	Qīngmíng (清明)	Seimei	Pure Brightness	15°	April 5
3.	**Gǔyǔ** (谷雨)	Kokuu	**Grain Rain**	**30°**	**April 20**
4.	Lìxià (立夏)	Rikka	Beginning of Summer	45°	May 6
4.	**Xiǎomǎn** (小满)	Shōman	**Grain Full**	**60°**	**May 21**
5.	Mángzhòng (芒种)	Bōshu	Grain in Ear	75°	June 6
5.	**Xiàzhì** (夏至)	Geshi	**Summer Solstice**	**90°**	**June 21**
6.	Xiǎoshǔ (小暑)	Shōsho	Slight Heat	105°	July 7
6.	**Dàshǔ** (大暑)	Taisho	**Great Heat**	**120°**	**July 23**
7.	Lìqiū (立秋)	Risshū	Beginning of Autumn	135°	August 8
7.	**Chǔshǔ** (处暑)	Shosho	**Limit of Heat**	**150°**	**August 23**
8.	Báilù (白露)	Hakuro	White Dew	165°	September 8
8.	**Qiūfēn** (秋分)	Shūbun	**Autumnal Equinox**	**180°**	**September 23**
9.	Hánlù (寒露)	Kanro	Cold Dew	195°	October 8
9.	**Shuāngjiàng** (霜降)	Sōkō	**Descent of Frost**	**210°**	**October 24**
10.	Lìdōng (立冬)	Rittō	Beginning of Winter	225°	November 8
10.	**Xiǎoxuě** (小雪)	Shōsetsu	**Slight Snow**	**240°**	**November 22**
11.	Dàxuě (大雪)	Taisetsu	Great Snow	255°	December 7
11.	**Dōngzhì** (冬至)	Tōji	**Winter Solstice**	**270°**	**December 22**
12.	Xiǎohán (小寒)	Shōkan	Slight Cold	285°	January 6
12.	**Dàhán** (大寒)	Taikan	**Great Cold**	**300°**	**January 20**

hours. After 1928, however, China adopted the standard time zone and calendar makers used the 120° meridian, or 8 hours after U.T.[5]

Although not needed for date conversion, a printed Chinese calendar usually indicates the major and minor solar terms. The solar longitude functions in Section 14.4 also allow us to calculate the moment after the start of a given R.D. date when the solar longitude will be a given value:

$$\textbf{chinese-solar-longitude-on-or-after}\,(\lambda, t) \stackrel{\text{def}}{=} \qquad (19.3)$$

$$\textbf{standard-from-universal}\,(sun, \textbf{chinese-location}\,(sun))$$

where

$$sun = \textbf{solar-longitude-after}\,(\lambda, \textbf{universal-from-standard}\,(t, \textbf{chinese-location}\,(t)))$$

from which we can determine the start of the major solar term on or after a given date:

$$\textbf{major-solar-term-on-or-after}\,(date) \stackrel{\text{def}}{=} \qquad (19.4)$$

$$\textbf{chinese-solar-longitude-on-or-after}\,(l, date)$$

where

$$s = \textbf{solar-longitude}\,(\textbf{midnight-in-china}\,(date))$$

$$l = \left(30 \times \left\lceil \frac{s}{30} \right\rceil\right) \bmod 360$$

We can also compute the index of the last minor solar term prior to a given date:

$$\textbf{current-minor-solar-term}\,(date) \stackrel{\text{def}}{=} \qquad (19.5)$$

$$\left(3 + \left\lfloor \frac{s - 15^\circ}{30^\circ} \right\rfloor\right) \bmod [1\,..\,12]$$

where

$$s = \textbf{solar-longitude}\,(\textbf{universal-from-standard}\,(date, \textbf{chinese-location}\,(date)))$$

and the date of the minor solar term on or after a given date:

$$\textbf{minor-solar-term-on-or-after}\,(date) \stackrel{\text{def}}{=} \qquad (19.6)$$

$$\textbf{chinese-solar-longitude-on-or-after}\,(l, date)$$

[5] Actual practice for 1928 is uncertain.

where

$$s = \textbf{solar-longitude}\,(\textbf{midnight-in-china}\,(date))$$

$$l = \left(30 \times \left\lceil \frac{s - 15^\circ}{30} \right\rceil + 15^\circ\right) \bmod 360$$

One of the solar terms, the winter solstice (dōngzhì), plays a dominant role in the calendar, and we need to determine the date it occurs; because days end at civil midnight, the U.T. moment of midnight is given by

$$\textbf{midnight-in-china}\,(date) \stackrel{\text{def}}{=} \tag{19.7}$$

$$\textbf{universal-from-standard}\,(date, \textbf{chinese-location}\,(date))$$

Now, using (14.43), we have

$$\textbf{chinese-winter-solstice-on-or-before}\,(date) \stackrel{\text{def}}{=} \tag{19.8}$$

$$\underset{day \geqslant \lfloor approx \rfloor - 1}{\textbf{MIN}} \left\{ \textbf{winter} < \textbf{solar-longitude}\,(\textbf{midnight-in-china}\,(day + 1)) \right\}$$

where

$$approx = \textbf{estimate-prior-solar-longitude}\,(\textbf{winter}, \textbf{midnight-in-china}\,(date + 1))$$

19.2 Months

Although there is a very large literature, still growing almost daily, on the Chinese calendar, its interest is, we suggest, much more archaeological and historical than scientific. A calendar is only a method of combining days into periods suitable for civil life and religious or cultural observances.

Joseph Needham: *Science and Civilisation in China* (1959)

Chinese months begin on the day of the new moon in Beijing, and thus we must be able to calculate that. We use the function **new-moon-at-or-after** (see page 231) to tell us the moment in universal time of the first new moon on or after a given date and the function **standard-from-universal** to convert to standard Beijing time (Section 14.2). With these functions we can write

$$\textbf{chinese-new-moon-on-or-after}\,(date) \stackrel{\text{def}}{=} \tag{19.9}$$

$$\lfloor \textbf{standard-from-universal}\,(t, \textbf{chinese-location}\,(t)) \rfloor$$

where

$$t = \textbf{new-moon-at-or-after}\,(\textbf{midnight-in-china}\,(date))$$

Similarly, we use **new-moon-before** (page 230) in

$$\textbf{chinese-new-moon-before}\,(date) \stackrel{\text{def}}{=} \qquad (19.10)$$

$$\lfloor \textbf{standard-from-universal}\,(t, \textbf{chinese-location}\,(t)) \rfloor$$

where

$$t = \textbf{new-moon-before}\,(\textbf{midnight-in-china}\,(date))$$

Once we can calculate the solar terms and new moons, we are ready to compute the arrangement of months in a Chinese year. The basic rule that determines the calendar is

> *The winter solstice (dōngzhì) always occurs during the eleventh month of the year.*

To enforce this rule for a given Chinese year, we must examine the winter-solstice-to-winter-solstice period, called a *suì* (岁). Hence, we must compute the dates of two successive winter solstices. For example, in 1989 the winter solstice occurred at 9:23 p.m. U.T. on December 21, which was December 22 (R.D. 726458) in Beijing. The next winter solstice was at 3:08 a.m. U.T. on December 22, 1990 (R.D. 726823), which was the same date in Beijing. The list of the new moons in Beijing with R.D. dates d such that $726458 < d \leqslant 726823$ is

(i)	R.D. 726464	(December 28, 1989)
(ii)	R.D. 726494	(January 27, 1990)
(iii)	R.D. 726523	(February 25, 1990)
(iv)	R.D. 726553	(March 27, 1990)
(v)	R.D. 726582	(April 25, 1990)
(vi)	R.D. 726611	(May 24, 1990)
(vii)	R.D. 726641	(June 23, 1990)
(viii)	R.D. 726670	(July 22, 1990)
(ix)	R.D. 726699	(August 20, 1990)
(x)	R.D. 726729	(September 19, 1990)
(xi)	R.D. 726758	(October 18, 1990)
(xii)	R.D. 726788	(November 17, 1990)
(xiii)	R.D. 726818	(December 17, 1990)

These 13 dates are the beginnings of months on the Chinese calendar during the suì from December 23, 1989 to December 22, 1990.

The average length of a lunar month is about 29.53 days; the length varies from approximately 29.27 to 29.84. Because there can be 365 or 366 days between successive solstices, there will be either 12 or 13 new moons. To have fewer than 12 new moons is impossible because the longest period containing at most 11 new moons is just short of 12 consecutive lunar months and considerably less than 365 days; more than 13 new moons is also impossible because the shortest period containing at least 14 new moons contains 13 full lunar months, which is much more than 366 days. The 12 or 13 months thus found form the months following the eleventh month of the preceding Chinese year to the eleventh month of the Chinese year in question.

Months on the Chinese calendar are numbered 1 to 12; a leap month duplicates the number of the preceding month. The possible numberings of the 12 or 13 months from a winter solstice to the following winter solstice are thus as shown in Figure 19.1. It is clear from this figure that if there are only 12 new moons, they must be numbered $12, 1, 2, \ldots, 11$; but if there are 13 new moons, which one is the leap month? The answer follows from the rule that

> *The leap month of a 13-month winter-solstice-to-winter-solstice period is the first month that does not contain a major solar term—that is, the first lunar month that is wholly within a solar month.*

There *must* be such a lunar month because the period from one winter solstice to the next contains only 12 major solar terms, yet there are 13 lunar months. (This is an application of the famous "Dirichlet box principle" or "pigeonhole principle"—see, for example, [16, sec. 4.8].) A solar month can also fall entirely within a lunar month—that is, a lunar month can contain *two* major solar terms. Such an occurrence in a 13-month Chinese year can cause two or more lunar months without major solar terms; in a 12-month Chinese year it can cause one or more months without major solar terms.

We can test for a leap year by computing the year's first new moon, computing its last new moon, and rounding

$$\frac{\textit{last-new-moon} - \textit{first-new-moon}}{29.53}$$

to the nearest integer; if the value obtained is 12, the year is a leap year with 13 months.

There cannot be more than one leap month in a suì, but how do we know that a Chinese year cannot require two leap months? That is impossible because the two-solar-year period between the winter solstice of year $y - 2$ and the winter solstice of year y can contain either 24 or 25 lunar months; since the period from the winter solstice of year $y - 1$ to the winter solstice of year y has 13 months, the period from the winter solstice of year $y - 2$ to the winter solstice of year $y - 1$ can have only 12 lunar months and hence no leap month. Thus, the first month in a winter-solstice-to-winter-solstice period without a major solar term will be the leap month, and no second leap month is possible.

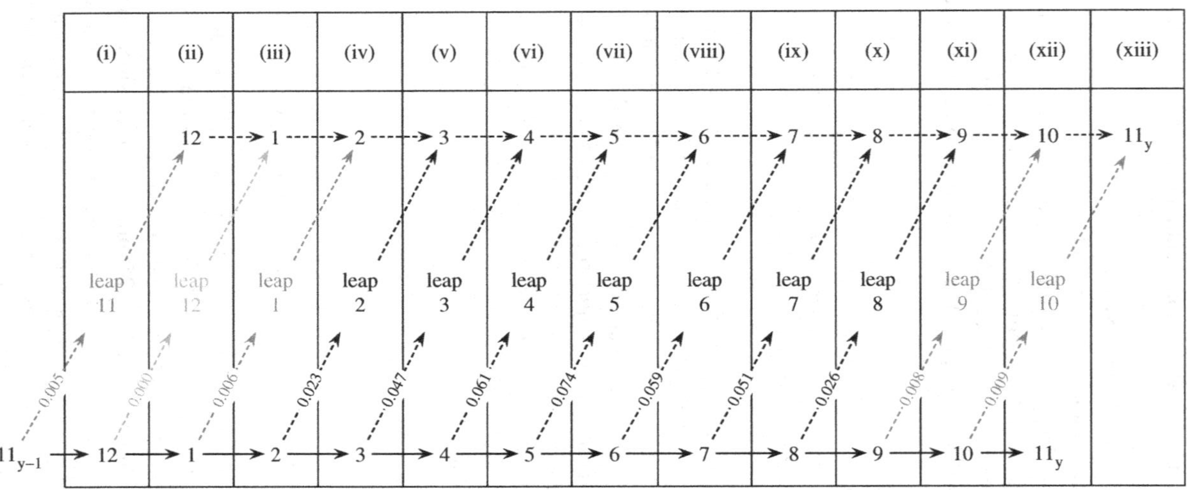

Figure 19.1 The theoretical possible numberings of the lunar months (i)–(xiii) for the Chinese calendar in the solstice-to-solstice period of year y. Each column corresponds to the new moon beginning a lunar month and contains the number of that lunar month. The winter solstice of Gregorian year $y-1$ occurs in the lunar month numbered 11_{y-1}, that is, in the month before the new moon (i), and the winter solstice for Gregorian year y occurs in the lunar month numbered 11_y, that is, in the month of the new moon (xii) or (xiii). The solid arrows show the only possible numbering when there are 12 new moons between the successive solstices. The dashed lines show possible numberings when there are 13 new moons between successive solstices. Before 1645, when *mean* solar terms were used, any month could be followed by a leap month. The relatively swift movement of the sun in the winter means that in current practice, because *true* solar terms are used, leap months 9, 10, 11, or 1 are rare (these numberings are shown in gray); leap month 12 is exceptionally rare (this rare numbering is shown in light gray). The dashed lines from a month i to a following leap month i are labeled with the approximate probability that a randomly chosen month i is followed by a leap month; these probabilities are based on data from [3] for the Chinese calendar for the thousand years 1645–2644.

To determine whether a given month lacks a major solar term, we write a function that compares the major solar term at a given date with that at the beginning of the next month:

$$\textbf{chinese-no-major-solar-term?}\,(date) \stackrel{\text{def}}{=} \qquad (19.11)$$

$$\textbf{current-major-solar-term}\,(date)$$
$$= \textbf{current-major-solar-term}\,(\textbf{chinese-new-moon-on-or-after}\,(date + 1))$$

Applying this function to the first day of a month tells us whether the month lacks a solar term. Because we want only the first month missing a major term to be a leap month, we also need the following function:

$$\textbf{chinese-prior-leap-month?}\,(m', m) \stackrel{\text{def}}{=} \qquad (19.12)$$

$$m \geqslant m' \text{ and}$$
$$\{\, \textbf{chinese-no-major-solar-term?}\,(m) \text{ or}$$
$$\textbf{chinese-prior-leap-month?}\,(m', \textbf{chinese-new-moon-before}\,(m)) \,\}$$

which determines (recursively) whether there is a Chinese leap month on or after the lunar month starting on fixed day m' and at or before the lunar month starting at fixed date m.

Figure 19.2 shows the structure of the Chinese calendar for a hypothetical year. Notice that the winter solstice is in the eleventh month, as required, and the month following the tenth month is a leap month containing no major solar term. Major terms and new moons are considered *without regard to their time of day.* Thus, for example, even if the major term, dōngzhì, occurred in Beijing *before* the new moon on that date, dōngzhì is considered to be in that month, not the previous month. In contrast, in the modern Hindu calendars (Chapter 20) the predicted time of day of an event is critical.

Continuing our example of 1989–90, we have the following dates for the major solar terms:

12.	Dàhán	R.D. 726487	(January 20, 1990)
1.	Yǔshuǐ	R.D. 726517	(February 19, 1990)
2.	Chūnfēn	R.D. 726547	(March 21, 1990)
3.	Gǔyǔ	R.D. 726577	(April 20, 1990)
4.	Xiǎomǎn	R.D. 726608	(May 21, 1990)
5.	Xiàzhì	R.D. 726639	(June 21, 1990)
6.	Dàshǔ	R.D. 726671	(July 23, 1990)
7.	Chǔshǔ	R.D. 726702	(August 23, 1990)
8.	Qiūfēn	R.D. 726733	(September 23, 1990)
9.	Shuāngjiàng	R.D. 726764	(October 24, 1990)
10.	Xiǎoxuě	R.D. 726793	(November 22, 1990)
11.	Dōngzhì	R.D. 726823	(December 22, 1990)

Collating this list with the list of new moons, we find

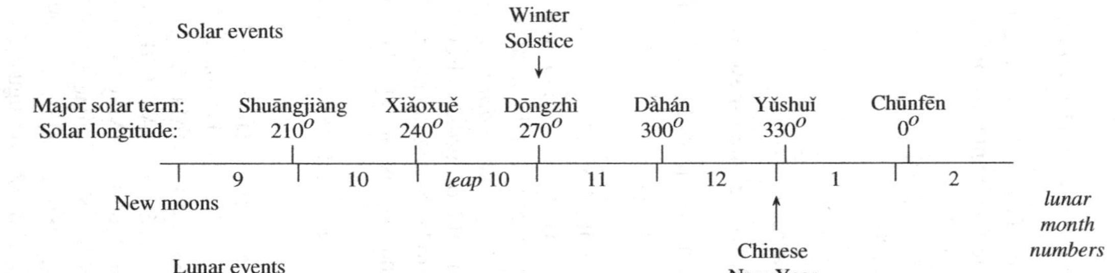

Figure 19.2 The Chinese calendar for a hypothetical year. Division into the major solar terms is shown above the time line and new moons are shown below. Solar and lunar events are specified by the day of occurrence irrespective of the exact time of day. Chinese month numbers are in italic.

	(i)	R.D. 726464	(December 28, 1989)
12.	Dàhán	R.D. 726487	(January 20, 1990)
	(ii)	R.D. 726494	(January 27, 1990)
1.	Yǔshuǐ	R.D. 726517	(February 19, 1990)
	(iii)	R.D. 726523	(February 25, 1990)
2.	Chūnfēn	R.D. 726547	(March 21, 1990)
	(iv)	R.D. 726553	(March 27, 1990)
3.	Gǔyǔ	R.D. 726577	(April 20, 1990)
	(v)	R.D. 726582	(April 25, 1990)
4.	Xiǎomǎn	R.D. 726608	(May 21, 1990)
	(vi)	R.D. 726611	(May 24, 1990)
5.	Xiàzhì	R.D. 726639	(June 21, 1990)
	(vii)	R.D. 726641	(June 23, 1990)
	(viii)	R.D. 726670	(July 22, 1990)
6.	Dàshǔ	R.D. 726671	(July 23, 1990)
	(ix)	R.D. 726699	(August 20, 1990)
7.	Chǔshǔ	R.D. 726702	(August 23, 1990)
	(x)	R.D. 726729	(September 19, 1990)
8.	Qiūfēn	R.D. 726733	(September 23, 1990)
	(xi)	R.D. 726758	(October 18, 1990)
9.	Shuāngjiàng	R.D. 726764	(October 24, 1990)
	(xii)	R.D. 726788	(November 17, 1990)
10.	Xiǎoxuě	R.D. 726793	(November 22, 1990)
	(xiii)	R.D. 726818	(December 17, 1990)
11.	Dōngzhì	R.D. 726823	(December 22, 1990)

Hence month (vii), from June 23 to July 21, 1990, is a leap month; that is, the numbering of the 13 months (i)–(xiii) must be (see Figure 19.1)

Month 12	R.D. 726464	(December 28, 1989)
Month 1	R.D. 726494	(January 27, 1990)
Month 2	R.D. 726523	(February 25, 1990)
Month 3	R.D. 726553	(March 27, 1990)
Month 4	R.D. 726582	(April 25, 1990)
Month 5	R.D. 726611	(May 24, 1990)
Leap month 5	R.D. 726641	(June 23, 1990)
Month 6	R.D. 726670	(July 22, 1990)
Month 7	R.D. 726699	(August 20, 1990)
Month 8	R.D. 726729	(September 19, 1990)
Month 9	R.D. 726758	(October 18, 1990)
Month 10	R.D. 726788	(November 17, 1990)
Month 11	R.D. 726818	(December 17, 1990)

Thus the date of the Chinese New Year in this suì is found to be R.D. 726494.

Describing the process outlined above algorithmically, we find the Chinese New Year in the suì containing *date*:

chinese-new-year-in-sui (*date*) $\stackrel{\text{def}}{=}$ (19.13)

$$\begin{cases} \textbf{chinese-new-moon-on-or-after}\,(m_{13}+1) \\ \qquad \textbf{if}\ \text{round}\left(\dfrac{\textit{next-}m_{11}-m_{12}}{\textbf{mean-synodic-month}}\right)=12\ \text{and} \\ \qquad\quad \{\,\textbf{chinese-no-major-solar-term?}\,(m_{12})\ \text{or} \\ \qquad\quad\ \ \textbf{chinese-no-major-solar-term?}\,(m_{13})\,\} \\ m_{13} \quad \textbf{otherwise} \end{cases}$$

where

$$\begin{aligned} s_1 &= \textbf{chinese-winter-solstice-on-or-before}\,(\textit{date}) \\ s_2 &= \textbf{chinese-winter-solstice-on-or-before}\,(s_1+370) \\ m_{12} &= \textbf{chinese-new-moon-on-or-after}\,(s_1+1) \\ m_{13} &= \textbf{chinese-new-moon-on-or-after}\,(m_{12}+1) \\ \textit{next-}m_{11} &= \textbf{chinese-new-moon-before}\,(s_2+1) \end{aligned}$$

This latter function allows us to find the Chinese New Year on or before a given *date*:

$$\textbf{chinese-new-year-on-or-before}\,(\textit{date}) \stackrel{\text{def}}{=} \tag{19.14}$$

$$\begin{cases} \textit{new-year} & \textbf{if}\ \textit{date} \geqslant \textit{new-year} \\ \textbf{chinese-new-year-in-sui}\,(\textit{date}-180) & \textbf{otherwise} \end{cases}$$

where

$$\textit{new-year} = \textbf{chinese-new-year-in-sui}\,(\textit{date})$$

We first find the Chinese New Year in the suì containing the given *date*; if that New Year is after *date* (which can happen if *date* is late in the Chinese year), we go back to the previous suì.

19.3 Conversions to and from Fixed Dates

Ancient Chinese texts say that "the calendar and the pitch pipes have such a close fit, that you could not slip a hair between them."

Giorgio de Santillana and Hertha von Dechend: *Hamlet's Mill* (1969)

By tradition, Chinese years go in cycles of 60, each year having a special sexagenary name (discussed in the next section); the first year of the first cycle commences in year −2636 (Gregorian). Thus we define

$$\textbf{chinese-epoch} \stackrel{\text{def}}{=} \tag{19.15}$$

$$\textbf{fixed-from-gregorian}\left(\boxed{-2636 \mid \textbf{february} \mid 15}\right)$$

This is the traditional date of the first use of the sexagesimal cycle, February 15, −2636 (Gregorian) = March 8, 2637 B.C.E. (Julian).

Although it is not traditional to count these cycles, we do so for convenience to identify a year uniquely. The conversion between Chinese dates and R.D. dates can now be done by a method nearly identical to our function **chinese-new-year-in-sui**. Notice that most of the work lies in determining the month number and whether it is a leap month:

$$\textbf{chinese-from-fixed}\,(\mathit{date}) \stackrel{\text{def}}{=} \tag{19.16}$$

cycle	*year*	*month*	*leap-month*	*day*

where

$$
\begin{aligned}
s_1 &= \textbf{chinese-winter-solstice-on-or-before}\,(\mathit{date})\\
s_2 &= \textbf{chinese-winter-solstice-on-or-before}\,(s_1 + 370)\\
m_{12} &= \textbf{chinese-new-moon-on-or-after}\,(s_1 + 1)\\
\mathit{next}\text{-}m_{11} &= \textbf{chinese-new-moon-before}\,(s_2 + 1)\\
m &= \textbf{chinese-new-moon-before}\,(\mathit{date} + 1)\\
\mathit{leap}\text{-}\mathit{year} &= \text{round}\left(\frac{\mathit{next}\text{-}m_{11} - m_{12}}{\textbf{mean-synodic-month}}\right) = 12\\
\mathit{month} &= \left(\text{round}\left(\frac{m - m_{12}}{\textbf{mean-synodic-month}}\right) - \begin{cases} 1 & \textbf{if } \mathit{leap}\text{-}\mathit{year} \text{ and } \textbf{chinese-prior-leap-month?}\,(m_{12}, m)\\ 0 & \textbf{otherwise}\end{cases}\right) \bmod [1\,..\,12]\\
\mathit{leap}\text{-}\mathit{month} &= \mathit{leap}\text{-}\mathit{year} \text{ and } \textbf{chinese-no-major-solar-term?}\,(m) \text{ and}\\
&\quad\ \text{not } \textbf{chinese-prior-leap-month?}\,(m_{12}, \textbf{chinese-new-moon-before}\,(m))\\
\mathit{elapsed}\text{-}\mathit{years} &= \left\lfloor 1.5 - \frac{\mathit{month}}{12} + \frac{\mathit{date} - \textbf{chinese-epoch}}{\textbf{mean-tropical-year}} \right\rfloor\\
\mathit{cycle} &= \left\lfloor \frac{1}{60} \times (\mathit{elapsed}\text{-}\mathit{years} - 1) \right\rfloor + 1\\
\mathit{year} &= \mathit{elapsed}\text{-}\mathit{years} \bmod [1\,..\,60]\\
\mathit{day} &= \mathit{date} - m + 1
\end{aligned}
$$

The calculation of *elapsed-years* is done by finding the elapsed years to the midsummer of the desired Chinese year so that the irregular character of leap years cannot affect the truncation.

Finally, to convert a Chinese date to an R.D. date, we find a midyear date of the given cycle and year, then find the prior Chinese New Year, go forward to the appropriate month, and add the day of the month:

$$\textbf{fixed-from-chinese}\left(\boxed{\mathit{cycle} \mid \mathit{year} \mid \mathit{month} \mid \mathit{leap} \mid \mathit{day}}\right) \stackrel{\text{def}}{=} \qquad (19.17)$$

$$\mathit{prior\text{-}new\text{-}moon} + \mathit{day} - 1$$

where

$$\mathit{mid\text{-}year} = \left\lfloor \textbf{chinese-epoch} + \left((\mathit{cycle} - 1) \times 60 + \mathit{year} - 1 + \frac{1}{2}\right) \times \textbf{mean-tropical-year} \right\rfloor$$

$$\mathit{new\text{-}year} = \textbf{chinese-new-year-on-or-before}\,(\mathit{mid\text{-}year})$$

$$p = \textbf{chinese-new-moon-on-or-after}\,(\mathit{new\text{-}year} + (\mathit{month} - 1) \times 29)$$

$$d = \textbf{chinese-from-fixed}\,(p)$$

$$\mathit{prior\text{-}new\text{-}moon} = \begin{cases} p & \textbf{if } \mathit{month} = d_{\textbf{month}} \text{ and } \mathit{leap} = d_{\textbf{leap}} \\ \textbf{chinese-new-moon-on-or-after}\,(p + 1) & \textbf{otherwise} \end{cases}$$

19.4 Sexagesimal Cycle of Names

The learned and indefatigable missionaries in China, to whose labours and researches the history and antiquities of that country are so much indebted ... have taken it for granted, that the lunar calendar, of the time of Confucius, or of the times to which these observations refer, and the sexagesimal cycle also, mutatis mutandis *were absolutely one and the same with the lunar calendar, and with the sexagesimal cycle, of their own time. This assumption was a great mistake: and it could not fail to lead them wrong, in their attempts to verify and confirm these eclipses in particular.*

Edward Greswell: *On the Two Miracles, Affecting the Sun, in the Time of Joshua, and in the Time of Hezekiah, Respectively: and on their Effect upon the Measures of Time in General, and on the Lunar Measure of Time in Particular, and on the Precession of the Equinoxes* (1847)

The Chinese calendar uses a cycle of 60 names (see [26] for a history of their ritual foundations) for years. The name is formed by combining a *celestial stem*, tiān gān (天干), with a *terrestrial branch*, dì zhī (地支). The celestial stems,

(1) Jiǎ (甲)	(6) Jǐ (己)
(2) Yǐ (乙)	(7) Gēng (庚)
(3) Bǐng (丙)	(8) Xīn (辛)
(4) Dīng (丁)	(9) Rén (壬)
(5) Wù (戊)	(10) Guǐ (癸)

are untranslatable, though they are sometimes associated with the 5 elements (tree, fire, earth, metal, and water), each in its male and female form. These stems have another use as well—they correspond to "A, B, C, D, ..." For example, because written Chinese uses word symbols, rather than an alphabet, jiǎ, yǐ, bǐng, and dīng are used as letter grades on Chinese exam papers.

The terrestrial branches

(1) Zǐ (子)	(Rat)	(7) Wǔ (午)	(Horse)
(2) Chǒu (丑)	(Ox)	(8) Wèi (未)	(Sheep)
(3) Yín (寅)	(Tiger)	(9) Shēn (申)	(Monkey)
(4) Mǎo (卯)	(Hare)	(10) Yǒu (酉)	(Fowl)
(5) Chén (辰)	(Dragon)	(11) Xū (戌)	(Dog)
(6) Sì (巳)	(Snake)	(12) Hài (亥)	(Pig)

are also untranslatable; the English names—traditional animal totems—given for the 12 branches corresponding to the years of the Chinese "Zodiac" are not translations from the Chinese.

The names are assigned sequentially, running through the decimal and duodenary lists simultaneously. The first name is jiǎzǐ, the second is yǐchǒu, the third is bǐngyín, and so on. Because the least common multiple of 10 and 12 is 60, the cycle of names repeats after the sixtieth name, guǐhài. Representing the name as a pair of numbers giving the celestial stem and the terrestrial branch (which must have the same parity), respectively, and using equation (1.70), we can thus obtain the nth name of the sexagenary cycle of names by means of the function

$$\textbf{chinese-sexagesimal-name}\,(n) \stackrel{\text{def}}{=} \boxed{n \bmod [1\,..\,10]}\boxed{n \bmod [1\,..\,12]} \tag{19.18}$$

Determining the number of names from the sexagesimal name $\boxed{\mathit{stem}_1 \mid \mathit{branch}_1}$ to the next occurrence of the sexagesimal name $\boxed{\mathit{stem}_2 \mid \mathit{branch}_2}$ is an instance of formula (1.74):

$$\textbf{chinese-name-difference}\left(\boxed{\mathit{stem}_1 \mid \mathit{branch}_1}, \boxed{\mathit{stem}_2 \mid \mathit{branch}_2}\right) \stackrel{\text{def}}{=} \tag{19.19}$$

$$(\,\mathit{stem\text{-}difference} + 25 \times (\mathit{branch\text{-}difference} - \mathit{stem\text{-}difference})\,) \bmod [1\,..\,60]$$

where

$$\mathit{stem\text{-}difference} = \mathit{stem}_2 - \mathit{stem}_1$$
$$\mathit{branch\text{-}difference} = \mathit{branch}_2 - \mathit{branch}_1$$

Because the name of the first year of any cycle is jiǎzǐ, the name of the Chinese *year* in any cycle is given by

$$\textbf{chinese-year-name}\,(\mathit{year}) \stackrel{\text{def}}{=} \qquad (19.20)$$

$$\textbf{chinese-sexagesimal-name}\,(\mathit{year})$$

This representation can be inverted to give the year within a cycle corresponding to a given sexagesimal name by using formula (1.74).

At one time the Chinese used the same sequence of 60 names to name months and days as well. Extrapolating backward from known dates, we find the number of elapsed months on the Chinese calendar at the start of a name cycle to be

$$\textbf{chinese-month-name-epoch} \stackrel{\text{def}}{=} 57 \qquad (19.21)$$

Because leap months were unnamed, we can write

$$\textbf{chinese-month-name}\,(\mathit{month}, \mathit{year}) \stackrel{\text{def}}{=} \qquad (19.22)$$

$$\textbf{chinese-sexagesimal-name}\\ (\mathit{elapsed\text{-}months} - \textbf{chinese-month-name-epoch})$$

where

$$\mathit{elapsed\text{-}months} = 12 \times (\mathit{year} - 1) + \mathit{month} - 1$$

For days, the repeating sequence of 60 names acts like a "week." We find that a day-cycle began on R.D. 46, so that day 0 (or, 60) of the cycle is:

$$\textbf{chinese-day-name-epoch} \stackrel{\text{def}}{=} \text{R.D. } 45 \qquad (19.23)$$

which allows us to write

$$\textbf{chinese-day-name}\,(\mathit{date}) \stackrel{\text{def}}{=} \qquad (19.24)$$

$$\textbf{chinese-sexagesimal-name}\,(\mathit{date} - \textbf{chinese-day-name-epoch})$$

Just as we did for the 7-day week in **kday-on-or-before**, we can apply formula (1.63) to compute the R.D. date of the last date with a given sexagesimal name on or before a given R.D. date:

$$\textbf{chinese-day-name-on-or-before}\,(\mathit{name}, \mathit{date}) \stackrel{\text{def}}{=} \qquad (19.25)$$

$$\textbf{chinese-name-difference}\,(\textbf{chinese-day-name}\,(0), \mathit{name})\\ \bmod [\mathit{date} \mathinner{\ldotp\ldotp} \mathit{date} - 60)$$

The 60-element cycle of stem-branch combinations is applied to Chinese hours as well as to years, months, and days. Because the Chinese hours are intervals that are 2 ordinary hours in length (from odd hour to odd hour), the 60-element cycle repeats in 5 days, and the 12-element cycle of branches repeats daily from 11 p.m. to 11 p.m. The 12 branches are therefore used on Chinese medicine labels—the herbalist tells the patient to take the medicine every day in time slots yín and shēn, for example.

19.5 Common Misconceptions

Cuiusvis hominis est errare; nullius nisi insipientis in errore perseverare. [*Any man can make a mistake; only a fool keeps making the same one.*]

Attributed to Cicero

Not much has been written in Western languages about the Chinese calendar, but much of what has been written is ill-informed, out of date, oversimplified, or wrong.

For instance, it is not true that the 19-year Metonic cycle is used to determine leap years; for example, the Chinese year 4664 (overlapping Gregorian years 1966–67) was a leap year but, 19 years later, the Chinese year 4683 (overlapping Gregorian years 1985–86) was a common year. Since 1645 the true, not the mean, behavior of the moon and sun is used in calculations and, as a consequence, months 11 and 12 can be followed by a leap month (rarely—but it can happen: in 2033 on the Chinese calendar there will be a leap month 11 and in 1890 on the Japanese lunisolar calendar, identical to the Chinese except for the location at which the calculations are done, there was a leap month 12). Thus, Chinese New Year is *not* always the second new moon after the winter solstice, as is sometimes claimed (in [33], for example). Far enough in the future, as the perihelion moves, winter leap months will become more and more common, including leap twelfth months.

There is a popular "rule" that says that Chinese New Year is the new moon closest to lìchūn (the beginning of spring), which occurs on approximately February 4 (see, for example, [22]). Most of the time this is true, but if there is a new moon around January 21 (and hence again around February 20), the rule is difficult to apply. In such close situations the rule can fail, as it did for 1985.

It is not traditional to count cycles or years; years are generally given as regnal years and by sexagesimal name. Our code describes the Chinese New Year that began on January 28, 1998 as year 15 in cycle 78, making it year $60\times(78-1)+15 = 4635$ in Chinese chronology. This era agrees with that used in Fritsche [8]. However, the popular press at the time described that new Chinese year as year 4696. The difference in year numbers stems from different choices of epoch and a likely error in calculation. We chose the traditional date of the first use of the sexagesimal cycle, February 15, −2636 (Gregorian) = March 8, 2637 B.C.E. (Julian); hence $1998 - (-2636) = 4634$ Chinese years elapsed prior to January 28, 1998. Others, including Sun Yat-sen, choose to number years from 2697 B.C.E., the first year of Emperor Huángdì, the traditional ancestor of the Chinese nation; this starting point would correctly give 4694 elapsed years as of January 28, 1998. Then, erroneously adding 1 to compensate for a year 0 on the Gregorian calendar gives 4695 elapsed years and hence year number 4696, as reported in the press. In any case, because the epoch in 2637 B.C.E. corresponds to year 61 of Huángdì, the sexagesimal name of a Chinese year is independent of the epoch.

The calculations are done for the 120° east meridian (after 1928). Calendars for other Asian countries may use other points of reference—see Section 19.9, for example.

19.6 Holidays

Please note ... Islamic and Chinese new year dates are approximate.[6]
American Express Publishing Company: *1995 Pocket Diary*

The last day of the Chinese lunisolar year, followed by the first day of the next year, is a major celebration on the Chinese calendar. We have already seen how to determine the Chinese New Year on or before a given fixed date. It is easy to use this to determine Chinese New Year in a given Gregorian year:

$$\textbf{chinese-new-year}\,(g\text{-}year) \stackrel{\text{def}}{=} \tag{19.26}$$

$$\textbf{chinese-new-year-on-or-before}\left(\textbf{fixed-from-gregorian}\left(\boxed{g\text{-}year \mid \textbf{july} \mid 1}\right)\right)$$

We ask for the New Year on or before a summer date because that New Year is the one found in the first suì examined in **chinese-new-year-on-or-before**. The more obvious choice of asking for the New Year on or before December 31 results in two suìs being examined because December 31 always falls at the end of the Chinese year.

Chinese New Year falls in the range January 21 through February 21 on the Gregorian calendar. Figure 19.3 shows the relative frequency with which it falls on the various Gregorian dates for 1645–2644.

Because the Chinese calendar is consistently aligned with the sufficiently accurate Gregorian calendar, the determination of holidays is handled, as on the Hebrew calendar, by observing that fixed dates on the Chinese calendar occur in fixed seasons of the year. Specifically,

$$\begin{aligned}&\text{Chinese New Year occurring in the winter of Gregorian year } y\\ &\qquad = y + 1 - \textbf{gregorian-year-from-fixed}(\textbf{chinese-epoch})\end{aligned}$$

For example, the Chinese year that began in the winter of year 0 (Gregorian) was 2637 (cycle 44, year 57). This means that holidays occurring in the spring, summer, and fall of Gregorian year y occur in the Chinese year $y+2637$, whereas holidays in the winter occur in either Chinese year $y+2637$ or $y+2636$, depending on whether they are before or after January 1; such holidays need to be handled like Islamic holidays (Section 7.2).

---

[6] In the next section we will see that Chinese New Year can be determined exactly, in contrast with the observation-based Islamic New Year (Section 18.3), which cannot.

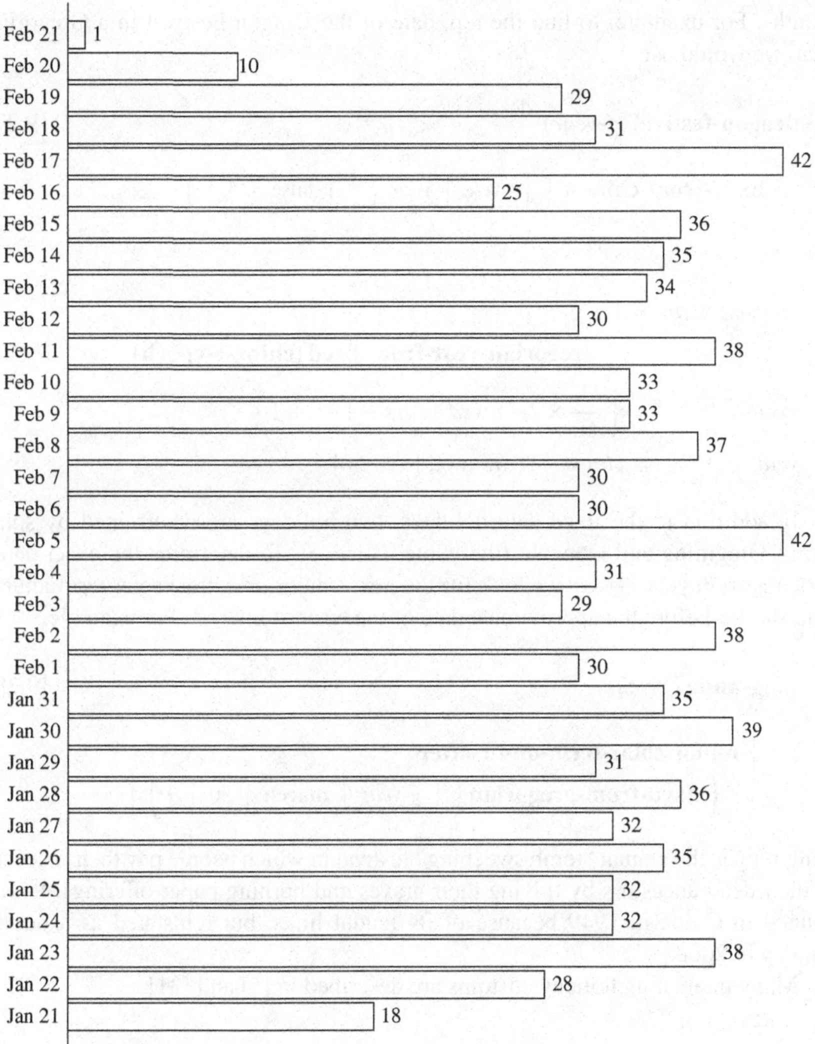

Figure 19.3 Distribution of Chinese New Year dates, 1645–2644 (suggested by Helmer Aslaksen). The single year that has Chinese New Year on February 21 is 2319.

Aside from Chinese New Year, the main fixed-Chinese-date holidays on the Chinese calendar are the Lantern Festival (fifteenth day of first month); the Dragon Festival (fifth day of the fifth month); Qǐqiǎo or Qīxī, called "Chinese Valentine's Day" (seventh day of the seventh month); Hungry Ghosts (fifteenth day of the seventh month); the Mid-Autumn Festival (fifteenth day of the eighth month); and the Double-Ninth Festival (ninth day of the ninth month). Buddha's Birthday is celebrated in many Asian countries on the eighth day of the fourth month of the Chinese calendar, but the date of observance is not uniform (in Japan, for instance, it is celebrated as the "Flower Festival" on April 8). Holidays are never observed in leap months. For example, to find the R.D. date of the Dragon Festival in a Gregorian year, we would use

$$\textbf{dragon-festival}\,(\textit{g-year}) \stackrel{\text{def}}{=} \tag{19.27}$$

$$\textbf{fixed-from-chinese}\left(\boxed{\textit{cycle} \mid \textit{year} \mid 5 \mid \text{false} \mid 5}\right)$$

where

$$\begin{aligned}
\textit{elapsed-years} &= 1 + \textit{g-year} \\
&\quad - \textbf{gregorian-year-from-fixed}\,(\textbf{chinese-epoch}) \\
\textit{cycle} &= \left\lfloor \frac{1}{60} \times (\textit{elapsed-years} - 1) \right\rfloor + 1 \\
\textit{year} &= \textit{elapsed-years} \bmod [1 \,..\, 60]
\end{aligned}$$

In addition to the fixed-date holidays, two holidays are determined by solar terms, Qīngmíng and Dōngzhì (the winter solstice). To determine the exact dates for Gregorian year *g-year* we look for the next (major or minor) solar term after a date shortly before the approximate date of the term of interest. For example,

$$\textbf{qing-ming}\,(\textit{g-year}) \stackrel{\text{def}}{=} \tag{19.28}$$

$$\left\lfloor \textbf{minor-solar-term-on-or-after} \left(\textbf{fixed-from-gregorian}\left(\boxed{\textit{g-year} \mid \textbf{march} \mid 30}\right)\right)\right\rfloor$$

Qīngmíng is the annual "tomb sweeping" festival in which people pay their respects to their dead ancestors by tidying their graves and burning paper offerings. It was banned in China in 1949 because of its feudal links, but reinstated as a public holiday in 2008.

Many interesting holiday customs are described in [5] and [31].

19.7 Chinese Age

Since the system of counting age differs in English and Chinese, "-years old" is only an approximate rendering.

Elizabeth Latimore Boyle and Pauline Ng Delbridge:
Cantonese: Basic Course

According to the Chinese custom, a person's age is considered to be 1 immediately at birth; a person becomes a year older with each subsequent Chinese New Year, and thus a child born a week before the New Year is considered to be age 2 a week after birth! This difference in the meaning of "age" has caused difficulties in gathering and interpreting sociological data [23]. To compute the age of a person according to this custom, given the Chinese date of birth and the present fixed *date*, we would use

$$\textbf{chinese-age}\,(\mathit{birthdate}, \mathit{date}) \stackrel{\text{def}}{=} \tag{19.29}$$

$$\begin{cases} 60 \times (\mathit{today}_{\textbf{cycle}} - \mathit{birthdate}_{\textbf{cycle}}) + \mathit{today}_{\textbf{year}} - \mathit{birthdate}_{\textbf{year}} + 1 \\ \qquad \textbf{if } \mathit{date} \geqslant \textbf{fixed-from-chinese}\,(\mathit{birthdate}) \\ \textbf{bogus} \quad \textbf{otherwise} \end{cases}$$

where

$$\mathit{today} = \textbf{chinese-from-fixed}\,(\mathit{date})$$

19.8 Chinese Marriage Auguries

I am only sorry that my daughter has so little merit, and that she has not had all the education desirable. I fear she is good for nothing, yet, nevertheless, since the augury is favourable, I dare not disobey you, and I accept your present, I salute you, and I consent to the day appointed for the wedding.

The Guernsey Magazine: A Monthly Illustrated Journal of Useful Information, Instruction, and Entertainment (1877)

Chinese years that do not contain the minor term Lìchūn ("Beginning of Spring" around February 4) are called "widow" years or "double-blind" years and are deemed unlucky for marriage. Because of the lunisolar nature of the Chinese calendar, widow years occur about 7 times in 19 years, mimicking the Metonic cycle; for example, 2005, 2008, and 2010 are widow years. By contrast, years in which Lìchūn occurs both at the start of the year and at the end (which also happens about 7 times in 19 years) are "double-bright" years and offer "double happiness" for newlyweds; 2004, 2006, and 2009 are such years, for example. Years missing the first Lìchūn but containing the second are "blind"; years containing the first but not the second are called "bright." Let 3 mean a double-bright year, 2 a bright year, 1 a blind year, and 0 a widow year:

$$\textbf{double-bright} \stackrel{\text{def}}{=} 3 \tag{19.30}$$

$$\textbf{bright} \stackrel{\text{def}}{=} 2 \tag{19.31}$$

$$\textbf{blind} \stackrel{\text{def}}{=} 1 \tag{19.32}$$

$$\textbf{widow} \stackrel{\text{def}}{=} 0 \tag{19.33}$$

We can determine the character of a year on the Chinese calendar from

$$\textbf{chinese-year-marriage-augury}\,(\mathit{cycle}, \mathit{year}) \stackrel{\text{def}}{=} \tag{19.34}$$

$$\begin{cases} \textbf{widow} & \textbf{if } \mathit{first\text{-}minor\text{-}term} = 1 \text{ and } \mathit{next\text{-}first\text{-}minor\text{-}term} = 12 \\ \textbf{blind} & \textbf{if } \mathit{first\text{-}minor\text{-}term} = 1 \text{ and } \mathit{next\text{-}first\text{-}minor\text{-}term} \neq 12 \\ \textbf{bright} & \textbf{if } \mathit{first\text{-}minor\text{-}term} \neq 1 \text{ and } \mathit{next\text{-}first\text{-}minor\text{-}term} = 12 \\ \textbf{double-bright} & \textbf{otherwise} \end{cases}$$

where

$$\begin{aligned}
\textit{new-year} &= \textbf{fixed-from-chinese}\left(\boxed{\textit{cycle} \mid \textit{year} \mid 1 \mid \text{false} \mid 1}\right) \\
c &= \begin{cases} \textit{cycle} + 1 & \textbf{if } \textit{year} = 60 \\ \textit{cycle} & \textbf{otherwise} \end{cases} \\
y &= \begin{cases} 1 & \textbf{if } \textit{year} = 60 \\ \textit{year} + 1 & \textbf{otherwise} \end{cases} \\
\textit{next-new-year} &= \textbf{fixed-from-chinese}\left(\boxed{c \mid y \mid 1 \mid \text{false} \mid 1}\right) \\
\textit{first-minor-term} &= \textbf{current-minor-solar-term}\,(\textit{new-year}) \\
\textit{next-first-minor-term} &= \textbf{current-minor-solar-term}\,(\textit{next-new-year})
\end{aligned}$$

19.9 The Japanese Calendar

It has often been remarked that the Japanese do many things in a way that runs directly counter to European ideas of what is natural and proper. To the Japanese themselves our ways appear equally unaccountable.

B. H. Chamberlain:: *Things Japanese* (1911)[7]

The development of calendars in Japan closely paralleled that in China with similar improvements to the traditional Japanese calendar in years following those improvements to the Chinese calendar. For example, the use of true new moons began in China in 619 C.E., but in Japan in 697 C.E.; true solar months have been used in the Chinese calendar since 1645 and in the Japanese calendar since 1798. Since 1844, the traditional Japanese calendar has followed the principles described in this chapter except that the calculations are based on locations in Japan. Although Japan officially changed over to the Gregorian calendar in 1873, the traditional calendar continues to be published and used, if only for astrological purposes. During 1873–1887 calculations were done using Tokyo's longitude, 139°46′ east, which is $9^{h}19^{m}4^{s}$ ($= 9\frac{143}{450}$) after U.T. Since 1888, longitude 135° east (9 hours after U.T.) has been used. Thus, we define

$$\textbf{japanese-location}\,(t) \stackrel{\text{def}}{=} \qquad (19.35)$$

$$\begin{cases} \boxed{35.7^\circ \mid 139^\circ 46' \mid 24\text{ m} \mid 9\frac{143}{450}^{\text{h}}} & \textbf{if } \textit{year} < 1888 \\ \boxed{35^\circ \mid 135^\circ \mid 0\text{ m} \mid 9^{\text{h}}} & \textbf{otherwise} \end{cases}$$

where

$$\textit{year} = \textbf{gregorian-year-from-fixed}\,(\lfloor t \rfloor)$$

As with the Chinese calendar, the sexagesimal cycles are not numbered. Rather, years are given according to the *nengō system*; this is a system of eras, the most recent of which are

[7] 筆者らは，必ずしも引用に同意というわけではない．

Heisei (平成)	January 8, 1989–
Showa (昭和)	December 26, 1925–January 7, 1989
Taisho (大正)	July 31, 1912–December 25, 1925
Meiji (明治)	January 1, 1869–July 30, 1912
Keio (慶應)	April 7, 1865–December 31, 1868

The nengō changes when the emperor dies, even if that occurs in the middle of the year. Some tables (like [18]) give not only nengō years but also the *kigen*, a count of years since the mythological founding of the Japanese empire in 660 B.C.E. by Emperor Jimmu Tennō. Months are numbered as in Chinese; solar terms are given by the Chinese ideograms in Table 19.1, but they are pronounced using Japanese pronunciation of the Chinese characters.

To calculate the Japanese calendar, we just replace **chinese-location** with **japanese-location** throughout our functions for the Chinese calendar and change the epoch. The results match those in [20], which covers the period 1873–2050.[8] For earlier years, our results approximate those in [32] for 1844–1872 fairly well.[9] The Japanese dates given in [34] are untrustworthy.

The function **chinese-age** also conforms to the Japanese system of determining age in the "kazoe doshi" (literally, "counted-year") system.

19.10 The Korean Calendar[10]

This information is, of course, partially erroneous, since the Korean calendar conformed precisely with the Chinese.

George McAfee McCune: *Korean Relations with China and Japan, 1800–1864* (1941)

During the Chosun dynasty, 1392–1897, Korea used the Chinese calendar for reference but did their own independent calculations. In 1896 Korea adopted the Gregorian calendar, but a Korean form of the Chinese calendar is still used traditionally.[11] The geographic location currently used for computations of solar terms and lunar phases is the Seoul City Hall at latitude 37°34′ north and longitude 126°58′ east (9 hours after U.T.). Prior to April 1, 1908 local mean time was used;

---

[8] Except for 1947; Nishizawa [20] follows the published calendar for 1947, which erroneously had a leap month 3 instead of a leap month 2 as the rules would dictate (in fact, the correct time is given for Gŭyŭ in [20] but is inconsistent with the calendar there!). Nishizawa [21] suggests that the erroneous calendar occurred because of post-war confusion. Our algorithms give the "correct" calendar.

[9] Perfectly from 1860 onward but with occasional minor errors in 1844–1859, except for a major disagreement from the end of 1851 to the spring of 1852. Such disagreement is not surprising because, during 1844–1872, the Japanese calendar was based on *apparent time* whereas our functions use *local mean time*. Furthermore, as with the Chinese calendar before the twentieth century, the astronomical models used for the Japanese calendar in the nineteenth century are less accurate than our astronomical functions.

[10] Based on information provided by S. Sohn [27] of the Korea Astronomy & Space Science Institute.

[11] The most reliable tables of the Korean calendar for the modern era are found in [1]. These tables, however have two peculiarities. All calculations for years after 1911 were made using the time zone U.T.+9. For 1900–1911 the tables were taken from calendars of that period, but all times given for solar terms were computed using U.T.+9 (rather than either local mean time or U.T.+8.5), except for eight scattered dates in 1903–1911 in which U.T.+8 was used to give agreement with old records. Because of this situation, the calendar as computed by our Chinese calendar functions together with **korean-location** gives perfect agreement with [1] for all dates after 1911 until August 9, 1961 *except* March 21, 1954.

for some intervals since then, 8.5 hours after U.T. was used as the time zone (from April 1, 1908 to December 31, 1911 and from March 21, 1954 until August 9, 1961). Thus, to implement the Korean calendar we use

$$\textbf{korean-location}\,(t) \stackrel{\text{def}}{=} \boxed{37°34' \mid 126°58' \mid 0\text{ m} \mid z^{\text{h}}} \tag{19.36}$$

where

$$z = \begin{cases} \frac{3809}{450} & \textbf{if } t < \textbf{fixed-from-gregorian}\left(\boxed{1908 \mid \textbf{april} \mid 1}\right) \\ 8.5 & \textbf{if } t < \textbf{fixed-from-gregorian}\left(\boxed{1912 \mid \textbf{january} \mid 1}\right) \\ 9 & \textbf{if } t < \textbf{fixed-from-gregorian}\left(\boxed{1954 \mid \textbf{march} \mid 21}\right) \\ 8.5 & \textbf{if } t < \textbf{fixed-from-gregorian}\left(\boxed{1961 \mid \textbf{august} \mid 10}\right) \\ 9 & \textbf{otherwise} \end{cases}$$

Years on the Korean calendar are counted on the "Danki system," counting from 2333 B.C.E., the traditional year of the founding of Go-Chosun, the first Korean nation. In terms of the Chinese cycle and year numbers, the Danki year number is given by

$$\textbf{korean-year}\,(cycle, year) \stackrel{\text{def}}{=} 60 \times cycle + year - 364 \tag{19.37}$$

The solar terms are as follows in Korean (the translations are the same as those given in Table 19.1 on page 307):

1.	Ip-Chun (입춘)	315°	7.	Ip-Choo (입추)	135°
1.	**Woo-Soo** (우수)	**330°**	**7.**	**Chu-Suh** (처서)	**150°**
2.	Kyung-Chip (경칩)	345°	8.	Bak-Roo (백로)	165°
2.	**Chun-Bun** (춘분)	**0°**	**8.**	**Chu-Bun** (추분)	**180°**
3.	Chyng-Myung (청명)	15°	9.	Han-Roo (한로)	195°
3.	**Gok-Woo** (곡우)	**30°**	**9.**	**Sang-Kang** (상강)	**210°**
4.	Ip-Ha (입하)	45°	10.	Ip-Dong (입동)	225°
4.	**So-Man** (소만)	**60°**	**10.**	**So-Sul** (소설)	**240°**
5.	Mang-Jong (망종)	75°	11.	Dae-Sul (대설)	255°
5.	**Ha-Ji** (하지)	**90°**	**11.**	**Dong-Ji** (동지)	**270°**
6.	So-Suh (소서)	105°	12.	So-Han (소한)	285°
6.	**Dae-Suh** (대서)	**120°**	**12.**	**Dae-Han** (대한)	**300°**

The Korean calendar names years, months, and days according to the same sexagesimal system use in the Chinese calendar, with stems

(1) Kap (갑)	(6) Ki (기)
(2) El (을)	(7) Kyung (경)
(3) Byung (병)	(8) Shin (신)
(4) Jung (정)	(9) Im (임)
(5) Mu (무)	(10) Gye (계)

and branches

(1) Ja (자) (Rat)	(7) Oh (오) (Horse)
(2) Chuk (축) (Ox)	(8) Mi (미) (Sheep)
(3) In (인) (Tiger)	(9) Shin (신) (Monkey)
(4) Myo (묘) (Hare)	(10) Yoo (유) (Fowl)
(5) Jin (진) (Dragon)	(11) Sool (술) (Dog)
(6) Sa (사) (Snake)	(12) Hae (해) (Pig)

The main Korean holidays are Gregorian New Year (신정), Korean New Year (설날; computed like Chinese New Year), and Thanksgiving (한식 or 추석; day 15 of the eighth month). In addition, the dates of solar longitudes 297° (January 17–18), 27° (April 17–18), 117° (July 20–21), and 207° (October 20–21) are called *Toe-Wang-Yong-Sa* (토왕용사); on these days, the energy from the soil is thought to dominate, so traditionally no work related to the soil is done. Our function **chinese-solar-longitude-on-or-after** makes the determination of the toe-wang-yong-sa an easy matter.

19.11 The Vietnamese Calendar[12]

Minister Tranh gazed ahead at the far wall, as though divining some message from the mildewed wallpaper. "Are you familiar with the Vietnamese calendar, Miss Maitland?" he asked quietly. "Your calendar?" She frowned, puzzled by the new twist of conversation. "It—it's the same as the Chinese, isn't it?"

Tess Gerritsen: *Never Say Die* (1996)

The traditional Vietnamese calendar used today is the Chinese calendar computed for Hanoi (Vietnam Standard Time, U.T. + 8 before 1968, U.T. + 7 since 1968):[13]

$$\textbf{vietnamese-location}\,(t) \stackrel{\text{def}}{=} \boxed{21°2' \mid 105°51' \mid 12\text{ m} \mid z^{\text{h}}} \qquad (19.38)$$

where

$$z = \begin{cases} 8 & \textbf{if } t < \textbf{gregorian-new-year}\,(1968) \\ 7 & \textbf{otherwise} \end{cases}$$

It was adopted in 1967 in North Vietnam and in 1976 in the whole country. Between 1813 and 1967 the Chinese calendar was used. Before 1813 the Vietnamese calendar was computed with slightly different formulas and tables, so it differs occasionally from the Chinese calendar, especially in the period 1645–1813.[14] See [12] and [13] for the full history of Vietnamese calendars.

---

[12] Based on information provided by Hồ Ngọc Đức [9] of the Institut für Informationssysteme, Universität zu Lübeck.

[13] Historical time-zone use in Vietnam is extremely complex, varying geographically (North versus South, before unification versus after), as well as historically (under the French, the Japanese, and after independence). What we use is simplistic but follows the TZ database and gives agreement with [29], as detailed in the following note.

[14] Our functions have complete agreement with [29] for 1999–2100. For 1901–1998 historical practice differed from our calculated values for six scattered months as given in Table 10 of [29, p. 69]

The years are not counted, but are named. The names of the stems and branches are translations of the Chinese names, but the animal totems are different from those of Chinese calendar in some cases: Water buffalo instead of Ox; Cat instead of Rabbit. In Vietnamese the names of the stems are:

(1) Giáp	(6) Kỷ
(2) Ất	(7) Canh
(3) Bính	(8) Tân
(4) Đinh	(9) Nhâm
(5) Mậu	(10) Quý

and the names of the branches are:

(1) Tý	(Rat)	(7) Ngọ	(Horse)
(2) Sửu	(Water buffalo)	(8) Mùi	(Goat)
(3) Dần	(Tiger)	(9) Thân	(Monkey)
(4) Mão	(Cat)	(10) Dậu	(Chicken)
(5) Thìn	(Dragon)	(11) Tuất	(Dog)
(6) Tỵ	(Snake)	(12) Hợi	(Pig)

Months are named in two ways, using the sexagesimal system as in the Chinese calendar or by the name of the month in the year only. The names are:

(1) Tháng Giêng	(7) Tháng Bảy
(2) Tháng Hai	(8) Tháng Tám
(3) Tháng Ba	(9) Tháng Chín
(4) Tháng Tư	(10) Tháng Mười
(5) Tháng Năm	(11) Tháng Một
(6) Tháng Sáu	(12) Tháng Chạp

Months 1, 11, and 12 have proper names; the other names are just numbers: "hai" is "second," . . . , "mười" is "tenth," and "tháng" is "month." Month 12 (Tháng Chạp) is sometimes called "Tháng Mười Hai" (the twelfth month), but Month 11 (Tháng Một) is almost never called "the eleventh month." The first month (Tháng Giêng) is never called "the first month." Leap months are indicated with "nhuận," for example "Tháng Tám nhuận."

References

[1] Korea Astronomy Observatory, *Man Se Ryuk* (*Perpetual Calendar*), Myung Mun Dang, Seoul, 2004.

but, with those corrections to [29], our functions also agree for 1901–1998. For the years after 1890, except for those six months, our calculations agree with [12], on which [29] is based for 1901–2010. Our functions are also in complete agreement with the calculations of Hồ Ngọc Đức [9] for 1891–2100.

[2] Purple Mountain Observatory, *Xīn biān wàn nián lì* (*The Newly Compiled Perpetual Chinese Calendar*) *1840–2050*, Kē xué pǔ jí chū bǎn shè (Popular Science Press), Beijing, 1984. Third and subsequent printings correct the structure of the year 2033.

[3] H. Aslaksen, "When is Chinese New Year?," *Griffith Observer*, vol. 66, no. 2, pp. 1–17, February 2002. An extended version can be found at `www.math.nus.edu.sg/aslaksen/calendar/cal.pdf`.

[4] W. Bramsen, *Japanese Chronological Tables*, Seishi Bunsha, Tokyo, 1880.

[5] J. Bredon and I. Mitrophanow, *The Moon Year*, Kelly & Walsh, Shanghai, 1927.

[6] J. Chen, "Chinese Calendars," in *Ancient China's Technology and Science*, compiled by the Institute of the History of Natural Sciences, Chinese Academy of Sciences, Foreign Language Press, Beijing, pp. 33–49, 1983.

[7] L. E. Doggett, "Calendars," *Explanatory Supplement to the Astronomical Almanac*, P. K. Seidelmann, ed., University Science Books, Mill Valley, CA, pp. 575–608, 1992.

[8] H. Fritsche, *On Chronology and the Construction of the Calendar with Special Regard to the Chinese Computation of Time Compared with the European*, R. Laverentz, St. Petersburg, 1886.

[9] N. Đ. Hồ, Institut für Informationssysteme, Universität zu Lübeck, personal communication, March 2005.

[10] P. Hoang, *A Notice of the Chinese Calendar and a Concordance with the European Calendar*, 2nd edn., Catholic Mission Press, Shanghai, 1904.

[11] P. Hoang, *Concordance des Chronologies Néoméniques Chinoise et Européene*, 12th edn., Kuangchi Press, Taiwan, 1968.

[12] L. T. Lân, *Lịch và niên biểu lịch sử 20 thế kỷ 0001–2010* (*The Cumulative Calendar and the Historical Chronology of Twenty Centuries (0001–2010)*, Nhà xuất bản Thống Kê, Hanoi, 2000.

[13] L. T. Lân, *Vietnamese Old-Time Calendars*, Band 6, SEACOM Studien zur Südostasienkunde, SEACOM, Berlin, 2003.

[14] Y. Lǐ and S. Dù, *Chinese Mathematics: A Concise History*, translated by J. N. Crossley and A. W.-C. Lun, Oxford University Press, Oxford, 1987.

[15] B. Liú and F. R. Stephenson, "The Chinese Calendar and Its Operational Rules," manuscript, 1990.

[16] C. L. Liu, *Elements of Discrete Mathematics*, 2nd. edn., McGraw-Hill, New York, 1985.

[17] J.-C. Martzloff, *Le calendrier chinois: structure et calculs (104 av. J.-C.–1644)*, Éditions Champion, Paris, 2009.

[18] S. Nakayama, *A History of Japanese Astronomy: Chinese Background and Western Impact*, Harvard University Press, Cambridge, MA, 1969.

[19] J. Needham, *Science and Civilisation in China, vol. 3, Mathematics and the Sciences of the Heavens and the Earth*, Cambridge University Press, Cambridge, 1959.

[20] Y. Nishizawa, *Rekijitsu Taikan* (*Treatise on the Japanese Calendar*), Shinjinbutsu-Ōraisha, Tokyo, 1994.

[21] Y. Nishizawa, personal communication, September 3, 1999.

[22] F. Parise, ed., *The Book of Calendars*, Facts on File, New York, 1982.

[23] S.-H. Saw, "Errors in Chinese Age Statistics," *Demography*, vol. 4, pp. 859–875, 1967.

[24] N. Sivin, *Granting the Seasons*, Springer, New York, 2009.

[25] N. Sivin, "Mathematical Astronomy and the Chinese Calendar," *Calendars and Years, vol. II*, J. M. Steele, ed., Oxbow Books, Oxford and Oakville, CT, pp. 39–51, 2011.

[26] A. Smith, "The Chinese Sexagenary Cycle and the Ritual Foundations of the Calendar," *Calendars and Years, vol. II*, J. M. Steele, ed., Oxbow Books, Oxford and Oakville, CT, pp. 1–37, 2011.

[27] S. Sohn, Korea Astronomy & Space Science Institute, personal communications, February–April, 2005.

[28] F. R. Stephenson and B. Liú, "A Brief Contemporary History of the Chinese Calendar," manuscript, 1990.

[29] T. B. Trần, *Lịch Việt Nam Thế kỷ XX–XXI (1901–2100)* (*Vietnamese Calendar XX–XXI Centuries (1901–2100)*), Nhà xuất bản Văn Hóa—Thông Tin, Hanoi, 2005.

[30] P. Y. Tsuchihashi, *Japanese Chronological Tables from 601 to 1872*, Monumenta Nipponica Monograph 11, Sophia University, Tokyo, 1988.

[31] L.-C. Tun, *Annual Customs and Festivals in Peking*, translated and annotated by Derk Bodde, Henri Vetch, Peiping, 1936.

[32] M. Uchida, *Nihon Rekijitsu Genten* (*Sourcebook for the Japanese Calendar System*), Yūzankaku-Shuppan, Tokyo, 1994.

[33] W. C. Welch, *Chinese-American Calendar for the 102 Chinese Years Commencing January 24, 1849 and Ending February 5, 1951*, U.S. Department

of Labor, Bureau of Immigration, United States Government Printing Office, Washington, D.C., 1928.

[34] H. C. Xú, *Xīn biān Zhōng-guó sān qiān nián lì rì jiǎn suǒ biǎo* (*The Newly Compiled Chinese 3000-Year Calendar Indexing Table*), Rén mín jiào yù chū bǎn shè (People's Education Press), Beijing, 1992.

Twelfth-century black stone slab from Andhra Pradesh, India, depicting the 12 signs of the zodiac surrounding a lotus in full bloom representing the sun. (Courtesy of the Prince of Wales Museum of Western India, Bombay.)

20

The Modern Hindu Calendars

From a chronological point of view the substitution for the mean calendric system of one based on the true movements of the sun and moon, was anything but an improvement, as it destabilized the foundations of the time reckoning. Indeed, the system may have had the charm of adapting daily life as nearly as the astronomical knowledge permitted to the movement of the heavenly bodies, but on the other hand it broke ties with history, as there was no unity of elements or systems. The very complexity of the system is proof of its primitiveness.

W. E. van Wijk: *Decimal Tables for the Reduction of Hindu Dates from the Data of the Sūrya-Siddhānta* (1938)[1]

Numerous calendars are used in India for different purposes. The Gregorian calendar is used by the government for civil matters; the Islamic calendar is used by Muslims; the Hindus employ both solar and lunisolar calendars. Indeed, there are over 30 variations of the Hindu calendar in active use. In March 1957, an attempt was made to revise the traditional calendar to follow the pattern of the Gregorian leap-year structure [1]. The proposed reform has not, however, been widely accepted, though the new National Calendar dates appear in published calendars. An excellent description of many Indian calendars, together with extensive tables, is given in [6].

The best known of several related systems used on the Indian subcontinent is the classical Hindu calendar of the (present) *Sūrya-Siddhānta* (circa 1000), said to have been revealed to Asura Maya the Assyrian at the end of the last "Golden Age," in the year 2163154 B.C.E.[2] al-Bīrūnī attributes the book to Lata. This work introduced a calendar based on approximations to the true times of astronomical events rather than the mean values used in the earlier, simpler, calendar described in Chapter 10. This calendar is somewhat similar to the Chinese, beginning its months according to the actual time of new moon; however, the Chinese calendar today uses modern astronomical methods to determine these times whereas the Hindu calendar applies fixed, ancient methods to approximate the true positions of the sun and moon.

[1] यह आवश्यक नहीं है कि सुक्तियाँ लेखक के विचारों को ही प्रकट करे

[2] Not 2163102 B.C.E., as stated in [2, p. ix], on account of the discrepancy between the Julian and Hindu average year lengths.

In the mean Hindu calendar, (Chapter 10) the calculations are simple. The necessary computational mechanisms for the true system are, by contrast, very complex; experts have attempted over the centuries to reduce hand calculations to table lookup and the very simplest arithmetical operations, avoiding nuisances like large numbers or even signed numbers but requiring logarithms and a multiplicity of tables covering various periods of time. However, shortcuts for humans are unnecessary complications for computers, and so we will avoid all of them. Unlike table-based methods, the use of rational numbers gives perfect fidelity to the sources. We believe that an algorithmic description is the simplest and most concise way of expressing the rules; it allows us to condense many pages of words and tables into a few hundred lines of computer code.

The modern Hindu calendar depends on computed positions of the sun and moon, taking into account that the solar and lunar motions vary in speed across the celestial sphere. We refer to these computed positions as "true," though they are not true in the astronomical sense but rather approximate the irregular apparent motions of the sun and moon. The Hindu sidereal year is the time it takes for the position of the sun to return to the constellation Aries; its length averages $365.25875648\cdots$ days. The length of a solar month varies from 29.318 days to 31.644; that of a Hindu lunar month varies from 29.305 to 29.812 days. The sidereal month is the mean time it takes for the moon to return to the same (longitudinal) point vis-à-vis the stars and is given as $27.321674\cdots$ days. The synodic month takes the motion of the sun into account; it is the mean time between new moons (lunar conjunctions) and is taken to be $29.5305879\cdots$ days. (See Section 14.6.) The mean values for years and months are given in the *Sūrya-Siddhānta* as rational numbers:

$$\textbf{hindu-sidereal-year} \stackrel{\text{def}}{=} 365\tfrac{279457}{1080000} \tag{20.1}$$

$$\textbf{hindu-sidereal-month} \stackrel{\text{def}}{=} 27\tfrac{4644439}{14438334} \tag{20.2}$$

$$\textbf{hindu-synodic-month} \stackrel{\text{def}}{=} 29\tfrac{7087771}{13358334} \tag{20.3}$$

The modern and old Hindu solar calendars have the same basic structure and are based on the sidereal year rather than the more commonly used tropical year. Each solar month begins when the sun enters a new sign of the zodiac. Hindu longitudes are sidereal (they are relative to the fixed stars, not to the precessing equinoctial point) and have as their origin a point near ζ Piscium (Revatī, the sixth brightest star—actually a binary star—in the constellation Pisces, near the ecliptic), or, according to other opinions, 180° from the star Spica (= α Virginis), rather than from the equinoctial point—but this has no impact on the calculations. (See Section 14.1.) If the sign is entered before some critical time (see page 348 for details), then that day is day 1 of a new month; otherwise, it is the last day of the previous month. However, because the solar months vary in length, we cannot know when successive months begin without calculating the position of the sun. The result is that a solar month can have 29, 30, 31, or 32 days. The (solar) day begins at sunrise. Because, in the variant we implement, it is the zodiacal position of the sun at sunrise that determines the month name, we will have to compute sunrise as well.

As with the old Hindu calendar (Chapter 10), lunar month names are determined by the (first) zodiacal sign entered by the sun during the month. When no sign is entered, the month is considered leap; leap months take the same name as the following month. This method of reckoning also leads occasionally to lost months. When, very rarely, a solar month elapses with no new moon, a lunar month is skipped (called *kshaya*). There is a 19- to 141-year gap between occurrences of skipped months; they occur in the winter, near perihelion, when the apparent motion of the sun is fastest. See Figure 20.1.

As in the Chinese calendar with its similar leap-month scheme (see page 310), a lunisolar year must have either 12 or 13 months. Thus, a year with a skipped month perforce contains either 1 leap month or (extremely rarely) 2 leap months. An example of a nonleap year with a leap month was the Hindu year beginning in 1963, with leap Āśvina and expunged Pauṣa, for a total of 12 months.[3] Examples of leap years with 2 leap months include 4576 K.Y. (1475–1476 Gregorian) and 5083 K.Y. (1982–1983 Gregorian).[4]

The Hindu lunar month is either 29 or 30 civil days long, but always comprises 30 "lunar" days. As explained in Section 10.3, each lunar month is split into a bright, waxing (*suddha*), half and a dark, waning (*bahula*), half. We follow the *amānta* scheme in which months begin and end with new moons; in the alternative *pūrṇimānta* scheme (used primarily in the states of Bihar, Uttar Pradesh, Madhya Pradesh, Rajasthan, Haryana, and Kashmir), months go from full moon to full moon. In the latter scheme, the dark half of each month is given the name of the following bright fortnight. When a leap month is inserted, it runs from new moon to new moon, and is thus sandwiched between the dark and light halves of the similarly named nonleap month. (In an alternative scheme, the first dark and light halves constitute the leap month.) The difference between the two schemes is only one of naming, since the rules governing the determination of months and leap months are unchanged [12, art. 51]. A peculiarity of the second method is that the New Year begins with the new moon in the middle of the first month, the same day as with the first method [3], [14].

The usual month names for both the solar and lunisolar calendars are the same as those given on page 160, namely:

---

[3] In 1897, Sewell and Dîkshit [12] wrote, "We are led by these peculiarities to suppose that there will be no suppressed month till at earliest A.D. 1944, and possibly not till A.D. 1963." Pillai's [8] reaction was that "there is no reason why this matter should be treated as one for conjecture, since anybody familiar with the present method can calculate that the next *Kshaya* month will be in A.D. 1963."

[4] From 1300 until 1980 (Gregorian), only Mārgaśīrṣa (in the years beginning in 1315, 1380, 1521), Pauṣa (1334, 1399, 1540, 1681, 1822, 1963), and Māgha (1418, 1475) have been skipped. The omission of Māgha (and the concomitant intercalation of Phālguna) in 1418 is not listed in [12] (only 4 minutes separate the start of the solar and lunar months). Also, according to our calculations Māgha should have been omitted in 5083 K.Y. This is a close call, for the sun entered Māgha on February 13, 1983 (Gregorian) at 4:10:18 a.m., and the new moon occurred half an hour later at 4:43:56. The prior new moon was on January 14 at 9:03:53 a.m., which was before the sun entered Makara at 5:26:14 p.m.; Āśvina and Phālguna were leap.

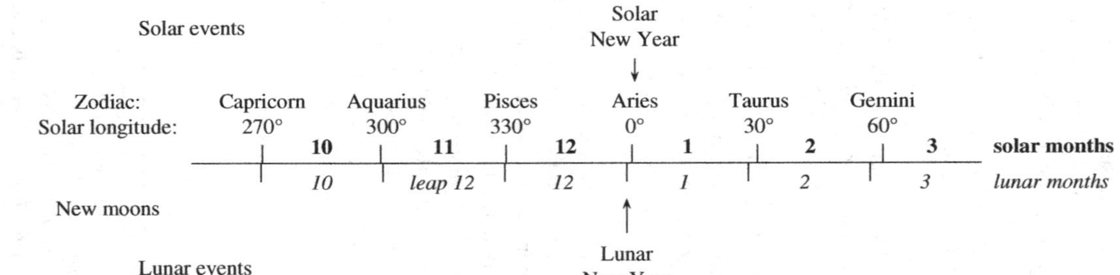

Figure 20.1 The modern Hindu lunisolar calendar. Solar events (entry into zodiac constellations) are shown above the time line; lunar events (lunar conjunctions) are shown below; the longitudes are sidereal. The solar months are shown in boldface numbers; the lunar months, in italic numbers. Note the expunged eleventh lunar month.

(1) Caitra	चैत्र	(7) Āśvina	आश्विन
(2) Vaiśākha	वैशाख	(8) Kārtika	कार्तिक
(3) Jyeṣṭha	ज्येष्ठ	(9) Mārgaśīrṣa	मार्गशीर्ष
(4) Āṣāḍha	आषाढ	(10) Pauṣa	पौष
(5) Śrāvaṇa	श्रावण	(11) Māgha	माघ
(6) Bhādrapada	भाद्रपद	(12) Phālguna	फाल्गुन

but the solar year typically begins with Vaiśākha, corresponding to the second month of the lunar year. The names are derived from asterisms (star groups) along the ecliptic. They are a subset of the original names for the (unequal) division of the ecliptic into 27 or 28 lunar stations or "mansions," one for each day of the sidereal month. The lunar month name is that of the asterism in which the full moon occurs. The exact star groups were already uncertain in the time of al-Bīrūnī; one suggestion is given in Table 20.1.

Day numbers are determined by the lunar phase, or *tithi*, current at sunrise (see Chapter 10). The days of the two halves of a month, each consisting of 15 lunar days, are usually numbered separately from 1 to 15, except that new-moon day (*tithi* 30) is numbered 30 in both the new-moon and full-moon schemes. The varying motion of the moon—a "lunar day" ranges in length from 21.5 to 26.2 hours—can cause two sunrises to fall within 1 lunar day, or (every 2 months, or so) for a lunar day to begin and end between one sunrise and the next. This situation leads to a unique aspect of the Hindu scheme: consecutive days can bear the *same* ordinal number (an "intercalated" day), and any number can be skipped (an "extracalated" day). In the case of days, the second of 2 days with the same number is considered extra (*adhika*). A day may therefore be named "Second 7 in the dark half of the first Mārgaśīrṣa."

Suppose that we can determine the sidereal longitudes of the sun and moon at any given time. To determine the Hindu lunar date of any given day, we perform the following sequence of operations:

1. The phase of the moon at sunrise of the given day is determined by taking the difference in longitudes between the positions of the sun and moon. Dividing this difference in degrees by 12 gives an integer in the range 0 .. 29, corresponding to (one less than) the ordinal number of the lunar day current at sunrise.
2. The current day number is compared with that of the previous day. If they are the same then it is a leap day (and "*adhika*" is appended to the number).
3. The time when the last new moon at or before sunrise of the current day occurred is determined.
4. The position of the sun (which is the same as that of the moon) at that new moon is determined. The zodiacal sign in which it occurs establishes the name (that of the next sign) of the current month.
5. The current month name is compared with that of the next new moon. If they are the same, then it is a leap month (and "*adhika*" is appended to the month's name).

Table 20.1 Suggested correspondence of the lunar stations and asterisms. Boldface indicates the stations after which the lunar months are named. The Greek letters (and the number 35) in the middle column indicate the relative brightness of the star in its constellation. (Popular names are given in parentheses.) Thus, α Tauri is the brightest star in Taurus, called Aldebaran ("the follower" in Arabic, a red star of first magnitude in the eye of the bull and part of the Hyades). A 28th station, omitted from some lists, is unnumbered.

	Lunar station		Prominent star	Associated deity
1.	**Aśvinī**	अश्विनी	α Arietis (Hamal)	Aśvinau
2.	Bharaṇī	भरणी	35 Arietis	Yama
3.	**Kṛttikā**	कृत्तिका	η Tauri (Alcyone)	Agni
4.	Rohiṇī	रोहिणी	α Tauri (Aldebaran)	Prajāpati
5.	**Mṛigaśiras**	मृगशिरस्	λ Orionis (Meissa)	Soma
6.	Ārdrā	आर्द्रा	α Orionis (Betelgeuse)	Rudra
7.	Punarvasu	पुनर्वसु	β Geminorum (Pollux)	Aditi
8.	**Puṣya**	पुष्य	δ Cancri (Asellus Australis)	Bṛhaspati
9.	Āśleṣā	आश्लेषा	α Cancri (Acubens)	Sarpāḥ
10.	**Maghā**	मघा	α Leonis (Regulus)	Pitaraḥ
11.	Pūrva-Phalgunī	पूर्व-फल्गुनी	δ Leonis (Zosma)	Aryaman
12.	**Uttara-Phalgunī**	उत्तर-फल्गुनी	β Leonis (Denebola)	Bhaga
13.	Hasta	हस्त	γ Corvi (Gienah)	Savitṛ
14.	**Citrā**	चित्रा	α Virginis (Spica)	Indra
15.	Svāti	स्वाती	α Bootis (Arcturus)	Vāyu
16.	**Viśākhā**	विशाखा	α Libræ (Zubenelgenubi)	Indrāgni
17.	Anṙādhā	अनूराधा	δ Scorpii (Dschubba)	Mitra
18.	**Jyeṣṭhā**	ज्येष्ठा	α Scorpii (Antares)	Indra
19.	Mūla	मूला	γ Scorpii	Pitaraḥ
20.	Pūrva-Āṣāḍhā	पूर्व-आषाढा	δ Sagittarii (Kaus Media)	Āpaḥ
21.	**Uttara-Āṣāḍhā**	उत्तर-आषाढा	σ Sagittarii (Nunki)	Viśve devāḥ
	Abhijit	अभिजित्	α Lyræ (Vega)	Brahmā
22.	**Śravaṇā**	श्रवण	α Aquilæ (Altair)	Viṣṇu
23.	Dhaniṣṭhā	धनिष्ठा	α Delphini (Sualocin)	Vasavaḥ
24.	Śatatārakā	शतभिषक्	λ Aquarii	Indra
25.	Pūrva-Bhādrapadā	पूर्व-भाद्रपद	α Pegasi (Markab)	Aja Ekapād
26.	**Uttara-Bhādrapadā**	उत्तर-भाद्रपद	α Andromedæ (Alpheratz)	Ahirbudhnya
27.	Revatī	रेवती	ζ Piscium	

Consider the unusual lunar year that began on March 26, 1982. The sequence of solar entries into zodiacal signs and new moons in that year are shown in Table 20.2. There were two new moons between the sun's reaching 150° and 180°, and between 300° and 330°, so both the seventh and twelfth months are leap. Because there was no new moon between 270° and 300°, month 11 is expunged. See Figure 20.1.

In contrast, the calculations of the old (mean) Hindu lunisolar calendar can result in added months and lost days but not lost months or added days. Because the mean lunar month is shorter than the mean solar month, there is never a situation on the mean calendar in which an expunged lunar month is called for. Similarly, because a civil day is longer than a 30th of a mean synodic month, leap days were never needed.

Table 20.2 The sequence of solar entries into zodiacal signs (bold) and new moons (italics) in 1982.

Date	Moment	Event
March 14, 1982	17:39:48	**330°**
March 25, 1982	15:21:52	*month 1*
April 14, 1982	2:08:34	**0°**
April 24, 1982	1:55:58	*month 2*
May 15, 1982	0:33:27	**30°**
May 23, 1982	10:18:42	*month 3*
June 15, 1982	10:38:20	**60°**
June 21, 1982	17:20:29	*month 4*
July 17, 1982	2:06:17	**90°**
July 21, 1982	0:01:51	*month 5*
August 17, 1982	13:30:07	**120°**
August 19, 1982	7:31:17	*month 6*
September 17, 1982	13:58:01	**150°**
September 17, 1982	16:46:25	*leap month 7*
October 17, 1982	4:35:29	*month 7*
October 18, 1982	0:34:25	**180°**
November 15, 1982	19:28:07	*month 8*
November 16, 1982	22:01:12	**210°**
December 15, 1982	13:18:01	*month 9*
December 16, 1982	9:48:12	**240°**
January 14, 1983	9:03:50	*month 10*
January 14, 1983	17:26:14	**270°**
February 13, 1983	4:10:17	**300°**
February 13, 1983	4:45:34	*leap month 12*
March 14, 1983	22:26:19	*month 12*
March 14, 1983	23:52:24	**330°**
April 13, 1983	13:06:31	*month 1*

20.1 Hindu Astronomy

I dare not hope that I have made myself quite clear, simply because [my explanation] involves too many fractions and details. To tell the truth it took me several days to get familiar with the [calendar] system ... Several of my Brahmin friends themselves were unable to explain the intricacies of the Hindu calendar ... But let me not leave the impression that these attempts on the part of the Brahmins of old to reconcile the seemingly irreconcilable have been futile ... There can be no doubt that, from the point of view of correctness and exactitude, the Hindu calendars are by far the nearest approaches to the actual machinery of astronomical phenomena governing life on our planet. The only fault of the Hindu calendars is that they are unintelligible to the common man.

Hashim Amir Ali: *Facts and Fancies* (1946)

From the time of Ptolemy's *Almagest* in the second century until the Keplerian revolution of the seventeenth century, it was well known that the motions of the seven heavenly bodies visible to the naked eye (the sun, the moon, Mercury, Venus, Mars, Jupiter, and Saturn) can best be described by combinations of circular motions, that is, cycles and epicycles.[5] The Hindu calendar approximations are based on such epicycles.

To find the true positions of the sun and moon we need to adjust their mean (sidereal) longitudes by the contribution of the epicycle. The heavenly body is assumed to remain on the *deferent* (the main circle) but to be "pulled" in one direction or the other by "winds" and "cords of air" originating on the epicycle. If we assume the center of the epicycle is at longitude β and the *anomaly* (the angle of the heavenly body around the epicycle, measured from the point farthest from Earth along the epicycle) is α, the angular position is approximately

$$\beta - \arcsin(r \sin \alpha)$$

where r is the ratio of the radii of the epicycle and the deferent. Figure 20.2 illustrates this arrangement.

The *Sūrya-Siddhānta* and earlier Hindu astronomical tracts give a table of sines for angles of 0° to 90°, in increments of 225 minutes of arc, and interpolation is used for intermediate values. The sines, shown in Table 20.3, are given as integers in the range 0 . . 3438 (that is, in terms of a radius of 3438 units) and serve as close approximations to the true sine.[6] We implement the table by means of the following ad hoc function, which returns an amplitude in the range [0 . . 1] for angles given in units of 225′:

$$\textbf{hindu-sine-table}\,(\mathit{entry}) \stackrel{\text{def}}{=} \frac{1}{3438} \times \text{round}\,(\mathit{exact} + \mathit{error}) \tag{20.4}$$

where

$$\mathit{exact} = 3438 \times \sin\,(\mathit{entry} \times 225')$$
$$\mathit{error} = 0.215 \times \text{sign}\,(\mathit{exact}) \times \text{sign}\,(|\mathit{exact}| - 1716)$$

Linear interpolation is used for in-between values:[7]

$$\textbf{hindu-sine}\,(\theta) \stackrel{\text{def}}{=} \tag{20.5}$$

$$\mathit{fraction} \times \textbf{hindu-sine-table}\,(\lceil \mathit{entry} \rceil) + (1 - \mathit{fraction}) \times \textbf{hindu-sine-table}\,(\lfloor \mathit{entry} \rfloor)$$

[5] Elliptical motion is indeed exactly characterized by one retrograde epicycle, on which the motion is in the opposite direction to the motion along the deferent and the period is double (see Figure 20.2); the distinction between elliptical motion and epicyclical motion is conceptual. Kepler's second law of 1609 explains that the motion is not uniform. Ptolemaic astronomy also included eccentric orbits to account for the off-center position of Earth and equants to model the uneven speeds.

[6] A radius of 3438 and a quadrant comprising 5400 minutes imply a value of $\frac{5400\times4}{3438\times2} \approx 3.141361$ for π. A recurrence is given in the *Sūrya-Siddhānta* for producing the data in this table of sines, namely

$$\sin(n\alpha) = n\alpha - \frac{1}{225} \sum_{i<n} (n - i) \sin(i\alpha)$$

where $\alpha = 225'$. The table given in *Sūrya-Siddhānta*, however, is more accurate than this formula and, as seen in Table 20.3, is correct except for erratic rounding. The recurrence would be quite accurate with $(225/3438)^2 \approx 1/233.5$ instead of 1/225. See Burgess's comments in [2, p. 335].

[7] The stepped sign function is not detrimental to the overall accuracy of the Hindu calendar. See [4].

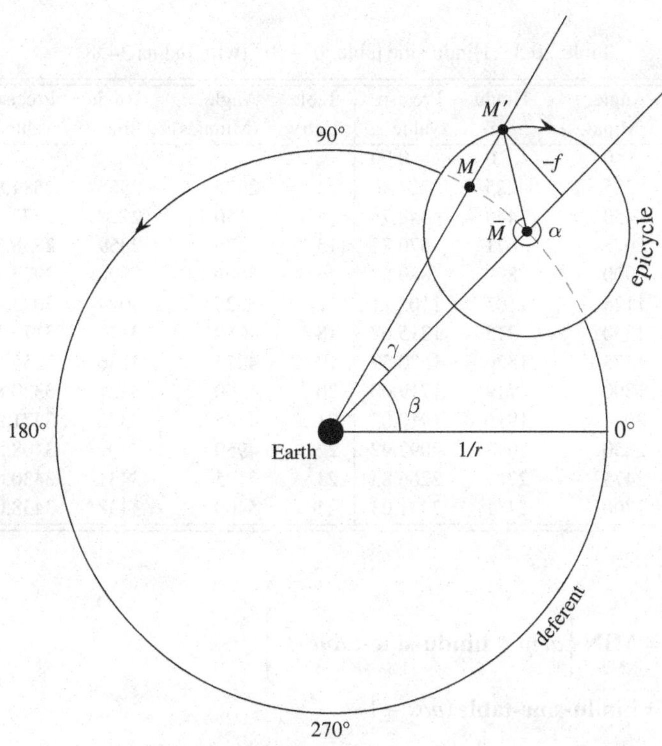

Figure 20.2 The motion of the moon viewed from above the North Pole. The mean position $\overline{M}$ of the moon revolves in a circle, called the *deferent*, of radius $1/r$, at a steady rate (once every mean sidereal month). At the same time, a hypothetical being M' rotates around an epicycle of unit radius centered at $\overline{M}$ in the opposite direction to the motion of $\overline{M}$ in such a way that it returns to the apogee (the point at which it is farthest from Earth) in a period called the *anomalistic month*. Let β be the longitude of $\overline{M}$, α be the angle of M' from the apogee, called the *anomaly*, and f be sin α, which we call the *offset*. The true longitude of the moon, M, on the deferent along a radius from Earth to M', is $\beta + \gamma$, where $\sin\gamma \approx -fr = -(\sin\alpha)r$. Thus we have for the *equation of center* $\gamma = 360° - \arcsin(r \sin\alpha) = -\arcsin(r \sin\alpha)$. In addition, the ratio r changes as $\overline{M}$ revolves around Earth (see the text). The figure is not drawn to scale.

where

$$\begin{aligned} \textit{entry} &= \frac{\theta}{225'} \\ \textit{fraction} &= \textit{entry} \bmod 1 \end{aligned}$$

To invert **hindu-sine** we use

$$\textbf{hindu-arcsin}\,(\textit{amp}) \stackrel{\text{def}}{=} \tag{20.6}$$

$$\begin{cases} -\,\textbf{hindu-arcsin}\,(-\,\textit{amp}) & \textbf{if } \textit{amp} < 0 \\ 225' \times \left(\textit{pos} - 1 + \dfrac{\textit{amp} - \textit{below}}{\textbf{hindu-sine-table}\,(\textit{pos}) - \textit{below}}\right) & \textbf{otherwise} \end{cases}$$

Table 20.3 Hindu sine table, 0°–90° (with radius 3438).

Table Entry	Angle (Minutes)	Hindu Sine	Precise Value	Table Entry	Angle (Minutes)	Hindu Sine	Precise Value
0	0	0	0.00				
1	225	225	224.86	13	2925	2585	2584.83
2	450	449	448.75	14	3150	2728	2727.55
3	675	671	670.72	15	3375	2859	2858.59
4	900	890	889.82	16	3600	2978	2977.40
5	1125	1105	1105.11	17	3825	3084	3083.45
6	1350	1315	1315.67	18	4050	3177	3176.30
7	1575	1520	1520.59	19	4275	3256	3255.55
8	1800	1719	1719.00	20	4500	3321	3320.85
9	2025	1910	1910.05	21	4725	3372	3371.94
10	2250	2093	2092.92	22	4950	3409	3408.59
11	2475	2267	2266.83	23	5175	3431	3430.64
12	2700	2431	2431.03	24	5400	3438	3438.00

where

$$pos = \underset{k \geqslant 0}{\mathbf{MIN}} \left\{ amp \leqslant \textbf{hindu-sine-table}\,(k) \right\}$$

$$below = \textbf{hindu-sine-table}\,(pos - 1)$$

Again, interpolation is used for intermediate values not appearing in the table.

To determine the position of the mean sun or moon, we have the generic function

$$\textbf{hindu-mean-position}\,(t, period) \stackrel{\text{def}}{=} \qquad (20.7)$$

$$360° \times \left(\frac{t - \textbf{hindu-creation}}{period} \bmod 1 \right)$$

which calculates the longitude (in degrees) at a given moment t when the period of rotation is *period* days. The visible planets, according to the *Sūrya-Siddhānta*, were in mean conjunction at the epoch but in *true* conjunction at the end of creation, 1955880000 years (sidereal, not tropical—the difference is slight; see Section 14.4) prior to the onset of the Kali Yuga:

$$\textbf{hindu-creation} \stackrel{\text{def}}{=} \qquad (20.8)$$

$$\textbf{hindu-epoch} - 1955880000 \times \textbf{hindu-sidereal-year}$$

Thus, the anomaly is taken to be 0° at (the end of) creation. The size of the sun's epicycle is 14/360 of its deferent; for the moon the ratio is larger: 32/360. The period of revolution of the (cords of air around the) epicycles are

$$\textbf{hindu-anomalistic-year} \stackrel{\text{def}}{=} \frac{1577917828000}{4320000000 - 387} \qquad (20.9)$$

$$\textbf{hindu-anomalistic-month} \stackrel{\text{def}}{=} \frac{1577917828}{57753336 - 488199} \tag{20.10}$$

for the sun and moon, respectively. These values, of approximately 365.258789 and 27.554598, respectively, are derived from the stated speed of rotation of the apsides (the extreme points of the orbit), 387/1000 times in 4320000 years (= 1577917828 days) for the sun and 488199 times in the same period for the moon.[8] The anomalistic month is the corrected (*bija*) value introduced in the mid-sixteenth century by Gaṇesa Daivajna and still in use today, not that originally given in the *Sūrya-Siddhānta*.

To complicate matters, in the scheme of *Sūrya-Siddhānta* the epicycle actually shrinks as it revolves (almost as if there were an epicycle on the epicycle). For both the sun and moon, the change amounts to 20′ and reaches its minimum value when entering the even quadrants. Changes in the size of the epicycle are reflected in the following function:

$$\textbf{hindu-true-position}\,(t, \textit{period}, \textit{size}, \textit{anomalistic}, \textit{change}) \stackrel{\text{def}}{=} \tag{20.11}$$

$$(\lambda - \textit{equation}) \bmod 360$$

where

$$\begin{aligned}
\lambda &= \textbf{hindu-mean-position}\,(t, \textit{period}) \\
\textit{offset} &= \textbf{hindu-sine}\,(\textbf{hindu-mean-position}\,(t, \textit{anomalistic})) \\
\textit{contraction} &= |\textit{offset}| \times \textit{change} \times \textit{size} \\
\textit{equation} &= \textbf{hindu-arcsin}\,(\textit{offset} \times (\textit{size} - \textit{contraction}))
\end{aligned}$$

which adjusts the mean longitudinal position (the center of the epicycle) by the equation of motion (the longitudinal displacement caused by epicyclic motion), calculated from creation and normalizes the resultant angle by using the modulus function.[9]

Substituting the relevant constants, we have

$$\textbf{hindu-solar-longitude}\,(t) \stackrel{\text{def}}{=} \tag{20.12}$$

$$\textbf{hindu-true-position}\left(t, \textbf{hindu-sidereal-year}, \frac{14}{360}, \textbf{hindu-anomalistic-year}, \frac{1}{42}\right)$$

from which the zodiacal position follows:

$$\textbf{hindu-zodiac}\,(t) \stackrel{\text{def}}{=} \left\lfloor \frac{\textbf{hindu-solar-longitude}\,(t)}{30^\circ} \right\rfloor + 1 \tag{20.13}$$

---

[8] Whereas we compute the anomaly from creation, traditionally one precomputes the position of perihelion at some base date, and the time between true and mean New Year for that base, called *sodhya*, because the solar anomaly changes very slowly. "The difference in the sun's equation of the centre and true longitude, caused by the shift of the apsin, is exceedingly small and may well be ignored" [11, p. 55].

[9] The fluctuating epicycle does not improve the accuracy of the Hindu calendar. See [4].

The position of the moon is calculated in a similar fashion:

$$\textbf{hindu-lunar-longitude}\,(t) \stackrel{\text{def}}{=} \tag{20.14}$$

$$\textbf{hindu-true-position}\left(t, \textbf{hindu-sidereal-month}, \frac{32}{360}, \textbf{hindu-anomalistic-month}, \frac{1}{96}\right)$$

Now we have all the information needed to determine the phase of the moon at any given time. It is simply the difference in longitudes:

$$\textbf{hindu-lunar-phase}\,(t) \stackrel{\text{def}}{=} \tag{20.15}$$

$$(\,\textbf{hindu-lunar-longitude}\,(t) - \textbf{hindu-solar-longitude}\,(t)\,) \bmod 360$$

This translates into the number of the lunar day if the difference is divided by one-thirtieth of a full circle (that is, 12°):

$$\textbf{hindu-lunar-day-from-moment}\,(t) \stackrel{\text{def}}{=} \tag{20.16}$$

$$\left\lfloor \frac{\textbf{hindu-lunar-phase}\,(t)}{12^\circ} \right\rfloor + 1$$

To find the zodiacal sign at the time of a new moon, we first use the following function to get a close enough approximation to the time of the last new moon preceding moment t:

$$\textbf{hindu-new-moon-before}\,(t) \stackrel{\text{def}}{=} \tag{20.17}$$

$$\underset{x\in[\tau-1..\min\{t,\tau+1\})}{\overset{p(l,u)}{\text{MIN}}} \left\{ \textbf{hindu-lunar-phase}\,(x) < 180^\circ \right\}$$

where

$$\varepsilon = 2^{-1000}$$

$$\tau = t - \frac{1}{360^\circ} \times \textbf{hindu-lunar-phase}\,(t) \times \textbf{hindu-synodic-month}$$

$$p\,(l, u) = \textbf{hindu-zodiac}\,(l) = \textbf{hindu-zodiac}\,(u) \text{ or } u - l < \varepsilon$$

Beginning with an interval of (up to) one day before and after the time τ of the last *mean* new moon, we perform a binary search (see page 24) for the moment when the moon's phase goes from 360° to 0°. The search is terminated as soon as the search interval is narrow enough to determine the sign of the zodiac. Additionally, to prevent any possibility of an infinite loop, the process is limited here to 1000 bisections.[10]

[10] The value $\epsilon = 2^{-1000}$ should be replaced by a very small, but representable, positive real number when used in a programming environment that does not support arbitrary-precision rational arithmetic.

Table 20.4 Śaka offsets for various eras.

Era	Current year	Elapsed year
Vikrama	+136	+135
Kali Yuga	+3180	+3179
Śaka	+1	0
Bengal		−515
Kollam	+901	
Nepalese		+955

20.2 Calendars

Adhika *months are the cream of the Indian Calendar, while* kshaya *are its* crème de la crème. *Figures of speech apart, it is certainly true that the success or failure of any computer in deducing* adhika *and* kshaya *months is the measure of the success or failure, as a whole, with the Indian Calendar. How far the present method satisfies this ordeal, will be for competent judges to decide.*

Dewan Bahadur L. D. Swamikannu Pillai:
Indian Chronology (1911)

To determine the Hindu year for a given R.D. date (or time), it is not enough to take the quotient of the number of days elapsed with the mean length of a year. A correction, based on where the sun actually is vis-à-vis the start of the zodiac, must be applied.

$$\textbf{hindu-calendar-year}\,(t) \stackrel{\text{def}}{=} \tag{20.18}$$

$$\text{round}\left(\frac{t - \textbf{hindu-epoch}}{\textbf{hindu-sidereal-year}} - \frac{\textbf{hindu-solar-longitude}\,(t)}{360^\circ}\right)$$

If the true solar longitude at the given time is a bit less than 360°, then the mean value of the quotient is decreased by 1.

The Kali Yuga Era is used today only for calculations. Instead, one commonly used starting point is the Śaka Era in which (elapsed) year 0 began in the spring of 78 C.E., or 3179 K.Y.:

$$\textbf{hindu-solar-era} \stackrel{\text{def}}{=} 3179 \tag{20.19}$$

In West Bengal an era that began in 593 C.E. is used instead. The year number of the major eras can be calculated using Table 20.4 of offsets from the Śaka. A detailed discussion of Indian dates and eras may be found in [13, chap. VII].

The solar date is determined by approximation followed by search:

$$\textbf{hindu-solar-from-fixed}\,(date) \stackrel{\text{def}}{=} \boxed{\,year \mid month \mid day\,} \tag{20.20}$$

where

$$critical = \textbf{hindu-sunrise}\,(date + 1)$$
$$month = \textbf{hindu-zodiac}\,(critical)$$

$$\begin{aligned}
year &= \textbf{hindu-calendar-year}\,(critical) - \textbf{hindu-solar-era}\\
approx &= date - 3 - (\lfloor \textbf{hindu-solar-longitude}\,(critical)\rfloor \bmod 30^\circ)\\
start &= \underset{i \geqslant approx}{\textbf{MIN}} \left\{ \textbf{hindu-zodiac}\,(\textbf{hindu-sunrise}\,(i+1)) = month \right\}\\
day &= date - start + 1
\end{aligned}$$

To determine the day of the month, we underestimate the day when the sun entered the current zodiacal sign (*approx*) and search forward for the start of the month, *begin*. The calculation of **hindu-sunrise** is given in the next section.

For example, R.D. 0 is Makara 20 of year −78 S.E.,[11] the same month but a day later than the mean solar calendar (page 158).

The preceding function follows the Orissa rule, according to which the solar month of a given day is determined by the zodiacal position of the sun at sunrise the following morning. This is just one of various critical times that have been used (see [12, pp. 12–13] and [3, p. 282]):

- According to the Orissa rule, sunrise of the following morning is used.
- According to the Tamil rule, sunset of the current day is used.
- According to the Malayali rule, 1:12 p.m. (seasonal time) on the current day is used.
- According to some calendars from Madras, apparent midnight of the next night is used.
- According to the Bengal rule, midnight at the start of the day is normally used unless the zodiac sign changes between 11:36 p.m. and 12:24 a.m., in which case various special rules apply.

Unlike for the mean calendar, determining the R.D. date now requires a search:

$$\textbf{fixed-from-hindu-solar}\left(\boxed{year \mid month \mid day}\right) \stackrel{\text{def}}{=} \tag{20.21}$$

$$day - 1 + \underset{d \geqslant start-3}{\textbf{MIN}} \left\{ \textbf{hindu-zodiac}\,(\textbf{hindu-sunrise}\,(d+1)) = month \right\}$$

where

$$start = \left\lfloor \left(year + \textbf{hindu-solar-era} + \frac{month-1}{12} \right) \times \textbf{hindu-sidereal-year} \right\rfloor + \textbf{hindu-epoch}$$

This function begins its linear search for the fixed date corresponding to the start of the Hindu solar month from the R.D. date *begin* − 3, where the estimate *begin*

[11] Śaka (Scythian) Era (expired).

is obtained by calculating the mean time of entrance into the month's (sidereal) zodiacal sign.

As explained earlier, there are both leap months and leap days on the true Hindu lunisolar calendar; hence, we use quintuples

year	*month*	*leap-month*	*day*	*leap-day*

for lunisolar dates. For the lunisolar year, we use another common era, the Vikrama, which began in 58 B.C.E. and differs from the Kali Yuga by 3044 years:

$$\textbf{hindu-lunar-era} \stackrel{\text{def}}{=} 3044 \tag{20.22}$$

Thus we have

$$\textbf{hindu-lunar-from-fixed}\,(\mathit{date}) \stackrel{\text{def}}{=} \tag{20.23}$$

year	*month*	*leap-month*	*day*	*leap-day*

where

$$\begin{aligned}
\mathit{critical} &= \textbf{hindu-sunrise}\,(\mathit{date})\\
\mathit{day} &= \textbf{hindu-lunar-day-from-moment}\,(\mathit{critical})\\
\mathit{leap\text{-}day} &= \mathit{day} = \textbf{hindu-lunar-day-from-moment}\\
&\qquad (\textbf{hindu-sunrise}\,(\mathit{date}-1))\\
\mathit{last\text{-}new\text{-}moon} &= \textbf{hindu-new-moon-before}\,(\mathit{critical})\\
\mathit{next\text{-}new\text{-}moon} &= \textbf{hindu-new-moon-before}\,(\lfloor \mathit{last\text{-}new\text{-}moon} \rfloor + 35)\\
\mathit{solar\text{-}month} &= \textbf{hindu-zodiac}\,(\mathit{last\text{-}new\text{-}moon})\\
\mathit{leap\text{-}month} &= \mathit{solar\text{-}month} = \textbf{hindu-zodiac}\,(\mathit{next\text{-}new\text{-}moon})\\
\mathit{month} &= (\mathit{solar\text{-}month} + 1) \bmod [1\,..\,12]\\
\mathit{year} &= \textbf{hindu-calendar-year}\left(\begin{cases} \mathit{date} + 180 & \textbf{if } \mathit{month} \leqslant 2\\ \mathit{date} & \textbf{otherwise}\end{cases}\right)\\
&\qquad - \textbf{hindu-lunar-era}
\end{aligned}$$

This function uses the Hindu approximations to the true times of new moons, the true position of the sun at new moon, and the true phase of the moon at sunrise (*critical*) to determine the *month* and *day*. The lunisolar month name and year number are those of the solar month and year, in effect 1 solar month after the beginning (*last-new-moon*) of the current lunar month. The function checks whether it is a leap month (*leap-month*), with the same name as the following month (*next-new-moon*), or a leap day (*leap-day*) with the same ordinal number as the previous day. Our fixed date R.D. 0 is the fourth day of the dark half (that is, lunar day 19) of Māgha (the eleventh month) in year 57 V.E.;[12] neither the day nor month is leap. This date is 1 month later than on the mean calendar (see page 162).

[12] Vikrama Era (expired).

To invert the process and derive the R.D. date from a lunar date, we first find a lower bound on the possible R.D. date and then search forward for the exact correspondence. As Jacobi [5, p. 409] explains: "The problem must be solved indirectly, *i.e.,* we must ascertain approximately the day on which the given *tithi* was likely to end, and then calculate ... the *tithi* that really ends on that day."

We can convert to a fixed date by means of a search:

$$\textbf{fixed-from-hindu-lunar}\left(\boxed{\textit{year} \mid \textit{month} \mid \textit{leap-month} \mid \textit{day} \mid \textit{leap-day}}\right) \stackrel{\text{def}}{=} \qquad (20.24)$$

$$\begin{cases} \textit{date} + 1 & \textbf{if } \textit{leap-day} \\ \textit{date} & \textbf{otherwise} \end{cases}$$

where

$$\textit{approx} = \textbf{hindu-epoch} + \textbf{hindu-sidereal-year} \times \left(\textit{year} + \textbf{hindu-lunar-era} + \frac{\textit{month} - 1}{12}\right)$$

$$s = \left\lfloor \textit{approx} - \textbf{hindu-sidereal-year} \times \left(\left(\frac{\textbf{hindu-solar-longitude}(\textit{approx})}{360^\circ} - \frac{\textit{month}-1}{12}\right) \bmod \left[-\frac{1}{2} \,..\, \frac{1}{2}\right)\right)\right\rfloor$$

$$k = \textbf{hindu-lunar-day-from-moment}\left(s + 6^{\text{h}}\right)$$

$$\textit{est} = s + \textit{day} - \begin{cases} k & \textbf{if } 3 < k < 27 \\ k \bmod [-15 \,..\, 15) & \textbf{if } \textit{mid}_{\textbf{month}} \neq \textit{month} \text{ or } \{\textit{mid}_{\textbf{leap-month}} \text{ and not } \textit{leap-month}\} \\ k \bmod [15 \,..\, 45) & \textbf{otherwise} \end{cases}$$

$$\tau = \textit{est} - \left(\left(\textbf{hindu-lunar-day-from-moment}\left(\textit{est} + 6^{\text{h}}\right) - \textit{day}\right) \bmod [-15 \,..\, 15)\right)$$

$$\textit{date} = \underset{d \geqslant \tau - 1}{\text{MIN}} \left\{ \textbf{hindu-lunar-day-from-moment}\left(\textbf{hindu-sunrise}(d)\right) \in \{\textit{day}, (\textit{day}+1) \bmod [1 \,..\, 30]\} \right\}$$

$$\textit{mid} = \textbf{hindu-lunar-from-fixed}(s - 15)$$

So as not to take an inordinate amount of time, this function performs a three-stage estimate before searching. First it uses mean solar months to estimate the fixed date s of the start of the lunar month. That estimate may be a month off in either direction because a true new moon might occur near the start of the true solar month. So we first check whether s is within 3 (lunar) days of the start of the lunar month. If it is, we look back 15 days and see whether *month* had already begun, in which case we need to go back a month for large k and forward a month for small k, giving an estimate *est* within the correct month. After the correct month is determined, a small search is still necessary because of the variability in month length. The search begins at $\tau - 1$, where τ is *est*, adjusted for the desired lunar *day* and taking the actual lunar day of *est* into account. All three estimates use an interval modulus (1.24). Since the given lunar date might have been expunged, the search ends when either the desired day or the following one is encountered. An adjustment of one day is made when a second leap day is sought.

The Nepalese calendar has the same structure as the Hindu solar calendar, each month beginning on the day when the sun's sidereal longitude reaches a multiple of 30°. The determining location is Kathmundu, and the critical time of day is midnight for most months but is sunrise or sunset for two of the months to accommodate traditional holidays. The month names are similar to those of the Indian calendar.

20.3 Sunrise

It should, however, be remarked that if the interval between true sunrise and the end of a tithi, *&c.* is very *small … the case must be regarded as doubtful; though our calculations materially agree with those of the Hindus, still an almanac-maker avails himself of abbreviations which in the end may slightly influence the result.*

Hermann Jacobi: "The Computation of Hindu Dates in Inscriptions, &c.," *Epigraphia Indica* (1892)

It remains to compute the actual time of sunrise for any particular day. We use the standard location, Ujjain, a city holy to the Hindus situated at 23°9′ north, 75°46′6″ east:

$$\textbf{ujjain} \stackrel{\text{def}}{=} \boxed{23°9' \mid 75°46'6'' \mid 0\text{ m} \mid 5\tfrac{461}{9000}\text{ h}} \tag{20.25}$$

with

$$\textbf{hindu-location} \stackrel{\text{def}}{=} \textbf{ujjain} \tag{20.26}$$

Other locales employ local variants of the calendar that depend on the zodiacal constellation and the lunar phase that are in effect at true local sunrise. Despite the comment of van Wijk [16, p. 24], that "the rules the Sūrya-Siddhānta gives for calculating the time of true sunrise are exceedingly complicated, and inapplicable in practice," so that no one seems to bother with all the corrections mandated for the calculation of local sunrise, and the inaccuracy of the methods, we include them here exactly as ordained by the *Sūrya-Siddhānta* (see [18]).

Four corrections to mean sunrise (6 a.m.) are necessary:

1. The latitude of the location affects the time of sunrise by an amount that also depends on the season. This is called the "ascensional difference":

$$\textbf{hindu-ascensional-difference}\,(date, location) \stackrel{\text{def}}{=} \qquad (20.27)$$

$$\textbf{hindu-arcsin}\left(-\frac{\textit{earth-sine}}{\textit{diurnal-radius}} \right)$$

where

$$\begin{aligned}
sin_\delta &= \frac{1397}{3438} \times \textbf{hindu-sine}\,(\textbf{hindu-tropical-longitude}\,(date)) \\
\varphi &= location_{\textbf{latitude}} \\
\textit{diurnal-radius} &= \textbf{hindu-sine}\,(90^\circ + \textbf{hindu-arcsin}\,(sin_\delta)) \\
tan_\varphi &= \frac{\textbf{hindu-sine}\,(\varphi)}{\textbf{hindu-sine}\,(90^\circ + \varphi)} \\
\textit{earth-sine} &= sin_\delta \times tan_\varphi
\end{aligned}$$

This computation requires *tropical longitude*, which is affected by precession of the equinoxes. The value given in the *Sūrya-Siddhānta* for the maximum precession is 27°, and it is said to cycle once every 7200 years:[13]

$$\textbf{hindu-tropical-longitude}\,(date) \stackrel{\text{def}}{=} \qquad (20.28)$$

$$\left(\textbf{hindu-solar-longitude}\,(date) - precession \right) \bmod 360$$

where

$$\begin{aligned}
days &= date - \textbf{hindu-epoch} \\
precession &= 27^\circ \\
&\quad - \left| 108^\circ \times \left(\left(\frac{600}{1577917828} \times days - \frac{1}{4} \right) \bmod \left[-\frac{1}{2} \,..\, \frac{1}{2} \right) \right) \right|
\end{aligned}$$

2. There is a small difference between the length of the sidereal day (one rotation of the Earth) and the solar day (from midnight to midnight), which amounts to almost a minute in a quarter of a day (see page 218). The function

$$\textbf{hindu-solar-sidereal-difference}\,(date) \stackrel{\text{def}}{=} \qquad (20.29)$$

$$\textbf{hindu-daily-motion}\,(date) \times \textbf{hindu-rising-sign}\,(date)$$

[13] The correct value is about 26000 years with no maximum; see page 219. It was a common pre-Newtonian misconception, called "trepidation," that the precession cycles in this way.

comprises a factor that depends on the solar anomaly for the varying speed of the sun along the ecliptic:

$$\textbf{hindu-daily-motion}\,(\textit{date}) \stackrel{\text{def}}{=} \textit{mean-motion} \times (\textit{factor} + 1) \tag{20.30}$$

where

$$\begin{aligned}
\textit{mean-motion} &= \frac{360^\circ}{\textbf{hindu-sidereal-year}}\\
\textit{anomaly} &= \textbf{hindu-mean-position}\\
&\quad\;(\textit{date}, \textbf{hindu-anomalistic-year})\\
\textit{epicycle} &= \frac{14}{360} - \frac{1}{1080} \times |\textbf{hindu-sine}\,(\textit{anomaly})|\\
\textit{entry} &= \left\lfloor \frac{\textit{anomaly}}{225'} \right\rfloor\\
\textit{sine-table-step} &= \textbf{hindu-sine-table}\,(\textit{entry} + 1)\\
&\quad - \textbf{hindu-sine-table}\,(\textit{entry})\\
\textit{factor} &= -\frac{3438}{225} \times \textit{sine-table-step} \times \textit{epicycle}
\end{aligned}$$

as well as a tabulated factor that depends on the distance of the sun from the celestial equator:

$$\textbf{hindu-rising-sign}\,(\textit{date}) \stackrel{\text{def}}{=} \tag{20.31}$$

$$\left\langle \frac{1670}{1800}, \frac{1795}{1800}, \frac{1935}{1800}, \frac{1935}{1800}, \frac{1795}{1800}, \frac{1670}{1800} \right\rangle_{[i \bmod 6]}$$

where

$$i = \left\lfloor \frac{\textbf{hindu-tropical-longitude}\,(\textit{date})}{30^\circ} \right\rfloor$$

3. The *equation of time* gives the difference between local and apparent midnight caused by the uneven (apparent) motion of the sun through the seasons (see page 215). The *Sūrya-Siddhānta* uses the following very rough approximation:

$$\textbf{hindu-equation-of-time}\,(\textit{date}) \stackrel{\text{def}}{=} \tag{20.32}$$

$$\frac{\textbf{hindu-daily-motion}\,(\textit{date})}{360^\circ} \times \frac{\textit{equation-sun}}{360^\circ} \times \textbf{hindu-sidereal-year}$$

where

$$\begin{aligned} \textit{offset} &= \textbf{hindu-sine}\big(\,\textbf{hindu-mean-position} \\ &\qquad\qquad (\textit{date}, \textbf{hindu-anomalistic-year})\,\big) \\ \textit{equation-sun} &= \textit{offset} \times 57^\circ 18' \times \left(\frac{14}{360} - \frac{|\textit{offset}|}{1080}\right) \end{aligned}$$

4. For locations other than Ujjain, the difference in longitude affects the local time of astronomical events by 4 minutes for every degree of longitude. Compare our **zone-from-longitude** (page 208).

Putting the preceding corrections together, we have

$$\textbf{hindu-sunrise}\,(\textit{date}) \stackrel{\text{def}}{=} \tag{20.33}$$

$$\begin{aligned} &\textit{date} + 6^{\text{h}} + \frac{\textbf{ujjain}_{\textbf{longitude}} - \textbf{hindu-location}_{\textbf{longitude}}}{360^\circ} \\ &- \textbf{hindu-equation-of-time}\,(\textit{date}) \\ &+ \frac{1577917828}{1582237828 \times 360^\circ} \\ &\quad \times \Big(\textbf{hindu-ascensional-difference}\,(\textit{date}, \textbf{hindu-location}) \\ &\qquad + \frac{1}{4} \times \textbf{hindu-solar-sidereal-difference}\,(\textit{date})\Big) \end{aligned}$$

The factor $1577917828/1582237828 \approx 0.9972697$ converts a sidereal hour angle to solar time. The definition of **hindu-location** must be changed to obtain the time of sunrise at other locations.

20.4 Alternatives

The months of the Hindus are lunar, their years are solar; therefore their new year's day must in each solar year fall by so much earlier as the lunar year is shorter than the solar ... If this precession makes up one complete month, they act in the same way as the Jews, who make the year a leap year of thirteen months ... and in a similar way to the heathen Arabs.

Abū-Raiḥān Muḥammad ibn 'Aḥmad al-Bīrūnī: *India* (circa 1030)

As mentioned above, the formulas we gave in Section 20.2 for the solar calendar are predicated on the Orissa rule. For the Tamil rule, we would need to use the function

$$\textbf{hindu-sunset}\,(\textit{date}) \stackrel{\text{def}}{=} \tag{20.34}$$

$$
\begin{aligned}
& date + 18^{\text{h}} + \frac{\textbf{ujjain}_{\textbf{longitude}} - \textbf{hindu-location}_{\textbf{longitude}}}{360^\circ} \\
& \quad - \textbf{hindu-equation-of-time}\,(date) \\
& \quad + \frac{1577917828}{1582237828 \times 360^\circ} \\
& \qquad \times \Big(- \textbf{hindu-ascensional-difference}\,(date, \textbf{hindu-location}) \\
& \qquad\qquad + \frac{3}{4} \times \textbf{hindu-solar-sidereal-difference}\,(date) \Big)
\end{aligned}
$$

defined analogously to **hindu-sunrise**, in the definition *critical* in (20.20). For the Malayali rule, we first define

$$
\textbf{hindu-standard-from-sundial}\,(t) \stackrel{\text{def}}{=} \tag{20.35}
$$

$$
a + 2 \times (b - a) \times \left(time - \begin{cases} 18^{\text{h}} & \textbf{if } q = 3 \\ -6^{\text{h}} & \textbf{if } q = 0 \\ 6^{\text{h}} & \textbf{otherwise} \end{cases} \right)
$$

where

$$
\begin{aligned}
date &= \textbf{fixed-from-moment}\,(t) \\
time &= \textbf{time-from-moment}\,(t) \\
q &= \lfloor 4 \times time \rfloor \\
a &= \begin{cases} \textbf{hindu-sunset}\,(date - 1) & \textbf{if } q = 0 \\ \textbf{hindu-sunset}\,(date) & \textbf{if } q = 3 \\ \textbf{hindu-sunrise}\,(date) & \textbf{otherwise} \end{cases} \\
b &= \begin{cases} \textbf{hindu-sunrise}\,(date) & \textbf{if } q = 0 \\ \textbf{hindu-sunrise}\,(date + 1) & \textbf{if } q = 3 \\ \textbf{hindu-sunset}\,(date) & \textbf{otherwise} \end{cases}
\end{aligned}
$$

which is analogous to **standard-from-sundial** (14.91), to determine the temporal time, and then use

hindu-standard-from-sundial (*date*, 13:12))

For Madras, the rule would be

hindu-standard-from-sundial (*date* + 1, 0:00)

The Bengal rule is more complicated.

To implement the full-moon-to-full-moon version of the lunisolar calendar, we need only change the month number during the second half of each nonleap month to that of the following month in the new-moon-to-new-moon scheme:

$$\textbf{hindu-fullmoon-from-fixed}\,(date) \stackrel{\text{def}}{=} \qquad (20.36)$$

$$\boxed{year \mid m \mid leap\text{-}month \mid day \mid leap\text{-}day}$$

where

$$\begin{aligned}
l\text{-}date &= \textbf{hindu-lunar-from-fixed}\,(date)\\
year &= l\text{-}date_{\textbf{year}}\\
month &= l\text{-}date_{\textbf{month}}\\
leap\text{-}month &= l\text{-}date_{\textbf{leap-month}}\\
day &= l\text{-}date_{\textbf{day}}\\
leap\text{-}day &= l\text{-}date_{\textbf{leap-day}}\\
m &= \begin{cases} (\textbf{hindu-lunar-from-fixed}\,(date+20))_{\textbf{month}} & \textbf{if } day \geqslant 16\\ month & \textbf{otherwise}\end{cases}
\end{aligned}$$

In the other direction, we have

$$\textbf{fixed-from-hindu-fullmoon}\left(\boxed{year \mid month \mid leap\text{-}month \mid day \mid leap\text{-}day}\right) \stackrel{\text{def}}{=} \qquad (20.37)$$

$$\textbf{fixed-from-hindu-lunar}\left(\boxed{year \mid m \mid leap\text{-}month \mid day \mid leap\text{-}day}\right)$$

where

$$m = \begin{cases} month & \textbf{if } leap\text{-}month \text{ or } day \leqslant 15\\ (month-2) \bmod [1\,..\,12] & \\ \qquad \textbf{if hindu-expunged?}\,(year, (month-1) \bmod [1\,..\,12]) & \\ (month-1) \bmod [1\,..\,12] & \\ \qquad \textbf{otherwise} & \end{cases}$$

This uses a simple test for expunged months:

$$\textbf{hindu-expunged?}\,(l\text{-}year, l\text{-}month) \stackrel{\text{def}}{=} \qquad (20.38)$$

$$\begin{aligned}
&l\text{-}month\\
&\neq \big(\textbf{hindu-lunar-from-fixed}\\
&\qquad \big(\textbf{fixed-from-hindu-lunar}\,(\langle l\text{-}year, l\text{-}month, \text{false}, 15, \text{false}\rangle)\big)\big)_{\textbf{month}}
\end{aligned}$$

which converts the date back and forth.

Though it is generally agreed that one should follow the rules dictated by the *Sūrya-Siddhānta* for calculating lunar days, for sunrise it seems that most calendars use tabulated times, not the approximate values obtained by following the strictures of the *Sūrya-Siddhānta*, which can be off by more than 16 minutes.[14] Thus, one would get better agreement with published Hindu calendars by incorporating modern computations of local sunrise in place of those we gave in the previous section. To use astronomical sunrise at the Hindu "prime meridian," or elsewhere, we would need to substitute the following calculation for **hindu-sunrise**:

$$\textbf{alt-hindu-sunrise}\,(\textit{date}) \stackrel{\text{def}}{=} \frac{1/60}{24} \times \text{round}\,(\textit{rise} \times 24 \times 60) \tag{20.39}$$

where

$$\textit{rise} = \textbf{dawn}\,(\textit{date}, \textbf{hindu-location}, 47')$$

The depression angle is $47'$, as used by Lahiri; many other almanac makers prefer to use $0'$, contending that "geometric" sunrise is what was intended by traditional reckoning. The calculated moment of sunrise is rounded to the nearest minute and left as a rational number.

The main source of the discrepancy in sunrise time is the very rough traditional approximation for the equation of time; see Figure 20.3. Using an accurate equation of time, but otherwise following the siddhāntic method for sunrise, gives close agreement with geometric sunrise.

We should also point out that the "infinite" precision of our algorithms is, from a mathematical point of view, specious, because the "true" motions are only approximations, and the sine table used to calculate the epicyclic adjustments is accurate to only three decimal places. There is therefore nothing gained by our keeping the fractions obtained by interpolation and calculation to greater accuracy than the table lookup methods other than fidelity to the traditional sources. Our formulas, as stated, can involve numbers with hundreds of digits! For example, sunrise on July 31, 2000 (Gregorian) is calculated to be at R.D. moment

$$\frac{\begin{array}{l}1615633889615837580262179821926100162403902884959403092965 21\\ 481871576370976411058660592363336648805753383863 52129\end{array}}{\begin{array}{l}2212190337338360601196433358868895705361302755736607228219 02\\ 3760238765247646791922950084531325000000000000000\end{array}}$$

which is 5:22:58.45 a.m. (about 7 minutes before the actual sunrise). At that time, the phase of the moon is

$$\frac{\begin{array}{l}130476405403393501333219102287451063244648251594485763252 6629\\ 588426416714918765030017854219532444517606402131450403859 1557\\ 906588786591176270882742899001396773289605388020533521537 0439\\ 828249210439506621297156609225428632978116179459316866370 391\end{array}}{\begin{array}{l}363636225691106036607102243341138046718454751726906416692 9050\\ 985824785417994335416309926443827777315979918609611333072 835\\ 787967997157291004542100003252314115653371401789668379531 2265\\ 275794619694772930360937500000000000000000000000000000000 0\end{array}}$$

[14] P. S. Purewal [10]: "Most Indian almanac editors give and advocate the use of [the] centre of [the] solar disk for sunrise without refraction."

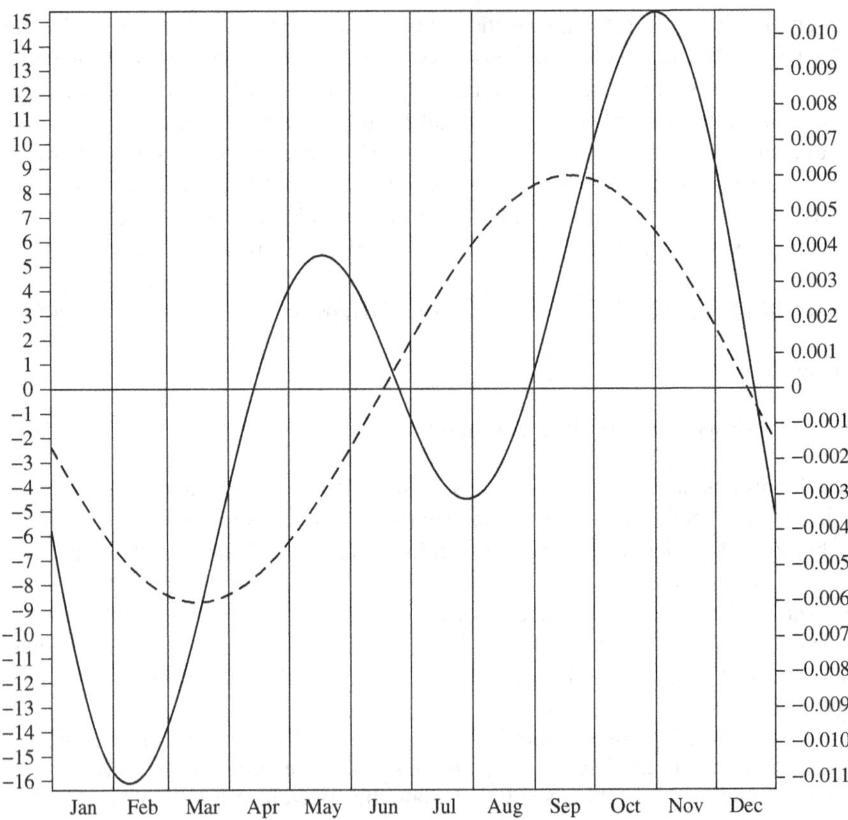

Figure 20.3 The equation of time in 1000 C.E. The astronomical version is shown as the solid line; the traditional Hindu version is shown as the dashed line. The left-hand vertical axis is marked in minutes and the right-hand vertical axis is marked in fractions of a day.

which is just shy of 359° (whereas it is actually a bit past new moon). Double-precision arithmetic suffices for all practical purposes.

20.5 Astronomical Versions

Every year a great number of pañcāṅgs [almanacs] is still printed all over India, and some are calculated entirely after the prescriptions of the Sūrya-Siddhānta *(or of another Siddhānta or Karaṇa), and some take their astronomical data from the Greenwich Nautical Almanac. Now there is something in favour of both ways, and one who wishes to know the exact moment of conjunctions, &c., must certainly use the second type. But that which is won on the one side is lost on the other: the Indians are possessors of an old tradition, and they ought to preserve that and glorify it . . .*

Walther E. van Wijk: "On Hindu Chronology IV: Decimal Tables for Calculating the Exact Moments of Beginning of Mean and True Tithis, Karaṇas, Nakṣatras and Yogas, According to the Sūrya-Siddhānta; Together with Some Miscellaneous Notes on the Subject of Hindu Chronology," *Acta Orientalia*, vol. IV (1926)

Another alternative to the calculations we have presented would be to utilize the same accurate astronomical functions as are used for the Chinese calendar. Indeed, some Indian calendar makers have replaced the traditional methods with such ephemeris data, but they are the minority.

All one needs to do to obtain astronomical Hindu calendars is to substitute the **sidereal-solar-longitude** (14.40) and **lunar-phase** (14.56) functions of Chapter 14 for those based on the *Sūrya-Siddhānta*. Calendar makers (as well as astrologers) typically apply a sidereal correction, called *ayanāmsha*, to the tropical values of modern astronomical tables or programs:

$$\textbf{ayanamsha}\,(t) \stackrel{\text{def}}{=} \quad \textbf{solar-longitude}\,(t) - \textbf{sidereal-solar-longitude}\,(t) \tag{20.40}$$

Different values for this correction have been proposed; they amount to choosing the moment at which tropical and sidereal values coincided, such as

$$\textbf{sidereal-start} \stackrel{\text{def}}{=} \quad \textbf{precession}\,(\textbf{universal-from-local}\,(\textbf{mesha-samkranti}\,(285\ \text{C.E.}), \textbf{hindu-location})) \tag{20.41}$$

The function **mesha-samkranti** (page 364) gives the time of the Hindu sidereal spring equinox (see Section 20.6), and **hindu-location** (page 351) is the city of Ujjain.

The difference between the equinoctial and sidereal longitudes (the *ayanamsha*) changes with time, as a direct consequence of the precession of the equinoxes. It is uncertain what the zero point of Indian sidereal longitude is, but it is customary to say that the two measurements coincided circa 285 C.E., the so-called "Lahiri *ayanamsha*." The average difference between this sidereal longitude and the astronomical value was 2°3′ during 1000–1002 C.E.; see [4]. Others (for example [15, sec. 18]) suggest that the two measurements coincided around 560 C.E. Either way, the overestimate of the length of the mean sidereal year used by the siddhantas leads to a slowly growing discrepancy in the calculation of solar longitude. (The length of the sidereal year is increasing by about 10^{-4} seconds per year.)

The discrepancy in the solar calendar grows noticeably with time, on account of the inaccuracy in the traditional value of the sidereal year. On the one hand, the difference in the lunisolar calendar can be on the order of a month—when a new moon occurs close to the border between zodiacal signs. On the other hand, neither the interpolated stepped sine function used traditionally nor the fluctuating epicycle of Indian theory makes a noticeable difference for the sun. In other words, the tabular sine and arcsine functions (see Table 20.3) are precise enough for the purpose, while the theory of changing epicycles (see Figure 20.2) is unnecessary for the sun. See [4].

For the solar calendar, suppose that we wish to implement the Tamil rule, for which the critical moment for measuring the sun's sidereal longitude is local sunset, and suppose we use geometric sunset, as is often done. We have

$$\textbf{astro-hindu-sunset}\,(\mathit{date}) \stackrel{\text{def}}{=} \textbf{dusk}\,(\mathit{date}, \textbf{hindu-location}, 0^\circ) \tag{20.42}$$

Then, we have the following set of functions:

$$\textbf{sidereal-zodiac}\,(t) \stackrel{\text{def}}{=} \left\lfloor \frac{\textbf{sidereal-solar-longitude}\,(t)}{30^\circ} \right\rfloor + 1 \tag{20.43}$$

$$\textbf{astro-hindu-calendar-year}\,(t) \stackrel{\text{def}}{=} \tag{20.44}$$

$$\text{round}\left(\frac{t - \textbf{hindu-epoch}}{\textbf{mean-sidereal-year}} - \frac{\textbf{sidereal-solar-longitude}\,(t)}{360^\circ}\right)$$

$$\textbf{astro-hindu-solar-from-fixed}\,(\mathit{date}) \stackrel{\text{def}}{=} \boxed{\mathit{year} \mid \mathit{month} \mid \mathit{day}} \tag{20.45}$$

where

$$\begin{aligned}
\mathit{critical} &= \textbf{astro-hindu-sunset}\,(\mathit{date})\\
\mathit{month} &= \textbf{sidereal-zodiac}\,(\mathit{critical})\\
\mathit{year} &= \textbf{astro-hindu-calendar-year}\,(\mathit{critical}) - \textbf{hindu-solar-era}\\
\mathit{approx} &= \mathit{date} - 3 - \left(\lfloor \textbf{sidereal-solar-longitude}\,(\mathit{critical}) \rfloor \bmod 30^\circ\right)\\
\mathit{start} &= \underset{i \geqslant \mathit{approx}}{\text{MIN}} \left\{ \textbf{sidereal-zodiac}\,(\textbf{astro-hindu-sunset}\,(i)) = \mathit{month} \right\}\\
\mathit{day} &= \mathit{date} - \mathit{start} + 1
\end{aligned}$$

$$\textbf{fixed-from-astro-hindu-solar}\left(\boxed{\mathit{year} \mid \mathit{month} \mid \mathit{day}}\right) \stackrel{\text{def}}{=} \tag{20.46}$$

$$\mathit{start} + \mathit{day} - 1$$

where

$$\begin{aligned}
\mathit{approx} &= \textbf{hindu-epoch} - 3\\
&\quad + \left\lfloor \left(\mathit{year} + \textbf{hindu-solar-era} + \frac{\mathit{month} - 1}{12}\right) \right.\\
&\qquad \left. \times\, \textbf{mean-sidereal-year} \right\rfloor\\
\mathit{start} &= \underset{i \geqslant \mathit{approx}}{\text{MIN}} \left\{ \textbf{sidereal-zodiac}\,(\textbf{astro-hindu-sunset}\,(i)) = \mathit{month} \right\}
\end{aligned}$$

For the lunar calendar, we need

$$\textbf{astro-lunar-day-from-moment}\,(t) \stackrel{\text{def}}{=} \left\lfloor \frac{\textbf{lunar-phase}\,(t)}{12^\circ} \right\rfloor + 1 \tag{20.47}$$

The conversions are analogous to the nonastronomical versions:

$$\textbf{astro-hindu-lunar-from-fixed}\,(date) \stackrel{\text{def}}{=} \tag{20.48}$$

$$\boxed{\mathit{year} \mid \mathit{month} \mid \mathit{leap\text{-}month} \mid \mathit{day} \mid \mathit{leap\text{-}day}}$$

where

$$\begin{aligned}
\mathit{critical} &= \textbf{alt-hindu-sunrise}\,(\mathit{date})\\
\mathit{day} &= \textbf{astro-lunar-day-from-moment}\,(\mathit{critical})\\
\mathit{leap\text{-}day} &= \mathit{day} = \textbf{astro-lunar-day-from-moment}\\
&\qquad\qquad (\textbf{alt-hindu-sunrise}\,(\mathit{date}-1))\\
\mathit{last\text{-}new\text{-}moon} &= \textbf{new-moon-before}\,(\mathit{critical})\\
\mathit{next\text{-}new\text{-}moon} &= \textbf{new-moon-at-or-after}\,(\mathit{critical})\\
\mathit{solar\text{-}month} &= \textbf{sidereal-zodiac}\,(\mathit{last\text{-}new\text{-}moon})\\
\mathit{leap\text{-}month} &= \mathit{solar\text{-}month} = \textbf{sidereal-zodiac}\,(\mathit{next\text{-}new\text{-}moon})\\
\mathit{month} &= (\mathit{solar\text{-}month}+1) \bmod [1 \,..\, 12]\\
\mathit{year} &= \textbf{astro-hindu-calendar-year}\\
&\qquad \left(\begin{cases} \mathit{date}+180 & \textbf{if } \mathit{month} \leqslant 2\\ \mathit{date} & \textbf{otherwise}\end{cases}\right)\\
&\qquad - \textbf{hindu-lunar-era}
\end{aligned}$$

In the other direction, we have

$$\textbf{fixed-from-astro-hindu-lunar} \tag{20.49}$$

$$\left(\boxed{\mathit{year} \mid \mathit{month} \mid \mathit{leap\text{-}month} \mid \mathit{day} \mid \mathit{leap\text{-}day}}\right) \stackrel{\text{def}}{=}$$

$$\begin{cases} \mathit{date}+1 & \textbf{if } \mathit{leap\text{-}day}\\ \mathit{date} & \textbf{otherwise}\end{cases}$$

where

$$\begin{aligned}
\mathit{approx} = {} & \textbf{hindu-epoch} + \textbf{mean-sidereal-year}\\
& \times \left(\mathit{year} + \textbf{hindu-lunar-era} + \frac{\mathit{month}-1}{12}\right)
\end{aligned}$$

$$
\begin{aligned}
s &= \Big\lfloor approx \\
&\quad - \textbf{hindu-sidereal-year} \\
&\quad \times \left(\left(\frac{\textbf{sidereal-solar-longitude}\,(approx)}{360^\circ} - \frac{month - 1}{12} \right) \right. \\
&\quad \left. \bmod \left[-\frac{1}{2} \,..\, \frac{1}{2}\right) \right) \Big\rfloor \\
k &= \textbf{astro-lunar-day-from-moment}\,(s + 6^{\text{h}}) \\
est &= s + day \\
&\quad - \left\{ \begin{array}{ll} k & \textbf{if } 3 < k < 27 \\ k \bmod [-15\,..\,15) & \textbf{if } mid_{\textbf{month}} \neq month \text{ or} \\ & \quad \{mid_{\textbf{leap-month}} \text{ and not } leap\text{-}month\} \\ k \bmod [15\,..\,45) & \textbf{otherwise} \end{array} \right\} \\
\tau &= est - \Big(\big(\textbf{astro-lunar-day-from-moment}\,(est + 6^{\text{h}}) - day \big) \\
&\quad \bmod [-15\,..\,15) \Big) \\
date &= \underset{d \geqslant \tau - 1}{\text{MIN}} \left\{ \begin{array}{l} \textbf{astro-lunar-day-from-moment}\,(\textbf{alt-hindu-sunrise}\,(d)) \\ \in \{day, (day + 1) \bmod [1\,..\,30]\} \end{array} \right\} \\
mid &= \textbf{astro-hindu-lunar-from-fixed}\,(s - 15)
\end{aligned}
$$

Though the mean time of the *tithis* differs only slightly between the traditional and astronomical calculations, the margin of error can be several hours; see Figure 20.4. Hence, the astronomical dates often differ by a day from the traditionally calculated ones for dates near the present. See Appendix C (page 451). Like for the solar calendar, varying the size of the epicycle does not have a noticeable effect. Similarly, the use of the *bija* correction for the length of the anomalistic months is of no consequence. See [4] for more details.

20.6 Holidays

In what manner the Hindus *contrive so far to reconcile the lunar and solar years, as to make them proceed concurrently in their ephemerides, might easily have been shown by exhibiting a version of their* Nadíyu *or* Varánes *almanack; but their modes of intercalation form no part of my present subject, and would injure the simplicity of my work, without throwing any light on the religion of the* Hindus.

Sir William Jones: "Asiatick Researches," *Transactions of the Bengal Society* (1801)

As with the Hindu calendars, so too with the holidays: there is a plethora of regional holidays and local variants of widespread holidays. The most complete reference in English is [14], but sufficient details to handle exceptional circumstances (leap months, skipped months, leap days, omitted days, and borderline cases) are lacking.

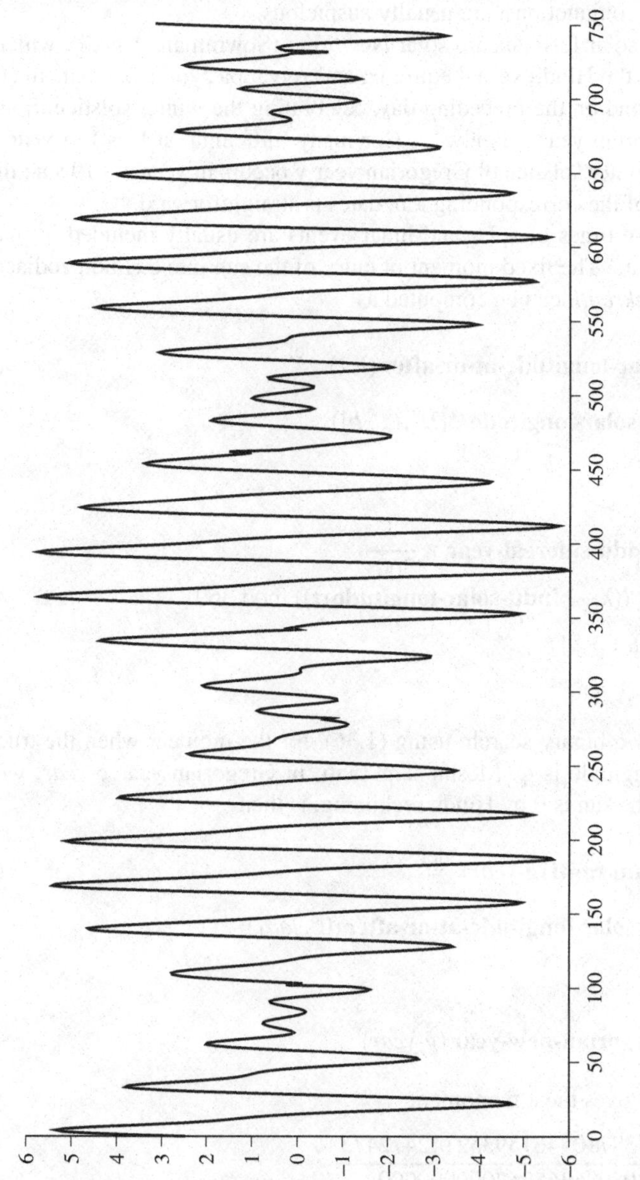

Figure 20.4 Tithi time differences, 1000–1001 C.E., in hours.

Certain hours, days, and months are more auspicious than others. For example, Wednesday and Saturday are "unlucky" days, as is the dark half of each month. Leap months and civil days containing lost lunar days are considered inauspicious. Astronomical events, such as actual or computed solar and lunar eclipses and planetary conjunctions, are usually auspicious.

The chief solar festivals are solar New Year (Sowramana Ugadi), which is the day following the Hindu vernal equinox, and Ayyappa Jyothi Darshanam (Pongal) on Makara 1 and on the preceding day, celebrating the winter solstice. Solar New Year in Gregorian year y is always (for many millennia, at least) in year $y - 78$ S.E., and the winter solstice of Gregorian year y occurs in year $y - 79$ S.E.; thus, the computation of the corresponding R.D. dates is straightforward.

The precise times of solar and lunar events are usually included in published Indian calendars. The fixed moment of entry of the sun into a Hindu zodiacal sign, called the *saṃkrānti*, can be computed as

$$\textbf{hindu-solar-longitude-at-or-after}\,(\lambda, t) \stackrel{\text{def}}{=} \qquad (20.50)$$

$$\textbf{hindu-solar-longitude}^{-1}(\lambda, [a \,..\, b])$$

where

$$\tau = t + \textbf{hindu-sidereal-year} \times \frac{1}{360^\circ}$$
$$\times\ ((\lambda - \textbf{hindu-solar-longitude}\,(t)) \bmod 360)$$
$$a = \max\{t, \tau - 5\}$$
$$b = \tau + 5$$

This is simply a binary search, using (1.36), for the moment when the true (sidereal) solar longitude is φ. Mesha saṃkrānti, in Gregorian year *g-year*, when the longitude of the sun is 0 by Hindu reckoning, is then

$$\textbf{mesha-samkranti}\,(\textit{g-year}) \stackrel{\text{def}}{=} \qquad (20.51)$$

$$\textbf{hindu-solar-longitude-at-or-after}\,(0^\circ, \textit{jan}_1)$$

where

$$\textit{jan}_1 = \textbf{gregorian-new-year}\,(\textit{g-year})$$

This function gives the R.D. moment

$$\frac{304233775871094675935214247247 3}{416630898636595200000000 0}$$

as the time of Mesha saṃkrānti in the Gregorian year 2000, which is 5:55:58 p.m. on April 13.

Most Indian holidays, however, depend on the lunar date. Festivals are usually celebrated on the day when a specified lunar day is current at sunrise; other events may depend on the phase of the moon at noon, sunset, or midnight. Some lunar holidays require that the specified lunar day be current at noon rather than at sunrise. Sometimes, if the lunar day in question begins at least 1/15 of a day before sunset of one day and ends before sunset of the next, the corresponding holiday is celebrated on the first day [8, sec. 113]. For example, Nāga Panchamī (a day of snake worship) is normally celebrated on Śrāvaṇa, 5 but is advanced by 1 day if lunar day 5 begins in the first 1.2 temporal hours of day 4 and ends within the first tenth of day 5. Technically, such determinations require the computation of the time of sunset in a manner analogous to that of sunrise.

The search for the new moon, given as **hindu-new-moon** (page 346), is halted once the position of the moon (and sun) at the time of conjunction has been narrowed to a particular constellation on the zodiac. When greater accuracy is needed, and for the arbitrary phases needed for holiday calculations, we use the following function—the inverse of equation (20.15)—which gives the moment at which the kth lunar day occurred after moment t:

$$\textbf{hindu-lunar-day-at-or-after}\,(k, t) \stackrel{\text{def}}{=} \qquad (20.52)$$

$$\textbf{hindu-lunar-phase}^{-1}(\mathit{phase}, [a \mathinner{..} b])$$

where

$$\begin{aligned} \mathit{phase} &= (k-1) \times 12^{\circ} \\ \tau &= t + \frac{1}{360^{\circ}} \times ((\mathit{phase} - \textbf{hindu-lunar-phase}\,(t)) \bmod 360) \\ &\quad \times \textbf{hindu-synodic-month} \\ a &= \max\,\{t, \tau - 2\} \\ b &= \tau + 2 \end{aligned}$$

The value of τ is the most recent mean moment when $k - 1$ thirtieths of a lunar month have elapsed. For the time of new moon, k should be 1; k should be 16 for the time of full moon.

The beginning of the lunisolar New Year (Chandramana Ugadi), usually Caitra 1, is the day of the first sunrise after the new moon preceding Mesha saṃkrānti, or the prior new moon in the case when the first month of the lunar year is leap:

$$\textbf{hindu-lunar-new-year}\,(\textit{g-year}) \stackrel{\text{def}}{=} \qquad (20.53)$$

$$\textit{h-day} + \left\{ \begin{array}{ll} 0 & \textbf{if } \mathit{new\text{-}moon} < \mathit{critical} \text{ or} \\ & \quad \textbf{hindu-lunar-day-from-moment} \\ & \qquad (\textbf{hindu-sunrise}\,(\textit{h-day} + 1)) = 2 \\ 1 & \textbf{otherwise} \end{array} \right\}$$

where

$$
\begin{aligned}
jan_1 &= \textbf{gregorian-new-year}\,(g\text{-}year)\\
mina &= \textbf{hindu-solar-longitude-at-or-after}\,(330^\circ, jan_1)\\
new\text{-}moon &= \textbf{hindu-lunar-day-at-or-after}\,(1, mina)\\
h\text{-}day &= \lfloor new\text{-}moon \rfloor\\
critical &= \textbf{hindu-sunrise}\,(h\text{-}day)
\end{aligned}
$$

If the first lunar day of the New Year is wholly contained in the interval between one sunrise and the next, then this function returns the fixed date on which the new moon occurs, which is also the last day of the previous lunisolar year, Phālguna 30.[15]

The major Hindu lunar holidays include the Birthday of Rāma (Rāma Navamī), celebrated on Caitra 9; Varalakshmi Vratam on the Friday prior to Śrāvaṇa 15; the Birthday of Krishna (Janmāshṭamī) on Śrāvaṇa 23; Ganēśa Chaturthī, held on Bhādrapada 4;[16] Durgā Ashtami on Āśvina 8; Sarasvatī Puja on Āśvina 9, when books are worshipped in honor of the goddess of eloquence and arts, Sarasvatī; Dasra on Āśvina 10; Diwali, a major autumn festival celebrated over the period Āśvina 29–Kārtika 1 (Kārtika 1 is the main day of festivity and marks the beginning of the year in some regions); the festival Karthikai Deepam on Kārtika 15; the main festival of the year, Vaikunta Ekadashi on Mārgaśīrṣa 11, honoring Vishnu; Maha Shivaratri, the Great Night of Shiva, celebrated on the day that lunar day Māgha 29 is current at midnight, and preceded by a day of fasting by devotees of Shiva; and the spring festival, Holi, which takes place in the evening of lunar day Phālguna 15. Buddha's Birthday is celebrated on the fifteenth of Vaiśākha, but the exact date depends on which lunar calendar is followed.

In general, holidays are not held in leap months. When a month is skipped, its holidays are usually celebrated in the following month. Festivals are generally celebrated on the first of two days with the same lunar day number; if a day is expunged, the festival takes place on the civil day containing that lunar day.

---

[15] The results obtained with our functions are in complete agreement with Sewell's and Dîkshit's tables [12] for the added and expunged months from 1500 to 1900. Furthermore, our functions are in agreement with the calculations in [8, pp. 97–101] for the earlier disputed years considered there. They also agree on the date of the lunisolar New Years in the period 1500–1900, except for spring 1600, when the first new moon of 1657 V.E. occurred on March 5, 1600 C.E. (Julian) after sunrise but the second lunar day began at 6:07 a.m. on March 6. Reckoning with mean sunrise, as in [12, p. lxxxii], March 6 is the first day of the New Year because at 6 a.m. that day the new moon was still in its first tithi. However, at the true time of sunrise, 6:13 according to the *Sūrya-Siddhānta*, or 6:08 using our astronomical code, lunar day 1 had already ended and, therefore, the New Year is considered to have started on the previous day.

[16] According to [7], the precise rule is that Ganēśa Chaturthī is celebrated on the day in which lunar day 4 is current in whole or in part during the midday period that extends from 1.2 temporal hours before noon until 1.2 temporal hours after noon. If, however, that lunar day is current during midday on 2 consecutive days, or if it extends from after midday on one day until before midday of the next, then it is celebrated on the former day.

We will need to compare the five components of lunar dates lexicographically:

hindu-lunar-on-or-before? (20.54)

$$\left(\boxed{year_1 \mid month_1 \mid leap_1 \mid day_1 \mid leap\text{-}day_1}, \boxed{year_2 \mid month_2 \mid leap_2 \mid day_2 \mid leap\text{-}day_2}\right) \stackrel{\text{def}}{=}$$

$$\begin{array}{l} year_1 < year_2 \text{ or} \\ \{ year_1 = year_2 \text{ and} \\ \quad \{ month_1 < month_2 \text{ or} \\ \quad\quad \{ month_1 = month_2 \text{ and} \\ \quad\quad\quad \{ \{leap_1 \text{ and not } leap_2\} \text{ or} \\ \quad\quad\quad\quad \{ leap_1 = leap_2 \text{ and} \\ \quad\quad\quad\quad\quad \{ day_1 < day_2 \text{ or} \\ \quad\quad\quad\quad\quad\quad \{day_1 = day_2 \text{ and } \{\text{not } leap\text{-}day_1 \text{ or } leap\text{-}day_2\}\} \} \} \} \} \} \end{array}$$

Taking into account the fact that **fixed-from-hindu-lunar** returns the day following an expunged day and a date in the month following an expunged month, we can compute the day on which an event is celebrated in this way:

hindu-date-occur (*l-year, l-month, l-day*) $\stackrel{\text{def}}{=}$ (20.55)

$$\begin{cases} \underset{d \geqslant try}{\mathbf{MIN}} \left\{ \begin{array}{l} \text{not } \mathbf{hindu\text{-}lunar\text{-}on\text{-}or\text{-}before?} \\ \quad (\mathbf{hindu\text{-}lunar\text{-}from\text{-}fixed}\,(d),\ l\text{-}date) \end{array} \right\} - 1 & \\ \quad\quad \mathbf{if}\ expunged? & \\ try - 1 \quad \mathbf{if}\ l\text{-}day \neq (\mathbf{hindu\text{-}lunar\text{-}from\text{-}fixed}\,(try))_{\mathbf{day}} & \\ try \quad \mathbf{otherwise} & \end{cases}$$

where

$$lunar = \boxed{l\text{-}year \mid l\text{-}month \mid \text{false} \mid l\text{-}day \mid \text{false}}$$

$$try = \mathbf{fixed\text{-}from\text{-}hindu\text{-}lunar}\,(lunar)$$

$$mid = \mathbf{hindu\text{-}lunar\text{-}from\text{-}fixed}\left(\begin{cases} try - 5 & \mathbf{if}\ l\text{-}day > 15 \\ try & \mathbf{otherwise} \end{cases}\right)$$

$$expunged? = l\text{-}month \neq mid_{\mathbf{month}}$$

$$l\text{-}date = \boxed{mid_{\mathbf{year}} \mid mid_{\mathbf{month}} \mid mid_{\mathbf{leap\text{-}month}} \mid l\text{-}day \mid \text{false}}$$

We use this to write

hindu-lunar-holiday (*l-month, l-day, g-year*) $\stackrel{\text{def}}{=}$ (20.56)

$$\{date_0, date_1\} \cap \mathbf{gregorian\text{-}year\text{-}range}\,(g\text{-}year)$$

where

$$\begin{aligned}
\textit{l-year} &= (\textbf{hindu-lunar-from-fixed}\,(\textbf{gregorian-new-year}\,(\textit{g-year})))_{\textbf{year}}\\
\textit{date}_0 &= \textbf{hindu-date-occur}\,(\textit{l-year}, \textit{l-month}, \textit{l-day})\\
\textit{date}_1 &= \textbf{hindu-date-occur}\,(\textit{l-year}+1, \textit{l-month}, \textit{l-day})
\end{aligned}$$

Now, to compute the main day of Diwali, normally Kārtika 1 in a given Gregorian year, we have

$$\textbf{diwali}\,(\textit{g-year}) \stackrel{\text{def}}{=} \textbf{hindu-lunar-holiday}\,(8, 1, \textit{g-year}) \tag{20.57}$$

As mentioned above, many holidays depend on the precise time of a lunar event. For such events we first approximate the date, using **hindu-date-occur** below, and then search for when the event occurs at the proper time of day:

$$\textbf{hindu-tithi-occur}\,(\textit{l-month}, \textit{tithi}, t, \textit{l-year}) \stackrel{\text{def}}{=} \tag{20.58}$$

$$\begin{cases}
\textit{try} & \textbf{if } \textit{lunar} \leqslant t_h \textbf{ or}\\
& \quad \textbf{hindu-lunar-phase}\\
& \quad\quad (\textbf{standard-from-sundial}\,(\textit{try}+1+t, \textbf{ujjain}))\\
& \quad > 12 \times \textit{tithi}\\
\textit{try}+1 & \textbf{otherwise}
\end{cases}$$

where

$$\begin{aligned}
\textit{approx} &= \textbf{hindu-date-occur}\,(\textit{l-year}, \textit{l-month}, \lfloor \textit{tithi} \rfloor)\\
\textit{lunar} &= \textbf{hindu-lunar-day-at-or-after}\,(\textit{tithi}, \textit{approx}-2)\\
\textit{try} &= \textbf{fixed-from-moment}\,(\textit{lunar})\\
t_h &= \textbf{standard-from-sundial}\,(\textit{try}+t, \textbf{ujjain})
\end{aligned}$$

To search for the time of occurrence of the event, we use

$$\textbf{hindu-lunar-event}\,(\textit{l-month}, \textit{tithi}, t, \textit{g-year}) \stackrel{\text{def}}{=} \tag{20.59}$$

$$\{\textit{date}_0, \textit{date}_1\} \cap \textbf{gregorian-year-range}\,(\textit{g-year})$$

where

$$\begin{aligned}
\textit{l-year} &= (\textbf{hindu-lunar-from-fixed}\,(\textbf{gregorian-new-year}\,(\textit{g-year})))_{\textbf{year}}\\
\textit{date}_0 &= \textbf{hindu-tithi-occur}\,(\textit{l-month}, \textit{tithi}, t, \textit{l-year})\\
\textit{date}_1 &= \textbf{hindu-tithi-occur}\,(\textit{l-month}, \textit{tithi}, t, \textit{l-year}+1)
\end{aligned}$$

If the event occurs after the specified time but the relevant lunar day is no longer current at the critical time the following day, then the former day is chosen. With

hindu-lunar-event, we can determine the dates of the Great Night of Shiva and the Birthday of Rāma, as follows:

$$\textbf{shiva}\,(g\text{-}year) \stackrel{\text{def}}{=} \textbf{hindu-lunar-event}\left(11, 29, 24^{\text{h}}, g\text{-}year\right) \tag{20.60}$$

$$\textbf{rama}\,(g\text{-}year) \stackrel{\text{def}}{=} \textbf{hindu-lunar-event}\left(1, 9, 12^{\text{h}}, g\text{-}year\right) \tag{20.61}$$

For some holidays (and in some regions), the location of the moon may be more important than the lunar date. A lunar station, called *nakṣatra*, is associated with each civil day and is determined by the (sidereal) longitude of the moon at sunrise:

$$\textbf{hindu-lunar-station}\,(date) \stackrel{\text{def}}{=} \tag{20.62}$$

$$\left\lfloor \frac{\textbf{hindu-lunar-longitude}\,(critical)}{800'} \right\rfloor + 1$$

where

$$critical = \textbf{hindu-sunrise}\,(date)$$

The names of the 27 stations are given in Table 20.1.

The function **hindu-lunar-day-at-or-after** can also be used to determine the time of onset of *karaṇas*, which are each a lunar half-day in duration, by using fractions for k. The most recent occurrence of the nth karaṇa ($1 \leqslant n \leqslant 60$), prior to day d, begins (very close to) **hindu-lunar-day-at-or-after**$((n+1)/2, d)$. The names of the karaṇas and their repeating pattern are shown in Table 20.5; the following function gives the column number of the nth karaṇa:

$$\textbf{karana}\,(n) \stackrel{\text{def}}{=} \begin{cases} 0 & \textbf{if } n = 1 \\ n - 50 & \textbf{if } n > 57 \\ (n-1) \bmod [1\,..\,7] & \textbf{otherwise} \end{cases} \tag{20.63}$$

A *yoga* (meaning "addition") is the varying period of time during which the solar and lunar longitudes increase by a *total* of 800 arc minutes (13°20′). A full circle contains 27 segments of 800′, corresponding to the 27 yogas given in Table 20.6. Because a full revolution of the sun or moon has no net effect on the yogas, we need only consider their longitudes, counted in increments of 800′ modulo 27:

$$\textbf{yoga}\,(date) \stackrel{\text{def}}{=} \tag{20.64}$$

$$1 + \left\lfloor \frac{\textbf{hindu-solar-longitude}\,(date) + \textbf{hindu-lunar-longitude}\,(date)}{800'} \bmod 27 \right\rfloor$$

Table 20.5 The cycle of 60 *karaṇas* (lunar half-days). The number and name for each half-day are given to the left of each row. Four special names apply at the beginning and end of a month; the other seven names repeat regularly during mid-month. The function **karana** returns the number in the leftmost column.

Karaṇa			Sequence							
Number	Name		1–8	9–15	16–22	23–29	30–36	37–43	44–50	51–60
0	Kiṃstughna	किंस्तुघ्न	1							
1	Bava	बव	2	9	16	23	30	37	44	51
2	Vālava	बालव	3	10	17	24	31	38	45	52
3	Kaulava	कौलव	4	11	18	25	32	39	46	53
4	Taitila	तैतिल	5	12	19	26	33	40	47	54
5	Gara	गर	6	13	20	27	34	41	48	55
6	Vaṇija	वणिज्	7	14	21	28	35	42	49	56
7	Viṣṭi	विष्टि	8	15	22	29	36	43	50	57
8	Śakuni	शकुनि								58
9	Catuṣpada	चतुष्पद								59
10	Nāga	नाग								60

Table 20.6 The cycle of 27 yogas corresponding to segments of 800′ of arc.

(1) Viṣkambha	विष्कम्भ	(15) Vajra	वज्र
(2) Prīti	प्रीति	(16) Siddhi	सिद्धि
(3) Ayuṣmān	आयुष्मान्	(17) Vyatīpāta	व्यतीपात
(4) Saubhāgya	सौभाग्य	(18) Varīyas	वरीयस्
(5) Śobhana	शोभन	(19) Parigha	परिघ
(6) Atigaṇḍa	अतिगण्ड	(20) Śiva	शिव
(7) Sukarman	सुकर्मन्	(21) Siddha	सिद्ध
(8) Dhṛti	धृति	(22) Sādhya	साध्य
(9) Śūla	शूल	(23) Śubha	शुभ
(10) Gaṇḍa	गण्ड	(24) Śukla	शुक्ल
(11) Vṛddhi	वृद्धि	(25) Brahman	ब्रह्मन्
(12) Dhruva	ध्रुव	(26) Indra	इन्द्र
(13) Vyāghāta	व्याघात	(27) Vaidhṛti	वैधृति
(14) Harṣaṇa	हर्षण		

Inverting this function to determine the time of the last occurrence of a given yoga is similar to **hindu-lunar-day-at-or-after**.
Certain other conjunctions of calendrical and astronomical events are also termed *yogas*.

There are numerous days of lesser importance that depend on the lunisolar calendar. Certain combinations of events are also significant. As a relatively insignificant example, whenever lunar day 8 falls on Wednesday, the day is sacred:

sacred-wednesdays (*g-year*) $\stackrel{\text{def}}{=}$ (20.65)

sacred-wednesdays-in-range (**gregorian-year-range** (*g-year*))

This uses the following function, parallel to (2.44), to collect all such Wednesdays within a range of fixed dates:

$$\textbf{sacred-wednesdays-in-range}\,([a\,..\,b)) \stackrel{\text{def}}{=} \tag{20.66}$$
$$\begin{cases} \begin{Bmatrix} \langle wed \rangle & \textbf{if } h\text{-}date_{\textbf{day}} = 8 \\ \langle\,\rangle & \textbf{otherwise} \end{Bmatrix} & \textbf{if } wed \in range \\ \parallel \textbf{sacred-wednesdays-in-range}\,([wed+1\,..\,b)) & \\ \langle\,\rangle & \textbf{otherwise} \end{cases}$$

where

$$\begin{aligned} range &= [a\,..\,b) \\ wed &= \textbf{kday-on-or-after}\,(\textbf{wednesday}, a) \\ h\text{-}date &= \textbf{hindu-lunar-from-fixed}\,(wed) \end{aligned}$$

There are various auspicious and inauspicious days that depend on the positions of the planets. All of these can be calculated in much the same way as that of the moon but with an additional epicyclic motion; see [9].

The *panchang* is the traditional five-part Hindu calendar comprising for each civil day its lunar day (*tithi*), day of the week, *nakṣatra* (stellar position of the moon), *yoga*, and *karaṇa* (based on the lunar phase). We have provided functions above for each component.

References

[1] Calendar Reform Committee, *Report of the Calendar Reform Committee*, New Delhi, 1955.

[2] *Sūrya-Siddhānta*, circa 1000. Translated by E. Burgess with notes by W. D. Whitney, *Journal of the American Oriental Society*, vol. 6, 1860. A new edition, edited by P. Gangooly with an introduction by P. Sengupta, was published by Calcutta University, 1935. Reprinted by Indological Book House, Varanasi, India, 1977; also reprinted by Wizards Book Shelf, Minneapolis, 1978.

[3] S. K. Chatterjee and A. K. Chakravarty, "Indian Calendar from Post-Vedic Period to A.D. 1900," *Indian Journal of History of Science*, vol. 20, pp. 252–308, 1985.

[4] N. Dershowitz and E. M. Reingold, "Indian Calendrical Calculations," *Ancient Indian Leaps in the Advent of Mathematics*, B. S. Yadav and M. Mohan, eds., Birkhäuser, Boston, pp. 1–32, 2011.

[5] H. G. Jacobi, "The Computation of Hindu Dates in Inscriptions, &c.," J. Burgess, ed., *Epigraphia Indica*: *A Collection of Inscriptions Supplementary to the Corpus Inscriptionum Indicarum of the Archæological Survey of India*, Calcutta, pp. 403–460 and 481, 1892.

[6] J. G. Jethabhai, *100 Years' Indian Calendar: Containing Christian, Samvat, Saka, Bengali, Mulki, Mugee, Burmese, Yazdejardi, Fasli, Nauroz and Hizri eras with their corresponding dates from 1845 to 1944 A.D.*, Limbdi, Kathiawar, Printed at the Jashvantsinhji printing press, 1912. (Reprinted by University of Michigan Library).

[7] F. Kielhorn, "Festal Days of the Hindu Lunar Calendar," *The Indian Antiquary*, vol. XXVI, pp. 177–187, 1897.

[8] D. B. L. D. S. Pillai, *Indian Chronology, Solar, Lunar, and Planetary. A Practical Guide*, Madras, 1911.

[9] D. Pingree, "History of Mathematical Astronomy in India," C. C. Gillispie, ed., *Dictionary of Scientific Biography*, vol. XV, suppl. I, pp. 533–633, 1978.

[10] P. S. Purewal, personal communication, April, 2002.

[11] R. Sewell, *The Siddhantas and the Indian Calendar*, Government of India Central Publication Branch, Calcutta, 1924.

[12] R. Sewell and S. B. Dîkshit, *The Indian Calendar, with Tables for the Conversion of Hindu and Muhammadan into* A.D. *Dates, and Vice Versa, with Tables of Eclipses Visible in India by R. Schram*, Motilal Banarsidass Publishers, Delhi, 1995. Originally published in 1896.

[13] D. C. Sircar, *Indian Epigraphy*, Motilal Banarsidass, Delhi, 1965.

[14] M. M. Underhill, *The Hindu Religious Year*, Association Press, Calcutta and Oxford University Press, London, 1921.

[15] Usha–Shashi, "Hindu Astrological Calculations (According to Modern Methods) with Complete Tables for Casting the Horoscope, and for Calculating the Graha and Bhava Balas," Sagar Publications, New Delhi, 1978.

[16] W. E. van Wijk, *Decimal Tables for the Reduction of Hindu Dates from the Data of the Sūrya-Siddhānta*, Martinus Nijhoff, The Hague, 1938.

[17] W. E. van Wijk, "On Hindu Chronology IV: Decimal Tables for Calculating the Exact Moments of Beginning of Mean and True Tithis, Karaṇas, Nakṣatras and Yogas, According to the Sūrya-Siddhānta; Together with Some Miscellaneous Notes on the Subject of Hindu Chronology," *Acta Orientalia*, vol. IV, pp. 55–80, 1926.

[18] W. E. van Wijk, "On Hindu Chronology V: Decimal Tables for Calculating True Local Time, According to the Sūrya-Siddhānta," *Acta Orientalia*, vol. V, pp. 1–27, 1927.

Hand-carved wall hanging from Nepal with a “Blessing Buddha” central image surrounded by the twelve animal totems of the Tibetan calendar. (Collection of E.M.R.)

21

The Tibetan Calendar[1]

The Tibetan system of astronomy and astrology is extremely complex. It takes five years to study and master it at the Astro Division of the Tibetan Medical and Astro Institute in Dharamsala, India. Students learn to calculate everything by hand in the traditional manner, on a wooden board covered with soot upon which one writes with a stylus. There is no complete ephemeris compiled in which to look up figures. One of the main aspects of the training is the mathematics involved in all the calculations.

Alexander Berzin (1986)[2]

21.1 Calendar

Brown's tables fill 650 quarto pages, and even with the tables a man working full time could extract the data just fast enough to keep up with the moon. The advent of the electronic calculator made feasible the direct evaluation of the formulas and ... improved accuracy.

Wallace J. Eckert: *Encyclopædia Britannica* (1964)

Several calendars are in use in Tibet. In this chapter we discuss the official *Phug-lugs* (or *Phug-pa* or *Phukluk*) version of the Kālacakra ("Wheel of Time") calendar, derived from the *Kālacakra Tantra*, translated into Tibetan from the Sanskrit in the eleventh century, used by the majority of Tibetans today, and sanctioned by the Dalai Lama. (The other widely used version is the *Tsurphu*.) The calendar is similar to the Hindu lunisolar calendars, somewhere between the arithmetic simplicity of the old Hindu version, and the astronomical complexity of the modern Hindu. There are also regional variants, because the calculated astronomical events are in terms of local time. The Bhutan, Mongolian, and Sherpa calendars are very similar.

Months are lunar; their length is based on an approximation to the varying length of the true synodic month, and can be 29 or 30 civil days long. Months are numbered consecutively, except for leap months, which *precede* their ordinary counterparts, as on the Hindu lunisolar calendar, and are named and numbered the same. The month names in Tibetan are:

---

[1] This chapter benefited from an implementation by Svante Janson [4]. Edward Henning kindly provided preprints of parts of [3].

[2] ཁུངས་སུ་དྲངས་འདི་དག་རྩོམ་པ་པོའི་བསམ་འཆར་བསྟན་པའི་ངེས་པ་མེད་

(1) dbo	(7) khrums
(2) nag pa	(8) tha skar
(3) sa ga	(9) smin drug
(4) snron	(10) mgo
(5) chu stod	(11) rgyal
(6) gro bzhin	(12) mchu

Weekdays are named in Tibetan as follows:

Sunday	gza' nyi ma
Monday	gza' zla ba
Tuesday	gza' mig dmar
Wednesday	gza' lhag pa
Thursday	gza' phur bu
Friday	gza' pa sangs
Saturday	gza' spen pa

There are several conventions for naming years. The most common is to use a 60-year cycle, naming them either like the Hindu Jovian years (Section 10.1), or using simultaneous 12-totem and 5-element cycles, in the fashion of the Chinese calendar (Section 19.4). The 5 elements, and their associated colors, are:

(1–2)	Wood	shing	Green
(3–4)	Fire	me	Red
(5–6)	Earth	sa	Yellow
(7–8)	Iron	lcags	White
(9–10)	Water	chu	Blue

The 12 animal totems are:

(1) Mouse	byi ba	(7) Horse	rta
(2) Ox	glang	(8) Sheep	lug
(3) Tiger	stag	(9) Monkey	spre'u
(4) Hare	yos	(10) Bird	bya
(5) Dragon	'brug	(11) Dog	khyi
(6) Snake	sbrul	(12) Pig	phag

The two cycles run in parallel, except that each element applies twice in a row, once "male" and once "female."

The sexagesimal cycles are counted starting from 1027 C.E., but the sexagesimal names are often coordinated with the Chinese.[3] However, we just number years, as in some variants, and choose as epoch the traditional year of ascension of the first Yarlung King, Nyatri Tsenpo:

$$\textbf{tibetan-epoch} \stackrel{\text{def}}{=} \quad (21.1)$$

$$\textbf{fixed-from-gregorian}\left(\boxed{-127 \mid \textbf{december} \mid 7}\right)$$

[3] Alexander Csoma de Kőrös [2, p. 148] wrongly fixed the first year of the first Rabbyuñ-cycle as 1026 instead of 1027. This was corrected in [5], [6]. Other important references are [1], [7], and [9].

Historically, many other variants have been used, posing similar problems to the historian as do Hindu dates.

Years follow a regular mean pattern, with 24 out of 65 years having a leap month. The year begins in late winter or early spring. Any month of the year can be leap, with leap months occurring at alternating fixed intervals of 33 and 34 months. Like the modern Hindu lunisolar calendar, there are also leap and expunged "lunar" days; unlike the modern Hindu calendar, but like most lunisolar calendars, there are no expunged months. So a date is a quintuple

year	*month*	*leap-month*	*day*	*leap-day*

The "true" time of solar and lunar events is obtained from their mean values by adding or subtracting an amount proportional to the sine of their anomaly. The sun's anomaly increases by about 0.97° per day, and the moon's by 12.86°. (The moon's anomaly is measured from apogee, the point at which it is farthest from Earth. In our **lunar-anomaly** function (14.52), it is measured from perigee; see page 234.) The mean year length is $365\frac{4975}{18382} \approx 365.270645$ days; the mean month is $29\frac{3001}{5656} \approx 29.530587$ days. Though traditional calendarists use mixed radix fractions in their calculations, we convert everything to ordinary rational numbers, as we have done for other calendars in this book.

The solar and lunar adjustments are computed by interpolating in tables for each heavenly body. The solar adjustment is

$$\textbf{tibetan-sun-equation}\,(\alpha) \stackrel{\text{def}}{=} \tag{21.2}$$

$$\begin{cases} -\,\textbf{tibetan-sun-equation}\,(\alpha - 6) & \textbf{if } \alpha > 6 \\ \textbf{tibetan-sun-equation}\,(6 - \alpha) & \textbf{if } \alpha > 3 \\ \langle 0', 6', 10', 11' \rangle_{[\alpha]} & \textbf{if } \alpha \in \mathbf{Z} \\ (\alpha \bmod 1) \times \textbf{tibetan-sun-equation}\,(\lceil \alpha \rceil) & \textbf{otherwise} \\ \quad +\,((-\alpha) \bmod 1) \times \textbf{tibetan-sun-equation}\,(\lfloor \alpha \rfloor) & \end{cases}$$

and for the lunar adjustment we have

$$\textbf{tibetan-moon-equation}\,(\alpha) \stackrel{\text{def}}{=} \tag{21.3}$$

$$\begin{cases} -\,\textbf{tibetan-moon-equation}\,(\alpha - 14) & \textbf{if } \alpha > 14 \\ \textbf{tibetan-moon-equation}\,(14 - \alpha) & \textbf{if } \alpha > 7 \\ \left\langle 0', 5', 10', 15', 19', 22', 24', 25' \right\rangle_{[\alpha]} & \textbf{if } \alpha \in \mathbf{Z} \\ (\alpha \bmod 1) \times \textbf{tibetan-moon-equation}\,(\lceil \alpha \rceil) & \textbf{otherwise} \\ \quad +\,((-\alpha) \bmod 1) \times \textbf{tibetan-moon-equation}\,(\lfloor \alpha \rfloor) & \end{cases}$$

For the solar equation, explicit values are given for 12 points in the full circle; for the lunar equation, for 28 points.

To convert from a Tibetan date to an R.D. date, we first use our cycle formulas (1.85) to determine how many (ordinary and leap) months have elapsed, then use that information to calculate how many mean lunar *days* and *mean* civil days have elapsed, and, lastly, make the solar and lunar adjustments:[4]

$$\textbf{fixed-from-tibetan}\left(\boxed{\textit{year} \mid \textit{month} \mid \textit{leap-month} \mid \textit{day} \mid \textit{leap-day}}\right) \stackrel{\text{def}}{=} \tag{21.4}$$

$$\lfloor \textbf{tibetan-epoch} + \textit{mean} + \textit{sun} + \textit{moon} \rfloor$$

where

$$\begin{aligned}
\textit{months} &= \left\lfloor \frac{804}{65} \times (\textit{year} - 1) + \frac{67}{65} \times \textit{month} \right. \\
&\qquad \left. + \begin{cases} -1 & \textbf{if } \textit{leap-month} \\ 0 & \textbf{otherwise} \end{cases} + \frac{64}{65} \right\rfloor \\
\textit{days} &= 30 \times \textit{months} + \textit{day} \\
\textit{mean} &= \textit{days} \times \frac{11135}{11312} - 30 + \begin{cases} 0 & \textbf{if } \textit{leap-day} \\ -1 & \textbf{otherwise} \end{cases} + \frac{1071}{1616} \\
\textit{solar-anomaly} &= \left(\textit{days} \times \frac{13}{4824} + \frac{2117}{4824}\right) \bmod 1 \\
\textit{lunar-anomaly} &= \left(\textit{days} \times \frac{3781}{105840} + \frac{2837}{15120}\right) \bmod 1 \\
\textit{sun} &= -\,\textbf{tibetan-sun-equation}\,(12 \times \textit{solar-anomaly}) \\
\textit{moon} &= \textbf{tibetan-moon-equation}\,(28 \times \textit{lunar-anomaly})
\end{aligned}$$

For the other direction, we simply estimate when the year begins, then search for the *year*, *month*, and *day* in turn, adjusting them as necessary in the case of a *leap-month*:

$$\textbf{tibetan-from-fixed}\,(\textit{date}) \stackrel{\text{def}}{=} \tag{21.5}$$

$$\boxed{\textit{year} \mid \textit{month} \mid \textit{leap-month} \mid \textit{day} \mid \textit{leap-day}}$$

where

$$\begin{aligned}
Y &= 365\tfrac{4975}{18382} \\
\textit{years} &= \left\lceil \frac{\textit{date} - \textbf{tibetan-epoch}}{Y} \right\rceil \\
\textit{year}_0 &= \underset{y \geqslant \textit{years}}{\textbf{MAX}} \left\{ \begin{array}{l} \textit{date} \\ \geqslant \textbf{fixed-from-tibetan}\left(\boxed{y \mid 1 \mid \text{false} \mid 1 \mid \text{false}}\right) \end{array} \right\}
\end{aligned}$$

---

[4] It is traditional to perform these astronomical calculations for the end of the lunar day, unlike our algorithm, which is based on the beginning of the given day.

$$month_0 = \underset{m \geqslant 1}{\mathbf{MAX}} \left\{ date \geqslant \textbf{fixed-from-tibetan}\left(\boxed{year_0 \mid m \mid \text{false} \mid 1 \mid \text{false}} \right) \right\}$$

$$est = date - \textbf{fixed-from-tibetan}\left(\boxed{year_0 \mid month_0 \mid \text{false} \mid 1 \mid \text{false}} \right)$$

$$day_0 = \underset{d \geqslant est-2}{\mathbf{MAX}} \left\{ date \geqslant \textbf{fixed-from-tibetan}\left(\boxed{year_0 \mid month_0 \mid \text{false} \mid d \mid \text{false}} \right) \right\}$$

$$leap\text{-}month = day_0 > 30$$

$$day = day_0 \bmod [1 \,..\, 30]$$

$$month = \left\{ \begin{array}{ll} month_0 - 1 & \textbf{if } day > day_0 \\ month_0 + 1 & \textbf{if } leap\text{-}month \\ month_0 & \textbf{otherwise} \end{array} \right\} \bmod [1 \,..\, 12]$$

$$year = \begin{cases} year_0 - 1 & \textbf{if } day > day_0 \text{ and } month_0 = 1 \\ year_0 + 1 & \textbf{if } leap\text{-}month \text{ and } month_0 = 12 \\ year_0 & \textbf{otherwise} \end{cases}$$

$$leap\text{-}day = date = \textbf{fixed-from-tibetan}\left(\boxed{year \mid month \mid leap\text{-}month \mid day \mid \text{true}} \right)$$

This algorithm relies on the fact that **fixed-from-tibetan** gives the fixed date of the following day when a day is expunged. The efficiency of the search for the month could be improved by starting from an underestimate.

21.2 Holidays

What the Yoga or 27 constellations of the zodiac are to the Indians also does not seem obscure to me.

Leonhard Euler: "On the Solar Astronomical Year of the Indians," from an appendix by Euler (translated by Kim Plofker) to two appendices [by C. T. Walther, Hebrew scholar and Danish missionary in Tranquebar, and T. S. Bayer, Euler's friend and Imperial Academy colleague] to a book by T. S. Bayer, *Historia regni Graecorum Bactriani* (1738)[5]

Yogas (combined motions of sun and moon), *nakṣatras* (lunar stations), and *karaṇas* (lunar half-days) follow the same patterns as on the Hindu calendar. One version of the 27 yoga names is as follows:

[5] This great mathematician, Leonhard Euler, was quite interested in Indian astronomy and developed calendrical formulas for the Indian calendars. See K. Plofker, "Euler and Indian Astronomy," *Leonhard Euler: Life, Work and Legacy*, R. E. Bradley and C. E. Sandifer, eds., Elsevier, New York, pp. 147–166, 2007.

(1) sel ba	(15) rdo rje
(2) mdza' ba	(16) grub pa
(3) tshe dang ldan pa	(17) shin tu lhung
(4) skal bzang	(18) mchog can
(5) bzang po	(19) yongs 'joms
(6) shin tu skrang	(20) zhi ba
(7) las bzang	(21) grub pa
(8) 'dzin pa	(22) bsgrub bya
(9) zug rngu	(23) dge ba
(10) skrang	(24) dkar po
(11) 'phel ba	(25) tshangs pa
(12) nges pa	(26) dbang po
(13) kun 'joms	(27) khon 'dzin
(14) dga' ba	

The 28 *nakṣatras* are:

(1) tha skar	(15) sa ri
(2) bra nye	(16) sa ga
(3) smin drug	(17) lha mtshams
(4) snar ma	(18) snron
(5) mgo	(19) snrubs
(6) lag	(20) chu stod
(7) nabs so	(21) chu smad
(8) rgyal	(22) gro bzhin
(9) skag	(23) byi bzhin
(10) mchu	(24) mon gre
(11) gre	(25) mon gru
(12) dbo	(26) khrums stod
(13) me bzhi	(27) khrums smad
(14) nag pa	(28) nam gru

The *karaṇa* names follow the same pattern as those of the Hindu calendar (Table 20.5):

(0) mi sdug pa	(6) tshong ba
(1) gdab pa	(7) vishti
(2) byis pa	(8) bkra shis
(3) rigs can	(9) rkang bzhi
(4) til rdung	(10) klu
(5) khyim skyes	

To determine whether a month is leap, we can check that inverting a leap-month date gives the same month:

$$\textbf{tibetan-leap-month?}\,(\textit{t-year}, \textit{t-month}) \stackrel{\text{def}}{=} \tag{21.6}$$

$$\textit{t-month} = \left(\textbf{tibetan-from-fixed}\left(\textbf{fixed-from-tibetan}\left(\boxed{\textit{t-year} \mid \textit{t-month} \mid \text{true} \mid 2 \mid \text{false}}\right)\right)\right)_{\textbf{month}}$$

It is also a simple matter to check whether a given Tibetan historical date might actually be a leap day with the following:

$$\textbf{tibetan-leap-day?}\,(\textit{t-year}, \textit{t-month}, \textit{t-day}) \stackrel{\text{def}}{=} \tag{21.7}$$

$$\textit{t-day} = \left(\textbf{tibetan-from-fixed}\left(\textbf{fixed-from-tibetan}\left(\boxed{\textit{t-year} \mid \textit{t-month} \mid \text{false} \mid \textit{t-day} \mid \text{true}}\right)\right)\right)_{\textbf{day}} \text{ or}$$

$$\textit{t-day} = \left(\textbf{tibetan-from-fixed}\left(\textbf{fixed-from-tibetan}\left(\boxed{\textit{t-year} \mid \textit{t-month} \mid \begin{array}{c}\textbf{tibetan-}\\ \textbf{leap-month?}\\ (\textit{t-year}, \textit{t-month})\end{array} \mid \textit{t-day} \mid \text{true}}\right)\right)\right)_{\textbf{day}}$$

The rules for holidays are similar to those of the Hindu calendar. The new year is called *Losar*; it is the first day of the year, even when the first month of the year is a leap month—other holidays are celebrated only in nonleap months. The leap day is preferred for day-specific Buddhist religious practices; in the event of an expunged day, the practice is performed on the prior day. Various days of the month may be auspicious or inauspicious for specific activities: especially inauspicious is the period from noon on the sixth day of the eleventh month until noon on the seventh day; the immediately following 24-hour period is particularly auspicious.

We can determine the fixed date of *Losar*, as follows:

$$\textbf{losar}\,(\textit{t-year}) \stackrel{\text{def}}{=} \tag{21.8}$$

$$\textbf{fixed-from-tibetan}\left(\boxed{\textit{t-year} \mid 1 \mid \textit{t-leap} \mid 1 \mid \text{false}}\right)$$

where

$$\textit{t-leap} = \textbf{tibetan-leap-month?}\,(\textit{t-year}, 1)$$

Celebration of the new year lasts three days. Since in the distant past and future there are Gregorian years with no occurrence of *Losar* (the last was in 719 C.E., long before this calendar was instituted, and next is in 12698), or with two occurrences (as in 718 C.E. and 12699), we need to check for the onset of two Tibetan years in each Gregorian year:

$$\textbf{tibetan-new-year}\,(\textit{g-year}) \stackrel{\text{def}}{=} \tag{21.9}$$

$$\{\textbf{losar}\,(\textit{t-year} - 1), \textbf{losar}\,(\textit{t-year})\} \cap \textbf{gregorian-year-range}\,(\textit{g-year})$$

where

$$\textit{dec}_{31} = \textbf{gregorian-year-end}\,(\textit{g-year})$$
$$\textit{t-year} = (\textbf{tibetan-from-fixed}\,(\textit{dec}_{31}))_{\textbf{year}}$$

For example, according to this function, *Losar* was on March 3, 2003 (Gregorian). In the *Tsurphu* version, however, it was on February 2.

Vesak or *Vaisakha*, Gautama Buddha's Birthday, is celebrated on different dates on different calendars, including: the seventh, eighth, or fifteenth day of the fourth month on the Tibetan calendar, the fifteenth of Vaiśākha on the Hindu calendar, the eighth day of the fourth month on the Chinese calendar, April 8 on the Gregorian calendar, or on the full moon day of May.

The whole first half of the first month of the year is significant, commemorating miracles performed by the Buddha. Buddha's Enlightenment (*nirvāṇa*) is celebrated on the fifteenth day of the fourth lunar month. The Turning of the Wheel of Dharma is celebrated on the fourth day of the sixth month; Buddha's Descent is celebrated on the twenty-second day of the ninth month.

References

[1] *The Kalachakra Tantra, Geshe Ngawang Dhargyey*, A. Wallace, translator, Library of Tibetan Works and Archives, Dharamsala, 1986.

[2] A. Csoma de Kőrös, *A Grammar of the Tibetan Language in English*, Calcutta, 1834.

[3] E. Henning, *Kalacakra and the Tibetan Calendar*, American Institute of Buddhist Studies, 2007.

[4] S. Janson, "Tibetan Calendar Mathematics," *ArXiv*, 1401.6285, 2014. Available at `arxiv.org/pdf/1401.6285v1.pdf`.

[5] B. Laufer, "The Application of the Tibetan Sexagenary Cycle," *T'oung Pao*, vol. 14, pp. 569–596, 1913.

[6] P. Pelliot, "Le Cycle sexagénaire dans la chronologie tibétaine," *Journal Asiatique*, vol. 1, pp. 633–667, 1913.

[7] W. Petri, *Indo-tibetische Astronomie*, Habilitationsschrift, Ludwig Maximilians Universität München, Munich, 1966.

[8] D. Schuh, *Untersuchungen zur Geschichte der Tibetischen Kalenderrechnung*, Franz Steiner Verlag, Wiesbaden, 1973.

[9] T. Tseng, *Sino-Tibetische Divinationskalkulationen (Nag-rtsis) dargestellt anhand des Werkes dPag-bsam ljon-šiṅ von Blo-bzaṅ tshul-khrims rgya-mtsho*, Halle, 2005.

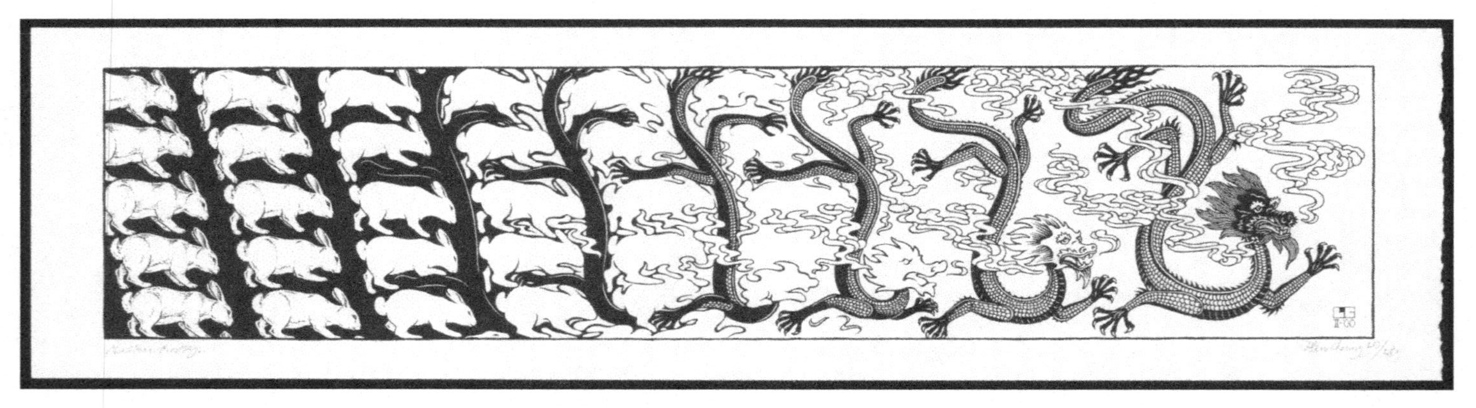

Chinese New Year greeting card by D. Bowyer from Lawrence Cheung Ltd. Inspired by M. C. Escher, the scroll shows rabbits morphing into a dragon as the year of the rabbit gives way to the year of the dragon on February 5, 2000. (Courtesy of the Victoria & Albert Museum, London.)

Coda

I hate quotations. Tell me what you know.
Ralph Waldo Emerson: *Journal* (May, 1849)

The following description of the presentation of the annual calendar in China is taken from Peter (Pierre) Hoang (*A Notice of the Chinese Calendar and a Concordance with the European Calendar*, 2nd edn., Catholic Mission Press, Shanghai, 1904):

> Every year, on the 1st of the 2nd month, the Board of Mathematics presents to the Emperor three copies of the *Annual Calendar* for the following year, namely in Chinese, in Manchou and in Mongolian. Approbation being given, it is engraved and printed. Then on the 1st of the 4th month, two printed copies in Chinese are sent to the *Fan-t'ai* (Treasurer) of each province, that of Chih li excepted; one of which, stamped with the seal of the Board of Mathematics, is to be preserved in the archives of the Treasury, while the other is used for engraving and printing for public use in the province.
>
> On the 1st day of the 10th month, early in the morning, the Board of Mathematics goes to offer Calendars to the Imperial court. The copies destined to the Emperor and Empresses are borne upon a sedan-like stand painted with figures of dragons (*Lung t'ing*), those for the Princes, the Ministers and officers of the court being carried on eight similar stands decorated with silk ornaments (*Ts'ai-t'ing*). They are accompanied by the officers of the Board with numerous attendants and the Imperial band of music. On arriving at the first entrance of the palace, the Calendars for the Emperor are placed upon an ornamented stand, those for other persons being put upon two other stands on each side. The copies for the Emperor and his family are not stamped with the seal of the Board of Mathematics, while the others are. The middle stand is taken into the palace, where the officers of the Board make three genuflections, each followed by three prostrations, after which the Calendars are handed to the eunuchs who present them to the Emperor, the Empress-mother, the Empress and other persons of the seraglio, two copies being given to

each, viz. one in Chinese and one in Manchou. The master of ceremonies then proceeds to the entrance of the palace where the two other stands were left, and where the Princes, the Ministers with the civil and military mandarins, both Manchous and Mongols all in robes of state are in attendance. The master of ceremonies reads the Imperial decree of publication of the Calendars, namely: "The Emperor presents you all with the Annual Calendar of the year, and promulgates it throughout the Empire," which proclamation is heard kneeling. Then follow three genuflections and nine prostrations, after which all receive the Calendar on their knees, the Princes two copies, one in Chinese and one in Manchou, the ministers and other officers only one, each in his own language. Lastly the Corean envoy, who must attend every year on that day, is presented kneeling with one hundred Chinese copies, to take home with him.

In the provinces, the *Fan-t'ai* (Treasurer), after getting some printed copies of the Calendar stamped with a special seal, also on the 1st of the 10th month, sends them on a sedan-like stand to the Viceroy or Governor, accompanied by the mandarin called *Li-wen-t'ing*, who is instructed with the printing of the Calendar. The Viceroy or Governor receives them to the sound of music and of three cannon shots. The Calendars being set upon a stand between two tapers in the tribunal, the Viceroy or Governor, in robes of state, approaches the stand, and turning towards that quarter where Peking is situated, makes three genuflections and nine prostrations, after which ceremony he reverently receives the Calendars. The Treasurer sends the Calendar to all the civil and military Mandarins, all of whom, except those of inferior degree, receive it with the same forms. Any copies left are sold to the people. The reprinting of the Calendar is forbidden under a penalty (except in *Fu-chien* and *Kuang-tong* where it is tolerated). If therefore any copy is found without seal or with a false one, its author is sought after and punished. Falsification of the Calendar is punished with death; whoever reprints the *Annual Calendar* is liable to 100 blows and two months cangue.

Now that's a society that took calendars (and copyrights) seriously!

Part III

Appendices

Page from a 1911 Turkish calendar. The uppermost portion gives the Islamic date, followed by dates in Arabic and Turkish; below that is the Gregorian date in Russian; below that on the left is the Julian date in Greek and the Gregorian date in French—the time of midday in Turkey is given at the left- and right-hand edges and the date of the full moon is given at the middle edges; below that are entries giving the time of sunset in Armenian on the left and French on the right; below that is the Hebrew date, with the day of the week given in Ladino. (Courtesy of Nicholas Stavroulakis and the Etz Hayyim Synagogue, Hania, Crete.)

Appendix A

Function, Parameter, and Constant Types

You must never forget that programs will be read by people as well as machines. Write them carefully.

George E. Forsythe: Remark to Alan George (1967)

In this appendix we list all the types of objects used in our calendar functions. The major categories of objects are numbers and lists. The *real* numbers serve to indicate *moments* of time, as well as *durations* of time. Similarly, an *angle* is a subtype of *real*. Conversely, *real* is a supertype of *angle*. The *integers* are used for fixed dates, among other purposes. Dates on most calendars are *lists* of numbers; in particular, *standard-date* has three components: *standard-year*, *standard-month*, and *standard-day*. Lists are also used for intervals. One type is often a subtype of another; for example, the type *rational* is a subtype of *real*, *integer* is a subtype of *rational*, *nonnegative-integer* is a subtype of *integer*, and *positive-integer* is a subtype of *nonnegative-integer*.

After giving a list of the types themselves, we list, for each function, the types of its parameters and of its result. Then, we give a similar list for all constants. In these latter two tables we include the page on which the definition is given, using *italic* page numbers for functions needed for typesetting purposes, mostly constructors and selectors, which appear only in the Lisp code of Appendix D. (This follows the convention used for page numbers in the index.)

A.1 Types

Type name	Type or range	Supertype
akan-name	⟨*akan-prefix*, *akan-stem*⟩	*list-of-nonnegative-integers*
akan-prefix	1 . . 6	*positive-integer*
akan-stem	1 . . 7	*positive-integer*
amplitude	[−1 . . 1]	*real*
angle	[0 . . 360)	*real*

continued

Type name	Type or range	Supertype
armenian-date	⟨*armenian-year*, *armenian-month*, *armenian-day*⟩	*standard-date*
armenian-day	1 .. 30	*positive-integer*
armenian-month	1 .. 13	*positive-integer*
armenian-year	*integer*	
auc-year	*nonzero-integer*	
augury	0 .. 3	*nonnegative-integer*
aztec-tonalpohualli-date	⟨*aztec-tonalpohualli-number*, *aztec-tonalpohualli-name*⟩	*list-of-nonnegative-integers*
aztec-tonalpohualli-name	1 .. 20	*nonnegative-integer*
aztec-tonalpohualli-number	1 .. 13	*nonnegative-integer*
aztec-xihuitl-date	⟨*aztec-xihuitl-month*, *aztec-xihuitl-day*⟩	*list-of-nonnegative-integers*
aztec-xihuitl-day	1 .. 20	*nonnegative-integer*
aztec-xihuitl-month	1 .. 19	*positive-integer*
aztec-xiuhmolpilli-designation	⟨*aztec-xiuhmolpilli-number*, *aztec-xiuhmolpilli-name*⟩	*list-of-nonnegative-integers*
aztec-xiuhmolpilli-name	{1, 8, 13, 18}	*positive-integer*
aztec-xiuhmolpilli-number	1 .. 13	*positive-integer*
babylonian-date	⟨*babylonian-year*, *babylonian-month*, *babylonian-leap*, *babylonian-day*⟩	*list*
babylonian-day	1 .. 30	*positive-integer*
babylonian-leap	*boolean*	
babylonian-month	1 .. 12	*positive-integer*
babylonian-year	*integer*	
bahai-cycle	1 .. 19	*positive-integer*
bahai-date	⟨*bahai-major*, *bahai-cycle*, *bahai-year*, *bahai-month*, *bahai-day*⟩	*list-of-integers*
bahai-day	1 .. 19	*positive-integer*
bahai-major	*integer*	
bahai-month	0 .. 19	*nonnegative-integer*
bahai-year	1 .. 19	*positive-integer*
boolean	*true*, *false*	
century	*real*	
chinese-branch	1 .. 12	*positive-integer*
chinese-cycle	*integer*	
chinese-date	⟨*chinese-cycle*, *chinese-year*, *chinese-month*, *chinese-leap-month*, *chinese-day*⟩	*list*
chinese-day	1 .. 31	*positive-integer*
chinese-leap	*boolean*	
chinese-month	1 .. 12	*positive-integer*
chinese-name	⟨*chinese-stem*, *chinese-branch*⟩	*list-of-nonnegative-integers*
chinese-stem	1 .. 10	*positive-integer*
chinese-year	1 .. 60	*positive-integer*

continued

Type name	Type or range	Supertype
circle	[−180 .. 180]	*angle*
clock-time	⟨*hour, minute, second*⟩	*list-of-reals*
coptic-date	⟨*coptic-year, coptic-month, coptic-day*⟩	*standard-date*
coptic-day	1 .. 31	*positive-integer*
coptic-month	1 .. 13	*positive-integer*
coptic-year	*integer*	
day-of-week	0 .. 6	*nonnegative-integer*
distance	*real*	
duration	*real*	
egyptian-date	⟨*egyptian-year, egyptian-month, egyptian-day*⟩	*standard-date*
egyptian-day	1 .. 30	*positive-integer*
egyptian-month	1 .. 13	*positive-integer*
egyptian-year	*integer*	
ethiopic-date	⟨*ethiopic-year, ethiopic-month, ethiopic-day*⟩	*standard-date*
ethiopic-day	1 .. 31	*positive-integer*
ethiopic-month	1 .. 13	*positive-integer*
ethiopic-year	*integer*	
fixed-date	*integer*	
fraction-of-day	[−0.5 .. 0.5]	*real*
french-date	⟨*french-year, french-month, french-day*⟩	*standard-date*
french-day	1 .. 30	*positive-integer*
french-month	1 .. 13	*positive-integer*
french-year	*integer*	
gregorian-date	⟨*gregorian-year, gregorian-month, gregorian-day*⟩	*standard-date*
gregorian-day	1 .. 31	*positive-integer*
gregorian-month	1 .. 12	*positive-integer*
gregorian-year	*integer*	
half-circle	[−90 .. 90]	*circle*
hebrew-date	⟨*hebrew-year, hebrew-month, hebrew-day*⟩	*standard-date*
hebrew-day	1 .. 30	*positive-integer*
hebrew-month	1 .. 13	*positive-integer*
hebrew-year	*integer*	
hindu-lunar-date	⟨*hindu-lunar-year, hindu-lunar-month, hindu-lunar-leap-month, hindu-lunar-day, hindu-lunar-leap-day*⟩	*list*
hindu-lunar-day	1 .. 30	*positive-integer*
hindu-lunar-leap-day	*boolean*	
hindu-lunar-leap-month	*boolean*	
hindu-lunar-month	1 .. 12	*positive-integer*
hindu-lunar-year	*integer*	
hindu-solar-date	⟨*hindu-solar-year, hindu-solar-month, hindu-solar-day*⟩	*standard-date*

continued

Type name	Type or range	Supertype
hindu-solar-day	1 .. 32	*positive-integer*
hindu-solar-month	1 .. 12	*positive-integer*
hindu-solar-year	*integer*	
hindu-year	*integer*	
hour	0 .. 23	*nonnegative-integer*
icelandic-date	⟨*icelandic-year*, *icelandic-season*, *icelandic-week*, *icelandic-weekday*⟩	*list*
icelandic-month	0 .. 6	*nonnegative-integer*
icelandic-season	*season*	*angle*
icelandic-week	1 .. 27	*positive-integer*
icelandic-weekday	*day-of-week*	*nonnegative-integer*
icelandic-year	*integer*	
ides	13,15	*roman-count*
integer		*rational*
interval	⟨*moment*, *moment*⟩	*list-of-moments*
islamic-date	⟨*islamic-year*, *islamic-month*, *islamic-day*⟩	*standard-date*
islamic-day	1 .. 30	*positive-integer*
islamic-month	1 .. 12	*positive-integer*
islamic-year	*integer*	
iso-date	⟨*iso-year*, *iso-week*, *iso-day*⟩	*list-of-integers*
iso-day	1 .. 7	*positive-integer*
iso-week	1 .. 53	*positive-integer*
iso-year	*integer*	
julian-date	⟨*julian-year*, *julian-month*, *julian-day*⟩	*standard-date*
julian-day	1 .. 31	*positive-integer*
julian-day-number	*real*	
julian-month	1 .. 12	*positive-integer*
julian-year	*nonzero-integer*	
list		
list-of-angles		*list-of-reals*
list-of-fixed-dates	*list-of-integers*	
list-of-integers		*list*
list-of-moments	*list-of-reals*	
list-of-nonnegative-integers		*list-of-integers*
list-of-pairs		*list*
list-of-reals		*list*
list-of-weekdays		*list-of-nonnegative-integers*
location	⟨*angle*, *angle*, *distance*, *fraction-of-day*⟩	*list*
mayan-baktun	*integer*	
mayan-haab-date	⟨*mayan-haab-month*, *mayan-haab-day*⟩	*list-of-nonnegative-integers*
mayan-haab-day	0 .. 19	*nonnegative-integer*
mayan-haab-month	1 .. 19	*positive-integer*
mayan-katun	0 .. 19	*nonnegative-integer*

continued

Type name	Type or range	Supertype
mayan-kin	0 .. 19	*nonnegative-integer*
mayan-long-count-date	⟨*mayan-baktun*, *mayan-katun*, *mayan-tun*, *mayan-uinal*, *mayan-kin*⟩	*list-of-integers*
mayan-tun	0 .. 17	*nonnegative-integer*
mayan-tzolkin-date	⟨*mayan-tzolkin-number*, *mayan-tzolkin-name*⟩	*list-of-nonnegative-integers*
mayan-tzolkin-name	1 .. 20	*nonnegative-integer*
mayan-tzolkin-number	1 .. 13	*nonnegative-integer*
mayan-uinal	0 .. 19	*nonnegative-integer*
minute	0 .. 59	*nonnegative-integer*
moment	*real*	
nakshatra	1 .. 27	*positive-integer*
nones	5, 7	*roman-count*
nonnegative-integer	0, 1, . . .	*integer*
nonzero-integer	. . . , −2, −1, 1, 2, . . .	*integer*
nonzero-real	$(-\infty \,..\, 0) \cup (0 \,..\, \infty)$	*real*
old-hindu-lunar-date	⟨*old-hindu-lunar-year*, *old-hindu-lunar-month*, *old-hindu-lunar-leap*, *old-hindu-lunar-day*⟩	*list*
old-hindu-lunar-day	1 .. 30	*positive-integer*
old-hindu-lunar-leap	*boolean*	
old-hindu-lunar-month	1 .. 12	*positive-integer*
old-hindu-lunar-year	*integer*	
old-hindu-month	1 .. 12	*positive-integer*
old-hindu-year	*integer*	
olympiad	⟨*olympiad-cycle*, *olympiad-year*⟩	*list-of-nonnegative-integers*
olympiad-cycle	*integer*	
olympiad-year	1 .. 4	*positive-integer*
omer-count	⟨0 .. 7, 0 .. 6⟩	*list-of-nonnegative-integers*
part	0 .. 1079	*nonnegative-integer*
persian-date	⟨*persian-year*, *persian-month*, *persian-day*⟩	*standard-date*
persian-day	1 .. 31	*positive-integer*
persian-month	1 .. 12	*positive-integer*
persian-year	*nonzero-integer*	
phase	[0 .. 360)	*angle*
positive-integer	1, 2, . . .	*nonnegative-integer*
radian	$[0 \,..\, 2\pi)$	*real*
range	⟨*fixed-date*, *fixed-date*⟩	*interval*
rational		*real*
rational-amplitude	[−1 .. 1]	*rational*
rational-angle	[0 .. 360)	*rational*
rational-moment	*rational*	*moment*

continued

Type name	Type or range	Supertype
real	$(-\infty\,..\,\infty)$	
roman-count	1 .. 19	*positive-integer*
roman-date	⟨*roman-year*, *roman-month*, *roman-event*, *roman-count*, *roman-leap*⟩	*list*
roman-event	1 .. 3	*positive-integer*
roman-leap	*boolean*	
roman-month	1 .. 12	*positive-integer*
roman-year	*nonzero-integer*	
season	[0 .. 360)	*angle*
second	[0 .. 60)	*duration*
standard-date	⟨*standard-year*, *standard-month*, *standard-day*⟩	*list-of-integers*
standard-day	1 .. 31	*positive-integer*
standard-month	1 .. 13	*positive-integer*
standard-year	*integer*	
string		
tibetan-date	⟨*tibetan-year*, *tibetan-month*, *tibetan-leap-month*, *tibetan-day*, *tibetan-leap-day*⟩	*list*
tibetan-day	1 .. 30	*positive-integer*
tibetan-leap-day	*boolean*	
tibetan-leap-month	*boolean*	
tibetan-month	1 .. 12	*positive-integer*
tibetan-year	*integer*	
time	[0 .. 1)	*duration*

A.2 Function Types

Function	Parameter type(s)	Result type
aberration (p. 223)	*moment*	*circle*
adda-season-in-gregorian (p. 133)	⟨*season*, *gregorian-year*, *positive-real*⟩	*list-of-moments*
advent (p. 70)	*gregorian-year*	*fixed-date*
akan-day-name (p. 38)	*integer*	*akan-name*
akan-day-name-on-or-before (p. 38)	⟨*akan-name*, *fixed-date*⟩	*fixed-date*
akan-name (p. *478*)	⟨*akan-prefix*, *akan-stem*⟩	*akan-name*
akan-name-difference (p. 38)	⟨*akan-name*, *akan-name*⟩	*nonnegative-integer*
akan-name-from-fixed (p. 38)	*fixed-date*	*akan-name*
akan-prefix (p. *478*)	*akan-name*	*akan-prefix*
akan-stem (p. *478*)	*akan-name*	*akan-stem*
alt-asr (p. 249)	⟨*fixed-date*, *location*⟩	*moment*
alt-birkath-ha-hama (p. 132)	*gregorian-year*	*list-of-fixed-dates*
alt-fixed-from-egyptian (p. 31)	*egyptian-date*	*fixed-date*
alt-fixed-from-gregorian (p. 65)	*gregorian-date*	*fixed-date*

continued

Function	Parameter type(s)	Result type
alt-fixed-from-observational-hebrew (p. 299)	*hebrew-date*	*fixed-date*
alt-fixed-from-observational-islamic (p. 295)	*islamic-date*	*fixed-date*
alt-gregorian-from-fixed (p. 66)	*fixed-date*	*gregorian-date*
alt-gregorian-year-from-fixed (p. 67)	*fixed-date*	*gregorian-year*
alt-hindu-sunrise (p. 357)	*fixed-date*	*rational-moment*
alt-observational-hebrew-from-fixed (p. 299)	*fixed-date*	*hebrew-date*
alt-observational-islamic-from-fixed (p. 295)	*fixed-date*	*islamic-date*
alt-orthodox-easter (p. 147)	*gregorian-year*	*fixed-date*
amod (p. 22)	⟨*integer, nonzero-integer*⟩	*integer*
angle (p. *514*)	⟨*nonnegative-integer, nonnegative-integer, real*⟩	*angle*
angle-from-degrees (p. 29)	*angle*	*list-of-reals*
apparent-from-local (p. 217)	⟨*moment, location*⟩	*moment*
apparent-from-universal (p. 218)	⟨*moment, location*⟩	*moment*
approx-moment-of-depression (p. 240)	⟨*moment, location, half-circle, boolean*⟩	*moment* (or **bogus**)
arccos-degrees (p. *514*)	*amplitude*	*angle*
arc-of-light (p. 250)	*moment*	*half-circle*
arc-of-vision (p. 251)	⟨*moment, location*⟩	*half-circle*
arcsin-degrees (p. *513*)	*amplitude*	*angle*
arctan (p. *205*)	⟨*real, real*⟩	*angle* (or **bogus**)
arctan-degrees (p. 205)	⟨*real, real*⟩	*angle* (or **bogus**)
arithmetic-french-from-fixed (p. 285)	*fixed-date*	*french-date*
arithmetic-french-leap-year? (p. 285)	*french-year*	*boolean*
arithmetic-persian-from-fixed (p. 263)	*fixed-date*	*persian-date*
arithmetic-persian-leap-year? (p. 262)	*persian-year*	*boolean*
arithmetic-persian-year-from-fixed (p. 263)	*fixed-date*	*persian-year*
armenian-date (p. *477*)	⟨*armenian-year, armenian-month, armenian-day*⟩	*armenian-date*
armenian-from-fixed (p. 31)	*fixed-date*	*armenian-date*
asr (p. 249)	⟨*fixed-date, location*⟩	*moment*
astro-bahai-from-fixed (p. 275)	*fixed-date*	*bahai-date*
astro-bahai-new-year-on-or-before (p. 274)	*fixed-date*	*fixed-date*
astro-hindu-calendar-year (p. 360)	*moment*	*hindu-solar-year*
astro-hindu-lunar-from-fixed (p. 361)	*fixed-date*	*hindu-lunar-date*
astro-hindu-solar-from-fixed (p. 360)	*fixed-date*	*hindu-solar-date*
astro-hindu-sunset (p. 360)	*fixed-date*	*moment*
astro-lunar-day-from-moment (p. 361)	*moment*	*hindu-lunar-day*
astronomical-easter (p. 292)	*gregorian-year*	*fixed-date*

continued

Function	Parameter type(s)	Result type
auc-year-from-julian (p. 81)	*julian-year*	*auc-year*
ayanamsha (p. 359)	*moment*	*angle*
aztec-tonalpohualli-date (p. *509*)	⟨*aztec-tonalpohualli-number*, *aztec-tonalpohualli-name*⟩	*aztec-tonalpohualli-date*
aztec-tonalpohualli-from-fixed (p. 179)	*fixed-date*	*aztec-tonalpohualli-date*
aztec-tonalpohualli-name (p. *509*)	*aztec-tonalpohualli-date*	*aztec-tonalpohualli-name*
aztec-tonalpohualli-number (p. *509*)	*aztec-tonalpohualli-date*	*aztec-tonalpohualli-number*
aztec-tonalpohualli-on-or-before (p. 180)	⟨*aztec-tonalpohualli-date*, *fixed-date*⟩	*fixed-date*
aztec-tonalpohualli-ordinal (p. 179)	*aztec-tonalpohualli-date*	*nonnegative-integer*
aztec-xihuitl-date (p. *508*)	⟨*aztec-xihuitl-month*, *aztec-xihuitl-day*⟩	*aztec-xihuitl-date*
aztec-xihuitl-day (p. *508*)	*aztec-xihuitl-date*	*aztec-xihuitl-day*
aztec-xihuitl-from-fixed (p. 178)	*fixed-date*	*aztec-xihuitl-date*
aztec-xihuitl-month (p. *508*)	*aztec-xihuitl-date*	*aztec-xihuitl-month*
aztec-xihuitl-on-or-before (p. 179)	⟨*aztec-xihuitl-date*, *fixed-date*⟩	*fixed-date*
aztec-xihuitl-ordinal (p. 178)	*aztec-xihuitl-date*	*nonnegative-integer*
aztec-xihuitl-tonalpohualli-on-or-before 180	⟨*aztec-xihuitl-date*, *aztec-tonalpohualli-date*, *fixed-date*⟩	*fixed-date* (or **bogus**)
aztec-xiuhmolpilli-designation (p. *509*)	⟨*aztec-tonalpohualli-number*, *aztec-tonalpohualli-name*⟩	*aztec-xiuhmolpilli-designation*
aztec-xiuhmolpilli-from-fixed (p. 180)	*fixed-date*	*aztec-xiuhmolpilli-designation* (or **bogus**)
aztec-xiuhmolpilli-name (p. *509*)	*aztec-xiuhmolpilli-designation*	*aztec-xiuhmolpilli-name*
aztec-xiuhmolpilli-number (p. *509*)	*aztec-xiuhmolpilli-designation*	*aztec-xiuhmolpilli-number*
babylonian-criterion (p. 290)	*fixed-date*	*boolean*
babylonian-date (p. *543*)	⟨*babylonian-year*, *babylonian-month*, *babylonian-leap*, *babylonian-day*⟩	*babylonian-date*
babylonian-day (p. *543*)	*babylonian-date*	*babylonian-day*
babylonian-leap (p. *543*)	*babylonian-date*	*babylonian-leap*
babylonian-month (p. *543*)	*babylonian-date*	*babylonian-month*
babylonian-year (p. *543*)	*babylonian-date*	*babylonian-year*
babylonian-from-fixed (p. 291)	*fixed-date*	*babylonian-date*
babylonian-leap-year? (p. 291)	*babylonian-year*	*boolean*
babylonian-new-month-on-or-before (p. 290)	*fixed-date*	*fixed-date*
bahai-cycle (p. *538*)	*bahai-date*	*bahai-cycle*

continued

Function	Parameter type(s)	Result type
bahai-date (p. *538*)	⟨*bahai-major, bahai-cycle, bahai-year, bahai-month, bahai-day*⟩	*bahai-date*
bahai-day (p. *538*)	*bahai-date*	*bahai-day*
bahai-from-fixed (p. 272)	*fixed-date*	*bahai-date*
bahai-major (p. *538*)	*bahai-date*	*bahai-major*
bahai-month (p. *538*)	*bahai-date*	*bahai-month*
bahai-new-year (p. 277)	*gregorian-year*	*fixed-date*
bahai-sunset (p. 274)	*fixed-date*	*moment*
bahai-year (p. *538*)	*bahai-date*	*bahai-year*
bali-asatawara (p. *511*)	*balinese-date*	1 . . 8
bali-asatawara-from-fixed (p. 188)	*fixed-date*	1 . . 8
bali-caturwara (p. *510*)	*balinese-date*	1 . . 4
bali-caturwara-from-fixed (p. 189)	*fixed-date*	1 . . 4
bali-dasawara (p. *511*)	*balinese-date*	0 . . 9
bali-dasawara-from-fixed (p. 188)	*fixed-date*	0 . . 9
bali-day-from-fixed (p. 187)	*fixed-date*	0 . . 209
bali-dwiwara (p. *510*)	*balinese-date*	1 . . 2
bali-dwiwara-from-fixed (p. 188)	*fixed-date*	1 . . 2
bali-luang (p. *510*)	*balinese-date*	*boolean*
bali-luang-from-fixed (p. 188)	*fixed-date*	*boolean*
balinese-date (p. *510*)	⟨*boolean*, 1 . . 2, 1 . . 3, 1 . . 4, 1 . . 5, 1 . . 6, 1 . . 7, 1 . . 8, 1 . . 9, 0 . . 9⟩	*balinese-date*
bali-on-or-before (p. 189)	⟨*balinese-date, fixed-date*⟩	*fixed-date*
bali-pancawara (p. *510*)	*balinese-date*	1 . . 5
bali-pancawara-from-fixed (p. 187)	*fixed-date*	1 . . 5
bali-pawukon-from-fixed (p. 185)	*fixed-date*	*balinese-date*
bali-sadwara (p. *510*)	*balinese-date*	1 . . 6
bali-sadwara-from-fixed (p. 187)	*fixed-date*	1 . . 6
bali-sangawara (p. *511*)	*balinese-date*	1 . . 9
bali-sangawara-from-fixed (p. 188)	*fixed-date*	1 . . 9
bali-saptawara (p. *510*)	*balinese-date*	1 . . 7
bali-saptawara-from-fixed (p. 187)	*fixed-date*	1 . . 7
bali-triwara (p. *510*)	*balinese-date*	1 . . 3
bali-triwara-from-fixed (p. 187)	*fixed-date*	1 . . 3
bali-week-from-fixed (p. 187)	*fixed-date*	1 . . 30
bce (p. *484*)	*standard-year*	*julian-year*
begin (p. *475*)	*interval*	*moment*
binary-search (p. 24)	⟨—, *real*, —, *real*, —, *real*→*boolean*, ⟨*real, real*⟩→*boolean*⟩	*real*
birkath-ha-hama (p. 131)	*gregorian-year*	*list-of-fixed-dates*
birth-of-the-bab (p. 278)	*gregorian-year*	*fixed-date*
bruin-best-view (p. 251)	⟨*fixed-date, location*⟩	*moment*
ce (p. *484*)	*standard-year*	*julian-year*

continued

Function	Parameter type(s)	Result type
chinese-age (p. 325)	⟨*chinese-date*, *fixed-date*⟩	*nonnegative-integer* (or **bogus**)
chinese-branch (p. *554*)	*chinese-name*	*chinese-branch*
chinese-cycle (p. *549*)	*chinese-date*	*chinese-cycle*
chinese-date (p. *549*)	⟨*chinese-cycle*, *chinese-year*, *chinese-month*, *chinese-leap*, *chinese-day*⟩	*chinese-date*
chinese-day (p. *550*)	*chinese-date*	*chinese-day*
chinese-day-name (p. 320)	*fixed-date*	*chinese-name*
chinese-day-name-on-or-before (p. 320)	⟨*chinese-name*, *fixed-date*⟩	*fixed-date*
chinese-from-fixed (p. 317)	*fixed-date*	*chinese-date*
chinese-leap (p. *550*)	*chinese-date*	*chinese-leap*
chinese-location (p. 306)	*moment*	*location*
chinese-month (p. *550*)	*chinese-date*	*chinese-month*
chinese-month-name (p. 320)	⟨*chinese-month*, *chinese-year*⟩	*chinese-name*
chinese-name (p. *553*)	⟨*chinese-stem*, *chinese-branch*⟩	*chinese-name* (or **bogus**)
chinese-name-difference (p. 319)	⟨*chinese-name*, *chinese-name*⟩	*nonnegative-integer*
chinese-new-moon-before (p. 310)	*fixed-date*	*fixed-date*
chinese-new-moon-on-or-after (p. 309)	*fixed-date*	*fixed-date*
chinese-new-year (p. 322)	*gregorian-year*	*fixed-date*
chinese-new-year-in-sui (p. 315)	*fixed-date*	*fixed-date*
chinese-new-year-on-or-before (p. 316)	*fixed-date*	*fixed-date*
chinese-no-major-solar-term? (p. 313)	*fixed-date*	*boolean*
chinese-prior-leap-month? (p. 313)	⟨*fixed-date*, *fixed-date*⟩	*boolean*
chinese-sexagesimal-name (p. 319)	*integer*	*chinese-name*
chinese-solar-longitude-on-or-after (p. 308)	⟨*season*, *moment*⟩	*moment*
chinese-stem (p. *553*)	*chinese-name*	*chinese-stem*
chinese-winter-solstice-on-or-before (p. 309)	*fixed-date*	*fixed-date*
chinese-year (p. *550*)	*chinese-date*	*chinese-year*
chinese-year-marriage-augury (p. 325)	⟨*chinese-cycle*, *chinese-year*⟩	*augury*
chinese-year-name (p. 320)	*chinese-year*	*chinese-name*
christmas (p. 70)	*gregorian-year*	*fixed-date*
classical-passover-eve (p. 298)	*gregorian-year*	*fixed-date*
clock-from-moment (p. 28)	*moment*	*clock-time*
coptic-christmas (p. 93)	*gregorian-year*	*list-of-fixed-dates*
coptic-date (p. *489*)	⟨*coptic-year*, *coptic-month*, *coptic-day*⟩	*coptic-date*
coptic-from-fixed (p. 91)	*fixed-date*	*coptic-date*
coptic-in-gregorian (p. 92)	⟨*coptic-month*, *coptic-day*, *gregorian-year*⟩	*list-of-fixed-dates*

continued

Function	Parameter type(s)	Result type
coptic-leap-year? (p. 90)	*coptic-year*	*boolean*
cos-degrees (p. *513*)	*angle*	*amplitude*
current-major-solar-term (p. 306)	*fixed-date*	*integer*
current-minor-solar-term (p. 308)	*fixed-date*	*integer*
cycle-in-gregorian (p. 83)	⟨*season, gregorian-year, moment*⟩	*list-of-moments*
dawn (p. 241)	⟨*fixed-date, location, angle*⟩	*moment* (or **bogus**)
daylight-saving-end (p. 70)	*gregorian-year*	*fixed-date*
daylight-saving-start (p. 70)	*gregorian-year*	*fixed-date*
day-number (p. 62)	*gregorian-date*	*positive-integer*
day-of-week-from-fixed (p. 33)	*fixed-date*	*day-of-week*
days-in-hebrew-year (p. 123)	*hebrew-year*	353,354,355,383,384,385
days-remaining (p. 62)	*gregorian-date*	*nonnegative-integer*
daytime-temporal-hour (p. 247)	⟨*fixed-date, location*⟩	*real* (or **bogus**)
declination (p. 220)	⟨*moment, angle, angle*⟩	*angle*
deg (p. *514*)	*real*	*angle*
	list-of-reals	*list-of-angles*
degrees-from-radians (p. *513*)	*radian*	*angle*
degrees-minutes-seconds (p. *514*)	⟨*degree, minute, real*⟩	*angle*
direction (p. 205)	⟨*location, location*⟩	*angle*
diwali (p. 368)	*gregorian-year*	*list-of-fixed-dates*
dragon-festival (p. 324)	*gregorian-year*	*fixed-date*
dusk (p. 242)	⟨*fixed-date, location, angle*⟩	*moment* (or **bogus**)
dynamical-from-universal (p. 212)	*moment*	*moment*
early-month? (p. 294)	⟨*fixed-date, location*⟩	boolean
easter (p. 148)	*gregorian-year*	*fixed-date*
eastern-orthodox-christmas (p. 85)	*gregorian-year*	*list-of-fixed-dates*
egyptian-date (p. *476*)	⟨*egyptian-year, egyptian-month, egyptian-day*⟩	*egyptian-date*
egyptian-from-fixed (p. 31)	*fixed-date*	*egyptian-date*
election-day (p. 70)	*gregorian-year*	*fixed-date*
elevation (p. *515*)	*location*	*distance*
end (p. *475*)	*interval*	*moment*
ephemeris-correction (p. 210)	*moment*	*fraction-of-day*
epiphany (p. 71)	*gregorian-year*	*fixed-date*
equation-of-time (p. 215)	*moment*	*fraction-of-day*
estimate-prior-solar-longitude (p. 226)	⟨*season, moment*⟩	*moment*
ethiopic-date (p. *490*)	⟨*ethiopic-year, ethiopic-month, ethiopic-day*⟩	*ethiopic-date*
ethiopic-from-fixed (p. 92)	*fixed-date*	*ethiopic-date*
feast-of-ridvan (p. 277)	*gregorian-year*	*fixed-date*
final (p. 24)	⟨*—, integer, integer→boolean*⟩	*integer*
first-kday (p. 69)	⟨*day-of-week, gregorian-date*⟩	*fixed-date*
fixed-from-arithmetic-french (p. 285)	*french-date*	*fixed-date*
fixed-from-arithmetic-persian (p. 262)	*persian-date*	*fixed-date*
fixed-from-armenian (p. 31)	*armenian-date*	*fixed-date*
fixed-from-astro-bahai (p. 275)	*bahai-date*	*fixed-date*

continued

Function	Parameter type(s)	Result type
fixed-from-astro-hindu-lunar (p. 361)	*hindu-lunar-date*	*fixed-date*
fixed-from-astro-hindu-solar (p. 360)	*hindu-solar-date*	*fixed-date*
fixed-from-babylonian (p. 291)	*babylonian-date*	*fixed-date*
fixed-from-bahai (p. 271)	*bahai-date*	*fixed-date*
fixed-from-chinese (p. 318)	*chinese-date*	*fixed-date*
fixed-from-coptic (p. 90)	*coptic-date*	*fixed-date*
fixed-from-egyptian (p. 30)	*egyptian-date*	*fixed-date*
fixed-from-ethiopic (p. 92)	*ethiopic-date*	*fixed-date*
fixed-from-french (p. 284)	*french-date*	*fixed-date*
fixed-from-gregorian (p. 60)	*gregorian-date*	*fixed-date*
fixed-from-hebrew (p. 123)	*hebrew-date*	*fixed-date*
fixed-from-hindu-fullmoon (p. 356)	*hindu-lunar-date*	*fixed-date*
fixed-from-hindu-lunar (p. 350)	*hindu-lunar-date*	*fixed-date*
fixed-from-hindu-solar (p. 348)	*hindu-solar-date*	*fixed-date*
fixed-from-icelandic (p. 100)	*icelandic-date*	*fixed-date*
fixed-from-islamic (p. 107)	*islamic-date*	*fixed-date*
fixed-from-iso (p. 95)	*iso-date*	*fixed-date*
fixed-from-jd (p. 20)	*julian-day-number*	*fixed-date*
fixed-from-julian (p. 76)	*julian-date*	*fixed-date*
fixed-from-mayan-long-count (p. 171)	*mayan-long-count-date*	*fixed-date*
fixed-from-mjd (p. 19)	*julian-day-number*	*fixed-date*
fixed-from-molad (p. 126)	*duration*	*fixed-date*
fixed-from-moment (p. 20)	*moment*	*fixed-date*
fixed-from-observational-hebrew (p. 298)	*hebrew-date*	*fixed-date*
fixed-from-observational-islamic (p. 293)	*islamic-date*	*fixed-date*
fixed-from-old-hindu-lunar (p. 165)	*old-hindu-lunar-date*	*fixed-date*
fixed-from-old-hindu-solar (p. 158)	*hindu-solar-date*	*fixed-date*
fixed-from-persian (p. 260)	*persian-date*	*fixed-date*
fixed-from-roman (p. 80)	*roman-date*	*fixed-date*
fixed-from-samaritan (p. 301)	*hebrew-date*	*fixed-date*
fixed-from-saudi-islamic (p. 296)	*islamic-date*	*fixed-date*
fixed-from-tibetan (p. 378)	*tibetan-date*	*fixed-date*
french-date (p. *541*)	⟨*french-year*, *french-month*, *french-day*⟩	*french-date*
french-from-fixed (p. 284)	*fixed-date*	*french-date*
french-leap-year? (p. 284)	*french-year*	*boolean*
french-new-year-on-or-before (p. 283)	*fixed-date*	*fixed-date*
from-radix (p. 27)	⟨*list-of-reals*, *list-of-rationals*, *list-of-rationals*⟩	*real*
gregorian-date (p. *479*)	⟨*gregorian-year*, *gregorian-month*, *gregorian-day*⟩	*gregorian-date*
gregorian-date-difference (p. 62)	⟨*gregorian-date*, *gregorian-date*⟩	*integer*
gregorian-from-fixed (p. 62)	*fixed-date*	*gregorian-date*

continued

Function	Parameter type(s)	Result type
gregorian-leap-year? (p. 59)	*gregorian-year*	*boolean*
gregorian-new-year (p. 60)	*gregorian-year*	*fixed-date*
gregorian-year-end (p. 60)	*gregorian-year*	*fixed-date*
gregorian-year-from-fixed (p. 61)	*fixed-date*	*gregorian-year*
gregorian-year-range (p. 60)	*gregorian-year*	*range*
hanukkah (p. 134)	*gregorian-year*	*list-of-fixed-dates*
hebrew-birthday (p. 135)	⟨*hebrew-date, hebrew-year*⟩	*fixed-date*
hebrew-birthday-in-gregorian (p. 135)	⟨*hebrew-date, gregorian-year*⟩	*list-of-fixed-dates*
hebrew-calendar-elapsed-days (p. 121)	*hebrew-year*	*integer*
hebrew-date (p. *494*)	⟨*hebrew-year, hebrew-month, hebrew-day*⟩	*hebrew-date*
hebrew-from-fixed (p. 123)	*fixed-date*	*hebrew-date*
hebrew-in-gregorian (p. 133)	⟨*hebrew-month, hebrew-day, gregorian-year*⟩	*list-of-fixed-dates*
hebrew-leap-year? (p. 115)	*hebrew-year*	*boolean*
hebrew-new-year (p. 122)	*hebrew-year*	*fixed-date*
hebrew-sabbatical-year? (p. 115)	*hebrew-year*	*boolean*
hebrew-year-length-correction (p. 122)	*hebrew-year*	0 . . 2
hindu-arcsin (p. 343)	*rational-amplitude*	*rational-angle*
hindu-ascensional-difference (p. 352)	⟨*fixed-date, location*⟩	*rational-angle*
hindu-calendar-year (p. 347)	*rational-moment*	*hindu-solar-year*
hindu-daily-motion (p. 353)	*fixed-date*	*rational-angle*
hindu-date-occur (p. 367)	⟨*hindu-lunar-year, hindu-lunar-month, hindu-lunar-day*⟩	*fixed-date*
hindu-day-count (p. 156)	*fixed-date*	*integer*
hindu-equation-of-time (p. 353)	*fixed-date*	*rational-moment*
hindu-expunged? (p. 356)	⟨*hindu-lunar-year, hindu-lunar-month*⟩	*boolean*
hindu-fullmoon-from-fixed (p. 356)	*fixed-date*	*hindu-lunar-date*
hindu-lunar-date (p. *560*)	⟨*hindu-lunar-year, hindu-lunar-month, hindu-lunar-leap-month, hindu-lunar-day, hindu-lunar-leap-day*⟩	*hindu-lunar-date*
hindu-lunar-day (p. *560*)	*hindu-lunar-date*	*hindu-lunar-day*
hindu-lunar-day-at-or-after (p. 365)	⟨*rational, rational-moment*⟩	*rational-moment*
hindu-lunar-day-from-moment (p. 346)	*rational-moment*	*hindu-lunar-day*
hindu-lunar-event (p. 368)	⟨*hindu-lunar-month, rational, rational, gregorian-year*⟩	*list-of-fixed-dates*
hindu-lunar-from-fixed (p. 349)	*fixed-date*	*hindu-lunar-date*
hindu-lunar-holiday (p. 367)	⟨*hindu-lunar-month, hindu-lunar-day, gregorian-year*⟩	*list-of-fixed-dates*

continued

Function	Parameter type(s)	Result type
hindu-lunar-leap-day (p. *560*)	*hindu-lunar-date*	*hindu-lunar-leap-day*
hindu-lunar-leap-month (p. *560*)	*hindu-lunar-date*	*hindu-lunar-leap-month*
hindu-lunar-longitude (p. 346)	*rational-moment*	*rational-angle*
hindu-lunar-month (p. *560*)	*hindu-lunar-date*	*hindu-lunar-month*
hindu-lunar-new-year (p. 365)	*gregorian-year*	*fixed-date*
hindu-lunar-on-or-before? (p. 367)	⟨*hindu-lunar-date*, *hindu-lunar-date*⟩	*boolean*
hindu-lunar-phase (p. 346)	*rational-moment*	*rational-angle*
hindu-lunar-station (p. 369)	*fixed-date*	*nakshatra*
hindu-lunar-year (p. *560*)	*hindu-lunar-date*	*hindu-lunar-year*
hindu-mean-position (p. 344)	⟨*rational-moment*, *rational*⟩	*rational-angle*
hindu-new-moon-before (p. 346)	*rational-moment*	*rational-moment*
hindu-rising-sign (p. 353)	*fixed-date*	*rational-amplitude*
hindu-sine (p. 342)	*angle*	*rational-amplitude*
hindu-sine-table (p. 342)	*integer*	*rational-amplitude*
hindu-solar-date (p. *559*)	⟨*hindu-solar-year*, *hindu-solar-month*, *hindu-solar-day*⟩	*hindu-solar-date*
hindu-solar-from-fixed (p. 347)	*fixed-date*	*hindu-solar-date*
hindu-solar-longitude (p. 345)	*rational-moment*	*rational-angle*
hindu-solar-longitude-at-or-after (p. 364)	⟨*season*, *moment*⟩	*moment*
hindu-solar-sidereal-difference (p. 352)	*fixed-date*	*rational-angle*
hindu-standard-from-sundial (p. 355)	*rational-moment*	*rational-moment*
hindu-sunrise (p. 354)	*fixed-date*	*rational-moment*
hindu-sunset (p. 354)	*fixed-date*	*rational-moment*
hindu-tithi-occur (p. 368)	⟨*hindu-lunar-month*, *rational*, *rational*, *hindu-lunar-year*⟩	*fixed-date*
hindu-tropical-longitude (p. 352)	*fixed-date*	*rational-angle*
hindu-true-position (p. 345)	⟨*rational-moment*, *rational*, *rational*, *rational*, *rational*⟩	*rational-angle*
hindu-zodiac (p. 345)	*rational-moment*	*hindu-solar-month*
hour (p. *474*)	*clock-time*	*hour*
hr (p. *514*)	*real*	*duration*
icelandic-date (p. *491*)	⟨*icelandic-year*, *icelandic-season*, *icelandic-week*, *icelandic-weekday*⟩	*icelandic-date*
icelandic-from-fixed (p. 101)	*fixed-date*	*icelandic-date*
icelandic-leap-year? (p. 101)	*icelandic-year*	*boolean*
icelandic-month (p. 101)	*icelandic-date*	*icelandic-month*
icelandic-season (p. *491*)	*icelandic-date*	*icelandic-season*
icelandic-summer (p. 100)	*gregorian-year*	*fixed-date*
icelandic-week (p. *491*)	*icelandic-date*	*icelandic-week*
icelandic-weekday (p. *491*)	*icelandic-date*	*icelandic-weekday*

continued

Function	Parameter type(s)	Result type
icelandic-winter (p. 100)	*gregorian-year*	*fixed-date*
icelandic-year (p. *491*)	*icelandic-date*	*icelandic-year*
ides-of-month (p. 77)	*roman-month*	*ides*
independence-day (p. 69)	*gregorian-year*	*fixed-date*
in-range? (p. 26)	⟨*moment, interval*⟩	*boolean*
interval (p. *475*)	⟨*moment, moment*⟩	*interval*
interval-closed (p. *475*)	⟨*moment, moment*⟩	*interval*
invert-angular (p. 25)	⟨*real→angle, real, interval*⟩	*real*
islamic-date (p. *493*)	⟨*islamic-year, islamic-month, islamic-day*⟩	*islamic-date*
islamic-from-fixed (p. 108)	*fixed-date*	*islamic-date*
islamic-in-gregorian (p. 108)	⟨*islamic-month, islamic-day, gregorian-year*⟩	*list-of-fixed-dates*
islamic-leap-year? (p. 107)	*islamic-year*	*boolean*
iso-date (p. *490*)	⟨*iso-year, iso-week, iso-day*⟩	*iso-date*
iso-day (p. *490*)	*iso-date*	*day-of-week*
iso-from-fixed (p. 96)	*fixed-date*	*iso-date*
iso-long-year? (p. 97)	*iso-year*	*boolean*
iso-week (p. *490*)	*iso-date*	*iso-week*
iso-year (p. *491*)	*iso-date*	*iso-year*
italian-from-local (p. 247)	*moment*	*moment*
japanese-location (p. 326)	*moment*	*location*
jd-from-fixed (p. 20)	*fixed-date*	*julian-day-number*
jd-from-moment (p. 18)	*moment*	*julian-day-number*
jewish-dusk (p. 243)	⟨*fixed-date, location*⟩	*moment*
jewish-morning-end (p. 248)	⟨*fixed-date, location*⟩	*moment*
jewish-sabbath-ends (p. 243)	⟨*fixed-date, location*⟩	*moment*
jovian-year (p. 157)	*fixed-date*	1 .. 60
julian-centuries (p. 212)	*moment*	*century*
julian-date (p. *484*)	⟨*julian-year, julian-month, julian-day*⟩	*julian-date*
julian-from-fixed (p. 76)	*fixed-date*	*julian-date*
julian-in-gregorian (p. 85)	⟨*julian-month, julian-day, gregorian-year*⟩	*list-of-fixed-dates*
julian-leap-year? (p. 75)	*julian-year*	*boolean*
julian-season-in-gregorian (p. 84)	⟨*season, gregorian-year*⟩	*list-of-moments*
julian-year-from-auc (p. 81)	*auc-year*	*julian-year*
julian-year-from-olympiad (p. 82)	*olympiad*	*julian-year*
kajeng-keliwon (p. 190)	*gregorian-year*	*list-of-fixed-dates*
karana (p. 369)	1 .. 60	0 .. 10
kday-after (p. 34)	⟨*day-of-week, fixed-date*⟩	*fixed-date*
kday-before (p. 34)	⟨*day-of-week, fixed-date*⟩	*fixed-date*
kday-nearest (p. 34)	⟨*day-of-week, fixed-date*⟩	*fixed-date*
kday-on-or-after (p. 34)	⟨*day-of-week, fixed-date*⟩	*fixed-date*
kday-on-or-before (p. 34)	⟨*day-of-week, fixed-date*⟩	*fixed-date*
korean-location (p. 328)	*moment*	*location*
korean-year (p. 328)	⟨*chinese-cycle, chinese-year*⟩	*integer*

continued

Function	Parameter type(s)	Result type
labor-day (p. 69)	*gregorian-year*	*fixed-date*
last-day-of-gregorian-month (p. 63)	⟨*gregorian-year*, *gregorian-month*⟩	*gregorian-day*
last-day-of-hebrew-month (p. 122)	⟨*hebrew-year*, *hebrew-month*⟩	*hebrew-day*
last-kday (p. 69)	⟨*day-of-week*, *gregorian-date*⟩	*fixed-date*
last-month-of-hebrew-year (p. 115)	*hebrew-year*	*hebrew-month*
latitude (p. *514*)	*location*	*half-circle*
list-of-fixed-from-moments (p. 26)	*list-of-moments*	*list-of-fixed-dates*
list-range (p. 26)	⟨*list-of-moments*, *interval*⟩	*list-of-moments*
local-from-apparent (p. 218)	⟨*moment*, *location*⟩	*moment*
local-from-italian (p. 247)	*moment*	*moment*
local-from-standard (p. 208)	⟨*moment*, *location*⟩	
local-from-universal (p. 208)	⟨*moment*, *location*⟩	*moment*
local-zero-hour (p. 246)	*moment*	*moment*
location (p. *514*)	⟨*half-circle*, *circle*, *distance*, *fraction-of-day*⟩	*location*
longitude (p. *515*)	*location*	*circle*
long-marheshvan? (p. 122)	*hebrew-year*	*boolean*
losar (p. 381)	*tibetan-year*	*fixed-date*
lunar-altitude (p. 237)	⟨*moment*, *location*⟩	*half-circle*
lunar-anomaly (p. 234)	*century*	*angle*
lunar-diameter (p. 252)	*moment*	*angle*
lunar-distance (p. 238)	*moment*	*distance*
lunar-elongation (p. 234)	*century*	*angle*
lunar-latitude (p. 236)	*moment*	*angle*
lunar-longitude (p. 232)	*moment*	*angle*
lunar-node (p. 234)	*fixed-date*	*angle*
lunar-parallax (p. 238)	⟨*moment*, *location*⟩	*angle*
lunar-phase (p. 235)	*moment*	*phase*
lunar-phase-at-or-after (p. 235)	⟨*phase*, *moment*⟩	*moment*
lunar-phase-at-or-before (p. 235)	⟨*phase*, *moment*⟩	*moment*
lunar-semi-diameter (p. 251)	⟨*moment*, *location*⟩	*half-circle*
major-solar-term-on-or-after (p. 308)	*fixed-date*	*moment*
mawlid (p. 109)	*gregorian-year*	*list-of-fixed-dates*
mayan-baktun (p. *505*)	*mayan-long-count-date*	*mayan-baktun*
mayan-calendar-round-on-or-before (p. 176)	⟨*mayan-haab-date*, *mayan-tzolkin-date*, *fixed-date*⟩	*fixed-date* (or **bogus**)
mayan-haab-date (p. *506*)	⟨*mayan-haab-month*, *mayan-haab-day*⟩	*mayan-haab-date*
mayan-haab-day (p. *506*)	*mayan-haab-date*	*mayan-haab-day*
mayan-haab-from-fixed (p. 173)	*fixed-date*	*mayan-haab-date*
mayan-haab-month (p. *506*)	*mayan-haab-date*	*mayan-haab-month*
mayan-haab-on-or-before (p. 173)	⟨*mayan-haab-date*, *fixed-date*⟩	*fixed-date*
mayan-haab-ordinal (p. 173)	*mayan-haab-date*	*nonnegative-integer*
mayan-katun (p. *506*)	*mayan-long-count-date*	*mayan-katun*
mayan-kin (p. *506*)	*mayan-long-count-date*	*mayan-kin*

continued

Function	Parameter type(s)	Result type
mayan-long-count-date (p. *505*)	⟨*mayan-baktun, mayan-katun, mayan-tun, mayan-uinal, mayan-kin*⟩	*mayan-long-count-date*
mayan-long-count-from-fixed (p. 171)	*fixed-date*	*mayan-long-count-date*
mayan-tun (p. *506*)	*mayan-long-count-date*	*mayan-tun*
mayan-tzolkin-date (p. *507*)	⟨*mayan-tzolkin-number, mayan-tzolkin-name*⟩	*mayan-tzolkin-date*
mayan-tzolkin-from-fixed (p. 175)	*fixed-date*	*mayan-tzolkin-date*
mayan-tzolkin-name (p. *507*)	*mayan-tzolkin-date*	*mayan-tzolkin-name*
mayan-tzolkin-number (p. *507*)	*mayan-tzolkin-date*	*mayan-tzolkin-number*
mayan-tzolkin-on-or-before (p. 175)	⟨*mayan-tzolkin-date, fixed-date*⟩	*fixed-date*
mayan-tzolkin-ordinal (p. 175)	*mayan-tzolkin-date*	*nonnegative-integer*
mayan-uinal (p. *506*)	*mayan-long-count-date*	*mayan-uinal*
mayan-year-bearer-from-fixed (p. 176)	*fixed-date*	*mayan-tzolkin-name* (or **bogus**)
mean-lunar-longitude (p. 233)	*century*	*angle*
memorial-day (p. 70)	*gregorian-year*	*fixed-date*
mesha-samkranti (p. 364)	*gregorian-year*	*rational-moment*
midday (p. 218)	⟨*fixed-date, location*⟩	*moment*
midday-in-tehran (p. 259)	*fixed-date*	*moment*
midnight (p. 218)	⟨*fixed-date, location*⟩	*moment*
midnight-in-china (p. 309)	*fixed-date*	*moment*
midnight-in-paris (p. 283)	*fixed-date*	*moment*
minor-solar-term-on-or-after (p. 308)	*fixed-date*	*moment*
mins (p. *514*)	*real*	*angle*
minute (p. *474*)	*clock-time*	*minute*
mjd-from-fixed (p. 19)	*fixed-date*	*julian-day-number*
mn (p. *514*)	*real*	*duration*
mod3 (p. 22)	⟨*real, real, real*⟩	*real*
molad (p. 119)	⟨*hebrew-year, hebrew-month*⟩	*rational-moment*
moment-from-jd (p. 18)	*julian-day-number*	*moment*
moment-from-unix (p. 19)	*second*	*moment*
moment-of-depression (p. 241)	⟨*moment, location, half-circle, boolean*⟩	*moment* (or **bogus**)
month-length (p. 294)	⟨*fixed-date, location*⟩	1 . . 31
moonlag (p. 290)	⟨*fixed-date, location*⟩	*duration*
moon-node (p. 234)	*century*	*angle*
moonrise (p. 244)	⟨*fixed-date, location*⟩	*moment* (or **bogus**)
moonset (p. 245)	⟨*fixed-date, location*⟩	*moment* (or **bogus**)
mt (p. *514*)	*real*	*distance*
naw-ruz (p. 277)	*gregorian-year*	*fixed-date*
new-moon-at-or-after (p. 231)	*moment*	*moment*
new-moon-before (p. 230)	*moment*	*moment*
next (p. 23)	⟨—, *integer, integer→boolean*⟩	*integer*
nighttime-temporal-hour (p. 248)	⟨*fixed-date, location*⟩	*real* (or **bogus**)

continued

Function	Parameter type(s)	Result type
nones-of-month (p. 78)	*roman-month*	*nones*
nowruz (p. 265)	*gregorian-year*	*fixed-date*
nth-kday (p. 69)	⟨*integer, day-of-week, gregorian-date*⟩	*fixed-date*
nth-new-moon (p. 229)	*integer*	*moment*
nutation (p. 223)	*moment*	*angle*
obliquity (p. 220)	*moment*	*angle*
observational-hebrew-first-of-nisan (p. 297)	*gregorian-year*	*fixed-date*
observational-hebrew-from-fixed (p. 298)	*fixed-date*	*hebrew-date*
observational-islamic-from-fixed (p. 294)	*fixed-date*	*islamic-date*
observed-lunar-altitude (p. 243)	⟨*moment, location*⟩	*angle*
old-hindu-lunar-date (p. *504*)	⟨*old-hindu-lunar-year, old-hindu-lunar-month, old-hindu-lunar-leap, old-hindu-lunar-day*⟩	*old-hindu-lunar-date*
old-hindu-lunar-day (p. *504*)	*old-hindu-lunar-date*	*old-hindu-lunar-day*
old-hindu-lunar-from-fixed (p. 165)	*fixed-date*	*old-hindu-lunar-date*
old-hindu-lunar-leap (p. *504*)	*old-hindu-lunar-date*	*old-hindu-lunar-leap*
old-hindu-lunar-leap-year? (p. 163)	*old-hindu-lunar-year*	*boolean*
old-hindu-lunar-month (p. *504*)	*old-hindu-lunar-date*	*old-hindu-lunar-month*
old-hindu-lunar-year (p. *504*)	*old-hindu-lunar-date*	*old-hindu-lunar-year*
old-hindu-solar-from-fixed (p. 159)	*fixed-date*	*hindu-solar-date*
olympiad (p. *487*)	⟨*olympiad-cycle, olympiad-year*⟩	*olympiad*
olympiad-cycle (p. *487*)	*olympiad*	*olympiad-cycle*
olympiad-from-julian-year (p. 82)	*julian-year*	*olympiad*
olympiad-year (p. *487*)	*olympiad*	*olympiad-year*
omer (p. 129)	*fixed-date*	*omer-count* (or **bogus**)
orthodox-easter (p. 146)	*gregorian-year*	*fixed-date*
passover (p. 129)	*gregorian-year*	*fixed-date*
pentecost (p. 152)	*gregorian-year*	*fixed-date*
persian-date (p. *535*)	⟨*persian-year, persian-month, persian-day*⟩	*persian-date*
persian-from-fixed (p. 260)	*fixed-date*	*persian-date*
persian-new-year-on-or-before (p. 259)	*fixed-date*	*fixed-date*
phasis-on-or-after (p. 252)	⟨*fixed-date, location*⟩	*fixed-date*
phasis-on-or-before (p. 252)	⟨*fixed-date, location*⟩	*fixed-date*
poly (p. *473*)	⟨*real, list-of-reals*⟩	*real*
positions-in-range (p. 27)	⟨*nonnegative-real, positive-real, nonnegative-real, interval*⟩	*list-of-fixed-dates*
possible-hebrew-days (p. 139)	⟨*hebrew-month, hebrew-day*⟩	*list-of-weekdays*

continued

Function	Parameter type(s)	Result type
precession (p. 225)	*moment*	*angle*
prod (p. 23)	⟨*integer→real*, —, *integer*, *integer→boolean*⟩	*real*
purim (p. 129)	*gregorian-year*	*fixed-date*
qing-ming (p. 324)	*gregorian-year*	*fixed-date*
quotient (p. *472*)	⟨*real*, *nonzero-real*⟩	*integer*
radians-from-degrees (p. *513*)	*real*	*radian*
rama (p. 369)	*gregorian-year*	*list-of-fixed-dates*
rd (p. 12)	*moment*	*moment*
refraction (p. 242)	⟨*moment*, *location*⟩	*angle*
right-ascension (p. 220)	⟨*moment*, *angle*, *angle*⟩	*angle*
roman-count (p. *486*)	*roman-date*	*roman-count*
roman-date (p. *486*)	⟨*roman-year*, *roman-month*, *roman-event*, *roman-count*, *roman-leap*⟩	*roman-date*
roman-event (p. *486*)	*roman-date*	*roman-event*
roman-from-fixed (p. 80)	*fixed-date*	*roman-date*
roman-leap (p. *486*)	*roman-date*	*roman-leap*
roman-month (p. *486*)	*roman-date*	*roman-month*
roman-year (p. *486*)	*roman-date*	*roman-year*
sacred-wednesdays (p. 370)	*gregorian-year*	*list-of-fixed-dates*
sacred-wednesdays-in-range (p. 371)	*range*	*list-of-fixed-dates*
samaritan-from-fixed (p. 302)	*fixed-date*	*hebrew-date*
samaritan-new-moon-after (p. 300)	*moment*	*fixed-date*
samaritan-new-moon-at-or-before (p. 300)	*moment*	*fixed-date*
samaritan-new-year-on-or-before (p. 301)	*fixed-date*	*fixed-date*
samaritan-noon (p. 300)	*fixed-date*	*moment*
samuel-season-in-gregorian (p. 132)	⟨*season*, *gregorian-year*⟩	*list-of-moments*
saudi-criterion (p. 296)	*fixed-date*	*boolean*
saudi-islamic-from-fixed (p. 296)	*fixed-date*	*islamic-date*
saudi-new-month-on-or-before (p. 296)	*fixed-date*,	*fixed-date*
season-in-gregorian (p. 224)	⟨*season*, *gregorian-year*⟩	*moment*
sec (p. *514*)	*real*	*duration*
seconds (p. *474*)	*clock-time*	*second*
secs (p. *514*)	*real*	*angle*
shaukat-criterion (p. 250)	⟨*fixed-date*, *location*⟩	*boolean*
sh-ela (p. 131)	*gregorian-year*	*list-of-fixed-dates*
shift-days (p. 138)	⟨*list-of-weekdays*, *integer*⟩	*list-of-weekdays*
shiva (p. 369)	*gregorian-year*	*list-of-fixed-dates*
short-kislev? (p. 122)	*hebrew-year*	*boolean*
sidereal-from-moment (p. 219)	*moment*	*angle*
sidereal-lunar-longitude (p. 234)	*moment*	*angle*
sidereal-solar-longitude (p. 225)	*moment*	*angle*
sidereal-zodiac (p. 360)	*moment*	*hindu-solar-month*

continued

Function	Parameter type(s)	Result type
sigma (p. *473*)	⟨*list-of-pairs, list-of-reals→real*⟩	*real*
sign (p. 20)	*real*	{−1, 0, +1}
simple-best-view (p. 250)	⟨*fixed-date, location*⟩	*moment*
sin-degrees (p. *513*)	*angle*	*amplitude*
sine-offset (p. 241)	⟨*moment, location, circle* ⟩	*real*
solar-altitude (p. 226)	⟨*moment, location*⟩	*half-circle*
solar-anomaly (p. 234)	*century*	*angle*
solar-longitude (p. 223)	*moment*	*season*
solar-longitude-after (p. 224)	⟨*season, moment*⟩	*moment*
standard-day (p. *474*)	*standard-date*	*standard-day*
standard-from-local (p. 208)	⟨*moment, location*⟩	*moment*
standard-from-sundial (p. 248)	⟨*moment, location*⟩	*moment* (or **bogus**)
standard-from-universal (p. 208)	⟨*moment, location*⟩	*moment*
standard-month (p. *474*)	*standard-date*	*standard-month*
standard-year (p. *474*)	*standard-date*	*standard-year*
sum (p. 23)	⟨*integer→real, —, integer, integer→boolean*⟩	*real*
sunrise (p. 242)	⟨*fixed-date, location*⟩	*moment*
sunset (p. 242)	⟨*fixed-date, location*⟩	*moment*
ta-anit-esther (p. 130)	*gregorian-year*	*fixed-date*
tan-degrees (p. *513*)	*angle*	*real*
tibetan-date (p. *570*)	⟨*tibetan-year, tibetan-month, tibetan-leap-month, tibetan-day, tibetan-leap-day*⟩	*tibetan-date*
tibetan-day (p. *570*)	*tibetan-date*	*tibetan-day*
tibetan-from-fixed (p. 378)	*fixed-date*	*tibetan-date*
tibetan-leap-day (p. 381)	*tibetan-date*	*tibetan-leap-day*
tibetan-leap-day? (p. 381)	⟨*tibetan-year, tibetan-month, tibetan-day*⟩	*boolean*
tibetan-leap-month (p. 380)	*tibetan-date*	*tibetan-leap-month*
tibetan-leap-month? (p. 380)	⟨*tibetan-year, tibetan-month*⟩	*boolean*
tibetan-month (p. *570*)	*tibetan-date*	*tibetan-month*
tibetan-moon-equation (p. 377)	*rational-angle*	*rational*
tibetan-new-year (p. 381)	*gregorian-year*	*list-of-fixed-dates*
tibetan-sun-equation (p. 377)	*rational-angle*	*rational*
tibetan-year (p. *570*)	*tibetan-date*	*tibetan-year*
time-from-clock (p. 28)	*clock-time*	*time*
time-from-moment (p. 21)	*moment*	*time*
time-of-day (p. *474*)	⟨*hour, minute, second*⟩	*clock-time*
tishah-be-av (p. 130)	*gregorian-year*	*fixed-date*
topocentric-lunar-altitude (p. 239)	⟨*moment, location*⟩	*half-circle*
to-radix (p. 28)	⟨*real, list-of-rationals, list-of-rationals*⟩	*list-of-reals*
tumpek (p. 190)	*gregorian-year*	*list-of-fixed-dates*
universal-from-apparent (p. 218)	⟨*moment, location*⟩	*moment*
universal-from-dynamical (p. 212)	*moment*	*moment*

continued

Function	Parameter type(s)	Result type
universal-from-local (p. 208)	⟨*moment, location*⟩	*moment*
universal-from-standard (p. 208)	⟨*moment, location*⟩	*moment*
unix-from-moment (p. 19)	*moment*	*second*
unlucky-fridays (p. 71)	*gregorian-year*	*list-of-fixed-dates*
unlucky-fridays-in-range (p. 71)	*range*	*list-of-fixed-dates*
vietnamese-location (p. 329)	*moment*	*location*
visible-crescent (p. 252)	⟨*fixed-date, location*⟩	*boolean*
yahrzeit (p. 136)	⟨*hebrew-date, hebrew-year*⟩	*fixed-date*
yahrzeit-in-gregorian (p. 137)	⟨*hebrew-date, gregorian-year*⟩	*list-of-fixed-dates*
yallop-criterion (p. 251)	⟨*fixed-date, location*⟩	*boolean*
yoga (p. 369)	*fixed-date*	1 . . 27
yom-ha-zikkaron (p. 131)	*gregorian-year*	*fixed-date*
yom-kippur (p. 128)	*gregorian-year*	*fixed-date*
zone (p. *515*)	*location*	*real*
zone-from-longitude (p. 208)	*angle*	*duration*

A.3 Constant Types and Values

Constant	Type	Value
acre (p. 204)	*location*	⟨32.94, 35.09, 22, 1/12⟩
adar (p. 115)	*hebrew-month*	12
adarii (p. 115)	*hebrew-month*	13
akan-day-name-epoch (p. 38)	*fixed-date*	37
april (p. 59)	*standard-month*	4
armenian-epoch (p. 31)	*fixed-date*	201443
arya-jovian-period (p. 157)	*rational*	131493125/30352
arya-lunar-day (p. 160)	*rational*	26298625/26716668
arya-lunar-month (p. 160)	*rational*	131493125/4452778
arya-solar-month (p. 158)	*rational*	210389/6912
arya-solar-year (p. 157)	*rational*	210389/576
august (p. 59)	*standard-month*	8
autumn (p. 83)	*season*	180
av (p. 114)	*hebrew-month*	5
ayyam-i-ha (p. 271)	*bahai-month*	0
aztec-correlation (p. 177)	*fixed-date*	555403
aztec-tonalpohualli-correlation (p. 179)	*fixed-date*	555299
aztec-xihuitl-correlation (p. 178)	*fixed-date*	555202
babylon (p. 290)	*location*	⟨32.4794, 44.4328, 26, 7/2⟩
babylonian-epoch (p. 291)	*fixed-date*	−113502
bahai-epoch (p. 271)	*fixed-date*	673222
bahai-location (p. 274)	*location*	⟨35.696111, 51.423055999999974, 0, 7/48⟩

continued

Constant	Type	Value
bali-epoch (p. 187)	*fixed-date*	−1721279
blind (p. 325)	*augury*	1
bogus (p. 47)	*string*	"bogus"
bright (p. 325)	*augury*	2
chinese-day-name-epoch (p. 320)	*integer*	45
chinese-epoch (p. 316)	*fixed-date*	−963099
chinese-month-name-epoch (p. 320)	*integer*	57
coptic-epoch (p. 90)	*fixed-date*	103605
december (p. 59)	*standard-month*	12
double-bright (p. 325)	*augury*	3
egyptian-epoch (p. 30)	*fixed-date*	−272787
elul (p. 115)	*hebrew-month*	6
ethiopic-epoch (p. 92)	*fixed-date*	2430
evening (p. 241)	*boolean*	false
false (p. *470*)	*boolean*	false
february (p. 59)	*standard-month*	2
first-quarter (p. 236)	*phase*	90
french-epoch (p. 283)	*fixed-date*	654415
friday (p. 33)	*day-of-week*	5
full (p. 236)	*phase*	180
gregorian-epoch (p. 58)	*fixed-date*	1
hebrew-epoch (p. 119)	*fixed-date*	−1373427
hebrew-location (p. 297)	*location*	⟨32.82, 35, 0, 1/12⟩
hindu-anomalistic-month (p. 345)	*rational*	1577917828/57265137
hindu-anomalistic-year (p. 344)	*rational*	1577917828000/4319999613
hindu-creation (p. 344)	*fixed-date*	−714403429586
hindu-epoch (p. 156)	*fixed-date*	−1132959
hindu-location (p. 351)	*location*	⟨463/20, 2273/30, 0, 383/75⟩
hindu-lunar-era (p. 349)	*standard-year*	3044
hindu-sidereal-month (p. 336)	*rational*	394479457/14438334
hindu-sidereal-year (p. 336)	*rational*	394479457/1080000
hindu-solar-era (p. 347)	*standard-year*	3179
hindu-synodic-month (p. 336)	*rational*	394479457/13358334
icelandic-epoch (p. 100)	*fixed-date*	109
ides (p. 77)	*roman-event*	3
islamic-epoch (p. 106)	*fixed-date*	227015
islamic-location (p. 293)	*location*	⟨30.1, 31.3, 200, 1/12⟩
iyyar (p. 114)	*hebrew-month*	2
j2000 (p. 212)	*moment*	730120.5
january (p. 59)	*standard-month*	1
jd-epoch (p. 18)	*moment*	−1721424.5
jerusalem (p. 204)	*location*	⟨31.78, 35.24, 740, 1/12⟩
julian-epoch (p. 76)	*fixed-date*	−1
july (p. 59)	*standard-month*	7
june (p. 59)	*standard-month*	6
kalends (p. 77)	*roman-event*	1

continued

Constant	Type	Value
kislev (p. 115)	*hebrew-month*	9
last-quarter (p. 236)	*phase*	270
march (p. 59)	*standard-month*	3
marheshvan (p. 115)	*hebrew-month*	8
may (p. 59)	*standard-month*	5
mayan-epoch (p. 171)	*fixed-date*	−1137142
mayan-haab-epoch (p. 173)	*fixed-date*	−1137490
mayan-tzolkin-epoch (p. 175)	*fixed-date*	−1137302
mean-sidereal-year (p. 221)	*duration*	365.25636
mean-synodic-month (p. 227)	*duration*	29.530588853
mean-tropical-year (p. 221)	*duration*	365.242189
mecca (p. 204)	*location*	⟨6427/300, 11947/300, 298, 1/8⟩
mjd-epoch (p. 19)	*fixed-date*	678576
monday (p. 33)	*day-of-week*	1
morning (p. 241)	*boolean*	true
new (p. 236)	*phase*	0
nisan (p. 114)	*hebrew-month*	1
nones (p. 77)	*roman-event*	2
november (p. 59)	*standard-month*	11
october (p. 59)	*standard-month*	10
olympiad-start (p. 82)	*julian-year*	−776
padua (p. 246)	*location*	⟨40867/900, 14263/1200, 18, 1/24⟩
paris (p. 283)	*location*	⟨175811/3600, 187/80, 27, 1/24⟩
persian-epoch (p. 258)	*fixed-date*	226896
samaritan-epoch (p. 301)	*fixed-date*	−598573
samaritan-location (p. 300)	*location*	⟨32.1994, 35.2728, 881, 1/12⟩
saturday (p. 33)	*day-of-week*	6
september (p. 59)	*standard-month*	9
shevat (p. 115)	*hebrew-month*	11
sidereal-start (p. 359)	*angle*	156.13605090692624
sivan (p. 114)	*hebrew-month*	3
spring (p. 83)	*season*	0
summer (p. 83)	*season*	90
sunday (p. 33)	*day-of-week*	0
tammuz (p. 114)	*hebrew-month*	4
tehran (p. 259)	*location*	⟨35.68, 51.42, 1100, 7/48⟩
tevet (p. 115)	*hebrew-month*	10
thursday (p. 33)	*day-of-week*	4
tibetan-epoch (p. 376)	*fixed-date*	294075
tishri (p. 115)	*hebrew-month*	7
true (p. *470*)	*boolean*	true
tuesday (p. 33)	*day-of-week*	2
ujjain (p. 351)	*location*	⟨463/20, 45461/600, 0, 45461/216000⟩

continued

Constant	Type	Value
unix-epoch (p. 19)	*fixed-date*	719163
wednesday (p. 33)	*day-of-week*	3
winter (p. 83)	*season*	270
year-rome-founded (p. 81)	*julian-year*	−753

Sixteenth-century astrolabe, with zodiac and star names inscribed in Hebrew. (Courtesy of Adler Planetarium & Astronomy Museum, Chicago.)

Sixteenth-century astrolabe, with zodiac and star names inscribed in Hebrew. (Courtesy of Adler Planetarium & Astronomy Museum, Chicago.)

Appendix B

Cross References for Functions and Constants

When the true Number of Days cannot be found at one View in this Table, then both them and their Decimals must be taken out of the Table at twice or thrice, as their Number requires, and added together.

Thomas Dilworth: *The Schoolmaster's Assistant, Being a Compendium of Arithmetic both Practical and Theoretical* (1743)

In this appendix we list all dependencies among the calendar functions.

Function/constant	Used by
aberration (p. 223)	**solar-longitude** (p. 223)
adar (p. 115)	**adda-season-in-gregorian** (p. 133) **last-day-of-hebrew-month** (p. 122) **last-month-of-hebrew-year** (p. 115) **possible-hebrew-days** (p. 139) **samuel-season-in-gregorian** (p. 132) **yahrzeit** (p. 136)
adarii (p. 115)	**last-day-of-hebrew-month** (p. 122) **last-month-of-hebrew-year** (p. 115) **yahrzeit** (p. 136)
akan-day-name (p. 38)	**akan-name-from-fixed** (p. 38)
akan-day-name-epoch (p. 38)	**akan-name-from-fixed** (p. 38)
akan-name-difference (p. 38)	**akan-day-name-on-or-before** (p. 38)
akan-name-from-fixed (p. 38)	**akan-day-name-on-or-before** (p. 38)
alt-hindu-sunrise (p. 357)	**astro-hindu-lunar-from-fixed** (p. 361) **fixed-from-astro-hindu-lunar** (p. 362)
apparent-from-local (p. 217)	**apparent-from-universal** (p. 218)
apparent-from-universal (p. 218)	**astronomical-easter** (p. 292) **samaritan-new-moon-after** (p. 300) **samaritan-new-moon-at-or-before** (p. 300)

continued

Function/constant	Used by
approx-moment-of-depression (p. 240)	**moment-of-depression** (p. 241)
april (p. 59)	**babylonian-epoch** (p. 291) **easter** (p. 148) **icelandic-epoch** (p. 100) **korean-location** (p. 328) **orthodox-easter** (p. 146)
arc-of-light (p. 250)	**shaukat-criterion** (p. 250) **yallop-criterion** (p. 251)
arc-of-vision (p. 251)	**yallop-criterion** (p. 251)
arithmetic-persian-year-from-fixed (p. 263)	**arithmetic-persian-from-fixed** (p. 263)
armenian-epoch (p. 31)	**armenian-from-fixed** (p. 31) **fixed-from-armenian** (p. 31)
arya-jovian-period (p. 157)	**jovian-year** (p. 158)
arya-lunar-day (p. 160)	**fixed-from-old-hindu-lunar** (p. 165) **old-hindu-lunar-from-fixed** (p. 165)
arya-lunar-month (p. 160)	**arya-lunar-day** (p. 160) **fixed-from-old-hindu-lunar** (p. 166) **old-hindu-lunar-from-fixed** (p. 165) **old-hindu-lunar-leap-year?** (p. 163)
arya-solar-month (p. 158)	**fixed-from-old-hindu-lunar** (p. 166) **fixed-from-old-hindu-solar** (p. 158) **old-hindu-lunar-from-fixed** (p. 165) **old-hindu-lunar-leap-year?** (p. 163) **old-hindu-solar-from-fixed** (p. 159)
arya-solar-year (p. 157)	**arya-solar-month** (p. 158) **fixed-from-old-hindu-solar** (p. 158) **old-hindu-lunar-from-fixed** (p. 165) **old-hindu-lunar-leap-year?** (p. 163) **old-hindu-solar-from-fixed** (p. 159)
astro-bahai-new-year-on-or-before (p. 274)	**astro-bahai-from-fixed** (p. 275) **fixed-from-astro-bahai** (p. 275) **naw-ruz** (p. 277)
astro-hindu-calendar-year (p. 360)	**astro-hindu-lunar-from-fixed** (p. 361) **astro-hindu-solar-from-fixed** (p. 360)
astro-hindu-lunar-from-fixed (p. 361)	**fixed-from-astro-hindu-lunar** (p. 362)
astro-hindu-sunset (p. 360)	**astro-hindu-solar-from-fixed** (p. 360) **fixed-from-astro-hindu-solar** (p. 360)
astro-lunar-day-from-moment (p. 361)	**astro-hindu-lunar-from-fixed** (p. 361) **fixed-from-astro-hindu-lunar** (p. 362)

continued

Function/constant	Used by
august (p. 59)	**aztec-correlation** (p. 177) **coptic-epoch** (p. 90) **ethiopic-epoch** (p. 92) **korean-location** (p. 328)
autumn (p. 83)	**french-new-year-on-or-before** (p. 283)
av (p. 114)	**tishah-be-av** (p. 130)
ayyam-i-ha (p. 271)	**astro-bahai-from-fixed** (p. 276) **bahai-from-fixed** (p. 272) **fixed-from-astro-bahai** (p. 275) **fixed-from-bahai** (p. 271)
aztec-correlation (p. 177)	**aztec-tonalpohualli-correlation** (p. 179) **aztec-xihuitl-correlation** (p. 178)
aztec-tonalpohualli-correlation (p. 179)	**aztec-tonalpohualli-from-fixed** (p. 180) **aztec-tonalpohualli-on-or-before** (p. 180) **aztec-xihuitl-tonalpohualli-on-or-before** (p. 181)
aztec-tonalpohualli-from-fixed (p. 179)	**aztec-xiuhmolpilli-from-fixed** (p. 180)
aztec-tonalpohualli-ordinal (p. 179)	**aztec-tonalpohualli-correlation** (p. 179) **aztec-tonalpohualli-on-or-before** (p. 180) **aztec-xihuitl-tonalpohualli-on-or-before** (p. 181)
aztec-xihuitl-correlation (p. 178)	**aztec-xihuitl-from-fixed** (p. 178) **aztec-xihuitl-on-or-before** (p. 179) **aztec-xihuitl-tonalpohualli-on-or-before** (p. 181)
aztec-xihuitl-from-fixed (p. 178)	**aztec-xiuhmolpilli-from-fixed** (p. 180)
aztec-xihuitl-on-or-before (p. 179)	**aztec-xiuhmolpilli-from-fixed** (p. 180)
aztec-xihuitl-ordinal (p. 178)	**aztec-xihuitl-correlation** (p. 178) **aztec-xihuitl-on-or-before** (p. 179) **aztec-xihuitl-tonalpohualli-on-or-before** (p. 181)
babylon (p. 290)	**babylonian-criterion** (p. 290)
babylonian-criterion (p. 290)	**babylonian-new-month-on-or-before** (p. 291)
babylonian-epoch (p. 291)	**babylonian-from-fixed** (p. 292) **fixed-from-babylonian** (p. 291)
babylonian-new-month-on-or-before (p. 290)	**babylonian-from-fixed** (p. 292) **fixed-from-babylonian** (p. 291)
bahai-epoch (p. 271)	**astro-bahai-from-fixed** (p. 275) **bahai-from-fixed** (p. 272) **fixed-from-astro-bahai** (p. 275) **fixed-from-bahai** (p. 272)

continued

Function/constant	Used by
bahai-location (p. 274)	**bahai-sunset** (p. 274)
bahai-sunset (p. 274)	**astro-bahai-new-year-on-or-before** (p. 274) **birth-of-the-bab** (p. 278)
bali-asatawara-from-fixed (p. 188)	**bali-caturwara-from-fixed** (p. 189) **bali-pawukon-from-fixed** (p. 185)
bali-caturwara-from-fixed (p. 189)	**bali-pawukon-from-fixed** (p. 185)
bali-dasawara-from-fixed (p. 188)	**bali-dwiwara-from-fixed** (p. 188) **bali-luang-from-fixed** (p. 188) **bali-pawukon-from-fixed** (p. 185)
bali-day-from-fixed (p. 187)	**bali-asatawara-from-fixed** (p. 189) **bali-on-or-before** (p. 189) **bali-pancawara-from-fixed** (p. 187) **bali-sadwara-from-fixed** (p. 187) **bali-sangawara-from-fixed** (p. 188) **bali-saptawara-from-fixed** (p. 187) **bali-triwara-from-fixed** (p. 187) **bali-week-from-fixed** (p. 187) **kajeng-keliwon** (p. 190) **tumpek** (p. 190)
bali-dwiwara-from-fixed (p. 188)	**bali-pawukon-from-fixed** (p. 185)
bali-epoch (p. 187)	**bali-day-from-fixed** (p. 187)
bali-luang-from-fixed (p. 188)	**bali-pawukon-from-fixed** (p. 185)
bali-pancawara-from-fixed (p. 187)	**bali-dasawara-from-fixed** (p. 188) **bali-pawukon-from-fixed** (p. 185)
bali-sadwara-from-fixed (p. 187)	**bali-pawukon-from-fixed** (p. 185)
bali-sangawara-from-fixed (p. 188)	**bali-pawukon-from-fixed** (p. 185)
bali-saptawara-from-fixed (p. 187)	**bali-dasawara-from-fixed** (p. 188) **bali-pawukon-from-fixed** (p. 185)
bali-triwara-from-fixed (p. 187)	**bali-pawukon-from-fixed** (p. 185)
blind (p. 325)	**chinese-year-marriage-augury** (p. 325)
bogus (p. 47)	**alt-asr** (p. 249) **approx-moment-of-depression** (p. 240) **arctan-degrees** (p. 205) **asr** (p. 249) **aztec-xihuitl-tonalpohualli-on-or-before** (p. 181) **aztec-xiuhmolpilli-from-fixed** (p. 180) **bruin-best-view** (p. 251) **chinese-age** (p. 325) **dawn** (p. 241)

continued

Function/constant	Used by
	daytime-temporal-hour (p. 247) **dusk** (p. 242) **mayan-calendar-round-on-or-before** (p. 176) **mayan-year-bearer-from-fixed** (p. 176) **moment-of-depression** (p. 241) **moonlag** (p. 290) **moonrise** (p. 244) **moonset** (p. 245) **nighttime-temporal-hour** (p. 248) **nth-kday** (p. 69) **omer** (p. 129) **simple-best-view** (p. 250) **standard-from-sundial** (p. 248)
bright (p. 325)	**chinese-year-marriage-augury** (p. 325)
bruin-best-view (p. 251)	**yallop-criterion** (p. 251)
chinese-day-name (p. 320)	**chinese-day-name-on-or-before** (p. 320)
chinese-day-name-epoch (p. 320)	**chinese-day-name** (p. 320)
chinese-epoch (p. 316)	**chinese-from-fixed** (p. 317) **dragon-festival** (p. 324) **fixed-from-chinese** (p. 318)
chinese-from-fixed (p. 317)	**chinese-age** (p. 325) **fixed-from-chinese** (p. 318)
chinese-location (p. 306)	**chinese-new-moon-before** (p. 310) **chinese-new-moon-on-or-after** (p. 309) **chinese-solar-longitude-on-or-after** (p. 308) **current-major-solar-term** (p. 306) **current-minor-solar-term** (p. 308) **midnight-in-china** (p. 309)
chinese-month-name-epoch (p. 320)	**chinese-month-name** (p. 320)
chinese-name-difference (p. 319)	**chinese-day-name-on-or-before** (p. 320)
chinese-new-moon-before (p. 310)	**chinese-from-fixed** (p. 317) **chinese-new-year-in-sui** (p. 316) **chinese-prior-leap-month?** (p. 313)
chinese-new-moon-on-or-after (p. 309)	**chinese-from-fixed** (p. 317) **chinese-new-year-in-sui** (p. 316) **chinese-no-major-solar-term?** (p. 313) **fixed-from-chinese** (p. 318)
chinese-new-year-in-sui (p. 315)	**chinese-new-year-on-or-before** (p. 316)
chinese-new-year-on-or-before (p. 316)	**chinese-new-year** (p. 322) **fixed-from-chinese** (p. 318)

continued

Function/constant	Used by
chinese-no-major-solar-term? (p. 313)	**chinese-from-fixed** (p. 317) **chinese-new-year-in-sui** (p. 316) **chinese-prior-leap-month?** (p. 313)
chinese-prior-leap-month? (p. 313)	**chinese-from-fixed** (p. 317)
chinese-sexagesimal-name (p. 319)	**chinese-day-name** (p. 320) **chinese-month-name** (p. 320) **chinese-year-name** (p. 320)
chinese-solar-longitude-on-or-after (p. 308)	**major-solar-term-on-or-after** (p. 308) **minor-solar-term-on-or-after** (p. 308)
chinese-winter-solstice-on-or-before (p. 309)	**chinese-from-fixed** (p. 317) **chinese-new-year-in-sui** (p. 316)
coptic-epoch (p. 90)	**coptic-from-fixed** (p. 91) **ethiopic-from-fixed** (p. 92) **fixed-from-coptic** (p. 90) **fixed-from-ethiopic** (p. 92)
coptic-from-fixed (p. 91)	**birkath-ha-hama** (p. 131) **coptic-in-gregorian** (p. 93) **ethiopic-from-fixed** (p. 92)
coptic-in-gregorian (p. 92)	**birkath-ha-hama** (p. 132) **coptic-christmas** (p. 93) **sh-ela** (p. 131)
current-major-solar-term? (p. 306)	**chinese-no-major-solar-term?** (p. 313)
current-minor-solar-term (p. 308)	**chinese-year-marriage-augury** (p. 326)
cycle-in-gregorian (p. 83)	**adda-season-in-gregorian** (p. 133) **julian-season-in-gregorian** (p. 84) **samuel-season-in-gregorian** (p. 132)
dawn (p. 241)	**alt-hindu-sunrise** (p. 357) **sunrise** (p. 242)
day-of-week-from-fixed (p. 33)	**alt-birkath-ha-hama** (p. 132) **icelandic-from-fixed** (p. 101) **iso-long-year?** (p. 97) **kday-on-or-before** (p. 34) **ta-anit-esther** (p. 130) **tishah-be-av** (p. 130) **yom-ha-zikkaron** (p. 131)
days-in-hebrew-year (p. 123)	**long-marheshvan?** (p. 122) **short-kislev?** (p. 122)
daytime-temporal-hour (p. 247)	**standard-from-sundial** (p. 248)
december (p. 59)	**christmas** (p. 70)

continued

Function/constant	Used by
	day-number (p. 62) **days-remaining** (p. 63) **eastern-orthodox-christmas** (p. 85) **fixed-from-iso** (p. 96) **gregorian-year-end** (p. 60) **julian-epoch** (p. 76) **tibetan-epoch** (p. 376)
declination (p. 220)	**alt-asr** (p. 249) **asr** (p. 249) **lunar-altitude** (p. 238) **sine-offset** (p. 241) **solar-altitude** (p. 226)
double-bright (p. 325)	**chinese-year-marriage-augury** (p. 325)
dusk (p. 242)	**alt-asr** (p. 249) **asr** (p. 249) **astro-hindu-sunset** (p. 360) **jewish-dusk** (p. 243) **jewish-sabbath-ends** (p. 243) **local-zero-hour** (p. 246) **simple-best-view** (p. 250) **sunset** (p. 242)
dynamical-from-universal (p. 212)	**julian-centuries** (p. 212)
early-month? (p. 294)	**alt-fixed-from-observational-hebrew** (p. 299) **alt-fixed-from-observational-islamic** (p. 295) **alt-observational-hebrew-from-fixed** (p. 299) **alt-observational-islamic-from-fixed** (p. 295)
easter (p. 148)	**pentecost** (p. 152)
egyptian-epoch (p. 30)	**alt-fixed-from-egyptian** (p. 31) **armenian-from-fixed** (p. 31) **egyptian-from-fixed** (p. 31) **fixed-from-armenian** (p. 31) **fixed-from-egyptian** (p. 30)
egyptian-from-fixed (p. 31)	**armenian-from-fixed** (p. 31)
elul (p. 115)	**last-day-of-hebrew-month** (p. 122) **possible-hebrew-days** (p. 139)
ephemeris-correction (p. 210)	**dynamical-from-universal** (p. 212) **universal-from-dynamical** (p. 212)
equation-of-time (p. 215)	**apparent-from-local** (p. 217) **local-from-apparent** (p. 218)
estimate-prior-solar-longitude (p. 226)	**astro-bahai-new-year-on-or-before** (p. 274) **chinese-winter-solstice-on-or-before** (p. 309)

continued

Function/constant	Used by
	french-new-year-on-or-before (p. 283) **persian-new-year-on-or-before** (p. 259)
ethiopic-epoch (p. 92)	**ethiopic-from-fixed** (p. 92) **fixed-from-ethiopic** (p. 92)
evening (p. 241)	**dusk** (p. 242)
february (p. 59)	**chinese-epoch** (p. 316) **hindu-epoch** (p. 156) **roman-from-fixed** (p. 80)
first-kday (p. 69)	**daylight-saving-end** (p. 70) **election-day** (p. 70) **epiphany** (p. 71) **labor-day** (p. 69)
first-quarter (p. 236)	**babylonian-criterion** (p. 290) **saudi-criterion** (p. 296) **shaukat-criterion** (p. 250) **yallop-criterion** (p. 251)
fixed-from-arithmetic-french (p. 285)	**arithmetic-french-from-fixed** (p. 286)
fixed-from-arithmetic-persian (p. 262)	**arithmetic-persian-from-fixed** (p. 264) **arithmetic-persian-year-from-fixed** (p. 263)
fixed-from-astro-bahai (p. 275)	**astro-bahai-from-fixed** (p. 276)
fixed-from-bahai (p. 271)	**bahai-from-fixed** (p. 273)
fixed-from-chinese (p. 318)	**chinese-age** (p. 325) **chinese-year-marriage-augury** (p. 326) **dragon-festival** (p. 324)
fixed-from-coptic (p. 90)	**coptic-from-fixed** (p. 91) **coptic-in-gregorian** (p. 93) **fixed-from-ethiopic** (p. 92)
fixed-from-egyptian (p. 30)	**fixed-from-armenian** (p. 31)
fixed-from-french (p. 284)	**french-leap-year?** (p. 284)
fixed-from-gregorian (p. 60)	**advent** (p. 70) **alt-gregorian-from-fixed** (p. 66) **bahai-epoch** (p. 271) **bahai-from-fixed** (p. 272) **bahai-new-year** (p. 277) **chinese-epoch** (p. 316) **chinese-new-year** (p. 322) **christmas** (p. 70) **easter** (p. 148) **fixed-from-bahai** (p. 271) **french-epoch** (p. 283)

continued

Function/constant	Used by
	gregorian-date-difference (p. 62)
	gregorian-from-fixed (p. 62)
	gregorian-new-year (p. 60)
	gregorian-year-end (p. 60)
	icelandic-epoch (p. 100)
	independence-day (p. 69)
	julian-epoch (p. 76)
	korean-location (p. 328)
	nth-kday (p. 69)
	qing-ming (p. 324)
	tibetan-epoch (p. 376)
fixed-from-hebrew (p. 123)	**adda-season-in-gregorian** (p. 133)
	alt-fixed-from-observational-hebrew (p. 300)
	fixed-from-observational-hebrew (p. 298)
	hebrew-birthday (p. 135)
	hebrew-from-fixed (p. 123)
	hebrew-in-gregorian (p. 133)
	passover (p. 129)
	possible-hebrew-days (p. 139)
	purim (p. 129)
	samuel-season-in-gregorian (p. 132)
	tishah-be-av (p. 130)
	yahrzeit (p. 136)
	yom-ha-zikkaron (p. 131)
	yom-kippur (p. 128)
fixed-from-hindu-lunar (p. 350)	**fixed-from-hindu-fullmoon** (p. 356)
	hindu-date-occur (p. 367)
	hindu-expunged? (p. 356)
fixed-from-icelandic (p. 100)	**icelandic-month** (p. 101)
fixed-from-islamic (p. 107)	**islamic-from-fixed** (p. 108)
	islamic-in-gregorian (p. 109)
fixed-from-iso (p. 95)	**iso-from-fixed** (p. 96)
fixed-from-jd (p. 20)	**bali-epoch** (p. 187)
	egyptian-epoch (p. 30)
	mayan-epoch (p. 171)
fixed-from-julian (p. 76)	**aztec-correlation** (p. 177)
	babylonian-epoch (p. 291)
	coptic-epoch (p. 90)
	ethiopic-epoch (p. 92)
	fixed-from-roman (p. 80)
	hebrew-epoch (p. 119)
	hindu-epoch (p. 156)
	islamic-epoch (p. 106)

continued

Function/constant	Used by
	julian-from-fixed (p. 77) **julian-in-gregorian** (p. 85) **julian-season-in-gregorian** (p. 84) **orthodox-easter** (p. 146) **persian-epoch** (p. 258) **samaritan-epoch** (p. 301)
fixed-from-moment (p. 20)	**alt-birkath-ha-hama** (p. 132) **approx-moment-of-depression** (p. 240) **babylonian-new-month-on-or-before** (p. 290) **birth-of-the-bab** (p. 278) **fixed-from-molad** (p. 126) **hindu-standard-from-sundial** (p. 355) **hindu-tithi-occur** (p. 368) **italian-from-local** (p. 247) **list-of-fixed-from-moments** (p. 26) **local-from-italian** (p. 247) **local-zero-hour** (p. 247) **phasis-on-or-after** (p. 252) **phasis-on-or-before** (p. 252) **saudi-new-month-on-or-before** (p. 296) **standard-from-sundial** (p. 248)
fixed-from-persian (p. 260)	**nowruz** (p. 265) **persian-from-fixed** (p. 260)
fixed-from-roman (p. 80)	**roman-from-fixed** (p. 81)
fixed-from-tibetan (p. 378)	**losar** (p. 381) **tibetan-from-fixed** (p. 379) **tibetan-leap-day?** (p. 381) **tibetan-leap-month?** (p. 380)
french-epoch (p. 283)	**arithmetic-french-from-fixed** (p. 285) **fixed-from-arithmetic-french** (p. 285) **fixed-from-french** (p. 284) **french-from-fixed** (p. 284)
french-new-year-on-or-before (p. 283)	**fixed-from-french** (p. 284) **french-from-fixed** (p. 284)
friday (p. 33)	**possible-hebrew-days** (p. 139) **unlucky-fridays-in-range** (p. 71) **yom-ha-zikkaron** (p. 131)
full (p. 236)	**astronomical-easter** (p. 292)
gregorian-date-difference (p. 62)	**day-number** (p. 62) **days-remaining** (p. 63) **ephemeris-correction** (p. 210) **last-day-of-gregorian-month** (p. 63)

continued

Function/constant	Used by
gregorian-epoch (p. 58)	**alt-fixed-from-gregorian** (p. 65) **alt-gregorian-from-fixed** (p. 66) **alt-gregorian-year-from-fixed** (p. 67) **alt-orthodox-easter** (p. 147) **fixed-from-gregorian** (p. 60) **gregorian-year-from-fixed** (p. 61)
gregorian-from-fixed (p. 62)	**unlucky-fridays-in-range** (p. 71)
gregorian-leap-year? (p. 59)	**fixed-from-bahai** (p. 271) **fixed-from-gregorian** (p. 60) **gregorian-from-fixed** (p. 62)
gregorian-new-year (p. 60)	**coptic-in-gregorian** (p. 93) **gregorian-from-fixed** (p. 62) **gregorian-year-range** (p. 60) **hebrew-birthday-in-gregorian** (p. 135) **hebrew-in-gregorian** (p. 133) **hindu-lunar-event** (p. 368) **hindu-lunar-holiday** (p. 368) **hindu-lunar-new-year** (p. 366) **islamic-in-gregorian** (p. 108) **iso-long-year?** (p. 97) **j2000** (p. 212) **julian-in-gregorian** (p. 85) **mesha-samkranti** (p. 364) **naw-ruz** (p. 277) **season-in-gregorian** (p. 225) **vietnamese-location** (p. 329) **yahrzeit-in-gregorian** (p. 137)
gregorian-year-end (p. 60)	**iso-long-year?** (p. 97) **tibetan-new-year** (p. 381)
gregorian-year-from-fixed (p. 61)	**alt-fixed-from-observational-hebrew** (p. 300) **alt-gregorian-from-fixed** (p. 66) **alt-observational-hebrew-from-fixed** (p. 299) **bahai-from-fixed** (p. 272) **chinese-location** (p. 306) **dragon-festival** (p. 324) **ephemeris-correction** (p. 210) **fixed-from-bahai** (p. 272) **fixed-from-observational-hebrew** (p. 298) **gregorian-from-fixed** (p. 62) **iso-from-fixed** (p. 96) **japanese-location** (p. 326) **nowruz** (p. 265) **observational-hebrew-from-fixed** (p. 298) **omer** (p. 129)

continued

Function/constant	Used by
	passover (p. 129) **purim** (p. 129) **samaritan-new-year-on-or-before** (p. 301) **tishah-be-av** (p. 130) **yom-ha-zikkaron** (p. 131) **yom-kippur** (p. 128)
gregorian-year-range (p. 60)	**coptic-in-gregorian** (p. 92) **cycle-in-gregorian** (p. 83) **hebrew-birthday-in-gregorian** (p. 135) **hebrew-in-gregorian** (p. 133) **hindu-lunar-event** (p. 368) **hindu-lunar-holiday** (p. 367) **islamic-in-gregorian** (p. 108) **julian-in-gregorian** (p. 85) **kajeng-keliwon** (p. 190) **sacred-wednesdays** (p. 370) **tibetan-new-year** (p. 381) **tumpek** (p. 190) **unlucky-fridays** (p. 71) **yahrzeit-in-gregorian** (p. 137)
hebrew-birthday (p. 135)	**hebrew-birthday-in-gregorian** (p. 135)
hebrew-calendar-elapsed-days (p. 121)	**hebrew-new-year** (p. 122) **hebrew-year-length-correction** (p. 122)
hebrew-epoch (p. 119)	**hebrew-from-fixed** (p. 123) **hebrew-new-year** (p. 122) **molad** (p. 119) **passover** (p. 129) **purim** (p. 129) **tishah-be-av** (p. 130) **yom-ha-zikkaron** (p. 131) **yom-kippur** (p. 128)
hebrew-from-fixed (p. 123)	**alt-observational-hebrew-from-fixed** (p. 299) **hebrew-birthday-in-gregorian** (p. 135) **hebrew-in-gregorian** (p. 133) **observational-hebrew-from-fixed** (p. 298) **yahrzeit-in-gregorian** (p. 137)
hebrew-in-gregorian (p. 133)	**hanukkah** (p. 134)
hebrew-leap-year? (p. 115)	**last-day-of-hebrew-month** (p. 122) **last-month-of-hebrew-year** (p. 115) **yahrzeit** (p. 136)
hebrew-location (p. 297)	**alt-fixed-from-observational-hebrew** (p. 300) **alt-observational-hebrew-from-fixed** (p. 299) **fixed-from-observational-hebrew** (p. 298)

continued

Function/constant	Used by
	observational-hebrew-first-of-nisan (p. 297) **observational-hebrew-from-fixed** (p. 298)
hebrew-new-year (p. 122)	**days-in-hebrew-year** (p. 123) **fixed-from-hebrew** (p. 123) **hebrew-from-fixed** (p. 123)
hebrew-year-length-correction (p. 122)	**hebrew-new-year** (p. 122)
hindu-anomalistic-month (p. 345)	**hindu-lunar-longitude** (p. 346)
hindu-anomalistic-year (p. 344)	**hindu-daily-motion** (p. 353) **hindu-equation-of-time** (p. 354) **hindu-solar-longitude** (p. 345)
hindu-arcsin (p. 343)	**hindu-ascensional-difference** (p. 352) **hindu-true-position** (p. 345)
hindu-ascensional-difference (p. 352)	**hindu-sunrise** (p. 354) **hindu-sunset** (p. 355)
hindu-calendar-year (p. 347)	**hindu-lunar-from-fixed** (p. 349) **hindu-solar-from-fixed** (p. 348)
hindu-creation (p. 344)	**hindu-mean-position** (p. 344)
hindu-daily-motion (p. 353)	**hindu-equation-of-time** (p. 353) **hindu-solar-sidereal-difference** (p. 352)
hindu-date-occur (p. 367)	**hindu-lunar-holiday** (p. 368) **hindu-tithi-occur** (p. 368)
hindu-day-count (p. 156)	**jovian-year** (p. 158) **old-hindu-lunar-from-fixed** (p. 165) **old-hindu-solar-from-fixed** (p. 159)
hindu-epoch (p. 156)	**astro-hindu-calendar-year** (p. 360) **fixed-from-astro-hindu-lunar** (p. 361) **fixed-from-astro-hindu-solar** (p. 360) **fixed-from-hindu-lunar** (p. 350) **fixed-from-hindu-solar** (p. 348) **fixed-from-old-hindu-lunar** (p. 165) **fixed-from-old-hindu-solar** (p. 158) **hindu-calendar-year** (p. 347) **hindu-creation** (p. 344) **hindu-day-count** (p. 156) **hindu-tropical-longitude** (p. 352)
hindu-equation-of-time (p. 353)	**hindu-sunrise** (p. 354) **hindu-sunset** (p. 355)
hindu-expunged? (p. 356)	**fixed-from-hindu-fullmoon** (p. 356)
hindu-location (p. 351)	**alt-hindu-sunrise** (p. 357)

continued

Function/constant	Used by
	astro-hindu-sunset (p. 360) **hindu-sunrise** (p. 354) **hindu-sunset** (p. 355) **sidereal-start** (p. 359)
hindu-lunar-day-at-or-after (p. 365)	**hindu-lunar-new-year** (p. 366) **hindu-tithi-occur** (p. 368)
hindu-lunar-day-from-moment (p. 346)	**fixed-from-hindu-lunar** (p. 350) **hindu-lunar-from-fixed** (p. 349) **hindu-lunar-new-year** (p. 365)
hindu-lunar-era (p. 349)	**astro-hindu-lunar-from-fixed** (p. 361) **fixed-from-astro-hindu-lunar** (p. 361) **fixed-from-hindu-lunar** (p. 350) **hindu-lunar-from-fixed** (p. 349)
hindu-lunar-event (p. 368)	**rama** (p. 369) **shiva** (p. 369)
hindu-lunar-from-fixed (p. 349)	**fixed-from-hindu-lunar** (p. 350) **hindu-date-occur** (p. 367) **hindu-expunged?** (p. 356) **hindu-fullmoon-from-fixed** (p. 356) **hindu-lunar-event** (p. 368) **hindu-lunar-holiday** (p. 368) **sacred-wednesdays-in-range** (p. 371)
hindu-lunar-holiday (p. 367)	**diwali** (p. 368)
hindu-lunar-longitude (p. 346)	**hindu-lunar-phase** (p. 346) **hindu-lunar-station** (p. 369) **yoga** (p. 369)
hindu-lunar-on-or-before? (p. 367)	**hindu-date-occur** (p. 367)
hindu-lunar-phase (p. 346)	**hindu-lunar-day-at-or-after** (p. 365) **hindu-lunar-day-from-moment** (p. 346) **hindu-new-moon-before** (p. 346) **hindu-tithi-occur** (p. 368)
hindu-mean-position (p. 344)	**hindu-daily-motion** (p. 353) **hindu-equation-of-time** (p. 354) **hindu-true-position** (p. 345)
hindu-new-moon-before (p. 346)	**hindu-lunar-from-fixed** (p. 349)
hindu-rising-sign (p. 353)	**hindu-solar-sidereal-difference** (p. 352)
hindu-sidereal-month (p. 336)	**hindu-lunar-longitude** (p. 346)
hindu-sidereal-year (p. 336)	**fixed-from-astro-hindu-lunar** (p. 362) **fixed-from-hindu-lunar** (p. 350) **fixed-from-hindu-solar** (p. 348)

continued

Function/constant	Used by
	hindu-calendar-year (p. 347)
	hindu-creation (p. 344)
	hindu-daily-motion (p. 353)
	hindu-equation-of-time (p. 353)
	hindu-solar-longitude (p. 345)
	hindu-solar-longitude-at-or-after (p. 364)
hindu-sine (p. 342)	**hindu-ascensional-difference** (p. 352)
	hindu-daily-motion (p. 353)
	hindu-equation-of-time (p. 354)
	hindu-true-position (p. 345)
hindu-sine-table (p. 342)	**hindu-arcsin** (p. 344)
	hindu-daily-motion (p. 353)
	hindu-sine (p. 342)
hindu-solar-era (p. 347)	**astro-hindu-solar-from-fixed** (p. 360)
	fixed-from-astro-hindu-solar (p. 360)
	fixed-from-hindu-solar (p. 348)
	hindu-solar-from-fixed (p. 348)
hindu-solar-longitude (p. 345)	**fixed-from-hindu-lunar** (p. 350)
	hindu-calendar-year (p. 347)
	hindu-lunar-phase (p. 346)
	hindu-solar-from-fixed (p. 348)
	hindu-solar-longitude-at-or-after (p. 364)
	hindu-tropical-longitude (p. 352)
	hindu-zodiac (p. 345)
	yoga (p. 369)
hindu-solar-longitude-at-or-after (p. 364)	**hindu-lunar-new-year** (p. 366)
	mesha-samkranti (p. 364)
hindu-solar-sidereal-difference (p. 352)	**hindu-sunrise** (p. 354)
	hindu-sunset (p. 355)
hindu-sunrise (p. 354)	**fixed-from-hindu-lunar** (p. 350)
	fixed-from-hindu-solar (p. 348)
	hindu-lunar-from-fixed (p. 349)
	hindu-lunar-new-year (p. 366)
	hindu-lunar-station (p. 369)
	hindu-solar-from-fixed (p. 348)
	hindu-standard-from-sundial (p. 355)
hindu-sunset (p. 354)	**hindu-standard-from-sundial** (p. 355)
hindu-synodic-month (p. 336)	**hindu-lunar-day-at-or-after** (p. 365)
	hindu-new-moon-before (p. 346)
hindu-tithi-occur (p. 368)	**hindu-lunar-event** (p. 368)
hindu-tropical-longitude (p. 352)	**hindu-ascensional-difference** (p. 352)

continued

Function/constant	Used by
	hindu-rising-sign (p. 353)
hindu-true-position (p. 345)	**hindu-lunar-longitude** (p. 346) **hindu-solar-longitude** (p. 345)
hindu-zodiac (p. 345)	**fixed-from-hindu-solar** (p. 348) **hindu-lunar-from-fixed** (p. 349) **hindu-new-moon-before** (p. 346) **hindu-solar-from-fixed** (p. 348)
icelandic-epoch (p. 100)	**icelandic-from-fixed** (p. 101) **icelandic-summer** (p. 100)
icelandic-summer (p. 100)	**fixed-from-icelandic** (p. 101) **icelandic-from-fixed** (p. 101) **icelandic-leap-year?** (p. 101) **icelandic-month** (p. 102) **icelandic-winter** (p. 100)
icelandic-winter (p. 100)	**fixed-from-icelandic** (p. 101) **icelandic-from-fixed** (p. 101) **icelandic-month** (p. 102)
ides (p. 77)	**fixed-from-roman** (p. 80) **roman-from-fixed** (p. 80)
ides-of-month (p. 77)	**fixed-from-roman** (p. 80) **nones-of-month** (p. 78) **roman-from-fixed** (p. 80)
islamic-epoch (p. 106)	**alt-fixed-from-observational-islamic** (p. 295) **alt-observational-islamic-from-fixed** (p. 295) **fixed-from-islamic** (p. 107) **fixed-from-observational-islamic** (p. 293) **fixed-from-saudi-islamic** (p. 296) **islamic-from-fixed** (p. 108) **observational-islamic-from-fixed** (p. 294) **saudi-islamic-from-fixed** (p. 297)
islamic-from-fixed (p. 108)	**islamic-in-gregorian** (p. 109)
islamic-in-gregorian (p. 108)	**mawlid** (p. 109)
islamic-location (p. 293)	**alt-fixed-from-observational-islamic** (p. 295) **alt-observational-islamic-from-fixed** (p. 295) **fixed-from-observational-islamic** (p. 293) **observational-islamic-from-fixed** (p. 294)
iyyar (p. 114)	**last-day-of-hebrew-month** (p. 122) **yom-ha-zikkaron** (p. 131)
january (p. 59)	**ephemeris-correction** (p. 210) **epiphany** (p. 71)

continued

Function/constant	Used by
	gregorian-new-year (p. 60) **julian-from-fixed** (p. 76) **korean-location** (p. 328)
jd-epoch (p. 18)	**jd-from-moment** (p. 18) **moment-from-jd** (p. 18)
jd-from-moment (p. 18)	**jd-from-fixed** (p. 20)
jerusalem (p. 204)	**astronomical-easter** (p. 292)
julian-centuries (p. 212)	**aberration** (p. 223) **equation-of-time** (p. 215) **lunar-distance** (p. 238) **lunar-latitude** (p. 236) **lunar-longitude** (p. 232) **lunar-node** (p. 234) **nutation** (p. 223) **obliquity** (p. 220) **precession** (p. 225) **solar-longitude** (p. 223)
julian-epoch (p. 76)	**fixed-from-julian** (p. 76) **julian-from-fixed** (p. 76)
julian-from-fixed (p. 76)	**julian-in-gregorian** (p. 85) **roman-from-fixed** (p. 80)
julian-in-gregorian (p. 85)	**eastern-orthodox-christmas** (p. 85) **samaritan-new-year-on-or-before** (p. 301)
julian-leap-year? (p. 75)	**fixed-from-julian** (p. 76) **fixed-from-roman** (p. 80) **julian-from-fixed** (p. 77) **roman-from-fixed** (p. 80)
july (p. 59)	**chinese-new-year** (p. 322) **ephemeris-correction** (p. 210) **ides-of-month** (p. 77) **independence-day** (p. 69) **islamic-epoch** (p. 106)
kalends (p. 77)	**fixed-from-roman** (p. 80) **roman-from-fixed** (p. 81)
kday-after (p. 34)	**alt-orthodox-easter** (p. 147) **astronomical-easter** (p. 292) **easter** (p. 148) **nth-kday** (p. 69) **orthodox-easter** (p. 146)
kday-before (p. 34)	**nth-kday** (p. 69) **yom-ha-zikkaron** (p. 131)

continued

Function/constant	Used by
kday-nearest (p. 34)	**advent** (p. 70)
kday-on-or-after (p. 34)	**icelandic-summer** (p. 100) **sacred-wednesdays-in-range** (p. 371) **unlucky-fridays-in-range** (p. 71)
kday-on-or-before (p. 34)	**kday-after** (p. 34) **kday-before** (p. 34) **kday-nearest** (p. 34) **kday-on-or-after** (p. 34)
kislev (p. 115)	**hanukkah** (p. 134) **last-day-of-hebrew-month** (p. 122) **possible-hebrew-days** (p. 139) **yahrzeit** (p. 136)
last-day-of-hebrew-month (p. 122)	**fixed-from-hebrew** (p. 123) **hebrew-from-fixed** (p. 123)
last-kday (p. 69)	**memorial-day** (p. 70)
last-month-of-hebrew-year (p. 115)	**fixed-from-hebrew** (p. 123) **hebrew-birthday** (p. 135) **purim** (p. 129) **yahrzeit** (p. 136)
local-from-apparent (p. 218)	**approx-moment-of-depression** (p. 240) **universal-from-apparent** (p. 218)
local-from-standard (p. 208)	**local-zero-hour** (p. 246)
local-from-universal (p. 208)	**apparent-from-universal** (p. 218) **local-from-standard** (p. 208)
local-zero-hour (p. 246)	**italian-from-local** (p. 247) **local-from-italian** (p. 247)
long-marheshvan? (p. 122)	**last-day-of-hebrew-month** (p. 122) **yahrzeit** (p. 136)
losar (p. 381)	**tibetan-new-year** (p. 381)
lunar-altitude (p. 237)	**arc-of-vision** (p. 251) **lunar-parallax** (p. 238) **lunar-semi-diameter** (p. 252) **shaukat-criterion** (p. 250) **topocentric-lunar-altitude** (p. 239)
lunar-anomaly (p. 234)	**lunar-distance** (p. 238) **lunar-latitude** (p. 236) **lunar-longitude** (p. 232)
lunar-distance (p. 238)	**lunar-diameter** (p. 252) **lunar-parallax** (p. 238)

continued

Function/constant	Used by
lunar-elongation (p. 234)	**lunar-distance** (p. 238) **lunar-latitude** (p. 236) **lunar-longitude** (p. 232)
lunar-latitude (p. 236)	**arc-of-light** (p. 250) **lunar-altitude** (p. 238)
lunar-longitude (p. 232)	**lunar-altitude** (p. 238) **lunar-phase** (p. 235) **sidereal-lunar-longitude** (p. 234)
lunar-parallax (p. 238)	**lunar-semi-diameter** (p. 252) **topocentric-lunar-altitude** (p. 239)
lunar-phase (p. 235)	**arc-of-light** (p. 250) **astro-lunar-day-from-moment** (p. 361) **babylonian-criterion** (p. 290) **lunar-phase-at-or-after** (p. 235) **lunar-phase-at-or-before** (p. 235) **moonrise** (p. 244) **moonset** (p. 245) **new-moon-at-or-after** (p. 232) **new-moon-before** (p. 231) **saudi-criterion** (p. 296) **shaukat-criterion** (p. 250) **yallop-criterion** (p. 251)
lunar-phase-at-or-after (p. 235)	**astronomical-easter** (p. 292)
lunar-phase-at-or-before (p. 235)	**babylonian-new-month-on-or-before** (p. 290) **phasis-on-or-after** (p. 252) **phasis-on-or-before** (p. 252) **saudi-new-month-on-or-before** (p. 296)
lunar-semi-diameter (p. 251)	**yallop-criterion** (p. 251)
march (p. 59)	**alt-gregorian-from-fixed** (p. 66) **bahai-epoch** (p. 271) **bahai-from-fixed** (p. 272) **bahai-new-year** (p. 277) **daylight-saving-start** (p. 70) **fixed-from-bahai** (p. 271) **fixed-from-roman** (p. 80) **gregorian-from-fixed** (p. 62) **ides-of-month** (p. 77) **julian-from-fixed** (p. 77) **julian-season-in-gregorian** (p. 84) **korean-location** (p. 328) **persian-epoch** (p. 258) **qing-ming** (p. 324)

continued

Function/constant	Used by
	roman-from-fixed (p. 80) **samaritan-epoch** (p. 301) **samaritan-new-year-on-or-before** (p. 301)
marheshvan (p. 115)	**last-day-of-hebrew-month** (p. 122) **possible-hebrew-days** (p. 139) **yahrzeit** (p. 136)
may (p. 59)	**ides-of-month** (p. 77) **memorial-day** (p. 70)
mayan-epoch (p. 171)	**fixed-from-mayan-long-count** (p. 171) **mayan-haab-epoch** (p. 173) **mayan-long-count-from-fixed** (p. 171) **mayan-tzolkin-epoch** (p. 175)
mayan-haab-epoch (p. 173)	**mayan-calendar-round-on-or-before** (p. 177) **mayan-haab-from-fixed** (p. 173) **mayan-haab-on-or-before** (p. 173)
mayan-haab-from-fixed (p. 173)	**mayan-year-bearer-from-fixed** (p. 176)
mayan-haab-on-or-before (p. 173)	**mayan-year-bearer-from-fixed** (p. 176)
mayan-haab-ordinal (p. 173)	**mayan-calendar-round-on-or-before** (p. 177) **mayan-haab-epoch** (p. 173) **mayan-haab-on-or-before** (p. 173)
mayan-tzolkin-epoch (p. 175)	**mayan-calendar-round-on-or-before** (p. 177) **mayan-tzolkin-from-fixed** (p. 175) **mayan-tzolkin-on-or-before** (p. 176)
mayan-tzolkin-from-fixed (p. 175)	**mayan-year-bearer-from-fixed** (p. 176)
mayan-tzolkin-ordinal (p. 175)	**mayan-calendar-round-on-or-before** (p. 177) **mayan-tzolkin-epoch** (p. 175) **mayan-tzolkin-on-or-before** (p. 176)
mean-lunar-longitude (p. 233)	**lunar-latitude** (p. 236) **lunar-longitude** (p. 232)
mean-sidereal-year (p. 221)	**astro-hindu-calendar-year** (p. 360) **fixed-from-astro-hindu-lunar** (p. 361) **fixed-from-astro-hindu-solar** (p. 360)
mean-synodic-month (p. 227)	**alt-fixed-from-observational-islamic** (p. 295) **alt-observational-islamic-from-fixed** (p. 295) **babylonian-from-fixed** (p. 292) **chinese-from-fixed** (p. 317) **chinese-new-year-in-sui** (p. 316) **fixed-from-babylonian** (p. 291) **fixed-from-observational-islamic** (p. 293) **fixed-from-saudi-islamic** (p. 296)

continued

Function/constant	Used by
	lunar-phase (p. 235) **lunar-phase-at-or-after** (p. 235) **lunar-phase-at-or-before** (p. 235) **new-moon-at-or-after** (p. 232) **new-moon-before** (p. 231) **nth-new-moon** (p. 229) **observational-islamic-from-fixed** (p. 294) **saudi-islamic-from-fixed** (p. 297)
mean-tropical-year (p. 221)	**astro-bahai-from-fixed** (p. 275) **chinese-from-fixed** (p. 317) **estimate-prior-solar-longitude** (p. 226) **fixed-from-astro-bahai** (p. 275) **fixed-from-chinese** (p. 318) **fixed-from-french** (p. 284) **fixed-from-persian** (p. 260) **french-from-fixed** (p. 284) **persian-from-fixed** (p. 260) **solar-longitude-after** (p. 224)
mecca (p. 204)	**saudi-criterion** (p. 296)
mesha-samkranti (p. 364)	**sidereal-start** (p. 359)
midday (p. 218)	**alt-asr** (p. 249) **asr** (p. 249) **midday-in-tehran** (p. 259) **samaritan-noon** (p. 300)
midday-in-tehran (p. 259)	**persian-new-year-on-or-before** (p. 259)
midnight (p. 218)	**midnight-in-paris** (p. 283)
midnight-in-china (p. 309)	**chinese-new-moon-before** (p. 310) **chinese-new-moon-on-or-after** (p. 309) **chinese-winter-solstice-on-or-before** (p. 309) **major-solar-term-on-or-after** (p. 308) **minor-solar-term-on-or-after** (p. 309)
midnight-in-paris (p. 283)	**french-new-year-on-or-before** (p. 283)
minor-solar-term-on-or-after (p. 308)	**qing-ming** (p. 324)
mjd-epoch (p. 19)	**fixed-from-mjd** (p. 19) **mjd-from-fixed** (p. 19)
molad (p. 119)	**fixed-from-molad** (p. 126)
moment-from-jd (p. 18)	**fixed-from-jd** (p. 20)
moment-of-depression (p. 241)	**dawn** (p. 241) **dusk** (p. 242)
monday (p. 33)	**labor-day** (p. 69)

continued

Function/constant	Used by
	memorial-day (p. 70) **possible-hebrew-days** (p. 139)
month-length (p. 294)	**alt-observational-hebrew-from-fixed** (p. 299) **alt-observational-islamic-from-fixed** (p. 295) **early-month?** (p. 295)
moon-node (p. 234)	**lunar-distance** (p. 238) **lunar-latitude** (p. 236) **lunar-longitude** (p. 232) **lunar-node** (p. 234)
moonlag (p. 290)	**babylonian-criterion** (p. 290) **saudi-criterion** (p. 296)
moonset (p. 245)	**bruin-best-view** (p. 251) **moonlag** (p. 290)
morning (p. 241)	**dawn** (p. 241)
naw-ruz (p. 277)	**birth-of-the-bab** (p. 278) **feast-of-ridvan** (p. 277)
new (p. 236)	**babylonian-criterion** (p. 290) **babylonian-new-month-on-or-before** (p. 290) **phasis-on-or-after** (p. 252) **phasis-on-or-before** (p. 252) **saudi-criterion** (p. 296) **saudi-new-month-on-or-before** (p. 296) **shaukat-criterion** (p. 250) **yallop-criterion** (p. 251)
new-moon-at-or-after (p. 231)	**astro-hindu-lunar-from-fixed** (p. 361) **birth-of-the-bab** (p. 278) **chinese-new-moon-on-or-after** (p. 309) **samaritan-new-moon-after** (p. 300)
new-moon-before (p. 230)	**astro-hindu-lunar-from-fixed** (p. 361) **babylonian-criterion** (p. 290) **chinese-new-moon-before** (p. 310) **samaritan-new-moon-at-or-before** (p. 300)
nighttime-temporal-hour (p. 248)	**standard-from-sundial** (p. 248)
nisan (p. 114)	**alt-fixed-from-observational-hebrew** (p. 300) **fixed-from-hebrew** (p. 123) **fixed-from-observational-hebrew** (p. 298) **hebrew-from-fixed** (p. 123) **passover** (p. 129) **possible-hebrew-days** (p. 139)
nones (p. 77)	**fixed-from-roman** (p. 80) **roman-from-fixed** (p. 80)

continued

Function/constant	Used by
nones-of-month (p. 78)	**fixed-from-roman** (p. 80)
	roman-from-fixed (p. 80)
november (p. 59)	**advent** (p. 70)
	daylight-saving-end (p. 70)
	election-day (p. 70)
nth-kday (p. 69)	**daylight-saving-start** (p. 70)
	first-kday (p. 69)
	fixed-from-iso (p. 96)
	last-kday (p. 69)
nth-new-moon (p. 229)	**lunar-phase** (p. 235)
	new-moon-at-or-after (p. 232)
	new-moon-before (p. 231)
nutation (p. 223)	**lunar-longitude** (p. 232)
	solar-longitude (p. 223)
obliquity (p. 220)	**declination** (p. 220)
	equation-of-time (p. 216)
	right-ascension (p. 220)
observational-hebrew-first-of-nisan (p. 297)	**alt-fixed-from-observational-hebrew** (p. 300)
	alt-observational-hebrew-from-fixed (p. 299)
	classical-passover-eve (p. 298)
	fixed-from-observational-hebrew (p. 298)
	observational-hebrew-from-fixed (p. 298)
observed-lunar-altitude (p. 243)	**moonrise** (p. 244)
	moonset (p. 245)
october (p. 59)	**hebrew-epoch** (p. 119)
	ides-of-month (p. 77)
olympiad-start (p. 82)	**julian-year-from-olympiad** (p. 82)
	olympiad-from-julian-year (p. 82)
padua (p. 246)	**local-zero-hour** (p. 246)
paris (p. 283)	**midnight-in-paris** (p. 283)
passover (p. 129)	**omer** (p. 129)
persian-epoch (p. 258)	**fixed-from-arithmetic-persian** (p. 262)
	fixed-from-persian (p. 260)
	nowruz (p. 265)
	persian-from-fixed (p. 260)
persian-new-year-on-or-before (p. 259)	**fixed-from-persian** (p. 260)
	persian-from-fixed (p. 260)
phasis-on-or-after (p. 252)	**month-length** (p. 294)
	observational-hebrew-first-of-nisan (p. 297)

continued

Function/constant	Used by
phasis-on-or-before (p. 252)	**alt-fixed-from-observational-hebrew** (p. 300) **alt-fixed-from-observational-islamic** (p. 295) **alt-observational-hebrew-from-fixed** (p. 299) **alt-observational-islamic-from-fixed** (p. 295) **early-month?** (p. 295) **fixed-from-observational-hebrew** (p. 298) **fixed-from-observational-islamic** (p. 293) **month-length** (p. 294) **observational-hebrew-from-fixed** (p. 298) **observational-islamic-from-fixed** (p. 294)
positions-in-range (p. 27)	**cycle-in-gregorian** (p. 83) **kajeng-keliwon** (p. 190) **tumpek** (p. 190)
precession (p. 225)	**sidereal-lunar-longitude** (p. 234) **sidereal-solar-longitude** (p. 225) **sidereal-start** (p. 359)
purim (p. 129)	**ta-anit-esther** (p. 130)
refraction (p. 242)	**observed-lunar-altitude** (p. 243) **sunrise** (p. 242) **sunset** (p. 243)
right-ascension (p. 220)	**lunar-altitude** (p. 238) **solar-altitude** (p. 226)
sacred-wednesdays-in-range (p. 371)	**sacred-wednesdays** (p. 370)
samaritan-epoch (p. 301)	**fixed-from-samaritan** (p. 301) **samaritan-from-fixed** (p. 302)
samaritan-location (p. 300)	**samaritan-new-moon-after** (p. 300) **samaritan-new-moon-at-or-before** (p. 300) **samaritan-noon** (p. 300)
samaritan-new-moon-after (p. 300)	**samaritan-new-year-on-or-before** (p. 301)
samaritan-new-moon-at-or-before (p. 300)	**fixed-from-samaritan** (p. 301) **samaritan-from-fixed** (p. 302)
samaritan-new-year-on-or-before (p. 301)	**fixed-from-samaritan** (p. 301) **samaritan-from-fixed** (p. 302)
samaritan-noon (p. 300)	**samaritan-from-fixed** (p. 302) **samaritan-new-year-on-or-before** (p. 301)
samuel-season-in-gregorian (p. 132)	**alt-birkath-ha-hama** (p. 132)
saturday (p. 33)	**fixed-from-icelandic** (p. 101) **possible-hebrew-days** (p. 139) **tishah-be-av** (p. 130)

continued

Function/constant	Used by
saudi-criterion (p. 296)	**saudi-new-month-on-or-before** (p. 296)
saudi-new-month-on-or-before (p. 296)	**fixed-from-saudi-islamic** (p. 296) **saudi-islamic-from-fixed** (p. 297)
season-in-gregorian (p. 224)	**astronomical-easter** (p. 292) **observational-hebrew-first-of-nisan** (p. 297)
september (p. 59)	**french-epoch** (p. 283) **labor-day** (p. 69)
shaukat-criterion (p. 250)	**visible-crescent** (p. 252)
shevat (p. 115)	**possible-hebrew-days** (p. 139) **yahrzeit** (p. 136)
shift-days (p. 138)	**possible-hebrew-days** (p. 139)
short-kislev? (p. 122)	**last-day-of-hebrew-month** (p. 122) **yahrzeit** (p. 136)
sidereal-from-moment (p. 219)	**lunar-altitude** (p. 238) **solar-altitude** (p. 226)
sidereal-solar-longitude (p. 225)	**astro-hindu-calendar-year** (p. 360) **astro-hindu-solar-from-fixed** (p. 360) **ayanamsha** (p. 359) **fixed-from-astro-hindu-lunar** (p. 362) **sidereal-zodiac** (p. 360)
sidereal-start (p. 359)	**sidereal-lunar-longitude** (p. 234) **sidereal-solar-longitude** (p. 225)
sidereal-zodiac (p. 360)	**astro-hindu-lunar-from-fixed** (p. 361) **astro-hindu-solar-from-fixed** (p. 360) **fixed-from-astro-hindu-solar** (p. 360)
simple-best-view (p. 250)	**shaukat-criterion** (p. 250)
sine-offset (p. 241)	**approx-moment-of-depression** (p. 240)
solar-altitude (p. 226)	**arc-of-vision** (p. 251)
solar-anomaly (p. 234)	**lunar-distance** (p. 238) **lunar-latitude** (p. 236) **lunar-longitude** (p. 232)
solar-longitude (p. 223)	**alt-asr** (p. 249) **asr** (p. 249) **astro-bahai-new-year-on-or-before** (p. 274) **ayanamsha** (p. 359) **chinese-winter-solstice-on-or-before** (p. 309) **current-major-solar-term** (p. 306) **current-minor-solar-term** (p. 308)

continued

Function/constant	Used by
	estimate-prior-solar-longitude (p. 226)
	french-new-year-on-or-before (p. 283)
	lunar-phase (p. 235)
	major-solar-term-on-or-after (p. 308)
	minor-solar-term-on-or-after (p. 309)
	persian-new-year-on-or-before (p. 259)
	sidereal-solar-longitude (p. 225)
	sine-offset (p. 241)
	solar-altitude (p. 226)
	solar-longitude-after (p. 224)
solar-longitude-after (p. 224)	**chinese-solar-longitude-on-or-after** (p. 308)
	season-in-gregorian (p. 224)
spring (p. 83)	**alt-birkath-ha-hama** (p. 132)
	astro-bahai-new-year-on-or-before (p. 274)
	astronomical-easter (p. 292)
	observational-hebrew-first-of-nisan (p. 297)
	persian-new-year-on-or-before (p. 259)
standard-from-local (p. 208)	**dawn** (p. 241)
	dusk (p. 242)
standard-from-sundial (p. 248)	**hindu-tithi-occur** (p. 368)
	jewish-morning-end (p. 248)
standard-from-universal (p. 208)	**chinese-new-moon-before** (p. 310)
	chinese-new-moon-on-or-after (p. 309)
	chinese-solar-longitude-on-or-after (p. 308)
	moonrise (p. 244)
	moonset (p. 245)
	standard-from-local (p. 208)
summer (p. 83)	**fixed-from-icelandic** (p. 101)
	icelandic-from-fixed (p. 101)
sunday (p. 33)	**advent** (p. 70)
	alt-orthodox-easter (p. 147)
	astronomical-easter (p. 292)
	day-of-week-from-fixed (p. 33)
	daylight-saving-end (p. 70)
	daylight-saving-start (p. 70)
	easter (p. 148)
	epiphany (p. 71)
	fixed-from-iso (p. 96)
	orthodox-easter (p. 146)
	possible-hebrew-days (p. 139)
	ta-anit-esther (p. 130)
	yom-ha-zikkaron (p. 131)
sunrise (p. 242)	**daytime-temporal-hour** (p. 247)

continued

Function/constant	Used by
	nighttime-temporal-hour (p. 248) **standard-from-sundial** (p. 248)
sunset (p. 242)	**babylonian-criterion** (p. 290) **bahai-sunset** (p. 274) **bruin-best-view** (p. 251) **daytime-temporal-hour** (p. 247) **moonlag** (p. 290) **nighttime-temporal-hour** (p. 248) **observational-hebrew-first-of-nisan** (p. 297) **saudi-criterion** (p. 296) **standard-from-sundial** (p. 248)
tammuz (p. 114)	**last-day-of-hebrew-month** (p. 122)
tehran (p. 259)	**midday-in-tehran** (p. 259)
tevet (p. 115)	**last-day-of-hebrew-month** (p. 122) **possible-hebrew-days** (p. 139) **yahrzeit** (p. 136)
thursday (p. 33)	**fixed-from-icelandic** (p. 101) **icelandic-summer** (p. 100) **iso-long-year?** (p. 97) **possible-hebrew-days** (p. 139) **yom-ha-zikkaron** (p. 131)
tibetan-epoch (p. 376)	**fixed-from-tibetan** (p. 378) **tibetan-from-fixed** (p. 378)
tibetan-from-fixed (p. 378)	**tibetan-leap-day?** (p. 381) **tibetan-leap-month?** (p. 380) **tibetan-new-year** (p. 381)
tibetan-leap-month? (p. 380)	**losar** (p. 381) **tibetan-leap-day?** (p. 381)
tibetan-moon-equation (p. 377)	**fixed-from-tibetan** (p. 378)
tibetan-sun-equation (p. 377)	**fixed-from-tibetan** (p. 378)
time-from-moment (p. 21)	**alt-birkath-ha-hama** (p. 132) **hindu-standard-from-sundial** (p. 355) **standard-from-sundial** (p. 248)
tishri (p. 115)	**alt-fixed-from-observational-hebrew** (p. 299) **alt-observational-hebrew-from-fixed** (p. 299) **fixed-from-hebrew** (p. 123) **fixed-from-molad** (p. 126) **fixed-from-observational-hebrew** (p. 298) **hebrew-from-fixed** (p. 123) **molad** (p. 120) **observational-hebrew-from-fixed** (p. 298)

continued

Function/constant	Used by
	yom-kippur (p. 128)
topocentric-lunar-altitude (p. 239)	**observed-lunar-altitude** (p. 243)
tuesday (p. 33)	**election-day** (p. 70) **possible-hebrew-days** (p. 139)
ujjain (p. 351)	**hindu-location** (p. 351) **hindu-sunrise** (p. 354) **hindu-sunset** (p. 355) **hindu-tithi-occur** (p. 368)
universal-from-apparent (p. 218)	**midday** (p. 218) **midnight** (p. 218)
universal-from-dynamical (p. 212)	**nth-new-moon** (p. 229)
universal-from-local (p. 208)	**apparent-from-local** (p. 217) **local-from-apparent** (p. 218) **sidereal-start** (p. 359) **sine-offset** (p. 241) **standard-from-local** (p. 208) **universal-from-apparent** (p. 218)
universal-from-standard (p. 208)	**babylonian-criterion** (p. 290) **bahai-sunset** (p. 274) **bruin-best-view** (p. 251) **chinese-solar-longitude-on-or-after** (p. 308) **current-major-solar-term** (p. 306) **current-minor-solar-term** (p. 308) **local-from-standard** (p. 208) **midnight-in-china** (p. 309) **moonrise** (p. 244) **moonset** (p. 245) **observational-hebrew-first-of-nisan** (p. 297) **saudi-criterion** (p. 296) **simple-best-view** (p. 250)
unix-epoch (p. 19)	**moment-from-unix** (p. 19) **unix-from-moment** (p. 19)
unlucky-fridays-in-range (p. 71)	**unlucky-fridays** (p. 71)
visible-crescent (p. 252)	**phasis-on-or-after** (p. 253) **phasis-on-or-before** (p. 252)
wednesday (p. 33)	**alt-birkath-ha-hama** (p. 132) **possible-hebrew-days** (p. 139) **sacred-wednesdays-in-range** (p. 371) **yom-ha-zikkaron** (p. 131)
widow (p. 325)	**chinese-year-marriage-augury** (p. 325)

continued

Function/constant	Used by
winter (p. 83)	**chinese-winter-solstice-on-or-before** (p. 309) **icelandic-from-fixed** (p. 101) **icelandic-month** (p. 102)
yahrzeit (p. 136)	**yahrzeit-in-gregorian** (p. 137)
year-rome-founded (p. 81)	**auc-year-from-julian** (p. 81) **julian-year-from-auc** (p. 81)
zone-from-longitude (p. 208)	**local-from-universal** (p. 208) **universal-from-local** (p. 208)

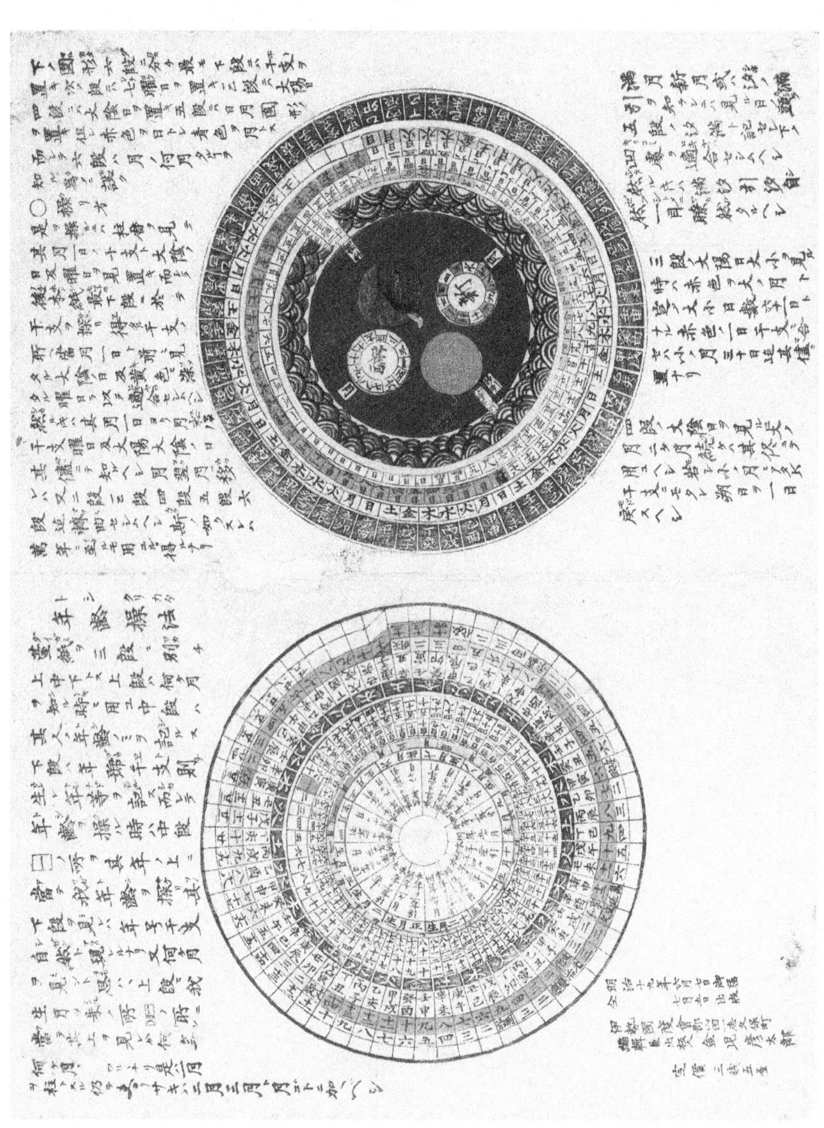

Hand-printed volvelles (chart dials) for the Japanese calendar by Hikotaro Kaneko, Ise, Japan, 1886. The wheels on the left calculate one's age; those on the right show lunar and solar months, tides, and so on. (Collection of E.M.R.)

Appendix C

Sample Data

I admit that it is not farfetched that I might err, that some analysis or source elude me—this is not a big matter. I am elated that I am being scrutinized so carefully; whosoever does so merits reward and gratitude. For either he is correct in his critique and I benefit thereby, or, if he is in error, he will derive benefit.

Maimonides: Letter to Joseph ben Judah Ibn Simeon, to whom *The Guide to the Perplexed* was addressed (1191)

To aid the reader interested in implementing our functions, we give two sets of tables in this appendix. First, we give tables of 33 dates from the years −1000 to 2100 with their equivalents on all the calendars discussed in the book. For each date we also give the dates of Easter that same year (Orthodox, Gregorian, and astronomical); the ephemeris correction, equation of time, and solar longitude at 12:00:00 U.T.; the moment of the next solstice or equinox (U.T.); the standard times of astronomical dawn in Paris, astronomical midday in Tehran, and astronomical sunset for Jerusalem; the lunar longitude, latitude, and altitude at 00:00:00 U.T.; the moment of the next new moon (U.T.), and the standard times of moonrise and moonset in Mecca. At the bottom of each column in the tables is the equation number and corresponding page of the function used to compute that column. Changes in the hardware and software since the preparation of the third edition have caused minor changes in some sample values compared with that edition; the revision of what we called the "future Bahá'í calendar" (now the astronomical calendar) has caused significant changes to some of those sample values. The second set of tables gives the Gregorian dates in 2000–2103 of many holidays and other calendrical events as calculated by the functions in this book.

All dates and values given in this appendix are as computed by our functions and hence may not represent historical reality; furthermore, some dates are not meaningful for all calendars. Though times are reported down to the second, the astronomical algorithms that we use do not promise such accuracy.

As pointed out in Section 1.16, the precise values of floating-point calculations may differ depending on the programming language, implementation, and platform. For example, with 64-bit (double precision) calculations, the solar longitude at midnight for the first date, R.D. −214193, computed with the expression

solar-longitude(−214193)

differs slightly from one implementation and computer to another:

- Allegro Common Lisp on a Sun Blade gives 118.98911336371384°;
- LispWorks on a MacBook Air with Intel Core i5 and GNU Common Lisp on an Intel Xeon E5410 and on an Intel Core i3-530 give 118.98911336367019°;
- CLisp on an HP Compaq PC gives 118.98911336376116°; and
- GNU Common Lisp on an Intel Xeon E5-2680 v2 gives 118.9891133637611631°.

Such small differences, in this case about $1^\circ \times 10^{-10}$ of arc or 8×10^{-6} seconds of time, are highly unlikely to affect the computations of dates. However, single precision yields a noticeably different value, 119.00391°.

All the values in this appendix were computed in double precision on an Intel® Xeon® E5-2680 v2 at 2.80 GHz and required about 208 seconds to produce.

But go thou thy way till the end be; and thou shalt rest, and shalt stand up to thy lot, at the end of the days.

Daniel 12:13

R.D.	Weekday	Julian day	Modified Julian day	Unix	Gregorian	Julian[1] Date	Julian[1] Roman name	Julian[1] Olympiad	Egyptian	Armenian
−214193	Sunday	1507231.5	−892769	−80641958400	−586 7 24	−587 7 30	−587 8 1 3 f	48 2	161 7 15	−1138 4 10
−61387	Wednesday	1660037.5	−739963	−67439520000	−168 12 5	−169 12 8	−169 12 3 6 f	152 4	580 3 6	−720 12 6
25469	Wednesday	1746893.5	−653107	−59935161600	70 9 24	70 9 26	70 10 1 6 f	212 2	818 2 22	−482 11 22
49217	Sunday	1770641.5	−629359	−57883334400	135 10 2	135 10 3	135 10 2 5 f	228 3	883 3 15	−417 12 15
171307	Wednesday	1892731.5	−507269	−47334758400	470 1 8	470 1 7	470 1 3 7 f	312 2	1217 9 15	−82 6 10
210155	Monday	1931579.5	−468421	−43978291200	576 5 20	576 5 18	576 6 1 15 f	338 4	1324 2 18	24 11 18
253427	Saturday	1974851.5	−425149	−40239590400	694 11 10	694 11 7	694 11 3 7 f	368 2	1442 9 10	143 6 5
369740	Sunday	2091164.5	−308836	−30190147200	1013 4 25	1013 4 19	1013 5 1 13 f	448 1	1761 5 8	462 2 3
400085	Sunday	2121509.5	−278491	−27568339200	1096 5 24	1096 5 18	1096 6 1 15 f	468 4	1844 6 28	545 3 23
434355	Friday	2155779.5	−244221	−24607411200	1190 3 23	1190 3 16	1190 4 1 17 f	492 2	1938 5 18	639 2 13
452605	Saturday	2174029.5	−225971	−23030611200	1240 3 10	1240 3 3	1240 3 2 5 f	504 4	1988 5 18	689 2 13
470160	Friday	2191584.5	−208416	−21513859200	1288 4 2	1288 3 26	1288 4 1 7 f	516 4	2036 6 23	737 3 18
473837	Sunday	2195261.5	−204739	−21196166400	1298 4 27	1298 4 20	1298 5 1 12 f	519 2	2046 7 20	747 4 15
507850	Sunday	2229274.5	−170726	−18257443200	1391 6 12	1391 6 4	1391 6 2 2 f	542 3	2139 9 28	840 6 23
524156	Wednesday	2245580.5	−154420	−16848604800	1436 2 3	1436 1 25	1436 2 1 8 f	553 4	2184 5 29	885 2 24
544676	Saturday	2266100.5	−133900	−15075676800	1492 4 9	1492 3 31	1492 4 1 2 f	567 4	2240 8 19	941 5 14
567118	Saturday	2288542.5	−111458	−13136688000	1553 9 19	1553 9 9	1553 9 3 5 f	583 1	2302 2 11	1002 11 11
569477	Saturday	2290901.5	−109099	−12932870400	1560 3 5	1560 2 24	1560 3 1 6 f	584 4	2308 7 30	1009 4 25
601716	Wednesday	2323140.5	−76860	−10147420800	1648 6 10	1648 5 31	1648 6 1 2 f	606 4	2396 11 29	1097 8 24
613424	Sunday	2334848.5	−65152	−9135849600	1680 6 30	1680 6 20	1680 7 1 12 f	614 4	2428 12 27	1129 9 22
626596	Friday	2348020.5	−51980	−7997788800	1716 7 24	1716 7 13	1716 7 3 3 f	623 4	2465 1 24	1165 10 24
645554	Sunday	2366978.5	−33022	−6359817600	1768 6 19	1768 6 8	1768 6 3 6 f	636 4	2517 1 2	1217 10 2
664224	Monday	2385648.5	−14352	−4746729600	1819 8 2	1819 7 21	1819 8 1 12 f	649 3	2568 2 27	1268 11 27
671401	Wednesday	2392825.5	−7175	−4126636800	1839 3 27	1839 3 15	1839 3 3 1 f	654 3	2587 10 29	1288 7 24
694799	Sunday	2416223.5	16223	−2105049600	1903 4 19	1903 4 6	1903 4 3 8 f	670 3	2651 12 7	1352 9 2
704424	Sunday	2425848.5	25848	−1273449600	1929 8 25	1929 8 12	1929 8 3 2 f	677 1	2678 4 17	1379 1 12
708842	Monday	2430266.5	30266	−891734400	1941 9 29	1941 9 16	1941 10 1 16 f	680 1	2690 5 25	1391 2 20
709409	Monday	2430833.5	30833	−842745600	1943 4 19	1943 4 6	1943 4 3 8 f	680 3	2691 12 17	1392 9 12
709580	Thursday	2431004.5	31004	−827971200	1943 10 7	1943 9 24	1943 10 1 8 f	680 3	2692 6 3	1393 2 28
727274	Tuesday	2448698.5	48698	700790400	1992 3 17	1992 3 4	1992 3 2 4 f	692 4	2740 11 27	1441 8 22
728714	Sunday	2450138.5	50138	825206400	1996 2 25	1996 2 12	1996 2 3 2 f	693 4	2744 11 7	1445 8 2
744313	Wednesday	2465737.5	65737	2172960000	2038 11 10	2038 10 28	2038 11 1 5 f	704 2	2787 8 1	1488 4 26
764652	Sunday	2486076.5	86076	3930249600	2094 7 18	2094 7 5	2094 7 2 3 f	718 2	2843 4 20	1544 1 15
Function	(1.60)	(1.5)	(1.8)	(1.11)	(2.23)	(3.4)	(3.11)	(3.17)	(1.49)	(1.52)
Page	33	18	19	19	62	76	80	82	31	31

[1] The negative years in the first two lines of the columns for the Julian date and the Roman name are B.C.E. years, 587 B.C.E. and 169 B.C.E., respectively. They appear as negative numbers because the table consists of raw output from the Lisp functions.

						Islamic			Hebrew	
R.D.	Akan	Coptic	Ethiopic	ISO	Icelandic	Arithmetic	Observational	Umm al-Qura	Standard	Observational
−214193	6 5	−870 12 6	−594 12 6	−586 29 7	−586 90 14 0	−1245 12 9	−1245 12 11	−1245 12 11	3174 5 10	3174 5 11
−61387	4 1	−451 4 12	−175 4 12	−168 49 3	−168 270 6 3	−813 2 23	−813 2 25	−813 2 26	3593 9 25	3593 9 24
25469	4 1	−213 1 29	63 1 29	70 39 3	70 90 22 3	−568 4 1	−568 4 2	−568 4 3	3831 7 3	3831 7 2
49217	4 5	−148 2 5	128 2 5	135 39 7	135 90 24 0	−501 4 6	−501 4 7	−501 4 8	3896 7 9	3896 7 7
171307	6 1	186 5 12	462 5 12	470 2 3	469 270 11 3	−157 10 17	−157 10 18	−157 10 18	4230 10 18	4230 10 18
210155	4 6	292 9 23	568 9 23	576 21 1	576 90 4 1	−47 6 3	−47 6 3	−47 6 4	4336 3 4	4336 3 3
253427	4 4	411 3 11	687 3 11	694 45 6	694 270 3 6	75 7 13	75 7 13	75 7 14	4455 8 13	4455 9 13
369740	1 5	729 8 24	1005 8 24	1013 16 7	1013 90 1 0	403 10 5	403 10 5	403 10 6	4773 2 6	4773 2 5
400085	4 5	812 9 23	1088 9 23	1096 21 7	1096 90 5 0	489 5 22	489 5 22	489 5 23	4856 2 23	4856 2 22
434355	2 3	906 7 20	1182 7 20	1190 12 5	1189 270 22 5	586 2 7	586 2 7	586 2 8	4950 1 7	4950 1 7
452605	6 4	956 7 7	1232 7 7	1240 10 6	1239 270 21 6	637 8 7	637 8 7	637 8 8	5000 13 8	5000 13 7
470160	5 3	1004 7 30	1280 7 30	1288 14 5	1287 270 23 5	687 2 20	687 2 21	687 2 22	5048 1 21	5048 1 21
473837	4 5	1014 8 25	1290 8 25	1298 17 7	1298 90 1 0	697 7 7	697 7 7	697 7 8	5058 2 7	5058 2 7
507850	3 5	1107 10 10	1383 10 10	1391 23 7	1391 90 8 0	793 7 1	793 6 30	793 7 1	5151 4 1	5151 3 30
524156	1 1	1152 5 29	1428 5 29	1436 5 3	1435 270 15 3	839 7 6	839 7 6	839 7 7	5196 11 7	5196 12 6
544676	1 4	1208 8 5	1484 8 5	1492 14 6	1491 270 25 6	897 6 1	897 6 2	897 6 3	5252 1 3	5252 2 2
567118	3 4	1270 1 12	1546 1 12	1553 38 6	1553 90 22 6	960 9 30	960 9 30	960 10 1	5314 7 1	5313 6 30
569477	4 4	1276 6 29	1552 6 29	1560 9 6	1559 270 20 6	967 5 27	967 5 27	967 5 28	5320 12 27	5320 12 27
601716	5 1	1364 10 6	1640 10 6	1648 24 3	1648 90 7 3	1058 5 18	1058 5 18	1058 5 19	5408 3 20	5408 3 18
613424	1 5	1396 10 26	1672 10 26	1680 26 7	1680 90 10 0	1091 6 2	1091 6 3	1091 6 4	5440 4 3	5440 4 3
626596	3 3	1432 11 19	1708 11 19	1716 30 5	1716 90 14 5	1128 8 4	1128 8 4	1128 8 5	5476 5 5	5476 5 4
645554	1 5	1484 10 14	1760 10 14	1768 24 7	1768 90 9 0	1182 2 3	1182 2 4	1182 2 4	5528 4 4	5528 4 4
664224	5 6	1535 11 27	1811 11 27	1819 31 1	1819 90 15 1	1234 10 10	1234 10 10	1234 10 11	5579 5 11	5579 5 10
671401	6 1	1555 7 19	1831 7 19	1839 13 3	1838 270 22 3	1255 1 11	1255 1 11	1255 1 11	5599 1 12	5599 1 11
694799	4 5	1619 8 11	1895 8 11	1903 16 7	1902 270 26 0	1321 1 21	1321 1 20	1321 1 21	5663 1 22	5663 1 20
704424	5 5	1645 12 19	1921 12 19	1929 34 7	1929 90 18 0	1348 3 19	1348 3 19	1348 3 20	5689 5 19	5689 6 19
708842	1 6	1658 1 19	1934 1 19	1941 40 1	1941 90 23 1	1360 9 8	1360 9 7	1360 9 8	5702 7 8	5702 7 7
709409	4 6	1659 8 11	1935 8 11	1943 16 1	1942 270 26 1	1362 4 13	1362 4 14	1362 4 14	5703 1 14	5703 2 14
709580	1 2	1660 1 26	1936 1 26	1943 40 4	1943 90 25 4	1362 10 7	1362 10 7	1362 10 8	5704 7 8	5704 8 7
727274	1 7	1708 7 8	1984 7 8	1992 12 2	1991 270 21 2	1412 9 13	1412 9 12	1412 9 12	5752 13 12	5752 1 12
728714	1 5	1712 6 17	1988 6 17	1996 8 7	1995 270 18 0	1416 10 5	1416 10 5	1416 10 6	5756 12 5	5756 12 5
744313	6 1	1755 3 1	2031 3 1	2038 45 3	2038 270 3 3	1460 10 12	1460 10 12	1460 10 13	5799 8 12	5799 9 12
764652	5 5	1810 11 11	2086 11 11	2094 28 7	2094 90 13 0	1518 3 5	1518 3 5	1518 3 6	5854 5 5	5854 5 5
Function	(1.79)	(4.4)	(4.7)	(5.2)	(6.5)	(7.4)	(18.12)	(18.20)	(8.28)	(18.23)
Page	38	91	92	96	101	108	294	296	123	298

R.D.	Persian		Bahá'í		French Revolutionary		Easter (same year)		
	Astronomical	Arithmetic	Western	Astronomical	Original	Modified	Julian	Gregorian	Astronomical
−214193	−1208 5 1	−1208 5 1	−6 6 3 7 12	−6 6 3 7 11	−2378 11 5	−2378 11 4	−586 4 3	−586 4 3	−586 4 3
−61387	−790 9 14	−790 9 14	−5 9 3 14 13	−5 9 3 14 13	−1959 3 14	−1959 3 13	−168 4 1	−168 4 8	−168 4 8
25469	−552 7 2	−552 7 2	−4 2 13 10 17	−4 2 13 10 17	−1721 1 2	−1721 1 2	70 4 13	70 4 13	70 4 13
49217	−487 7 9	−487 7 9	−4 6 2 11 6	−4 6 2 11 6	−1656 1 10	−1656 1 10	135 4 17	135 4 17	135 4 17
171307	−153 10 19	−153 10 18	−3 4 13 16 9	−3 4 13 16 10	−1322 4 19	−1322 4 18	470 4 6	470 4 6	470 4 6
210155	−46 2 31	−46 2 30	−3 10 6 4 4	−3 10 6 4 5	−1216 9 1	−1216 9 1	576 4 7	576 4 7	576 4 7
253427	73 8 19	73 8 19	−3 16 10 13 7	−3 16 10 13 7	−1097 2 19	−1097 2 19	694 4 22	694 4 22	694 4 22
369740	392 2 5	392 2 5	−2 14 6 2 17	−2 14 6 2 17	−779 8 5	−779 8 4	1013 4 11	1013 4 11	1013 4 11
400085	475 3 4	475 3 3	−2 18 13 4 8	−2 18 13 4 9	−696 9 5	−696 9 5	1096 4 19	1096 4 19	1096 4 19
434355	569 1 3	569 1 3	−1 4 12 1 3	−1 4 12 1 3	−602 7 2	−602 7 1	1190 4 1	1190 4 1	1190 4 1
452605	618 12 20	618 12 20	−1 7 4 19 9	−1 7 4 19 10	−552 6 20	−552 6 20	1240 4 22	1240 4 22	1240 4 22
470160	667 1 14	667 1 14	−1 9 15 1 13	−1 9 15 1 14	−504 7 13	−504 7 13	1288 4 4	1288 3 28	1288 3 28
473837	677 2 8	677 2 8	−1 10 6 2 19	−1 10 6 3 1	−494 8 8	−494 8 8	1298 4 13	1298 4 6	1298 4 6
507850	770 3 22	770 3 22	−1 15 4 5 8	−1 15 4 5 8	−401 9 23	−401 9 23	1391 4 3	1391 4 3	1391 4 3
524156	814 11 13	814 11 13	−1 17 10 17 16	−1 17 10 17 16	−356 5 14	−356 5 13	1436 4 17	1436 4 17	1436 4 17
544676	871 1 21	871 1 21	0 1 10 2 1	0 1 10 2 2	−300 7 20	−300 7 19	1492 5 1	1492 3 27	1492 3 27
567118	932 6 28	932 6 28	0 4 14 10 12	0 4 14 10 12	−239 13 2	−239 13 1	1553 4 12	1553 4 12	1553 4 12
569477	938 12 14	938 12 14	0 5 1 19 4	0 5 1 19 4	−232 6 15	−232 6 14	1560 4 24	1560 3 27	1560 3 27
601716	1027 3 21	1027 3 21	0 9 14 5 6	0 9 14 5 7	−144 9 22	−144 9 22	1648 4 12	1648 4 12	1648 4 12
613424	1059 4 10	1059 4 10	0 11 8 6 7	0 11 8 6 8	−112 10 12	−112 10 12	1680 4 21	1680 4 21	1680 4 21
626596	1095 5 2	1095 5 2	0 13 6 7 12	0 13 6 7 13	−76 11 6	−76 11 6	1716 4 12	1716 4 12	1716 4 12
645554	1147 3 30	1147 3 30	0 16 1 5 15	0 16 1 5 16	−24 10 1	−24 10 1	1768 4 10	1768 4 3	1768 4 3
664224	1198 5 10	1198 5 10	0 18 14 8 2	0 18 14 8 2	27 11 14	27 11 14	1819 4 18	1819 4 11	1819 4 11
671401	1218 1 7	1218 1 7	0 19 15 1 7	0 19 15 1 7	47 7 6	47 7 6	1839 4 7	1839 3 31	1839 3 31
694799	1282 1 29	1282 1 29	1 4 3 2 11	1 4 3 2 10	111 7 28	111 7 29	1903 4 19	1903 4 12	1903 4 19
704424	1308 6 3	1308 6 3	1 5 10 9 6	1 5 10 9 6	137 12 7	137 12 7	1929 5 5	1929 3 31	1929 3 31
708842	1320 7 7	1320 7 7	1 6 3 11 3	1 6 3 11 3	150 1 7	150 1 7	1941 4 20	1941 4 13	1941 4 13
709409	1322 1 29	1322 1 29	1 6 5 2 11	1 6 5 2 11	151 7 29	151 7 29	1943 4 25	1943 4 25	1943 3 28
709580	1322 7 14	1322 7 14	1 6 5 11 11	1 6 5 11 11	152 1 15	152 1 15	1943 4 25	1943 4 25	1943 3 28
727274	1370 12 27	1370 12 27	1 8 15 19 16	1 8 15 19 17	200 6 27	200 6 27	1992 4 26	1992 4 19	1992 4 19
728714	1374 12 6	1374 12 6	1 8 19 18 19	1 8 19 18 19	204 6 6	204 6 7	1996 4 14	1996 4 7	1996 4 7
744313	1417 8 19	1417 8 19	1 11 5 13 7	1 11 5 13 8	247 2 20	247 2 20	2038 4 25	2038 4 25	2038 3 28
764652	1473 4 28	1473 4 28	1 14 4 7 6	1 14 4 7 7	302 10 30	302 11 1	2094 4 11	2094 4 4	2094 4 4
Function	(15.6)	(15.10)	(16.4)	(16.9)	(17.6)	(17.10)	(9.1)	(9.3)	(18.9)
Page	260	263	272	275	284	285	146	148	292

	Mayan									Aztec																				
R.D.	Long Count					Haab		Tzolkin		Xihuitl		Tonalp.		Balinese Pawukon										Babylonian				Samaritan		
−214193	6	8	3	13	9	11	12	5	9	2	6	5	9	*f*	1	1	1	3	1	1	5	7	3	−275	4	*f*	10	1052	5	12
−61387	7	9	8	3	15	5	3	9	15	14	2	9	15	*t*	2	2	1	4	5	4	5	5	2	143	8	*f*	24	1471	9	27
25469	8	1	9	8	11	4	9	12	11	13	8	12	11	*t*	2	2	1	5	5	4	1	5	6	381	7	*f*	1	1709	7	4
49217	8	4	15	7	19	5	12	9	19	14	11	9	19	*f*	1	2	3	3	5	1	3	5	3	446	7	*f*	7	1774	7	9
171307	9	1	14	10	9	14	12	3	9	5	6	3	9	*f*	1	1	3	3	1	4	3	1	5	780	10	*f*	17	2108	10	19
210155	9	7	2	8	17	4	5	7	17	13	4	7	17	*t*	2	2	1	1	5	2	1	8	0	887	2	*f*	3	2214	3	5
253427	9	13	2	12	9	14	7	2	9	5	1	2	9	*f*	1	2	3	3	5	7	3	2	7	1005	8	*f*	13	2333	8	14
369740	10	9	5	14	2	8	5	4	2	17	4	4	2	*f*	1	2	2	1	2	1	2	2	1	1324	1	*f*	5	2651	2	7
400085	10	13	10	1	7	10	15	7	7	1	9	7	7	*f*	1	2	1	1	5	1	1	8	1	1407	2	*f*	22	2734	2	24
434355	10	18	5	4	17	8	15	9	17	17	14	9	17	*t*	2	3	1	1	3	6	1	3	2	1500	12	*f*	7	2828	13	9
452605	11	0	15	17	7	8	15	7	7	17	14	7	7	*f*	1	1	1	1	1	7	5	1	5	1550	12	*f*	7	2878	12	8
470160	11	3	4	13	2	10	10	12	2	1	4	12	2	*t*	2	3	4	1	6	6	8	6	2	1598	12	*f*	21	2926	13	23
473837	11	3	14	16	19	11	17	10	19	2	11	10	19	*f*	1	2	3	3	5	1	3	5	3	1609	1	*f*	7	2936	2	8
507850	11	8	9	7	12	15	5	2	12	5	19	2	12	*f*	1	1	4	1	4	1	4	7	1	1702	2	*f*	29	3029	3	2
524156	11	10	14	12	18	9	6	6	18	18	5	6	18	*f*	1	2	2	2	2	4	2	5	7	1746	11	*f*	6	3074	11	7
544676	11	13	11	12	18	13	6	12	18	3	20	12	18	*f*	1	2	4	2	2	7	8	8	9	1803	1	*f*	2	3130	1	4
567118	11	16	14	1	0	3	18	3	20	12	17	3	20	*t*	2	1	4	4	4	7	4	7	4	1864	5	*f*	30	3192	7	2
569477	11	17	0	10	19	12	7	9	19	3	1	9	19	*f*	1	2	3	3	5	7	3	2	7	1870	11	*f*	27	3198	11	28
601716	12	1	10	2	18	18	6	8	18	8	20	8	18	*f*	1	3	4	2	6	4	8	3	7	1959	2	*f*	18	3286	3	19
613424	12	3	2	12	6	1	9	3	6	10	8	3	6	*t*	2	2	4	5	2	1	4	5	4	1991	4	*f*	2	3318	4	4
626596	12	4	19	4	18	3	1	6	18	11	20	6	18	*t*	2	1	2	2	4	6	2	1	6	2027	4	*f*	4	3354	5	6
645554	12	7	11	16	16	1	19	10	16	10	18	10	16	*t*	2	2	4	5	2	1	4	5	4	2079	3	*f*	3	3406	3	5
664224	12	10	3	14	6	4	14	12	6	13	13	12	6	*f*	1	3	4	5	6	2	8	3	3	2130	4	*f*	10	3457	5	12
671401	12	11	3	13	3	16	16	13	3	7	10	13	3	*f*	1	1	1	2	1	4	5	4	7	2149	12	*f*	11	3477	13	12
694799	12	14	8	13	1	18	14	11	1	9	8	11	1	*t*	2	2	1	5	5	1	5	8	4	2213	12	*t*	20	3541	1	22
704424	12	15	15	8	6	7	4	3	6	16	3	3	6	*t*	2	3	2	5	6	1	2	3	4	2240	5	*f*	19	3567	5	21
708842	12	16	7	13	4	9	2	1	4	18	1	1	4	*t*	2	2	2	3	2	2	2	1	2	2252	6	*f*	7	3580	7	9
709409	12	16	9	5	11	19	4	9	11	9	18	9	11	*f*	1	2	3	5	5	2	3	2	3	2254	1	*f*	13	3581	1	15
709580	12	16	9	14	2	9	10	11	2	18	9	11	2	*t*	2	2	4	1	2	5	4	8	4	2254	7	*f*	7	3582	7	8
727274	12	18	18	16	16	18	4	12	16	8	18	12	16	*t*	2	2	2	5	2	3	2	8	2	2302	12	*f*	12	3630	12	13
728714	12	19	2	16	16	17	4	9	16	7	18	9	16	*t*	2	2	4	5	2	1	4	5	4	2306	12	*f*	5	3634	12	7
744313	13	1	6	4	15	12	8	8	15	3	2	8	15	*t*	2	1	3	4	1	4	7	1	2	2349	8	*f*	12	3677	8	14
764652	13	4	2	13	14	7	7	2	14	16	6	2	14	*f*	1	3	4	3	6	1	8	6	3	2405	4	*f*	5	3732	4	6
Function	(11.3)					(11.6)		(11.9)		(11.17)		(11.21)		(12.1)										(18.8)				(18.35)		
Page	171					173		175		178		179		185										291				302		

R.D.	Chinese			Hindu Solar			Hindu Lunisolar			Tibetan
	Date	Name	Next Zhongqi	Old	Modern	Astronomical	Old	Modern	Astronomical	
−214193	35 11 6 *f* 12	2 10	−214191.633133	2515 5 19	−664 5 19	−664 5 13	2515 6 *f* 11	−529 6 *f* 11 *f*	−529 6 *t* 11 *f*	−459 8 *f* 11 *f*
−61387	42 9 10 *f* 27	8 8	−61370.729673	2933 9 26	−246 9 26	−246 9 21	2933 9 *f* 26	−111 9 *f* 27 *f*	−111 9 *f* 27 *f*	−41 12 *f* 27 *f*
25469	46 7 8 *f* 4	4 8	25498.215092	3171 7 11	−8 7 9	−8 7 5	3171 8 *f* 3	127 8 *f* 3 *f*	127 8 *f* 3 *t*	197 10 *f* 3 *f*
49217	47 12 8 *f* 9	2 8	49239.004860	3236 7 17	57 7 16	57 7 11	3236 8 *f* 9	192 8 *f* 9 *f*	192 8 *f* 9 *f*	262 10 *f* 9 *f*
171307	52 46 11 *f* 20	2 10	171318.588098	3570 10 19	391 10 21	391 10 17	3570 11 *t* 19	526 11 *f* 19 *f*	526 10 *f* 20 *f*	596 12 *f* 19 *f*
210155	54 33 4 *f* 5	10 2	210156.745715	3677 2 28	498 2 31	498 2 27	3677 3 *f* 5	633 3 *f* 5 *f*	633 3 *f* 5 *f*	703 5 *f* 4 *f*
253427	56 31 10 *f* 15	2 2	253439.318423	3795 8 17	616 8 16	616 8 13	3795 9 *f* 15	751 9 *f* 15 *f*	751 8 *f* 15 *f*	821 10 *f* 15 *f*
369740	61 50 3 *f* 7	5 11	369767.423610	4114 1 26	935 1 28	935 1 26	4114 2 *f* 7	1070 2 *f* 6 *f*	1070 2 *f* 6 *f*	1140 4 *f* 6 *f*
400085	63 13 4 *f* 24	10 8	400113.941895	4197 2 24	1018 2 26	1018 2 24	4197 2 *f* 24	1153 3 *t* 23 *f*	1153 2 *f* 23 *f*	1223 4 *f* 23 *f*
434355	64 47 2 *f* 9	10 6	434384.035740	4290 12 20	1111 12 23	1111 12 21	4291 1 *f* 9	1247 1 *f* 8 *f*	1247 1 *f* 8 *f*	1317 3 *f* 8 *f*
452605	65 37 2 *f* 9	10 4	452615.458234	4340 12 7	1161 12 10	1161 12 8	4340 12 *f* 9	1297 1 *f* 8 *f*	1296 12 *f* 8 *f*	1367 2 *f* 8 *f*
470160	66 25 2 *f* 23	5 3	470177.759817	4388 12 30	1210 1 2	1209 12 31	4389 1 *f* 23	1345 1 *f* 22 *f*	1345 1 *f* 23 *f*	1415 2 *f* 22 *f*
473837	66 35 3 *f* 9	2 8	473861.324287	4399 1 24	1220 1 27	1220 1 25	4399 2 *f* 8	1355 2 *f* 8 *f*	1355 2 *f* 8 *f*	1425 4 *f* 8 *f*
507850	68 8 5 *f* 2	5 1	507860.235360	4492 3 7	1313 3 8	1313 3 7	4492 4 *f* 2	1448 4 *f* 1 *f*	1448 4 *f* 1 *f*	1518 5 *f* 1 *f*
524156	68 53 1 *f* 8	1 11	524172.836499	4536 10 28	1357 10 30	1357 10 28	4536 11 *f* 7	1492 11 *f* 7 *f*	1492 11 *f* 7 *f*	1563 1 *f* 7 *f*
544676	69 49 3 *f* 4	1 11	544687.134951	4593 1 3	1414 1 5	1414 1 4	4593 1 *f* 3	1549 2 *t* 3 *f*	1549 2 *t* 4 *f*	1619 3 *f* 3 *f*
567118	70 50 8 *f* 2	3 1	567122.835546	4654 6 12	1475 6 10	1475 6 9	4654 7 *f* 2	1610 7 *f* 2 *f*	1610 7 *f* 2 *f*	1680 8 *f* 2 *f*
569477	70 57 1 *f* 29	2 8	569492.996631	4660 11 27	1481 11 29	1481 11 28	4660 11 *f* 29	1616 11 *f* 28 *t*	1616 11 *f* 29 *f*	1687 1 *f* 29 *f*
601716	72 25 4 *t* 20	1 3	601727.342101	4749 3 1	1570 3 3	1570 3 2	4749 3 *f* 20	1705 3 *f* 20 *f*	1705 3 *f* 20 *f*	1775 4 *f* 20 *f*
613424	72 57 6 *f* 5	9 11	613446.520844	4781 3 21	1602 3 22	1602 3 22	4781 4 *f* 4	1737 4 *f* 4 *f*	1737 4 *f* 5 *f*	1807 6 *t* 4 *f*
626596	73 33 6 *f* 6	1 7	626626.467423	4817 4 13	1638 4 13	1638 4 13	4817 5 *f* 6	1773 5 *f* 6 *f*	1773 5 *f* 6 *f*	1843 6 *f* 6 *f*
645554	74 25 5 *f* 5	9 5	645556.325334	4869 3 8	1690 3 10	1690 3 9	4869 4 *f* 5	1825 4 *f* 5 *f*	1825 4 *f* 5 *f*	1895 5 *f* 5 *f*
664224	75 16 6 *f* 12	9 3	664246.376294	4920 4 20	1741 4 20	1741 4 20	4920 5 *f* 12	1876 5 *f* 11 *f*	1876 5 *f* 11 *f*	1946 6 *f* 11 *f*
671401	75 36 2 *f* 13	6 4	671426.124336	4939 12 13	1760 12 16	1760 12 15	4940 1 *t* 13	1896 1 *f* 13 *f*	1896 1 *f* 13 *f*	1966 2 *f* 13 *f*
694799	76 40 3 *f* 22	4 2	694801.614262	5004 1 4	1825 1 7	1825 1 7	5004 1 *f* 23	1960 1 *f* 22 *f*	1960 1 *f* 22 *f*	2030 2 *f* 22 *f*
704424	77 6 7 *f* 21	9 3	704453.869487	5030 5 11	1851 5 10	1851 5 10	5030 5 *f* 21	1986 5 *f* 20 *f*	1986 5 *f* 20 *f*	2056 7 *f* 20 *f*
708842	77 18 8 *f* 9	7 5	708867.143728	5042 6 15	1863 6 14	1863 6 14	5042 7 *f* 9	1998 7 *f* 9 *f*	1998 7 *f* 9 *f*	2068 8 *f* 9 *f*
709409	77 20 3 *f* 15	4 8	709411.313394	5044 1 4	1865 1 7	1865 1 6	5044 1 *f* 15	2000 1 *f* 14 *f*	2000 1 *f* 14 *f*	2070 3 *t* 14 *f*
709580	77 20 9 *f* 9	5 11	709597.630490	5044 6 23	1865 6 21	1865 6 21	5044 7 *f* 9	2000 7 *f* 8 *f*	2000 7 *f* 8 *f*	2070 8 *f* 8 *f*
727274	78 9 2 *f* 14	9 5	727277.699910	5092 12 2	1913 12 4	1913 12 4	5092 12 *f* 14	2048 12 *f* 14 *f*	2048 12 *f* 14 *f*	2119 1 *f* 14 *f*
728714	78 13 1 *f* 7	9 5	728738.668683	5096 11 11	1917 11 13	1917 11 13	5096 12 *f* 7	2052 12 *f* 7 *f*	2052 12 *f* 7 *f*	2123 1 *f* 7 *f*
744313	78 55 10 *f* 14	8 4	744325.563213	5139 7 26	1960 7 24	1960 7 25	5139 8 *f* 14	2095 8 *f* 14 *f*	2095 8 *f* 14 *f*	2165 9 *f* 14 *f*
764652	79 51 6 *f* 7	7 3	764656.564371	5195 4 2	2016 4 2	2016 4 2	5195 4 *f* 6	2151 4 *f* 6 *f*	2151 4 *f* 6 *f*	2221 6 *f* 6 *f*
Function	(19.16)	(19.24)	(19.4)	(10.8)	(20.20)	(20.45)	(10.13)	(20.23)	(20.48)	(21.5)
Page	317	320	308	159	347	360	165	349	361	378

R.D.	Ephemeris Correction	Equation of Time	Solar Longitude at 12:00:00 U.T. (Degrees)	Next Solstice/Equinox (R.D.)	Dawn in Paris 48.84° N, 2.34° E, 27m (Standard Time)	Midday in Tehran 21.42° N, 39.82° E, 298m (Standard Time)	Sunset in Jerusalem 31.8° N, 35.2° E, 800m (Standard Time)
−214193	0.214169	−0.001190	119.473431	−214131.147334	0.095285 = 02:17:13	0.504216 = 12:06:04	0.780556 = 18:44:00
−61387	0.143632	0.003159	254.248961	−61371.053052	0.277372 = 06:39:25	0.499952 = 11:59:56	0.697324 = 16:44:09
25469	0.114444	0.005373	181.435996	25556.789090	0.203569 = 04:53:08	0.497556 = 11:56:29	0.734889 = 17:38:14
49217	0.107183	0.006791	188.663922	49297.584568	0.212231 = 05:05:37	0.496143 = 11:54:27	0.728514 = 17:29:04
171307	0.069498	−0.007231	289.091566	171378.539292	0.286370 = 06:52:22	0.510331 = 12:14:53	0.708788 = 17:00:39
210155	0.057506	0.004410	59.119741	210187.908137	0.096280 = 02:18:39	0.498595 = 11:57:59	0.774201 = 18:34:51
253427	0.044758	0.009897	228.314554	253468.413001	0.253730 = 06:05:22	0.493137 = 11:50:07	0.700877 = 16:49:16
369740	0.017397	0.001987	34.460769	369798.559125	0.149472 = 03:35:14	0.500958 = 12:01:23	0.762736 = 18:18:20
400085	0.012796	0.003478	63.187995	400113.618511	0.088486 = 02:07:25	0.499538 = 11:59:20	0.776777 = 18:38:34
434355	0.008869	−0.004947	2.457591	434446.328561	0.209217 = 05:01:16	0.507865 = 12:11:20	0.748088 = 17:57:15
452605	0.007262	−0.007588	350.475934	452615.134851	0.228552 = 05:29:07	0.510516 = 12:15:09	0.742536 = 17:49:15
470160	0.005979	−0.002369	13.498220	470240.017391	0.189859 = 04:33:24	0.505289 = 12:07:37	0.753102 = 18:04:28
473837	0.005740	0.002140	37.403920	473892.432571	0.143920 = 03:27:15	0.500814 = 12:01:10	0.764402 = 18:20:44
507850	0.003875	0.001195	81.028130	507859.911980	**bogus**	0.501853 = 12:02:40	0.784041 = 18:49:01
524156	0.003157	−0.010356	313.860498	524202.622400	0.272361 = 06:32:12	0.513383 = 12:19:16	0.722535 = 17:20:27
544676	0.002393	−0.001013	19.954430	544749.318739	0.178067 = 04:16:25	0.503941 = 12:05:41	0.756134 = 18:08:50
567118	0.001731	0.004277	176.059431	567122.512168	0.196839 = 04:43:27	0.498637 = 11:58:02	0.739658 = 17:45:06
569477	0.001669	−0.008429	344.922951	569492.673245	0.236578 = 05:40:40	0.511368 = 12:16:22	0.739663 = 17:45:07
601716	0.000615	0.000943	79.964921	601727.018725	0.045748 = 01:05:53	0.502105 = 12:03:02	0.784057 = 18:49:03
613424	0.000177	−0.002039	99.302317	613508.259061	**bogus**	0.505088 = 12:07:20	0.787086 = 18:53:24
626596	0.000101	−0.004076	121.535304	626656.970915	0.105595 = 02:32:03	0.507082 = 12:10:12	0.781969 = 18:46:02
645554	0.000171	−0.000541	88.567428	645556.001954	**bogus**	0.503594 = 12:05:11	0.786308 = 18:52:17
664224	0.000136	−0.004143	129.289884	664276.907718	0.122462 = 02:56:21	0.507129 = 12:10:16	0.778132 = 18:40:31
671401	0.000061	−0.004008	6.146910	671488.166885	0.202856 = 04:52:07	0.506931 = 12:09:59	0.749687 = 17:59:33
694799	0.000014	0.000392	28.251993	694863.628311	0.162579 = 03:54:07	0.502551 = 12:03:40	0.760231 = 18:14:44
704424	0.000276	−0.001555	151.780633	704453.536160	0.163289 = 03:55:08	0.504488 = 12:06:28	0.761909 = 18:17:09
708842	0.000296	0.006529	185.945867	708926.239052	0.208698 = 05:00:32	0.496387 = 11:54:48	0.730647 = 17:32:08
709409	0.000302	0.000427	28.555607	709473.300039	0.162020 = 03:53:19	0.502516 = 12:03:37	0.760390 = 18:14:58
709580	0.000302	0.008180	193.347892	709656.728163	0.216912 = 05:12:21	0.494746 = 11:52:26	0.724012 = 17:22:35
727274	0.000675	−0.005843	357.151254	727277.366581	0.217687 = 05:13:28	0.508771 = 12:12:38	0.745361 = 17:53:19
728714	0.000712	−0.009214	336.170692	728738.335351	0.247980 = 05:57:06	0.512176 = 12:17:32	0.734750 = 17:38:02
744313	0.000963	0.011238	228.184879	744354.792807	0.251890 = 06:02:43	0.491786 = 11:48:10	0.699821 = 16:47:45
764652	0.002913	−0.004466	116.439352	764718.468836	0.094955 = 02:16:44	0.507483 = 12:10:47	0.784480 = 18:49:39
Function	(14.15)	(14.20)	(14.33)	(14.36)	(14.72)	(14.26)	(14.77)
Page	210	215	223	224	241	218	242

	Lunar Position at 00:00:00 U.T.			Next	In Mecca (21.42° N, 39.82° E, 298m)	
	Longitude	Latitude	Altitude	New Moon	Moonrise	Moonset
R.D.	(Degrees)	(Degrees)	(Degrees)	(R.D.)	(Standard Time)	(Standard Time)
−214193	244.853905	2.452759	−13.163184	−214174.605828	0.645260 = 15:29:10	0.084225 = 02:01:17
−61387	208.856738	−4.902230	−7.281426	−61382.995328	0.146650 = 03:31:11	0.627607 = 15:03:45
25469	213.746842	−2.939469	−77.149900	25495.809776	0.365595 = 08:46:27	0.842646 = 20:13:25
49217	292.046243	5.001904	−30.401178	49238.502448	0.582553 = 13:58:53	0.030307 = 00:43:39
171307	156.819014	−3.208909	71.848578	171318.435313	0.926722 = 22:14:29	0.419886 = 10:04:38
210155	108.055632	0.894361	−43.798579	210180.691849	0.391565 = 09:23:51	0.965784 = 23:10:44
253427	39.356097	−3.863335	40.653204	253442.859367	0.737227 = 17:41:36	0.252852 = 06:04:06
369740	98.565851	−2.522444	−40.278725	369763.746413	0.434271 = 10:25:21	**bogus**
400085	332.958296	1.032069	29.611156	400091.578343	0.028119 = 00:40:30	0.528119 = 12:40:30
434355	92.259651	3.005689	−19.973178	434376.578106	0.501712 = 12:02:28	0.052493 = 01:15:35
452605	78.132029	1.613843	−23.740743	452627.191972	0.494050 = 11:51:26	0.037996 = 00:54:43
470160	274.946995	4.766741	30.956688	470167.578360	0.013196 = 00:19:00	0.493177 = 11:50:11
473837	128.362844	4.899203	−18.888690	473858.853276	0.519306 = 12:27:48	0.060322 = 01:26:52
507850	89.518450	4.838474	−32.161162	507878.666842	0.259826 = 06:14:09	0.856017 = 20:32:40
524156	24.607322	2.301475	−45.680919	524179.247062	0.452190 = 10:51:09	**bogus**
544676	53.485956	−0.890563	−50.292110	544702.753873	0.343276 = 08:14:19	0.908706 = 21:48:32
567118	187.898520	4.765784	−54.345305	567146.513181	0.300431 = 07:12:37	0.818009 = 19:37:56
569477	320.172362	−2.737358	−34.566000	569479.203258	0.231763 = 05:33:44	0.714185 = 17:08:26
601716	314.042566	−4.035652	44.131989	601727.033557	0.973015 = 23:21:09	0.416862 = 10:00:17
613424	145.474065	−3.157214	−57.539862	613449.762129	0.394417 = 09:27:58	0.932503 = 22:22:48
626596	185.030507	−1.879614	−62.082439	626620.369801	0.450518 = 10:48:45	0.956378 = 22:57:11
645554	142.189132	−3.379519	−54.072091	645579.076748	0.416008 = 09:59:03	0.952629 = 22:51:47
664224	253.743375	−4.398341	−16.120452	664242.886718	0.657391 = 15:46:39	0.070965 = 01:42:11
671401	151.648685	2.099198	23.864594	671418.970538	0.686259 = 16:28:13	0.200419 = 04:48:36
694799	287.987743	5.268746	32.950146	694807.563371	0.008243 = 00:11:52	0.489200 = 11:44:27
704424	25.626707	−1.672299	72.691651	704433.491182	0.916779 = 22:00:10	0.429962 = 10:19:09
708842	290.288300	4.682012	−29.849481	708863.597000	0.586590 = 14:04:41	0.031414 = 00:45:14
709409	189.913142	3.705518	31.610644	709424.404929	0.742587 = 17:49:20	0.224521 = 05:23:19
709580	284.931730	2.493964	−42.219689	709602.082686	0.555246 = 13:19:33	**bogus**
727274	152.339044	−4.167774	28.647809	727291.209400	0.719220 = 17:15:41	0.214825 = 05:09:21
728714	51.662265	−2.873757	−38.950553	728737.447691	0.466211 = 11:11:21	**bogus**
744313	26.682060	−4.667251	27.601977	744329.573999	0.705999 = 16:56:38	0.211858 = 05:05:05
764652	175.500822	5.138562	−54.854681	764676.191273	0.436806 = 10:29:00	0.963174 = 23:06:58
Function	(14.48)	(14.63)	(14.64)	(14.47)	(14.83)	(14.84)
Page	232	236	237	231	244	245

Holiday	Func., page	2000	2001	2002	2003	2004	2005	2006	2007
Advent Sunday	(2.42), 70	12/3	12/2	12/1	11/30	11/28	11/27	12/3	12/2
Bahá'í New Year	(16.10), 277	3/21	3/21	3/21	3/21	3/21	3/21	3/21	3/21
Birkath ha-Hama	(8.38), 131	*none*	*none*	*none*	*none*	*none*	*none*	*none*	*none*
Birth of the Bāb	(16.13), 278	10/28	10/18	11/6	10/26	10/15	11/3	10/23	11/11
Birthday of Rama	(20.61), 369	4/12	4/2	4/21	4/10	3/30	4/17	4/6	3/27
Chinese New Year	(19.26), 322	2/5	1/24	2/12	2/1	1/22	2/9	1/29	2/18
Christmas	(2.41), 70	12/25	12/25	12/25	12/25	12/25	12/25	12/25	12/25
Christmas (Coptic)	(4.9), 93	1/8	1/7	1/7	1/7	1/8	1/7	1/7	1/7
Christmas (Orthodox)	(3.25), 85	1/7	1/7	1/7	1/7	1/7	1/7	1/7	1/7
Diwali	(20.57), 368	10/28	11/16	11/5	10/26	11/13	11/2	10/23	11/10
Dragon Festival	(19.27), 324	6/6	6/25	6/15	6/4	6/22	6/11	5/31	6/19
Easter	(9.3), 148	4/23	4/15	3/31	4/20	4/11	3/27	4/16	4/8
Easter (Astronomical)	(18.9), 292	4/23	4/15	3/31	4/20	4/11	3/27	4/16	4/8
Easter (Orthodox)	(9.1), 146	4/30	4/15	5/5	4/27	4/11	5/1	4/23	4/8
Epiphany	(2.43), 71	1/2	1/7	1/6	1/5	1/4	1/2	1/8	1/7
Feast of Naw-Rūz	(16.11), 277	3/20	3/20	3/21	3/21	3/20	3/20	3/21	3/21
Feast of Riḍvān	(16.12), 277	4/20	4/20	4/21	4/21	4/20	4/20	4/21	4/21
Friday the 13th (first)	(2.45), 71	10/13	4/13	9/13	6/13	2/13	5/13	1/13	4/13
Great Night of Shiva	(20.60), 369	3/4	2/21	3/12	3/1	2/18	3/8	2/26	2/16
Hanukkah (first day)	(8.43), 134	12/22	12/10	11/30	12/20	12/8	12/26	12/16	12/5
Hindu Lunar New Year	(20.53), 365	4/5	3/25	4/13	4/2	3/21	4/9	3/30	3/19
Icelandic Summer	(6.2), 100	4/20	4/19	4/25	4/24	4/22	4/21	4/20	4/19
Icelandic Winter	(6.3), 100	10/21	10/27	10/26	10/25	10/23	10/22	10/21	10/27
Kajeng Keliwon (first)	(12.16), 190	1/15	1/9	1/4	1/14	1/9	1/3	1/13	1/8
Losar	(21.9), 381	2/6	2/24	2/13	3/3	2/21	2/9	2/28	2/18
Mawlid	(7.6), 109	6/15	6/4	5/24	5/14	5/2	4/21	4/11	3/31
Mesha Saṃkrānti (date)	(20.51), 364	4/13	4/14	4/14	4/14	4/13	4/14	4/14	4/14
Nowruz	(15.11), 265	3/20	3/21	3/21	3/21	3/20	3/21	3/21	3/21
Observ. Hebrew 1 Nisan	(18.22), 297	3/8	3/27	3/16	4/4	3/23	3/12	3/31	3/21
Passover	(8.31), 129	4/20	4/8	3/28	4/17	4/6	4/24	4/13	4/3
Passover Eve (Classical)	(18.25), 298	3/21	4/9	3/29	4/17	4/5	3/25	4/13	4/3
Pentecost	(9.4), 152	6/11	6/3	5/19	6/8	5/30	5/15	6/4	5/27
Purim	(8.33), 129	3/21	3/9	2/26	3/18	3/7	3/25	3/14	3/4
Qīngmíng	(19.28), 324	4/4	4/5	4/5	4/5	4/4	4/5	4/5	4/5
Sacred Wednesday (first)	(20.65), 370	4/12	1/3	2/20	12/31	4/28	2/16	8/2	9/19
Sh'ela	(8.37), 131	12/5	12/5	12/5	12/6	12/5	12/5	12/5	12/6
Ta'anit Esther	(8.34), 130	3/20	3/8	2/25	3/17	3/4	3/24	3/13	3/1
Tishah be-Av	(8.35), 130	8/10	7/29	7/18	8/7	7/27	8/14	8/3	7/24
Tumpek (first)	(12.17), 190	1/15	2/3	1/19	1/4	1/24	1/8	1/28	1/13
U.S. Daylight Saving End	(2.40), 70	11/5	11/4	11/3	11/2	11/7	11/6	11/5	11/4
U.S. Daylight Saving Start	(2.39), 70	3/12	3/11	3/10	3/9	3/14	3/13	3/12	3/11
U.S. Election Day	(2.38), 70	11/7	11/6	11/5	11/4	11/2	11/8	11/7	11/6
U.S. Independence Day	(2.32), 69	7/4	7/4	7/4	7/4	7/4	7/4	7/4	7/4
U.S. Labor Day	(2.36), 69	9/4	9/3	9/2	9/1	9/6	9/5	9/4	9/3
U.S. Memorial Day	(2.37), 70	5/29	5/28	5/27	5/26	5/31	5/30	5/29	5/28
Yom ha-Zikkaron	(8.36), 131	5/9	4/25	4/16	5/6	4/26	5/11	5/2	4/23
Yom Kippur	(8.30), 128	10/9	9/27	9/16	10/6	9/25	10/13	10/2	9/22

Holiday	Func., page	2008	2009	2010	2011	2012	2013	2014	2015
Advent Sunday	(2.42), 70	11/30	11/29	11/28	11/27	12/2	12/1	11/30	11/29
Bahá'í New Year	(16.10), 277	3/21	3/21	3/21	3/21	3/21	3/21	3/21	3/21
Birkath ha-Hama	(8.38), 131	*none*	4/8	*none*	*none*	*none*	*none*	*none*	*none*
Birth of the Bāb	(16.13), 278	10/30	10/19	11/7	10/28	10/16	11/4	10/25	11/13
Birthday of Rama	(20.61), 369	4/14	4/3	3/24	4/12	3/31	4/19	4/8	3/28
Chinese New Year	(19.26), 322	2/7	1/26	2/14	2/3	1/23	2/10	1/31	2/19
Christmas	(2.41), 70	12/25	12/25	12/25	12/25	12/25	12/25	12/25	12/25
Christmas (Coptic)	(4.9), 93	1/8	1/7	1/7	1/7	1/8	1/7	1/7	1/7
Christmas (Orthodox)	(3.25), 85	1/7	1/7	1/7	1/7	1/7	1/7	1/7	1/7
Diwali	(20.57), 368	10/29	10/19	11/7	10/27	11/14	11/4	10/24	11/12
Dragon Festival	(19.27), 324	6/8	5/28	6/16	6/6	6/23	6/12	6/2	6/20
Easter	(9.3), 148	3/23	4/12	4/4	4/24	4/8	3/31	4/20	4/5
Easter (Astronomical)	(18.9), 292	3/23	4/12	4/4	4/24	4/8	3/31	4/20	4/5
Easter (Orthodox)	(9.1), 146	4/27	4/19	4/4	4/24	4/15	5/5	4/20	4/12
Epiphany	(2.43), 71	1/6	1/4	1/3	1/2	1/8	1/6	1/5	1/4
Feast of Naw-Rūz	(16.11), 277	3/20	3/20	3/21	3/21	3/20	3/20	3/21	3/21
Feast of Riḍvān	(16.12), 277	4/20	4/20	4/21	4/21	4/20	4/20	4/21	4/21
Friday the 13th (first)	(2.45), 71	6/13	2/13	8/13	5/13	1/13	9/13	6/13	2/13
Great Night of Shiva	(20.60), 369	3/5	2/23	2/12	3/2	2/20	3/10	2/27	2/17
Hanukkah (first day)	(8.43), 134	12/22	12/12	12/2	12/21	12/9	11/28	12/17	12/7
Hindu Lunar New Year	(20.53), 365	4/7	3/27	3/16	4/4	3/23	4/11	3/31	3/21
Icelandic Summer	(6.2), 100	4/24	4/23	4/22	4/21	4/19	4/25	4/24	4/23
Icelandic Winter	(6.3), 100	10/25	10/24	10/23	10/22	10/27	10/26	10/25	10/24
Kajeng Keliwon (first)	(12.16), 190	1/3	1/12	1/7	1/2	1/12	1/6	1/1	1/11
Losar	(21.9), 381	2/7	2/25	2/14	3/5	2/22	2/11	3/2	2/19
Mawlid	(7.6), 109	3/20	3/9	2/26	2/16	2/5	1/24	1/14	1/3
Mesha Saṃkrānti (date)	(20.51), 364	4/13	4/14	4/14	4/14	4/13	4/14	4/14	4/14
Nowruz	(15.11), 265	3/20	3/21	3/21	3/21	3/20	3/21	3/21	3/21
Observ. Hebrew 1 Nisan	(18.22), 297	3/9	3/28	3/18	3/7	3/24	3/13	4/1	3/22
Passover	(8.31), 129	4/20	4/9	3/30	4/19	4/7	3/26	4/15	4/4
Passover Eve (Classical)	(18.25), 298	3/22	4/10	3/31	3/20	4/6	3/26	4/14	4/4
Pentecost	(9.4), 152	5/11	5/31	5/23	6/12	5/27	5/19	6/8	5/24
Purim	(8.33), 129	3/21	3/10	2/28	3/20	3/8	2/24	3/16	3/5
Qīngmíng	(19.28), 324	4/4	4/4	4/5	4/5	4/4	4/4	4/5	4/5
Sacred Wednesday (first)	(20.65), 370	1/16	3/4	9/15	1/12	6/27	3/20	1/8	6/24
Sh'ela	(8.37), 131	12/5	12/5	12/5	12/6	12/5	12/5	12/5	12/6
Ta'anit Esther	(8.34), 130	3/20	3/9	2/25	3/17	3/7	2/21	3/13	3/4
Tishah be-Av	(8.35), 130	8/10	7/30	7/20	8/9	7/29	7/16	8/5	7/26
Tumpek (first)	(12.17), 190	2/2	1/17	1/2	1/22	1/7	1/26	1/11	1/31
U.S. Daylight Saving End	(2.40), 70	11/2	11/1	11/7	11/6	11/4	11/3	11/2	11/1
U.S. Daylight Saving Start	(2.39), 70	3/9	3/8	3/14	3/13	3/11	3/10	3/9	3/8
U.S. Election Day	(2.38), 70	11/4	11/3	11/2	11/8	11/6	11/5	11/4	11/3
U.S. Independence Day	(2.32), 69	7/4	7/4	7/4	7/4	7/4	7/4	7/4	7/4
U.S. Labor Day	(2.36), 69	9/1	9/7	9/6	9/5	9/3	9/2	9/1	9/7
U.S. Memorial Day	(2.37), 70	5/26	5/25	5/31	5/30	5/28	5/27	5/26	5/25
Yom ha-Zikkaron	(8.36), 131	5/7	4/28	4/19	5/9	4/25	4/15	5/5	4/22
Yom Kippur	(8.30), 128	10/9	9/28	9/18	10/8	9/26	9/14	10/4	9/23

Holiday	Func., page	2016	2017	2018	2019	2020	2021	2022	2023
Advent Sunday	(2.42), 70	11/27	12/3	12/2	12/1	11/29	11/28	11/27	12/3
Bahá'í New Year	(16.10), 277	3/21	3/21	3/21	3/21	3/21	3/21	3/21	3/21
Birkath ha-Hama	(8.38), 131	*none*	*none*	*none*	*none*	*none*	*none*	*none*	*none*
Birth of the Bāb	(16.13), 278	11/1	10/21	11/9	10/29	10/18	11/6	10/26	10/16
Birthday of Rama	(20.61), 369	4/15	4/5	3/25	4/13	4/2	4/21	4/10	3/30
Chinese New Year	(19.26), 322	2/8	1/28	2/16	2/5	1/25	2/12	2/1	1/22
Christmas	(2.41), 70	12/25	12/25	12/25	12/25	12/25	12/25	12/25	12/25
Christmas (Coptic)	(4.9), 93	1/8	1/7	1/7	1/7	1/8	1/7	1/7	1/7
Christmas (Orthodox)	(3.25), 85	1/7	1/7	1/7	1/7	1/7	1/7	1/7	1/7
Diwali	(20.57), 368	10/31	10/20	11/8	10/29	11/16	11/5	10/26	11/14
Dragon Festival	(19.27), 324	6/9	5/30	6/18	6/7	6/25	6/14	6/3	6/22
Easter	(9.3), 148	3/27	4/16	4/1	4/21	4/12	4/4	4/17	4/9
Easter (Astronomical)	(18.9), 292	3/27	4/16	4/1	3/24	4/12	4/4	4/17	4/9
Easter (Orthodox)	(9.1), 146	5/1	4/16	4/8	4/28	4/19	5/2	4/24	4/16
Epiphany	(2.43), 71	1/3	1/8	1/7	1/6	1/5	1/3	1/2	1/8
Feast of Naw-Rūz	(16.11), 277	3/20	3/20	3/21	3/21	3/20	3/20	3/21	3/21
Feast of Riḍvān	(16.12), 277	4/20	4/20	4/21	4/21	4/20	4/20	4/21	4/21
Friday the 13th (first)	(2.45), 71	5/13	1/13	4/13	9/13	3/13	8/13	5/13	1/13
Great Night of Shiva	(20.60), 369	3/7	2/24	2/13	3/4	2/21	3/11	3/1	2/18
Hanukkah (first day)	(8.43), 134	12/25	12/13	12/3	12/23	12/11	11/29	12/19	12/8
Hindu Lunar New Year	(20.53), 365	4/8	3/29	3/18	4/6	3/25	4/13	4/2	3/22
Icelandic Summer	(6.2), 100	4/21	4/20	4/19	4/25	4/23	4/22	4/21	4/20
Icelandic Winter	(6.3), 100	10/22	10/21	10/27	10/26	10/24	10/23	10/22	10/28
Kajeng Keliwon (first)	(12.16), 190	1/6	1/15	1/10	1/5	1/15	1/9	1/4	1/14
Losar	(21.9), 381	2/9	2/27	2/16	2/5	2/24	2/12	3/3	2/21
Mawlid	(7.6), 109	12/12	12/1	11/21	11/10	10/29	10/19	10/8	9/27
Mesha Saṃkrānti (date)	(20.51), 364	4/13	4/14	4/14	4/14	4/13	4/14	4/14	4/14
Nowruz	(15.11), 265	3/20	3/21	3/21	3/21	3/20	3/21	3/21	3/21
Observ. Hebrew 1 Nisan	(18.22), 297	3/11	3/30	3/19	3/8	3/26	3/15	4/3	3/23
Passover	(8.31), 129	4/23	4/11	3/31	4/20	4/9	3/28	4/16	4/6
Passover Eve (Classical)	(18.25), 298	3/24	4/12	4/1	3/21	4/8	3/28	4/16	4/5
Pentecost	(9.4), 152	5/15	6/4	5/20	6/9	5/31	5/23	6/5	5/28
Purim	(8.33), 129	3/24	3/12	3/1	3/21	3/10	2/26	3/17	3/7
Qīngmíng	(19.28), 324	4/4	4/4	4/5	4/5	4/4	4/4	4/5	4/5
Sacred Wednesday (first)	(20.65), 370	3/16	5/3	10/17	2/13	4/1	10/13	2/9	3/29
Sh'ela	(8.37), 131	12/5	12/5	12/5	12/6	12/5	12/5	12/5	12/6
Ta'anit Esther	(8.34), 130	3/23	3/9	2/28	3/20	3/9	2/25	3/16	3/6
Tishah be-Av	(8.35), 130	8/14	8/1	7/22	8/11	7/30	7/18	8/7	7/27
Tumpek (first)	(12.17), 190	1/16	2/4	1/20	1/5	1/25	1/9	1/29	1/14
U.S. Daylight Saving End	(2.40), 70	11/6	11/5	11/4	11/3	11/1	11/7	11/6	11/5
U.S. Daylight Saving Start	(2.39), 70	3/13	3/12	3/11	3/10	3/8	3/14	3/13	3/12
U.S. Election Day	(2.38), 70	11/8	11/7	11/6	11/5	11/3	11/2	11/8	11/7
U.S. Independence Day	(2.32), 69	7/4	7/4	7/4	7/4	7/4	7/4	7/4	7/4
U.S. Labor Day	(2.36), 69	9/5	9/4	9/3	9/2	9/7	9/6	9/5	9/4
U.S. Memorial Day	(2.37), 70	5/30	5/29	5/28	5/27	5/25	5/31	5/30	5/29
Yom ha-Zikkaron	(8.36), 131	5/11	5/1	4/18	5/8	4/28	4/14	5/4	4/25
Yom Kippur	(8.30), 128	10/12	9/30	9/19	10/9	9/28	9/16	10/5	9/25

Holiday	Func., page	2024	2025	2026	2027	2028	2029	2030	2031
Advent Sunday	(2.42), 70	12/1	11/30	11/29	11/28	12/3	12/2	12/1	11/30
Bahá'í New Year	(16.10), 277	3/21	3/21	3/21	3/21	3/21	3/21	3/21	3/21
Birkath ha-Hama	(8.38), 131	*none*	*none*	*none*	*none*	*none*	*none*	*none*	*none*
Birth of the Bāb	(16.13), 278	11/2	10/22	11/10	10/30	10/19	11/7	10/28	10/17
Birthday of Rama	(20.61), 369	4/17	4/6	3/26	4/15	4/3	4/22	4/12	4/1
Chinese New Year	(19.26), 322	2/10	1/29	2/17	2/6	1/26	2/13	2/3	1/23
Christmas	(2.41), 70	12/25	12/25	12/25	12/25	12/25	12/25	12/25	12/25
Christmas (Coptic)	(4.9), 93	1/8	1/7	1/7	1/7	1/8	1/7	1/7	1/7
Christmas (Orthodox)	(3.25), 85	1/7	1/7	1/7	1/7	1/7	1/7	1/7	1/7
Diwali	(20.57), 368	11/2	10/22	11/10	10/30	11/17	11/7	10/27	11/15
Dragon Festival	(19.27), 324	6/10	5/31	6/19	6/9	5/28	6/16	6/5	6/24
Easter	(9.3), 148	3/31	4/20	4/5	3/28	4/16	4/1	4/21	4/13
Easter (Astronomical)	(18.9), 292	3/31	4/20	4/5	3/28	4/16	4/1	4/21	4/13
Easter (Orthodox)	(9.1), 146	5/5	4/20	4/12	5/2	4/16	4/8	4/28	4/13
Epiphany	(2.43), 71	1/7	1/5	1/4	1/3	1/2	1/7	1/6	1/5
Feast of Naw-Rūz	(16.11), 277	3/20	3/20	3/20	3/21	3/20	3/20	3/20	3/21
Feast of Riḍvān	(16.12), 277	4/20	4/20	4/20	4/21	4/20	4/20	4/20	4/21
Friday the 13th (first)	(2.45), 71	9/13	6/13	2/13	8/13	10/13	4/13	9/13	6/13
Great Night of Shiva	(20.60), 369	3/8	2/26	2/15	3/6	2/23	2/11	3/2	2/20
Hanukkah (first day)	(8.43), 134	12/26	12/15	12/5	12/25	12/13	12/2	12/21	12/10
Hindu Lunar New Year	(20.53), 365	4/9	3/30	3/19	4/7	3/27	3/16	4/3	3/24
Icelandic Summer	(6.2), 100	4/25	4/24	4/23	4/22	4/20	4/19	4/25	4/24
Icelandic Winter	(6.3), 100	10/26	10/25	10/24	10/23	10/21	10/27	10/26	10/25
Kajeng Keliwon (first)	(12.16), 190	1/9	1/3	1/13	1/8	1/3	1/12	1/7	1/2
Losar	(21.9), 381	2/10	2/28	2/18	2/7	2/26	2/14	3/5	2/22
Mawlid	(7.6), 109	9/16	9/5	8/26	8/15	8/3	7/24	7/13	7/2
Mesha Saṃkrānti (date)	(20.51), 364	4/13	4/14	4/14	4/14	4/13	4/14	4/14	4/14
Nowruz	(15.11), 265	3/20	3/21	3/21	3/21	3/20	3/20	3/21	3/21
Observ. Hebrew 1 Nisan	(18.22), 297	3/12	3/31	3/21	3/10	3/28	3/17	3/6	3/25
Passover	(8.31), 129	4/23	4/13	4/2	4/22	4/11	3/31	4/18	4/8
Passover Eve (Classical)	(18.25), 298	3/25	4/13	4/3	3/23	4/10	3/30	3/19	4/7
Pentecost	(9.4), 152	5/19	6/8	5/24	5/16	6/4	5/20	6/9	6/1
Purim	(8.33), 129	3/24	3/14	3/3	3/23	3/12	3/1	3/19	3/9
Qīngmíng	(19.28), 324	4/4	4/4	4/5	4/5	4/4	4/4	4/5	4/5
Sacred Wednesday (first)	(20.65), 370	9/11	2/5	7/22	4/14	1/5	2/21	8/7	1/1
Sh'ela	(8.37), 131	12/5	12/5	12/5	12/6	12/5	12/5	12/5	12/6
Ta'anit Esther	(8.34), 130	3/21	3/13	3/2	3/22	3/9	2/28	3/18	3/6
Tishah be-Av	(8.35), 130	8/13	8/3	7/23	8/12	8/1	7/22	8/8	7/29
Tumpek (first)	(12.17), 190	2/3	1/18	1/3	1/23	1/8	1/27	1/12	2/1
U.S. Daylight Saving End	(2.40), 70	11/3	11/2	11/1	11/7	11/5	11/4	11/3	11/2
U.S. Daylight Saving Start	(2.39), 70	3/10	3/9	3/8	3/14	3/12	3/11	3/10	3/9
U.S. Election Day	(2.38), 70	11/5	11/4	11/3	11/2	11/7	11/6	11/5	11/4
U.S. Independence Day	(2.32), 69	7/4	7/4	7/4	7/4	7/4	7/4	7/4	7/4
U.S. Labor Day	(2.36), 69	9/2	9/1	9/7	9/6	9/4	9/3	9/2	9/1
U.S. Memorial Day	(2.37), 70	5/27	5/26	5/25	5/31	5/29	5/28	5/27	5/26
Yom ha-Zikkaron	(8.36), 131	5/13	4/30	4/21	5/11	5/1	4/18	5/7	4/28
Yom Kippur	(8.30), 128	10/12	10/2	9/21	10/11	9/30	9/19	10/7	9/27

Holiday	Func., page	2032	2033	2034	2035	2036	2037	2038	2039
Advent Sunday	(2.42), 70	11/28	11/27	12/3	12/2	11/30	11/29	11/28	11/27
Bahá'í New Year	(16.10), 277	3/21	3/21	3/21	3/21	3/21	3/21	3/21	3/21
Birkath ha-Hama	(8.38), 131	*none*	*none*	*none*	*none*	*none*	4/8	*none*	*none*
Birth of the Bāb	(16.13), 278	11/4	10/24	11/12	11/1	10/20	11/8	10/29	10/19
Birthday of Rama	(20.61), 369	4/18	4/8	3/28	4/16	4/5	3/25	4/13	4/2
Chinese New Year	(19.26), 322	2/11	1/31	2/19	2/8	1/28	2/15	2/4	1/24
Christmas	(2.41), 70	12/25	12/25	12/25	12/25	12/25	12/25	12/25	12/25
Christmas (Coptic)	(4.9), 93	1/8	1/7	1/7	1/7	1/8	1/7	1/7	1/7
Christmas (Orthodox)	(3.25), 85	1/7	1/7	1/7	1/7	1/7	1/7	1/7	1/7
Diwali	(20.57), 368	11/4	10/24	11/11	11/1	10/20	11/8	10/29	11/17
Dragon Festival	(19.27), 324	6/12	6/1	6/20	6/10	5/30	6/18	6/7	5/27
Easter	(9.3), 148	3/28	4/17	4/9	3/25	4/13	4/5	4/25	4/10
Easter (Astronomical)	(18.9), 292	3/28	4/17	4/9	3/25	4/13	4/5	3/28	4/10
Easter (Orthodox)	(9.1), 146	5/2	4/24	4/9	4/29	4/20	4/5	4/25	4/17
Epiphany	(2.43), 71	1/4	1/2	1/8	1/7	1/6	1/4	1/3	1/2
Feast of Naw-Rūz	(16.11), 277	3/20	3/20	3/20	3/21	3/20	3/20	3/20	3/21
Feast of Riḍvān	(16.12), 277	4/20	4/20	4/20	4/21	4/20	4/20	4/20	4/21
Friday the 13th (first)	(2.45), 71	2/13	5/13	1/13	4/13	6/13	2/13	8/13	5/13
Great Night of Shiva	(20.60), 369	3/10	2/27	2/17	3/8	2/25	2/13	3/4	2/21
Hanukkah (first day)	(8.43), 134	11/28	12/17	12/7	12/26	12/14	12/3	12/22	12/12
Hindu Lunar New Year	(20.53), 365	4/11	3/31	3/21	4/9	3/28	3/17	4/5	3/25
Icelandic Summer	(6.2), 100	4/22	4/21	4/20	4/19	4/24	4/23	4/22	4/21
Icelandic Winter	(6.3), 100	10/23	10/22	10/21	10/27	10/25	10/24	10/23	10/22
Kajeng Keliwon (first)	(12.16), 190	1/12	1/6	1/1	1/11	1/6	1/15	1/10	1/5
Losar	(21.9), 381	2/12	3/2	2/19	2/9	2/27	2/15	3/6	2/23
Mawlid	(7.6), 109	6/21	6/10	5/30	5/20	5/8	4/28	4/17	4/6
Mesha Saṃkrānti (date)	(20.51), 364	4/14	4/14	4/14	4/14	4/14	4/14	4/14	4/14
Nowruz	(15.11), 265	3/20	3/20	3/21	3/21	3/20	3/20	3/21	3/21
Observ. Hebrew 1 Nisan	(18.22), 297	3/13	4/1	3/22	3/12	3/30	3/19	3/8	3/26
Passover	(8.31), 129	3/27	4/14	4/4	4/24	4/12	3/31	4/20	4/9
Passover Eve (Classical)	(18.25), 298	3/26	4/14	4/4	3/25	4/12	4/1	3/21	4/8
Pentecost	(9.4), 152	5/16	6/5	5/28	5/13	6/1	5/24	6/13	5/29
Purim	(8.33), 129	2/26	3/15	3/5	3/25	3/13	3/1	3/21	3/10
Qīngmíng	(19.28), 324	4/4	4/4	4/5	4/5	4/4	4/4	4/5	4/5
Sacred Wednesday (first)	(20.65), 370	2/18	8/3	4/26	1/17	7/30	3/25	1/13	6/29
Sh'ela	(8.37), 131	12/5	12/5	12/5	12/6	12/5	12/5	12/5	12/6
Ta'anit Esther	(8.34), 130	2/25	3/14	3/2	3/22	3/12	2/26	3/18	3/9
Tishah be-Av	(8.35), 130	7/18	8/4	7/25	8/14	8/3	7/21	8/10	7/31
Tumpek (first)	(12.17), 190	1/17	1/1	1/21	1/6	1/26	1/10	1/30	1/15
U.S. Daylight Saving End	(2.40), 70	11/7	11/6	11/5	11/4	11/2	11/1	11/7	11/6
U.S. Daylight Saving Start	(2.39), 70	3/14	3/13	3/12	3/11	3/9	3/8	3/14	3/13
U.S. Election Day	(2.38), 70	11/2	11/8	11/7	11/6	11/4	11/3	11/2	11/8
U.S. Independence Day	(2.32), 69	7/4	7/4	7/4	7/4	7/4	7/4	7/4	7/4
U.S. Labor Day	(2.36), 69	9/6	9/5	9/4	9/3	9/1	9/7	9/6	9/5
U.S. Memorial Day	(2.37), 70	5/31	5/30	5/29	5/28	5/26	5/25	5/31	5/30
Yom ha-Zikkaron	(8.36), 131	4/14	5/3	4/24	5/14	4/30	4/20	5/10	4/27
Yom Kippur	(8.30), 128	9/15	10/3	9/23	10/13	10/1	9/19	10/9	9/28

Holiday	Func., page	2040	2041	2042	2043	2044	2045	2046	2047
Advent Sunday	(2.42), 70	12/2	12/1	11/30	11/29	11/27	12/3	12/2	12/1
Bahá'í New Year	(16.10), 277	3/21	3/21	3/21	3/21	3/21	3/21	3/21	3/21
Birkath ha-Hama	(8.38), 131	*none*	*none*	*none*	*none*	*none*	*none*	*none*	*none*
Birth of the Bāb	(16.13), 278	11/6	10/26	10/15	11/3	10/22	11/10	10/30	10/20
Birthday of Rama	(20.61), 369	4/20	4/9	3/29	4/17	4/6	3/27	4/15	4/4
Chinese New Year	(19.26), 322	2/12	2/1	1/22	2/10	1/30	2/17	2/6	1/26
Christmas	(2.41), 70	12/25	12/25	12/25	12/25	12/25	12/25	12/25	12/25
Christmas (Coptic)	(4.9), 93	1/8	1/7	1/7	1/7	1/8	1/7	1/7	1/7
Christmas (Orthodox)	(3.25), 85	1/7	1/7	1/7	1/7	1/7	1/7	1/7	1/7
Diwali	(20.57), 368	11/5	10/25	11/13	11/2	10/21	11/9	10/30	10/20
Dragon Festival	(19.27), 324	6/14	6/3	6/22	6/11	5/31	6/19	6/8	5/29
Easter	(9.3), 148	4/1	4/21	4/6	3/29	4/17	4/9	3/25	4/14
Easter (Astronomical)	(18.9), 292	4/1	4/21	4/6	3/29	4/17	4/2	3/25	4/14
Easter (Orthodox)	(9.1), 146	5/6	4/21	4/13	5/3	4/24	4/9	4/29	4/21
Epiphany	(2.43), 71	1/8	1/6	1/5	1/4	1/3	1/8	1/7	1/6
Feast of Naw-Rūz	(16.11), 277	3/20	3/20	3/20	3/21	3/20	3/20	3/20	3/21
Feast of Riḍvān	(16.12), 277	4/20	4/20	4/20	4/21	4/20	4/20	4/20	4/21
Friday the 13th (first)	(2.45), 71	1/13	9/13	6/13	2/13	5/13	1/13	4/13	9/13
Great Night of Shiva	(20.60), 369	3/11	3/1	2/18	3/9	2/27	2/15	3/5	2/22
Hanukkah (first day)	(8.43), 134	11/30	12/18	12/8	12/27	12/15	12/4	12/24	12/13
Hindu Lunar New Year	(20.53), 365	4/12	4/1	3/22	4/10	3/30	3/19	4/7	3/27
Icelandic Summer	(6.2), 100	4/19	4/25	4/24	4/23	4/21	4/20	4/19	4/25
Icelandic Winter	(6.3), 100	10/27	10/26	10/25	10/24	10/22	10/21	10/27	10/26
Kajeng Keliwon (first)	(12.16), 190	1/15	1/9	1/4	1/14	1/9	1/3	1/13	1/8
Losar	(21.9), 381	2/13	3/3	2/21	2/10	2/29	2/17	2/6	2/25
Mawlid	(7.6), 109	3/26	3/15	3/4	2/22	2/11	1/31	1/20	1/9
Mesha Saṃkrānti (date)	(20.51), 364	4/14	4/14	4/14	4/14	4/14	4/14	4/14	4/14
Nowruz	(15.11), 265	3/20	3/20	3/21	3/21	3/20	3/20	3/21	3/21
Observ. Hebrew 1 Nisan	(18.22), 297	3/15	4/3	3/23	3/13	3/31	3/20	3/10	3/28
Passover	(8.31), 129	3/29	4/16	4/5	4/25	4/12	4/2	4/21	4/11
Passover Eve (Classical)	(18.25), 298	3/28	4/16	4/5	3/26	4/13	4/2	3/23	4/10
Pentecost	(9.4), 152	5/20	6/9	5/25	5/17	6/5	5/28	5/13	6/2
Purim	(8.33), 129	2/28	3/17	3/6	3/26	3/13	3/3	3/22	3/12
Qīngmíng	(19.28), 324	4/4	4/4	4/4	4/5	4/4	4/4	4/4	4/5
Sacred Wednesday (first)	(20.65), 370	3/21	5/8	1/29	3/18	*none*	5/24	2/14	4/3
Sh'ela	(8.37), 131	12/5	12/5	12/5	12/6	12/5	12/5	12/5	12/6
Ta'anit Esther	(8.34), 130	2/27	3/14	3/5	3/25	3/10	3/2	3/21	3/11
Tishah be-Av	(8.35), 130	7/19	8/6	7/27	8/16	8/2	7/23	8/12	8/1
Tumpek (first)	(12.17), 190	2/4	1/19	1/4	1/24	1/9	1/28	1/13	2/2
U.S. Daylight Saving End	(2.40), 70	11/4	11/3	11/2	11/1	11/6	11/5	11/4	11/3
U.S. Daylight Saving Start	(2.39), 70	3/11	3/10	3/9	3/8	3/13	3/12	3/11	3/10
U.S. Election Day	(2.38), 70	11/6	11/5	11/4	11/3	11/8	11/7	11/6	11/5
U.S. Independence Day	(2.32), 69	7/4	7/4	7/4	7/4	7/4	7/4	7/4	7/4
U.S. Labor Day	(2.36), 69	9/3	9/2	9/1	9/7	9/5	9/4	9/3	9/2
U.S. Memorial Day	(2.37), 70	5/28	5/27	5/26	5/25	5/30	5/29	5/28	5/27
Yom ha-Zikkaron	(8.36), 131	4/17	5/6	4/23	5/13	5/2	4/19	5/9	4/30
Yom Kippur	(8.30), 128	9/17	10/5	9/24	10/14	10/1	9/21	10/10	9/30

Holiday	Func., page	2048	2049	2050	2051	2052	2053	2054	2055
Advent Sunday	(2.42), 70	11/29	11/28	11/27	12/3	12/1	11/30	11/29	11/28
Bahá'í New Year	(16.10), 277	3/21	3/21	3/21	3/21	3/21	3/21	3/21	3/21
Birkath ha-Hama	(8.38), 131	*none*	*none*	*none*	*none*	*none*	*none*	*none*	*none*
Birth of the Bāb	(16.13), 278	11/7	10/28	10/17	11/5	10/24	11/11	11/1	10/21
Birthday of Rama	(20.61), 369	4/22	4/11	3/31	4/19	4/7	3/28	4/16	4/6
Chinese New Year	(19.26), 322	2/14	2/2	1/23	2/11	2/1	2/19	2/8	1/28
Christmas	(2.41), 70	12/25	12/25	12/25	12/25	12/25	12/25	12/25	12/25
Christmas (Coptic)	(4.9), 93	1/8	1/7	1/7	1/7	1/8	1/7	1/7	1/7
Christmas (Orthodox)	(3.25), 85	1/7	1/7	1/7	1/7	1/7	1/7	1/7	1/7
Diwali	(20.57), 368	11/7	10/27	11/15	11/4	10/23	11/11	10/31	10/21
Dragon Festival	(19.27), 324	6/15	6/4	6/23	6/13	6/1	6/20	6/10	5/30
Easter	(9.3), 148	4/5	4/18	4/10	4/2	4/21	4/6	3/29	4/18
Easter (Astronomical)	(18.9), 292	4/5	4/25	4/10	4/2	4/21	4/6	3/29	4/18
Easter (Orthodox)	(9.1), 146	4/5	4/25	4/17	5/7	4/21	4/13	5/3	4/18
Epiphany	(2.43), 71	1/5	1/3	1/2	1/8	1/7	1/5	1/4	1/3
Feast of Naw-Rūz	(16.11), 277	3/20	3/20	3/20	3/21	3/20	3/20	3/20	3/21
Feast of Riḍvān	(16.12), 277	4/20	4/20	4/20	4/21	4/20	4/20	4/20	4/21
Friday the 13th (first)	(2.45), 71	3/13	8/13	5/13	1/13	9/13	6/13	2/13	8/13
Great Night of Shiva	(20.60), 369	2/12	3/2	2/20	3/11	2/28	2/16	3/7	2/24
Hanukkah (first day)	(8.43), 134	11/30	12/20	12/10	11/29	12/16	12/6	12/26	12/15
Hindu Lunar New Year	(20.53), 365	4/14	4/3	3/23	4/11	3/31	3/21	4/9	3/29
Icelandic Summer	(6.2), 100	4/23	4/22	4/21	4/20	4/25	4/24	4/23	4/22
Icelandic Winter	(6.3), 100	10/24	10/23	10/22	10/28	10/26	10/25	10/24	10/23
Kajeng Keliwon (first)	(12.16), 190	1/3	1/12	1/7	1/2	1/12	1/6	1/1	1/11
Losar	(21.9), 381	2/14	3/4	2/22	2/12	3/2	2/19	2/8	2/27
Mawlid	(7.6), 109	12/18	12/7	11/27	11/16	11/4	10/25	10/14	10/4
Mesha Saṃkrānti (date)	(20.51), 364	4/14	4/14	4/14	4/14	4/14	4/14	4/14	4/14
Nowruz	(15.11), 265	3/20	3/20	3/21	3/21	3/20	3/20	3/21	3/21
Observ. Hebrew 1 Nisan	(18.22), 297	3/16	3/6	3/25	3/14	4/1	3/22	3/11	3/30
Passover	(8.31), 129	3/29	4/17	4/7	3/28	4/14	4/3	4/23	4/13
Passover Eve (Classical)	(18.25), 298	3/29	3/19	4/7	3/27	4/14	4/4	3/24	4/12
Pentecost	(9.4), 152	5/24	6/6	5/29	5/21	6/9	5/25	5/17	6/6
Purim	(8.33), 129	2/28	3/18	3/8	2/26	3/15	3/4	3/24	3/14
Qīngmíng	(19.28), 324	4/4	4/4	4/4	4/5	4/4	4/4	4/4	4/5
Sacred Wednesday (first)	(20.65), 370	*none*	2/10	3/30	9/13	*none*	2/26	4/15	1/6
Sh'ela	(8.37), 131	12/5	12/5	12/5	12/6	12/5	12/5	12/5	12/6
Ta'anit Esther	(8.34), 130	2/27	3/17	3/7	2/23	3/14	3/3	3/23	3/11
Tishah be-Av	(8.35), 130	7/19	8/8	7/28	7/18	8/4	7/24	8/13	8/3
Tumpek (first)	(12.17), 190	1/18	1/2	1/22	1/7	1/27	1/11	1/31	1/16
U.S. Daylight Saving End	(2.40), 70	11/1	11/7	11/6	11/5	11/3	11/2	11/1	11/7
U.S. Daylight Saving Start	(2.39), 70	3/8	3/14	3/13	3/12	3/10	3/9	3/8	3/14
U.S. Election Day	(2.38), 70	11/3	11/2	11/8	11/7	11/5	11/4	11/3	11/2
U.S. Independence Day	(2.32), 69	7/4	7/4	7/4	7/4	7/4	7/4	7/4	7/4
U.S. Labor Day	(2.36), 69	9/7	9/6	9/5	9/4	9/2	9/1	9/7	9/6
U.S. Memorial Day	(2.37), 70	5/25	5/31	5/30	5/29	5/27	5/26	5/25	5/31
Yom ha-Zikkaron	(8.36), 131	4/15	5/5	4/26	4/17	5/1	4/22	5/12	5/3
Yom Kippur	(8.30), 128	9/17	10/6	9/26	9/16	10/3	9/22	10/12	10/2

Holiday	Func., page	2056	2057	2058	2059	2060	2061	2062	2063
Advent Sunday	(2.42), 70	12/3	12/2	12/1	11/30	11/28	11/27	12/3	12/2
Bahá'í New Year	(16.10), 277	3/21	3/21	3/21	3/21	3/21	3/21	3/21	3/21
Birkath ha-Hama	(8.38), 131	*none*	*none*	*none*	*none*	*none*	*none*	*none*	*none*
Birth of the Bāb	(16.13), 278	11/8	10/29	10/18	11/6	10/25	10/14	11/2	10/23
Birthday of Rama	(20.61), 369	3/25	4/13	4/2	4/21	4/9	3/29	4/17	4/7
Chinese New Year	(19.26), 322	2/15	2/4	1/24	2/12	2/2	1/21	2/9	1/29
Christmas	(2.41), 70	12/25	12/25	12/25	12/25	12/25	12/25	12/25	12/25
Christmas (Coptic)	(4.9), 93	1/8	1/7	1/7	1/7	1/8	1/7	1/7	1/7
Christmas (Orthodox)	(3.25), 85	1/7	1/7	1/7	1/7	1/7	1/7	1/7	1/7
Diwali	(20.57), 368	11/8	10/29	11/17	11/6	10/25	11/13	11/2	10/22
Dragon Festival	(19.27), 324	6/17	6/6	6/25	6/14	6/3	6/22	6/11	6/1
Easter	(9.3), 148	4/2	4/22	4/14	3/30	4/18	4/10	3/26	4/15
Easter (Astronomical)	(18.9), 292	4/2	3/25	4/14	3/30	4/18	4/10	3/26	4/15
Easter (Orthodox)	(9.1), 146	4/9	4/29	4/14	5/4	4/25	4/10	4/30	4/22
Epiphany	(2.43), 71	1/2	1/7	1/6	1/5	1/4	1/2	1/8	1/7
Feast of Naw-Rūz	(16.11), 277	3/20	3/20	3/20	3/20	3/20	3/20	3/20	3/20
Feast of Riḍvān	(16.12), 277	4/20	4/20	4/20	4/20	4/20	4/20	4/20	4/20
Friday the 13th (first)	(2.45), 71	10/13	4/13	9/13	6/13	2/13	5/13	1/13	4/13
Great Night of Shiva	(20.60), 369	2/13	3/3	2/21	3/12	3/1	2/18	3/9	2/26
Hanukkah (first day)	(8.43), 134	12/3	12/22	12/11	11/30	12/18	12/8	12/27	12/16
Hindu Lunar New Year	(20.53), 365	3/17	4/4	3/25	4/13	4/1	3/22	4/10	3/30
Icelandic Summer	(6.2), 100	4/20	4/19	4/25	4/24	4/22	4/21	4/20	4/19
Icelandic Winter	(6.3), 100	10/21	10/27	10/26	10/25	10/23	10/22	10/21	10/27
Kajeng Keliwon (first)	(12.16), 190	1/6	1/15	1/10	1/5	1/15	1/9	1/4	1/14
Losar	(21.9), 381	2/16	3/6	2/23	2/13	3/3	2/21	2/10	3/1
Mawlid	(7.6), 109	9/22	9/11	9/1	8/21	8/9	7/30	7/19	7/8
Mesha Saṃkrānti (date)	(20.51), 364	4/14	4/14	4/14	4/15	4/14	4/14	4/14	4/15
Nowruz	(15.11), 265	3/20	3/20	3/21	3/21	3/20	3/20	3/20	3/21
Observ. Hebrew 1 Nisan	(18.22), 297	3/18	3/7	3/26	3/16	4/3	3/23	3/13	4/1
Passover	(8.31), 129	4/1	4/19	4/9	3/29	4/15	4/5	4/25	4/14
Passover Eve (Classical)	(18.25), 298	3/31	3/20	4/8	3/29	4/16	4/5	3/26	4/14
Pentecost	(9.4), 152	5/21	6/10	6/2	5/18	6/6	5/29	5/14	6/3
Purim	(8.33), 129	3/2	3/20	3/10	2/27	3/16	3/6	3/26	3/15
Qīngmíng	(19.28), 324	4/4	4/4	4/4	4/5	4/4	4/4	4/4	4/5
Sacred Wednesday (first)	(20.65), 370	2/23	8/8	1/2	6/18	8/4	4/27	1/18	11/28
Sh'ela	(8.37), 131	12/5	12/5	12/5	12/6	12/5	12/5	12/5	12/6
Ta'anit Esther	(8.34), 130	3/1	3/19	3/7	2/26	3/15	3/3	3/23	3/14
Tishah be-Av	(8.35), 130	7/23	8/9	7/30	7/20	8/5	7/26	8/15	8/5
Tumpek (first)	(12.17), 190	1/1	1/20	1/5	1/25	1/10	1/29	1/14	2/3
U.S. Daylight Saving End	(2.40), 70	11/5	11/4	11/3	11/2	11/7	11/6	11/5	11/4
U.S. Daylight Saving Start	(2.39), 70	3/12	3/11	3/10	3/9	3/14	3/13	3/12	3/11
U.S. Election Day	(2.38), 70	11/7	11/6	11/5	11/4	11/2	11/8	11/7	11/6
U.S. Independence Day	(2.32), 69	7/4	7/4	7/4	7/4	7/4	7/4	7/4	7/4
U.S. Labor Day	(2.36), 69	9/4	9/3	9/2	9/1	9/6	9/5	9/4	9/3
U.S. Memorial Day	(2.37), 70	5/29	5/28	5/27	5/26	5/31	5/30	5/29	5/28
Yom ha-Zikkaron	(8.36), 131	4/19	5/8	4/29	4/16	5/4	4/25	5/15	5/2
Yom Kippur	(8.30), 128	9/20	10/8	9/28	9/17	10/4	9/24	10/14	10/3

Holiday	Func., page	2064	2065	2066	2067	2068	2069	2070	2071
Advent Sunday	(2.42), 70	11/30	11/29	11/28	11/27	12/2	12/1	11/30	11/29
Bahá'í New Year	(16.10), 277	3/21	3/21	3/21	3/21	3/21	3/21	3/21	3/21
Birkath ha-Hama	(8.38), 131	*none*	4/8	*none*	*none*	*none*	*none*	*none*	*none*
Birth of the Bāb	(16.13), 278	11/10	10/30	10/20	11/8	10/27	10/16	11/4	10/24
Birthday of Rama	(20.61), 369	3/26	4/14	4/4	4/22	4/10	3/31	4/19	4/8
Chinese New Year	(19.26), 322	2/17	2/5	1/26	2/14	2/3	1/23	2/11	1/31
Christmas	(2.41), 70	12/25	12/25	12/25	12/25	12/25	12/25	12/25	12/25
Christmas (Coptic)	(4.9), 93	1/8	1/7	1/7	1/7	1/8	1/7	1/7	1/7
Christmas (Orthodox)	(3.25), 85	1/7	1/7	1/7	1/7	1/7	1/7	1/7	1/7
Diwali	(20.57), 368	11/9	10/30	10/19	11/7	10/27	11/14	11/3	10/24
Dragon Festival	(19.27), 324	6/19	6/8	5/28	6/16	6/4	6/23	6/13	6/2
Easter	(9.3), 148	4/6	3/29	4/11	4/3	4/22	4/14	3/30	4/19
Easter (Astronomical)	(18.9), 292	4/6	3/29	4/11	4/3	4/22	4/7	3/30	4/19
Easter (Orthodox)	(9.1), 146	4/13	4/26	4/18	4/10	4/29	4/14	5/4	4/19
Epiphany	(2.43), 71	1/6	1/4	1/3	1/2	1/8	1/6	1/5	1/4
Feast of Naw-Rūz	(16.11), 277	3/20	3/20	3/20	3/20	3/20	3/20	3/20	3/20
Feast of Riḍvān	(16.12), 277	4/20	4/20	4/20	4/20	4/20	4/20	4/20	4/20
Friday the 13th (first)	(2.45), 71	6/13	2/13	8/13	5/13	1/13	9/13	6/13	2/13
Great Night of Shiva	(20.60), 369	2/15	3/5	2/22	2/12	3/2	2/19	3/10	2/28
Hanukkah (first day)	(8.43), 134	12/4	12/23	12/13	12/2	12/19	12/9	11/28	12/17
Hindu Lunar New Year	(20.53), 365	3/18	4/6	3/26	4/14	4/3	3/23	4/11	4/1
Icelandic Summer	(6.2), 100	4/24	4/23	4/22	4/21	4/19	4/25	4/24	4/23
Icelandic Winter	(6.3), 100	10/25	10/24	10/23	10/22	10/27	10/26	10/25	10/24
Kajeng Keliwon (first)	(12.16), 190	1/9	1/3	1/13	1/8	1/3	1/12	1/7	1/2
Losar	(21.9), 381	2/18	2/6	2/25	2/14	3/4	2/22	2/11	3/2
Mawlid	(7.6), 109	6/27	6/16	6/6	5/26	5/14	5/4	4/23	4/12
Mesha Saṃkrānti (date)	(20.51), 364	4/14	4/14	4/14	4/15	4/14	4/14	4/14	4/15
Nowruz	(15.11), 265	3/20	3/20	3/20	3/21	3/20	3/20	3/20	3/21
Observ. Hebrew 1 Nisan	(18.22), 297	3/20	3/9	3/28	3/17	4/4	3/25	3/14	4/2
Passover	(8.31), 129	4/1	4/21	4/10	3/31	4/17	4/6	3/27	4/14
Passover Eve (Classical)	(18.25), 298	4/2	3/22	4/10	3/30	4/17	4/7	3/27	4/15
Pentecost	(9.4), 152	5/25	5/17	5/30	5/22	6/10	6/2	5/18	6/7
Purim	(8.33), 129	3/2	3/22	3/11	3/1	3/18	3/7	2/25	3/15
Qīngmíng	(19.28), 324	4/4	4/4	4/4	4/5	4/4	4/4	4/4	4/5
Sacred Wednesday (first)	(20.65), 370	3/26	1/14	11/24	3/23	5/9	1/30	*none*	4/8
Sh'ela	(8.37), 131	12/5	12/5	12/5	12/6	12/5	12/5	12/5	12/6
Ta'anit Esther	(8.34), 130	2/28	3/19	3/10	2/28	3/15	3/6	2/24	3/12
Tishah be-Av	(8.35), 130	7/22	8/11	8/1	7/21	8/7	7/28	7/17	8/4
Tumpek (first)	(12.17), 190	1/19	1/3	1/23	1/8	1/28	1/12	2/1	1/17
U.S. Daylight Saving End	(2.40), 70	11/2	11/1	11/7	11/6	11/4	11/3	11/2	11/1
U.S. Daylight Saving Start	(2.39), 70	3/9	3/8	3/14	3/13	3/11	3/10	3/9	3/8
U.S. Election Day	(2.38), 70	11/4	11/3	11/2	11/8	11/6	11/5	11/4	11/3
U.S. Independence Day	(2.32), 69	7/4	7/4	7/4	7/4	7/4	7/4	7/4	7/4
U.S. Labor Day	(2.36), 69	9/1	9/7	9/6	9/5	9/3	9/2	9/1	9/7
U.S. Memorial Day	(2.37), 70	5/26	5/25	5/31	5/30	5/28	5/27	5/26	5/25
Yom ha-Zikkaron	(8.36), 131	4/21	5/11	4/28	4/19	5/7	4/24	4/15	5/4
Yom Kippur	(8.30), 128	9/20	10/10	9/29	9/19	10/6	9/25	9/15	10/3

Holiday	Func., page	2072	2073	2074	2075	2076	2077	2078	2079
Advent Sunday	(2.42), 70	11/27	12/3	12/2	12/1	11/29	11/28	11/27	12/3
Bahá'í New Year	(16.10), 277	3/21	3/21	3/21	3/21	3/21	3/21	3/21	3/21
Birkath ha-Hama	(8.38), 131	*none*	*none*	*none*	*none*	*none*	*none*	*none*	*none*
Birth of the Bāb	(16.13), 278	11/11	11/1	10/21	11/9	10/29	10/18	11/6	10/26
Birthday of Rama	(20.61), 369	3/28	4/16	4/5	3/25	4/12	4/1	4/20	4/9
Chinese New Year	(19.26), 322	2/19	2/7	1/27	2/15	2/5	1/24	2/12	2/2
Christmas	(2.41), 70	12/25	12/25	12/25	12/25	12/25	12/25	12/25	12/25
Christmas (Coptic)	(4.9), 93	1/8	1/7	1/7	1/7	1/8	1/7	1/7	1/7
Christmas (Orthodox)	(3.25), 85	1/7	1/7	1/7	1/7	1/7	1/7	1/7	1/7
Diwali	(20.57), 368	11/11	10/31	10/21	11/9	10/28	11/16	11/5	10/25
Dragon Festival	(19.27), 324	6/20	6/10	5/30	6/17	6/6	6/24	6/14	6/4
Easter	(9.3), 148	4/10	3/26	4/15	4/7	4/19	4/11	4/3	4/23
Easter (Astronomical)	(18.9), 292	4/10	3/26	4/15	4/7	3/22	4/11	4/3	4/23
Easter (Orthodox)	(9.1), 146	4/10	4/30	4/22	4/7	4/26	4/18	5/8	4/23
Epiphany	(2.43), 71	1/3	1/8	1/7	1/6	1/5	1/3	1/2	1/8
Feast of Naw-Rūz	(16.11), 277	3/20	3/20	3/20	3/20	3/20	3/20	3/20	3/20
Feast of Riḍvān	(16.12), 277	4/20	4/20	4/20	4/20	4/20	4/20	4/20	4/20
Friday the 13th (first)	(2.45), 71	5/13	1/13	4/13	9/13	3/13	8/13	5/13	1/13
Great Night of Shiva	(20.60), 369	2/17	3/6	2/24	2/13	3/3	2/21	3/12	3/1
Hanukkah (first day)	(8.43), 134	12/5	12/25	12/14	12/2	12/21	12/11	11/30	12/18
Hindu Lunar New Year	(20.53), 365	3/20	4/8	3/28	3/17	4/4	3/25	4/13	4/2
Icelandic Summer	(6.2), 100	4/21	4/20	4/19	4/25	4/23	4/22	4/21	4/20
Icelandic Winter	(6.3), 100	10/22	10/21	10/27	10/26	10/24	10/23	10/22	10/28
Kajeng Keliwon (first)	(12.16), 190	1/12	1/6	1/1	1/11	1/6	1/15	1/10	1/5
Losar	(21.9), 381	2/19	2/7	2/26	2/16	3/6	2/23	2/13	3/4
Mawlid	(7.6), 109	4/1	3/21	3/11	2/28	2/17	2/6	1/26	1/15
Mesha Saṃkrānti (date)	(20.51), 364	4/14	4/14	4/14	4/15	4/14	4/14	4/14	4/15
Nowruz	(15.11), 265	3/20	3/20	3/20	3/21	3/20	3/20	3/20	3/21
Observ. Hebrew 1 Nisan	(18.22), 297	3/22	3/11	3/29	3/18	3/7	3/26	3/16	4/4
Passover	(8.31), 129	4/3	4/22	4/12	3/31	4/18	4/8	3/29	4/16
Passover Eve (Classical)	(18.25), 298	4/4	3/24	4/11	3/31	3/20	4/8	3/29	4/17
Pentecost	(9.4), 152	5/29	5/14	6/3	5/26	6/7	5/30	5/22	6/11
Purim	(8.33), 129	3/4	3/23	3/13	3/1	3/19	3/9	2/27	3/17
Qīngmíng	(19.28), 324	4/4	4/4	4/4	4/4	4/4	4/4	4/4	4/4
Sacred Wednesday (first)	(20.65), 370	5/25	2/15	*none*	9/18	2/12	3/31	9/14	1/11
Sh'ela	(8.37), 131	12/5	12/5	12/5	12/6	12/5	12/5	12/5	12/6
Ta'anit Esther	(8.34), 130	3/3	3/22	3/12	2/28	3/18	3/8	2/24	3/16
Tishah be-Av	(8.35), 130	7/24	8/13	8/2	7/21	8/9	7/29	7/19	8/6
Tumpek (first)	(12.17), 190	1/2	1/21	1/6	1/26	1/11	1/30	1/15	2/4
U.S. Daylight Saving End	(2.40), 70	11/6	11/5	11/4	11/3	11/1	11/7	11/6	11/5
U.S. Daylight Saving Start	(2.39), 70	3/13	3/12	3/11	3/10	3/8	3/14	3/13	3/12
U.S. Election Day	(2.38), 70	11/8	11/7	11/6	11/5	11/3	11/2	11/8	11/7
U.S. Independence Day	(2.32), 69	7/4	7/4	7/4	7/4	7/4	7/4	7/4	7/4
U.S. Labor Day	(2.36), 69	9/5	9/4	9/3	9/2	9/7	9/6	9/5	9/4
U.S. Memorial Day	(2.37), 70	5/30	5/29	5/28	5/27	5/25	5/31	5/30	5/29
Yom ha-Zikkaron	(8.36), 131	4/20	5/10	5/1	4/17	5/6	4/27	4/18	5/3
Yom Kippur	(8.30), 128	9/22	10/11	10/1	9/19	10/7	9/27	9/17	10/5

Holiday	Func., page	2080	2081	2082	2083	2084	2085	2086	2087
Advent Sunday	(2.42), 70	12/1	11/30	11/29	11/28	12/3	12/2	12/1	11/30
Bahá'í New Year	(16.10), 277	3/21	3/21	3/21	3/21	3/21	3/21	3/21	3/21
Birkath ha-Hama	(8.38), 131	*none*	*none*	*none*	*none*	*none*	*none*	*none*	*none*
Birth of the Bāb	(16.13), 278	10/14	11/2	10/23	11/11	10/30	10/20	11/7	10/27
Birthday of Rama	(20.61), 369	3/29	4/17	4/7	3/27	4/14	4/3	4/22	4/11
Chinese New Year	(19.26), 322	1/22	2/9	1/29	2/17	2/6	1/26	2/14	2/3
Christmas	(2.41), 70	12/25	12/25	12/25	12/25	12/25	12/25	12/25	12/25
Christmas (Coptic)	(4.9), 93	1/8	1/7	1/7	1/7	1/8	1/7	1/7	1/7
Christmas (Orthodox)	(3.25), 85	1/7	1/7	1/7	1/7	1/7	1/7	1/7	1/7
Diwali	(20.57), 368	11/12	11/1	10/22	11/10	10/30	11/18	11/7	10/27
Dragon Festival	(19.27), 324	6/22	6/11	6/1	6/19	6/7	5/27	6/15	6/5
Easter	(9.3), 148	4/7	3/30	4/19	4/4	3/26	4/15	3/31	4/20
Easter (Astronomical)	(18.9), 292	4/7	3/30	4/19	4/4	3/26	4/15	3/31	4/20
Easter (Orthodox)	(9.1), 146	4/14	5/4	4/19	4/11	4/30	4/15	4/7	4/27
Epiphany	(2.43), 71	1/7	1/5	1/4	1/3	1/2	1/7	1/6	1/5
Feast of Naw-Rūz	(16.11), 277	3/20	3/20	3/20	3/20	3/20	3/20	3/20	3/20
Feast of Riḍvān	(16.12), 277	4/20	4/20	4/20	4/20	4/20	4/20	4/20	4/20
Friday the 13th (first)	(2.45), 71	9/13	6/13	2/13	8/13	10/13	4/13	9/13	6/13
Great Night of Shiva	(20.60), 369	2/18	3/8	2/25	2/15	3/5	2/22	2/12	3/3
Hanukkah (first day)	(8.43), 134	12/7	12/27	12/16	12/5	12/23	12/12	12/1	12/20
Hindu Lunar New Year	(20.53), 365	3/22	4/10	3/30	3/19	4/6	3/26	4/14	4/4
Icelandic Summer	(6.2), 100	4/25	4/24	4/23	4/22	4/20	4/19	4/25	4/24
Icelandic Winter	(6.3), 100	10/26	10/25	10/24	10/23	10/21	10/27	10/26	10/25
Kajeng Keliwon (first)	(12.16), 190	1/15	1/9	1/4	1/14	1/9	1/3	1/13	1/8
Losar	(21.9), 381	2/21	2/9	2/28	2/17	2/7	2/25	2/14	3/5
Mawlid	(7.6), 109	1/5	12/13	12/3	11/22	11/11	10/31	10/20	10/10
Mesha Saṃkrānti (date)	(20.51), 364	4/14	4/14	4/14	4/15	4/14	4/14	4/14	4/15
Nowruz	(15.11), 265	3/20	3/20	3/20	3/21	3/20	3/20	3/20	3/21
Observ. Hebrew 1 Nisan	(18.22), 297	3/23	3/12	3/31	3/20	3/8	3/27	3/17	3/7
Passover	(8.31), 129	4/4	4/24	4/14	4/3	4/20	4/10	3/30	4/17
Passover Eve (Classical)	(18.25), 298	4/5	3/25	4/13	4/2	3/21	4/9	3/30	3/20
Pentecost	(9.4), 152	5/26	5/18	6/7	5/23	5/14	6/3	5/19	6/8
Purim	(8.33), 129	3/5	3/25	3/15	3/4	3/21	3/11	2/28	3/18
Qīngmíng	(19.28), 324	4/4	4/4	4/4	4/4	4/4	4/4	4/4	4/4
Sacred Wednesday (first)	(20.65), 370	2/28	9/10	1/7	6/23	8/9	1/3	6/19	3/12
Sh'ela	(8.37), 131	12/5	12/5	12/5	12/6	12/5	12/5	12/5	12/6
Ta'anit Esther	(8.34), 130	3/4	3/24	3/12	3/3	3/20	3/8	2/27	3/17
Tishah be-Av	(8.35), 130	7/25	8/14	8/4	7/25	8/10	7/31	7/21	8/7
Tumpek (first)	(12.17), 190	1/20	1/4	1/24	1/9	1/29	1/13	2/2	1/18
U.S. Daylight Saving End	(2.40), 70	11/3	11/2	11/1	11/7	11/5	11/4	11/3	11/2
U.S. Daylight Saving Start	(2.39), 70	3/10	3/9	3/8	3/14	3/12	3/11	3/10	3/9
U.S. Election Day	(2.38), 70	11/5	11/4	11/3	11/2	11/7	11/6	11/5	11/4
U.S. Independence Day	(2.32), 69	7/4	7/4	7/4	7/4	7/4	7/4	7/4	7/4
U.S. Labor Day	(2.36), 69	9/2	9/1	9/7	9/6	9/4	9/3	9/2	9/1
U.S. Memorial Day	(2.37), 70	5/27	5/26	5/25	5/31	5/29	5/28	5/27	5/26
Yom ha-Zikkaron	(8.36), 131	4/23	5/13	5/4	4/21	5/9	4/30	4/17	5/6
Yom Kippur	(8.30), 128	9/23	10/13	10/3	9/22	10/9	9/29	9/18	10/6

Holiday	Func., page	2088	2089	2090	2091	2092	2093	2094	2095
Advent Sunday	(2.42), 70	11/28	11/27	12/3	12/2	11/30	11/29	11/28	11/27
Bahá'í New Year	(16.10), 277	3/21	3/21	3/21	3/21	3/21	3/21	3/21	3/21
Birkath ha-Hama	(8.38), 131	*none*	*none*	*none*	*none*	*none*	4/8	*none*	*none*
Birth of the Bāb	(16.13), 278	10/16	11/3	10/24	11/12	11/1	10/21	11/9	10/29
Birthday of Rama	(20.61), 369	3/30	4/18	4/8	3/29	4/16	4/5	3/25	4/12
Chinese New Year	(19.26), 322	1/24	2/10	1/30	2/18	2/7	1/27	2/15	2/5
Christmas	(2.41), 70	12/25	12/25	12/25	12/25	12/25	12/25	12/25	12/25
Christmas (Coptic)	(4.9), 93	1/8	1/7	1/7	1/7	1/8	1/7	1/7	1/7
Christmas (Orthodox)	(3.25), 85	1/7	1/7	1/7	1/7	1/7	1/7	1/7	1/7
Diwali	(20.57), 368	11/14	11/3	10/23	11/12	10/31	10/21	11/9	10/29
Dragon Festival	(19.27), 324	6/23	6/13	6/2	6/21	6/9	5/29	6/17	6/6
Easter	(9.3), 148	4/11	4/3	4/16	4/8	3/30	4/12	4/4	4/24
Easter (Astronomical)	(18.9), 292	4/11	3/27	4/16	4/8	3/30	4/12	4/4	3/27
Easter (Orthodox)	(9.1), 146	4/18	5/1	4/23	4/8	4/27	4/19	4/11	4/24
Epiphany	(2.43), 71	1/4	1/2	1/8	1/7	1/6	1/4	1/3	1/2
Feast of Naw-Rūz	(16.11), 277	3/20	3/20	3/20	3/20	3/19	3/20	3/20	3/20
Feast of Riḍvān	(16.12), 277	4/20	4/20	4/20	4/20	4/19	4/20	4/20	4/20
Friday the 13th (first)	(2.45), 71	2/13	5/13	1/13	4/13	6/13	2/13	8/13	5/13
Great Night of Shiva	(20.60), 369	2/20	3/10	2/27	2/16	3/6	2/23	2/13	3/4
Hanukkah (first day)	(8.43), 134	12/8	11/28	12/17	12/6	12/24	12/14	12/3	12/21
Hindu Lunar New Year	(20.53), 365	3/23	4/11	4/1	3/21	4/7	3/28	3/17	4/5
Icelandic Summer	(6.2), 100	4/22	4/21	4/20	4/19	4/24	4/23	4/22	4/21
Icelandic Winter	(6.3), 100	10/23	10/22	10/21	10/27	10/25	10/24	10/23	10/22
Kajeng Keliwon (first)	(12.16), 190	1/3	1/12	1/7	1/2	1/12	1/6	1/1	1/11
Losar	(21.9), 381	2/23	2/11	3/2	2/19	2/8	2/26	2/16	3/7
Mawlid	(7.6), 109	9/28	9/17	9/7	8/27	8/15	8/5	7/25	7/15
Mesha Saṃkrānti (date)	(20.51), 364	4/14	4/14	4/15	4/15	4/14	4/14	4/15	4/15
Nowruz	(15.11), 265	3/20	3/20	3/20	3/20	3/20	3/20	3/20	3/20
Observ. Hebrew 1 Nisan	(18.22), 297	3/25	3/14	4/2	3/22	3/10	3/29	3/18	3/8
Passover	(8.31), 129	4/6	3/26	4/15	4/3	4/22	4/11	4/1	4/19
Passover Eve (Classical)	(18.25), 298	4/7	3/27	4/15	4/4	3/23	4/11	3/31	3/21
Pentecost	(9.4), 152	5/30	5/22	6/4	5/27	5/18	5/31	5/23	6/12
Purim	(8.33), 129	3/7	2/24	3/16	3/4	3/23	3/12	3/2	3/20
Qīngmíng	(19.28), 324	4/4	4/4	4/4	4/4	4/4	4/4	4/4	4/4
Sacred Wednesday (first)	(20.65), 370	4/28	*none*	11/29	3/28	5/14	*none*	3/24	5/11
Sh'ela	(8.37), 131	12/5	12/5	12/5	12/6	12/5	12/5	12/5	12/6
Ta'anit Esther	(8.34), 130	3/4	2/23	3/15	3/1	3/20	3/11	3/1	3/17
Tishah be-Av	(8.35), 130	7/27	7/17	8/6	7/24	8/12	8/2	7/22	8/9
Tumpek (first)	(12.17), 190	1/3	1/22	1/7	1/27	1/12	1/31	1/16	1/1
U.S. Daylight Saving End	(2.40), 70	11/7	11/6	11/5	11/4	11/2	11/1	11/7	11/6
U.S. Daylight Saving Start	(2.39), 70	3/14	3/13	3/12	3/11	3/9	3/8	3/14	3/13
U.S. Election Day	(2.38), 70	11/2	11/8	11/7	11/6	11/4	11/3	11/2	11/8
U.S. Independence Day	(2.32), 69	7/4	7/4	7/4	7/4	7/4	7/4	7/4	7/4
U.S. Labor Day	(2.36), 69	9/6	9/5	9/4	9/3	9/1	9/7	9/6	9/5
U.S. Memorial Day	(2.37), 70	5/31	5/30	5/29	5/28	5/26	5/25	5/31	5/30
Yom ha-Zikkaron	(8.36), 131	4/26	4/13	5/3	4/23	5/12	4/29	4/20	5/9
Yom Kippur	(8.30), 128	9/25	9/14	10/4	9/22	10/11	9/30	9/20	10/8

Holiday	Func., page	2096	2097	2098	2099	2100	2101	2102	2103
Advent Sunday	(2.42), 70	12/2	12/1	11/30	11/29	11/28	11/27	12/3	12/2
Bahá'í New Year	(16.10), 277	3/21	3/21	3/21	3/21	3/21	3/21	3/21	3/21
Birkath ha-Hama	(8.38), 131	*none*	*none*	*none*	*none*	*none*	*none*	*none*	*none*
Birth of the Bāb	(16.13), 278	10/17	11/5	10/25	10/15	11/3	10/24	11/12	11/1
Birthday of Rama	(20.61), 369	4/1	4/20	4/9	3/30	4/18	4/7	3/27	4/15
Chinese New Year	(19.26), 322	1/25	2/12	2/1	1/21	2/9	1/29	2/17	2/7
Christmas	(2.41), 70	12/25	12/25	12/25	12/25	12/25	12/25	12/25	12/25
Christmas (Coptic)	(4.9), 93	1/8	1/7	1/7	1/7	1/8	1/8	1/8	1/8
Christmas (Orthodox)	(3.25), 85	1/7	1/7	1/7	1/7	1/7	1/8	1/8	1/8
Diwali	(20.57), 368	11/15	11/4	10/25	11/13	11/2	10/23	11/11	10/31
Dragon Festival	(19.27), 324	6/24	6/14	6/4	6/23	6/12	6/1	6/20	6/9
Easter	(9.3), 148	4/15	3/31	4/20	4/12	3/28	4/17	4/9	3/25
Easter (Astronomical)	(18.9), 292	4/8	3/31	4/20	4/12	3/28	4/17	4/9	3/25
Easter (Orthodox)	(9.1), 146	4/15	5/5	4/27	4/12	5/2	4/24	4/9	4/29
Epiphany	(2.43), 71	1/8	1/6	1/5	1/4	1/3	1/2	1/8	1/7
Feast of Naw-Rūz	(16.11), 277	3/19	3/20	3/20	3/20	3/20	3/21	3/21	3/21
Feast of Riḍvān	(16.12), 277	4/19	4/20	4/20	4/20	4/20	4/21	4/21	4/21
Friday the 13th (first)	(2.45), 71	1/13	9/13	6/13	2/13	8/13	5/13	1/13	4/13
Great Night of Shiva	(20.60), 369	2/22	3/12	3/1	2/18	3/9	2/26	2/15	3/7
Hanukkah (first day)	(8.43), 134	12/10	11/30	12/19	12/7	12/27	12/17	12/6	12/24
Hindu Lunar New Year	(20.53), 365	3/25	4/13	4/2	3/22	4/10	3/30	3/19	4/7
Icelandic Summer	(6.2), 100	4/19	4/25	4/24	4/23	4/22	4/21	4/20	4/19
Icelandic Winter	(6.3), 100	10/27	10/26	10/25	10/24	10/23	10/22	10/21	10/27
Kajeng Keliwon (first)	(12.16), 190	1/6	1/15	1/10	1/5	1/15	1/10	1/5	1/15
Losar	(21.9), 381	2/24	2/13	3/3	2/20	2/10	2/28	2/18	3/9
Mawlid	(7.6), 109	7/3	6/22	6/12	6/1	5/21	5/11	4/30	4/20
Mesha Saṃkrānti (date)	(20.51), 364	4/14	4/14	4/15	4/15	4/15	4/15	4/16	4/16
Nowruz	(15.11), 265	3/20	3/20	3/20	3/20	3/21	3/21	3/21	3/21
Observ. Hebrew 1 Nisan	(18.22), 297	3/26	3/16	4/4	3/24	3/13	3/31	3/21	3/10
Passover	(8.31), 129	4/7	3/28	4/17	4/5	4/24	4/14	4/4	4/22
Passover Eve (Classical)	(18.25), 298	4/8	3/29	4/17	4/6	3/26	4/13	4/3	3/23
Pentecost	(9.4), 152	6/3	5/19	6/8	5/31	5/16	6/5	5/28	5/13
Purim	(8.33), 129	3/8	2/26	3/18	3/6	3/25	3/15	3/5	3/23
Qīngmíng	(19.28), 324	4/4	4/4	4/4	4/4	4/5	4/5	4/5	4/5
Sacred Wednesday (first)	(20.65), 370	2/1	*none*	4/9	5/27	2/17	8/3	9/20	2/14
Sh'ela	(8.37), 131	12/5	12/5	12/5	12/6	12/6	12/6	12/6	12/7
Ta'anit Esther	(8.34), 130	3/7	2/25	3/17	3/5	3/24	3/14	3/2	3/22
Tishah be-Av	(8.35), 130	7/29	7/18	8/7	7/26	8/15	8/4	7/25	8/12
Tumpek (first)	(12.17), 190	1/21	1/5	1/25	1/10	1/30	1/15	2/4	1/20
U.S. Daylight Saving End	(2.40), 70	11/4	11/3	11/2	11/1	11/7	11/6	11/5	11/4
U.S. Daylight Saving Start	(2.39), 70	3/11	3/10	3/9	3/8	3/14	3/13	3/12	3/11
U.S. Election Day	(2.38), 70	11/6	11/5	11/4	11/3	11/2	11/8	11/7	11/6
U.S. Independence Day	(2.32), 69	7/4	7/4	7/4	7/4	7/4	7/4	7/4	7/4
U.S. Labor Day	(2.36), 69	9/3	9/2	9/1	9/7	9/6	9/5	9/4	9/3
U.S. Memorial Day	(2.37), 70	5/28	5/27	5/26	5/25	5/31	5/30	5/29	5/28
Yom ha-Zikkaron	(8.36), 131	4/25	4/16	5/6	4/22	5/12	5/3	4/24	5/9
Yom Kippur	(8.30), 128	9/26	9/16	10/6	9/24	10/13	10/3	9/23	10/11

המבין יבין

Abraham ben David of Posquieres: *Strictures to Maimonides' Mishneh Torah, Gifts to the Poor* (circa 1195)

References

[1] A. P. Bloch, *Day by Day in Jewish History: A Chronology and Calendar of Historic Events*, Ktav Publishing House, New York, 1983.

[2] M. Gilbert, *Atlas of the Holocaust*, Pergamon Press, New York, 1988.

[3] H. H. Graetz, *History of the Jews*, Jewish Publication Society, Philadelphia, 1891.

[4] F. E. Peters, *Jerusalem: The Holy City in the Eyes of Chroniclers, Visitors, Pilgrims, and Prophets from the Days of Abraham to the Beginnings of Modern Times*, Princeton University Press, Princeton, NJ, 1985.

[5] C. Roth, ed., *Encyclopædia Judaica*, Macmillan, New York, 1971.

[6] C. Roth, *A Jewish Book of Days*, Goldston Ltd., London, 1931.

[7] I. Singer, ed., *The Jewish Encyclopedia*, Funk and Wagnalls, New York, 1906.

Astronomical clock (number 3) designed and made in Norway by Rasmus Sørnes. Finished in 1954, it computes a large number of time/astronomical values including sidereal time, sunsets and sunrises, Gregorian date, solar and lunar eclipses, precession, tides, the positions of the planets, and many other things. (Courtesy of the Borgarsyssel Museum, Sarpsborg, Norway.)

Appendix D

Lisp Implementation

> *It has been often said that a person does not really understand something until he teaches it to someone else. Actually a person does not* really *understand something until he can teach it to a* computer, *i.e., express it as an algorithm.*
>
> Donald E. Knuth: "Computer Science and its Relation to Mathematics," *American Mathematical Monthly* (1974)

This appendix contains the complete Common Lisp implementation of the calendar functions described in the main text; the equation numbers given here are those of the corresponding functions in the text. Some Lisp functions have no corresponding equation in the text—these are constructors, selectors, and standard mathematical operations that are also used to control the typesetting: the functions in the main text were automatically typeset from the definitions in this appendix. The Lisp functions are available over the World Wide Web at

`www.cambridge.org/calendricalcalculations`

Please bear in mind the limits of the License and that the copyright on this book includes the code. *Also please keep in mind that if the result of any calculation is critical, it should be verified by independent means.*

For licensing information about nonpersonal and other uses, contact the authors. The code is distributed in the hope that it may be useful but without any warranty as to the accuracy of its output and with liability limited to return of the price of this book, which restrictions are set forth on page xli.

D.1 Basics

D.1.1 Lisp Preliminaries

For readers unfamiliar with Lisp, this section provides the bare necessities. A complete description can be found in [2].

All functions in Lisp are written in prefix notation. If `f` is a defined function, then

```
(f e0 e1 e2 ... en)
```

applies `f` to the $n + 1$ arguments `e0`, `e1`, `e2`, ..., `en`. Thus, for example, `+` adds up a list of numbers; for example,

```
(+ 1 -2 3)
```

adds the three numbers and returns the value 2. The Lisp functions `-`, `*`, and `/` work similarly, to subtract, multiply, and divide, respectively, a list of numbers. In a similar fashion, `<=` ($\leqslant$) checks that the numbers are in nondecreasing order and yields true (`t` in Lisp) if the relations hold. For instance,

```
(<= 1 2 3)
```

evaluates to `t`. The Lisp functions `=`, `/=` (not equal), `<`, `>`, and `>=` (greater than or equal) are similar. The predicate `evenp` tests whether an integer is even.

Lists are Lisp's main data structure. To construct a list `(e0 e1 e2 ... en)` the expression

```
(list e0 e1 e2 ... en)
```

is used. The function `nth`, used as `(nth i l)`, extracts the ith element of the list `l`, indexing from 0; the predicate `member`, used as `(member x l)`, tests whether `x` is an element of `l`. To get the first (indexed 0), second, and so on, through tenth elements of a list, we use the functions `first`, `second`, `third`, `fourth`, `fifth`, `sixth`, `seventh`, `eighth`, `ninth`, and `tenth`. The tail of the list, consisting of all the elements but the first, is obtained using `rest`. The empty list is represented by `nil`.

Constants are defined with the `defconstant` command, which has the syntax

```
(defconstant constant-name
  expression)
```

For example,

```
(defconstant sunday                                   (1.53)
  ;; TYPE day-of-week
  ;; Residue class for Sunday.
  0)
```

(1.54)

```
(defconstant monday
  ;; TYPE day-of-week
  ;; Residue class for Monday.
  1)
```

(1.55)

```
(defconstant tuesday
  ;; TYPE day-of-week
  ;; Residue class for Tuesday.
  2)
```

(1.56)

```
(defconstant wednesday
  ;; TYPE day-of-week
  ;; Residue class for Wednesday.
  3)
```

(1.57)

```
(defconstant thursday
  ;; TYPE day-of-week
  ;; Residue class for Thursday.
  4)
```

(1.58)

```
(defconstant friday
  ;; TYPE day-of-week
  ;; Residue class for Friday.
  5)
```

(1.59)

```
(defconstant saturday
  ;; TYPE day-of-week
  ;; Residue class for Saturday.
  6)
```

Notice that semicolons mark the start of comments. "Type" information is given in comments for each function. Although Common Lisp has its own system of type declarations, we prefered the simpler, untyped, Lisp, but we annotate each function and constant to aid the reader in translating our code into a typed language. The base types are defined in Table A.1, beginning on page 389.

To distinguish in the code between empty lists (`nil`) and the truth value "false," we define

```
(defconstant false
  ;; TYPE boolean
  ;; Constant representing false.
  nil)
```

For "true," we define

```
(defconstant true
  ;; TYPE boolean
  ;; Constant representing true.
  t)
```

We also use a string constant to signify an error value:

(1.97)

```
(defconstant bogus
  ;; TYPE string
  ;; Used to denote nonexistent dates.
  "bogus")
```

The function `equal` can be used to check lists and strings for equality.

Functions are defined using the `defun` command, which has the following syntax:

```
(defun function-name (param1 ... paramn)
  expression)
```

For example, we compute the day of the week of an R.D. date (page 33) with

(1.60)

```
(defun day-of-week-from-fixed (date)
  ;; TYPE fixed-date -> day-of-week
  ;; The residue class of the day of the week of date.
  (mod (- date (rd 0) sunday) 7))
```

and we implement julian day calculations by writing

```
1   (defconstant jd-epoch                                        (1.3)
2     ;; TYPE moment
3     ;; Fixed time of start of the julian day number.
4     (rd -1721424.5L0))
```

Common Lisp uses `L0` after a number to specify unscaled maximum-precision (at least 50-bit) constants.

We use the identity function

```
1   (defun rd (tee)                                              (1.1)
2     ;; TYPE moment -> moment
3     ;; Identity function for fixed dates/moments.  If internal
4     ;; timekeeping is shifted, change epoch to be RD date of
5     ;; origin of internal count.  epoch should be an integer.
6     (let* ((epoch 0))
7       (- tee epoch)))
```

to make it easy to adapt the code to an alternate fixed-date enumeration—all that is needed is to change the value of `epoch` in line 6 of `rd`. The Common Lisp construct `let*` defines a sequence of constants (possibly in terms of previously defined constants) and ends with an expression whose value is returned by the construct.

```
1   (defun moment-from-jd (jd)                                   (1.4)
2     ;; TYPE julian-day-number -> moment
3     ;; Moment of julian day number jd.
4     (+ jd jd-epoch))
```

```
1   (defun jd-from-moment (tee)                                  (1.5)
2     ;; TYPE moment -> julian-day-number
3     ;; Julian day number of moment tee.
4     (- tee jd-epoch))
```

```
1   (defconstant mjd-epoch                                       (1.6)
2     ;; TYPE fixed-date
3     ;; Fixed time of start of the modified julian day number.
4     (rd 678576))
```

```
1   (defun fixed-from-mjd (mjd)                                  (1.7)
2     ;; TYPE julian-day-number -> fixed-date
3     ;; Fixed date of modified julian day number mjd.
4     (+ mjd mjd-epoch))
```

```
1   (defun mjd-from-fixed (date)                                 (1.8)
2     ;; TYPE fixed-date -> julian-day-number
3     ;; Modified julian day number of fixed date.
4     (- date mjd-epoch))
```

```
1   (defconstant unix-epoch                                      (1.9)
2     ;; TYPE fixed-date
3     ;; Fixed date of the start of the Unix second count.
4     (rd 719163))
```

```
1   (defun moment-from-unix (s)                                  (1.10)
2     ;; TYPE second -> moment
3     ;; Fixed date from Unix second count s
4     (+ unix-epoch (/ s 24 60 60)))
```

```
1   (defun unix-from-moment (tee)                                (1.11)
2     ;; TYPE moment -> second
3     ;; Unix second count from moment tee
4     (* 24 60 60 (- tee unix-epoch)))
```

```
1   (defun fixed-from-jd (jd)                                    (1.13)
2     ;; TYPE julian-day-number -> fixed-date
3     ;; Fixed date of julian day number jd.
4     (floor (moment-from-jd jd)))
```

```
1   (defun jd-from-fixed (date)                                  (1.14)
2     ;; TYPE fixed-date -> julian-day-number
3     ;; Julian day number of fixed date.
4     (jd-from-moment date))
```

As another example of a function definition, we can define a function (inconveniently named `floor` in Common Lisp) to return the (truncated) integer quotient of two integers, $\lfloor m/n \rfloor$:

```
(defun quotient (m n)
  ;; TYPE (real nonzero-real) -> integer
  ;; Whole part of m/n.
  (floor m n))
```

The `floor` function can also be called with one argument. Thus

```
(floor x)
```

is $\lfloor x \rfloor$, the greatest integer less than or equal to x.

As a final example of function definitions, note that the Common Lisp function `mod` *always returns a nonnegative value for a positive divisor*; we use this property occasionally, but we also need a function like `mod` with its values adjusted in such a way that the modulus of a multiple of the divisor is the divisor itself rather than 0. To define this function, we write

```
(defun amod (x y)                                           (1.29)
  ;; TYPE (integer nonzero-integer) -> integer
  ;; The value of (x mod y) with y instead of 0.
  (+ y (mod x (- y))))
```

This is typeset as x mod $[1 \,..\, y]$ in the main text.

More generally, we use a function that shifts the modulus into a specified range of values [1]:

```
(defun mod3 (x a b)                                         (1.24)
  ;; TYPE (real real real) -> real
  ;; The value of x shifted into the range
  ;; [a..b). Returns x if a=b.
  (if (= a b)
      x
    (+ a (mod (- x a) (- b a)))))
```

This is typeset as x mod $[a \,..\, b)$; see page 22.

The function `if` has three arguments: a boolean condition, a then-expression, and an else-expression. The `cond` statement, also used in what follows, lists a sequence of tests and values and serves as a generalized case statement.

For convenience in expressing our calendar functions in Lisp, we introduce a macro to compute sums. The expression

```
(sum f i k p)
```

computes

$$\sum_{k \leqslant i < \min_{j \geq k}\{\neg p(j)\}} f(i);$$

that is, the expression $f(i)$ is summed for all $i = k, k+1, \ldots$, continuing only as long as the condition $p(i)$ holds. The sum is 0 if $p(k)$ is false. Our Common Lisp definition of **sum** uses the versatile `loop` construct and is as follows:

```
(defmacro sum (expression index initial condition)          (1.30)
  ;; TYPE ((integer->real) * integer (integer->boolean))
  ;; TYPE  -> real
  ;; Sum expression for index = initial and successive
  ;; integers, as long as condition holds.
  `(loop for ,index from ,initial
         while ,condition
         sum ,expression))
```

This is the first of the few instances in which we use macros and not functions; it allows us to avoid the issue of passing functions to functions.

A similar macro, **prod**, is used for products:

```
(defmacro prod (expression index initial condition)         (1.31)
  ;; TYPE ((integer->real) * integer (integer->boolean))
  ;; TYPE  -> real
  ;; Product of expression for index = initial and successive
  ;; integers, as long as condition holds.
  `(apply '*
          (loop for ,index from ,initial
                while ,condition
                collect ,expression)))
```

The `collect` construct gathers a list of factors and the function `apply` applies the multiplication operation to that list.

A summation macro **sigma** and a summation function **poly** for polynomials are used mainly in the astronomical code:

```
(defmacro sigma (list body)
  ;; TYPE (list-of-pairs (list-of-reals->real))
  ;; TYPE  -> real
  ;; list is of the form ((i1 l1)...(in ln)).
  ;; Sum of body for indices i1...in
  ;; running simultaneously thru lists l1...ln.
  `(apply '+ (mapcar (function (lambda
                                  ,(mapcar 'car list)
                                  ,body))
                     ,@(mapcar 'cadr list))))
```

```
(defun poly (x a)
  ;; TYPE (real list-of-reals) -> real
  ;; Sum powers of x with coefficients (from order 0 up)
  ;; in list a.
  (if (equal a nil)
      0
    (+ (first a) (* x (poly x (rest a))))))
```

The function `mapcar` applies a function (expressed by means of `function` and `lambda`) to each element of a list.

Two additional **sum**-like macros are used for searching; the first implements the **MIN** function, equation (1.32), and the second implements **MAX**, equation (1.33):

```
(defmacro next (index initial condition)                         (1.32)
  ;; TYPE (* integer (integer->boolean)) -> integer
  ;; First integer greater or equal to initial such that
  ;; condition holds.
  `(loop for ,index from ,initial
         when ,condition
         return ,index))
```

```
(defmacro final (index initial condition)                        (1.33)
  ;; TYPE (* integer (integer->boolean)) -> integer
  ;; Last integer greater or equal to initial such that
  ;; condition holds.
  `(loop for ,index from ,initial
         when (not ,condition)
         return (1- ,index)))
```

The function `1-` decrements a number by one; the similar function `1+` increments by one.

We also use binary search—see equation (1.35)—expressed as the macro **binary-search**:

```
(defmacro binary-search (l lo h hi x test end)                   (1.35)
  ;; TYPE (* real * real * (real->boolean)
  ;; TYPE  ((real real)->boolean)) -> real
  ;; Bisection search for x in [lo..hi] such that
  ;; end holds.  test determines when to go left.
  (let* ((left (gensym)))
    `(do* ((,x false (/ (+ ,h ,l) 2))
           (,left false ,test)
           (,l ,lo (if ,left ,l ,x))
           (,h ,hi (if ,left ,x ,h)))
          (,end (/ (+ ,h ,l) 2)))))
```

The construct `do*` is a form of loop.

Binary search is used mainly for function inversion:

```
(defmacro invert-angular (f y r)                                 (1.36)
  ;; TYPE (real->angle real interval) -> real
  ;; Use bisection to find inverse of angular function
  ;; f at y within interval r.
  (let* ((varepsilon 1/100000)); Desired accuracy
    `(binary-search l (begin ,r) u (end ,r) x
                    (< (mod (- (,f x) ,y) 360) (deg 180))
                    (< (- u l) ,varepsilon))))
```

The interval selectors, **begin** and **end**, are defined below.

D.1.2 Basic Code

To extract a particular component from a date, we use, when necessary, the functions **standard-month**, **standard-day**, and **standard-year**. For example:

```
(defun standard-month (date)
  ;; TYPE standard-date -> standard-month
  ;; Month field of date = (year month day).
  (second date))
```

```
(defun standard-day (date)
  ;; TYPE standard-date -> standard-day
  ;; Day field of date = (year month day).
  (third date))
```

```
(defun standard-year (date)
  ;; TYPE standard-date -> standard-year
  ;; Year field of date = (year month day).
  (first date))
```

Such constructors and selectors could be defined as macros or Lisp structures. In languages like C or C++, these would more naturally be field selection in fixed-length records rather than lists.

We also have

```
(defun hour (clock)
  ;; TYPE clock-time -> hour
  (first clock))
```

```
(defun minute (clock)
  ;; TYPE clock-time -> minute
  (second clock))
```

```
(defun seconds (clock)
  ;; TYPE clock-time -> second
  (third clock))
```

```
(defun time-of-day (hour minute second)
  ;; TYPE (hour minute second) -> clock-time
  (list hour minute second))
```

(1.12)

```
(defun fixed-from-moment (tee)
  ;; TYPE moment -> fixed-date
  ;; Fixed-date from moment tee.
  (floor tee))
```

(1.16)

```
(defun sign (y)
  ;; TYPE real -> {-1,0,+1}
  ;; Sign of y.
  (cond
   ((< y 0) -1)
   ((> y 0) +1)
   (t 0)))
```

(1.18)

```
(defun time-from-moment (tee)
  ;; TYPE moment -> time
  ;; Time from moment tee.
  (mod tee 1))
```

(1.37)

```
(defun list-of-fixed-from-moments (ell)
  ;; TYPE list-of-moments -> list-of-fixed-dates
  ;; List of fixed dates corresponding to list ell
  ;; of moments.
  (if (equal ell nil)
      nil
    (append (list (fixed-from-moment (first ell)))
            (list-of-fixed-from-moments (rest ell)))))
```

```
(defun interval (t0 t1)
  ;; TYPE (moment moment) -> interval
  ;; Half-open interval [t0..t1).
  (list t0 t1))
```

```
(defun interval-closed (t0 t1)
  ;; TYPE (moment moment) -> interval
  ;; Closed interval [t0..t1].
  (list t0 t1))
```

```
(defun begin (range)
  ;; TYPE interval -> moment
  ;; Start t0 of range [t0..t1) or [t0..t1].
  (first range))
```

```
(defun end (range)
  ;; TYPE interval -> moment
  ;; End t1 of range [t0..t1) or [t0..t1].
  (second range))
```

(1.38)

```
(defun in-range? (tee range)
  ;; TYPE (moment interval) -> boolean
  ;; True if tee is in half-open range.
  (and (<= (begin range) tee) (< tee (end range))))
```

(1.39)

```
(defun list-range (ell range)
  ;; TYPE (list-of-moments interval) -> list-of-moments
  ;; Those moments in list ell that occur in range.
  (if (equal ell nil)
      nil
    (let* ((r (list-range (rest ell) range)))
      (if (in-range? (first ell) range)
          (append (list (first ell)) r)
        r))))
```

(1.40)

```
(defun positions-in-range (p c cap-Delta range)
  ;; TYPE (nonnegative-real positive-real
  ;; TYPE  nonnegative-real interval) -> list-of-moments
  ;; List of occurrences of moment p of c-day cycle
  ;; within range.
  ;; cap-Delta is position in cycle of RD moment 0.
  (let* ((a (begin range))
         (b (end range))
         (date (mod3 (- p cap-Delta) a (+ a c))))
    (if (>= date b)
        nil
      (append (list date)
              (positions-in-range p c cap-Delta
                                  (interval (+ a c) b))))))
```

The following two functions for mixed-radix conversions (see Section 1.10) take an optional third parameter for the fractional part of the basis:

(1.41)

```
(defun from-radix (a b &optional c)
  ;; TYPE (list-of-reals list-of-rationals list-of-rationals)
  ;; TYPE  -> real
  ;; The number corresponding to a in radix notation
  ;; with base b for whole part and c for fraction.
  (/ (sum (* (nth i a)
             (prod (nth j (append b c))
                   j i (< j (+ (length b) (length c)))))
          i 0 (< i (length a)))
     (apply '* c)))
```

where `length` measures the length of a list; and

(1.42)

```
(defun to-radix (x b &optional c)
  ;; TYPE (real list-of-rationals list-of-rationals)
  ;; TYPE  -> list-of-reals
  ;; The radix notation corresponding to x
  ;; with base b for whole part and c for fraction.
  (if (null c)
      (if (null b)
          (list x)
        (append (to-radix (quotient x (nth (1- (length b)) b))
                          (butlast b) nil)
                (list (mod x (nth (1- (length b)) b)))))
    (to-radix (* x (apply '* c)) (append b c))))
```

which is implemented recursively.

(1.43)

```
(defun time-from-clock (hms)
  ;; TYPE clock-time -> time
  ;; Time of day from hms = hour:minute:second.
  (/ (from-radix hms nil (list 24 60 60)) 24))
```

(1.44)

```
(defun clock-from-moment (tee)
  ;; TYPE moment -> clock-time
  ;; Clock time hour:minute:second from moment tee.
  (rest (to-radix tee nil (list 24 60 60))))
```

(1.45)

```
(defun angle-from-degrees (alpha)
  ;; TYPE angle -> list-of-reals
  ;; List of degrees-arcminutes-arcseconds from angle alpha
  ;; in degrees.
  (let* ((dms (to-radix (abs alpha) nil (list 60 60))))
    (if (>= alpha 0)
        dms
      (list ; degrees-minutes-seconds
       (- (first dms)) (- (second dms)) (- (third dms))))))
```

D.1.3 The Egyptian and Armenian Calendars

```
(defun egyptian-date (year month day)
  ;; TYPE (egyptian-year egyptian-month egyptian-day)
  ;; TYPE  -> egyptian-date
  (list year month day))
```

(1.46)

```
(defconstant egyptian-epoch
  ;; TYPE fixed-date
  ;; Fixed date of start of the Egyptian (Nabonasser)
  ;; calendar.
  ;; JD 1448638 = February 26, 747 BCE (Julian).
  (fixed-from-jd 1448638))
```

(1.47)

```
(defun fixed-from-egyptian (e-date)
  ;; TYPE egyptian-date -> fixed-date
  ;; Fixed date of Egyptian date e-date.
  (let* ((month (standard-month e-date))
         (day (standard-day e-date))
         (year (standard-year e-date)))
    (+ egyptian-epoch   ; Days before start of calendar
       (* 365 (1- year)); Days in prior years
       (* 30 (1- month)); Days in prior months this year
       day -1)))        ; Days so far this month
```

(1.48)

```
(defun alt-fixed-from-egyptian (e-date)
  ;; TYPE egyptian-date -> fixed-date
  ;; Fixed date of Egyptian date e-date.
  (+ egyptian-epoch
     (sigma ((a (list 365 30 1))
             (e-date e-date))
            (* a (1- e-date)))))
```

(1.49)

```
(defun egyptian-from-fixed (date)
  ;; TYPE fixed-date -> egyptian-date
  ;; Egyptian equivalent of fixed date.
  (let* ((days ; Elapsed days since epoch.
          (- date egyptian-epoch))
         (year ; Year since epoch.
          (1+ (quotient days 365)))
         (month; Calculate the month by division.
          (1+ (quotient (mod days 365)
                        30)))
         (day  ; Calculate the day by subtraction.
          (- days
             (* 365 (1- year))
             (* 30 (1- month))
             -1)))
    (egyptian-date year month day)))
```

```
(defun armenian-date (year month day)
  ;; TYPE (armenian-year armenian-month armenian-day)
  ;; TYPE  -> armenian-date
  (list year month day))
```

(1.50)

```
(defconstant armenian-epoch
  ;; TYPE fixed-date
  ;; Fixed date of start of the Armenian calendar.
  ;; = July 11, 552 CE (Julian).
  (rd 201443))
```

(1.51)

```
(defun fixed-from-armenian (a-date)
  ;; TYPE armenian-date -> fixed-date
  ;; Fixed date of Armenian date a-date.
  (let* ((month (standard-month a-date))
         (day (standard-day a-date))
         (year (standard-year a-date)))
    (+ armenian-epoch
       (- (fixed-from-egyptian
           (egyptian-date year month day))
          egyptian-epoch))))
```

(1.52)

```
(defun armenian-from-fixed (date)
  ;; TYPE fixed-date -> armenian-date
  ;; Armenian equivalent of fixed date.
  (egyptian-from-fixed
   (+ date (- egyptian-epoch armenian-epoch))))
```

D.1.4 Cycles of Days

(1.62)

```
(defun kday-on-or-before (k date)
  ;; TYPE (day-of-week fixed-date) -> fixed-date
  ;; Fixed date of the k-day on or before fixed date.
  ;; k=0 means Sunday, k=1 means Monday, and so on.
  (- date (day-of-week-from-fixed (- date k))))
```

(1.65)

```
(defun kday-on-or-after (k date)
  ;; TYPE (day-of-week fixed-date) -> fixed-date
  ;; Fixed date of the k-day on or after fixed date.
  ;; k=0 means Sunday, k=1 means Monday, and so on.
  (kday-on-or-before k (+ date 6)))
```

(1.66)

```
(defun kday-nearest (k date)
  ;; TYPE (day-of-week fixed-date) -> fixed-date
  ;; Fixed date of the k-day nearest fixed date.
  ;; k=0 means Sunday, k=1 means Monday, and so on.
  (kday-on-or-before k (+ date 3)))
```

(1.67)
```
(defun kday-before (k date)
  ;; TYPE (day-of-week fixed-date) -> fixed-date
  ;; Fixed date of the k-day before fixed date.
  ;; k=0 means Sunday, k=1 means Monday, and so on.
  (kday-on-or-before k (- date 1)))
```

(1.68)
```
(defun kday-after (k date)
  ;; TYPE (day-of-week fixed-date) -> fixed-date
  ;; Fixed date of the k-day after fixed date.
  ;; k=0 means Sunday, k=1 means Monday, and so on.
  (kday-on-or-before k (+ date 7)))
```

D.1.5 Akan Calendar

(1.76)
```
(defun akan-day-name (n)
  ;; TYPE integer -> akan-name
  ;; The n-th name of the Akan cycle.
  (akan-name (amod n 6)
             (amod n 7)))
```

```
(defun akan-name (prefix stem)
  ;; TYPE (akan-prefix akan-stem) -> akan-name
  (list prefix stem))
```

```
(defun akan-prefix (name)
  ;; TYPE akan-name -> akan-prefix
  (first name))
```

```
(defun akan-stem (name)
  ;; TYPE akan-name -> akan-stem
  (second name))
```

(1.77)
```
(defun akan-name-difference (a-name1 a-name2)
  ;; TYPE (akan-name akan-name) -> nonnegative-integer
  ;; Number of names from Akan name a-name1 to the
  ;; next occurrence of Akan name a-name2.
  (let* ((prefix1 (akan-prefix a-name1))
         (prefix2 (akan-prefix a-name2))
         (stem1 (akan-stem a-name1))
         (stem2 (akan-stem a-name2))
         (prefix-difference (- prefix2 prefix1))
         (stem-difference (- stem2 stem1)))
    (amod (+ prefix-difference
             (* 36 (- stem-difference
                      prefix-difference)))
          42)))
```

(1.78)
```
(defconstant akan-day-name-epoch
  ;; TYPE fixed-date
  ;; RD date of an epoch (day 0)  of Akan day cycle.
  (rd 37))
```

(1.79)
```
(defun akan-name-from-fixed (date)
  ;; TYPE fixed-date -> akan-name
  ;; Akan name for date.
  (akan-day-name (- date akan-day-name-epoch)))
```

(1.80)
```
(defun akan-day-name-on-or-before (name date)
  ;; TYPE (akan-name fixed-date) -> fixed-date
  ;; Fixed date of latest date on or before fixed date
  ;; that has Akan name.
  (mod3
   (akan-name-difference (akan-name-from-fixed 0) name)
   date (- date 42)))
```

D.2 The Gregorian Calendar

```
(defun gregorian-date (year month day)
  ;; TYPE (gregorian-year gregorian-month gregorian-day)
  ;; TYPE  -> gregorian-date
  (list year month day))
```

(2.3)
```
(defconstant gregorian-epoch
  ;; TYPE fixed-date
  ;; Fixed date of start of the (proleptic) Gregorian
  ;; calendar.
  (rd 1))
```

(2.4)
```
(defconstant january
  ;; TYPE standard-month
  ;; January on Julian/Gregorian calendar.
  1)
```

(2.5)
```
(defconstant february
  ;; TYPE standard-month
  ;; February on Julian/Gregorian calendar.
  2)
```

(2.6)
```
(defconstant march
  ;; TYPE standard-month
  ;; March on Julian/Gregorian calendar.
  3)
```

(2.7)
```
(defconstant april
  ;; TYPE standard-month
  ;; April on Julian/Gregorian calendar.
  4)
```

(2.8)
```
(defconstant may
  ;; TYPE standard-month
  ;; May on Julian/Gregorian calendar.
  5)
```

(2.9)
```
(defconstant june
  ;; TYPE standard-month
  ;; June on Julian/Gregorian calendar.
  6)
```

(2.10)
```
(defconstant july
  ;; TYPE standard-month
  ;; July on Julian/Gregorian calendar.
  7)
```

(2.11)
```
(defconstant august
  ;; TYPE standard-month
  ;; August on Julian/Gregorian calendar.
  8)
```

(2.12)
```
(defconstant september
  ;; TYPE standard-month
  ;; September on Julian/Gregorian calendar.
  9)
```

(2.13)
```
(defconstant october
  ;; TYPE standard-month
  ;; October on Julian/Gregorian calendar.
  10)
```

(2.14)

```
(defconstant november
  ;; TYPE standard-month
  ;; November on Julian/Gregorian calendar.
  11)
```

(2.15)

```
(defconstant december
  ;; TYPE standard-month
  ;; December on Julian/Gregorian calendar.
  12)
```

(2.16)

```
(defun gregorian-leap-year? (g-year)
  ;; TYPE gregorian-year -> boolean
  ;; True if g-year is a leap year on the Gregorian
  ;; calendar.
  (and (= (mod g-year 4) 0)
       (not (member (mod g-year 400)
                    (list 100 200 300)))))
```

(2.17)

```
(defun fixed-from-gregorian (g-date)
  ;; TYPE gregorian-date -> fixed-date
  ;; Fixed date equivalent to the Gregorian date g-date.
  (let* ((month (standard-month g-date))
         (day (standard-day g-date))
         (year (standard-year g-date)))
    (+ (1- gregorian-epoch); Days before start of calendar
       (* 365 (1- year)); Ordinary days since epoch
       (quotient (1- year)
                 4); Julian leap days since epoch...
       (-          ; ...minus century years since epoch...
        (quotient (1- year) 100))
       (quotient   ; ...plus years since epoch divisible...
        (1- year) 400)  ; ...by 400.
       (quotient        ; Days in prior months this year...
        (- (* 367 month) 362); ...assuming 30-day Feb
        12)
       (if (<= month 2) ; Correct for 28- or 29-day Feb
           0
         (if (gregorian-leap-year? year)
             -1
           -2))
       day)))           ; Days so far this month.
```

(2.18)

```
(defun gregorian-new-year (g-year)
  ;; TYPE gregorian-year -> fixed-date
  ;; Fixed date of January 1 in g-year.
  (fixed-from-gregorian
   (gregorian-date g-year january 1)))
```

(2.19)

```
(defun gregorian-year-end (g-year)
  ;; TYPE gregorian-year -> fixed-date
  ;; Fixed date of December 31 in g-year.
  (fixed-from-gregorian
   (gregorian-date g-year december 31)))
```

(2.20)

```
(defun gregorian-year-range (g-year)
  ;; TYPE gregorian-year -> range
  ;; The range of moments in Gregorian year g-year.
  (interval (gregorian-new-year g-year)
            (gregorian-new-year (1+ g-year))))
```

(2.21)

```
(defun gregorian-year-from-fixed (date)
  ;; TYPE fixed-date -> gregorian-year
  ;; Gregorian year corresponding to the fixed date.
  (let* ((d0        ; Prior days.
          (- date gregorian-epoch))
         (n400      ; Completed 400-year cycles.
          (quotient d0 146097))
```

```
        (d1        ; Prior days not in n400.
         (mod d0 146097))
        (n100      ; 100-year cycles not in n400.
         (quotient d1 36524))
        (d2        ; Prior days not in n400 or n100.
         (mod d1 36524))
        (n4        ; 4-year cycles not in n400 or n100.
         (quotient d2 1461))
        (d3        ; Prior days not in n400, n100, or n4.
         (mod d2 1461))
        (n1        ; Years not in n400, n100, or n4.
         (quotient d3 365))
        (year (+ (* 400 n400)
                 (* 100 n100)
                 (* 4 n4)
                 n1)))
    (if (or (= n100 4) (= n1 4))
        year      ; Date is day 366 in a leap year.
      (1+ year)))); Date is ordinal day (1+ (mod d3 365))
                                     ; in (1+ year).
```

(2.23)

```
(defun gregorian-from-fixed (date)
  ;; TYPE fixed-date -> gregorian-date
  ;; Gregorian (year month day) corresponding to fixed date.
  (let* ((year (gregorian-year-from-fixed date))
        (prior-days; This year
         (- date (gregorian-new-year year)))
        (correction; To simulate a 30-day Feb
         (if (< date (fixed-from-gregorian
                       (gregorian-date year march 1)))
             0
           (if (gregorian-leap-year? year)
               1
             2)))
        (month     ; Assuming a 30-day Feb
         (quotient
          (+ (* 12 (+ prior-days correction)) 373)
          367))
        (day       ; Calculate the day by subtraction.
         (1+ (- date
                (fixed-from-gregorian
                 (gregorian-date year month 1))))))
    (gregorian-date year month day)))
```

(2.24)

```
(defun gregorian-date-difference (g-date1 g-date2)
  ;; TYPE (gregorian-date gregorian-date) -> integer
  ;; Number of days from Gregorian date g-date1 until
  ;; g-date2.
  (- (fixed-from-gregorian g-date2)
     (fixed-from-gregorian g-date1)))
```

(2.25)

```
(defun day-number (g-date)
  ;; TYPE gregorian-date -> positive-integer
  ;; Day number in year of Gregorian date g-date.
  (gregorian-date-difference
   (gregorian-date (1- (standard-year g-date)) december 31)
   g-date))
```

(2.26)

```
(defun days-remaining (g-date)
  ;; TYPE gregorian-date -> nonnegative-integer
  ;; Days remaining in year after Gregorian date g-date.
  (gregorian-date-difference
   g-date
   (gregorian-date (standard-year g-date) december 31)))
```

(2.27)

```
(defun last-day-of-gregorian-month (g-year g-month)
  ;; TYPE (gregorian-year gregorian-month) -> gregorian-day
  ;; Last day of month g-month in Gregorian year g-year.
  (gregorian-date-difference
```

```
    (gregorian-date g-year g-month 1)
    (gregorian-date (if (= g-month 12)
                        (1+ g-year)
                      g-year)
                    (amod (1+ g-month) 12)
                    1)))
```

```
(defun alt-fixed-from-gregorian (g-date)                    (2.28)
  ;; TYPE gregorian-date -> fixed-date
  ;; Alternative calculation of fixed date equivalent to the
  ;; Gregorian date g-date.
  (let* ((month (standard-month g-date))
         (day (standard-day g-date))
         (year (standard-year g-date))
         (m-prime (mod (- month 3) 12))
         (y-prime (- year (quotient m-prime 10))))
    (+ (1- gregorian-epoch)
       -306          ; Days in March...December.
       (* 365 y-prime); Ordinary days.
       (sigma ((y (to-radix y-prime (list 4 25 4)))
               (a (list 97 24 1 0)))
              (* y a))
       (quotient   ; Days in prior months.
        (+ (* 3 m-prime) 2)
        5)
       (* 30 m-prime)
       day)))       ; Days so far this month.
```

```
(defun alt-gregorian-from-fixed (date)                      (2.29)
  ;; TYPE fixed-date -> gregorian-date
  ;; Alternative calculation of Gregorian (year month day)
  ;; corresponding to fixed date.
  (let* ((y (gregorian-year-from-fixed
             (+ (1- gregorian-epoch)
                date
                306)))
         (prior-days
          (- date (fixed-from-gregorian
                   (gregorian-date (1- y) march 1))))
         (month
          (amod (+ (quotient
                    (+ (* 5 prior-days) 2)
                    153)
                   3)
                12))
         (year (- y (quotient (+ month 9) 12)))
         (day
          (1+ (- date
                 (fixed-from-gregorian
                  (gregorian-date year month 1))))))
    (gregorian-date year month day)))
```

```
(defun alt-gregorian-year-from-fixed (date)                 (2.30)
  ;; TYPE fixed-date -> gregorian-year
  ;; Gregorian year corresponding to the fixed date.
  (let* ((approx ; approximate year
          (quotient (- date gregorian-epoch -2)
                    146097/400))
         (start  ; start of next year
          (+ gregorian-epoch
             (* 365 approx)
             (sigma ((y (to-radix approx (list 4 25 4)))
                     (a (list 97 24 1 0)))
                    (* y a)))))
    (if (< date start)
        approx
      (1+ approx))))
```

```
(defun independence-day (g-year)                            (2.32)
  ;; TYPE gregorian-year -> fixed-date
```

```
  ;; Fixed date of United States Independence Day in
  ;; Gregorian year g-yaer.
  (fixed-from-gregorian (gregorian-date g-year july 4)))
```

(2.33)

```
(defun nth-kday (n k g-date)
  ;; TYPE (integer day-of-week gregorian-date) -> fixed-date
  ;; If n>0, return the n-th k-day on or after
  ;; g-date.  If n<0, return the n-th k-day on or
  ;; before g-date.  If n=0 return bogus.  A k-day of
  ;; 0 means Sunday, 1 means Monday, and so on.
  (cond ((> n 0)
         (+ (* 7 n)
            (kday-before k (fixed-from-gregorian g-date))))
        ((< n 0)
         (+ (* 7 n)
            (kday-after k (fixed-from-gregorian g-date))))
        (t bogus)))
```

(2.34)

```
(defun first-kday (k g-date)
  ;; TYPE (day-of-week gregorian-date) -> fixed-date
  ;; Fixed date of first k-day on or after Gregorian date
  ;; g-date. A k-day of 0 means Sunday, 1 means Monday,
  ;; and so on.
  (nth-kday 1 k g-date))
```

(2.35)

```
(defun last-kday (k g-date)
  ;; TYPE (day-of-week gregorian-date) -> fixed-date
  ;; Fixed date of last k-day on or before Gregorian date
  ;; g-date. A k-day of 0 means Sunday, 1 means Monday,
  ;; and so on.
  (nth-kday -1 k g-date))
```

(2.36)

```
(defun labor-day (g-year)
  ;; TYPE gregorian-year -> fixed-date
  ;; Fixed date of United States Labor Day in Gregorian
  ;; year g-year (the first Monday in September).
  (first-kday monday (gregorian-date g-year september 1)))
```

(2.37)

```
(defun memorial-day (g-year)
  ;; TYPE gregorian-year -> fixed-date
  ;; Fixed date of United States Memorial Day in Gregorian
  ;; year g-year (the last Monday in May).
  (last-kday monday (gregorian-date g-year may 31)))
```

(2.38)

```
(defun election-day (g-year)
  ;; TYPE gregorian-year -> fixed-date
  ;; Fixed date of United States Election Day in Gregorian
  ;; year g-year (the Tuesday after the first Monday in
  ;; November).
  (first-kday tuesday (gregorian-date g-year november 2)))
```

(2.39)

```
(defun daylight-saving-start (g-year)
  ;; TYPE gregorian-year -> fixed-date
  ;; Fixed date of the start of United States daylight
  ;; saving time in Gregorian year g-year (the second
  ;; Sunday in March).
  (nth-kday 2 sunday (gregorian-date g-year march 1)))
```

(2.40)

```
(defun daylight-saving-end (g-year)
  ;; TYPE gregorian-year -> fixed-date
  ;; Fixed date of the end of United States daylight saving
  ;; time in Gregorian year g-year (the first Sunday in
  ;; November).
  (first-kday sunday (gregorian-date g-year november 1)))
```

(2.41)
```
(defun christmas (g-year)
  ;; TYPE gregorian-year -> fixed-date
  ;; Fixed date of Christmas in Gregorian year g-year.
  (fixed-from-gregorian
   (gregorian-date g-year december 25)))
```

(2.42)
```
(defun advent (g-year)
  ;; TYPE gregorian-year -> fixed-date
  ;; Fixed date of Advent in Gregorian year g-year
  ;; (the Sunday closest to November 30).
  (kday-nearest sunday
                (fixed-from-gregorian
                 (gregorian-date g-year november 30))))
```

(2.43)
```
(defun epiphany (g-year)
  ;; TYPE gregorian-year -> fixed-date
  ;; Fixed date of Epiphany in U.S. in Gregorian year
  ;; g-year (the first Sunday after January 1).
  (first-kday sunday (gregorian-date g-year january 2)))
```

(2.44)
```
(defun unlucky-fridays-in-range (range)
  ;; TYPE range -> list-of-fixed-dates
  ;; List of Fridays within range of dates
  ;; that are day 13 of Gregorian months.
  (let* ((a (begin range))
         (b (end range))
         (fri (kday-on-or-after friday a))
         (date (gregorian-from-fixed fri)))
    (if (in-range? fri range)
        (append
         (if (= (standard-day date) 13)
             (list fri)
           nil)
         (unlucky-fridays-in-range
          (interval (1+ fri) b)))
      nil)))
```

(2.45)
```
(defun unlucky-fridays (g-year)
  ;; TYPE gregorian-year -> list-of-fixed-dates
  ;; List of Fridays within Gregorian year g-year
  ;; that are day 13 of Gregorian months.
  (unlucky-fridays-in-range
   (gregorian-year-range g-year)))
```

D.3 The Julian Calendar

In the Lisp code we use $-n$ for year n B.C.E. (Julian):

```
(defun bce (n)
  ;; TYPE standard-year -> julian-year
  ;; Negative value to indicate a BCE Julian year.
  (- n))
```

and positive numbers for C.E. (Julian) years:

```
(defun ce (n)
  ;; TYPE standard-year -> julian-year
  ;; Positive value to indicate a CE Julian year.
  n)
```

```
(defun julian-date (year month day)
  ;; TYPE (julian-year julian-month julian-day)
  ;; TYPE  -> julian-date
  (list year month day))
```

(3.1)
```
(defun julian-leap-year? (j-year)
  ;; TYPE julian-year -> boolean
  ;; True if j-year is a leap year on the Julian calendar.
  (= (mod j-year 4) (if (> j-year 0) 0 3)))
```

(3.2)

```
(defconstant julian-epoch
  ;; TYPE fixed-date
  ;; Fixed date of start of the Julian calendar.
  (fixed-from-gregorian (gregorian-date 0 december 30)))
```

(3.3)

```
(defun fixed-from-julian (j-date)
  ;; TYPE julian-date -> fixed-date
  ;; Fixed date equivalent to the Julian date j-date.
  (let* ((month (standard-month j-date))
         (day (standard-day j-date))
         (year (standard-year j-date))
         (y (if (< year 0)
                (1+ year) ; No year zero
              year)))
    (+ (1- julian-epoch)  ; Days before start of calendar
       (* 365 (1- y))     ; Ordinary days since epoch.
       (quotient (1- y) 4); Leap days since epoch...
       (quotient          ; Days in prior months this year...
        (- (* 367 month) 362); ...assuming 30-day Feb
        12)
       (if (<= month 2)   ; Correct for 28- or 29-day Feb
           0
         (if (julian-leap-year? year)
             -1
           -2))
       day)))             ; Days so far this month.
```

(3.4)

```
(defun julian-from-fixed (date)
  ;; TYPE fixed-date -> julian-date
  ;; Julian (year month day) corresponding to fixed date.
  (let* ((approx     ; Nominal year.
          (quotient (+ (* 4 (- date julian-epoch)) 1464)
                    1461))
         (year (if (<= approx 0)
                   (1- approx) ; No year 0.
                 approx))
         (prior-days; This year
          (- date (fixed-from-julian
                   (julian-date year january 1))))
         (correction; To simulate a 30-day Feb
          (if (< date (fixed-from-julian
                       (julian-date year march 1)))
              0
            (if (julian-leap-year? year)
                1
              2)))
         (month     ; Assuming a 30-day Feb
          (quotient
           (+ (* 12 (+ prior-days correction)) 373)
           367))
         (day       ; Calculate the day by subtraction.
          (1+ (- date
                 (fixed-from-julian
                  (julian-date year month 1))))))
    (julian-date year month day)))
```

(3.5)

```
(defconstant kalends
  ;; TYPE roman-event
  ;; Class of Kalends.
  1)
```

(3.6)

```
(defconstant nones
  ;; TYPE roman-event
  ;; Class of Nones.
  2)
```

(3.7)

```
(defconstant ides
  ;; TYPE roman-event
  ;; Class of Ides.
  3)
```

```
(defun roman-date (year month event count leap)
  ;; TYPE (roman-year roman-month roman-event roman-count
  ;; TYPE  roman-leap) -> roman-date
  (list year month event count leap))
```

```
(defun roman-year (date)
  ;; TYPE roman-date -> roman-year
  (first date))
```

```
(defun roman-month (date)
  ;; TYPE roman-date -> roman-month
  (second date))
```

```
(defun roman-event (date)
  ;; TYPE roman-date -> roman-event
  (third date))
```

```
(defun roman-count (date)
  ;; TYPE roman-date -> roman-count
  (fourth date))
```

```
(defun roman-leap (date)
  ;; TYPE roman-date -> roman-leap
  (fifth date))
```

(3.8)

```
(defun ides-of-month (month)
  ;; TYPE roman-month -> ides
  ;; Date of Ides in Roman month.
  (if (member month (list march may july october))
      15
    13))
```

(3.9)

```
(defun nones-of-month (month)
  ;; TYPE roman-month -> nones
  ;; Date of Nones in Roman month.
  (- (ides-of-month month) 8))
```

(3.10)

```
(defun fixed-from-roman (r-date)
  ;; TYPE roman-date -> fixed-date
  ;; Fixed date for Roman name r-date.
  (let* ((leap (roman-leap r-date))
         (count (roman-count r-date))
         (event (roman-event r-date))
         (month (roman-month r-date))
         (year (roman-year r-date)))
    (+ (cond
        ((= event kalends)
         (fixed-from-julian (julian-date year month 1)))
        ((= event nones)
         (fixed-from-julian
          (julian-date year month (nones-of-month month))))
        ((= event ides)
         (fixed-from-julian
          (julian-date year month (ides-of-month month)))))
       (- count)
       (if (and (julian-leap-year? year)
                (= month march)
                (= event kalends)
                (>= 16 count 6))
           0 ; After Ides until leap day
         1) ; Otherwise
       (if leap
           1 ; Leap day
         0)))) ; Non-leap day
```

```
(defun roman-from-fixed (date)                                    (3.11)
  ;; TYPE fixed-date -> roman-date
  ;; Roman name for fixed date.
  (let* ((j-date (julian-from-fixed date))
         (month (standard-month j-date))
         (day (standard-day j-date))
         (year (standard-year j-date))
         (month-prime (amod (1+ month) 12))
         (year-prime (if (/= month-prime 1)
                         year
                       (if (/= year -1)
                           (1+ year)
                         1)))
         (kalends1 (fixed-from-roman
                    (roman-date year-prime month-prime
                                kalends 1 false))))
    (cond
     ((= day 1) (roman-date year month kalends 1 false))
     ((<= day (nones-of-month month))
      (roman-date year month nones
                  (1+ (- (nones-of-month month) day)) false))
     ((<= day (ides-of-month month))
      (roman-date year month ides
                  (1+ (- (ides-of-month month) day)) false))
     ((or (/= month february)
          (not (julian-leap-year? year)))
      ;; After the Ides, in a month that is not February of a
      ;; leap year
      (roman-date year-prime month-prime kalends
                  (1+ (- kalends1 date)) false))
     ((< day 25)
      ;; February of a leap year, before leap day
      (roman-date year march kalends (- 30 day) false))
     (true
      ;; February of a leap year, on or after leap day
      (roman-date year march kalends
                  (- 31 day) (= day 25))))))
```

```
(defconstant year-rome-founded                                    (3.12)
  ;; TYPE julian-year
  ;; Year on the Julian calendar of the founding of Rome.
  (bce 753))
```

```
(defun julian-year-from-auc (year)                                (3.13)
  ;; TYPE auc-year -> julian-year
  ;; Julian year equivalent to AUC year
  (if (<= 1 year (- year-rome-founded))
      (+ year year-rome-founded -1)
    (+ year year-rome-founded)))
```

```
(defun auc-year-from-julian (year)                                (3.14)
  ;; TYPE julian-year -> auc-year
  ;; Year AUC equivalent to Julian year
  (if (<= year-rome-founded year -1)
      (- year year-rome-founded -1)
    (- year year-rome-founded)))
```

```
(defun olympiad (cycle year)
  ;; TYPE (olympiad-cycle olympiad-year) -> olympiad
  (list cycle year))
```

```
(defun olympiad-cycle (o-date)
  ;; TYPE olympiad -> olympiad-cycle
  (first o-date))
```

```
(defun olympiad-year (o-date)
  ;; TYPE olympiad -> olympiad-year
  (second o-date))
```

(3.15)

```
(defconstant olympiad-start
  ;; TYPE julian-year
  ;; Start of the Olympiads.
  (bce 776))
```

(3.16)

```
(defun julian-year-from-olympiad (o-date)
  ;; TYPE olympiad -> julian-year
  ;; Julian year corresponding to Olympian o-date.
  (let* ((cycle (olympiad-cycle o-date))
         (year (olympiad-year o-date))
         (years (+ olympiad-start
                   (* 4 (1- cycle))
                   year -1)))
    (if (< years 0)
        years
      (1+ years))))
```

(3.17)

```
(defun olympiad-from-julian-year (j-year)
  ;; TYPE julian-year -> olympiad
  ;; Olympiad corresponding to Julian year j-year.
  (let* ((years (- j-year olympiad-start
                   (if (< j-year 0) 0 1))))
    (olympiad (1+ (quotient years 4))
              (1+ (mod years 4)))))
```

(3.18)

```
(defconstant spring
  ;; TYPE season
  ;; Longitude of sun at vernal equinox.
  (deg 0))
```

(3.19)

```
(defconstant summer
  ;; TYPE season
  ;; Longitude of sun at summer solstice.
  (deg 90))
```

(3.20)

```
(defconstant autumn
  ;; TYPE season
  ;; Longitude of sun at autumnal equinox.
  (deg 180))
```

(3.21)

```
(defconstant winter
  ;; TYPE season
  ;; Longitude of sun at winter solstice.
  (deg 270))
```

(3.22)

```
(defun cycle-in-gregorian (season g-year cap-L start)
  ;; TYPE (season gregorian-year positive-real moment)
  ;; TYPE  -> list-of-moments
  ;; Moments of season in Gregorian year g-year.
  ;; Seasonal year is cap-L days, seasons are given as
  ;; longitudes and are of equal length,
  ;; and a seasonal year started at moment start.
  (let* ((year (gregorian-year-range g-year))
         (pos (* (/ season (deg 360)) cap-L))
         (cap-Delta (- pos (mod start cap-L))))
    (positions-in-range pos cap-L cap-Delta year)))
```

(3.23)

```
(defun julian-season-in-gregorian (season g-year)
  ;; TYPE (season gregorian-year) -> list-of-moments
  ;; Moment(s) of Julian season in Gregorian year g-year.
  (let* ((cap-Y (+ 365 (hr 6)))
         (offset ; season start
          (* (/ season (deg 360)) cap-Y)))
    (cycle-in-gregorian season g-year cap-Y
                        (+ (fixed-from-julian
                            (julian-date (bce 1) march 23))
                           offset))))
```

(3.24)

```
(defun julian-in-gregorian (j-month j-day g-year)
  ;; TYPE (julian-month julian-day gregorian-year)
  ;; TYPE  -> list-of-fixed-dates
  ;; List of the fixed dates of Julian month j-month, day
  ;; j-day that occur in Gregorian year g-year.
  (let* ((jan1 (gregorian-new-year g-year))
         (y (standard-year (julian-from-fixed jan1)))
         (y-prime (if (= y -1)
                      1
                    (1+ y)))
         ;; The possible occurrences in one year are
         (date0 (fixed-from-julian
                 (julian-date y j-month j-day)))
         (date1 (fixed-from-julian
                 (julian-date y-prime j-month j-day))))
    (list-range (list date0 date1)
                (gregorian-year-range g-year))))
```

(3.25)

```
(defun eastern-orthodox-christmas (g-year)
  ;; TYPE gregorian-year -> list-of-fixed-dates
  ;; List of zero or one fixed dates of Eastern Orthodox
  ;; Christmas in Gregorian year g-year.
  (julian-in-gregorian december 25 g-year))
```

In languages like Lisp that allow functions as parameters, one could write a generic version of this function to collect the holidays of any given calendar and pass `fixed-from-julian` to it as an additional parameter. We have deliberately avoided this and similar advanced language features in the interests of portability.

D.4 The Coptic and Ethiopic Calendars

```
(defun coptic-date (year month day)
  ;; TYPE (coptic-year coptic-month coptic-day) -> coptic-date
  (list year month day))
```

(4.1)

```
(defconstant coptic-epoch
  ;; TYPE fixed-date
  ;; Fixed date of start of the Coptic calendar.
  (fixed-from-julian (julian-date (ce 284) august 29)))
```

(4.2)

```
(defun coptic-leap-year? (c-year)
  ;; TYPE coptic-year -> boolean
  ;; True if c-year is a leap year on the Coptic calendar.
  (= (mod c-year 4) 3))
```

(4.3)

```
(defun fixed-from-coptic (c-date)
  ;; TYPE coptic-date -> fixed-date
  ;; Fixed date of Coptic date c-date.
  (let* ((month (standard-month c-date))
         (day (standard-day c-date))
         (year (standard-year c-date)))
    (+ coptic-epoch -1  ; Days before start of calendar
       (* 365 (1- year)); Ordinary days in prior years
       (quotient year 4); Leap days in prior years
       (* 30 (1- month)); Days in prior months this year
       day)))           ; Days so far this month
```

(4.4)

```
(defun coptic-from-fixed (date)
  ;; TYPE fixed-date -> coptic-date
  ;; Coptic equivalent of fixed date.
  (let* ((year ; Calculate the year by cycle-of-years formula
          (quotient (+ (* 4 (- date coptic-epoch)) 1463)
                    1461))
         (month; Calculate the month by division.
          (1+ (quotient
               (- date (fixed-from-coptic
                        (coptic-date year 1 1)))
               30)))
```

```
        (day  ; Calculate the day by subtraction.
         (- date -1
            (fixed-from-coptic
             (coptic-date year month 1)))))
    (coptic-date year month day)))
```

```
(defun ethiopic-date (year month day)
  ;; TYPE (ethiopic-year ethiopic-month ethiopic-day)
  ;; TYPE  -> ethiopic-date
  (list year month day))
```

(4.5)

```
(defconstant ethiopic-epoch
  ;; TYPE fixed-date
  ;; Fixed date of start of the Ethiopic calendar.
  (fixed-from-julian (julian-date (ce 8) august 29)))
```

(4.6)

```
(defun fixed-from-ethiopic (e-date)
  ;; TYPE ethiopic-date -> fixed-date
  ;; Fixed date of Ethiopic date e-date.
  (let* ((month (standard-month e-date))
         (day (standard-day e-date))
         (year (standard-year e-date)))
    (+ ethiopic-epoch
       (- (fixed-from-coptic
           (coptic-date year month day))
          coptic-epoch))))
```

(4.7)

```
(defun ethiopic-from-fixed (date)
  ;; TYPE fixed-date -> ethiopic-date
  ;; Ethiopic equivalent of fixed date.
  (coptic-from-fixed
   (+ date (- coptic-epoch ethiopic-epoch))))
```

(4.8)

```
(defun coptic-in-gregorian (c-month c-day g-year)
  ;; TYPE (coptic-month coptic-day gregorian-year)
  ;; TYPE  -> list-of-fixed-dates
  ;; List of the fixed dates of Coptic month c-month, day
  ;; c-day that occur in Gregorian year g-year.
  (let* ((jan1 (gregorian-new-year g-year))
         (y (standard-year (coptic-from-fixed jan1)))
         ;; The possible occurrences in one year are
         (date0 (fixed-from-coptic
                 (coptic-date y c-month c-day)))
         (date1 (fixed-from-coptic
                 (coptic-date (1+ y) c-month c-day))))
    (list-range (list date0 date1)
                (gregorian-year-range g-year))))
```

(4.9)

```
(defun coptic-christmas (g-year)
  ;; TYPE gregorian-year -> list-of-fixed-dates
  ;; List of zero or one fixed dates of Coptic Christmas
  ;; in Gregorian year g-year.
  (coptic-in-gregorian 4 29 g-year))
```

D.5 The ISO Calendar

```
(defun iso-date (year week day)
  ;; TYPE (iso-year iso-week iso-day) -> iso-date
  (list year week day))
```

```
(defun iso-week (date)
  ;; TYPE iso-date -> iso-week
  (second date))
```

```
(defun iso-day (date)
  ;; TYPE iso-date -> day-of-week
  (third date))
```

```
(defun iso-year (date)
  ;; TYPE iso-date -> iso-year
  (first date))
```

(5.1)

```
(defun fixed-from-iso (i-date)
  ;; TYPE iso-date -> fixed-date
  ;; Fixed date equivalent to ISO i-date.
  (let* ((week (iso-week i-date))
         (day (iso-day i-date))
         (year (iso-year i-date)))
    ;; Add fixed date of Sunday preceding date plus day
    ;; in week.
    (+ (nth-kday
        week sunday
        (gregorian-date (1- year) december 28)) day)))
```

(5.2)

```
(defun iso-from-fixed (date)
  ;; TYPE fixed-date -> iso-date
  ;; ISO (year week day) corresponding to the fixed date.
  (let* ((approx ; Year may be one too small.
          (gregorian-year-from-fixed (- date 3)))
         (year (if (>= date
                       (fixed-from-iso
                        (iso-date (1+ approx) 1 1)))
                   (1+ approx)
                 approx))
         (week (1+ (quotient
                    (- date
                       (fixed-from-iso (iso-date year 1 1)))
                    7)))
         (day (amod (- date (rd 0)) 7)))
    (iso-date year week day)))
```

(5.3)

```
(defun iso-long-year? (i-year)
  ;; TYPE iso-year -> boolean
  ;; True if i-year is a long (53-week) year.
  (let* ((jan1 (day-of-week-from-fixed
                (gregorian-new-year i-year)))
         (dec31 (day-of-week-from-fixed
                 (gregorian-year-end i-year))))
    (or (= jan1 thursday)
        (= dec31 thursday))))
```

D.6 The Icelandic Calendar

```
(defun icelandic-date (year season week weekday)
  ;; TYPE (icelandic-year icelandic-season
  ;; TYPE  icelandic-week icelandic-weekday) -> icelandic-date
  (list year season week weekday))
```

```
(defun icelandic-year (i-date)
  ;; TYPE icelandic-date -> icelandic-year
  (first i-date))
```

```
(defun icelandic-season (i-date)
  ;; TYPE icelandic-date -> icelandic-season
  (second i-date))
```

```
(defun icelandic-week (i-date)
  ;; TYPE icelandic-date -> icelandic-week
  (third i-date))
```

```
(defun icelandic-weekday (i-date)
  ;; TYPE icelandic-date -> icelandic-weekday
  (fourth i-date))
```

```
(defconstant icelandic-epoch                                        (6.1)
  ;; TYPE fixed-date
  ;; Fixed date of start of the Icelandic calendar.
  (fixed-from-gregorian (gregorian-date 1 april 19)))
```

```
(defun icelandic-summer (i-year)                                    (6.2)
  ;; TYPE icelandic-year -> fixed-date
  ;; Fixed date of start of Icelandic year i-year.
  (let* ((apr19 (+ icelandic-epoch (* 365 (1- i-year))
                 (sigma ((y (to-radix i-year (list 4 25 4)))
                         (a (list 97 24 1 0)))
                        (* y a)))))
    (kday-on-or-after thursday apr19)))
```

```
(defun icelandic-winter (i-year)                                    (6.3)
  ;; TYPE icelandic-year -> fixed-date
  ;; Fixed date of start of Icelandic winter season
  ;; in Icelandic year i-year.
  (- (icelandic-summer (1+ i-year)) 180))
```

```
(defun fixed-from-icelandic (i-date)                                (6.4)
  ;; TYPE icelandic-date -> fixed-date
  ;; Fixed date equivalent to Icelandic i-date.
  (let* ((year (icelandic-year i-date))
         (season (icelandic-season i-date))
         (week (icelandic-week i-date))
         (weekday (icelandic-weekday i-date))
         (start ; Start of season.
          (if (= season summer)
              (icelandic-summer year)
            (icelandic-winter year)))
         (shift ; First day of week in prior season.
          (if (= season summer) thursday saturday)))
    (+ start
       (* 7 (1- week)) ; Elapsed weeks.
       (mod (- weekday shift) 7))))
```

```
(defun icelandic-from-fixed (date)                                  (6.5)
  ;; TYPE fixed-date -> icelandic-date
  ;; Icelandic (year season week weekday) corresponding to
  ;; the fixed date.
  (let* ((approx ; approximate year
          (quotient (- date icelandic-epoch -369)
                    146097/400))
         (year (if (>= date (icelandic-summer approx))
                   approx
                 (1- approx)))
         (season (if (< date (icelandic-winter year))
                     summer
                   winter))
         (start ; Start of current season.
          (if (= season summer)
              (icelandic-summer year)
            (icelandic-winter year)))
         (week ; Weeks since start of season.
          (1+ (quotient (- date start) 7)))
         (weekday (day-of-week-from-fixed date)))
    (icelandic-date year season week weekday)))
```

```
(defun icelandic-leap-year? (i-year)                                (6.6)
  ;; TYPE icelandic-year -> boolean
  ;; True if Icelandic i-year is a leap year (53 weeks)
  ;; on the Icelandic calendar.
  (/= (- (icelandic-summer (1+ i-year))
         (icelandic-summer i-year))
      364))
```

(6.7)

```
(defun icelandic-month (i-date)
  ;; TYPE icelandic-date -> icelandic-month
  ;; Month of i-date on the Icelandic calendar.
  ;; Epagomenae are "month" 0.
  (let* ((date (fixed-from-icelandic i-date))
         (year (icelandic-year i-date))
         (season (icelandic-season i-date))
         (midsummer (- (icelandic-winter year) 90))
         (start (cond ((= season winter)
                       (icelandic-winter year))
                      ((>= date midsummer)
                       (- midsummer 90))
                      ((< date (+ (icelandic-summer year) 90))
                       (icelandic-summer year))
                      (t ; Epagomenae.
                       midsummer))))
    (1+ (quotient (- date start) 30))))
```

D.7 The Islamic Calendar

```
(defun islamic-date (year month day)
  ;; TYPE (islamic-year islamic-month islamic-day)
  ;; TYPE  -> islamic-date
  (list year month day))
```

(7.1)

```
(defconstant islamic-epoch
  ;; TYPE fixed-date
  ;; Fixed date of start of the Islamic calendar.
  (fixed-from-julian (julian-date (ce 622) july 16)))
```

(7.2)

```
(defun islamic-leap-year? (i-year)
  ;; TYPE islamic-year -> boolean
  ;; True if i-year is an Islamic leap year.
  (< (mod (+ 14 (* 11 i-year)) 30) 11))
```

(7.3)

```
(defun fixed-from-islamic (i-date)
  ;; TYPE islamic-date -> fixed-date
  ;; Fixed date equivalent to Islamic date i-date.
  (let* ((month (standard-month i-date))
         (day (standard-day i-date))
         (year (standard-year i-date)))
    (+ (1- islamic-epoch)     ; Days before start of calendar
       (* (1- year) 354)      ; Ordinary days since epoch.
       (quotient              ; Leap days since epoch.
        (+ 3 (* 11 year)) 30)
       (* 29 (1- month))      ; Days in prior months this year
       (quotient month 2)
       day)))                 ; Days so far this month.
```

(7.4)

```
(defun islamic-from-fixed (date)
  ;; TYPE fixed-date -> islamic-date
  ;; Islamic date (year month day) corresponding to fixed
  ;; date.
  (let* ((year
          (quotient
           (+ (* 30 (- date islamic-epoch)) 10646)
           10631))
         (prior-days
          (- date (fixed-from-islamic
                   (islamic-date year 1 1))))
         (month
          (quotient
           (+ (* 11 prior-days) 330)
           325))
         (day
          (1+ (- date (fixed-from-islamic
                       (islamic-date year month 1))))))
    (islamic-date year month day)))
```

(7.5)

```
(defun islamic-in-gregorian (i-month i-day g-year)
  ;; TYPE (islamic-month islamic-day gregorian-year)
  ;; TYPE  -> list-of-fixed-dates
  ;; List of the fixed dates of Islamic month i-month, day
  ;; i-day that occur in Gregorian year g-year.
  (let* ((jan1 (gregorian-new-year g-year))
         (y (standard-year (islamic-from-fixed jan1)))
         ;; The possible occurrences in one year are
         (date0 (fixed-from-islamic
                 (islamic-date y i-month i-day)))
         (date1 (fixed-from-islamic
                 (islamic-date (1+ y) i-month i-day)))
         (date2 (fixed-from-islamic
                 (islamic-date (+ y 2) i-month i-day))))
    ;; Combine in one list those that occur in current year
    (list-range (list date0 date1 date2)
                (gregorian-year-range g-year))))
```

(7.6)

```
(defun mawlid (g-year)
  ;; TYPE gregorian-year -> list-of-fixed-dates
  ;; List of fixed dates of Mawlid an-Nabi occurring in
  ;; Gregorian year g-year.
  (islamic-in-gregorian 3 12 g-year))
```

D.8 The Hebrew Calendar

```
(defun hebrew-date (year month day)
  ;; TYPE (hebrew-year hebrew-month hebrew-day) -> hebrew-date
  (list year month day))
```

(8.1)

```
(defconstant nisan
  ;; TYPE hebrew-month
  ;; Nisan is month number 1.
  1)
```

(8.2)

```
(defconstant iyyar
  ;; TYPE hebrew-month
  ;; Iyyar is month number 2.
  2)
```

(8.3)

```
(defconstant sivan
  ;; TYPE hebrew-month
  ;; Sivan is month number 3.
  3)
```

(8.4)

```
(defconstant tammuz
  ;; TYPE hebrew-month
  ;; Tammuz is month number 4.
  4)
```

(8.5)

```
(defconstant av
  ;; TYPE hebrew-month
  ;; Av is month number 5.
  5)
```

(8.6)

```
(defconstant elul
  ;; TYPE hebrew-month
  ;; Elul is month number 6.
  6)
```

(8.7)

```
(defconstant tishri
  ;; TYPE hebrew-month
  ;; Tishri is month number 7.
  7)
```

(8.8)
```
(defconstant marheshvan
  ;; TYPE hebrew-month
  ;; Marheshvan is month number 8.
  8)
```

(8.9)
```
(defconstant kislev
  ;; TYPE hebrew-month
  ;; Kislev is month number 9.
  9)
```

(8.10)
```
(defconstant tevet
  ;; TYPE hebrew-month
  ;; Tevet is month number 10.
  10)
```

(8.11)
```
(defconstant shevat
  ;; TYPE hebrew-month
  ;; Shevat is month number 11.
  11)
```

(8.12)
```
(defconstant adar
  ;; TYPE hebrew-month
  ;; Adar is month number 12.
  12)
```

(8.13)
```
(defconstant adarii
  ;; TYPE hebrew-month
  ;; Adar II is month number 13.
  13)
```

(8.14)
```
(defun hebrew-leap-year? (h-year)
  ;; TYPE hebrew-year -> boolean
  ;; True if h-year is a leap year on Hebrew calendar.
  (< (mod (1+ (* 7 h-year)) 19) 7))
```

(8.15)
```
(defun last-month-of-hebrew-year (h-year)
  ;; TYPE hebrew-year -> hebrew-month
  ;; Last month of Hebrew year h-year.
  (if (hebrew-leap-year? h-year)
      adarii
    adar))
```

(8.16)
```
(defun hebrew-sabbatical-year? (h-year)
  ;; TYPE hebrew-year -> boolean
  ;; True if h-year is a sabbatical year on the Hebrew
  ;; calendar.
  (= (mod h-year 7) 0))
```

(8.17)
```
(defconstant hebrew-epoch
  ;; TYPE fixed-date
  ;; Fixed date of start of the Hebrew calendar, that is,
  ;; Tishri 1, 1 AM.
  (fixed-from-julian (julian-date (bce 3761) october 7)))
```

(8.19)
```
(defun molad (h-year h-month)
  ;; TYPE (hebrew-year hebrew-month) -> rational-moment
  ;; Moment of mean conjunction of h-month in Hebrew
  ;; h-year.
  (let* ((y ;; Treat Nisan as start of year.
          (if (< h-month tishri)
              (1+ h-year)
            h-year))
```

```
          (months-elapsed
           (+ (- h-month tishri)  ;; Months this year.
              (quotient ;; Months until New Year.
               (- (* 235 y) 234)
               19))))
     (+ hebrew-epoch
        -876/25920
        (* months-elapsed (+ 29 (hr 12) 793/25920)))))
```

(8.20)

```
(defun hebrew-calendar-elapsed-days (h-year)
  ;; TYPE hebrew-year -> integer
  ;; Number of days elapsed from the (Sunday) noon prior
  ;; to the epoch of the Hebrew calendar to the mean
  ;; conjunction (molad) of Tishri of Hebrew year h-year,
  ;; or one day later.
  (let* ((months-elapsed  ; Since start of Hebrew calendar.
          (quotient (- (* 235 h-year) 234) 19))
         (parts-elapsed; Fractions of days since prior noon.
          (+ 12084 (* 13753 months-elapsed)))
         (days  ; Whole days since prior noon.
          (+ (* 29 months-elapsed)
             (quotient parts-elapsed 25920)))
         ;; If (* 13753 months-elapsed) causes integers that
         ;; are too large, use instead:
         ;; (parts-elapsed
         ;;  (+ 204 (* 793 (mod months-elapsed 1080))))
         ;; (hours-elapsed
         ;;  (+ 11 (* 12 months-elapsed)
         ;;     (* 793 (quotient months-elapsed 1080))
         ;;     (quotient parts-elapsed 1080)))
         ;; (days
         ;;  (+ (* 29 months-elapsed)
         ;;     (quotient hours-elapsed 24)))
         ;; If even larger integers aren't a problem, use just:
         ;; (days
         ;;  (quotient (+ 12084 (* months-elapsed 765433))
         ;;            25920)))
         )
    (if (< (mod (* 3 (1+ days)) 7) 3); Sun, Wed, or Fri
        (+ days 1) ; Delay one day.
      days)))
```

(8.21)

```
(defun hebrew-year-length-correction (h-year)
  ;; TYPE hebrew-year -> 0-2
  ;; Delays to start of Hebrew year h-year to keep ordinary
  ;; year in range 353-356 and leap year in range 383-386.
  (let* ((ny0 (hebrew-calendar-elapsed-days (1- h-year)))
         (ny1 (hebrew-calendar-elapsed-days h-year))
         (ny2 (hebrew-calendar-elapsed-days (1+ h-year))))
    (cond
     ((= (- ny2 ny1) 356) ; Next year would be too long.
      2)
     ((= (- ny1 ny0) 382) ; Previous year too short.
      1)
     (t 0))))
```

(8.22)

```
(defun hebrew-new-year (h-year)
  ;; TYPE hebrew-year -> fixed-date
  ;; Fixed date of Hebrew new year h-year.
  (+ hebrew-epoch
     (hebrew-calendar-elapsed-days h-year)
     (hebrew-year-length-correction h-year)))
```

(8.23)

```
(defun last-day-of-hebrew-month (h-year h-month)
  ;; TYPE (hebrew-year hebrew-month) -> hebrew-day
  ;; Last day of month h-month in Hebrew year h-year.
  (if (or (member h-month
                  (list iyyar tammuz elul tevet adarii))
          (and (= h-month adar)
               (not (hebrew-leap-year? h-year)))
```

```
          (and (= h-month marheshvan)
               (not (long-marheshvan? h-year)))
          (and (= h-month kislev)
               (short-kislev? h-year)))
      29
    30))
```

(8.24)

```
(defun long-marheshvan? (h-year)
  ;; TYPE hebrew-year -> boolean
  ;; True if Marheshvan is long in Hebrew year h-year.
  (member (days-in-hebrew-year h-year) (list 355 385)))
```

(8.25)

```
(defun short-kislev? (h-year)
  ;; TYPE hebrew-year -> boolean
  ;; True if Kislev is short in Hebrew year h-year.
  (member (days-in-hebrew-year h-year) (list 353 383)))
```

(8.26)

```
(defun days-in-hebrew-year (h-year)
  ;; TYPE hebrew-year -> {353,354,355,383,384,385}
  ;; Number of days in Hebrew year h-year.
  (- (hebrew-new-year (1+ h-year))
     (hebrew-new-year h-year)))
```

(8.27)

```
(defun fixed-from-hebrew (h-date)
  ;; TYPE hebrew-date -> fixed-date
  ;; Fixed date of Hebrew date h-date.
  (let* ((month (standard-month h-date))
         (day (standard-day h-date))
         (year (standard-year h-date)))
    (+ (hebrew-new-year year)
       day -1                 ; Days so far this month.
       (if ;; before Tishri
           (< month tishri)
           ;; Then add days in prior months this year before
           ;; and after Nisan.
           (+ (sum (last-day-of-hebrew-month year m)
                   m tishri
                   (<= m (last-month-of-hebrew-year year)))
              (sum (last-day-of-hebrew-month year m)
                   m nisan (< m month)))
         ;; Else add days in prior months this year
         (sum (last-day-of-hebrew-month year m)
              m tishri (< m month))))))
```

(8.28)

```
(defun hebrew-from-fixed (date)
  ;; TYPE fixed-date -> hebrew-date
  ;; Hebrew (year month day) corresponding to fixed date.
  ;; The fraction can be approximated by 365.25.
  (let* ((approx    ; Approximate year
          (1+
           (quotient (- date hebrew-epoch) 35975351/98496)))
         ;; The value 35975351/98496, the average length of
         ;; a Hebrew year, can be approximated by 365.25
         (year      ; Search forward.
          (final y (1- approx)
                 (<= (hebrew-new-year y) date)))
         (start     ; Starting month for search for month.
          (if (< date (fixed-from-hebrew
                       (hebrew-date year nisan 1)))
              tishri
            nisan))
         (month ; Search forward from either Tishri or Nisan.
          (next m start
                (<= date
                    (fixed-from-hebrew
                     (hebrew-date
                      year
```

```
                          m
                          (last-day-of-hebrew-month year m))))))
          (day   ; Calculate the day by subtraction.
           (1+ (- date (fixed-from-hebrew
                          (hebrew-date year month 1))))))
     (hebrew-date year month day)))
```

We are using Common Lisp exact arithmetic for rationals here (and elsewhere). Without that facility, one must rephrase all quotient operations to work with integers only.

The function hebrew-calendar-elapsed-days is called repeatedly during the calculations, often several times for the same year. A more efficient algorithm could avoid such repetition.

(8.29)

```
(defun fixed-from-molad (moon)
  ;; TYPE duration -> fixed-date
  ;; Fixed date of the molad that occurs moon days
  ;; and fractional days into the week.
  (let* ((r (mod (- (* 74377 moon) 2879/2160) 7)))
    (fixed-from-moment
     (+ (molad 1 tishri) (* r 765433)))))
```

(This latter function requires 64-bit integers.)

(8.30)

```
(defun yom-kippur (g-year)
  ;; TYPE gregorian-year -> fixed-date
  ;; Fixed date of Yom Kippur occurring in Gregorian year
  ;; g-year.
  (let* ((h-year
          (1+ (- g-year
                 (gregorian-year-from-fixed
                  hebrew-epoch)))))
    (fixed-from-hebrew (hebrew-date h-year tishri 10))))
```

(8.31)

```
(defun passover (g-year)
  ;; TYPE gregorian-year -> fixed-date
  ;; Fixed date of Passover occurring in Gregorian year
  ;; g-year.
  (let* ((h-year
          (- g-year
             (gregorian-year-from-fixed hebrew-epoch))))
    (fixed-from-hebrew (hebrew-date h-year nisan 15))))
```

(8.32)

```
(defun omer (date)
  ;; TYPE fixed-date -> omer-count
  ;; Number of elapsed weeks and days in the omer at date.
  ;; Returns bogus if that date does not fall during the
  ;; omer.
  (let* ((c (- date
               (passover
                (gregorian-year-from-fixed date)))))
    (if (<= 1 c 49)
        (list (quotient c 7) (mod c 7))
      bogus)))
```

(8.33)

```
(defun purim (g-year)
  ;; TYPE gregorian-year -> fixed-date
  ;; Fixed date of Purim occurring in Gregorian year g-year.
  (let* ((h-year
          (- g-year
             (gregorian-year-from-fixed hebrew-epoch)))
         (last-month  ; Adar or Adar II
          (last-month-of-hebrew-year h-year)))
    (fixed-from-hebrew
     (hebrew-date h-year last-month 14))))
```

(8.34)

```
(defun ta-anit-esther (g-year)
  ;; TYPE gregorian-year -> fixed-date
  ;; Fixed date of Ta'anit Esther occurring in
  ;; Gregorian year g-year.
  (let* ((purim-date (purim g-year)))
```

```
    (if ; Purim is on Sunday
        (= (day-of-week-from-fixed purim-date) sunday)
        ;; Then prior Thursday
        (- purim-date 3)
      ;; Else previous day
      (1- purim-date))))
```

(8.35)

```
(defun tishah-be-av (g-year)
  ;; TYPE gregorian-year -> fixed-date
  ;; Fixed date of Tishah be-Av occurring in
  ;; Gregorian year g-year.
  (let* ((h-year ; Hebrew year
          (- g-year
             (gregorian-year-from-fixed hebrew-epoch)))
         (av9
          (fixed-from-hebrew
           (hebrew-date h-year av 9))))
    (if ; Ninth of Av is Saturday
        (= (day-of-week-from-fixed av9) saturday)
        ;; Then the next day
        (1+ av9)
      av9)))
```

(8.36)

```
(defun yom-ha-zikkaron (g-year)
  ;; TYPE gregorian-year -> fixed-date
  ;; Fixed date of Yom ha-Zikkaron occurring in Gregorian
  ;; year g-year.
  (let* ((h-year ; Hebrew year
          (- g-year
             (gregorian-year-from-fixed hebrew-epoch)))
         (iyyar4; Ordinarily Iyyar 4
          (fixed-from-hebrew
           (hebrew-date h-year iyyar 4))))
    (cond ((member (day-of-week-from-fixed iyyar4)
                   (list thursday friday))
           ;; If Iyyar 4 is Thursday or Friday, then Wednesday
           (kday-before wednesday iyyar4))
          ;; If it's on Sunday, then Monday
          ((= sunday (day-of-week-from-fixed iyyar4))
           (1+ iyyar4))
          (t iyyar4))))
```

(8.37)

```
(defun sh-ela (g-year)
  ;; TYPE gregorian-year -> list-of-fixed-dates
  ;; List of fixed dates of Sh'ela occurring in
  ;; Gregorian year g-year.
  (coptic-in-gregorian 3 26 g-year))
```

(8.38)

```
(defun birkath-ha-hama (g-year)
  ;; TYPE gregorian-year -> list-of-fixed-dates
  ;; List of fixed date of Birkath ha-Hama occurring in
  ;; Gregorian year g-year, if it occurs.
  (let* ((dates (coptic-in-gregorian 7 30 g-year)))
    (if (and (not (equal dates nil))
             (= (mod (standard-year
                      (coptic-from-fixed (first dates)))
                     28)
                17))
        dates
      nil)))
```

(8.39)

```
(defun samuel-season-in-gregorian (season g-year)
  ;; TYPE (season gregorian-year) -> list-of-moments
  ;; Moment(s) of season in Gregorian year g-year
  ;; per Samuel.
  (let* ((cap-Y (+ 365 (hr 6)))
         (offset ; season start
```

```
          (* (/ season (deg 360)) cap-Y)))
    (cycle-in-gregorian season g-year cap-Y
                        (+ (fixed-from-hebrew
                            (hebrew-date 1 adar 21))
                           (hr 18)
                           offset))))
```

(8.40)

```
(defun alt-birkath-ha-hama (g-year)
  ;; TYPE gregorian-year -> list-of-fixed-dates
  ;; List of fixed date of Birkath ha-Hama occurring in
  ;; Gregorian year g-year, if it occurs.
  (let* ((cap-Y (+ 365 (hr 6))) ; year
         (season (+ spring (* (hr 6) (/ (deg 360) cap-Y))))
         (moments (samuel-season-in-gregorian season g-year)))
    (if (and (not (equal moments nil))
             (= (day-of-week-from-fixed (first moments))
                wednesday)
             (= (time-from-moment (first moments))
                (hr 0))) ; midnight
        (list (fixed-from-moment (first moments)))
      nil)))
```

(8.41)

```
(defun adda-season-in-gregorian (season g-year)
  ;; TYPE (season gregorian-year) -> list-of-moments
  ;; Moment(s) of season in Gregorian year g-year
  ;; per R. Adda bar Ahava.
  (let* ((cap-Y (+ 365 (hr (+ 5 3791/4104))))
         (offset ; season start
          (* (/ season (deg 360)) cap-Y)))
    (cycle-in-gregorian season g-year cap-Y
                        (+ (fixed-from-hebrew
                            (hebrew-date 1 adar 28))
                           (hr 18)
                           offset))))
```

(8.42)

```
(defun hebrew-in-gregorian (h-month h-day g-year)
  ;; TYPE (hebrew-month hebrew-day gregorian-year)
  ;; TYPE  -> list-of-fixed-dates
  ;; List of the fixed dates of Hebrew month h-month, day
  ;; h-day that occur in Gregorian year g-year.
  (let* ((jan1 (gregorian-new-year g-year))
         (y (standard-year (hebrew-from-fixed jan1)))
         ;; The possible occurrences in one year are
         (date0 (fixed-from-hebrew
                 (hebrew-date y h-month h-day)))
         (date1 (fixed-from-hebrew
                 (hebrew-date (1+ y) h-month h-day)))
         (date2 (fixed-from-hebrew
                 (hebrew-date (+ y 2) h-month h-day))))
    (list-range (list date0 date1 date2)
                (gregorian-year-range g-year))))
```

(8.43)

```
(defun hanukkah (g-year)
  ;; TYPE gregorian-year -> list-of-fixed-dates
  ;; Fixed date(s) of first day of Hanukkah
  ;; occurring in Gregorian year g-year.
  (hebrew-in-gregorian kislev 25 g-year))
```

(8.44)

```
(defun hebrew-birthday (birthdate h-year)
  ;; TYPE (hebrew-date hebrew-year) -> fixed-date
  ;; Fixed date of the anniversary of Hebrew birthdate
  ;; occurring in Hebrew h-year.
  (let* ((birth-day (standard-day birthdate))
         (birth-month (standard-month birthdate))
         (birth-year (standard-year birthdate)))
    (if ; It's Adar in a normal Hebrew year or Adar II
                                        ; in a Hebrew leap year,
        (= birth-month (last-month-of-hebrew-year birth-year))
        ;; Then use the same day in last month of Hebrew year.
```

```
        (fixed-from-hebrew
         (hebrew-date h-year (last-month-of-hebrew-year h-year)
                      birth-day))
      ;; Else use the normal anniversary of the birth date,
      ;; or the corresponding day in years without that date
      (+ (fixed-from-hebrew
           (hebrew-date h-year birth-month 1))
         birth-day -1))))
```

(8.45)

```
(defun hebrew-birthday-in-gregorian (birthdate g-year)
  ;; TYPE (hebrew-date gregorian-year)
  ;; TYPE  -> list-of-fixed-dates
  ;; List of the fixed dates of Hebrew birthday
  ;; that occur in Gregorian g-year.
  (let* ((jan1 (gregorian-new-year g-year))
         (y (standard-year (hebrew-from-fixed jan1)))
         ;; The possible occurrences in one year are
         (date0 (hebrew-birthday birthdate y))
         (date1 (hebrew-birthday birthdate (1+ y)))
         (date2 (hebrew-birthday birthdate (+ y 2))))
    ;; Combine in one list those that occur in current year.
    (list-range (list date0 date1 date2)
                (gregorian-year-range g-year))))
```

(8.46)

```
(defun yahrzeit (death-date h-year)
  ;; TYPE (hebrew-date hebrew-year) -> fixed-date
  ;; Fixed date of the anniversary of Hebrew death-date
  ;; occurring in Hebrew h-year.
  (let* ((death-day (standard-day death-date))
         (death-month (standard-month death-date))
         (death-year (standard-year death-date)))
    (cond
     ;; If it's Marheshvan 30 it depends on the first
     ;; anniversary; if that was not Marheshvan 30, use
     ;; the day before Kislev 1.
     ((and (= death-month marheshvan)
           (= death-day 30)
           (not (long-marheshvan? (1+ death-year))))
      (1- (fixed-from-hebrew
           (hebrew-date h-year kislev 1))))
     ;; If it's Kislev 30 it depends on the first
     ;; anniversary; if that was not Kislev 30, use
     ;; the day before Tevet 1.
     ((and (= death-month kislev)
           (= death-day 30)
           (short-kislev? (1+ death-year)))
      (1- (fixed-from-hebrew
           (hebrew-date h-year tevet 1))))
     ;; If it's Adar II, use the same day in last
     ;; month of Hebrew year (Adar or Adar II).
     ((= death-month adarii)
      (fixed-from-hebrew
       (hebrew-date
        h-year (last-month-of-hebrew-year h-year)
        death-day)))
     ;; If it's the 30th in Adar I and Hebrew year is not a
     ;; Hebrew leap year (so Adar has only 29 days), use the
     ;; last day in Shevat.
     ((and (= death-day 30)
           (= death-month adar)
           (not (hebrew-leap-year? h-year)))
      (fixed-from-hebrew (hebrew-date h-year shevat 30)))
     ;; In all other cases, use the normal anniversary of
     ;; the date of death.
     (t (+ (fixed-from-hebrew
             (hebrew-date h-year death-month 1))
           death-day -1)))))
```

(8.47)

```
(defun yahrzeit-in-gregorian (death-date g-year)
  ;; TYPE (hebrew-date gregorian-year)
```

```
  ;; TYPE  -> list-of-fixed-dates
  ;; List of the fixed dates of death-date (yahrzeit)
  ;; that occur in Gregorian year g-year.
  (let* ((jan1 (gregorian-new-year g-year))
         (y (standard-year (hebrew-from-fixed jan1)))
         ;; The possible occurrences in one year are
         (date0 (yahrzeit death-date y))
         (date1 (yahrzeit death-date (1+ y)))
         (date2 (yahrzeit death-date (+ y 2))))
    ;; Combine in one list those that occur in current year
    (list-range (list date0 date1 date2)
                (gregorian-year-range g-year))))
```

(8.49)

```
(defun shift-days (l cap-Delta)
  ;; TYPE (list-of-weekdays integer) -> list-of-weekdays
  ;; Shift each weekday on list l by cap-Delta days
  (if (equal l nil)
      nil
    (append (list (mod (+ (first l) cap-Delta) 7))
            (shift-days (rest l) cap-Delta))))
```

(8.50)

```
(defun possible-hebrew-days (h-month h-day)
  ;; TYPE (hebrew-month hebrew-day) -> list-of-weekdays
  ;; Possible days of week
  (let* ((h-date0 (hebrew-date 5 nisan 1))
         ;; leap year with full pattern
         (h-year (if (> h-month elul) 6 5))
         (h-date (hebrew-date h-year h-month h-day))
         (n (- (fixed-from-hebrew h-date)
               (fixed-from-hebrew h-date0)))
         (basic (list tuesday thursday saturday))
         (extra
          (cond
           ((and (= h-month marheshvan) (= h-day 30))
            nil)
           ((and (= h-month kislev) (< h-day 30))
            (list monday wednesday friday))
           ((and (= h-month kislev) (= h-day 30))
            (list monday))
           ((member h-month (list tevet shevat))
            (list sunday monday))
           ((and (= h-month adar) (< h-day 30))
            (list sunday monday))
           (t (list sunday)))))
    (shift-days (append basic extra) n)))
```

D.9 The Ecclesiastical Calendars

(9.1)

```
(defun orthodox-easter (g-year)
  ;; TYPE gregorian-year -> fixed-date
  ;; Fixed date of Orthodox Easter in Gregorian year g-year.
  (let* ((shifted-epact ; Age of moon for April 5.
          (mod (+ 14 (* 11 (mod g-year 19)))
               30))
         (j-year (if (> g-year 0); Julian year number.
                     g-year
                   (1- g-year)))
         (paschal-moon  ; Day after full moon on
                                        ; or after March 21.
          (- (fixed-from-julian (julian-date j-year april 19))
             shifted-epact)))
    ;; Return the Sunday following the Paschal moon.
    (kday-after sunday paschal-moon)))
```

(9.2)

```
(defun alt-orthodox-easter (g-year)
  ;; TYPE gregorian-year -> fixed-date
  ;; Alternative calculation of fixed date of Orthodox Easter
  ;; in Gregorian year g-year.
  (let* ((paschal-moon  ; Day after full moon on
```

```
                                        ; or after March 21.
          (+ (* 354 g-year)
             (* 30 (quotient (+ (* 7 g-year) 8) 19))
             (quotient g-year 4)
             (- (quotient g-year 19))
             -273
             gregorian-epoch)))
    ;; Return the Sunday following the Paschal moon.
    (kday-after sunday paschal-moon)))
```

```
(defun easter (g-year)                                         (9.3)
  ;; TYPE gregorian-year -> fixed-date
  ;; Fixed date of Easter in Gregorian year g-year.
  (let* ((century (1+ (quotient g-year 100)))
         (shifted-epact        ; Age of moon for April 5...
          (mod
           (+ 14 (* 11 (mod g-year 19));    ...by Nicaean rule
              (- ;...corrected for the Gregorian century rule
               (quotient (* 3 century) 4))
              (quotient; ...corrected for Metonic
                                        ; cycle inaccuracy.
               (+ 5 (* 8 century)) 25))
           30))
         (adjusted-epact        ;  Adjust for 29.5 day month.
          (if (or (= shifted-epact 0)
                  (and (= shifted-epact 1)
                       (< 10 (mod g-year 19))))
              (1+ shifted-epact)
            shifted-epact))
         (paschal-moon; Day after full moon on
                                        ; or after March 21.
          (- (fixed-from-gregorian
              (gregorian-date g-year april 19))
             adjusted-epact)))
    ;; Return the Sunday following the Paschal moon.
    (kday-after sunday paschal-moon)))
```

```
(defun pentecost (g-year)                                      (9.4)
  ;; TYPE gregorian-year -> fixed-date
  ;; Fixed date of Pentecost in Gregorian year g-year.
  (+ (easter g-year) 49))
```

D.10 The Old Hindu Calendars

```
(defconstant hindu-epoch                                       (10.1)
  ;; TYPE fixed-date
  ;; Fixed date of start of the Hindu calendar (Kali Yuga).
  (fixed-from-julian (julian-date (bce 3102) february 18)))
```

```
(defun hindu-day-count (date)                                  (10.2)
  ;; TYPE fixed-date -> integer
  ;; Elapsed days (Ahargana) to date since Hindu epoch (KY).
  (- date hindu-epoch))
```

```
(defconstant arya-solar-year                                   (10.3)
  ;; TYPE rational
  ;; Length of Old Hindu solar year.
  1577917500/4320000)
```

```
(defconstant arya-jovian-period                                (10.4)
  ;; TYPE rational
  ;; Number of days in one revolution of Jupiter around the
  ;; Sun.
  1577917500/364224)
```

```
(defun jovian-year (date)                                      (10.5)
  ;; TYPE fixed-date -> 1-60
  ;; Year of Jupiter cycle at fixed date.
  (amod (+ 27 (quotient (hindu-day-count date)
                        (/ arya-jovian-period 12)))
        60))
```

(10.6)
```
(defconstant arya-solar-month
  ;; TYPE rational
  ;; Length of Old Hindu solar month.
  (/ arya-solar-year 12))
```

(10.7)
```
(defun fixed-from-old-hindu-solar (s-date)
  ;; TYPE hindu-solar-date -> fixed-date
  ;; Fixed date corresponding to Old Hindu solar date s-date.
  (let* ((month (standard-month s-date))
         (day (standard-day s-date))
         (year (standard-year s-date)))
    (ceiling
     (+ hindu-epoch ; Since start of era.
        (* year arya-solar-year) ; Days in elapsed years
        (* (1- month) arya-solar-month) ; ...in months.
        day (hr -30)))))) ; Midnight of day.
```

(10.8)
```
(defun old-hindu-solar-from-fixed (date)
  ;; TYPE fixed-date -> hindu-solar-date
  ;; Old Hindu solar date equivalent to fixed date.
  (let* ((sun ; Sunrise on Hindu date.
          (+ (hindu-day-count date) (hr 6)))
         (year    ; Elapsed years.
          (quotient sun arya-solar-year))
         (month (1+ (mod (quotient sun arya-solar-month)
                         12)))
         (day (1+ (floor (mod sun arya-solar-month)))))
    (hindu-solar-date year month day)))
```

```
(defun old-hindu-lunar-date (year month leap day)
  ;; TYPE (old-hindu-lunar-year old-hindu-lunar-month
  ;; TYPE  old-hindu-lunar-leap old-hindu-lunar-day)
  ;; TYPE  -> old-hindu-lunar-date
  (list year month leap day))
```

```
(defun old-hindu-lunar-month (date)
  ;; TYPE old-hindu-lunar-date -> old-hindu-lunar-month
  (second date))
```

```
(defun old-hindu-lunar-leap (date)
  ;; TYPE old-hindu-lunar-date -> old-hindu-lunar-leap
  (third date))
```

```
(defun old-hindu-lunar-day (date)
  ;; TYPE old-hindu-lunar-date -> old-hindu-lunar-day
  (fourth date))
```

```
(defun old-hindu-lunar-year (date)
  ;; TYPE old-hindu-lunar-date -> old-hindu-lunar-year
  (first date))
```

(10.9)
```
(defconstant arya-lunar-month
  ;; TYPE rational
  ;; Length of Old Hindu lunar month.
  1577917500/53433336)
```

(10.10)
```
(defconstant arya-lunar-day
  ;; TYPE rational
  ;; Length of Old Hindu lunar day.
  (/ arya-lunar-month 30))
```

(10.11)

```
(defun old-hindu-lunar-leap-year? (l-year)
  ;; TYPE old-hindu-lunar-year -> boolean
  ;; True if l-year is a leap year on the
  ;; old Hindu calendar.
  (>= (mod (- (* l-year arya-solar-year)
              arya-solar-month)
           arya-lunar-month)
      23902504679/1282400064))
```

(10.13)

```
(defun old-hindu-lunar-from-fixed (date)
  ;; TYPE fixed-date -> old-hindu-lunar-date
  ;; Old Hindu lunar date equivalent to fixed date.
  (let* ((sun ; Sunrise on Hindu date.
          (+ (hindu-day-count date) (hr 6)))
         (new-moon ; Beginning of lunar month.
          (- sun (mod sun arya-lunar-month)))
         (leap ; If lunar contained in solar.
          (and (>= (- arya-solar-month arya-lunar-month)
                   (mod new-moon arya-solar-month))
               (> (mod new-moon arya-solar-month) 0)))
         (month ; Next solar month's name.
          (1+ (mod (ceiling (/ new-moon
                               arya-solar-month))
                   12)))
         (day ; Lunar days since beginning of lunar month.
          (1+ (mod (quotient sun arya-lunar-day) 30)))
         (year ; Solar year at end of lunar month(s).
          (1- (ceiling (/ (+ new-moon arya-solar-month)
                          arya-solar-year)))))
    (old-hindu-lunar-date year month leap day)))
```

(10.14)

```
(defun fixed-from-old-hindu-lunar (l-date)
  ;; TYPE old-hindu-lunar-date -> fixed-date
  ;; Fixed date corresponding to Old Hindu lunar date
  ;; l-date.
  (let* ((year (old-hindu-lunar-year l-date))
         (month (old-hindu-lunar-month l-date))
         (leap (old-hindu-lunar-leap l-date))
         (day (old-hindu-lunar-day l-date))
         (mina ; One solar month before solar new year.
          (* (1- (* 12 year)) arya-solar-month))
         (lunar-new-year ; New moon after mina.
          (* arya-lunar-month
             (1+ (quotient mina arya-lunar-month)))))
    (ceiling
     (+ hindu-epoch
        lunar-new-year
        (* arya-lunar-month
           (if ; If there was a leap month this year.
               (and (not leap)
                    (<= (ceiling (/ (- lunar-new-year mina)
                                    (- arya-solar-month
                                       arya-lunar-month)))
                        month))
               month
             (1- month)))
        (* (1- day) arya-lunar-day) ; Lunar days.
        (hr -6))))) ; Subtract 1 if phase begins before
                    ; sunrise.
```

D.11 The Mayan Calendars

```
(defun mayan-long-count-date (baktun katun tun uinal kin)
  ;; TYPE (mayan-baktun mayan-katun mayan-tun mayan-uinal
  ;; TYPE  mayan-kin) -> mayan-long-count-date
  (list baktun katun tun uinal kin))
```

```
(defun mayan-baktun (date)
  ;; TYPE mayan-long-count-date -> mayan-baktun
  (first date))
```

```
(defun mayan-katun (date)
  ;; TYPE mayan-long-count-date -> mayan-katun
  (second date))
```

```
(defun mayan-tun (date)
  ;; TYPE mayan-long-count-date -> mayan-tun
  (third date))
```

```
(defun mayan-uinal (date)
  ;; TYPE mayan-long-count-date -> mayan-uinal
  (fourth date))
```

```
(defun mayan-kin (date)
  ;; TYPE mayan-long-count-date -> mayan-kin
  (fifth date))
```

(11.1)
```
(defconstant mayan-epoch
  ;; TYPE fixed-date
  ;; Fixed date of start of the Mayan calendar, according
  ;; to the Goodman-Martinez-Thompson correlation.
  ;; That is, August 11, -3113.
  (fixed-from-jd 584283))
```

(11.2)
```
(defun fixed-from-mayan-long-count (count)
  ;; TYPE mayan-long-count-date -> fixed-date
  ;; Fixed date corresponding to the Mayan long count,
  ;; which is a list (baktun katun tun uinal kin).
  (+ mayan-epoch       ; Fixed date at Mayan 0.0.0.0.0
     (from-radix count (list 20 20 18 20))))
```

(11.3)
```
(defun mayan-long-count-from-fixed (date)
  ;; TYPE fixed-date -> mayan-long-count-date
  ;; Mayan long count date of fixed date.
  (to-radix (- date mayan-epoch) (list 20 20 18 20)))
```

```
(defun mayan-haab-date (month day)
  ;; TYPE (mayan-haab-month mayan-haab-day) -> mayan-haab-date
  (list month day))
```

```
(defun mayan-haab-day (date)
  ;; TYPE mayan-haab-date -> mayan-haab-day
  (second date))
```

```
(defun mayan-haab-month (date)
  ;; TYPE mayan-haab-date -> mayan-haab-month
  (first date))
```

(11.4)
```
(defun mayan-haab-ordinal (h-date)
  ;; TYPE mayan-haab-date -> nonnegative-integer
  ;; Number of days into cycle of Mayan haab date h-date.
  (let* ((day (mayan-haab-day h-date))
         (month (mayan-haab-month h-date)))
    (+ (* (1- month) 20) day)))
```

(11.5)
```
(defconstant mayan-haab-epoch
  ;; TYPE fixed-date
  ;; Fixed date of start of haab cycle.
  (- mayan-epoch
     (mayan-haab-ordinal (mayan-haab-date 18 8))))
```

```
(defun mayan-haab-from-fixed (date)                                    (11.6)
  ;; TYPE fixed-date -> mayan-haab-date
  ;; Mayan haab date of fixed date.
  (let* ((count
           (mod (- date mayan-haab-epoch) 365))
          (day (mod count 20))
          (month (1+ (quotient count 20))))
    (mayan-haab-date month day)))
```

```
(defun mayan-haab-on-or-before (haab date)                             (11.7)
  ;; TYPE (mayan-haab-date fixed-date) -> fixed-date
  ;; Fixed date of latest date on or before fixed date
  ;; that is Mayan haab date haab.
  (mod3 (+ (mayan-haab-ordinal haab) mayan-haab-epoch)
        date (- date 365)))
```

```
(defun mayan-tzolkin-date (number name)
  ;; TYPE (mayan-tzolkin-number mayan-tzolkin-name)
  ;; TYPE  -> mayan-tzolkin-date
  (list number name))
```

```
(defun mayan-tzolkin-number (date)
  ;; TYPE mayan-tzolkin-date -> mayan-tzolkin-number
  (first date))
```

```
(defun mayan-tzolkin-name (date)
  ;; TYPE mayan-tzolkin-date -> mayan-tzolkin-name
  (second date))
```

```
(defconstant mayan-tzolkin-epoch                                       (11.8)
  ;; TYPE fixed-date
  ;; Start of tzolkin date cycle.
  (- mayan-epoch
     (mayan-tzolkin-ordinal (mayan-tzolkin-date 4 20))))
```

```
(defun mayan-tzolkin-from-fixed (date)                                 (11.9)
  ;; TYPE fixed-date -> mayan-tzolkin-date
  ;; Mayan tzolkin date of fixed date.
  (let* ((count (- date mayan-tzolkin-epoch -1))
         (number (amod count 13))
         (name (amod count 20)))
    (mayan-tzolkin-date number name)))
```

```
(defun mayan-tzolkin-ordinal (t-date)                                  (11.10)
  ;; TYPE mayan-tzolkin-date -> nonnegative-integer
  ;; Number of days into Mayan tzolkin cycle of t-date.
  (let* ((number (mayan-tzolkin-number t-date))
         (name (mayan-tzolkin-name t-date)))
    (mod (+ number -1
            (* 39 (- number name)))
         260)))
```

```
(defun mayan-tzolkin-on-or-before (tzolkin date)                       (11.11)
  ;; TYPE (mayan-tzolkin-date fixed-date) -> fixed-date
  ;; Fixed date of latest date on or before fixed date
  ;; that is Mayan tzolkin date tzolkin.
  (mod3 (+ (mayan-tzolkin-ordinal tzolkin) mayan-tzolkin-epoch)
        date (- date 260)))
```

```
(defun mayan-year-bearer-from-fixed (date)                             (11.12)
  ;; TYPE fixed-date -> mayan-tzolkin-name
  ;; Year bearer of year containing fixed date.
  ;; Returns bogus for uayeb.
  (let* ((x (mayan-haab-on-or-before
              (mayan-haab-date 1 0)
              date)))
    (if (= (mayan-haab-month (mayan-haab-from-fixed date))
           19)
        bogus
      (mayan-tzolkin-name (mayan-tzolkin-from-fixed x)))))
```

(11.13)

```
(defun mayan-calendar-round-on-or-before (haab tzolkin date)
  ;; TYPE (mayan-haab-date mayan-tzolkin-date fixed-date)
  ;; TYPE  -> fixed-date
  ;; Fixed date of latest date on or before date, that is
  ;; Mayan haab date haab and tzolkin date tzolkin.
  ;; Returns bogus for impossible combinations.
  (let* ((haab-count
          (+ (mayan-haab-ordinal haab) mayan-haab-epoch))
         (tzolkin-count
          (+ (mayan-tzolkin-ordinal tzolkin)
             mayan-tzolkin-epoch))
         (diff (- tzolkin-count haab-count)))
    (if (= (mod diff 5) 0)
        (mod3 (+ haab-count (* 365 diff))
              date (- date 18980))
      bogus))); haab-tzolkin combination is impossible.
```

(11.14)

```
(defconstant aztec-correlation
  ;; TYPE fixed-date
  ;; Known date of Aztec cycles (Caso's correlation)
  (fixed-from-julian (julian-date 1521 August 13)))
```

```
(defun aztec-xihuitl-date (month day)
  ;; TYPE (aztec-xihuitl-month aztec-xihuitl-day) ->
  ;; TYPE  aztec-xihuitl-date
  (list month day))
```

```
(defun aztec-xihuitl-month (date)
  ;; TYPE aztec-xihuitl-date -> aztec-xihuitl-month
  (first date))
```

```
(defun aztec-xihuitl-day (date)
  ;; TYPE aztec-xihuitl-date -> aztec-xihuitl-day
  (second date))
```

(11.15)

```
(defun aztec-xihuitl-ordinal (x-date)
  ;; TYPE aztec-xihuitl-date -> nonnegative-integer
  ;; Number of elapsed days into cycle of Aztec xihuitl x-date.
  (let* ((day (aztec-xihuitl-day x-date))
         (month (aztec-xihuitl-month x-date)))
    (+ (* (1- month) 20) (1- day))))
```

(11.16)

```
(defconstant aztec-xihuitl-correlation
  ;; TYPE fixed-date
  ;; Start of a xihuitl cycle.
  (- aztec-correlation
     (aztec-xihuitl-ordinal (aztec-xihuitl-date 11 2))))
```

(11.17)

```
(defun aztec-xihuitl-from-fixed (date)
  ;; TYPE fixed-date -> aztec-xihuitl-date
  ;; Aztec xihuitl date of fixed date.
  (let* ((count (mod (- date aztec-xihuitl-correlation) 365))
         (day (1+ (mod count 20)))
         (month (1+ (quotient count 20))))
    (aztec-xihuitl-date month day)))
```

(11.18)

```
(defun aztec-xihuitl-on-or-before (xihuitl date)
  ;; TYPE (aztec-xihuitl-date fixed-date) -> fixed-date
  ;; Fixed date of latest date on or before fixed date
  ;; that is Aztec xihuitl date xihuitl.
  (mod3 (+ aztec-xihuitl-correlation
           (aztec-xihuitl-ordinal xihuitl))
        date (- date 365)))
```

```
(defun aztec-tonalpohualli-date (number name)
  ;; TYPE (aztec-tonalpohualli-number aztec-tonalpohualli-name)
  ;; TYPE  -> aztec-tonalpohualli-date
  (list number name))
```

```
(defun aztec-tonalpohualli-number (date)
  ;; TYPE aztec-tonalpohualli-date -> aztec-tonalpohualli-number
  (first date))
```

```
(defun aztec-tonalpohualli-name (date)
  ;; TYPE aztec-tonalpohualli-date -> aztec-tonalpohualli-name
  (second date))
```

```
(defun aztec-tonalpohualli-ordinal (t-date)                    (11.19)
  ;; TYPE aztec-tonalpohualli-date -> nonnegative-integer
  ;; Number of days into Aztec tonalpohualli cycle of t-date.
  (let* ((number (aztec-tonalpohualli-number t-date))
         (name (aztec-tonalpohualli-name t-date)))
    (mod (+ number -1
            (* 39 (- number name)))
         260)))
```

```
(defconstant aztec-tonalpohualli-correlation                   (11.20)
  ;; TYPE fixed-date
  ;; Start of a tonalpohualli date cycle.
  (- aztec-correlation
     (aztec-tonalpohualli-ordinal
      (aztec-tonalpohualli-date 1 5))))
```

```
(defun aztec-tonalpohualli-from-fixed (date)                   (11.21)
  ;; TYPE fixed-date -> aztec-tonalpohualli-date
  ;; Aztec tonalpohualli date of fixed date.
  (let* ((count (- date aztec-tonalpohualli-correlation -1))
         (number (amod count 13))
         (name (amod count 20)))
    (aztec-tonalpohualli-date number name)))
```

```
(defun aztec-tonalpohualli-on-or-before (tonalpohualli date)   (11.22)
  ;; TYPE (aztec-tonalpohualli-date fixed-date) -> fixed-date
  ;; Fixed date of latest date on or before fixed date
  ;; that is Aztec tonalpohualli date tonalpohualli.
  (mod3 (+ aztec-tonalpohualli-correlation
           (aztec-tonalpohualli-ordinal tonalpohualli))
        date (- date 260)))
```

```
(defun aztec-xiuhmolpilli-designation (number name)
  ;; TYPE (aztec-xiuhmolpilli-number aztec-xiuhmolpilli-name)
  ;; TYPE  -> aztec-xiuhmolpilli-designation
  (list number name))
```

```
(defun aztec-xiuhmolpilli-number (date)
  ;; TYPE aztec-xiuhmolpilli-designation -> aztec-xiuhmolpilli-number
  (first date))
```

```
(defun aztec-xiuhmolpilli-name (date)
  ;; TYPE aztec-xiuhmolpilli-designation -> aztec-xiuhmolpilli-name
  (second date))
```

```
(defun aztec-xiuhmolpilli-from-fixed (date)                    (11.23)
  ;; TYPE fixed-date -> aztec-xiuhmolpilli-designation
  ;; Designation of year containing fixed date.
  ;; Returns bogus for nemontemi.
```

```
  (let* ((x (aztec-xihuitl-on-or-before
             (aztec-xihuitl-date 18 20)
             (+ date 364)))
         (month (aztec-xihuitl-month
                 (aztec-xihuitl-from-fixed date))))
    (if (= month 19)
        bogus
      (aztec-tonalpohualli-from-fixed x))))
```

```
(defun aztec-xihuitl-tonalpohualli-on-or-before            (11.24)
  (xihuitl tonalpohualli date)
  ;; TYPE (aztec-xihuitl-date aztec-tonalpohualli-date
  ;; TYPE  fixed-date) -> fixed-date
  ;; Fixed date of latest xihuitl-tonalpohualli combination
  ;; on or before date.  That is the date on or before
  ;; date that is Aztec xihuitl date xihuitl and
  ;; tonalpohualli date tonalpohualli.
  ;; Returns bogus for impossible combinations.
  (let* ((xihuitl-count
          (+ (aztec-xihuitl-ordinal xihuitl)
             aztec-xihuitl-correlation))
         (tonalpohualli-count
          (+ (aztec-tonalpohualli-ordinal tonalpohualli)
             aztec-tonalpohualli-correlation))
         (diff (- tonalpohualli-count xihuitl-count)))
    (if (= (mod diff 5) 0)
        (mod3 (+ xihuitl-count (* 365 diff))
              date (- date 18980))
      bogus))); xihuitl-tonalpohualli combination is impossible.
```

D.12 The Balinese Pawukon Calendar

```
(defun balinese-date (b1 b2 b3 b4 b5 b6 b7 b8 b9 b0)
  ;; TYPE (boolean 1-2 1-3 1-4 1-5 1-6 1-7 1-8 1-9 0-9)
  ;; TYPE  -> balinese-date
  (list b1 b2 b3 b4 b5 b6 b7 b8 b9 b0))
```

```
(defun bali-luang (b-date)
  ;; TYPE balinese-date -> boolean
  (first b-date))
```

```
(defun bali-dwiwara (b-date)
  ;; TYPE balinese-date -> 1-2
  (second b-date))
```

```
(defun bali-triwara (b-date)
  ;; TYPE balinese-date -> 1-3
  (third b-date))
```

```
(defun bali-caturwara (b-date)
  ;; TYPE balinese-date -> 1-4
  (fourth b-date))
```

```
(defun bali-pancawara (b-date)
  ;; TYPE balinese-date -> 1-5
  (fifth b-date))
```

```
(defun bali-sadwara (b-date)
  ;; TYPE balinese-date -> 1-6
  (sixth b-date))
```

```
(defun bali-saptawara (b-date)
  ;; TYPE balinese-date -> 1-7
  (seventh b-date))
```

```
(defun bali-asatawara (b-date)
  ;; TYPE balinese-date -> 1-8
  (eighth b-date))
```

```
(defun bali-sangawara (b-date)
  ;; TYPE balinese-date -> 1-9
  (ninth b-date))
```

```
(defun bali-dasawara (b-date)
  ;; TYPE balinese-date -> 0-9
  (tenth b-date))
```

(12.1)

```
(defun bali-pawukon-from-fixed (date)
  ;; TYPE fixed-date -> balinese-date
  ;; Positions of date in ten cycles of Balinese Pawukon
  ;; calendar.
  (balinese-date (bali-luang-from-fixed date)
                 (bali-dwiwara-from-fixed date)
                 (bali-triwara-from-fixed date)
                 (bali-caturwara-from-fixed date)
                 (bali-pancawara-from-fixed date)
                 (bali-sadwara-from-fixed date)
                 (bali-saptawara-from-fixed date)
                 (bali-asatawara-from-fixed date)
                 (bali-sangawara-from-fixed date)
                 (bali-dasawara-from-fixed date)))
```

(12.2)

```
(defconstant bali-epoch
  ;; TYPE fixed-date
  ;; Fixed date of start of a Balinese Pawukon cycle.
  (fixed-from-jd 146))
```

(12.3)

```
(defun bali-day-from-fixed (date)
  ;; TYPE fixed-date -> 0-209
  ;; Position of date in 210-day Pawukon cycle.
  (mod (- date bali-epoch) 210))
```

(12.4)

```
(defun bali-triwara-from-fixed (date)
  ;; TYPE fixed-date -> 1-3
  ;; Position of date in 3-day Balinese cycle.
  (1+ (mod (bali-day-from-fixed date) 3)))
```

(12.5)

```
(defun bali-sadwara-from-fixed (date)
  ;; TYPE fixed-date -> 1-6
  ;; Position of date in 6-day Balinese cycle.
  (1+ (mod (bali-day-from-fixed date) 6)))
```

(12.6)

```
(defun bali-saptawara-from-fixed (date)
  ;; TYPE fixed-date -> 1-7
  ;; Position of date in Balinese week.
  (1+ (mod (bali-day-from-fixed date) 7)))
```

(12.7)

```
(defun bali-pancawara-from-fixed (date)
  ;; TYPE fixed-date -> 1-5
  ;; Position of date in 5-day Balinese cycle.
  (amod (+ (bali-day-from-fixed date) 2) 5))
```

(12.8)

```
(defun bali-week-from-fixed (date)
  ;; TYPE fixed-date -> 1-30
  ;; Week number of date in Balinese cycle.
  (1+ (quotient (bali-day-from-fixed date) 7)))
```

(12.9)

```
(defun bali-dasawara-from-fixed (date)
  ;; TYPE fixed-date -> 0-9
  ;; Position of date in 10-day Balinese cycle.
  (let* ((i ; Position in 5-day cycle.
          (1- (bali-pancawara-from-fixed date)))
         (j ; Weekday.
          (1- (bali-saptawara-from-fixed date))))
    (mod (+ 1 (nth i (list 5 9 7 4 8))
            (nth j (list 5 4 3 7 8 6 9)))
         10)))
```

(12.10)

```
(defun bali-dwiwara-from-fixed (date)
  ;; TYPE fixed-date -> 1-2
  ;; Position of date in 2-day Balinese cycle.
  (amod (bali-dasawara-from-fixed date) 2))
```

(12.11)

```
(defun bali-luang-from-fixed (date)
  ;; TYPE fixed-date -> boolean
  ;; Membership of date in "1-day" Balinese cycle.
  (evenp (bali-dasawara-from-fixed date)))
```

(12.12)

```
(defun bali-sangawara-from-fixed (date)
  ;; TYPE fixed-date -> 1-9
  ;; Position of date in 9-day Balinese cycle.
  (1+ (mod (max 0
                (- (bali-day-from-fixed date) 3))
           9)))
```

(12.13)

```
(defun bali-asatawara-from-fixed (date)
  ;; TYPE fixed-date -> 1-8
  ;; Position of date in 8-day Balinese cycle.
  (let* ((day (bali-day-from-fixed date)))
    (1+ (mod
         (max 6
              (+ 4 (mod (- day 70)
                        210)))
         8))))
```

(12.14)

```
(defun bali-caturwara-from-fixed (date)
  ;; TYPE fixed-date -> 1-4
  ;; Position of date in 4-day Balinese cycle.
  (amod (bali-asatawara-from-fixed date) 4))
```

(12.15)

```
(defun bali-on-or-before (b-date date)
  ;; TYPE (balinese-date fixed-date) -> fixed-date
  ;; Last fixed date on or before date with Pawukon b-date.
  (let* ((luang (bali-luang b-date))
         (dwiwara (bali-dwiwara b-date))
         (triwara (bali-triwara b-date))
         (caturwara (bali-caturwara b-date))
         (pancawara (bali-pancawara b-date))
         (sadwara (bali-sadwara b-date))
         (saptawara (bali-saptawara b-date))
         (asatawara (bali-asatawara b-date))
         (sangawara (bali-sangawara b-date))
         (dasawara (bali-dasawara b-date))
         (a5 ; Position in 5-day subcycle.
          (1- pancawara))
         (a6 ; Position in 6-day subcycle.
          (1- sadwara))
         (b7 ; Position in 7-day subcycle.
          (1- saptawara))
         (b35 ; Position in 35-day subcycle.
          (mod (+ a5 14 (* 15 (- b7 a5))) 35))
         (days ; Position in full cycle.
          (+ a6 (* 36 (- b35 a6))))
         (cap-Delta (bali-day-from-fixed (rd 0))))
    (- date (mod (- (+ date cap-Delta) days) 210))))
```

(12.16)

```
(defun kajeng-keliwon (g-year)
  ;; TYPE gregorian-year -> list-of-fixed-dates
  ;; Occurrences of Kajeng Keliwon (9th day of each
  ;; 15-day subcycle of Pawukon) in Gregorian year g-year.
  (let* ((year (gregorian-year-range g-year))
         (cap-Delta (bali-day-from-fixed (rd 0))))
    (positions-in-range 8 15 cap-Delta year)))
```

(12.17)

```
(defun tumpek (g-year)
  ;; TYPE gregorian-year -> list-of-fixed-dates
  ;; Occurrences of Tumpek (14th day of Pawukon and every
  ;; 35th subsequent day) within Gregorian year g-year.
  (let* ((year (gregorian-year-range g-year))
         (cap-Delta (bali-day-from-fixed (rd 0))))
    (positions-in-range 13 35 cap-Delta year)))
```

D.13 General Cyclical Calendars

No Lisp code is included for this chapter.

D.14 Time and Astronomy

Common Lisp's built-in trigonometric functions work with radians, whereas we have used degrees. The following functions do the necessary normalization and conversions:

```
(defun radians-from-degrees (theta)
  ;; TYPE real -> radian
  ;; Convert angle theta from degrees to radians.
  (* (mod theta 360) pi 1/180))
```

```
(defun degrees-from-radians (theta)
  ;; TYPE radian -> angle
  ;; Convert angle theta from radians to degrees.
  (mod (/ theta pi 1/180) 360))
```

```
(defun sin-degrees (theta)
  ;; TYPE angle -> amplitude
  ;; Sine of theta (given in degrees).
  (sin (radians-from-degrees theta)))
```

```
(defun cos-degrees (theta)
  ;; TYPE angle -> amplitude
  ;; Cosine of theta (given in degrees).
  (cos (radians-from-degrees theta)))
```

```
(defun tan-degrees (theta)
  ;; TYPE angle -> real
  ;; Tangent of theta (given in degrees).
  (tan (radians-from-degrees theta)))
```

(14.7)

```
(defun arctan-degrees (y x)
  ;; TYPE (real real) -> angle
  ;; Arctangent of y/x in degrees.
  ;; Returns bogus if x and y are both 0.
  (if (and (= x y 0))
      bogus
    (mod
     (if (= x 0)
         (* (sign y) (deg 90L0))
       (let* ((alpha (degrees-from-radians
                      (atan (/ y x)))))
         (if (>= x 0)
             alpha
           (+ alpha (deg 180L0)))))
     360)))
```

```
(defun arcsin-degrees (x)
  ;; TYPE amplitude -> angle
  ;; Arcsine of x in degrees.
  (degrees-from-radians (asin x)))
```

```
(defun arccos-degrees (x)
  ;; TYPE amplitude -> angle
  ;; Arccosine of x in degrees.
  (degrees-from-radians (acos x)))
```

We also use the following functions to indicate units; they are also used for typesetting:

```
(defun hr (x)
  ;; TYPE real -> duration
  ;; x hours.
  (/ x 24))
```

```
(defun mn (x)
  ;; TYPE real -> duration
  ;; x minutes.
  (/ x 24 60))
```

```
(defun sec (x)
  ;; TYPE real -> duration
  ;; x seconds.
  (/ x 24 60 60))
```

```
(defun mt (x)
  ;; TYPE real -> distance
  ;; x meters.
  ;; For typesetting purposes.
  x)
```

```
(defun deg (x)
  ;; TYPE real -> angle
  ;; TYPE list-of-reals -> list-of-angles
  ;; x degrees.
  ;; For typesetting purposes.
  x)
```

```
(defun mins (x)
  ;; TYPE real -> angle
  ;; x arcminutes
  (/ x 60))
```

```
(defun secs (x)
  ;; TYPE real -> angle
  ;; x arcseconds
  (/ x 3600))
```

```
(defun angle (d m s)
  ;; TYPE (integer integer real) -> angle
  ;; d degrees, m arcminutes, s arcseconds.
  (+ d (/ (+ m (/ s 60)) 60)))
```

```
(defun degrees-minutes-seconds (d m s)
  ;; TYPE (degree minute real) -> angle
  (list d m s))
```

The deg function is also applied to lists, to indicate that it is a list of angles.

The following allow us to specify locations and directions:

```
(defun location (latitude longitude elevation zone)
  ;; TYPE (half-circle circle distance real) -> location
  (list latitude longitude elevation zone))
```

```
(defun latitude (location)
  ;; TYPE location -> half-circle
  (first location))
```

```lisp
(defun longitude (location)
  ;; TYPE location -> circle
  (second location))
```

```lisp
(defun elevation (location)
  ;; TYPE location -> distance
  (third location))
```

```lisp
(defun zone (location)
  ;; TYPE location -> real
  (fourth location))
```

(14.3)

```lisp
(defconstant mecca
  ;; TYPE location
  ;; Location of Mecca.
  (location (angle 21 25 24) (angle 39 49 24)
            (mt 298) (hr 3)))
```

(14.4)

```lisp
(defconstant jerusalem
  ;; TYPE location
  ;; Location of Jerusalem.
  (location (deg 31.78L0) (deg 35.24L0) (mt 740) (hr 2)))
```

(14.5)

```lisp
(defconstant acre
  ;; TYPE location
  ;; Location of Acre.
  (location (deg 32.94L0) (deg 35.09L0) (mt 22) (hr 2)))
```

(14.6)

```lisp
(defun direction (location focus)
  ;; TYPE (location location) -> angle
  ;; Angle (clockwise from North) to face focus when
  ;; standing in location.  Subject to errors near focus and
  ;; its antipode.
  (let* ((phi (latitude location))
         (phi-prime (latitude focus))
         (psi (longitude location))
         (psi-prime (longitude focus))
         (y (sin-degrees (- psi-prime psi)))
         (x
          (- (* (cos-degrees phi)
                (tan-degrees phi-prime))
             (* (sin-degrees phi)
                (cos-degrees
                 (- psi psi-prime))))))
    (cond ((or (= x y 0) (= phi-prime (deg 90)))
           (deg 0))
          ((= phi-prime (deg -90))
           (deg 180))
          (t (arctan-degrees y x)))))
```

The following functions compute times:

(14.8)

```lisp
(defun zone-from-longitude (phi)
  ;; TYPE circle -> duration
  ;; Difference between UT and local mean time at longitude
  ;; phi as a fraction of a day.
  (/ phi (deg 360)))
```

(14.9)

```lisp
(defun universal-from-local (tee_ell location)
  ;; TYPE (moment location) -> moment
  ;; Universal time from local tee_ell at location.
  (- tee_ell (zone-from-longitude (longitude location))))
```

(14.10)

```
(defun local-from-universal (tee_rom-u location)
  ;; TYPE (moment location) -> moment
  ;; Local time from universal tee_rom-u at location.
  (+ tee_rom-u (zone-from-longitude (longitude location))))
```

(14.11)

```
(defun standard-from-universal (tee_rom-u location)
  ;; TYPE (moment location) -> moment
  ;; Standard time from tee_rom-u in universal time at
  ;; location.
  (+ tee_rom-u (zone location)))
```

(14.12)

```
(defun universal-from-standard (tee_rom-s location)
  ;; TYPE (moment location) -> moment
  ;; Universal time from tee_rom-s in standard time at
  ;; location.
  (- tee_rom-s (zone location)))
```

(14.13)

```
(defun standard-from-local (tee_ell location)
  ;; TYPE (moment location) -> moment
  ;; Standard time from local tee_ell at location.
  (standard-from-universal
   (universal-from-local tee_ell location)
   location))
```

(14.14)

```
(defun local-from-standard (tee_rom-s location)
  ;; TYPE (moment location) -> moment
  ;; Local time from standard tee_rom-s at location.
  (local-from-universal
   (universal-from-standard tee_rom-s location)
   location))
```

(14.15)

```
(defun ephemeris-correction (tee)
  ;; TYPE moment -> fraction-of-day
  ;; Dynamical Time minus Universal Time (in days) for
  ;; moment tee.  Adapted from "Astronomical Algorithms"
  ;; by Jean Meeus, Willmann-Bell (1991) for years
  ;; 1600-1986 and from polynomials on the NASA
  ;; Eclipse web site for other years.
  (let* ((year (gregorian-year-from-fixed (floor tee)))
         (c (/ (gregorian-date-difference
                (gregorian-date 1900 january 1)
                (gregorian-date year july 1))
               36525))
         (c2051 (* 1/86400
                   (+ -20 (* 32 (expt (/ (- year 1820) 100) 2))
                      (* 0.5628L0 (- 2150 year)))))
         (y2000 (- year 2000))
         (c2006 (* 1/86400
                   (poly y2000
                         (list 62.92L0 0.32217L0 0.005589L0))))
         (c1987 (* 1/86400
                   (poly y2000
                         (list 63.86L0 0.3345L0 -0.060374L0
                               0.0017275L0
                               0.000651814L0 0.00002373599L0))))
         (c1900 (poly c
                      (list -0.00002L0 0.000297L0 0.025184L0
                            -0.181133L0 0.553040L0 -0.861938L0
                            0.677066L0 -0.212591L0)))
         (c1800 (poly c
                      (list -0.000009L0 0.003844L0 0.083563L0
                            0.865736L0
                            4.867575L0 15.845535L0 31.332267L0
                            38.291999L0 28.316289L0 11.636204L0
                            2.043794L0)))
         (y1700 (- year 1700))
         (c1700 (* 1/86400
```

```
            (poly y1700
                  (list 8.118780842L0 -0.005092142L0
                        0.003336121L0 -0.0000266484L0))))
        (y1600 (- year 1600))
        (c1600 (* 1/86400
            (poly y1600
                  (list 120 -0.9808L0 -0.01532L0
                        0.000140272128L0))))
        (y1000 (/ (- year 1000) 100L0))
        (c500 (* 1/86400
           (poly y1000
                 (list 1574.2L0 -556.01L0 71.23472L0 0.319781L0
                       -0.8503463L0 -0.005050998L0
                       0.0083572073L0))))
        (y0 (/ year 100L0))
        (c0 (* 1/86400
          (poly y0
                (list 10583.6L0 -1014.41L0 33.78311L0
                      -5.952053L0 -0.1798452L0 0.022174192L0
                      0.0090316521L0))))
        (y1820 (/ (- year 1820) 100L0))
        (other (* 1/86400
            (poly y1820 (list -20 0 32)))))
    (cond ((<= 2051 year 2150) c2051)
          ((<= 2006 year 2050) c2006)
          ((<= 1987 year 2005) c1987)
          ((<= 1900 year 1986) c1900)
          ((<= 1800 year 1899) c1800)
          ((<= 1700 year 1799) c1700)
          ((<= 1600 year 1699) c1600)
          ((<= 500 year 1599) c500)
          ((< -500 year 500) c0)
          (t other))))
```

(14.16)

```
(defun dynamical-from-universal (tee_rom-u)
  ;; TYPE moment -> moment
  ;; Dynamical time at Universal moment tee_rom-u.
  (+ tee_rom-u (ephemeris-correction tee_rom-u)))
```

(14.17)

```
(defun universal-from-dynamical (tee)
  ;; TYPE moment -> moment
  ;; Universal moment from Dynamical time tee.
  (- tee (ephemeris-correction tee)))
```

(14.18)

```
(defun julian-centuries (tee)
  ;; TYPE moment -> century
  ;; Julian centuries since 2000 at moment tee.
  (/ (- (dynamical-from-universal tee) j2000)
     36525))
```

(14.19)

```
(defconstant j2000
  ;; TYPE moment
  ;; Noon at start of Gregorian year 2000.
  (+ (hr 12L0) (gregorian-new-year 2000)))
```

(14.20)

```
(defun equation-of-time (tee)
  ;; TYPE moment -> fraction-of-day
  ;; Equation of time (as fraction of day) for moment tee.
  ;; Adapted from "Astronomical Algorithms" by Jean Meeus,
  ;; Willmann-Bell, 2nd edn., 1998, p. 185.
  (let* ((c (julian-centuries tee))
         (lambda
           (poly c
                 (deg (list 280.46645L0 36000.76983L0
                            0.0003032L0))))
         (anomaly
          (poly c
                (deg (list 357.52910L0 35999.05030L0
                           -0.0001559L0 -0.00000048L0))))
```

```
       (eccentricity
        (poly c
              (list 0.016708617L0 -0.000042037L0
                    -0.0000001236L0)))
       (varepsilon (obliquity tee))
       (y (expt (tan-degrees (/ varepsilon 2)) 2))
       (equation
        (* (/ 1 2 pi)
           (+ (* y (sin-degrees (* 2 lambda)))
              (* -2 eccentricity (sin-degrees anomaly))
              (* 4 eccentricity y (sin-degrees anomaly)
                 (cos-degrees (* 2 lambda)))
              (* -0.5L0 y y (sin-degrees (* 4 lambda)))
              (* -1.25L0 eccentricity eccentricity
                 (sin-degrees (* 2 anomaly)))))))
  (* (sign equation) (min (abs equation) (hr 12L0)))))
```

(14.21)

```
(defun apparent-from-local (tee_ell location)
  ;; TYPE (moment location) -> moment
  ;; Sundial time from local time tee_ell at location.
  (+ tee_ell (equation-of-time
              (universal-from-local tee_ell location))))
```

(14.22)

```
(defun local-from-apparent (tee location)
  ;; TYPE (moment location) -> moment
  ;; Local time from sundial time tee at location.
  (- tee (equation-of-time (universal-from-local tee location))))
```

(14.23)

```
(defun apparent-from-universal (tee_rom-u location)
  ;; TYPE (moment location) -> moment
  ;; True (apparent) time at universal time tee at location.
  (apparent-from-local
   (local-from-universal tee_rom-u location)
   location))
```

(14.24)

```
(defun universal-from-apparent (tee location)
  ;; TYPE (moment location) -> moment
  ;; Universal time from sundial time tee at location.
  (universal-from-local
   (local-from-apparent tee location)
   location))
```

(14.25)

```
(defun midnight (date location)
  ;; TYPE (fixed-date location) -> moment
  ;; Universal time of true (apparent)
  ;; midnight of fixed date at location.
  (universal-from-apparent date location))
```

(14.26)

```
(defun midday (date location)
  ;; TYPE (fixed-date location) -> moment
  ;; Universal time on fixed date of midday at location.
  (universal-from-apparent (+ date (hr 12)) location))
```

(14.27)

```
(defun sidereal-from-moment (tee)
  ;; TYPE moment -> angle
  ;; Mean sidereal time of day from moment tee expressed
  ;; as hour angle.  Adapted from "Astronomical Algorithms"
  ;; by Jean Meeus, Willmann-Bell, Inc., 2nd edn., 1998, p. 88.
  (let* ((c (/ (- tee j2000) 36525)))
    (mod (poly c
               (deg (list 280.46061837L0
                          (* 36525 360.98564736629L0)
                          0.000387933L0 -1/38710000)))
         360)))
```

Additional solar and lunar astronomical functions are:

```
(defun obliquity (tee)                                          (14.28)
  ;; TYPE moment -> angle
  ;; Obliquity of ecliptic at moment tee.
  (let* ((c (julian-centuries tee)))
    (+ (angle 23 26 21.448L0)
       (poly c (list 0L0
                     (angle 0 0 -46.8150L0)
                     (angle 0 0 -0.00059L0)
                     (angle 0 0 0.001813L0))))))
```

```
(defun declination (tee beta lambda)                            (14.29)
  ;; TYPE (moment half-circle circle) -> angle
  ;; Declination at moment UT tee of object at
  ;; latitude beta and longitude lambda.
  (let* ((varepsilon (obliquity tee)))
    (arcsin-degrees (+ (* (sin-degrees beta)
                          (cos-degrees varepsilon))
                       (* (cos-degrees beta)
                          (sin-degrees varepsilon)
                          (sin-degrees lambda))))))
```

```
(defun right-ascension (tee beta lambda)                        (14.30)
  ;; TYPE (moment half-circle circle) -> angle
  ;; Right ascension at moment UT tee of object at
  ;; latitude beta and longitude lambda.
  (let* ((varepsilon (obliquity tee)))
    (arctan-degrees ; Cannot be bogus
     (- (* (sin-degrees lambda)
           (cos-degrees varepsilon))
        (* (tan-degrees beta)
           (sin-degrees varepsilon)))
     (cos-degrees lambda))))
```

```
(defconstant mean-tropical-year                                 (14.31)
  ;; TYPE duration
  365.242189L0)
```

```
(defconstant mean-sidereal-year                                 (14.32)
  ;; TYPE duration
  365.25636L0)
```

```
(defun solar-longitude (tee)                                    (14.33)
  ;; TYPE moment -> season
  ;; Longitude of sun at moment tee.
  ;; Adapted from "Planetary Programs and Tables from -4000
  ;; to +2800" by Pierre Bretagnon and Jean-Louis Simon,
  ;; Willmann-Bell, 1986.
  (let* ((c       ; moment in Julian centuries
          (julian-centuries tee))
         (coefficients
          (list 403406 195207 119433 112392 3891 2819 1721
                660 350 334 314 268 242 234 158 132 129 114
                99 93 86 78 72 68 64 46 38 37 32 29 28 27 27
                25 24 21 21 20 18 17 14 13 13 13 12 10 10 10
                10))
         (multipliers
          (list 0.9287892L0 35999.1376958L0 35999.4089666L0
                35998.7287385L0 71998.20261L0 71998.4403L0
                36000.35726L0 71997.4812L0 32964.4678L0
                -19.4410L0 445267.1117L0 45036.8840L0 3.1008L0
                22518.4434L0 -19.9739L0 65928.9345L0
                9038.0293L0 3034.7684L0 33718.148L0 3034.448L0
                -2280.773L0 29929.992L0 31556.493L0 149.588L0
                9037.750L0 107997.405L0 -4444.176L0 151.771L0
                67555.316L0 31556.080L0 -4561.540L0
                107996.706L0 1221.655L0 62894.167L0
                31437.369L0 14578.298L0 -31931.757L0
```

```
                34777.243L0 1221.999L0 62894.511L0
                -4442.039L0 107997.909L0 119.066L0 16859.071L0
                -4.578L0 26895.292L0 -39.127L0 12297.536L0
                90073.778L0))
         (addends
          (list 270.54861L0 340.19128L0 63.91854L0 331.26220L0
                317.843L0 86.631L0 240.052L0 310.26L0 247.23L0
                260.87L0 297.82L0 343.14L0 166.79L0 81.53L0
                3.50L0 132.75L0 182.95L0 162.03L0 29.8L0
                266.4L0 249.2L0 157.6L0 257.8L0 185.1L0 69.9L0
                8.0L0 197.1L0 250.4L0 65.3L0 162.7L0 341.5L0
                291.6L0 98.5L0 146.7L0 110.0L0 5.2L0 342.6L0
                230.9L0 256.1L0 45.3L0 242.9L0 115.2L0 151.8L0
                285.3L0 53.3L0 126.6L0 205.7L0 85.9L0
                146.1L0))
         (lambda
           (+ (deg 282.7771834L0)
              (* (deg 36000.76953744L0) c)
              (* (deg 0.000005729577951308232L0)
                 (sigma ((x coefficients)
                         (y addends)
                         (z multipliers))
                        (* x (sin-degrees (+ y (* z c)))))))))
    (mod (+ lambda (aberration tee) (nutation tee))
         360)))
```

(14.34)

```
(defun nutation (tee)
  ;; TYPE moment -> circle
  ;; Longitudinal nutation at moment tee.
  (let* ((c       ; moment in Julian centuries
          (julian-centuries tee))
         (cap-A (poly c (deg (list 124.90L0 -1934.134L0
                                   0.002063L0))))
         (cap-B (poly c (deg (list 201.11L0 72001.5377L0
                                   0.00057L0)))))
    (+ (* (deg -0.004778L0) (sin-degrees cap-A))
       (* (deg -0.0003667L0) (sin-degrees cap-B)))))
```

(14.35)

```
(defun aberration (tee)
  ;; TYPE moment -> circle
  ;; Aberration at moment tee.
  (let* ((c       ; moment in Julian centuries
          (julian-centuries tee)))
    (- (* (deg 0.0000974L0)
          (cos-degrees
           (+ (deg 177.63L0) (* (deg 35999.01848L0) c))))
       (deg 0.005575L0))))
```

(14.36)

```
(defun solar-longitude-after (lambda tee)
  ;; TYPE (season moment) -> moment
  ;; Moment UT of the first time at or after tee
  ;; when the solar longitude will be lambda degrees.
  (let* ((rate ; Mean days for 1 degree change.
          (/ mean-tropical-year (deg 360)))
         (tau ; Estimate (within 5 days).
          (+ tee
             (* rate
                (mod (- lambda (solar-longitude tee)) 360))))
         (a (max tee (- tau 5))) ; At or after tee.
         (b (+ tau 5)))
    (invert-angular solar-longitude lambda
                    (interval-closed a b))))
```

(14.37)

```
(defun season-in-gregorian (season g-year)
  ;; TYPE (season gregorian-year) -> moment
  ;; Moment UT of season in Gregorian year g-year.
  (let* ((jan1 (gregorian-new-year g-year)))
    (solar-longitude-after season jan1)))
```

```
(defun precession (tee)                                        (14.39)
  ;; TYPE moment -> angle
  ;; Precession at moment tee using 0,0 as J2000 coordinates.
  ;; Adapted from "Astronomical Algorithms" by Jean Meeus,
  ;; Willmann-Bell, 2nd edn., 1998, pp. 136-137.
  (let* ((c (julian-centuries tee))
         (eta (mod
               (poly c (list 0 (secs 47.0029L0)
                             (secs -0.03302L0)
                             (secs 0.000060L0)))
               360))
         (cap-P (mod (poly c (list (deg 174.876384L0)
                                   (secs -869.8089L0)
                                   (secs 0.03536L0)))
                     360))
         (p (mod (poly c (list 0 (secs 5029.0966L0)
                               (secs 1.11113L0)
                               (secs 0.000006L0)))
                 360))
         (cap-A (* (cos-degrees eta) (sin-degrees cap-P)))
         (cap-B (cos-degrees cap-P))
         (arg (arctan-degrees cap-A cap-B)))
    (mod (- (+ p cap-P) arg) 360)))
```

```
(defun sidereal-solar-longitude (tee)                          (14.40)
  ;; TYPE moment -> angle
  ;; Sidereal solar longitude at moment tee
  (mod (+ (solar-longitude tee)
          (- (precession tee))
          sidereal-start)
       360))
```

```
(defun solar-altitude (tee location)                           (14.41)
  ;; TYPE (moment location) -> half-circle
  ;; Geocentric altitude of sun at tee at location,
  ;; as a positive/negative angle in degrees, ignoring
  ;; parallax and refraction.
  (let* ((phi ; Local latitude.
          (latitude location))
         (psi ; Local longitude.
          (longitude location))
         (lambda ; Solar longitude.
          (solar-longitude tee))
         (alpha ; Solar right ascension.
          (right-ascension tee 0 lambda))
         (delta ; Solar declination.
          (declination tee 0 lambda))
         (theta0 ; Sidereal time.
          (sidereal-from-moment tee))
         (cap-H ; Local hour angle.
          (mod (- theta0 (- psi) alpha) 360))
         (altitude
          (arcsin-degrees (+ (* (sin-degrees phi)
                                (sin-degrees delta))
                             (* (cos-degrees phi)
                                (cos-degrees delta)
                                (cos-degrees cap-H))))))
    (mod3 altitude -180 180)))
```

```
(defun estimate-prior-solar-longitude (lambda tee)             (14.42)
  ;; TYPE (season moment) -> moment
  ;; Approximate moment at or before tee
  ;; when solar longitude just exceeded lambda degrees.
  (let* ((rate ; Mean change of one degree.
          (/ mean-tropical-year (deg 360)))
         (tau ; First approximation.
          (- tee
             (* rate (mod (- (solar-longitude tee)
                             lambda)
```

```
                        360))))
           (cap-Delta ; Difference in longitude.
            (mod3 (- (solar-longitude tau) lambda)
                  -180 180)))
      (min tee (- tau (* rate cap-Delta)))))
```

```
(defconstant mean-synodic-month                                    (14.44)
  ;; TYPE duration
  29.530588861L0)
```

```
(defun nth-new-moon (n)                                            (14.45)
  ;; TYPE integer -> moment
  ;; Moment of n-th new moon after (or before) the new moon
  ;; of January 11, 1.  Adapted from "Astronomical Algorithms"
  ;; by Jean Meeus, Willmann-Bell, corrected 2nd edn., 2005.
  (let* ((n0 24724) ; Months from RD 0 until j2000.
         (k (- n n0)) ; Months since j2000.
         (c (/ k 1236.85L0)) ; Julian centuries.
         (approx (+ j2000
                    (poly c (list 5.09766L0
                                  (* mean-synodic-month
                                     1236.85L0)
                                  0.00015437L0
                                  -0.000000150L0
                                  0.00000000073L0)))))
         (cap-E (poly c (list 1 -0.002516L0 -0.0000074L0)))
         (solar-anomaly
          (poly c (deg (list 2.5534L0
                             (* 1236.85L0 29.10535670L0)
                             -0.0000014L0 -0.00000011L0))))
         (lunar-anomaly
          (poly c (deg (list 201.5643L0 (* 385.81693528L0
                                           1236.85L0)
                             0.0107582L0 0.00001238L0
                             -0.000000058L0))))
         (moon-argument ; Moon's argument of latitude.
          (poly c (deg (list 160.7108L0 (* 390.67050284L0
                                           1236.85L0)
                             -0.0016118L0 -0.00000227L0
                             0.000000011L0))))
         (cap-omega ; Longitude of ascending node.
          (poly c (deg (list 124.7746L0 (* -1.56375588L0 1236.85L0)
                        0.0020672L0 0.00000215L0))))
         (E-factor (list 0 1 0 0 1 1 2 0 0 1 0 1 1 1 0 0 0 0
                         0 0 0 0 0 0))
         (solar-coeff (list 0 1 0 0 -1 1 2 0 0 1 0 1 1 -1 2
                            0 3 1 0 1 -1 -1 1 0))
         (lunar-coeff (list 1 0 2 0 1 1 0 1 1 2 3 0 0 2 1 2
                            0 1 2 1 1 1 3 4))
         (moon-coeff (list 0 0 0 2 0 0 0 -2 2 0 0 2 -2 0 0
                           -2 0 -2 2 2 2 -2 0 0))
         (sine-coeff
          (list -0.40720L0 0.17241L0 0.01608L0 0.01039L0
                0.00739L0 -0.00514L0 0.00208L0
                -0.00111L0 -0.00057L0 0.00056L0
                -0.00042L0 0.00042L0 0.00038L0
                -0.00024L0 -0.00007L0 0.00004L0
                0.00004L0 0.00003L0 0.00003L0
                -0.00003L0 0.00003L0 -0.00002L0
                -0.00002L0 0.00002L0))
         (correction
          (+ (* -0.00017L0 (sin-degrees cap-omega))
             (sigma ((v sine-coeff)
                     (w E-factor)
                     (x solar-coeff)
                     (y lunar-coeff)
                     (z moon-coeff))
                    (* v (expt cap-E w)
                       (sin-degrees
                        (+ (* x solar-anomaly)
```

```
                            (* y lunar-anomaly)
                            (* z moon-argument)))))))
        (add-const
         (list 251.88L0 251.83L0 349.42L0 84.66L0
               141.74L0 207.14L0 154.84L0 34.52L0 207.19L0
               291.34L0 161.72L0 239.56L0 331.55L0))
        (add-coeff
         (list 0.016321L0 26.651886L0
               36.412478L0 18.206239L0 53.303771L0
               2.453732L0 7.306860L0 27.261239L0 0.121824L0
               1.844379L0 24.198154L0 25.513099L0
               3.592518L0))
        (add-factor
         (list 0.000165L0 0.000164L0 0.000126L0
               0.000110L0 0.000062L0 0.000060L0 0.000056L0
               0.000047L0 0.000042L0 0.000040L0 0.000037L0
               0.000035L0 0.000023L0))
        (extra
         (* 0.000325L0
            (sin-degrees
             (poly c
                   (deg (list 299.77L0 132.8475848L0
                              -0.009173L0))))))
        (additional
         (sigma ((i add-const)
                 (j add-coeff)
                 (l add-factor))
                (* l (sin-degrees (+ i (* j k)))))))
   (universal-from-dynamical
    (+ approx correction extra additional))))
```

(14.46)

```
(defun new-moon-before (tee)
  ;; TYPE moment -> moment
  ;; Moment UT of last new moon before tee.
  (let* ((t0 (nth-new-moon 0))
         (phi (lunar-phase tee))
         (n (round (- (/ (- tee t0) mean-synodic-month)
                      (/ phi (deg 360))))))
    (nth-new-moon (final k (1- n) (< (nth-new-moon k) tee)))))
```

(14.47)

```
(defun new-moon-at-or-after (tee)
  ;; TYPE moment -> moment
  ;; Moment UT of first new moon at or after tee.
  (let* ((t0 (nth-new-moon 0))
         (phi (lunar-phase tee))
         (n (round (- (/ (- tee t0) mean-synodic-month)
                      (/ phi (deg 360))))))
    (nth-new-moon (next k n (>= (nth-new-moon k) tee)))))
```

(14.48)

```
(defun lunar-longitude (tee)
  ;; TYPE moment -> angle
  ;; Longitude of moon (in degrees) at moment tee.
  ;; Adapted from "Astronomical Algorithms" by Jean Meeus,
  ;; Willmann-Bell, 2nd edn., 1998, pp. 338-342.
  (let* ((c (julian-centuries tee))
         (cap-L-prime (mean-lunar-longitude c))
         (cap-D (lunar-elongation c))
         (cap-M (solar-anomaly c))
         (cap-M-prime (lunar-anomaly c))
         (cap-F (moon-node c))
         (cap-E (poly c (list 1 -0.002516L0 -0.0000074L0)))
         (args-lunar-elongation
          (list 0 2 2 0 0 0 2 2 2 2 0 1 0 2 0 0 4 0 4 2 2 1
                1 2 2 4 2 0 2 2 1 2 0 0 2 2 2 4 0 3 2 4 0 2
                2 2 4 0 4 1 2 0 1 3 4 2 0 1 2))
         (args-solar-anomaly
          (list 0 0 0 0 1 0 0 -1 0 -1 1 0 1 0 0 0 0 0 0 1 1
                0 1 -1 0 0 0 1 0 -1 0 -2 1 2 -2 0 0 -1 0 0 1
                -1 2 2 1 -1 0 0 -1 0 1 0 1 0 0 -1 2 1 0))
```

```
(args-lunar-anomaly
 (list 1 -1 0 2 0 0 -2 -1 1 0 -1 0 1 0 1 1 -1 3 -2
       -1 0 -1 0 1 2 0 -3 -2 -1 -2 1 0 2 0 -1 1 0
       -1 2 -1 1 -2 -1 -1 -2 0 1 4 0 -2 0 2 1 -2 -3
       2 1 -1 3))
(args-moon-node
 (list 0 0 0 0 0 2 0 0 0 0 0 0 0 -2 2 -2 0 0 0 0 0
       0 0 0 0 0 0 0 2 0 0 0 0 0 0 -2 2 0 2 0 0 0 0
       0 0 -2 0 0 0 0 -2 -2 0 0 0 0 0 0 0))
(sine-coeff
 (list 6288774 1274027 658314 213618 -185116 -114332
       58793 57066 53322 45758 -40923 -34720 -30383
       15327 -12528 10980 10675 10034 8548 -7888
       -6766 -5163 4987 4036 3994 3861 3665 -2689
       -2602 2390 -2348 2236 -2120 -2069 2048 -1773
       -1595 1215 -1110 -892 -810 759 -713 -700 691
       596 549 537 520 -487 -399 -381 351 -340 330
       327 -323 299 294))
(correction
 (* (deg 1/1000000)
    (sigma ((v sine-coeff)
            (w args-lunar-elongation)
            (x args-solar-anomaly)
            (y args-lunar-anomaly)
            (z args-moon-node))
           (* v (expt cap-E (abs x))
              (sin-degrees
               (+ (* w cap-D)
                  (* x cap-M)
                  (* y cap-M-prime)
                  (* z cap-F)))))))
(venus (* (deg 3958/1000000)
          (sin-degrees
           (+ (deg 119.75L0) (* c (deg 131.849L0))))))
(jupiter (* (deg 318/1000000)
            (sin-degrees
             (+ (deg 53.09L0)
                (* c (deg 479264.29L0))))))
(flat-earth
 (* (deg 1962/1000000)
    (sin-degrees (- cap-L-prime cap-F)))))
(mod (+ cap-L-prime correction venus jupiter flat-earth
        (nutation tee))
     360)))
```

(14.49)

```
(defun mean-lunar-longitude (c)
  ;; TYPE century -> angle
  ;; Mean longitude of moon (in degrees) at moment
  ;; given in Julian centuries c.
  ;; Adapted from "Astronomical Algorithms" by Jean Meeus,
  ;; Willmann-Bell, 2nd edn., 1998, pp. 337-340.
  (mod
   (poly c
         (deg (list 218.3164477L0 481267.88123421L0
                    -0.0015786L0 1/538841 -1/65194000)))
   360))
```

(14.50)

```
(defun lunar-elongation (c)
  ;; TYPE century -> angle
  ;; Elongation of moon (in degrees) at moment
  ;; given in Julian centuries c.
  ;; Adapted from "Astronomical Algorithms" by Jean Meeus,
  ;; Willmann-Bell, 2nd edn., 1998, p. 338.
  (mod
   (poly c
         (deg (list 297.8501921L0 445267.1114034L0
                    -0.0018819L0 1/545868 -1/113065000)))
   360))
```

(14.51)

```
(defun solar-anomaly (c)
  ;; TYPE century -> angle
  ;; Mean anomaly of sun (in degrees) at moment
```

```
  ;; given in Julian centuries c.
  ;; Adapted from "Astronomical Algorithms" by Jean Meeus,
  ;; Willmann-Bell, 2nd edn., 1998, p. 338.
  (mod
   (poly c
         (deg (list 357.5291092L0 35999.0502909L0
                    -0.0001536L0 1/24490000)))
   360))
```

(14.52)

```
(defun lunar-anomaly (c)
  ;; TYPE century -> angle
  ;; Mean anomaly of moon (in degrees) at moment
  ;; given in Julian centuries c.
  ;; Adapted from "Astronomical Algorithms" by Jean Meeus,
  ;; Willmann-Bell, 2nd edn., 1998, p. 338.
  (mod
   (poly c
         (deg (list 134.9633964L0 477198.8675055L0
                    0.0087414L0 1/69699 -1/14712000)))
   360))
```

(14.53)

```
(defun moon-node (c)
  ;; TYPE century -> angle
  ;; Moon's argument of latitude (in degrees) at moment
  ;; given in Julian centuries c.
  ;; Adapted from "Astronomical Algorithms" by Jean Meeus,
  ;; Willmann-Bell, 2nd edn., 1998, p. 338.
  (mod
   (poly c
         (deg (list 93.2720950L0 483202.0175233L0
                    -0.0036539L0 -1/3526000 1/863310000)))
   360))
```

(14.54)

```
(defun lunar-node (date)
  ;; TYPE fixed-date -> angle
  ;; Angular distance of the lunar node from the equinoctial
  ;; point on fixed date.
  (mod3 (+ (moon-node (julian-centuries date)))
        -90 90))
```

(14.55)

```
(defun sidereal-lunar-longitude (tee)
  ;; TYPE moment -> angle
  ;; Sidereal lunar longitude at moment tee.
  (mod (+ (lunar-longitude tee)
          (- (precession tee))
          sidereal-start)
       360))
```

(14.56)

```
(defun lunar-phase (tee)
  ;; TYPE moment -> phase
  ;; Lunar phase, as an angle in degrees, at moment tee.
  ;; An angle of 0 means a new moon, 90 degrees means the
  ;; first quarter, 180 means a full moon, and 270 degrees
  ;; means the last quarter.
  (let* ((phi (mod (- (lunar-longitude tee)
                      (solar-longitude tee))
                   360))
         (t0 (nth-new-moon 0))
         (n (round (/ (- tee t0) mean-synodic-month)))
         (phi-prime (* (deg 360)
                       (mod (/ (- tee (nth-new-moon n))
                               mean-synodic-month)
                            1))))
    (if (> (abs (- phi phi-prime)) (deg 180)) ; close call
        phi-prime
      phi)))
```

(14.57)
```
(defun lunar-phase-at-or-before (phi tee)
  ;; TYPE (phase moment) -> moment
  ;; Moment UT of the last time at or before tee
  ;; when the lunar-phase was phi degrees.
  (let* ((tau ; Estimate.
          (- tee
             (* mean-synodic-month (/ 1 (deg 360))
                (mod (- (lunar-phase tee) phi) 360))))
         (a (- tau 2))
         (b (min tee (+ tau 2)))) ; At or before tee.
    (invert-angular lunar-phase phi
                    (interval-closed a b))))
```

(14.58)
```
(defun lunar-phase-at-or-after (phi tee)
  ;; TYPE (phase moment) -> moment
  ;; Moment UT of the next time at or after tee
  ;; when the lunar-phase is phi degrees.
  (let* ((tau ; Estimate.
          (+ tee
             (* mean-synodic-month (/ 1 (deg 360))
                (mod (- phi (lunar-phase tee)) 360))))
         (a (max tee (- tau 2))) ; At or after tee.
         (b (+ tau 2)))
    (invert-angular lunar-phase phi
                    (interval-closed a b))))
```

(14.59)
```
(defconstant new
  ;; TYPE phase
  ;; Excess of lunar longitude over solar longitude at new
  ;; moon.
  (deg 0))
```

(14.61)
```
(defconstant full
  ;; TYPE phase
  ;; Excess of lunar longitude over solar longitude at full
  ;; moon.
  (deg 180))
```

(14.60)
```
(defconstant first-quarter
  ;; TYPE phase
  ;; Excess of lunar longitude over solar longitude at first
  ;; quarter moon.
  (deg 90))
```

(14.62)
```
(defconstant last-quarter
  ;; TYPE phase
  ;; Excess of lunar longitude over solar longitude at last
  ;; quarter moon.
  (deg 270))
```

(14.63)
```
(defun lunar-latitude (tee)
  ;; TYPE moment -> half-circle
  ;; Latitude of moon (in degrees) at moment tee.
  ;; Adapted from "Astronomical Algorithms" by Jean Meeus,
  ;; Willmann-Bell, 2nd edn., 1998, pp. 338-342.
  (let* ((c (julian-centuries tee))
         (cap-L-prime (mean-lunar-longitude c))
         (cap-D (lunar-elongation c))
         (cap-M (solar-anomaly c))
         (cap-M-prime (lunar-anomaly c))
         (cap-F (moon-node c))
         (cap-E (poly c (list 1 -0.002516L0 -0.0000074L0)))
         (args-lunar-elongation
          (list 0 0 0 2 2 2 2 0 2 0 2 2 2 2 2 2 2 0 4 0 0 0
                1 0 0 0 1 0 4 4 0 4 2 2 2 2 0 2 2 2 2 4 2 2
                0 2 1 1 0 2 1 2 0 4 4 1 4 1 4 2))
         (args-solar-anomaly
          (list 0 0 0 0 0 0 0 0 0 0 -1 0 0 1 -1 -1 -1 1 0 1
```

```
          0 1 0 1 1 1 0 0 0 0 0 0 0 -1 0 0 0 0 1 1
          0 -1 -2 0 1 1 1 1 1 0 -1 1 0 -1 0 0 0 -1 -2))
   (args-lunar-anomaly
    (list 0 1 1 0 -1 -1 0 2 1 2 0 -2 1 0 -1 0 -1 -1 -1
          0 0 -1 0 1 1 0 0 3 0 -1 1 -2 0 2 1 -2 3 2 -3
          -1 0 0 1 0 1 1 0 0 -2 -1 1 -2 2 -2 -1 1 1 -1
          0 0))
   (args-moon-node
    (list 1 1 -1 -1 1 -1 1 1 -1 -1 -1 -1 1 -1 1 1 -1 -1
          -1 1 3 1 1 1 -1 -1 -1 1 -1 1 -3 1 -3 -1 -1 1
          -1 1 -1 1 1 1 1 -1 3 -1 -1 1 -1 -1 1 -1 1 -1
          -1 -1 -1 -1 -1 1))
   (sine-coeff
    (list 5128122 280602 277693 173237 55413 46271 32573
          17198 9266 8822 8216 4324 4200 -3359 2463 2211
          2065 -1870 1828 -1794 -1749 -1565 -1491 -1475
          -1410 -1344 -1335 1107 1021 833 777 671 607
          596 491 -451 439 422 421 -366 -351 331 315
          302 -283 -229 223 223 -220 -220 -185 181
          -177 176 166 -164 132 -119 115 107))
   (beta
    (* (deg 1/1000000)
       (sigma ((v sine-coeff)
               (w args-lunar-elongation)
               (x args-solar-anomaly)
               (y args-lunar-anomaly)
               (z args-moon-node))
              (* v (expt cap-E (abs x))
                 (sin-degrees
                  (+ (* w cap-D)
                     (* x cap-M)
                     (* y cap-M-prime)
                     (* z cap-F)))))))
   (venus (* (deg 175/1000000)
             (+ (sin-degrees
                 (+ (deg 119.75L0) (* c (deg 131.849L0))
                    cap-F))
                (sin-degrees
                 (+ (deg 119.75L0) (* c (deg 131.849L0))
                    (- cap-F))))))
   (flat-earth
    (+ (* (deg -2235/1000000)
          (sin-degrees cap-L-prime))
       (* (deg 127/1000000) (sin-degrees
                             (- cap-L-prime cap-M-prime)))
       (* (deg -115/1000000) (sin-degrees
                              (+ cap-L-prime cap-M-prime)))))
   (extra (* (deg 382/1000000)
             (sin-degrees
              (+ (deg 313.45L0)
                 (* c (deg 481266.484L0)))))))
  (+ beta venus flat-earth extra)))
```

```
(defun lunar-altitude (tee location)                          (14.64)
  ;; TYPE (moment location) -> half-circle
  ;; Geocentric altitude of moon at tee at location,
  ;; as a small positive/negative angle in degrees, ignoring
  ;; parallax and refraction.  Adapted from "Astronomical
  ;; Algorithms" by Jean Meeus, Willmann-Bell, 2nd edn.,
  ;; 1998.
  (let* ((phi ; Local latitude.
          (latitude location))
         (psi ; Local longitude.
          (longitude location))
         (lambda ; Lunar longitude.
           (lunar-longitude tee))
         (beta ; Lunar latitude.
          (lunar-latitude tee))
         (alpha ; Lunar right ascension.
          (right-ascension tee beta lambda))
         (delta ; Lunar declination.
```

```
         (declination tee beta lambda))
        (theta0 ; Sidereal time.
         (sidereal-from-moment tee))
        (cap-H ; Local hour angle.
         (mod (- theta0 (- psi) alpha) 360))
        (altitude
         (arcsin-degrees (+ (* (sin-degrees phi)
                               (sin-degrees delta))
                            (* (cos-degrees phi)
                               (cos-degrees delta)
                               (cos-degrees cap-H))))))
    (mod3 altitude -180 180)))
```

(14.65)

```
(defun lunar-distance (tee)
  ;; TYPE moment -> distance
  ;; Distance to moon (in meters) at moment tee.
  ;; Adapted from "Astronomical Algorithms" by Jean Meeus,
  ;; Willmann-Bell, 2nd edn., 1998, pp. 338-342.
  (let* ((c (julian-centuries tee))
         (cap-D (lunar-elongation c))
         (cap-M (solar-anomaly c))
         (cap-M-prime (lunar-anomaly c))
         (cap-F (moon-node c))
         (cap-E (poly c (list 1 -0.002516L0 -0.0000074L0)))
         (args-lunar-elongation
          (list 0 2 2 0 0 0 2 2 2 2 0 1 0 2 0 0 4 0 4 2 2 1
                1 2 2 4 2 0 2 2 1 2 0 0 2 2 2 4 0 3 2 4 0 2
                2 2 4 0 4 1 2 0 1 3 4 2 0 1 2 2))
         (args-solar-anomaly
          (list 0 0 0 0 1 0 0 -1 0 -1 1 0 1 0 0 0 0 0 0 1 1
                0 1 -1 0 0 0 1 0 -1 0 -2 1 2 -2 0 0 -1 0 0 1
                -1 2 2 1 -1 0 0 -1 0 1 0 1 0 0 -1 2 1 0 0))
         (args-lunar-anomaly
          (list 1 -1 0 2 0 0 -2 -1 1 0 -1 0 1 0 1 1 -1 3 -2
                -1 0 -1 0 1 2 0 -3 -2 -1 -2 1 0 2 0 -1 1 0
                -1 2 -1 1 -2 -1 -1 -2 0 1 4 0 -2 0 2 1 -2 -3
                2 1 -1 3 -1))
         (args-moon-node
          (list 0 0 0 0 0 2 0 0 0 0 0 0 0 -2 2 -2 0 0 0 0 0
                0 0 0 0 0 0 0 2 0 0 0 0 0 0 -2 2 0 2 0 0 0 0
                0 0 -2 0 0 0 0 -2 -2 0 0 0 0 0 0 0 -2))
         (cosine-coeff
          (list -20905355 -3699111 -2955968 -569925 48888 -3149
                246158 -152138 -170733 -204586 -129620 108743
                104755 10321 0 79661 -34782 -23210 -21636 24208
                30824 -8379 -16675 -12831 -10445 -11650 14403
                -7003 0 10056 6322 -9884 5751 0 -4950 4130 0
                -3958 0 3258 2616 -1897 -2117 2354 0 0 -1423
                -1117 -1571 -1739 0 -4421 0 0 0 0 1165 0 0
                8752))
         (correction
          (sigma ((v cosine-coeff)
                  (w args-lunar-elongation)
                  (x args-solar-anomaly)
                  (y args-lunar-anomaly)
                  (z args-moon-node))
                 (* v (expt cap-E (abs x))
                    (cos-degrees
                     (+ (* w cap-D)
                        (* x cap-M)
                        (* y cap-M-prime)
                        (* z cap-F)))))))
    (+ (mt 385000560) correction)))
```

(14.66)

```
(defun lunar-parallax (tee location)
  ;; TYPE (moment location) -> angle
  ;; Parallax of moon at tee at location.
  ;; Adapted from "Astronomical Algorithms" by Jean Meeus,
  ;; Willmann-Bell, 2nd edn., 1998.
  (let* ((geo (lunar-altitude tee location))
```

```
        (cap-Delta (lunar-distance tee))
        (alt (/ (mt 6378140) cap-Delta))
        (arg (* alt (cos-degrees geo))))
    (arcsin-degrees arg)))
```

(14.67)

```
(defun topocentric-lunar-altitude (tee location)
  ;; TYPE (moment location) -> half-circle
  ;; Topocentric altitude of moon at tee at location,
  ;; as a small positive/negative angle in degrees,
  ;; ignoring refraction.
  (- (lunar-altitude tee location)
     (lunar-parallax tee location)))
```

Times of day are computed by the following functions:

(14.68)

```
(defun approx-moment-of-depression (tee location alpha early?)
  ;; TYPE (moment location half-circle boolean) -> moment
  ;; Moment in local time near tee when depression angle
  ;; of sun is alpha (negative if above horizon) at
  ;; location; early? is true when morning event is sought
  ;; and false for evening.  Returns bogus if depression
  ;; angle is not reached.
  (let* ((try (sine-offset tee location alpha))
         (date (fixed-from-moment tee))
         (alt (if (>= alpha 0)
                  (if early? date (1+ date))
                (+ date (hr 12))))
         (value (if (> (abs try) 1)
                    (sine-offset alt location alpha)
                  try)))
    (if (<= (abs value) 1) ; Event occurs
        (let* ((offset (mod3 (/ (arcsin-degrees value) (deg 360))
                             (hr -12) (hr 12))))
          (local-from-apparent
           (+ date
              (if early?
                  (- (hr 6) offset)
                (+ (hr 18) offset)))
           location))
      bogus)))
```

(14.69)

```
(defun sine-offset (tee location alpha)
  ;; TYPE (moment location half-circle) -> real
  ;; Sine of angle between position of sun at
  ;; local time tee and
  ;; when its depression is alpha at location.
  ;; Out of range when it does not occur.
  (let* ((phi (latitude location))
         (tee-prime (universal-from-local tee location))
         (delta ; Declination of sun.
          (declination tee-prime (deg 0L0)
                       (solar-longitude tee-prime))))
    (+ (* (tan-degrees phi)
          (tan-degrees delta))
       (/ (sin-degrees alpha)
          (* (cos-degrees delta)
             (cos-degrees phi))))))
```

(14.70)

```
(defun moment-of-depression (approx location alpha early?)
  ;; TYPE (moment location half-circle boolean) -> moment
  ;; Moment in local time near approx when depression
  ;; angle of sun is alpha (negative if above horizon) at
  ;; location; early? is true when morning event is
  ;; sought, and false for evening.
  ;; Returns bogus if depression angle is not reached.
  (let* ((tee (approx-moment-of-depression
               approx location alpha early?)))
    (if (equal tee bogus)
        bogus
```

```
      (if (< (abs (- approx tee))
             (sec 30))
          tee
        (moment-of-depression tee location alpha early?)))))
```

(14.71)

```
(defconstant morning
  ;; TYPE boolean
  ;; Signifies morning.
  true)
```

(14.72)

```
(defun dawn (date location alpha)
  ;; TYPE (fixed-date location half-circle) -> moment
  ;; Standard time in morning on fixed date at
  ;; location when depression angle of sun is alpha.
  ;; Returns bogus if there is no dawn on date.
  (let* ((result (moment-of-depression
                  (+ date (hr 6)) location alpha morning)))
    (if (equal result bogus)
        bogus
      (standard-from-local result location))))
```

(14.73)

```
(defconstant evening
  ;; TYPE boolean
  ;; Signifies evening.
  false)
```

(14.74)

```
(defun dusk (date location alpha)
  ;; TYPE (fixed-date location half-circle) -> moment
  ;; Standard time in evening on fixed date at
  ;; location when depression angle of sun is alpha.
  ;; Returns bogus if there is no dusk on date.
  (let* ((result (moment-of-depression
                  (+ date (hr 18)) location alpha evening)))
    (if (equal result bogus)
        bogus
      (standard-from-local result location))))
```

(14.75)

```
(defun refraction (tee location)
  ;; TYPE (moment location) -> half-circle
  ;; Refraction angle at moment tee at location.
  ;; The moment is not used.
  (let* ((h (max (mt 0) (elevation location)))
         (cap-R (mt 6.372d6)) ; Radius of Earth.
         (dip ; Depression of visible horizon.
          (arccos-degrees (/ cap-R (+ cap-R h)))))
    (+ (mins 34) dip
       (* (secs 19) (sqrt h)))))
```

(14.76)

```
(defun sunrise (date location)
  ;; TYPE (fixed-date location) -> moment
  ;; Standard time of sunrise on fixed date at
  ;; location.
  (let* ((alpha (+ (refraction (+ date (hr 6)) location)
                   (mins 16))))
    (dawn date location alpha)))
```

(14.77)

```
(defun sunset (date location)
  ;; TYPE (fixed-date location) -> moment
  ;; Standard time of sunset on fixed date at
  ;; location.
  (let* ((alpha (+ (refraction (+ date (hr 18)) location)
                   (mins 16))))
    (dusk date location alpha)))
```

(14.80)

```
(defun jewish-sabbath-ends (date location)
  ;; TYPE (fixed-date location) -> moment
  ;; Standard time of end of Jewish sabbath on fixed date
  ;; at location (as per Berthold Cohn).
  (dusk date location (angle 7 5 0)))
```

(14.81)

```
(defun jewish-dusk (date location)
  ;; TYPE (fixed-date location) -> moment
  ;; Standard time of Jewish dusk on fixed date
  ;; at location (as per Vilna Gaon).
  (dusk date location (angle 4 40 0)))
```

(14.82)

```
(defun observed-lunar-altitude (tee location)
  ;; TYPE (moment location) -> half-circle
  ;; Observed altitude of upper limb of moon at tee at location,
  ;; as a small positive/negative angle in degrees, including
  ;; refraction and elevation.
  (+ (topocentric-lunar-altitude tee location)
     (refraction tee location)
     (mins 16)))
```

(14.83)

```
(defun moonrise (date location)
  ;; TYPE (fixed-date location) -> moment
  ;; Standard time of moonrise on fixed date at location.
  ;; Returns bogus if there is no moonrise on date.
  (let* ((tee ; Midnight.
           (universal-from-standard date location))
          (waning (> (lunar-phase tee) (deg 180)))
          (alt ; Altitude at midnight.
           (observed-lunar-altitude tee location))
          (lat (latitude location))
          (offset (/ alt (* 4 (- (deg 90) (abs lat)))))
          (approx ; Approximate rising time.
           (if waning
               (if (> offset 0)
                   (- tee -1 offset)
                 (- tee offset))
             (+ tee 1/2 offset)))
          (rise (binary-search
                 l (- approx (hr 6))
                 u (+ approx (hr 6))
                 x (> (observed-lunar-altitude x location)
                      (deg 0))
                 (< (- u l) (mn 1)))))
    (if (< rise (1+ tee))
        (max (standard-from-universal rise location)
             date) ; May be just before to midnight.
      ;; Else no moonrise this day.
      bogus)))
```

(14.84)

```
(defun moonset (date location)
  ;; TYPE (fixed-date location) -> moment
  ;; Standard time of moonset on fixed date at location.
  ;; Returns bogus if there is no moonset on date.
  (let* ((tee ; Midnight.
           (universal-from-standard date location))
         (waxing (< (lunar-phase tee) (deg 180)))
         (alt ; Altitude at midnight.
          (observed-lunar-altitude tee location))
         (lat (latitude location))
         (offset (/ alt (* 4 (- (deg 90) (abs lat)))))
         (approx ; Approximate setting time.
          (if waxing
              (if (> offset 0)
                  (+ tee offset)
                (+ tee 1 offset))
            (- tee offset -1/2)))
         (set (binary-search
```

```
                 l (- approx (hr 6))
                 u (+ approx (hr 6))
                 x (< (observed-lunar-altitude x location) (deg 0))
                 (< (- u l) (mn 1)))))
    (if (< set (1+ tee))
        (max (standard-from-universal set location)
             date) ; May be just before to midnight.
      ;; Else no moonset this day.
      bogus)))
```

```
(defconstant padua                                              (14.85)
  ;; TYPE location
  ;; Location of Padua, Italy.
  (location (angle 45 24 28) (angle 11 53 9) (mt 18) (hr 1)))
```

```
(defun local-zero-hour (tee)                                    (14.86)
  ;; TYPE moment -> moment
  ;; Local time of dusk in Padua, Italy on date of moment tee.
  (let* ((date (fixed-from-moment tee)))
    (local-from-standard
     (+ (dusk date padua (angle 0 16 0)) ; Sunset.
        (mn 30)) ; Dusk.
     padua)))
```

```
(defun local-from-italian (tee)                                 (14.87)
  ;; TYPE moment -> moment
  ;; Local time corresponding to Italian time tee.
  (let* ((date (fixed-from-moment tee))
         (z (local-zero-hour (1- tee))))
    (- tee (- date z))))
```

```
(defun italian-from-local (tee_ell)                             (14.88)
  ;; TYPE moment -> moment
  ;; Italian time corresponding to local time tee_ell.
  (let* ((date (fixed-from-moment tee_ell))
         (z0 (local-zero-hour (1- tee_ell)))
         (z (local-zero-hour tee_ell)))
    (if (> tee_ell z) ; if after zero hour
        (+ tee_ell (- date -1 z)) ; then next day
      (+ tee_ell (- date z0)))))
```

```
(defun daytime-temporal-hour (date location)                    (14.89)
  ;; TYPE (fixed-date location) -> real
  ;; Length of daytime temporal hour on fixed date at location.
  ;; Returns bogus if there no sunrise or sunset on date.
  (if (or (equal (sunrise date location) bogus)
          (equal (sunset date location) bogus))
      bogus
    (/ (- (sunset date location)
          (sunrise date location))
       12)))
```

```
(defun nighttime-temporal-hour (date location)                  (14.90)
  ;; TYPE (fixed-date location) -> real
  ;; Length of nighttime temporal hour on fixed date at location.
  ;; Returns bogus if there no sunrise or sunset on date.
  (if (or (equal (sunrise (1+ date) location) bogus)
          (equal (sunset date location) bogus))
      bogus
    (/ (- (sunrise (1+ date) location)
          (sunset date location))
       12)))
```

```
(defun standard-from-sundial (tee location)                     (14.91)
  ;; TYPE (moment location) -> moment
  ;; Standard time of temporal moment tee at location.
  ;; Returns bogus if temporal hour is undefined that day.
```

```
  (let* ((date (fixed-from-moment tee))
         (hour (* 24 (time-from-moment tee)))
         (h (cond ((<= 6 hour 18); daytime today
                   (daytime-temporal-hour date location))
                  ((< hour 6)    ; early this morning
                   (nighttime-temporal-hour (1- date) location))
                  (t             ; this evening
                   (nighttime-temporal-hour date location)))))
    (cond ((equal h bogus) bogus)
          ((<= 6 hour 18); daytime today
           (+ (sunrise date location) (* (- hour 6) h)))
          ((< hour 6)    ; early this morning
           (+ (sunset (1- date) location) (* (+ hour 6) h)))
          (t             ; this evening
           (+ (sunset date location) (* (- hour 18) h))))))
```

(14.92)

```
(defun jewish-morning-end (date location)
  ;; TYPE (fixed-date location) -> moment
  ;; Standard time on fixed date at location of end of
  ;; morning according to Jewish ritual.
  (standard-from-sundial (+ date (hr 10)) location))
```

(14.93)

```
(defun asr (date location)
  ;; TYPE (fixed-date location) -> moment
  ;; Standard time of asr on fixed date at location.
  ;; According to Hanafi rule.
  ;; Returns bogus is no asr occurs.
  (let* ((noon ; Time when sun nearest zenith.
           (midday date location))
         (phi (latitude location))
         (delta ; Solar declination at noon.
          (declination noon (deg 0) (solar-longitude noon)))
         (altitude ; Solar altitude at noon.
          (arcsin-degrees
           (+ (* (cos-degrees delta) (cos-degrees phi))
              (* (sin-degrees delta) (sin-degrees phi)))))
         (h ; Sun's altitude when shadow increases by
          (mod3 (arctan-degrees ; ... double its length.
                 (tan-degrees altitude)
                 (1+ (* 2 (tan-degrees altitude))))
                -90 90)))
    (if (<= altitude (deg 0)) ; No shadow.
        bogus
      (dusk date location (- h)))))
```

(14.94)

```
(defun alt-asr (date location)
  ;; TYPE (fixed-date location) -> moment
  ;; Standard time of asr on fixed date at location.
  ;; According to Shafi'i rule.
  ;; Returns bogus is no asr occurs.
  (let* ((noon ; Time when sun nearest zenith.
           (midday date location))
         (phi (latitude location))
         (delta ; Solar declination at noon.
          (declination noon (deg 0) (solar-longitude noon)))
         (altitude ; Solar altitude at noon.
          (arcsin-degrees
           (+ (* (cos-degrees delta) (cos-degrees phi))
              (* (sin-degrees delta) (sin-degrees phi)))))
         (h ; Sun's altitude when shadow increases by
          (mod3 (arctan-degrees ; ... its length.
                 (tan-degrees altitude)
                 (1+ (tan-degrees altitude)))
                -90 90)))
    (if (<= altitude (deg 0)) ; No shadow.
        bogus
      (dusk date location (- h)))))
```

The functions for lunar visibility are:

```
(defun arc-of-light (tee)
  ;; TYPE moment -> half-circle
  ;; Angular separation of sun and moon
  ;; at moment tee.
  (arccos-degrees
   (* (cos-degrees (lunar-latitude tee))
      (cos-degrees (lunar-phase tee)))))
```
(14.95)

```
(defun simple-best-view (date location)
  ;; TYPE (fixed-date location) -> moment
  ;; Best viewing time (UT) in the evening.
  ;; Simple version.
  (let* ((dark ; Best viewing time prior evening.
          (dusk date location (deg 4.5L0)))
         (best (if (equal dark bogus)
                   (1+ date) ; An arbitrary time.
                 dark)))
    (universal-from-standard best location)))
```
(14.96)

```
(defun shaukat-criterion (date location)
  ;; TYPE (fixed-date location) -> boolean
  ;; S. K. Shaukat's criterion for likely
  ;; visibility of crescent moon on eve of date at location.
  ;; Not intended for high altitudes or polar regions.
  (let* ((tee (simple-best-view (1- date) location))
         (phase (lunar-phase tee))
         (h (lunar-altitude tee location))
         (cap-ARCL (arc-of-light tee)))
    (and (< new phase first-quarter)
         (<= (deg 10.6L0) cap-ARCL (deg 90))
         (> h (deg 4.1L0)))))
```
(14.97)

```
(defun arc-of-vision (tee location)
  ;; TYPE (moment location) -> half-circle
  ;; Angular difference in altitudes of sun and moon
  ;; at moment tee at location.
  (- (lunar-altitude tee location)
     (solar-altitude tee location)))
```
(14.98)

```
(defun bruin-best-view (date location)
  ;; TYPE (fixed-date location) -> moment
  ;; Best viewing time (UT) in the evening.
  ;; Yallop version, per Bruin (1977).
  (let* ((sun (sunset date location))
         (moon (moonset date location))
         (best ; Best viewing time prior evening.
          (if (or (equal sun bogus) (equal moon bogus))
              (1+ date) ; An arbitrary time.
            (+ (* 5/9 sun) (* 4/9 moon)))))
    (universal-from-standard best location)))
```
(14.99)

```
(defun yallop-criterion (date location)
  ;; TYPE (fixed-date location) -> boolean
  ;; B. D. Yallop's criterion for possible
  ;; visibility of crescent moon on eve of date at location.
  ;; Not intended for high altitudes or polar regions.
  (let* ((tee ; Best viewing time prior evening.
          (bruin-best-view (1- date) location))
         (phase (lunar-phase tee))
         (cap-D (lunar-semi-diameter tee location))
         (cap-ARCL (arc-of-light tee))
         (cap-W (* cap-D (- 1 (cos-degrees cap-ARCL))))
         (cap-ARCV (arc-of-vision tee location))
         (e -0.14L0) ; Crescent visible under perfect conditions.
         (q1 (poly cap-W
                   (list 11.8371L0 -6.3226L0 0.7319L0 -0.1018L0))))
    (and (< new phase first-quarter)
         (> cap-ARCV (+ q1 e)))))
```
(14.100)

```
(defun lunar-semi-diameter (tee location)                    (14.101)
  ;; TYPE (moment location) -> half-circle
  ;; Topocentric lunar semi-diameter at moment tee and location.
  (let* ((h (lunar-altitude tee location))
         (p (lunar-parallax tee location)))
    (* 0.27245L0 p (1+ (* (sin-degrees h) (sin-degrees p))))))
```

```
(defun lunar-diameter (tee)                                  (14.102)
  ;; TYPE moment -> angle
  ;; Geocentric apparent lunar diameter of the moon (in
  ;; degrees) at moment tee.  Adapted from "Astronomical
  ;; Algorithms" by Jean Meeus, Willmann-Bell, 2nd edn.,
  ;; 1998.
  (/ (deg 1792367000/9) (lunar-distance tee)))
```

```
(defun visible-crescent (date location)                      (14.103)
  ;; TYPE (fixed-date location) -> boolean
  ;; Criterion for possible visibility of crescent moon
  ;; on eve of date at location.
  ;; Shaukat's criterion may be replaced with another.
  (shaukat-criterion date location))
```

```
(defun phasis-on-or-before (date location)                   (14.104)
  ;; TYPE (fixed-date location) -> fixed-date
  ;; Closest fixed date on or before date when crescent
  ;; moon first became visible at location.
  (let* ((moon ; Prior new moon.
          (fixed-from-moment
           (lunar-phase-at-or-before new date)))
         (age (- date moon))
         (tau ; Check if not visible yet on eve of date.
          (if (and (<= age 3)
                   (not (visible-crescent date location)))
              (- moon 30) ; Must go back a month.
            moon)))
    (next d tau (visible-crescent d location))))
```

```
(defun phasis-on-or-after (date location)                    (14.105)
  ;; TYPE (fixed-date location) -> fixed-date
  ;; Closest fixed date on or after date on the eve
  ;; of which crescent moon first became visible at location.
  (let* ((moon ; Prior new moon.
          (fixed-from-moment
           (lunar-phase-at-or-before new date)))
         (age (- date moon))
         (tau ; Check if not visible yet on eve of date.
          (if (or (<= 4 age)
                  (visible-crescent (1- date) location))
              (+ moon 29) ; Next new moon
            date)))
    (next d tau (visible-crescent d location))))
```

D.15 The Persian Calendar

```
(defun persian-date (year month day)
  ;; TYPE (persian-year persian-month persian-day)
  ;; TYPE  -> persian-date
  (list year month day))
```

```
(defconstant persian-epoch                                   (15.1)
  ;; TYPE fixed-date
  ;; Fixed date of start of the Persian calendar.
  (fixed-from-julian (julian-date (ce 622) march 19)))
```

```
(defconstant tehran                                          (15.2)
  ;; TYPE location
  ;; Location of Tehran, Iran.
  (location (deg 35.68L0) (deg 51.42L0)
            (mt 1100) (hr (+ 3 1/2))))
```

(15.3)

```
(defun midday-in-tehran (date)
  ;; TYPE fixed-date -> moment
  ;; Universal time of true noon on fixed date in Tehran.
  (midday date tehran))
```

(15.4)

```
(defun persian-new-year-on-or-before (date)
  ;; TYPE fixed-date -> fixed-date
  ;; Fixed date of Astronomical Persian New Year on or
  ;; before fixed date.
  (let* ((approx ; Approximate time of equinox.
          (estimate-prior-solar-longitude
           spring (midday-in-tehran date))))
    (next day (- (floor approx) 1)
          (<= (solar-longitude (midday-in-tehran day))
              (+ spring (deg 2))))))
```

(15.5)

```
(defun fixed-from-persian (p-date)
  ;; TYPE persian-date -> fixed-date
  ;; Fixed date of Astronomical Persian date p-date.
  (let* ((month (standard-month p-date))
         (day (standard-day p-date))
         (year (standard-year p-date))
         (new-year
          (persian-new-year-on-or-before
           (+ persian-epoch 180; Fall after epoch.
              (floor
               (* mean-tropical-year
                  (if (< 0 year)
                      (1- year)
                    year))))))); No year zero.
    (+ (1- new-year)       ; Days in prior years.
       (if (<= month 7)   ; Days in prior months this year.
           (* 31 (1- month))
         (+ (* 30 (1- month)) 6))
       day)))              ; Days so far this month.
```

(15.6)

```
(defun persian-from-fixed (date)
  ;; TYPE fixed-date -> persian-date
  ;; Astronomical Persian date (year month day)
  ;; corresponding to fixed date.
  (let* ((new-year
          (persian-new-year-on-or-before date))
         (y (1+ (round (/ (- new-year persian-epoch)
                          mean-tropical-year))))
         (year (if (< 0 y)
                   y
                 (1- y))); No year zero
         (day-of-year (1+ (- date
                             (fixed-from-persian
                              (persian-date year 1 1)))))
         (month (if (<= day-of-year 186)
                    (ceiling (/ day-of-year 31))
                  (ceiling (/ (- day-of-year 6) 30))))
         (day             ; Calculate the day by subtraction
          (- date (1- (fixed-from-persian
                       (persian-date year month 1))))))
    (persian-date year month day)))
```

(15.7)

```
(defun arithmetic-persian-leap-year? (p-year)
  ;; TYPE persian-year -> boolean
  ;; True if p-year is a leap year on the Persian calendar.
  (let* ((y ; Years since start of 2820-year cycles
          (if (< 0 p-year)
              (- p-year 474)
            (- p-year 473))); No year zero
         (year ; Equivalent year in the range 474..3263
          (+ (mod y 2820) 474)))
    (< (mod (* (+ year 38)
               31)
            128)
       31)))
```

(15.8)

```
(defun fixed-from-arithmetic-persian (p-date)
  ;; TYPE persian-date -> fixed-date
  ;; Fixed date equivalent to Persian date p-date.
  (let* ((day (standard-day p-date))
         (month (standard-month p-date))
         (p-year (standard-year p-date))
         (y ; Years since start of 2820-year cycle
          (if (< 0 p-year)
              (- p-year 474)
            (- p-year 473))); No year zero
         (year ; Equivalent year in the range 474..3263
          (+ (mod y 2820) 474)))
    (+ (1- persian-epoch); Days before epoch
       (* 1029983        ; Days in 2820-year cycles
                                  ; before Persian year 474
          (quotient y 2820))
       (* 365 (1- year)) ; Nonleap days in prior years this
                                  ; 2820-year cycle
       (quotient         ; Leap days in prior years this
                                  ; 2820-year cycle
        (- (* 31 year) 5) 128)
       (if (<= month 7)  ; Days in prior months this year
           (* 31 (1- month))
         (+ (* 30 (1- month)) 6))
       day)))            ; Days so far this month
```

(15.9)

```
(defun arithmetic-persian-year-from-fixed (date)
  ;; TYPE fixed-date -> persian-year
  ;; Persian year corresponding to the fixed date.
  (let* ((d0      ; Prior days since start of 2820-year cycle
                  ; beginning in Persian year 474
          (- date (fixed-from-arithmetic-persian
                   (persian-date 475 1 1))))
         (n2820   ; Completed prior 2820-year cycles
          (quotient d0 1029983))
         (d1      ; Prior days not in n2820--that is, days
                  ; since start of last 2820-year cycle
          (mod d0 1029983))
         (y2820 ; Years since start of last 2820-year cycle
          (if (= d1 1029982)
              ;; Last day of 2820-year cycle
              2820
            ;; Otherwise use cycle of years formula
            (quotient (+ (* 128 d1) 46878)
                      46751)))
         (year    ; Years since Persian epoch
          (+ 474      ; Years before start of 2820-year cycles
             (* 2820 n2820) ; Years in prior 2820-year cycles
             y2820))); Years since start of last 2820-year
                                  ; cycle
    (if (< 0 year)
        year
      (1- year)))); No year zero
```

(15.10)

```
(defun arithmetic-persian-from-fixed (date)
  ;; TYPE fixed-date -> persian-date
  ;; Persian date corresponding to fixed date.
  (let* ((year (arithmetic-persian-year-from-fixed date))
         (day-of-year (1+ (- date
                             (fixed-from-arithmetic-persian
                              (persian-date year 1 1)))))
         (month (if (<= day-of-year 186)
                    (ceiling (/ day-of-year 31))
                  (ceiling (/ (- day-of-year 6) 30))))
         (day         ; Calculate the day by subtraction
          (- date (1- (fixed-from-arithmetic-persian
                       (persian-date year month 1))))))
    (persian-date year month day)))
```

(15.11)

```
(defun nowruz (g-year)
  ;; TYPE gregorian-year -> fixed-date
```

```
  ;; Fixed date of Persian New Year (Nowruz) in Gregorian
  ;; year g-year.
  (let* ((persian-year
          (1+ (- g-year
                 (gregorian-year-from-fixed
                  persian-epoch))))
         (y (if (<= persian-year 0)
                ;; No Persian year 0
                (1- persian-year)
              persian-year)))
    (fixed-from-persian (persian-date y 1 1))))
```

D.16 The Bahá'í Calendar

```
(defun bahai-date (major cycle year month day)
  ;; TYPE (bahai-major bahai-cycle bahai-year
  ;; TYPE  bahai-month bahai-day) -> bahai-date
  (list major cycle year month day))
```

```
(defun bahai-major (date)
  ;; TYPE bahai-date -> bahai-major
  (first date))
```

```
(defun bahai-cycle (date)
  ;; TYPE bahai-date -> bahai-cycle
  (second date))
```

```
(defun bahai-year (date)
  ;; TYPE bahai-date -> bahai-year
  (third date))
```

```
(defun bahai-month (date)
  ;; TYPE bahai-date -> bahai-month
  (fourth date))
```

```
(defun bahai-day (date)
  ;; TYPE bahai-date -> bahai-day
  (fifth date))
```

(16.1)

```
(defconstant ayyam-i-ha
  ;; TYPE bahai-month
  ;; Signifies intercalary period of 4 or 5 days.
  0)
```

(16.2)

```
(defconstant bahai-epoch
  ;; TYPE fixed-date
  ;; Fixed date of start of Baha'i calendar.
  (fixed-from-gregorian (gregorian-date 1844 march 21)))
```

(16.3)

```
(defun fixed-from-bahai (b-date)
  ;; TYPE bahai-date -> fixed-date
  ;; Fixed date equivalent to the Baha'i date b-date.
  (let* ((major (bahai-major b-date))
         (cycle (bahai-cycle b-date))
         (year (bahai-year b-date))
         (month (bahai-month b-date))
         (day (bahai-day b-date))
         (g-year; Corresponding Gregorian year.
          (+ (* 361 (1- major))
             (* 19 (1- cycle)) year -1
             (gregorian-year-from-fixed bahai-epoch))))
    (+ (fixed-from-gregorian ; Prior years.
        (gregorian-date g-year march 20))
```

```
        (cond ((= month ayyam-i-ha) ; Intercalary period.
               342) ; 18 months have elapsed.
              ((= month 19); Last month of year.
               (if (gregorian-leap-year? (1+ g-year))
                   347  ; Long ayyam-i-ha.
                 346)); Ordinary ayyam-i-ha.
              (t (* 19 (1- month)))); Elapsed months.
        day))) ; Days of current month.
```

(16.4)

```
(defun bahai-from-fixed (date)
  ;; TYPE fixed-date -> bahai-date
  ;; Baha'i (major cycle year month day) corresponding to fixed
  ;; date.
  (let* ((g-year (gregorian-year-from-fixed date))
         (start   ; 1844
          (gregorian-year-from-fixed bahai-epoch))
         (years ; Since start of Baha'i calendar.
          (- g-year start
             (if (<= date
                     (fixed-from-gregorian
                      (gregorian-date g-year march 20)))
                 1 0)))
         (major (1+ (quotient years 361)))
         (cycle (1+ (quotient (mod years 361) 19)))
         (year (1+ (mod years 19)))
         (days; Since start of year
          (- date (fixed-from-bahai
                   (bahai-date major cycle year 1 1))))
         (month
          (cond ((>= date
                     (fixed-from-bahai
                      (bahai-date major cycle year 19 1)))
                 19) ; Last month of year.
                ((>= date ; Intercalary days.
                     (fixed-from-bahai
                      (bahai-date major cycle year
                                  ayyam-i-ha 1)))
                 ayyam-i-ha) ; Intercalary period.
                (t (1+ (quotient days 19)))))
         (day (- date -1
                 (fixed-from-bahai
                  (bahai-date major cycle year month 1)))))
    (bahai-date major cycle year month day)))
```

(16.5)

```
(defconstant bahai-location
  ;; TYPE location
  ;; Location of Tehran for astronomical Baha'i calendar.
  (location (deg 35.696111L0) (deg 51.423056L0)
            (mt 0) (hr (+ 3 1/2))))
```

(16.6)

```
(defun bahai-sunset (date)
  ;; TYPE fixed-date -> moment
  ;; Universal time of sunset on fixed date
  ;; in Bahai-Location.
  (universal-from-standard
   (sunset date bahai-location)
   bahai-location))
```

(16.7)

```
(defun astro-bahai-new-year-on-or-before (date)
  ;; TYPE fixed-date -> fixed-date
  ;; Fixed date of astronomical Bahai New Year on or before fixed
  ;; date.
  (let* ((approx ; Approximate time of equinox.
          (estimate-prior-solar-longitude
           spring (bahai-sunset date))))
    (next day (1- (floor approx))
          (<= (solar-longitude (bahai-sunset day))
              (+ spring (deg 2))))))
```

(16.8)

```
(defun fixed-from-astro-bahai (b-date)
  ;; TYPE bahai-date -> fixed-date
  ;; Fixed date of Baha'i date b-date.
  (let* ((major (bahai-major b-date))
         (cycle (bahai-cycle b-date))
         (year (bahai-year b-date))
         (month (bahai-month b-date))
         (day (bahai-day b-date))
         (years; Years from epoch
          (+ (* 361 (1- major))
             (* 19 (1- cycle))
             year)))
    (cond ((= month 19); last month of year
           (+ (astro-bahai-new-year-on-or-before
               (+ bahai-epoch
                  (floor (* mean-tropical-year
                            (+ years 1/2)))))
              -20 day))
          ((= month ayyam-i-ha)
           ;; intercalary month, between 18th & 19th
           (+ (astro-bahai-new-year-on-or-before
               (+ bahai-epoch
                  (floor (* mean-tropical-year
                            (- years 1/2)))))
              341 day))
          (t (+ (astro-bahai-new-year-on-or-before
                 (+ bahai-epoch
                    (floor (* mean-tropical-year
                              (- years 1/2)))))
                (* (1- month) 19)
                day -1)))))
```

(16.9)

```
(defun astro-bahai-from-fixed (date)
  ;; TYPE fixed-date -> bahai-date
  ;; Astronomical Baha'i date corresponding to fixed date.
  (let* ((new-year (astro-bahai-new-year-on-or-before date))
         (years (round (/ (- new-year bahai-epoch)
                          mean-tropical-year)))
         (major (1+ (quotient years 361)))
         (cycle (1+ (quotient (mod years 361) 19)))
         (year (1+ (mod years 19)))
         (days; Since start of year
          (- date new-year))
         (month
          (cond
           ((>= date (fixed-from-astro-bahai
                      (bahai-date major cycle year 19 1)))
                                       ; last month of year
            19)
           ((>= date
                (fixed-from-astro-bahai
                 (bahai-date major cycle year ayyam-i-ha 1)))
                                       ; intercalary month
            ayyam-i-ha)
           (t (1+ (quotient days 19)))))
         (day (- date -1
                 (fixed-from-astro-bahai
                  (bahai-date major cycle year month 1)))))
    (bahai-date major cycle year month day)))
```

(16.10)

```
(defun bahai-new-year (g-year)
  ;; TYPE gregorian-year -> fixed-date
  ;; Fixed date of Baha'i New Year in Gregorian year g-year.
  (fixed-from-gregorian
   (gregorian-date g-year march 21)))
```

(16.11)

```
(defun naw-ruz (g-year)
  ;; TYPE gregorian-year -> fixed-date
  ;; Fixed date of Baha'i New Year (Naw-Ruz) in Gregorian
```

```
  ;; year g-year.
  (astro-bahai-new-year-on-or-before
   (gregorian-new-year (1+ g-year))))
```

```
(defun feast-of-ridvan (g-year)                                    (16.12)
  ;; TYPE gregorian-year -> fixed-date
  ;; Fixed date of Feast of Ridvan in Gregorian year g-year.
  (+ (naw-ruz g-year) 31))
```

```
(defun birth-of-the-bab (g-year)                                   (16.13)
  ;; TYPE gregorian-year -> fixed-date
  ;; Fixed date of the Birthday of the Bab
  ;; in Gregorian year g-year.
  (let* ((ny ; Beginning of Baha'i year.
          (naw-ruz g-year))
         (set1 (bahai-sunset ny))
         (m1 (new-moon-at-or-after set1))
         (m8 (new-moon-at-or-after (+ m1 190)))
         (day (fixed-from-moment m8))
         (set8 (bahai-sunset day)))
    (if (< m8 set8)
        (1+ day)
      (+ day 2))))
```

D.17 The French Revolutionary Calendar

```
(defun french-date (year month day)
  ;; TYPE (french-year french-month french-day) -> french-date
  (list year month day))
```

```
(defconstant paris                                                 (17.1)
  ;; TYPE location
  ;; Location of Paris Observatory.  Longitude corresponds
  ;; to difference of 9m 21s between Paris time zone and
  ;; Universal Time.
  (location (angle 48 50 11) (angle 2 20 15) (mt 27) (hr 1)))
```

```
(defun midnight-in-paris (date)                                    (17.2)
  ;; TYPE fixed-date -> moment
  ;; Universal time of true midnight at end of fixed date
  ;; in Paris.
  (midnight (+ date 1) paris))
```

```
(defun french-new-year-on-or-before (date)                         (17.3)
  ;; TYPE fixed-date -> fixed-date
  ;; Fixed date of French Revolutionary New Year on or
  ;; before fixed date.
  (let* ((approx ; Approximate time of solstice.
          (estimate-prior-solar-longitude
           autumn (midnight-in-paris date))))
    (next day (- (floor approx) 1)
          (<= autumn (solar-longitude
                      (midnight-in-paris day))))))
```

```
(defconstant french-epoch                                          (17.4)
  ;; TYPE fixed-date
  ;; Fixed date of start of the French Revolutionary
  ;; calendar.
  (fixed-from-gregorian (gregorian-date 1792 september 22)))
```

```
(defun fixed-from-french (f-date)                                  (17.5)
  ;; TYPE french-date -> fixed-date
  ;; Fixed date of French Revolutionary date.
  (let* ((month (standard-month f-date))
         (day (standard-day f-date))
         (year (standard-year f-date))
         (new-year
```

```
          (french-new-year-on-or-before
           (floor (+ french-epoch 180; Spring after epoch.
                     (* mean-tropical-year
                        (1- year))))))
    (+ new-year -1      ;  Days in prior years
       (* 30 (1- month));  Days in prior months
       day)))           ;  Days this month
```

(17.6)

```
(defun french-from-fixed (date)
  ;; TYPE fixed-date -> french-date
  ;; French Revolutionary date of fixed date.
  (let* ((new-year
          (french-new-year-on-or-before date))
         (year (1+ (round (/ (- new-year french-epoch)
                             mean-tropical-year))))
         (month (1+ (quotient (- date new-year) 30)))
         (day (1+ (mod (- date new-year) 30))))
    (french-date year month day)))
```

(17.7)

```
(defun french-leap-year? (f-year)
  ;; TYPE french-year -> boolean
  ;; True if f-year is a leap year on the
  ;; French Revolutionary calendar.
  (> (- (fixed-from-french
         (french-date (1+ f-year) 1 1))
        (fixed-from-french
         (french-date f-year 1 1)))
     365))
```

(17.8)

```
(defun arithmetic-french-leap-year? (f-year)
  ;; TYPE french-year -> boolean
  ;; True if f-year is a leap year on the
  ;; Arithmetic French Revolutionary calendar.
  (and (= (mod f-year 4) 0)
       (not (member (mod f-year 400) (list 100 200 300)))
       (not (= (mod f-year 4000) 0))))
```

(17.9)

```
(defun fixed-from-arithmetic-french (f-date)
  ;; TYPE french-date -> fixed-date
  ;; Fixed date of Arithmetic French Revolutionary
  ;; date f-date.
  (let* ((month (standard-month f-date))
         (day (standard-day f-date))
         (year (standard-year f-date)))
    (+ french-epoch -1; Days before start of calendar.
       (* 365 (1- year)); Ordinary days in prior years.
                        ; Leap days in prior years.
       (quotient (1- year) 4)
       (- (quotient (1- year) 100))
       (quotient (1- year) 400)
       (- (quotient (1- year) 4000))
       (* 30 (1- month)); Days in prior months this year.
       day))); Days this month.
```

(17.10)

```
(defun arithmetic-french-from-fixed (date)
  ;; TYPE fixed-date -> french-date
  ;; Arithmetic French Revolutionary date (year month day)
  ;; of fixed date.
  (let* ((approx   ; Approximate year (may be off by 1).
          (1+ (quotient (- date french-epoch -2)
                        1460969/4000)))
         (year (if (< date
                      (fixed-from-arithmetic-french
                       (french-date approx 1 1)))
                   (1- approx)
                 approx))
         (month    ; Calculate the month by division.
          (1+ (quotient
               (- date (fixed-from-arithmetic-french
```

```
                        (french-date year 1 1)))
                   30)))
            (day      ; Calculate the day by subtraction.
             (1+ (- date
                         (fixed-from-arithmetic-french
                          (french-date year month 1))))))
       (french-date year month day)))
```

D.18 Astronomical Lunar Calendars

```
(defun babylonian-date (year month leap day)
  ;; TYPE (babylonian-year babylonian-month
  ;; TYPE  babylonian-leap babylonian-day)
  ;; TYPE  -> babylonian-date
  (list year month leap day))
```

```
(defun babylonian-year (date)
  ;; TYPE babylonian-date -> babylonian-year
  (first date))
```

```
(defun babylonian-month (date)
  ;; TYPE babylonian-date -> babylonian-month
  (second date))
```

```
(defun babylonian-leap (date)
  ;; TYPE babylonian-date -> babylonian-leap
  (third date))
```

```
(defun babylonian-day (date)
  ;; TYPE babylonian-date -> babylonian-day
  (fourth date))
```

(18.1)

```
(defun moonlag (date location)
  ;; TYPE (fixed-date location) -> duration
  ;; Time between sunset and moonset on date at location.
  ;; Returns bogus if there is no sunset on date.
  (let* ((sun (sunset date location))
         (moon (moonset date location)))
    (cond ((equal sun bogus) bogus)
          ((equal moon bogus) (hr 24)) ; Arbitrary.
          (t (- moon sun)))))
```

(18.2)

```
(defconstant babylon
  ;; TYPE location
  ;; Location of Babylon.
  (location (deg 32.4794L0) (deg 44.4328L0)
            (mt 26) (hr (+ 3 1/2))))
```

(18.3)

```
(defun babylonian-criterion (date)
  ;; TYPE (fixed-date location) -> boolean
  ;; Moonlag criterion for visibility of crescent moon on
  ;; eve of date in Babylon.
  (let* ((set (sunset (1- date) babylon))
         (tee (universal-from-standard set babylon))
         (phase (lunar-phase tee)))
    (and (< new phase first-quarter)
         (<= (new-moon-before tee) (- tee (hr 24)))
         (> (moonlag (1- date) babylon) (mn 48)))))
```

(18.4)

```
(defun babylonian-new-month-on-or-before (date)
  ;; TYPE fixed-date -> fixed-date
  ;; Fixed date of start of Babylonian month on or before
  ;; Babylonian date.  Using lag of moonset criterion.
  (let* ((moon ; Prior new moon.
          (fixed-from-moment
           (lunar-phase-at-or-before new date)))
```

```
        (age (- date moon))
        (tau ; Check if not visible yet on eve of date.
         (if (and (<= age 3)
                  (not (babylonian-criterion date)))
             (- moon 30) ; Must go back a month.
           moon)))
    (next d tau (babylonian-criterion d))))
```

(18.5)

```
(defconstant babylonian-epoch
  ;; TYPE fixed-date
  ;; Fixed date of start of the Babylonian calendar
  ;; (Seleucid era).  April 3, 311 BCE (Julian).
  (fixed-from-julian (julian-date (bce 311) april 3)))
```

(18.6)

```
(defun babylonian-leap-year? (b-year)
  ;; TYPE babylonian-year -> boolean
  ;; True if b-year is a leap year on Babylonian calendar.
  (< (mod (+ (* 7 b-year) 13) 19) 7))
```

(18.7)

```
(defun fixed-from-babylonian (b-date)
  ;; TYPE babylonian-date -> fixed-date
  ;; Fixed date equivalent to Babylonian date.
  (let* ((month (babylonian-month b-date))
         (leap (babylonian-leap b-date))
         (day (babylonian-day b-date))
         (year (babylonian-year b-date))
         (month1 ;  Elapsed months this year.
          (if (or leap
                  (and (= (mod year 19) 18)
                       (> month 6)))
              month (1- month)))
         (months ; Elapsed months since epoch.
          (+ (quotient (+ (* (1- year) 235) 13) 19)
             month1))
         (midmonth ; Middle of given month.
          (+ babylonian-epoch
             (round (* mean-synodic-month months)) 15)))
    (+ (babylonian-new-month-on-or-before midmonth)
       day -1)))
```

(18.8)

```
(defun babylonian-from-fixed (date)
  ;; TYPE fixed-date -> babylonian-date
  ;; Babylonian date corresponding to fixed date.
  (let* ((crescent ; Most recent new month.
          (babylonian-new-month-on-or-before date))
         (months ; Elapsed months since epoch.
          (round (/ (- crescent babylonian-epoch)
                    mean-synodic-month)))
         (year (1+ (quotient (+ (* 19 months) 5) 235)))
         (approx ; Approximate date of new year.
          (+ babylonian-epoch
             (round (* (quotient (+ (* (1- year) 235) 13) 19)
                       mean-synodic-month))))
         (new-year (babylonian-new-month-on-or-before
                    (+ approx 15)))
         (month1 (1+ (round (/ (- crescent new-year) 29.5L0))))
         (special (= (mod year 19) 18))
         (leap (if special (= month1 7) (= month1 13)))
         (month (if (or leap (and special (> month1 6)))
                    (1- month1)
                  month1))
         (day (- date crescent -1)))
    (babylonian-date year month leap day)))
```

(18.9)

```
(defun astronomical-easter (g-year)
  ;; TYPE gregorian-year -> fixed-date
  ;; Date of (proposed) astronomical Easter in Gregorian
  ;; year g-year.
  (let* ((equinox ; Spring equinox.
```

```
        (season-in-gregorian spring g-year))
       (paschal-moon ; Date of next full moon.
        (floor (apparent-from-universal
                (lunar-phase-at-or-after full equinox)
                jerusalem))))
   ;; Return the Sunday following the Paschal moon.
   (kday-after sunday paschal-moon)))
```

```
(defconstant islamic-location                                    (18.10)
  ;; TYPE location
  ;; Sample location for Observational Islamic calendar
  ;; (Cairo, Egypt).
  (location (deg 30.1L0) (deg 31.3L0) (mt 200) (hr 2)))
```

```
(defun fixed-from-observational-islamic (i-date)                 (18.11)
  ;; TYPE islamic-date -> fixed-date
  ;; Fixed date equivalent to Observational Islamic date
  ;; i-date.
  (let* ((month (standard-month i-date))
         (day (standard-day i-date))
         (year (standard-year i-date))
         (midmonth ; Middle of given month.
          (+ islamic-epoch
             (floor (* (+ (* (1- year) 12)
                          month -1/2)
                       mean-synodic-month)))))
    (+ (phasis-on-or-before ; First day of month.
        midmonth islamic-location)
       day -1)))
```

```
(defun observational-islamic-from-fixed (date)                  (18.12)
  ;; TYPE fixed-date -> islamic-date
  ;; Observational Islamic date (year month day)
  ;; corresponding to fixed date.
  (let* ((crescent ; Most recent new moon.
          (phasis-on-or-before date islamic-location))
         (elapsed-months
          (round (/ (- crescent islamic-epoch)
                    mean-synodic-month)))
         (year (1+ (quotient elapsed-months 12)))
         (month (1+ (mod elapsed-months 12)))
         (day (1+ (- date crescent))))
    (islamic-date year month day)))
```

```
(defun month-length (date location)                              (18.13)
  ;; TYPE (fixed-date location) -> 1..31
  ;; Length of lunar month based on observability at location,
  ;; which includes date.
  (let* ((moon (phasis-on-or-after (1+ date) location))
         (prev (phasis-on-or-before date location)))
    (- moon prev)))
```

```
(defun early-month? (date location)                              (18.14)
  ;; TYPE (fixed-date location) -> boolean
  ;; Fixed date in location is in a month that was forced to
  ;; start early.
  (let* ((start (phasis-on-or-before date location))
         (prev (- start 15)))
    (or (>= (- date start) 30)
        (> (month-length prev location) 30)
        (and (= (month-length prev location) 30)
             (early-month? prev location)))))
```

```
(defun alt-fixed-from-observational-islamic (i-date)             (18.15)
  ;; TYPE islamic-date -> fixed-date
  ;; Fixed date equivalent to Observational Islamic i-date.
  ;; Months are never longer than 30 days.
  (let* ((month (standard-month i-date))
```

```
        (day (standard-day i-date))
        (year (standard-year i-date))
        (midmonth ; Middle of given month.
         (+ islamic-epoch
            (floor (* (+ (* (1- year) 12)
                         month -1/2)
                      mean-synodic-month))))
        (moon (phasis-on-or-before ; First day of month.
               midmonth islamic-location))
        (date (+ moon day -1)))
    (if (early-month? midmonth islamic-location) (1- date) date)))
```

```
(defun alt-observational-islamic-from-fixed (date)                (18.16)
  ;; TYPE fixed-date -> islamic-date
  ;; Observational Islamic date (year month day)
  ;; corresponding to fixed date.
  ;; Months are never longer than 30 days.
  (let* ((early (early-month? date islamic-location))
         (long (and early
                    (> (month-length date islamic-location) 29)))
         (date-prime
          (if long (1+ date) date))
         (moon ; Most recent new moon.
          (phasis-on-or-before date-prime islamic-location))
         (elapsed-months
          (round (/ (- moon islamic-epoch)
                    mean-synodic-month)))
         (year (1+ (quotient elapsed-months 12)))
         (month (1+ (mod elapsed-months 12)))
         (day (- date-prime moon
                 (if (and early (not long)) -2 -1))))
    (islamic-date year month day)))
```

```
(defun saudi-criterion (date)                                     (18.17)
  ;; TYPE fixed-date -> boolean
  ;; Saudi visibility criterion on eve of fixed date in Mecca.
  (let* ((set (sunset (1- date) mecca))
         (tee (universal-from-standard set mecca))
         (phase (lunar-phase tee)))
    (and (< new phase first-quarter)
         (> (moonlag (1- date) mecca) 0))))
```

```
(defun saudi-new-month-on-or-before (date)                        (18.18)
  ;; TYPE fixed-date -> fixed-date
  ;; Closest fixed date on or before date when Saudi
  ;; visibility criterion held.
  (let* ((moon ; Prior new moon.
          (fixed-from-moment
           (lunar-phase-at-or-before new date)))
         (age (- date moon))
         (tau ; Check if not visible yet on eve of date.
          (if (and (<= age 3)
                   (not (saudi-criterion date)))
              (- moon 30) ; Must go back a month.
            moon)))
    (next d tau (saudi-criterion d))))
```

```
(defun fixed-from-saudi-islamic (s-date)                          (18.19)
  ;; TYPE islamic-date -> fixed-date
  ;; Fixed date equivalent to Saudi Islamic date s-date.
  (let* ((month (standard-month s-date))
         (day (standard-day s-date))
         (year (standard-year s-date))
         (midmonth ; Middle of given month.
          (+ islamic-epoch
             (floor (* (+ (* (1- year) 12)
                          month -1/2)
                       mean-synodic-month)))))
    (+ (saudi-new-month-on-or-before ; First day of month.
        midmonth)
       day -1)))
```

(18.20)

```
(defun saudi-islamic-from-fixed (date)
  ;; TYPE fixed-date -> islamic-date
  ;; Saudi Islamic date (year month day) corresponding to
  ;; fixed date.
  (let* ((crescent ; Most recent new moon.
          (saudi-new-month-on-or-before date))
         (elapsed-months
          (round (/ (- crescent islamic-epoch)
                    mean-synodic-month)))
         (year (1+ (quotient elapsed-months 12)))
         (month (1+ (mod elapsed-months 12)))
         (day (1+ (- date crescent))))
    (islamic-date year month day)))
```

(18.21)

```
(defconstant hebrew-location
  ;; TYPE location
  ;; Sample location for Observational Hebrew calendar
  ;; (Haifa, Israel).
  (location (deg 32.82L0) (deg 35) (mt 0) (hr 2)))
```

(18.22)

```
(defun observational-hebrew-first-of-nisan (g-year)
  ;; TYPE gregorian-year -> fixed-date
  ;; Fixed date of Observational (classical)
  ;; Nisan 1 occurring in Gregorian year g-year.
  (let* ((equinox ; Spring equinox.
          (season-in-gregorian spring g-year))
         (set ; Moment (UT) of sunset on day of equinox.
          (universal-from-standard
           (sunset (floor equinox) hebrew-location)
           hebrew-location)))
    (phasis-on-or-after
     (- (floor equinox) ; Day of equinox
        (if ; Spring starts before sunset.
            (< equinox set) 14 13))
     hebrew-location)))
```

(18.23)

```
(defun observational-hebrew-from-fixed (date)
  ;; TYPE fixed-date -> hebrew-date
  ;; Observational Hebrew date (year month day)
  ;; corresponding to fixed date.
  (let* ((crescent ; Most recent new moon.
          (phasis-on-or-before date hebrew-location))
         (g-year (gregorian-year-from-fixed date))
         (ny (observational-hebrew-first-of-nisan g-year))
         (new-year (if (< date ny)
                       (observational-hebrew-first-of-nisan
                        (1- g-year))
                     ny))
         (month (1+ (round (/ (- crescent new-year) 29.5L0))))
         (year (+ (standard-year (hebrew-from-fixed new-year))
                  (if (>= month tishri) 1 0)))
         (day (- date crescent -1)))
    (hebrew-date year month day)))
```

(18.24)

```
(defun fixed-from-observational-hebrew (h-date)
  ;; TYPE hebrew-date -> fixed-date
  ;; Fixed date equivalent to Observational Hebrew date.
  (let* ((month (standard-month h-date))
         (day (standard-day h-date))
         (year (standard-year h-date))
         (year1 (if (>= month tishri) (1- year) year))
         (start (fixed-from-hebrew
                 (hebrew-date year1 nisan 1)))
         (g-year (gregorian-year-from-fixed
                  (+ start 60)))
         (new-year (observational-hebrew-first-of-nisan g-year))
         (midmonth ; Middle of given month.
          (+ new-year (round (* 29.5L0 (1- month))) 15)))
    (+ (phasis-on-or-before ; First day of month.
        midmonth hebrew-location)
       day -1)))
```

```
(defun classical-passover-eve (g-year)                          (18.25)
  ;; TYPE gregorian-year -> fixed-date
  ;; Fixed date of Classical (observational) Passover Eve
  ;; (Nisan 14) occurring in Gregorian year g-year.
  (+ (observational-hebrew-first-of-nisan g-year) 13))
```

```
(defun alt-observational-hebrew-from-fixed (date)               (18.26)
  ;; TYPE fixed-date -> hebrew-date
  ;; Observational Hebrew date (year month day)
  ;; corresponding to fixed date.
  ;; Months are never longer than 30 days.
  (let* ((early (early-month? date hebrew-location))
         (long (and early (> (month-length date hebrew-location) 29)))
         (date-prime
          (if long (1+ date) date))
         (moon ; Most recent new moon.
          (phasis-on-or-before date-prime hebrew-location))
         (g-year (gregorian-year-from-fixed date-prime))
         (ny (observational-hebrew-first-of-nisan g-year))
         (new-year (if (< date-prime ny)
                       (observational-hebrew-first-of-nisan
                        (1- g-year))
                     ny))
         (month (1+ (round (/ (- moon new-year) 29.5L0))))
         (year (+ (standard-year (hebrew-from-fixed new-year))
                  (if (>= month tishri) 1 0)))
         (day (- date-prime moon
                 (if (and early (not long)) -2 -1))))
    (hebrew-date year month day)))
```

```
(defun alt-fixed-from-observational-hebrew (h-date)             (18.27)
  ;; TYPE hebrew-date -> fixed-date
  ;; Fixed date equivalent to Observational Hebrew h-date.
  ;; Months are never longer than 30 days.
  (let* ((month (standard-month h-date))
         (day (standard-day h-date))
         (year (standard-year h-date))
         (year1 (if (>= month tishri) (1- year) year))
         (start (fixed-from-hebrew
                 (hebrew-date year1 nisan 1)))
         (g-year (gregorian-year-from-fixed
                  (+ start 60)))
         (new-year (observational-hebrew-first-of-nisan g-year))
         (midmonth ; Middle of given month.
          (+ new-year (round (* 29.5L0 (1- month))) 15))
         (moon (phasis-on-or-before ; First day of month.
                midmonth hebrew-location))
         (date (+ moon day -1)))
    (if (early-month? midmonth hebrew-location) (1- date) date)))
```

```
(defconstant samaritan-location                                 (18.28)
  ;; TYPE location
  ;; Location of Mt. Gerizim.
  (location (deg 32.1994) (deg 35.2728) (mt 881) (hr 2)))
```

```
(defun samaritan-noon (date)                                    (18.29)
  ;; TYPE fixed-date -> moment
  ;; Universal time of true noon on date at Samaritan location.
  (midday date samaritan-location))
```

```
(defun samaritan-new-moon-after (tee)                           (18.30)
  ;; TYPE moment -> fixed-date
  ;; Fixed date of first new moon after UT moment tee.
  ;; Modern calculation.
  (ceiling
   (- (apparent-from-universal (new-moon-at-or-after tee)
                               samaritan-location)
      (hr 12))))
```

```
(defun samaritan-new-moon-at-or-before (tee)                      (18.31)
  ;; TYPE moment -> fixed-date
  ;; Fixed-date of last new moon before UT moment tee.
  ;; Modern calculation.
  (ceiling
   (- (apparent-from-universal (new-moon-before tee)
                               samaritan-location)
      (hr 12))))
```

```
(defconstant samaritan-epoch                                      (18.32)
  ;; TYPE fixed-date
  ;; Fixed date of start of the Samaritan Entry Era.
  (fixed-from-julian (julian-date (bce 1639) march 15)))
```

```
(defun samaritan-new-year-on-or-before (date)                     (18.33)
  ;; TYPE fixed-date -> fixed-date
  ;; Fixed date of Samaritan New Year on or before fixed
  ;; date.
  (let* ((g-year (gregorian-year-from-fixed date))
         (dates ; All possible March 11's.
          (append
           (julian-in-gregorian march 11 (1- g-year))
           (julian-in-gregorian march 11 g-year)
           (list (1+ date)))) ; Extra to stop search.
         (n
          (final i 0
                 (<= (samaritan-new-moon-after
                      (samaritan-noon (nth i dates)))
                     date))))
    (samaritan-new-moon-after (samaritan-noon (nth n dates)))))
```

```
(defun fixed-from-samaritan (s-date)                              (18.34)
  ;; TYPE hebrew-date -> fixed-date
  ;; Fixed date of Samaritan date h-date.
  (let* ((month (standard-month s-date))
         (day (standard-day s-date))
         (year (standard-year s-date))
         (ny (samaritan-new-year-on-or-before
              (floor (+ samaritan-epoch 50
                        (* 365.25L0 (- year
                                       (ceiling (- month 5) 8)))))))
         (nm (samaritan-new-moon-at-or-before
              (+ ny (* 29.5L0 (1- month)) 15))))
    (+ nm day -1)))
```

```
(defun samaritan-from-fixed (date)                                (18.35)
  ;; TYPE fixed-date -> hebrew-date
  ;; Samaritan date corresponding to fixed date.
  (let* ((moon ; First of month
          (samaritan-new-moon-at-or-before
           (samaritan-noon date)))
         (new-year (samaritan-new-year-on-or-before moon))
         (month (1+ (round (/ (- moon new-year) 29.5L0))))
         (year (+ (round (/ (- new-year samaritan-epoch) 365.25L0))
                  (ceiling (- month 5) 8)))
         (day (- date moon -1)))
    (hebrew-date year month day)))
```

D.19 The Chinese Calendar

```
(defun chinese-date (cycle year month leap day)
  ;; TYPE (chinese-cycle chinese-year chinese-month
  ;; TYPE  chinese-leap chinese-day) -> chinese-date
  (list cycle year month leap day))
```

```
(defun chinese-cycle (date)
  ;; TYPE chinese-date -> chinese-cycle
  (first date))
```

```lisp
(defun chinese-year (date)
  ;; TYPE chinese-date -> chinese-year
  (second date))
```

```lisp
(defun chinese-month (date)
  ;; TYPE chinese-date -> chinese-month
  (third date))
```

```lisp
(defun chinese-leap (date)
  ;; TYPE chinese-date -> chinese-leap
  (fourth date))
```

```lisp
(defun chinese-day (date)
  ;; TYPE chinese-date -> chinese-day
  (fifth date))
```

(19.1)

```lisp
(defun current-major-solar-term (date)
  ;; TYPE fixed-date -> integer
  ;; Last Chinese major solar term (zhongqi) before fixed
  ;; date.
  (let* ((s (solar-longitude
             (universal-from-standard
              date
              (chinese-location date)))))
    (amod (+ 2 (quotient s (deg 30))) 12)))
```

(19.2)

```lisp
(defun chinese-location (tee)
  ;; TYPE moment -> location
  ;; Location of Beijing; time zone varies with tee.
  (let* ((year (gregorian-year-from-fixed (floor tee))))
    (if (< year 1929)
        (location (angle 39 55 0) (angle 116 25 0)
                  (mt 43.5) (hr 1397/180))
      (location (angle 39 55 0) (angle 116 25 0)
                (mt 43.5) (hr 8)))))
```

(19.3)

```lisp
(defun chinese-solar-longitude-on-or-after (lambda tee)
  ;; TYPE (season moment) -> moment
  ;; Moment (Beijing time) of the first time at or after
  ;; tee (Beijing time) when the solar longitude
  ;; will be lambda degrees.
  (let* ((sun (solar-longitude-after
               lambda
               (universal-from-standard
                tee
                (chinese-location tee)))))
    (standard-from-universal
     sun
     (chinese-location sun))))
```

(19.4)

```lisp
(defun major-solar-term-on-or-after (date)
  ;; TYPE fixed-date -> moment
  ;; Moment (in Beijing) of the first Chinese major
  ;; solar term (zhongqi) on or after fixed date.  The
  ;; major terms begin when the sun's longitude is a
  ;; multiple of 30 degrees.
  (let* ((s (solar-longitude (midnight-in-china date)))
         (l (mod (* 30 (ceiling (/ s 30))) 360)))
    (chinese-solar-longitude-on-or-after l date)))
```

(19.5)

```lisp
(defun current-minor-solar-term (date)
  ;; TYPE fixed-date -> integer
  ;; Last Chinese minor solar term (jieqi) before date.
  (let* ((s (solar-longitude
```

```
          (universal-from-standard
           date
           (chinese-location date)))))
   (amod (+ 3 (quotient (- s (deg 15)) (deg 30)))
         12)))
```

(19.6)

```
(defun minor-solar-term-on-or-after (date)
  ;; TYPE fixed-date -> moment
  ;; Moment (in Beijing) of the first Chinese minor solar
  ;; term (jieqi) on or after fixed date.  The minor terms
  ;; begin when the sun's longitude is an odd multiple of 15
  ;; degrees.
  (let* ((s (solar-longitude (midnight-in-china date)))
         (l (mod
             (+ (* 30
                   (ceiling
                    (/ (- s (deg 15)) 30)))
                (deg 15))
             360)))
    (chinese-solar-longitude-on-or-after l date)))
```

(19.7)

```
(defun midnight-in-china (date)
  ;; TYPE fixed-date -> moment
  ;; Universal time of (clock) midnight at start of fixed
  ;; date in China.
  (universal-from-standard date (chinese-location date)))
```

(19.8)

```
(defun chinese-winter-solstice-on-or-before (date)
  ;; TYPE fixed-date -> fixed-date
  ;; Fixed date, in the Chinese zone, of winter solstice
  ;; on or before fixed date.
  (let* ((approx ; Approximate time of solstice.
          (estimate-prior-solar-longitude
           winter (midnight-in-china (+ date 1)))))
    (next day (1- (floor approx))
          (< winter (solar-longitude
                     (midnight-in-china (1+ day)))))))
```

(19.9)

```
(defun chinese-new-moon-on-or-after (date)
  ;; TYPE fixed-date -> fixed-date
  ;; Fixed date (Beijing) of first new moon on or after
  ;; fixed date.
  (let* ((tee (new-moon-at-or-after
               (midnight-in-china date))))
    (floor
     (standard-from-universal
      tee
      (chinese-location tee)))))
```

(19.10)

```
(defun chinese-new-moon-before (date)
  ;; TYPE fixed-date -> fixed-date
  ;; Fixed date (Beijing) of first new moon before fixed
  ;; date.
  (let* ((tee (new-moon-before
               (midnight-in-china date))))
    (floor
     (standard-from-universal
      tee
      (chinese-location tee)))))
```

(19.11)

```
(defun chinese-no-major-solar-term? (date)
  ;; TYPE fixed-date -> boolean
  ;; True if Chinese lunar month starting on date
  ;; has no major solar term.
  (= (current-major-solar-term date)
     (current-major-solar-term
      (chinese-new-moon-on-or-after (+ date 1)))))
```

(19.12)

```
(defun chinese-prior-leap-month? (m-prime m)
  ;; TYPE (fixed-date fixed-date) -> boolean
  ;; True if there is a Chinese leap month on or after lunar
  ;; month starting on fixed day m-prime and at or before
  ;; lunar month starting at fixed date m.
  (and (>= m m-prime)
       (or (chinese-no-major-solar-term? m)
           (chinese-prior-leap-month?
            m-prime
            (chinese-new-moon-before m)))))
```

(19.13)

```
(defun chinese-new-year-in-sui (date)
  ;; TYPE fixed-date -> fixed-date
  ;; Fixed date of Chinese New Year in sui (period from
  ;; solstice to solstice) containing date.
  (let* ((s1; prior solstice
          (chinese-winter-solstice-on-or-before date))
         (s2; following solstice
          (chinese-winter-solstice-on-or-before
           (+ s1 370)))
         (m12 ; month after 11th month--either 12 or leap 11
          (chinese-new-moon-on-or-after (1+ s1)))
         (m13 ; month after m12--either 12 (or leap 12) or 1
          (chinese-new-moon-on-or-after (1+ m12)))
         (next-m11 ; next 11th month
          (chinese-new-moon-before (1+ s2))))
    (if ; Either m12 or m13 is a leap month if there are
        ; 13 new moons (12 full lunar months) and
        ; either m12 or m13 has no major solar term
        (and (= (round (/ (- next-m11 m12)
                          mean-synodic-month))
                12)
             (or (chinese-no-major-solar-term? m12)
                 (chinese-no-major-solar-term? m13)))
        (chinese-new-moon-on-or-after (1+ m13))
      m13)))
```

(19.14)

```
(defun chinese-new-year-on-or-before (date)
  ;; TYPE fixed-date -> fixed-date
  ;; Fixed date of Chinese New Year on or before fixed date.
  (let* ((new-year (chinese-new-year-in-sui date)))
    (if (>= date new-year)
        new-year
      ;; Got the New Year after--this happens if date is
      ;; after the solstice but before the new year.
      ;; So, go back half a year.
      (chinese-new-year-in-sui (- date 180)))))
```

(19.15)

```
(defconstant chinese-epoch
  ;; TYPE fixed-date
  ;; Fixed date of start of the Chinese calendar.
  (fixed-from-gregorian (gregorian-date -2636 february 15)))
```

(19.16)

```
(defun chinese-from-fixed (date)
  ;; TYPE fixed-date -> chinese-date
  ;; Chinese date (cycle year month leap day) of fixed date.
  (let* ((s1; Prior solstice
          (chinese-winter-solstice-on-or-before date))
         (s2; Following solstice
          (chinese-winter-solstice-on-or-before (+ s1 370)))
         (m12     ; month after last 11th month
          (chinese-new-moon-on-or-after (1+ s1)))
         (next-m11; next 11th month
          (chinese-new-moon-before (1+ s2)))
         (m       ; start of month containing date
          (chinese-new-moon-before (1+ date)))
         (leap-year; if there are 13 new moons (12 full
                                               ; lunar months)
          (= (round (/ (- next-m11 m12)
                       mean-synodic-month))
```

```
              12))
          (month  ; month number
           (amod
            (-
             ;; ordinal position of month in year
             (round (/ (- m m12) mean-synodic-month))
             ;; minus 1 during or after a leap month
             (if (and leap-year
                      (chinese-prior-leap-month? m12 m))
                 1
               0))
            12))
          (leap-month    ; it's a leap month if...
           (and
            leap-year; ...there are 13 months
            (chinese-no-major-solar-term?
             m)                              ; no major solar term
            (not (chinese-prior-leap-month? ; and no prior leap
                                             ; month
                  m12 (chinese-new-moon-before m)))))
          (elapsed-years  ; Approximate since the epoch
           (floor (+ 1.5L0  ; 18 months (because of truncation)
                     (- (/ month 12)); after at start of year
                     (/ (- date chinese-epoch)
                        mean-tropical-year))))
          (cycle (1+ (quotient (1- elapsed-years) 60)))
          (year (amod elapsed-years 60))
          (day (1+ (- date m))))
     (chinese-date cycle year month leap-month day)))
```

(19.17)

```
(defun fixed-from-chinese (c-date)
  ;; TYPE chinese-date -> fixed-date
  ;; Fixed date of Chinese date c-date.
  (let* ((cycle (chinese-cycle c-date))
         (year (chinese-year c-date))
         (month (chinese-month c-date))
         (leap (chinese-leap c-date))
         (day (chinese-day c-date))
         (mid-year      ;  Middle of the Chinese year
          (floor
           (+ chinese-epoch
              (* (+ (* (1- cycle) 60); years in prior cycles
                    (1- year)        ; prior years this cycle
                    1/2)             ; half a year
                 mean-tropical-year))))
         (new-year (chinese-new-year-on-or-before mid-year))
         (p  ; new moon before date--a month too early if
             ; there was prior leap month that year
          (chinese-new-moon-on-or-after
           (+ new-year (* (1- month) 29))))
         (d (chinese-from-fixed p))
         (prior-new-moon
          (if  ; If the months match...
              (and (= month (chinese-month d))
                   (equal leap (chinese-leap d)))
              p; ...that's the right month
            ;; otherwise, there was a prior leap month that
            ;; year, so we want the next month
            (chinese-new-moon-on-or-after (1+ p)))))
    (+ prior-new-moon day -1)))
```

```
(defun chinese-name (stem branch)
  ;; TYPE (chinese-stem chinese-branch) -> chinese-name
  ;; Combination is impossible if stem and branch
  ;; are not the equal mod 2.
  (list stem branch))
```

```
(defun chinese-stem (name)
  ;; TYPE chinese-name -> chinese-stem
  (first name))
```

```
(defun chinese-branch (name)
  ;; TYPE chinese-name -> chinese-branch
  (second name))
```

(19.18)

```
(defun chinese-sexagesimal-name (n)
  ;; TYPE integer -> chinese-name
  ;; The n-th name of the Chinese sexagesimal cycle.
  (chinese-name (amod n 10)
                (amod n 12)))
```

(19.19)

```
(defun chinese-name-difference (c-name1 c-name2)
  ;; TYPE (chinese-name chinese-name) -> nonnegative-integer
  ;; Number of names from Chinese name c-name1 to the
  ;; next occurrence of Chinese name c-name2.
  (let* ((stem1 (chinese-stem c-name1))
         (stem2 (chinese-stem c-name2))
         (branch1 (chinese-branch c-name1))
         (branch2 (chinese-branch c-name2))
         (stem-difference (- stem2 stem1))
         (branch-difference (- branch2 branch1)))
    (amod (+ stem-difference
             (* 25 (- branch-difference
                      stem-difference)))
          60)))
```

(19.20)

```
(defun chinese-year-name (year)
  ;; TYPE chinese-year -> chinese-name
  ;; Sexagesimal name for Chinese year of any cycle.
  (chinese-sexagesimal-name year))
```

(19.21)

```
(defconstant chinese-month-name-epoch
  ;; TYPE integer
  ;; Elapsed months at start of Chinese sexagesimal month
  ;; cycle.
  57)
```

(19.22)

```
(defun chinese-month-name (month year)
  ;; TYPE (chinese-month chinese-year) -> chinese-name
  ;; Sexagesimal name for month month of Chinese year
  ;; year.
  (let* ((elapsed-months (+ (* 12 (1- year))
                            (1- month))))
    (chinese-sexagesimal-name
     (- elapsed-months chinese-month-name-epoch))))
```

(19.23)

```
(defconstant chinese-day-name-epoch
  ;; TYPE integer
  ;; RD date of a start of Chinese sexagesimal day cycle.
  (rd 45))
```

(19.24)

```
(defun chinese-day-name (date)
  ;; TYPE fixed-date -> chinese-name
  ;; Chinese sexagesimal name for date.
  (chinese-sexagesimal-name
   (- date chinese-day-name-epoch)))
```

(19.25)

```
(defun chinese-day-name-on-or-before (name date)
  ;; TYPE (chinese-name fixed-date) -> fixed-date
  ;; Fixed date of latest date on or before fixed date
  ;; that has Chinese name.
  (mod3 (chinese-name-difference
         (chinese-day-name 0) name)
        date (- date 60)))
```

```
(defun chinese-new-year (g-year)                              (19.26)
  ;; TYPE gregorian-year -> fixed-date
  ;; Fixed date of Chinese New Year in Gregorian year g-year.
  (chinese-new-year-on-or-before
   (fixed-from-gregorian
    (gregorian-date g-year july 1))))
```

```
(defun dragon-festival (g-year)                               (19.27)
  ;; TYPE gregorian-year -> fixed-date
  ;; Fixed date of the Dragon Festival occurring in
  ;; Gregorian year g-year.
  (let* ((elapsed-years
          (1+ (- g-year
                 (gregorian-year-from-fixed
                  chinese-epoch))))
         (cycle (1+ (quotient (1- elapsed-years) 60)))
         (year (amod elapsed-years 60)))
    (fixed-from-chinese (chinese-date cycle year 5 false 5))))
```

```
(defun qing-ming (g-year)                                     (19.28)
  ;; TYPE gregorian-year -> fixed-date
  ;; Fixed date of Qingming occurring in Gregorian year
  ;; g-year.
  (floor
   (minor-solar-term-on-or-after
    (fixed-from-gregorian
     (gregorian-date g-year march 30)))))
```

```
(defun chinese-age (birthdate date)                           (19.29)
  ;; TYPE (chinese-date fixed-date) -> nonnegative-integer
  ;; Age at fixed date, given Chinese birthdate,
  ;; according to the Chinese custom.  Returns bogus if
  ;; date is before birthdate.
  (let* ((today (chinese-from-fixed date)))
    (if (>= date (fixed-from-chinese birthdate))
        (+ (* 60 (- (chinese-cycle today)
                    (chinese-cycle birthdate)))
           (- (chinese-year today)
              (chinese-year birthdate))
           1)
      bogus)))
```

```
(defconstant double-bright                                    (19.30)
  ;; TYPE augury
  ;; Lichun occurs twice (double-happiness).
  3)
```

```
(defconstant bright                                           (19.31)
  ;; TYPE augury
  ;; Lichun occurs once at the start.
  2)
```

```
(defconstant blind                                            (19.32)
  ;; TYPE augury
  ;; Lichun occurs once at the end.
  1)
```

```
(defconstant widow                                            (19.33)
  ;; TYPE augury
  ;; Lichun does not occur (double-blind year).
  0)
```

```
(defun chinese-year-marriage-augury (cycle year)              (19.34)
  ;; TYPE (chinese-cycle chinese-year) -> augury
  ;; The marriage augury type of Chinese year in cycle.
  (let* ((new-year (fixed-from-chinese
```

```
                  (chinese-date cycle year 1 false 1)))
         (c (if (= year 60); next year's cycle
                (1+ cycle)
              cycle))
         (y (if (= year 60); next year's number
                1
              (1+ year)))
         (next-new-year (fixed-from-chinese
                         (chinese-date c y 1 false 1)))
         (first-minor-term
          (current-minor-solar-term new-year))
         (next-first-minor-term
          (current-minor-solar-term next-new-year)))
    (cond
     ((and
       (= first-minor-term 1)        ; no lichun at start...
       (= next-first-minor-term 12)) ; ...or at end
      widow)
     ((and
       (= first-minor-term 1)        ; no lichun at start...
       (/= next-first-minor-term 12)); ...only at end
      blind)
     ((and
       (/= first-minor-term 1)       ; lichun at start...
       (= next-first-minor-term 12)) ; ... not at end
      bright)
     (t double-bright))))            ; lichun at start and end
```

(19.35)

```
(defun japanese-location (tee)
  ;; TYPE moment -> location
  ;; Location for Japanese calendar; varies with tee.
  (let* ((year (gregorian-year-from-fixed (floor tee))))
    (if (< year 1888)
        ;; Tokyo (139 deg 46 min east) local time
        (location (deg 35.7L0) (angle 139 46 0)
                  (mt 24) (hr (+ 9 143/450)))
                                             ; Longitude 135 time zone
      (location (deg 35) (deg 135) (mt 0) (hr 9)))))
```

(19.36)

```
(defun korean-location (tee)
  ;; TYPE moment -> location
  ;; Location for Korean calendar; varies with tee.
  ;; Seoul city hall at a varying time zone.
  (let* ((z (cond
             ((< tee
                 (fixed-from-gregorian
                  (gregorian-date 1908 april 1)))
              ;; local mean time for longitude 126 deg 58 min
              3809/450)
             ((< tee
                 (fixed-from-gregorian
                  (gregorian-date 1912 january 1)))
              8.5)
             ((< tee
                 (fixed-from-gregorian
                  (gregorian-date 1954 march 21)))
              9)
             ((< tee
                 (fixed-from-gregorian
                  (gregorian-date 1961 august 10)))
              8.5)
             (t 9))))
    (location (angle 37 34 0) (angle 126 58 0)
              (mt 0) (hr z))))
```

(19.37)

```
(defun korean-year (cycle year)
  ;; TYPE (chinese-cycle chinese-year) -> integer
  ;; Equivalent Korean year to Chinese cycle and year
  (+ (* 60 cycle) year -364))
```

(19.38)

```
(defun vietnamese-location (tee)
  ;; TYPE moment -> location
  ;; Location for Vietnamese calendar is Hanoi; varies with
  ;; tee.  Time zone has changed over the years.
  (let* ((z (if (< tee
                   (gregorian-new-year 1968))
                8
              7)))
    (location (angle 21 2 0) (angle 105 51 0)
              (mt 12) (hr z))))
```

D.20 The Modern Hindu Calendars

Common Lisp supplies arithmetic with arbitrary rational numbers, and we take advantage of this for implementing the Hindu calendars. With other languages, 64-bit arithmetic is required for many of the calculations.

(20.1)

```
(defconstant hindu-sidereal-year
  ;; TYPE rational
  ;; Mean length of Hindu sidereal year.
  (+ 365 279457/1080000))
```

(20.2)

```
(defconstant hindu-sidereal-month
  ;; TYPE rational
  ;; Mean length of Hindu sidereal month.
  (+ 27 4644439/14438334))
```

(20.3)

```
(defconstant hindu-synodic-month
  ;; TYPE rational
  ;; Mean time from new moon to new moon.
  (+ 29 7087771/13358334))
```

(20.4)

```
(defun hindu-sine-table (entry)
  ;; TYPE integer -> rational-amplitude
  ;; This simulates the Hindu sine table.
  ;; entry is an angle given as a multiplier of 225'.
  (let* ((exact (* 3438 (sin-degrees
                         (* entry (angle 0 225 0)))))
         (error (* 0.215L0 (sign exact)
                   (sign (- (abs exact) 1716)))))
    (/ (round (+ exact error)) 3438)))
```

(20.5)

```
(defun hindu-sine (theta)
  ;; TYPE rational-angle -> rational-amplitude
  ;; Linear interpolation for theta in Hindu table.
  (let* ((entry
          (/ theta (angle 0 225 0))); Interpolate in table.
         (fraction (mod entry 1)))
    (+ (* fraction
          (hindu-sine-table (ceiling entry)))
       (* (- 1 fraction)
          (hindu-sine-table (floor entry))))))
```

(20.6)

```
(defun hindu-arcsin (amp)
  ;; TYPE rational-amplitude -> rational-angle
  ;; Inverse of Hindu sine function of amp.
  (if (< amp 0) (- (hindu-arcsin (- amp)))
    (let* ((pos (next k 0 (<= amp (hindu-sine-table k))))
           (below ; Lower value in table.
            (hindu-sine-table (1- pos))))
      (* (angle 0 225 0)
         (+ pos -1  ; Interpolate.
            (/ (- amp below)
               (- (hindu-sine-table pos) below)))))))
```

(20.7)
```
(defun hindu-mean-position (tee period)
  ;; TYPE (rational-moment rational) -> rational-angle
  ;; Position in degrees at moment tee in uniform circular
  ;; orbit of period days.
  (* (deg 360) (mod (/ (- tee hindu-creation) period) 1)))
```

(20.8)
```
(defconstant hindu-creation
  ;; TYPE fixed-date
  ;; Fixed date of Hindu creation.
  (- hindu-epoch (* 1955880000 hindu-sidereal-year)))
```

(20.9)
```
(defconstant hindu-anomalistic-year
  ;; TYPE rational
  ;; Time from aphelion to aphelion.
  (/ 1577917828000 (- 4320000000 387)))
```

(20.10)
```
(defconstant hindu-anomalistic-month
  ;; TYPE rational
  ;; Time from apogee to apogee, with bija correction.
  (/ 1577917828 (- 57753336 488199)))
```

(20.11)
```
(defun hindu-true-position (tee period size anomalistic change)
  ;; TYPE (rational-moment rational rational rational
  ;; TYPE  rational) -> rational-angle
  ;; Longitudinal position at moment tee.  period is
  ;; period of mean motion in days.  size is ratio of
  ;; radii of epicycle and deferent.  anomalistic is the
  ;; period of retrograde revolution about epicycle.
  ;; change is maximum decrease in epicycle size.
  (let* ((lambda ; Position of epicycle center
           (hindu-mean-position tee period))
         (offset ; Sine of anomaly
           (hindu-sine (hindu-mean-position tee anomalistic)))
         (contraction (* (abs offset) change size))
         (equation ; Equation of center
           (hindu-arcsin (* offset (- size contraction)))))
    (mod (- lambda equation) 360)))
```

(20.12)
```
(defun hindu-solar-longitude (tee)
  ;; TYPE rational-moment -> rational-angle
  ;; Solar longitude at moment tee.
  (hindu-true-position tee hindu-sidereal-year
                       14/360 hindu-anomalistic-year 1/42))
```

(20.13)
```
(defun hindu-zodiac (tee)
  ;; TYPE rational-moment -> hindu-solar-month
  ;; Zodiacal sign of the sun, as integer in range 1..12,
  ;; at moment tee.
  (1+ (quotient (hindu-solar-longitude tee) (deg 30))))
```

(20.14)
```
(defun hindu-lunar-longitude (tee)
  ;; TYPE rational-moment -> rational-angle
  ;; Lunar longitude at moment tee.
  (hindu-true-position tee hindu-sidereal-month
                       32/360 hindu-anomalistic-month 1/96))
```

(20.15)
```
(defun hindu-lunar-phase (tee)
  ;; TYPE rational-moment -> rational-angle
  ;; Longitudinal distance between the sun and moon
  ;; at moment tee.
  (mod (- (hindu-lunar-longitude tee)
          (hindu-solar-longitude tee))
       360))
```

```
(defun hindu-lunar-day-from-moment (tee)                    (20.16)
  ;; TYPE rational-moment -> hindu-lunar-day
  ;; Phase of moon (tithi) at moment tee, as an integer in
  ;; the range 1..30.
  (1+ (quotient (hindu-lunar-phase tee) (deg 12))))
```

```
(defun hindu-new-moon-before (tee)                          (20.17)
  ;; TYPE rational-moment -> rational-moment
  ;; Approximate moment of last new moon preceding moment
  ;; tee, close enough to determine zodiacal sign.
  (let* ((varepsilon (expt 2 -1000)) ; Safety margin.
         (tau ; Can be off by almost a day.
          (- tee (* (/ 1 (deg 360)) (hindu-lunar-phase tee)
                    hindu-synodic-month))))
    (binary-search ; Search for phase start.
     l (1- tau)
     u (min tee (1+ tau))
     x (< (hindu-lunar-phase x) (deg 180))
     (or (= (hindu-zodiac l) (hindu-zodiac u))
         (< (- u l) varepsilon)))))
```

```
(defun hindu-solar-date (year month day)
  ;; TYPE (hindu-solar-year hindu-solar-month hindu-solar-day)
  ;; TYPE  -> hindu-solar-date
  (list year month day))
```

```
(defun hindu-calendar-year (tee)                            (20.18)
  ;; TYPE rational-moment -> hindu-solar-year
  ;; Determine solar year at given moment tee.
  (round (- (/ (- tee hindu-epoch)
               hindu-sidereal-year)
            (/ (hindu-solar-longitude tee)
               (deg 360)))))
```

```
(defconstant hindu-solar-era                                (20.19)
  ;; TYPE standard-year
  ;; Years from Kali Yuga until Saka era.
  3179)
```

```
(defun hindu-solar-from-fixed (date)                        (20.20)
  ;; TYPE fixed-date -> hindu-solar-date
  ;; Hindu (Orissa) solar date equivalent to fixed date.
  (let* ((critical    ; Sunrise on Hindu date.
          (hindu-sunrise (1+ date)))
         (month (hindu-zodiac critical))
         (year (- (hindu-calendar-year critical)
                  hindu-solar-era))
         (approx ; 3 days before start of mean month.
          (- date 3
             (mod (floor (hindu-solar-longitude critical))
                  (deg 30))))
         (start ; Search forward for beginning...
          (next i approx ; ... of month.
                (= (hindu-zodiac (hindu-sunrise (1+ i)))
                   month)))
         (day (- date start -1)))
    (hindu-solar-date year month day)))
```

```
(defun fixed-from-hindu-solar (s-date)                      (20.21)
  ;; TYPE hindu-solar-date -> fixed-date
  ;; Fixed date corresponding to Hindu solar date s-date
  ;; (Saka era; Orissa rule.)
  (let* ((month (standard-month s-date))
         (day (standard-day s-date))
         (year (standard-year s-date))
         (start ; Approximate start of month
                                          ; by adding days...
          (+ (floor (* (+ year hindu-solar-era
```

```
                        (/ (1- month) 12))    ; in months...
                     hindu-sidereal-year))    ; ... and years
               hindu-epoch)))    ; and days before RD 0.
    ;; Search forward to correct month
    (+ day -1
       (next d (- start 3)
             (= (hindu-zodiac (hindu-sunrise (1+ d)))
                month)))))
```

```
(defun hindu-lunar-date (year month leap-month day leap-day)
  ;; TYPE (hindu-lunar-year hindu-lunar-month
  ;; TYPE  hindu-lunar-leap-month hindu-lunar-day
  ;; TYPE  hindu-lunar-leap-day) -> hindu-lunar-date
  (list year month leap-month day leap-day))
```

```
(defun hindu-lunar-month (date)
  ;; TYPE hindu-lunar-date -> hindu-lunar-month
  (second date))
```

```
(defun hindu-lunar-leap-month (date)
  ;; TYPE hindu-lunar-date -> hindu-lunar-leap-month
  (third date))
```

```
(defun hindu-lunar-day (date)
  ;; TYPE hindu-lunar-date -> hindu-lunar-day
  (fourth date))
```

```
(defun hindu-lunar-leap-day (date)
  ;; TYPE hindu-lunar-date -> hindu-lunar-leap-day
  (fifth date))
```

```
(defun hindu-lunar-year (date)
  ;; TYPE hindu-lunar-date -> hindu-lunar-year
  (first date))
```

(20.22)

```
(defconstant hindu-lunar-era
  ;; TYPE standard-year
  ;; Years from Kali Yuga until Vikrama era.
  3044)
```

(20.23)

```
(defun hindu-lunar-from-fixed (date)
  ;; TYPE fixed-date -> hindu-lunar-date
  ;; Hindu lunar date, new-moon scheme,
  ;; equivalent to fixed date.
  (let* ((critical (hindu-sunrise date)) ; Sunrise that day.
         (day (hindu-lunar-day-from-moment
               critical)); Day of month.
         (leap-day         ; If previous day the same.
          (= day (hindu-lunar-day-from-moment
                  (hindu-sunrise (- date 1)))))
         (last-new-moon
          (hindu-new-moon-before critical))
         (next-new-moon
          (hindu-new-moon-before
           (+ (floor last-new-moon) 35)))
         (solar-month          ; Solar month name.
          (hindu-zodiac last-new-moon))
         (leap-month       ; If begins and ends in same sign.
          (= solar-month (hindu-zodiac next-new-moon)))
         (month                       ; Month of lunar year.
          (amod (1+ solar-month) 12))
         (year ; Solar year at end of month.
          (- (hindu-calendar-year
              (if (<= month 2) ; date might precede solar
                                                ; new year.
```

```
                (+ date 180)
              date))
           hindu-lunar-era)))
    (hindu-lunar-date year month leap-month day leap-day)))
```

(20.24)

```
(defun fixed-from-hindu-lunar (l-date)
  ;; TYPE hindu-lunar-date -> fixed-date
  ;; Fixed date corresponding to Hindu lunar date l-date.
  (let* ((year (hindu-lunar-year l-date))
         (month (hindu-lunar-month l-date))
         (leap-month (hindu-lunar-leap-month l-date))
         (day (hindu-lunar-day l-date))
         (leap-day (hindu-lunar-leap-day l-date))
         (approx
          (+ hindu-epoch
             (* hindu-sidereal-year
                (+ year hindu-lunar-era
                   (/ (1- month) 12)))))
         (s (floor
             (- approx
                (* hindu-sidereal-year
                   (mod3 (- (/ (hindu-solar-longitude approx)
                               (deg 360))
                            (/ (1- month) 12))
                         -1/2 1/2)))))
         (k (hindu-lunar-day-from-moment (+ s (hr 6))))
         (est
          (- s (- day)
             (cond
              ((< 3 k 27) ; Not borderline case.
               k)
              ((let* ((mid ; Middle of preceding solar month.
                       (hindu-lunar-from-fixed
                        (- s 15))))
                 (or ; In month starting near s.
                  (/= (hindu-lunar-month mid) month)
                  (and (hindu-lunar-leap-month mid)
                       (not leap-month))))
               (mod3 k -15 15))
              (t ; In preceding month.
               (mod3 k 15 45)))))
         (tau ; Refined estimate.
          (- est (mod3 (- (hindu-lunar-day-from-moment
                           (+ est (hr 6)))
                          day)
                       -15 15)))
         (date (next d (1- tau)
                     (member (hindu-lunar-day-from-moment
                              (hindu-sunrise d))
                             (list day (amod (1+ day) 30))))))
    (if leap-day (1+ date) date)))
```

(20.25)

```
(defconstant ujjain
  ;; TYPE location
  ;; Location of Ujjain.
  (location (angle 23 9 0) (angle 75 46 6)
            (mt 0) (hr (+ 5 461/9000))))
```

(20.26)

```
(defconstant hindu-location
  ;; TYPE location
  ;; Location (Ujjain) for determining Hindu calendar.
  ujjain)
```

(20.27)

```
(defun hindu-ascensional-difference (date location)
  ;; TYPE (fixed-date location) -> rational-angle
  ;; Difference between right and oblique ascension
  ;; of sun on date at location.
  (let* ((sin_delta
          (* 1397/3438 ; Sine of inclination.
             (hindu-sine (hindu-tropical-longitude date))))
```

```
         (phi (latitude location))
         (diurnal-radius
          (hindu-sine (+ (deg 90) (hindu-arcsin sin_delta))))
         (tan_phi ; Tangent of latitude as rational number.
          (/ (hindu-sine phi)
             (hindu-sine (+ (deg 90) phi))))
         (earth-sine (* sin_delta tan_phi)))
    (hindu-arcsin (- (/ earth-sine diurnal-radius)))))
```

(20.28)

```
(defun hindu-tropical-longitude (date)
  ;; TYPE fixed-date -> rational-angle
  ;; Hindu tropical longitude on fixed date.
  ;; Assumes precession with maximum of 27 degrees
  ;; and period of 7200 sidereal years
  ;; (= 1577917828/600 days).
  (let* ((days (- date hindu-epoch)) ; Whole days.
         (precession
          (- (deg 27)
             (abs
              (* (deg 108)
                 (mod3 (- (* 600/1577917828 days)
                          1/4)
                       -1/2 1/2))))))
    (mod (- (hindu-solar-longitude date) precession)
         360)))
```

(20.29)

```
(defun hindu-solar-sidereal-difference (date)
  ;; TYPE fixed-date -> rational-angle
  ;; Difference between solar and sidereal day on date.
  (* (hindu-daily-motion date) (hindu-rising-sign date)))
```

(20.30)

```
(defun hindu-daily-motion (date)
  ;; TYPE fixed-date -> rational-angle
  ;; Sidereal daily motion of sun on date.
  (let* ((mean-motion ; Mean daily motion in degrees.
           (/ (deg 360) hindu-sidereal-year))
         (anomaly
          (hindu-mean-position date hindu-anomalistic-year))
         (epicycle ; Current size of epicycle.
          (- 14/360 (/ (abs (hindu-sine anomaly)) 1080)))
         (entry (quotient anomaly (angle 0 225 0)))
         (sine-table-step ; Marginal change in anomaly
          (- (hindu-sine-table (1+ entry))
             (hindu-sine-table entry)))
         (factor
          (* -3438/225 sine-table-step epicycle)))
    (* mean-motion (1+ factor))))
```

(20.31)

```
(defun hindu-rising-sign (date)
  ;; TYPE fixed-date -> rational-amplitude
  ;; Tabulated speed of rising of current zodiacal sign on
  ;; date.
  (let* ((i  ; Index.
          (quotient (hindu-tropical-longitude date)
                    (deg 30))))
    (nth (mod i 6)
         (list 1670/1800 1795/1800 1935/1800 1935/1800
               1795/1800 1670/1800))))
```

(20.32)

```
(defun hindu-equation-of-time (date)
  ;; TYPE fixed-date -> rational-moment
  ;; Time from true to mean midnight of date.
  ;; (This is a gross approximation to the correct value.)
  (let* ((offset (hindu-sine
                  (hindu-mean-position
                   date
                   hindu-anomalistic-year)))
         (equation-sun ; Sun's equation of center
          ;; Arcsin is not needed since small
```

```
          (* offset (angle 57 18 0)
             (- 14/360 (/ (abs offset) 1080)))))
    (* (/ (hindu-daily-motion date) (deg 360))
       (/ equation-sun (deg 360))
       hindu-sidereal-year)))
```

(20.33)

```
(defun hindu-sunrise (date)
  ;; TYPE fixed-date -> rational-moment
  ;; Sunrise at hindu-location on date.
  (+ date (hr 6) ; Mean sunrise.
     (/ (- (longitude ujjain) (longitude hindu-location))
        (deg 360)) ; Difference from longitude.
     (- (hindu-equation-of-time date)) ; Apparent midnight.
     (* ; Convert sidereal angle to fraction of civil day.
      (/ 1577917828/1582237828 (deg 360))
      (+ (hindu-ascensional-difference date hindu-location)
         (* 1/4 (hindu-solar-sidereal-difference date))))))
```

(20.34)

```
(defun hindu-sunset (date)
  ;; TYPE fixed-date -> rational-moment
  ;; Sunset at hindu-location on date.
  (+ date (hr 18) ; Mean sunset.
     (/ (- (longitude ujjain) (longitude hindu-location))
        (deg 360)) ; Difference from longitude.
     (- (hindu-equation-of-time date)) ; Apparent midnight.
     (* ; Convert sidereal angle to fraction of civil day.
      (/ 1577917828/1582237828 (deg 360))
      (+ (- (hindu-ascensional-difference date hindu-location))
         (* 3/4 (hindu-solar-sidereal-difference date))))))
```

(20.35)

```
(defun hindu-standard-from-sundial (tee)
  ;; TYPE rational-moment -> rational-moment
  ;; Hindu local time of temporal moment tee.
  (let* ((date (fixed-from-moment tee))
         (time (time-from-moment tee))
         (q (floor (* 4 time))) ; quarter of day
         (a (cond ((= q 0)     ; early this morning
                   (hindu-sunset (1- date)))
                  ((= q 3)     ; this evening
                   (hindu-sunset date))
                  (t ;  daytime today
                   (hindu-sunrise date))))
         (b (cond ((= q 0) (hindu-sunrise date))
                  ((= q 3) (hindu-sunrise (1+ date)))
                  (t (hindu-sunset date)))))
    (+ a (* 2 (- b a) (- time
                         (cond ((= q 3) (hr 18))
                               ((= q 0) (hr -6))
                               (t (hr 6))))))))
```

(20.36)

```
(defun hindu-fullmoon-from-fixed (date)
  ;; TYPE fixed-date -> hindu-lunar-date
  ;; Hindu lunar date, full-moon scheme,
  ;; equivalent to fixed date.
  (let* ((l-date (hindu-lunar-from-fixed date))
         (year (hindu-lunar-year l-date))
         (month (hindu-lunar-month l-date))
         (leap-month (hindu-lunar-leap-month l-date))
         (day (hindu-lunar-day l-date))
         (leap-day (hindu-lunar-leap-day l-date))
         (m (if (>= day 16)
                (hindu-lunar-month
                 (hindu-lunar-from-fixed (+ date 20)))
              month)))
    (hindu-lunar-date year m leap-month day leap-day)))
```

(20.37)

```
(defun fixed-from-hindu-fullmoon (l-date)
  ;; TYPE hindu-lunar-date -> fixed-date
  ;; Fixed date equivalent to Hindu lunar l-date
```

```
  ;; in full-moon scheme.
  (let* ((year (hindu-lunar-year l-date))
         (month (hindu-lunar-month l-date))
         (leap-month (hindu-lunar-leap-month l-date))
         (day (hindu-lunar-day l-date))
         (leap-day (hindu-lunar-leap-day l-date))
         (m (cond ((or leap-month (<= day 15))
                   month)
                  ((hindu-expunged? year (amod (1- month) 12))
                   (amod (- month 2) 12))
                  (t (amod (1- month) 12)))))
    (fixed-from-hindu-lunar
     (hindu-lunar-date year m leap-month day leap-day))))
```

(20.38)

```
(defun hindu-expunged? (l-year l-month)
  ;; TYPE (hindu-lunar-year hindu-lunar-month) ->
  ;; TYPE  boolean
  ;; True of Hindu lunar month l-month in l-year
  ;; is expunged.
  (/= l-month
      (hindu-lunar-month
       (hindu-lunar-from-fixed
        (fixed-from-hindu-lunar
         (list l-year l-month false 15 false))))))
```

(20.39)

```
(defun alt-hindu-sunrise (date)
  ;; TYPE fixed-date -> rational-moment
  ;; Astronomical sunrise at Hindu location on date,
  ;; per Lahiri,
  ;; rounded to nearest minute, as a rational number.
  (let* ((rise (dawn date hindu-location (angle 0 47 0))))
    (* 1/24 1/60 (round (* rise 24 60)))))
```

(20.40)

```
(defun ayanamsha (tee)
  ;; TYPE moment -> angle
  ;; Difference between tropical and sidereal solar longitude.
  (- (solar-longitude tee)
     (sidereal-solar-longitude tee)))
```

(20.41)

```
(defconstant sidereal-start
  ;; TYPE angle
  (precession (universal-from-local
               (mesha-samkranti (ce 285))
               hindu-location)))
```

(20.42)

```
(defun astro-hindu-sunset (date)
  ;; TYPE fixed-date -> moment
  ;; Geometrical sunset at Hindu location on date.
  (dusk date hindu-location (deg 0)))
```

(20.43)

```
(defun sidereal-zodiac (tee)
  ;; TYPE moment -> hindu-solar-month
  ;; Sidereal zodiacal sign of the sun, as integer in range
  ;; 1..12, at moment tee.
  (1+ (quotient (sidereal-solar-longitude tee) (deg 30))))
```

(20.44)

```
(defun astro-hindu-calendar-year (tee)
  ;; TYPE moment -> hindu-solar-year
  ;; Astronomical Hindu solar year KY at given moment tee.
  (round (- (/ (- tee hindu-epoch)
               mean-sidereal-year)
            (/ (sidereal-solar-longitude tee)
               (deg 360)))))
```

(20.45)

```
(defun astro-hindu-solar-from-fixed (date)
  ;; TYPE fixed-date -> hindu-solar-date
  ;; Astronomical Hindu (Tamil) solar date equivalent to
  ;; fixed date.
  (let* ((critical    ; Sunrise on Hindu date.
           (astro-hindu-sunset date))
         (month (sidereal-zodiac critical))
         (year (- (astro-hindu-calendar-year critical)
                  hindu-solar-era))
         (approx ; 3 days before start of mean month.
          (- date 3
             (mod (floor (sidereal-solar-longitude critical))
                  (deg 30))))
         (start ; Search forward for beginning...
          (next i approx ; ... of month.
                (= (sidereal-zodiac (astro-hindu-sunset i))
                   month)))
         (day (- date start -1)))
    (hindu-solar-date year month day)))
```

(20.46)

```
(defun fixed-from-astro-hindu-solar (s-date)
  ;; TYPE hindu-solar-date -> fixed-date
  ;; Fixed date corresponding to Astronomical
  ;; Hindu solar date (Tamil rule; Saka era).
  (let* ((month (standard-month s-date))
         (day (standard-day s-date))
         (year (standard-year s-date))
         (approx ; 3 days before start of mean month.
          (+ hindu-epoch -3
             (floor (* (+ (+ year hindu-solar-era)
                          (/ (1- month) 12))
                       mean-sidereal-year))))
         (start ; Search forward for beginning...
          (next i approx ; ... of month.
                (= (sidereal-zodiac (astro-hindu-sunset i))
                   month))))
    (+ start day -1)))
```

(20.47)

```
(defun astro-lunar-day-from-moment (tee)
  ;; TYPE moment -> hindu-lunar-day
  ;; Phase of moon (tithi) at moment tee, as an integer in
  ;; the range 1..30.
  (1+ (quotient (lunar-phase tee) (deg 12))))
```

(20.48)

```
(defun astro-hindu-lunar-from-fixed (date)
  ;; TYPE fixed-date -> hindu-lunar-date
  ;; Astronomical Hindu lunar date equivalent to fixed date.
  (let* ((critical
           (alt-hindu-sunrise date)) ; Sunrise that day.
         (day
          (astro-lunar-day-from-moment critical)); Day of month
         (leap-day              ; If previous day the same.
          (= day (astro-lunar-day-from-moment
                  (alt-hindu-sunrise (- date 1)))))
         (last-new-moon
          (new-moon-before critical))
         (next-new-moon
          (new-moon-at-or-after critical))
         (solar-month          ; Solar month name.
          (sidereal-zodiac last-new-moon))
         (leap-month        ; If begins and ends in same sign.
          (= solar-month (sidereal-zodiac next-new-moon)))
         (month                          ; Month of lunar year.
          (amod (1+ solar-month) 12))
         (year ; Solar year at end of month.
          (- (astro-hindu-calendar-year
              (if (<= month 2) ; date might precede solar
                                ; new year.
                  (+ date 180)
```

```
                    date))
                hindu-lunar-era)))
    (hindu-lunar-date year month leap-month day leap-day)))
```

(20.49)

```
(defun fixed-from-astro-hindu-lunar (l-date)
  ;; TYPE hindu-lunar-date -> fixed-date
  ;; Fixed date corresponding to Hindu lunar date l-date.
  (let* ((year (hindu-lunar-year l-date))
         (month (hindu-lunar-month l-date))
         (leap-month (hindu-lunar-leap-month l-date))
         (day (hindu-lunar-day l-date))
         (leap-day (hindu-lunar-leap-day l-date))
         (approx
          (+ hindu-epoch
             (* mean-sidereal-year
                (+ year hindu-lunar-era
                   (/ (1- month) 12)))))
         (s (floor
             (- approx
                (* hindu-sidereal-year
                   (mod3 (- (/ (sidereal-solar-longitude approx)
                               (deg 360))
                            (/ (1- month) 12))
                         -1/2 1/2)))))
         (k (astro-lunar-day-from-moment (+ s (hr 6))))
         (est
          (- s (- day)
             (cond
              ((< 3 k 27) ; Not borderline case.
               k)
              ((let* ((mid ; Middle of preceding solar month.
                       (astro-hindu-lunar-from-fixed
                        (- s 15))))
                 (or ; In month starting near s.
                  (/= (hindu-lunar-month mid) month)
                  (and (hindu-lunar-leap-month mid)
                       (not leap-month))))
               (mod3 k -15 15))
              (t ; In preceding month.
               (mod3 k 15 45)))))
         (tau ; Refined estimate.
          (- est (mod3 (- (astro-lunar-day-from-moment
                           (+ est (hr 6)))
                          day)
                       -15 15)))
         (date (next d (1- tau)
                     (member (astro-lunar-day-from-moment
                              (alt-hindu-sunrise d))
                             (list day (amod (1+ day) 30))))))
    (if leap-day (1+ date) date)))
```

(20.50)

```
(defun hindu-solar-longitude-at-or-after (lambda tee)
  ;; TYPE (season moment) -> moment
  ;; Moment of the first time at or after tee
  ;; when Hindu solar longitude will be lambda degrees.
  (let* ((tau ; Estimate (within 5 days).
          (+ tee
             (* hindu-sidereal-year (/ 1 (deg 360))
                (mod (- lambda (hindu-solar-longitude tee))
                     360))))
         (a (max tee (- tau 5))) ; At or after tee.
         (b (+ tau 5)))
    (invert-angular hindu-solar-longitude lambda
                    (interval-closed a b))))
```

(20.51)

```
(defun mesha-samkranti (g-year)
  ;; TYPE gregorian-year -> rational-moment
  ;; Fixed moment of Mesha samkranti (Vernal equinox)
  ;; in Gregorian g-year.
```

```
  (let* ((jan1 (gregorian-new-year g-year)))
    (hindu-solar-longitude-at-or-after (deg 0) jan1)))
```

(20.52)

```
(defun hindu-lunar-day-at-or-after (k tee)
  ;; TYPE (rational rational-moment) -> rational-moment
  ;; Time lunar-day (tithi) number k begins at or after
  ;; moment tee.  k can be fractional (for karanas).
  (let* ((phase ; Degrees corresponding to k.
          (* (1- k) (deg 12)))
         (tau ; Mean occurrence of lunar-day.
          (+ tee (* (/ 1 (deg 360))
                    (mod (- phase (hindu-lunar-phase tee))
                         360)
                    hindu-synodic-month)))
         (a (max tee (- tau 2)))
         (b (+ tau 2)))
    (invert-angular hindu-lunar-phase phase
                    (interval-closed a b))))
```

(20.53)

```
(defun hindu-lunar-new-year (g-year)
  ;; TYPE gregorian-year -> fixed-date
  ;; Fixed date of Hindu lunisolar new year in Gregorian
  ;; g-year.
  (let* ((jan1 (gregorian-new-year g-year))
         (mina ; Fixed moment of solar longitude 330.
          (hindu-solar-longitude-at-or-after (deg 330) jan1))
         (new-moon ; Next new moon.
          (hindu-lunar-day-at-or-after 1 mina))
         (h-day (floor new-moon))
         (critical ; Sunrise that day.
          (hindu-sunrise h-day)))
    (+ h-day
       ;; Next day if new moon after sunrise,
       ;; unless lunar day ends before next sunrise.
       (if (or (< new-moon critical)
               (= (hindu-lunar-day-from-moment
                   (hindu-sunrise (1+ h-day))) 2))
           0 1))))
```

(20.54)

```
(defun hindu-lunar-on-or-before? (l-date1 l-date2)
  ;; TYPE (hindu-lunar-date hindu-lunar-date) -> boolean
  ;; True if Hindu lunar date l-date1 is on or before
  ;; Hindu lunar date l-date2.
  (let* ((month1 (hindu-lunar-month l-date1))
         (month2 (hindu-lunar-month l-date2))
         (leap1 (hindu-lunar-leap-month l-date1))
         (leap2 (hindu-lunar-leap-month l-date2))
         (day1 (hindu-lunar-day l-date1))
         (day2 (hindu-lunar-day l-date2))
         (leap-day1 (hindu-lunar-leap-day l-date1))
         (leap-day2 (hindu-lunar-leap-day l-date2))
         (year1 (hindu-lunar-year l-date1))
         (year2 (hindu-lunar-year l-date2)))
    (or (< year1 year2)
        (and (= year1 year2)
             (or (< month1 month2)
                 (and (= month1 month2)
                      (or (and leap1 (not leap2))
                          (and (equal leap1 leap2)
                               (or (< day1 day2)
                                   (and (= day1 day2)
                                        (or (not leap-day1)
                                            leap-day2)))))
                      ))))))
```

(20.55)

```
(defun hindu-date-occur (l-year l-month l-day)
  ;; TYPE (hindu-lunar-year hindu-lunar-month
  ;; TYPE  hindu-lunar-day) -> fixed-date
  ;; Fixed date of occurrence of Hindu lunar l-month,
  ;; l-day in Hindu lunar year l-year, taking leap and
```

```
  ;; expunged days into account.  When the month is
  ;; expunged, then the following month is used.
  (let* ((lunar (hindu-lunar-date l-year l-month false
                                  l-day false))
         (try (fixed-from-hindu-lunar lunar))
         (mid (hindu-lunar-from-fixed
               (if (> l-day 15) (- try 5) try)))
         (expunged? (/= l-month (hindu-lunar-month mid)))
         (l-date ; day in next month
          (hindu-lunar-date (hindu-lunar-year mid)
                            (hindu-lunar-month mid)
                            (hindu-lunar-leap-month mid)
                            l-day false)))
    (cond (expunged?
           (1- (next d try
                     (not
                      (hindu-lunar-on-or-before?
                       (hindu-lunar-from-fixed d) l-date)))))
          ((/= l-day (hindu-lunar-day
                      (hindu-lunar-from-fixed try)))
           (1- try))
          (t try))))
```

(20.56)

```
(defun hindu-lunar-holiday (l-month l-day g-year)
  ;; TYPE (hindu-lunar-month hindu-lunar-day
  ;; TYPE  gregorian-year) -> list-of-fixed-dates
  ;; List of fixed dates of occurrences of Hindu lunar
  ;; month, day in Gregorian year g-year.
  (let* ((l-year (hindu-lunar-year
                  (hindu-lunar-from-fixed
                   (gregorian-new-year g-year))))
         (date0 (hindu-date-occur l-year l-month l-day))
         (date1 (hindu-date-occur (1+ l-year) l-month l-day)))
    (list-range (list date0 date1)
                (gregorian-year-range g-year))))
```

(20.57)

```
(defun diwali (g-year)
  ;; TYPE gregorian-year -> list-of-fixed-dates
  ;; List of fixed date(s) of Diwali in Gregorian year
  ;; g-year.
  (hindu-lunar-holiday 8 1 g-year))
```

(20.58)

```
(defun hindu-tithi-occur (l-month tithi tee l-year)
  ;; TYPE (hindu-lunar-month rational rational
  ;; TYPE  hindu-lunar-year) -> fixed-date
  ;; Fixed date of occurrence of Hindu lunar tithi prior
  ;; to sundial time tee, in Hindu lunar l-month, l-year.
  (let* ((approx
          (hindu-date-occur l-year l-month (floor tithi)))
         (lunar
          (hindu-lunar-day-at-or-after tithi (- approx 2)))
         (try (fixed-from-moment lunar))
         (tee_h (standard-from-sundial (+ try tee) ujjain)))
    (if (or (<= lunar tee_h)
            (> (hindu-lunar-phase
                (standard-from-sundial (+ try 1 tee) ujjain))
               (* 12 tithi)))
        try
      (1+ try))))
```

(20.59)

```
(defun hindu-lunar-event (l-month tithi tee g-year)
  ;; TYPE (hindu-lunar-month rational rational
  ;; TYPE  gregorian-year) -> list-of-fixed-dates
  ;; List of fixed dates of occurrences of Hindu lunar tithi
  ;; prior to sundial time tee, in Hindu lunar l-month,
  ;; in Gregorian year g-year.
  (let* ((l-year (hindu-lunar-year
                  (hindu-lunar-from-fixed
                   (gregorian-new-year g-year))))
         (date0 (hindu-tithi-occur l-month tithi tee l-year))
```

```
      (date1 (hindu-tithi-occur
              l-month tithi tee (1+ l-year))))
  (list-range (list date0 date1)
              (gregorian-year-range g-year))))
```

(20.60)

```
(defun shiva (g-year)
  ;; TYPE gregorian-year -> list-of-fixed-dates
  ;; List of fixed date(s) of Night of Shiva in Gregorian
  ;; year g-year.
  (hindu-lunar-event 11 29 (hr 24) g-year))
```

(20.61)

```
(defun rama (g-year)
  ;; TYPE gregorian-year -> list-of-fixed-dates
  ;; List of fixed date(s) of Rama's Birthday in Gregorian
  ;; year g-year.
  (hindu-lunar-event 1 9 (hr 12) g-year))
```

(20.62)

```
(defun hindu-lunar-station (date)
  ;; TYPE fixed-date -> nakshatra
  ;; Hindu lunar station (nakshatra) at sunrise on date.
  (let* ((critical (hindu-sunrise date)))
    (1+ (quotient (hindu-lunar-longitude critical)
                  (angle 0 800 0)))))
```

(20.63)

```
(defun karana (n)
  ;; TYPE 1-60 -> 0-10
  ;; Number (0-10) of the name of the n-th (1-60) Hindu
  ;; karana.
  (cond ((= n 1) 0)
        ((> n 57) (- n 50))
        (t (amod (1- n) 7))))
```

(20.64)

```
(defun yoga (date)
  ;; TYPE fixed-date -> 1-27
  ;; Hindu yoga on date.
  (1+ (floor (mod (/ (+ (hindu-solar-longitude date)
                        (hindu-lunar-longitude date))
                     (angle 0 800 0))
                  27))))
```

(20.65)

```
(defun sacred-wednesdays (g-year)
  ;; TYPE gregorian-year -> list-of-fixed-dates
  ;; List of Wednesdays in Gregorian year g-year
  ;; that are day 8 of Hindu lunar months.
  (sacred-wednesdays-in-range
   (gregorian-year-range g-year)))
```

(20.66)

```
(defun sacred-wednesdays-in-range (range)
  ;; TYPE range -> list-of-fixed-dates
  ;; List of Wednesdays within range of dates
  ;; that are day 8 of Hindu lunar months.
  (let* ((a (begin range))
         (b (end range))
         (wed (kday-on-or-after wednesday a))
         (h-date (hindu-lunar-from-fixed wed)))
    (if (in-range? wed range)
        (append
         (if (= (hindu-lunar-day h-date) 8)
             (list wed)
           nil)
         (sacred-wednesdays-in-range
          (interval (1+ wed) b)))
      nil)))
```

D.21 The Tibetan Calendar

```
(defun tibetan-date (year month leap-month day leap-day)
  ;; TYPE (tibetan-year tibetan-month
  ;; TYPE  tibetan-leap-month tibetan-day
  ;; TYPE  tibetan-leap-day) -> tibetan-date
  (list year month leap-month day leap-day))
```

```
(defun tibetan-year (date)
  ;; TYPE tibetan-date -> tibetan-year
  (first date))
```

```
(defun tibetan-month (date)
  ;; TYPE tibetan-date -> tibetan-month
  (second date))
```

```
(defun tibetan-leap-month (date)
  ;; TYPE tibetan-date -> tibetan-leap-month
  (third date))
```

```
(defun tibetan-day (date)
  ;; TYPE tibetan-date -> tibetan-day
  (fourth date))
```

```
(defun tibetan-leap-day (date)
  ;; TYPE tibetan-date -> tibetan-leap-day
  (fifth date))
```

(21.1)

```
(defconstant tibetan-epoch
  ;; TYPE fixed-date
  (fixed-from-gregorian (gregorian-date -127 december 7)))
```

(21.2)

```
(defun tibetan-sun-equation (alpha)
  ;; TYPE rational-angle -> rational
  ;; Interpolated tabular sine of solar anomaly alpha.
  (cond ((> alpha 6) (- (tibetan-sun-equation (- alpha 6))))
        ((> alpha 3) (tibetan-sun-equation (- 6 alpha)))
        ((integerp alpha)
         (nth alpha (list (mins 0) (mins 6) (mins 10) (mins 11))))
        (t (+ (* (mod alpha 1)
                 (tibetan-sun-equation (ceiling alpha)))
              (* (mod (- alpha) 1)
                 (tibetan-sun-equation (floor alpha)))))))
```

(21.3)

```
(defun tibetan-moon-equation (alpha)
  ;; TYPE rational-angle -> rational
  ;; Interpolated tabular sine of lunar anomaly alpha.
  (cond ((> alpha 14) (- (tibetan-moon-equation (- alpha 14))))
        ((> alpha 7) (tibetan-moon-equation (- 14 alpha)))
        ((integerp alpha)
         (nth alpha
              (list (mins 0) (mins 5) (mins 10) (mins 15)
                    (mins 19) (mins 22) (mins 24) (mins 25))))
        (t (+ (* (mod alpha 1)
                 (tibetan-moon-equation (ceiling alpha)))
              (* (mod (- alpha) 1)
                 (tibetan-moon-equation (floor alpha)))))))
```

(21.4)

```
(defun fixed-from-tibetan (t-date)
  ;; TYPE tibetan-date -> fixed-date
  ;; Fixed date corresponding to Tibetan lunar date t-date.
  (let* ((year (tibetan-year t-date))
         (month (tibetan-month t-date))
         (leap-month (tibetan-leap-month t-date))
         (day (tibetan-day t-date))
         (leap-day (tibetan-leap-day t-date))
```

```
        (months ; Lunar month count.
         (floor (+ (* 804/65 (1- year)) (* 67/65 month)
                   (if leap-month -1 0) 64/65)))
        (days ; Lunar day count.
         (+ (* 30 months) day))
        (mean ; Mean civil days since epoch.
         (+ (* days 11135/11312) -30
            (if leap-day 0 -1) 1071/1616))
        (solar-anomaly
         (mod (+ (* days 13/4824) 2117/4824) 1))
        (lunar-anomaly
         (mod (+ (* days 3781/105840) 2837/15120) 1))
        (sun (- (tibetan-sun-equation (* 12 solar-anomaly))))
        (moon (tibetan-moon-equation (* 28 lunar-anomaly))))
    (floor (+ tibetan-epoch mean sun moon))))
```

```
(defun tibetan-from-fixed (date)
  ;; TYPE fixed-date -> tibetan-date
  ;; Tibetan lunar date corresponding to fixed date.
  (let* ((cap-Y (+ 365 4975/18382)) ; Average Tibetan year.
         (years (ceiling (/ (- date tibetan-epoch) cap-Y)))
         (year0 ; Search for year.
          (final y years
                 (>= date
                     (fixed-from-tibetan
                      (tibetan-date y 1 false 1 false)))))
         (month0 ; Search for month.
          (final m 1
                 (>= date
                     (fixed-from-tibetan
                      (tibetan-date year0 m false 1 false)))))
         (est ; Estimated day.
          (- date (fixed-from-tibetan
                   (tibetan-date year0 month0 false 1 false))))
         (day0 ; Search for day.
          (final
           d (- est 2)
           (>= date
               (fixed-from-tibetan
                (tibetan-date year0 month0 false d false)))))
         (leap-month (> day0 30))
         (day (amod day0 30))
         (month (amod (cond ((> day day0) (1- month0))
                            (leap-month (1+ month0))
                            (t month0))
                      12))
         (year (cond ((and (> day day0) (= month0 1))
                      (1- year0))
                     ((and leap-month (= month0 12))
                      (1+ year0))
                     (t year0)))
         (leap-day
          (= date
             (fixed-from-tibetan
              (tibetan-date year month leap-month day true)))))
    (tibetan-date year month leap-month day leap-day)))
```

(21.5)

```
(defun tibetan-leap-month? (t-year t-month)
  ;; TYPE (tibetan-year tibetan-month) -> boolean
  ;; True if t-month is leap in Tibetan year t-year.
  (= t-month
     (tibetan-month
      (tibetan-from-fixed
       (fixed-from-tibetan
        (tibetan-date t-year t-month true 2 false))))))
```

(21.6)

```
(defun tibetan-leap-day? (t-year t-month t-day)
  ;; TYPE (tibetan-year tibetan-month tibetan-day) -> boolean
  ;; True if t-day is leap in Tibetan
```

(21.7)

```
  ;; month t-month and year t-year.
  (or
   (= t-day
      (tibetan-day
       (tibetan-from-fixed
        (fixed-from-tibetan
         (tibetan-date t-year t-month false t-day true)))))
   ;; Check also in leap month if there is one.
   (= t-day
      (tibetan-day
       (tibetan-from-fixed
        (fixed-from-tibetan
         (tibetan-date t-year t-month
                       (tibetan-leap-month? t-year t-month)
                       t-day true)))))))
```

(21.8)

```
(defun losar (t-year)
  ;; TYPE tibetan-year -> fixed-date
  ;; Fixed date of Tibetan New Year (Losar)
  ;; in Tibetan year t-year.
  (let* ((t-leap (tibetan-leap-month? t-year 1)))
    (fixed-from-tibetan
     (tibetan-date t-year 1 t-leap 1 false))))
```

(21.9)

```
(defun tibetan-new-year (g-year)
  ;; TYPE gregorian-year -> list-of-fixed-dates
  ;; List of fixed dates of Tibetan New Year in
  ;; Gregorian year g-year.
  (let* ((dec31 (gregorian-year-end g-year))
         (t-year (tibetan-year (tibetan-from-fixed dec31))))
    (list-range
     (list (losar (1- t-year))
           (losar t-year))
     (gregorian-year-range g-year))))
```

References

[1] N. Dershowitz and E. M. Reingold, "Modulo Intervals: A Proposed Notation," *ACM SIGACT News*, vol. 43, no. 3, pp. 60–64, 2012.

[2] G. L. Steele, Jr., *Common LISP: The Language*, 2nd edn., Digital Press, Bedford, MA, 1990.

In octo libros De emendatione temporum Index.

A

Oo

First page of the index to Joseph Scaliger's *De Emendatione Temporum* (Frankfort edition, 1593). (Courtesy of the University of Illinois, Urbana, IL.)

Index

... there will be few who will consider the industry, labor, vigils which we have bestowed upon [the index], or the profit and utility that may be gathered from our labors. For it is the equivalent of a whole book.

Joseph Scaliger: Letter to Isaac Casaubon (January 7, 1604)

It requires more scholarship to make a good index than to write the book that is indexed.

George Foot Moore: Address at a reception of the Harvard Graduate School of Arts and Sciences (1925)

Names of functions and constants are given in **boldface**. Page numbers for a function are of four types: the page with the function definition is in **boldface**; the page with the type description in Appendix A is underlined; the page with the cross-references in Appendix B is in *italics*; the page with the corresponding Lisp code in Appendix D is shown in `typewriter font`.

Names of people are indexed according to the guidelines of *The Chicago Manual of Style*: *The Essential Guide for Writers, Editors, and Publishers*, 14th edn, The University of Chicago Press, Chicago, 1993.

Symbols

function definition function type *Cross references* `Lisp code`

function definition function type *Cross references* `Lisp code`

function definition function type *Cross references* `Lisp code`

function definition function type *Cross references* Lisp code

The covers of this book are too far apart.
Attributed to Ambrose Bierce

Blue and white glazed jar from the reign of Kāng Xī (1662–1722), showing plum blossoms against a background of melting ice and used to hold a gift of fragrant tea for New Year's Day. (Courtesy of the Victoria & Albert Museum, London.)

Envoi

Ohe, iam satis est, ohe, libelle,
Iam pervenimus usque ad umbilicos.
Tu procedere adhuc et ire quæris,
Nec summa potes in schida teneri,
Sic tamquam tibi res peracta non sit,
Quae prima quoque pagina peracta est.
Iam lector queriturque deficitque,
Iam librarius hoc et ipse dicit
"Ohe, iam satis est, ohe, libelle."

Martial: *Epigrams*, IV, 89 (circa 90 C.E.)

About the Cover

The cover shows the astronomical clock from the southern wall of the Prague Town Hall. This clock, dating back to 1410, is one of the oldest astronomical clocks in the world. It contains an astrolabe dial and displays a wide variety of temporal and calendrical data including times of sunrise/sunset/twilight, seasonal hours, Italian time, siderial time, the zodiac, the position on the ecliptic of the sun and moon, and the lunar phase.

Cover design by Hart McLeod Ltd.

Image courtesy of Future Light/DigitalVision/Getty Images.

Printed in the United States
By Bookmasters